Second Edition

fluency

with INFORMATION TECHNOLOGY

Skills, Concepts, & Capabilities

Lawrence Snyder

University of Washington

PEARSON

Addison
Wesley

Boston San Francisco New York
London Toronto Sydney Tokyo Singapore Madrid
Mexico City Munich Paris Cape Town Hong Kong Montreal

Senior Acquisitions Editor:	Michael Hirsch
Development Editor:	Pat Mahtani
Editorial Assistant:	Lindsey Triebel
Marketing Manager:	Michelle Brown
Marketing Assistant:	Dana Lopreato
Copyeditor:	Kathy Cantwell
Proofreader:	Holly McLean-Aldis
Indexer:	Jack Lewis
Senior Production Supervisor:	Meredith Gertz
Text Designers:	Joyce Cosentino Wells and Gillian Hall
Cover Designer:	Joyce Cosentino Wells
Supplements Supervisor:	Jason Miranda
Media Producer:	Bethany Tidd
Prepress and Manufacturing:	Caroline Fell
Rights and Permissions Advisor:	Dana Weightman
Production Coordination, Composition, and Illustrations:	Gillian Hall, The Aardvark Group
Text and Cover Image:	© 2005 Stockbyte

Access the latest information about Addison-Wesley titles from our World Wide Web site: http://www.aw.com/cs.

Many of the designations used by manufacturers and sellers to distinguish their products are claimed as trademarks. Where those designations appear in this book, and Addison-Wesley was aware of a trademark claim, the designations have been printed in initial caps or all caps.

Library of Congress Cataloging-in-Publication Data

Snyder, Lawrence.
    Fluency with information technology : skills, concepts, & capabilities /
Lawrence Snyder.-- 2nd ed.
        p. cm.
    Includes index.
    ISBN-13: 978-0-321-35782-5
    1. Information technology. I. Title.

    T58.5.S645 2005
    004--dc22

                                                    2005015969

ISBN 0-321-35782-5

2 3 4 5 6 7 8 9 10—VH—09 08 07 06

WELCOME to the Second Edition of *Fluency with Information Technology: Skills, Concepts, and Capabilities*. This book moves beyond the click here-click-there form of technology instruction to one firmly founded on ideas. As is demonstrated by the number of schools that have adopted this book, the time is right for a new introduction to IT. Today the majority of college and post-secondary students are already familiar with computers, the Internet, and the World Wide Web, and do not need rudimentary instruction in double-clicking and resizing windows. Rather, they need to be taught to be confident, in-control users of IT. They need to know how to navigate independently in the ever-changing worlds of information and technology, to solve their problems on their own, and to be capable of fully applying the power of IT tools in the service of their personal and career goals. They must be more than literate; they must be fluent with IT.

What's New in this Edition?

The revision was developed based on feedback we received from the thousands of professors and students who have used this book around the world; further we have responded to the rapid changes in IT since the first edition. The most obvious change is the new chapter covering Spreadsheets (Chapter 13) that shows readers how to do more than business applications with this tool. The chapter introduces all students to the power of spreadsheets, prepares business students for their more advanced business applications, and provides a smooth transition into the important topic of relational databases.

Privacy and security (Chapter 17) have been substantially updated, addressing the contemporary topics of identity theft, spamming, phishing, and other privacy issues. The treatment of functions (Chapter 20) has been completely revised resulting in a much more simplified presentation. Chapter 7 on debugging presents a new HTML troubleshooting scenario that emphasizes the use of multiple browsers. Information searching (Chapter 5) has been revised to reflect the maturity of the World Wide Web and tools such as Google™. Throughout the text examples and illustrations have been revised to reflect the latest features of Mac OS X and Windows® XP. Finally, the glossary has been expanded to better serve the reader.

What's Fluency with Information Technology?

This book is inspired by a report from the National Research Council (NRC), *Being Fluent with Information Technology*. In that study, commissioned by the National Science Foundation, the committee asserted that traditional computer literacy does not have the "staying power" students need to keep pace with the rapid changes in IT. The study concluded that the educational "bar needs to be raised" if students' knowledge is to evolve and adapt to that change. The recommended alternative, dubbed *fluency with information technology*, or *FIT*, was a package of skills, concepts, and capabilities wrapped in a project-oriented learning approach that ensures that the content is fully integrated. The goal is to help people become effective users immediately, and to prepare them for lifelong learning.

The Vision

Because fluency with information technology—I usually shorten it to *Fluency*—is still a new concept that largely implements the vision of the NRC committee, I'll introduce the main components: the three-part content, the integration mechanism of projects, and the role of programming.

Three-part Content

To make students immediately effective and launch them on the path of lifelong learning, they need to be taught three types of knowledge: Skills, Concepts, and Capabilities.

> *Skills* refers to proficiency with contemporary computer applications such as email, word processing, Web searching, etc. Skills make the technology immediately useful to students and give them practical experience on which to base other learning. The Skills component approximates traditional computer literacy content; that is, Fluency *includes* literacy.

> *Concepts* refers to the fundamental knowledge underpinning IT, such as how a computer works, digital representation of information, assessing information authenticity, etc. Concepts provide the principles on which students will build new understanding as IT evolves.

> *Capabilities* refers to higher-level thinking processes such as problem solving, reasoning, complexity management, troubleshooting, etc. Capabilities embody modes of thinking that are essential to exploiting IT, but they apply broadly. Reasoning, problem solving, etc. are standard components of education, their heavy use in IT makes them topics of emphasis in the Fluency approach.

For each component, the NRC report lists ten recommended items. These are shown in the accompanying table.

The NRC's List of Top Ten Skills, Concepts, and Capabilities

Fluency with Information Technology

Skills

1. Set-up a personal computer
2. Use basic operating system facilities
3. Use a word processor to create a document
4. Use a graphics or artwork package to manipulate an image
5. Connect a computer to the Internet
6. Use the Internet to locate information
7. Use a computer to communicate with others
8. Use a spreadsheet to model a simple process
9. Use a database to access information
10. Use on-line help and instructional materials

Concepts

1. Fundamentals of computers
2. Organization of information systems
3. Fundamentals of networks
4. Digital representation of information
5. Structuring information
6. Modeling and abstraction
7. Algorithmic thinking and programming
8. Universality
9. Limitations of Information Technology
10. Social impact of computers and technology

Capabilities

1. Engage in sustained reasoning
2. Manage complexity
3. Test a solution
4. Find problems in a faulty use of IT
5. Navigate a collection and assess quality of the information
6. Collaborate using IT
7. Communicate using IT about IT
8. Expect the unexpected
9. Anticipate technological change
10. Think abstractly about Information Technology

Projects

The Skills, Concepts, and Capabilities represent different kinds of knowledge that are co-equal in their contribution to IT fluency. They span separate dimensions of understanding. The overall strategy is to focus on the Skills instruction in the lab, the Concepts instruction in lecture/reading material, and the Capabilities instruction in lecture/lab demonstrations. The projects are the opportunity to use the three kinds of knowledge for a specific purpose. They illustrate IT as it is often applied in practice—to solve information processing tasks of a substantial nature.

A project is a multiweek assignment to achieve a specific IT goal. An example of a project is to create a database to track medical patients in a walk-in clinic, and to give a presentation to convince an audience that patient privacy has been preserved. Students apply a variety of Skills such as using database design software, Web searching, and presentation facilities. They rely on their understanding of Concepts such as database keys, table structure, and the Join query operator. And they use Capabilities such as reasoning, debugging, complexity management, testing, and others. The components are applied together to produce the final result, leading students to an integrated understanding of IT and preparing them for significant "real life" applications of IT. The labs can be found on the book's Web site.

The Programming Debate

Since the advent of computer literacy nearly three decades ago, there has been ongoing debate as to whether nonspecialists should be taught programming. Rational arguments have been offered on both sides, and thoughtful, well-intentioned adherents espouse each point of view. This book does *not* claim that one must be a professional programmer to be fluent. It sees programming's significance for the general population to be much more limited: to support algorithmic thinking, reasoning, debugging, and other components of Fluency. And learning the NRC committee's modest set of basic programming ideas—variable, conditional, iteration, etc.—won't make anyone a programmer. In the discussion following the publication of the report, the committee's "some, but not much" compromise on the programming question seems to have been widely accepted.

Fluency with Information Technology treats only the recommended handful of basic programming concepts. Nevertheless, the perception that programming is a difficult topic suitable only for mathematically strong "techies" raises the question of whether even this small set of concepts can be taught to a general student population. The answer is that it can and the students find it rewarding!

The programming can be found in Chapters 18, 20, and 21 (with case studies in Chapters 19 and 22).

Audience

This book is designed for freshmen "non-techies," students who will not be majoring in science, engineering, or math. ("Techies" benefit, too, but because "hot shots" can intimidate others, they should be discouraged from taking the class, or better, encouraged to join an accelerated track or honors section.) Except for one short paragraph about encryption, which can be skipped, no mathematical skills are required beyond arithmetic. There are no prerequisites.

Most students who take Fluency will have used email, surfed the Web, and perhaps word processed, and this is more than enough preparation to be successful. Students with no experience are advised to spend a few hours acquiring some exposure to IT prior to starting Fluency.

Chapter Dependencies

I have written *Fluency with Information Technology* so it can be taught in a variety of ways. In addition to the preliminary material in Chapters 1 and 2 and the wrap-up in Chapter 24, the overall structure of the book includes standalone chapters with few dependencies, as well as small chapter sequences devoted to a sustained topic. The sequences are:

> 3, 4, 5 networking, HTML, and information

> 8, 9, 10, 11 data representations, computers, and algorithms

> 13, 14, 15, 16 spreadsheets and database principles

> 18, 19, 20, 21 programming in JavaScript

One effective way to use this design is to present one of the chapter sequences as the basis for a project assignment. Then, while the students are working on the project—projects may span two or more weeks—material from standalone chapters is covered.

Though there are many sequences, three stand out to me as especially good ways to present the material:

> *Networking cycle.* The linear sequence of chapters is designed to begin with information and networking and progressively advance through computation and databases to JavaScript, where it returns to the networking theme. This is the basic Chapter 1 to Chapter 24 sequence, adjusted by local reordering to accommodate the timing of projects as needed.

> *Internet forward.* I teach Fluency in the 1–10, 18–22, 11–17, 23–24 order. This approach begins with information and HTML, progresses through to algorithms, then jumps to JavaScript to continue the Web page building theme, and finally wraps up with databases. The strategy is dictated to a large degree by the logistics of teaching the class in a quarter (10 weeks), and is recommended for that situation.

> *Traditional.* In this approach, the material is taught to parallel the time sequence of its creation. So, information representation and computers come well before networking. In this case, the order is 1–2, (23), 8–16, 3–7, 17–24. Chapter 23, which contains more philosophical content like the Turing test and Kasparov/Deep Blue chess tournament, might optionally be presented early for its foundational content.

Each of these strategies has a compelling pedagogical justification. Which is chosen depends more on instructor taste and class logistics than on any need to present material in a specific order.

Pedagogical Features

Learning Objectives: Each chapter opens with a list of the key concepts that readers should master after reading the chapter.

There are several boxed features that appear throughout the text to aid in your understanding of the material. They all begin with FIT, the acronym for Fluency with Information Technology. These are:

*fit*TIP: Practical hints and suggestions for every day computer use.

*fit*BYTE: Interesting facts and statistics.

*fit*CAUTION: Warnings and explanations of common mistakes.

Try It: Short, in-chapter exercises with solutions provided.

Checklists: A useful list of steps for completing a specific task.

Throughout the text, we also distinguish notable material by the following features:

Great *fit* Moments: A historical look at some of the major milestones in computing.

Great *fit* Minds: This feature takes a closer look at some of the influential pioneers in technology.

Reference material includes the following:

Glossary: Important words and phrases appear in boldface type throughout the text. A glossary of these terms is included at the end of the book.

Answers: Solutions are provided to the odd-numbered exercises for the multiple-choice and short-answer questions.

Appendix A: HTML reference including a chart of Web-safe colors.

Appendix B: JavaScript programming rules.

Appendix C: Bean Counter Program: A complete JavaScript and HTML example.

Appendix D: Memory Bank Program: A complete JavaScript and HTML example.

Appendix E: Smooth Motion Program: A complete JavaScript and HTML example.

Supplements

The companion Web site for *Fluency with Information Technology* at `www.aw.com/snyder/` is where you can find the various HTML sources, database designs, and JavaScript programs used in the textbook examples. Students are encouraged to retrieve these files to explore along with the text.

The following supplements are available to all users of this book:

> *Fluency Lab materials.* Learning Fluency is a hands-on activity, and so 14 complete laboratory exercises are available at the Web site.

> *JavaScript reference card*

> *Glossry flashcards.*

The following instructor supplements are available to qualified instructors only. Please contact your local Addison-Wesley sales representative, or send email to `aw.cse@aw.com` for information about how to access them.

> *PowerPoint slides.* A convenient resource for teaching Fluency is the collection of PowerPoint slides available online.

> *Instructor's manual with solutions.*

> *Test bank.*

> *Test generator.*

> *Excel labs with solutions.* Since understanding how to solve problems with Excel is an important skill, a series of problem-oriented labs using Excel are available.

In addition to the companion Web site, the course content is available in CourseCompass™, Blackboard™, and WebCT. CourseCompass is a nationally hosted, dynamic, interactive online course management system powered by Blackboard, leaders in the development of Internet-based learning tools. This easy-to-use and customizable program enables professors to tailor content and functionality to meet individual course needs. To see a demo, visit `www.coursecompass.com`. Please contact your local Addison-Wesley sales representative for more information on obtaining course content in these various formats.

Note to Students

Fluency is a somewhat unusual topic, making this a somewhat unusual book. There are two things that I think you should know about using this book.

> *Learn Skills in the lab.* Of the three kinds of knowledge that define Fluency—Skills, Concepts, and Capabilities—very little of the Skills material is included in this book. The Skills content, which is mostly about how to use contemporary computer applications, changes very rapidly, making it difficult to keep up to date. But the main reason few skills are included is that they are best learned in the lab, seated in front of a computer. The lab exercises, which are online and are up to date, provide an excellent introduction to contemporary applications. They provide great coverage of the Skills.

> *Study Fluency steadily.* If this book is successful, it will change the way you think, making you a better problem solver, better at reasoning, better at debugging, etc. These Capabilities are useful in IT and elsewhere

in life, so they make learning Fluency really worthwhile. But changing how you think won't happen by just putting the book under your pillow. It'll take some studying. To learn Fluency you must apply good study habits: read the book, do the end-of-chapter exercises (answers to odd-number exercises are printed at the back of the book), start on your assignments early, ask questions, etc. I think it's best if you spend some time in the lab studying Fluency (not reading email) *every day*, because it takes some time for the ideas to sink in. Students with good study habits tend to do well in Fluency class, and because it improves their problem-solving abilities, etc., they become even better students! It takes some discipline but it pays.

Finally, reading this book is enhanced by having a computer handy so you can try out examples. All files used here are available at `www.aw.com/snyder/`. Good luck! Writing this book has truly been a pleasure. I hope reading it is equally enjoyable.

Acknowledgments

Many people have contributed to this work. First to be thanked are my collaborators in the creation of the Fluency concept, the NRC Committee on Computer Literacy—Al Aho, Marcia Linn, Arnie Packer, Allen Tucker, Jeff Ullman, and Andy van Dam. Special thanks go to Herb Lin of the NRC staff who assisted throughout the Fluency effort, tirelessly and in his usual great good humor. Two enthusiastic supporters of Fluency—Bill Wulf of the National Academy of Engineering and John Cherniavski of the National Science Foundation—have continually supported this effort in more ways than I am aware. It has been a pleasure to know and work with this team.

As the material was developed for this book, many have contributed: Ken Yasuhara and Brian Bannon, teaching assistants on the first offering of CSE100, contributed in innumerable ways and injected a needed dose of practicality into my ideas. Grace Whiteaker, Alan Borning, and Batya Friedman have been generous with their ideas regarding Fluency. Martin Dickey of CSE and Mark Donovan of UWired have been constant sources of support. The original offerings of CSE100 benefited greatly from contributions by Nana Lowell, Anne Zald, Mike Eisenberg, and Fred Videon. Colleagues who have contributed include Frank Tompa, Martin Tompa, Carl Ebeling, Brian Kerninghan, Dotty Smith, Calvin Lin, and David Mizell.

I am particularly grateful for the keen insights and valuable feedback from the reviewers of this book. For this edition, my thanks go to: Steve Hodges, Cabrillo College; Thomas Parks, Colgate University; Roger Priebe, Univeristy of Texas; Glenn Ray, University of Pittsburgh, and Carol Schwartz, Rutgers University. Also, the following, who have provided helpful reviews: Nazih Abdallah, University of Central Florida; Robert M. Aiken, Temple University; Diane M. Cassidy, University of North Carolina at Charlotte; Anne Condon, University of British Columbia; Lee D. Cornell, Minnesota State University, Mankato; Nicholas Cravotta, University of

California, Berkeley; Gordon Davies, Open University; Peter J. Denning, George Mason University; Rory J. DeSimone, University of Florida; Richard C. Detmer, Middle Tennessee State University; David L. Doss, Illinois State University; John P. Dougherty, Haverford College; Philip East, University of Northern Iowa; Michael B. Eisenberg, University of Washington; Robert S. Fenchel, University of Wisconsin, Madison; Michael Gildersleeve, University of New Hampshire; Jennifer Golbeck; Michael H. Goldner; Esther Grassian, UCLA College Library; Raymond Greenlaw, Armstrong Atlantic State University; A. J. Hurst, Monash University, Australia; Malcolm G. Lane, James Madison University; Doris K. Lidtke, Towson University; Wen Liu, ITT Technical Institute; Daniela Marghitu, Auburn University; C. Dianne Martin, George Washington University; Peter B. Miller, University of Virginia; Namdar Mogharreban, Southern Illinois University, Carbondale; Paul M. Mullins, Slippery Rock University; David R. Musicant, Carleton College; Alexander Nakhimovsky, Colgate University; Brenda C. Parker, Middle Tennessee State University; Dee Parks, Appalachian State University; Laurie J. Patterson, University of North Carolina, Wilmington; Roger Priebe, University of Texas at Austin; Paul Quan, Albuquerque Technical Vocational Institute; John Rosenberg, Monash University, Australia; Robert T. Ross, California Polytechnic State University; Zhizhang Shen, Plymouth State College; Robert J. Shive, Jr., Millsaps College; Patrick Tantalo, University of California, Santa Cruz; and Mark Urban-Lurain, Michigan State University.

Thank you to Jim McKeown for contributing to the end of-chapter exercises.

The Fluency material has been a topic of discussion with many international colleagues. Discussions with Hans Hinterberger, John Rosenberg, and John Hirsch have been especially valuable in critiquing the material from an overseas perspective. Other helpful international commentary came from Anne Condon, Hannes Jonsson, Jerg Nievergelt, Clark Thomberson, Barbara Thomberson, Ewan Tempero, and Kazuo Iwama.

Among the many thoughtful computer users who have either generously described their misunderstandings about IT or patiently listened to my explanations about IT, I wish to thank Esther Snyder, Helene Fowler, Judy Watson, Brendan Healey, Victory Grund, Shelley Burr, Ken Burr, and Noelle Lamb.

It is my great pleasure to thank my editors, Michael Hirsch and Pat Mahtani. Their enthusiasm for the project and their devotion to perfection have been inspirational. And working with them is fun. Joyce Cosentino Wells has done a fantastic job with the design. Others of the Addison-Wesley team to whom I owe thanks are Michelle Brown, Meredith Gertz, Lindsey Triebel, and Dana Lopreato. And especially, thanks go to Gillian Hall.

Finally, my wife Julie, and sons, Dan and Dave, have been patient, encouraging, and, most important, a continual source of good humor throughout this effort. It is with my deepest appreciation that I thank them for everything.

—Larry Snyder
June 2005

For Julie Ann, Dan, and Dave

CONTENTS

The Master said: "To learn something and then put it into practice at the right time. Is this not a joy?"

—THE ANALECTS OF CONFUCIUS

part 1

BECOMING SKILLED AT INFORMATION TECHNOLOGY

OUR STUDY of information technology begins with an intro-duction to both information and technology. If your contact with computers has been limited, an introduction is essential. If you are like most readers, you've used computers enough to be familiar with email, Web surfing, and perhaps word processing; but, you think, there must be many other cool and interesting ways to use information technology. You're right! And establishing a firm foun-dation is the fastest way to move forward.

In Part 1 we focus on becoming skilled at using an Internet-connected personal computer. You will learn new applications—in fact, you will *learn how to learn* new applications—and you will dis-cover new ways to use the Internet and World Wide Web. By the end of Part 1 you will be able to apply information technology to your studies, work, and recreation.

Our goal is to become confident and skilled computer users. You can achieve this goal by combining the information in Part 1 with daily computer and Internet use. We present practical, useful information that requires practice and use, making Fluency a sub-ject in which you can immediately apply what you learn.

1

TERMS OF ENDEARMENT
Defining Information Technology

learning objectives

> Explain why it's important to know the right word

> Define basic hardware and software terms

> Describe how the mouse clicks a button

> Define and give examples of "idea" terms

> Develop the ability to think more analytically

  • Compare speed records

  • Express an improvement in speed as a factor

> Explain the benefits of analytical thinking

TERMS OF ENDEARMENT
Defining Information Technology

It would appear that we have [as a society] reached the limits of what it is possible to achieve with computer technology, although one should be careful with such statements as they tend to sound pretty silly in 5 years.

—JOHN VON NEUMANN,
COMPUTER PIONEER 1947

TO BECOME Fluent, we need to learn the language of information technology (IT). The people who create IT are notorious for using acronyms, jargon, and everyday words in unusual ways. Acronyms like WYSIWYG (WHIZ·zee·wig), "what you see is what you get," are often meaningless even after you learn what the letters stand for. (We'll come back to the WYSIWYG story later.) Jargon like "clicking around," for navigating through an application or a series of Web pages, is meaningful only after you have actually done it. And an everyday term like **window**, which was originally chosen to suggest the idea of a portal to the computer, may no longer be an appropriate metaphor for the sophisticated computer concept. It is not surprising that coming across these terms for the first time is confusing. But is such techno-speak any weirder than, say, medical or musical terms? (For example, *bili-rubin* and *hemi-demisemiquaver* are odd words unless you're a doctor or a musician.) Technology, like medicine and music, makes more sense when we are familiar with the vocabulary.

Our first goal is to understand why learning the right term is essential to any new endeavor. Next, we ask some simple questions about computers (like "Where's the Start button?") to review terms you may already know. But, for almost every familiar term, there is a new word or idea to learn. We also introduce some new words for the physical and computational parts of the computer. These are mostly terms you have probably heard before; but learning exactly what they mean will help you make them part of your everyday vocabulary. Along the way, we explain basic ideas like how buttons are created and how they are clicked. This starts to demystify the computer's virtual world and introduces the ideas of process and algorithm. Then we introduce the "idea" terms of IT, words like *abstraction* and *generalization*. These terms refer to deep concepts, and devoting a few minutes to understanding them will pay off throughout the rest of our Fluency study. Finally, we close with interesting stories about how people and computers have advanced, as we become more analytical thinkers.

WHY KNOW JUST THE RIGHT WORD

IT adopts many strange terms because it is filled with new ideas, concepts, and devices that never before existed. The inventors name them so they can describe and explain their ideas to others. Acronyms are common, because as engineers and scientists develop ideas, they often abbreviate them with the letters of the concept's description. The abbreviation sticks, and if the concept is important, its use extends beyond the laboratory. For example, when engineers invented the "small computer system interface," they abbreviated it SCSI. People began to pronounce it "skuzzy" rather than saying S-C-S-I. Naming-by-abbreviation creates a terminology full of acronyms. Critics call it "alphabet soup." But we can understand the terms once we understand what all the letters stand for. For example, ROM is short for "read-only memory." Even without knowing much about computers, you can guess that ROM is a special type of memory that can be read but not written to.

Using the right word at the right time is one characteristic of an educated person. Perhaps the best term to learn to use well is the French (now also English) term *le mot juste* (luh·MO·joost), which means the right word or exact phrasing.

There are two important reasons for knowing and using *le mot juste*. First, understanding the terminology is basic to learning any new subject. When we learn what new words mean, we learn the ideas and concepts that they stand for. Our brains seem to be organized so that when we name a thing or idea, we remember it. For example, in ice hockey, *icing* is the term for hitting the puck across the blue lines and the opponent's goal line. We might not even notice this amid all the passing and slap shots. By knowing this new definition for the familiar word *icing*, we start watching for it, increasing our understanding and enjoyment of the game. Precision in using the term means precision in understanding the idea. Eventually the word stops sounding weird and becomes a part of our vocabulary. At that point, we use the right word without even thinking about it.

The second reason for knowing and using the right word is to communicate with others. If we use terms properly, people understand us. We are able to ask questions and receive help—something everyone starting out in a field needs to do. When seeking help in information technology, using the right word is especially important because we often must rely on email, the telephone, or an online help facility. We have to be precise and articulate because no one is by our side to help us describe what we need. A goal of Fluency is to be able to get help from such resources. The ability to use *le mot juste* allows us to communicate, get help, and ultimately, be self-reliant.

You can learn vocabulary by reading a computer dictionary, of course, but that's *waaay* too boring. Instead, we introduce the basic terminology by asking some simple IT questions that have unexpected answers.

● WHERE'S THE START BUTTON?

Most computers are on all the time, which is why screen savers were invented. Screen savers—animations such as a kitten prancing around the screen or a changing geometric design—are programs that sleep when the computer is in use and wake up when the computer is idle. These moving images "save the screen." Without them, a single, unchanging image can "burn" into the screen, permanently changing the phosphorous surface and creating a "ghost" of the image, which interferes with viewing. (Recent technological advances have made burn-in less of a problem and many computers simply turn off the screen when the system is idle.) You can reactivate the computer by moving or clicking the mouse, or by pressing any key.

If computers are usually on, why bother to learn where the Start button is? Because sometimes they are off, and as we will see later, we might need to **cycle power**—turn the computer off and then back on. To know where to look for the power button, we need to know how a computer is organized.

Two Basic Organizations: Monolithic or Component

Some computers are sold as **components** with a separate monitor, computer and hard drive, speakers, and other devices. (We'll discuss the individual devices later.) Many desktop PCs are organized this way. The **monolithic** package, like an iMac or a laptop, has all the devices bundled together, as shown in Figure 1.1(a). The component approach lets you mix and match parts to fit your needs, as shown in Figure 1.1(b). The all-in-one monolithic design is simpler because manufacturers decide for you which components will form a balanced, effective system. Laptops are monolithic, of course, because it is inconvenient to carry around multiple parts.

In a monolithic design, the **power switch** (⏻) is on the chassis or, often with Macs, on the keyboard. For component systems, the power switch is usually on a separate box near the display containing the CD and/or floppy disk drives. Most

(a)   (b)

Figure 1.1. Examples of the (a) monolithic and (b) component systems.

component monitors also have their own power switch, but it controls power only for the monitor, not the whole computer.

The Monitor

The **monitor** is a video screen like a TV, of course, but there are many differences. Unlike passive TVs, computers are interactive, so the monitor becomes more like a blackboard showing the information created by both the computer and the user as they communicate. Modern monitors are **bit-mapped**, meaning that they display information stored in (the bits of) the computer's memory, as illustrated in Figure 1.2. TVs generally display images live or from recorded tape, captured with a camera. The big, bulky monitors are **cathode ray tubes** (CRTs), whereas the slim, flat displays are **liquid crystal displays** (LCDs).

To emphasize the contrast between TVs and computers, notice that television can only show "reality"—the images *recorded* through a camera's lens. A computer creates the images it displays in its memory; the images don't have to exist in physical reality. The world that a computer creates is called **virtual reality**.

Figure 1.2. An enlargement of a monitor's display of the word bitmap and the corresponding bits for each pixel.

Cables

The components and the computer must be connected to each other and they must be connected to an electrical power source. For power-hungry devices like monitors, separate **power cables** are usually used, which is why there is a separate power switch. For simple devices like the keyboard or mouse, the **signal** and power wires are combined into one cable. To help us plug in the cables correctly, the computer's sockets and the cable's plugs are usually labeled with icons, as shown in Figure 1.3. So, we simply match up the icons.

Computer component plugs fit into their sockets in only one way. After you figure out which way the plug goes in, insert it into the socket gently to make sure that the pins (the stiff wires making the connections) align and do not bend. Once the plug is inserted, push it in firmly.

*fit***CAUTION**

Damage Control. When connecting computer components (or other electronic devices), plug in the power connection last. When disconnecting, remove the power connection first. Remember PILPOF—plug in last, pull out first.

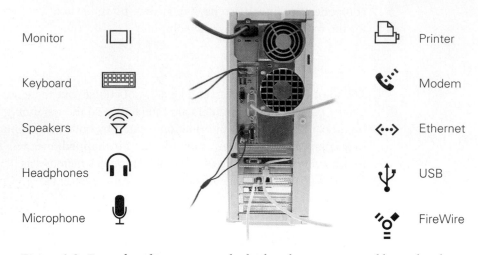

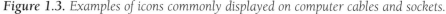

Figure 1.3. Examples of icons commonly displayed on computer cables and sockets.

Colors: RGB

Combining different amounts of three colors of light—red, green, and blue (RGB)—produces the colors you see on your computer monitor, as shown in Figure 1.4. The computer tells the monitor the right proportions of light to display with signals sent through the RGB cable. Any color can be created with some combination of intensities of these three colors. In computer applications, when we select a color from a "palette"—to change the color of text, for example—we are really telling the computer how much of these three colors of light to use.

Pixels

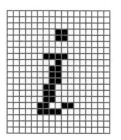

The monitor's screen is divided into a grid of small units called **picture elements** or **pixels**. A pixel is about the size of the dot on an *i* in 10-point type. (Check this out on your monitor.) The computer displays information on the screen by drawing each pixel in the color designated for the figure or image. For example, in text, the pixels forming the words are colored black and the surrounding pixels are colored white. The size of the grid in pixels—1024 × 768 is typical for a laptop—is important because the more pixels in each row and column, the higher the resolution of the screen image, and the smoother and crisper the result.

The computer must first create in its memory everything displayed on the screen, pixel by pixel. For computer-animated movies like *Toy Story*, creating images of dancing toys is extremely complex. But the appearance of reality that we see on a computer screen is much easier to generate, as we demonstrate in the *fit*BYTE beginning on the next page.

*fit*TIP   **Image Change.** The size of the pixel grid displayed on the screen can be increased or decreased using the Control Panel for the Display (Windows) or Monitor (Mac).

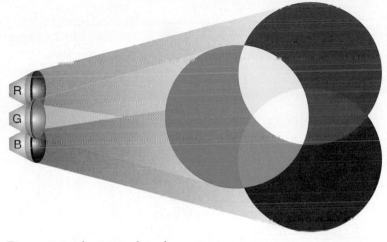

Figure 1.4. *The RGB color scheme.*

A Virtual Button >>

It is simple to color the screen's pixels to make a figure that looks like a believable button. On a medium-gray background, the designer colors the top and left sides of a rectangle white and the bottom and right sides black. This makes the interior of the rectangle appear to project out from the surface because the white part is highlighted and the dark part looks like a shadow from a light source at the upper left. (If the figure doesn't look much like a button, look at it from a distance.) There is nothing special about the medium-gray/white/black combination except that it gives the lighted/shadowed effect. Other colors work, too. And, by using colors with less contrast, it is possible to give the button a different "feel"; for example, less metallic, as shown in Figure 1.5.

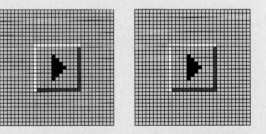

Figure 1.5. *Two virtual buttons with different "feels."*

THE ILLUSION OF BUTTON MOTION

To show that the button has been pressed, the designer reverses the black and white colors and translates the icon one position down and to the right. To **translate** a figure means to move it, unchanged, to a new position. Because our brains assume that the light source's position stays the same, the reversal of the colors changes the highlights and shadows to make the inside of the rectangle appear to be pushed in. The translation of the icon creates motion that our eyes notice, completing the illusion that the button is pressed, as shown in Figure 1.6. Notice however, that the translation of the icon down and to the right is not really a correct motion for a button "pushed into the screen." But accuracy is less important than the perception of motion.

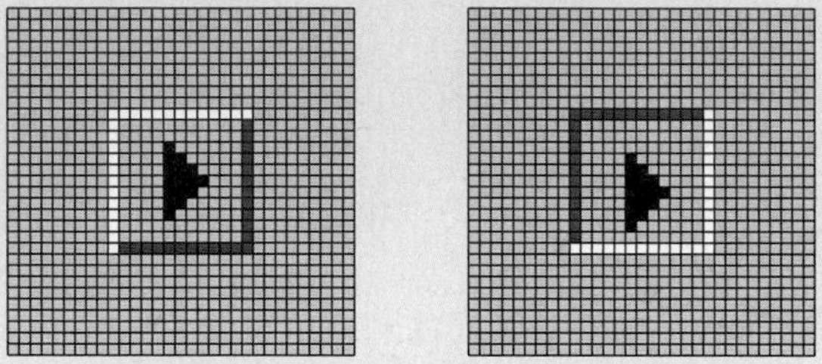

Figure 1.6. *Pushing a button.*

There is no real button anywhere inside the computer. The bits of the computer's memory have been set so that when they are displayed on the screen, the pixels appear to be a picture of a button. The computer can change the bits when necessary so that the next time they are displayed, the button looks as if it has been pushed in. The designer can add a "click" sound that makes the illusion even more real. But there is still no button.

PRESSING A VIRTUAL BUTTON

If there is only a picture of a button, how can we "click" it with the mouse? That's a good question, which we can answer without becoming too technical.

We begin with the mouse pointer. The mouse pointer is a white arrow point with a black border and, like the button, must be created by the computer. When we move the mouse, the computer determines which direction it is moving and redraws the pointer translated a short distance in that direction. By repeatedly redrawing the pointer in new positions that are redisplayed rapidly, the computer produces the illusion that the pointer moves smoothly across the screen. It's the same idea as cartoon flip-books or motion pictures: A series of still pictures, progressively different and rapidly displayed, creates the illusion of motion. The frequency of display changes is called the **refresh rate** and, like motion-picture frames, is typically 30 times per second. At that rate, the human eye sees the sequence of still frames as smooth motion.

As the mouse pointer moves across the screen, the computer keeps track of which pixel is at the point of the arrow. In Figure 1.7, the computer records the position by the row and column coordinates because the pixel grid is like graph paper. So (141, 1003) in Figure 1.7(a) means that the pixel pointed out is in the 141st pixel row from the top of the screen and at the 1003rd pixel column from the left side of the screen. With each new position, the coordinates are updated. When the mouse is clicked, as shown in Figure 1.7(d), the computer determines which button the mouse pointer is hovering over and then redraws the button to look pushed in.

COORDINATING THE BUTTON AND THE MOUSE

How does the computer know which button the mouse pointer is hovering over? It keeps a list of every button drawn on the screen, recording the coordinates of the but-

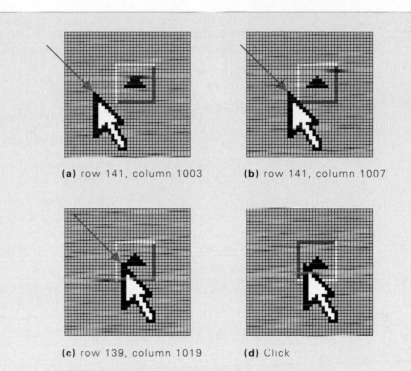

(a) row 141, column 1003   **(b)** row 141, column 1007

(c) row 139, column 1019   **(d)** Click

Figure 1.7. *Mouse pointer moving toward (a, b), pointing to (c), and then clicking (d), a button; the coordinates of the point of the pointer are given by their row, column positions.*

ton's upper-left and lower-right corners. In Figure 1.8, the button has its upper-left corner at pixel (132, 1010) and its lower-right corner at pixel (145, 1022). The two corners, call them (x_1, y_1) and (x_2, y_2), determine the position of the rectangle that defines the button: the top row of white pixels is in row x_1, the left-side column of white pixels is in column y_1, the bottom row of black pixels is in row x_2, and the right-side column of black pixels is in column y_2.

Now, if the mouse pointer's point has a row coordinate between x_1 and x_2, the pointer is somewhere between the top and bottom of the button, although it may be

$(x_1, y_1) = (132, 1010)$

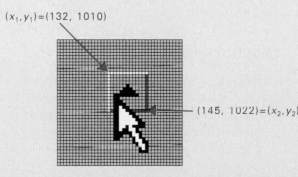

$(145, 1022) = (x_2, y_2)$

Figure 1.8. *A button's location is completely determined by the positions of its upper-left and lower-right corners.*

to the left or right of the button rather than on top of it. But if the pointer's point also has a column coordinate between y_1 and y_2, the pointer is between the left and right sides of the button; that is, it is somewhere on the button. So, for each button with coordinates (x_1, y_1) and (x_2, y_2), the computer tests whether

$$x_1 < \text{row coordinate of mouse pointer point} < x_2$$
and
$$y_1 < \text{column coordinate of mouse pointer point} < y_2$$

are *both* true. If so, the mouse pointer's point is over that button and the button is redrawn in the "clicked configuration." This tells the user that the command has been received and the program performs the appropriate action.

Creating a button and keeping track of the positions of the button and the mouse pointer may seem like a lot of work, but it makes using a computer easier (and more fun) for us. The metaphor of pressing a button to cause an action is so natural that software developers believe it's worth the trouble to make buttons.

WHERE IS THE COMPUTER?

This may seem like an odd question, but it's not. In casual conversation, most of us call the monitor "the computer." Technically speaking, we're usually wrong. If we are referring to a laptop or iMac, the part that actually does the computing *is* inside the same unit as the monitor, so in those cases we're right. But for component systems, the computer is not in the monitor unit, but rather in a separate box on the floor or somewhere else nearby. Calling the monitor the computer is not so much a mistake as an acknowledgment that the monitor is our interface to the computer, wherever it is.

In the component approach, the computer and most of its parts (for example, hard disk, floppy disk drive, and CD drive) are packaged together in a box called the **processor box**, though it often has a fancy marketing name (for example, mini-tower) that has no technical meaning; see Figure 1.9. In the monolithic approach, the associated disks and drives are in the same package as the monitor. It's as if the monitor were attached to the processor box. The information in this section applies to both component and monolithic systems.

Motherboard

Inside the processor box is the **motherboard**, a printed circuit board containing most of the circuitry of a personal computer system, as shown in Figure 1.10. The name comes from the fact that smaller printed circuit boards, sometimes called **daughter boards** but more often called **cards**, are plugged into the motherboard for added functionality. A motherboard is impressive to look at with all of its fine wire patterns, colorful resistors, economy of space, and so forth. (Ask your computer dealer to show you one—it's safer than looking at the one in your computer

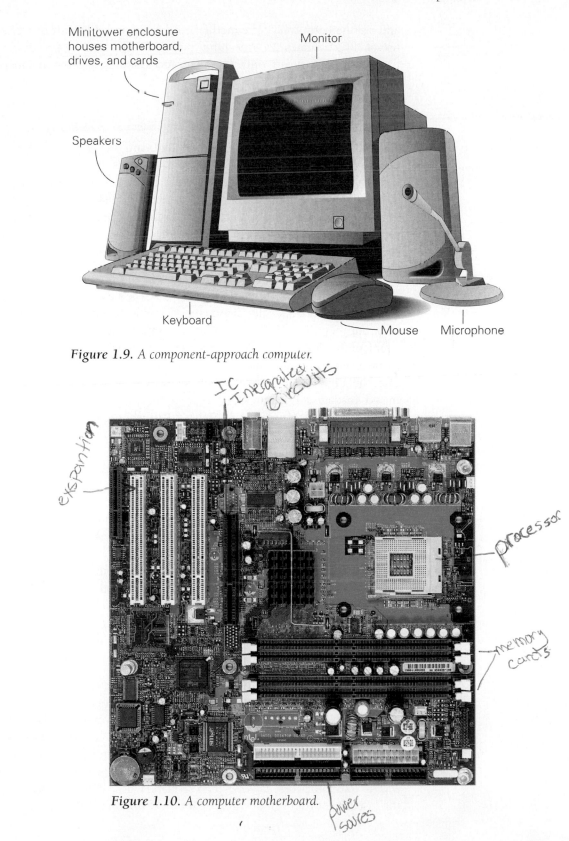

Minitower enclosure
houses motherboard,
drives, and cards

Monitor

Speakers

Keyboard

Mouse

Microphone

Figure 1.9. *A component-approach computer.*

IC Integrated Circuits

expansion

processor

memory cards

power source

Figure 1.10. *A computer motherboard.*

and risking harm to it.) The motherboard is a **printed circuit** or PC board. (This use of "PC" predates "PC" meaning "personal computer" by decades.) Of the many parts on this PC board, only the microprocessor chip and the memory interest us at the moment.

Microprocessor

The **microprocessor**, found on the motherboard, is the part of a personal computer system that computes. The microprocessor is involved in every activity of the system, everything from making the mouse pointer appear to move around the screen to locating information stored on the hard disk. The microprocessor is the "smart" part of the system, so engineers often describe the other parts of a computer as "dumb." It is surprisingly easy for a computer to be "smart," as we will see. Eventually, we will even ask, "Can a computer think?"

The "micro" part of microprocessor is archaic and no longer accurate. The term "microprocessor" was adopted around 1980 when all of the circuitry for a computer first fit onto a single silicon chip. These were technically computer processors, but they were small and primitive compared to the mainframes and the "minicomputers" of the day, so they were called *micro*processors. But improvements came so quickly that in a few years microprocessors were more powerful than the largest computers of 1980. Today's microprocessors are fast, highly optimized, loaded with features, and very sophisticated. In fact, microprocessors spend most of their time doing nothing, just waiting for us. Because there is nothing "micro" about today's microprocessors, we will simply use the term **processor** for the rest of this book.

Memory

The **memory** of a computer is where a program and its data are located while the program is running. For example, when you are using a word processor, the word processing program and the document being edited are stored in the computer's memory. (When they're not in memory, programs and data are stored on the hard disk; see the next section.) Computer memory is also called **RAM**, short for **random access memory**. The basic unit of memory is a **byte**, which is described in Chapter 8. Today's personal computers have millions of bytes of RAM memory, or **megabytes** (from the Greek prefix **mega-** meaning million). See Figure 9.9 in Chapter 9 for a list of prefixes.

There are two basic ways to locate and retrieve, or *access* information: sequential and random. Information stored sequentially is arranged in a line, so that when you want to find a specific item, you have to skip everything else stored before it, as shown in Figure 1.11. Cassette tapes, VCR tapes, etc. are examples of **sequential access**. **Random access** means that any item can be retrieved directly. Finding dictionary entries, library books, and phone numbers are examples of random access. Random access is faster than sequential access, as anyone trying to locate the last scene of a TV show on a VCR tape knows.

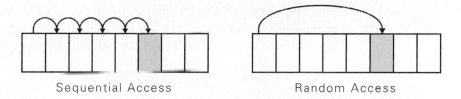

Sequential Access   Random Access

Figure 1.11. *Sequential versus random access.*

Hard Disk

The **hard disk** is not really part of the computer—technically it is a high-capacity, persistent storage peripheral device. But it is so fundamental to personal computer systems that it's helpful to think of it as a basic part. The hard disk is also referred to as the **hard drive**, and was once simply known as a **disk** before floppy disks were invented. The hard disk stores programs and data when they are not in immediate use by a computer. Disks are made from an iron compound that can be magnetized. Because the magnetism remains even when the power is off, the encoded information is still there when the power comes back on. So a disk is said to be *permanent* or *persistent* storage. A hard disk is usually located in the same box as the processor, because without access to permanent storage, the processor is crippled.

The hard disk looks like a small stack of metal washers with an arm that can sweep across and between them, as shown in Figure 1.12. The "popping" or "clicking" sound we sometimes hear is the arm moving back and forth as it accesses information on various tracks of the disk.

Figure 1.12. *A hard disk.*

`Saving from RAM to Hard Disk.` Successful computer users save their work regularly. For example, when writing a term paper using a word processor, run the **Save** command every half hour or perhaps after completing a few pages or a section. Saving moves the information, that is, your term paper, from the RAM memory to the hard disk memory. This action is important because of the differences between the two types of memory.

Recall that hard disk memory is made from a magnetic material that "remembers," even when the power is off. Today's RAM memory, however, is made from integrated circuit (IC) technology, informally called microchips. One property of IC memory is that it is volatile, meaning that the information is lost when the power is turned off. That is, when IC memory loses power, it "forgets." This difference wouldn't matter if computers didn't fail. But they do.

When a computer crashes, that is, when it no longer works correctly or it stops running entirely, it must be restarted, a process called rebooting. If the computer's not working correctly, the **Restart** command will run. The first step in restarting is to erase the memory, causing the information stored in the RAM to be lost. If it's not working at all, then the power must be cycled—turned off, and then turned on again—also causing the information stored in the RAM to be lost, because IC memory is volatile. Either way, anything that was in the RAM, such as the latest version of your term paper, will be lost. Only the copy that is on the hard disk, which is the copy from the last time it was saved, is available when the computer "comes up." All the work since the last save is lost.

Crashes are not common, but they happen. Frequently saving your file limits the amount of work you will have to redo if your computer crashes.

HOW SOFT IS SOFTWARE?

The term hardware predates computers by centuries. Originally it meant metal items used in construction, like hinges and nails. The word software did not exist until computers were invented.

Software

Software is a collective term for computer programs. The name contrasts with hardware, of course, but what does it mean for software to be "soft"? When a computer function is implemented in software, the computer performs the operation by following instructions. A program that figures out your income taxes is an example of software. If a computer function is implemented in **hardware**, the computer performs the operations directly with wires and transistors. (We say it is **hard-wired**.) The multiplication operation is an example of hardware implemented functions.

The difference between "hard" and "soft" is like the difference between an innate ability, such as coughing, and a learned ability, such as reading. Innate abilities are "built in" biologically, and they're impossible to change, like hardware. Learned abilities are easily changed and expanded, like software. Typically, only the most primitive operations like multiplication are implemented in hardware; everything else is software. (Computers don't *learn* to perform soft operations, of course, the way we learn to read. Rather, they are simply given the instructions and told to follow them.)

fit BYTE

> **The Hard Reality.** The difference between hardware and software was dramatically illustrated in 1994 when a bug was discovered in the hard-wired divide operation of Intel's Pentium processor, an approximately $200 chip. Though the wrong answers were rare and tiny, the error had to be fixed. If divide had been implemented in software, as had been the usual approach in computing's early years, Intel could have sent everyone a simple patch for $1 or $2. But hardware cannot be changed, so the Pentium chips had to be recalled at a total cost estimated at about $500 million.

Algorithms and Programs

An **algorithm** is a precise and systematic method for solving a problem. Another term for a systematic method is a **process**. Some familiar algorithms are arithmetic operations like addition, subtraction, multiplication, and division; the process for sending a greeting card; and searching for a phone number. The method used for determining when a mouse pointer hovers over a button is an algorithm. Because an algorithm's instructions are written down for some other agent (a person or a computer) to follow, precision is important.

We learn some algorithms, like arithmetic. Sometimes we figure out algorithms on our own, like finding phone numbers. In Chapter 10, we introduce **algorithmic thinking**, the act of thinking up algorithms. Writing out the steps of an algorithm is called **programming**. **Programs** are simply algorithms written in a specific programming language for a specific set of conditions.

When we ask a computer to do something for us, we ask it to **run** a program. This is literally what we ask when we click on the icon for an application like Internet Explorer. We are saying, "Run the program from the Microsoft company to browse the Internet." *Run* is a term that has been used since the invention of computers. But *execute* is a slightly better term because it emphasizes an important property of computing.

Execute

A computer **executes** a program when it *performs* instructions. The word **execute** means to follow a set of orders exactly as they are written. Computer pioneers used the word *orders* for what we now call instructions. Orders tell the computer to act in a specific way. When orders are given, the faithful agent is *not* supposed to think. "Following instructions literally" is what computers do when they run programs; it is that aspect that makes "execute" a slightly better term than "run."

In addition to run and execute, **interpret** is also a correct term for following a program's instructions, as explained in Chapter 9.

Boot

Finally, the term **booting** means to start a computer and **rebooting** means to restart it. Because booting most often happens after a catastrophic error or a crash, you might guess that the term is motivated by frustration—we want to kick the computer like a football. Actually, the term *booting* comes from *bootstrap*. Computers were originally started by an operator who entered a few instructions into the computer's empty memory using console push buttons. Those instructions told the computer to read in a few more instructions—a very simple operating system—from punch cards. This operating system could then read in the instructions of the real operating system from magnetic tape, similar to a VCR tape. Finally, the computer was able to start doing useful work. This incremental process was called **bootstrapping**, from the phrase "pulling yourself up by your bootstraps," because the computer basically started itself. Today the instructions to start a computer are stored on a microchip called the boot ROM.

● THE WORDS FOR IDEAS

Although understanding the physical parts of IT—monitors, motherboards, and memory—seems very important, we are not too concerned with them here. Instead, we will focus on *concept* words, such as those discussed in this section.

"Abstract"

One of the most important "idea" words used in this book is the verb *abstract*. It has several meanings. In British mysteries, *to abstract* means *to remove*, as in *to steal*: "The thief abstracted the pearl necklace while the jeweler looked at the diamond ring." In information technology, *to abstract* also means to remove, but the thing being removed is not physical. The thing being removed is an idea or a process, and it is extracted from some form of information.

To **abstract** is to remove the basic concept, idea, or process from a situation. The removed concept is usually expressed in another, more succinct and usually more general form, called an **abstraction**.

We are familiar with abstraction in this sense. Parables and fables, which teach lessons in the form of stories, require us to abstract the essential point of the story. When we are told about a fox who can't reach a bunch of grapes and so calls them sour, we abstract the idea from the story: When people fail to reach a goal, they often decide they didn't want to reach that goal in the first place.

Notice two key points here. First, many but not all of the details of the story are irrelevant to the concept. When abstracting, we must decide which details of the story are relevant and which are irrelevant. The "grapes" and the "fox" are unimportant, but "failure" is important. Being able to tell the difference between important and unimportant details is essential to understanding the point of a story, and to abstraction in general. Second, the idea—the abstraction—has meaning beyond the story. The point of repeating the parable, of course, is to convey an idea that applies to many situations.

"Generalize"

A process similar to abstraction is to recognize the common idea in two or more situations. Recognizing how different situations have something basic in common is why we create parables, rules, and so on.

To **generalize** is to express an idea, concept, or process that applies to many situations. The statement summing up that idea is called a **generalization**.

For example, most of us notice that twisting a faucet handle left turns water on and twisting it right turns it off. Not always—some water taps have only a single "joy stick" handle, and others have horizontal bars that pull forward. But since it's true most of the time, we generalize that "on" is to the left and "off" is to the right. Perhaps we also notice that twisting lids, caps, screws, and nuts to the left usually loosens them, and turning them to the right usually tightens them. Again, we generalize that left means loosen and right means tighten. We probably also generalize that both situations are examples of the same thing! A generalization of generalizations.

Noticing patterns and generalizing about them is a very valuable habit. Although generalizations do not always apply, recognizing them gives us a way to begin in a new, but similar situation.

"Operationally Attuned"

Another term related to extracting concepts and processes refers to being aware of how a gadget works. To be **operationally attuned** is to apply what we know about how a device or system works to simplify its use.

For example, we previously generalized that with few exceptions, all caps, lids, screws, and nuts tighten by turning right and loosen by turning left. We might know this intuitively, but knowing it *explicitly* makes us operationally attuned. Knowing this fact as a rule means that when a lid or nut is stuck, we can twist it very hard, certain that we are forcing it to loosen rather than tighten. Being operationally attuned makes us more effective.

The term operationally attuned is introduced here to emphasize that thinking about how IT works makes it simpler to use. We don't expect to be experts on all of the technology—few are. But by asking ourselves, "How does this work?" and using what we learn by thinking about the answer, we will be more successful at applying IT. Our Fluency study focuses on learning enough to answer many of the "How does this work?" questions well enough to succeed.

"Mnemonic"

Mnemonic is a rather unusual term that we use in IT and in other fields as well. The silent *m* implies that it's a word with an unusual past.

Tuning In >>

In our daily lives, we use hundreds of devices, systems, and processes. For some, like a car ignition, we quickly learn which way to turn the key because it only turns in one direction. We don't think about how it works. Using it becomes a habit. Other gadgets, however, have more leeway, and for them it helps to be attuned to their operation. One example is a deadbolt lock, which moves a metal bar from the door to the doorframe to lock the door. Thinking about how the lock works tells us whether the door is locked or not. Referring to Figure 1.13(a), notice which way the knob is turned. By visualizing the internal works of the lock, we can imagine that the top of the knob is attached to the bar. When the knob is pointing left, the bar must be pulled back—that is, unlocked. When the knob is pointing right, the bar is extended, so the door is locked. We may not know how the lock really works, but explaining its operation in our own terms means that we can see at a distance whether the door is locked or unlocked. It might save us from getting up from the sofa to check if the door is locked.

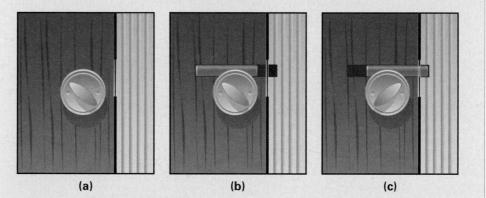

(a)   (b)   (c)

Figure 1.13. Deadbolt lock. (a) The external view. (b) Internal components, unlocked. (c) Internal components, locked. Thinking about how the deadbolt works allows us to see at a glance whether the door is locked or not.

A mnemonic (ni·MĂ·nik) is an aid for remembering something. The reminder can take many forms, such as pronounceable words or phrases. We remember the five Great Lakes with the acronym HOMES—Huron, Ontario, Michigan, Erie, and Superior. Earlier in this chapter, we mentioned PILPOF—plug in last, pull out first—for remembering when to connect and disconnect the power cable.

There are many IT details that we need to know only occasionally, like when to connect power. They're not worth memorizing, but they're inconvenient to look up. So, if we can think of a mnemonic that helps us remember the details when we need them, using technology is simpler.

ANALYTICAL THINKING

Using the right terms makes learning IT simpler. Becoming more analytical is an equally valuable habit to acquire. When we say that the world record in the mile run has improved or that computer performance has improved, we are making very weak statements. They simply assert that things have changed over time for the better. But has the change been infinitesimally small or gigantic? How does the change compare to other changes? Since we can easily find information on the Internet, we can compare an earlier measure of performance with a recent one. Thinking analytically is essential to becoming Fluent in IT, but it is also useful in our other studies, our careers, and our lives.

Mile Runs

When Moroccan runner Hicham El Guerrouj broke the world record on July 7, 1999, the news reports trumpeted that he "smashed," "eclipsed," and "shattered" the world record set six years earlier by Noureddine Moreceli of Algeria (see Figure 1.14). El Guerrouj had run a mile in an astonishing 3 minutes, 43.13 seconds, an impressive 1.26 seconds faster than Moreceli. The descriptions were not hyperbole. People around the world truly marveled at El Guerrouj's accomplishment, even though 1.26 seconds seems like an insignificant difference.

To put El Guerrouj's run into perspective, notice that 45 years had passed since Englishman Roger Bannister attracted world attention as the first man in recorded history to run a mile in less than 4 minutes (see Figure 1.14). His time was 3:59.4.

Figure 1.14. *The runners Hicham El Guerrouj (left) and Roger Bannister (right).*

In 45 years, the world's best runners improved the time for the mile by an astonishing 16.27 seconds. (Notice that El Guerrouj's 1.26 seconds was a large part of that.) As a rate, 16.27 seconds represents an improvement from 15.038 miles per hour to 16.134 miles per hour, or just over 7 percent. Given that Bannister's world-class time was the starting point, an improvement in human performance of that size is truly something to admire.

Comparing to 20-Year-Olds

How do these world champions compare to average people? Most healthy people in their early 20s—the age group of the world record setters—can run a mile in 7.5 minutes. This number was chosen because it covers the ability of a majority of the people in the age range, and is approximately twice the time El Guerrouj needed. To say El Guerrouj is twice as fast as an average person is to say he is faster by a factor of 2. (The factor relating two numbers is found by dividing one by the other; for example 7.5 / 3.45 = 2.)

This factor-of-2 difference is a rough rule for the performance gap between an average person and a world champion for most physical strength activities such as running, swimming, jumping, and pole vaulting. The factor-of-2 rule tells us that no matter how hard most people try at physical activities, their performance can improve by roughly twice. Of course, most of us can only dream of achieving even part of that factor-of-2 potential. Nevertheless, the factor-of-2 rule is an important benchmark.

Factor of Improvement

When we compared world champions, we said there was a 7 percent improvement and that El Guerrouj's speed was about a factor-of-2 times faster than the speed of an average person. There is a difference between expressing improvement as a *percentage* and expressing improvement as a *factor*. We find a **factor-of-improvement** by dividing the new rate by the old rate. So, to find El Guerrouj's improvement over Bannister's, we divide their rates (16.134 / 15.038) to get 1.07. Percentages are a closely related computation found by dividing the *amount of change* by the old rate (16.134 − 15.038) / 15.038 = 0.07 and multiplying the result by 100. The added complexity of percentage is potentially confusing, so we use the simpler factor-of-improvement method. El Guerrouj was a factor-of-1.07 times faster than Bannister and about a factor-of-2 times faster than an average person.

Super Computers

As another example of analytical thinking, let's compare computer speeds. The UNIVAC I, the first commercial computer, unveiled in 1951 (and current when Bannister set his record), operated at a rate of nearly 100,000 addition operations (adds) per second. By comparison, a typical PC today—say, the portable IBM ThinkPad—can perform a billion additions per second or so. This factor-of-10,000 improvement over UNIVAC I (1,000,000,000/100,000) is truly remarkable. But, consider this—the ThinkPad is no record setter. It's the sort of computer a college

> **try it**
>
> **Computing the Factor of Improvement.** Flyer 1, the aircraft Orville and Wilbur Wright flew at Kitty Hawk, North Carolina, traveled so slowly (10 mph) that the brother who wasn't piloting could run alongside as it flew just off the ground. The SR-71 Blackbird, probably the world's fastest plane, flies at 2200 mph, three times the speed of sound.
>
>   What is the factor of improvement between Blackbird and Flyer 1?
>
> Speed of Blackbird = 2200 mph
>
> Speed of Flyer 1 = 10 mph
>
> Factor of improvement = 2200 / 10 = 220
>
> *The Blackbird is a factor-of 220 faster than Flyer 1.*

student can afford to buy. Engineering workstations can easily do several billion adds per second, boosting the factor even higher. And an Intel computer called ASCI Red, built for Sandia National Laboratory, held the world record for computer speed in 1999, when El Guerrouj set his record. ASCI Red ran at an astonishing 2.1 trillion floating-point adds per second. (Floating-point adds are decimal arithmetic operations that are more complex than the additions used to measure the speed of the UNIVAC I.) Compared to the UNIVAC I, ASCI Red is a factor of 21 million times faster!

fit **TIP**

> **Faster Still.** ASCI Red was the fastest of its day, but its day has passed. Several computers have eclipsed its performance, and better designs continue to emerge. For the latest speed tests, see **www.netlib.org/benchmark/top500.html**.

Perhaps nothing else in human experience has improved so dramatically. In roughly the same time period that human performance improved by a factor of 1.07 as measured by the mile run, computer performance improved by a factor of 21,000,000. Can we comprehend such a huge factor of improvement, or even the raw speed of ASCI Red?

fit **BYTE**

> **Think About It.** Most of us can appreciate the 7 percent improvement of El Guerrouj's run over Bannister's, and probably the factor-of-2 improvement in average versus world champion performance. Those we can imagine. But factors of improvement in the thousands or millions are beyond our comprehension. Notice that if El Guerrouj had improved on Bannister by a factor of 21,000,000, he'd have run the mile in 11.4 microseconds. That's 11.4 millionths of a second. What does that mean?
>
> \> Human visual perception is so slow that El Guerrouj could run 3000 miles at that rate before anyone would even notice he had moved.
>
> \> The sound would still be "inside" the starting gun 11.4 microseconds after the trigger was pulled.
>
> \> Light travels only twice as fast.
>
> Both the raw power of today's computers and their improvement over the last half-century are almost beyond our comprehension.

Benefits of Analytical Thinking

To summarize, we have made our understanding of recent speed improvements crisper by applying simple analysis. Rather than accepting the statement that the mile run and computers have improved, we learned the facts given as two measurements of performance. But once we had the data, we did not leave it as two separate observations: 100,000 additions in 1951 versus 2.1 trillion additions in 1999. Instead, we analyzed their relationship by figuring the factor of improvement: 2,100,000,000,000/100,000. ASCI Red is faster by a factor of 21 million.

This analysis let us compare the improvement to other advancements, and to put them all into perspective. The mile run, improved by an apparently small factor of 1.07 times in 45 years, is still very impressive when we recall that champions are only about a factor-of-2 better than average people. Computer performance has improved by unimaginable amounts. Although our original statement, "the mile run and computers have improved," is correct, our analysis helps us to be much more expressive and precise. Analytical thinking helps us understand more clearly the world of information technology and the physical world in which we live.

Defining WYSIWYG

Our only remaining task is to define the first acronym mentioned in the chapter: **WYSIWYG**. Remember that it stands for "what you see is what you get." To understand the term, recall that the computer creates the virtual world we see on our monitors. The representation the computer uses to keep track of the things on the screen is very different from the picture it shows us. For example, the text you are reading was stored in the computer as one very long line of letters, numbers, punctuation, and special characters, but it is displayed to me as a nicely formatted page like the one you are reading. The computer processes its representation—the long sequence of letters—to create the nicely formatted page. Original text editing software couldn't do that, so users had to work with the long sequence. If you wanted to make a change to the document, you had to imagine what it would look like when printed.

Eventually text editing systems were programmed to show the user the page as it would appear when printed. Changing the text became much easier. This property was described as "what you see (when editing) is what you get (when it's printed)" or WYSIWYG. Text editors with the WYSIWYG property became known as **word processors**.

SUMMARY

In this chapter we focused on learning IT terms in context. We learned to:

> Know and use the right word because as we learn words, we learn ideas; knowing the right words helps us to communicate.

> Ask questions to review basic and familiar terms, such as monitor, screen saver, RAM, and software.

> Understand some new terms, such as sequential access, volatile, and motherboard.

> Consider a brief list of "idea" words, such as abstract and generalize.

> Save our work regularly.

> Think analytically by looking at improvements in the mile run and computer speed.

We're not done, however. All of the chapters introduce new terms when new ideas are discussed. Learning and remembering these key terms will help you learn and remember the ideas. Key terms appear in the glossary at the end of the book. Check the glossary when the meaning of a term slips your mind. In addition to the glossary in this book, there are several good online glossaries. It's a good idea to find one with your Web browser and bookmark it—that is, save its URL. We will discuss URLs in Chapter 3. Meanwhile, check the glossary to learn what the acronym URL means.

EXERCISES

Multiple Choice

1. Computer monitors are different from TVs because
   A. monitors are bit-mapped and TVs are not
   B. TVs are interactive and monitors are not
   C. monitors are CRTs and TVs are not
   D. more than one of the above

2. Screen savers
   A. are useful because they prevent burn-in
   B. save energy
   C. can be turned off with a key press or a mouse click
   D. all of the above

3. The display for a laptop is most likely a
   A. TV
   B. RGB display
   C. LCD
   D. CRT display

4. Mice and keyboards do not have separate power cords because
   A. they are not electrical
   B. the power and the signal wires are in one cable
   C. they run on batteries
   D. none of the above

5. The last cable you plug in should be the
   A. monitor cable
   B. keyboard cable
   C. printer cable
   D. power cable

6. RGB stands for
   A. red, green, black
   B. red, gray, blue
   C. rust, black, brown
   D. red, green, blue

7. A typical monitor
   A. has over a million pixels
   B. has exactly a million pixels
   C. displays pixels in only one color
   D. none of the above

8. How many pixels make up the button shown in Figure 1.8?
   A. 19×19
   B. 304
   C. 1024×768
   D. none of the above

9. How is the process for clicking a check box similar to clicking a button?
   A. The tip of the arrow must be inside the x, y coordinates that make up the check box.
   B. The user must click the mouse button.
   C. The configuration of the check box must change from unchecked to checked or vice versa.
   D. all of the above

Short Answer

1. The _____ is involved in every activity of the computer system.

2. Knowing _____ is important to understanding technology and being understood when talking about it.

3. A _____ saves a CRT monitor from "burn in" when it is not in use.

4. The last cable you should plug in should be the _____.

5. There are _____ pixels on a typical laptop.

6. The number of times per second that images on the screen are redrawn is called the _____.

7. The _____ is the active point of the mouse pointer.

8. A specified result sought through the use of a precise and systematic method is a(n) _____.

9. _____ is a proper term used when a computer performs the instructions in a program.

10. The process of starting a computer is called _____.

11. Gleaning the central idea or concept from a situation is called _____.

12. A device that helps you remember a fact or concept is a _____.

13. A WYSIWYG text editor is called a _____.

14. On the computer, programs and information are stored on the _____.

15. The formulation of an idea, concept, or process that can be applied in many situations is called a _____.

Exercises

1. Here are some of the acronyms found in this chapter. Next to each, write its name and its meaning.

   SCSI
   IT
   CRT
   LCD
   RGB
   CD
   RAM
   ROM
   PC
   IC

2. Create a list of mnemonics that you know and their meanings.

3. Find the details of the computer system you are using. If you do not have the manual, use an ad from a newspaper, flyer, or Web site. Write down your system specifications, paying close attention to the terms and specs that are unfamiliar. Make a note to learn more about these in further chapters.

4. It took Magellan's expedition three years to circumnavigate the globe. The space shuttle completes an orbit in about 90 minutes. Calculate the factor of improvement.

5. Ellery Clark of the United States won the long jump in the 1896 Olympiad in Athens, Greece with a jump of 20 feet 9 3/4 inches. The current world record is held by Mike Powell of the United States, who jumped a distance of 8.95 meters. What is the factor of improvement? Be sure to convert between feet and meters.

6. Ray Harroun won the first Indianapolis 500 in 1911 with a speed of 74.59 miles per hour. The 2004 race was won by Buddy Rice with a speed of 138.518 mph. What is the factor of improvement?

7. In 2003, Svetlana Feofanova set the world pole vault record at 4.76 meters. William Hoyt set the record in 1896 with a vault of 3.30 meters. What is the factor of improvement that Feofanova made over the men's record of 1896? What is the percentage increase?

2

WHAT THE DIGERATI KNOW
Exploring the Human–Computer Interface

learning objectives

> Explain key ideas familiar to experienced users (the digerati):
  - The advantages of having consistent features in information technology
  - The benefits of using feedback of clicking around and blazing away in exploring new applications
  - The basic principle of IT: Form follows function

> Explain how a basic search is done

> Use common methods to search and edit text:
  - Find (words, characters, spaces)
  - Shift-select
  - The placeholder technique
  - Search-and-replace (substitution)

chapter 2

WHAT THE DIGERATI KNOW
Exploring the Human–Computer Interface

Exploration is really the essence of the human spirit.
— FRANK BORMAN, US ASTRONAUT

Text processing has made it possible to right-justify any idea, even one which cannot be justified on any other grounds.
— J FINNEGAN, USC

PERHAPS the most uncomfortable part of being an inexperienced computer user is the suspicion that everyone but you knows how to use technology. They seem to know automatically what to do in any situation.

Of course, experienced users don't really have a technology gene. Through experience, however, they have learned a certain kind of knowledge that lets them figure out what to do in most situations. Most people don't "know" this information explicitly—it's not usually taught in class. They learn it through experience. But you can avoid long hours of stumbling around gaining experience. In this chapter, we reveal some secrets of the digerati so that you too, can "join the club." (Digerati, analogous to the word *literati*, means people who understand digital technology.)

Our major goal in this chapter is to show you how to think abstractly about technology. We do this by asking how people learn technical skills and by considering what technology developers expect from us as users. This chapter will also help you understand that:

> Computer systems use consistent interfaces, standard metaphors, and common operations.
> Computer systems always give feedback while they are working.
> Making mistakes does not break the computer.
> The best way to learn to use new computer software is to experiment with it.
> Asking questions of other computer users is not evidence of being a dummy, but proof of an inquiring mind.

These ideas can help you learn new software quickly. A key abstract idea about software is that it obeys fundamental laws. This core idea can help you in your everyday software use, as we illustrate when we explain the principle "form follows function." We show how this principle applies to basic text searching by teaching the subject without using any specific software. Such knowledge applies to every system and makes us versatile users. You too, can become one of the digerati.

LEARNING ABOUT TECHNOLOGY

Human beings are born knowing how to chew, cough, stand, blink, smile, and so forth. They are not born knowing how to ride a bicycle, drive a car, use a food processor, or start a lawnmower. For any tool more complicated than a stick, we need some explanation about how it works and possibly some training in how it's used. Parents teach their children how to ride bicycles and most products come with an owner's manual.

Some tools, such as portable CD players, are so intuitive that most people living in our technological society find their use "obvious." We don't need to refer to the owner's manual. We can guess what the controls do because we know what operations are needed to play music. (Without this knowledge, the icons on the buttons would probably be meaningless.) And we can usually recover from our mistakes. For example, if you were to insert a CD upside-down, it wouldn't work, so you'd turn it over and try again.

But the fact that we live in a technological society and can figure out how a CD player works doesn't mean that we have any innate technological abilities. Instead, it emphasizes two facts about technology that are key to our success:

> Our experience using (related) devices, including software, guides us in what to expect.

> Designers who create these devices, including software, know we have that experience and design products to match what we already know.

The Desktop

When a personal computer starts up, the image it displays on the monitor is called the **desktop**. It usually has a colored background, but photos, patterns, logos, etc. are also common background images. Information is displayed along the top, bottom, or side of the desktop. Small icons of three basic kinds are displayed on the "desk":

> Applications (programs), such as Internet Explorer, which are identified by their logos

> Folders (directories), which have icons like small file folders

> Files (documents), which are identified by an icon corresponding to the application, such as Adobe Acrobat, that created them

There are other icons too, such as the wastebasket for trash.

The image is called the desktop because it implies a metaphor. In software, a **metaphor** is an object or idea used as an analogy for computation. Working with a personal computer is analogous to working at a desk: You keep your work in files, you organize your files into folders, and you use applications (programs) such as a calculator or photo-editing tool to perform your tasks. The designers at

Xerox PARC and Apple Computer who created the idea of personal computing, wanted an analogy to represent the interaction between humans and computers. They chose the analogy of working at a desk; all personal computing software since is designed around that same metaphor.

*fit*BYTE

> **Desktop.** Many creative people have contributed to the invention of personal computing, beginning in the late 1960s with Douglas Englebart and his team at SRI who created devices such as the mouse. In the 1970s researchers at Xerox's Palo Alto Research Center (PARC) applied the ideas to office automation by creating the Alto, the first personal computer with the features we've come to expect: bit-mapped display, mouse, windows, desk-top metaphor, etc. Although it was never marketed, the Alto motivated Apple to create the Macintosh, launched in 1984. Eventually, Microsoft upgraded its DOS (disk operating system) to have these features, making them effectively universal.

Playing Recorded Music

To illustrate how metaphors are used, consider listening to music. When we listen to a CD on a computer, we control the software that plays the CD using a graphic user interface (GUI), as shown in Figure 2.1. This GUI (GOO·ey) is for the iTunes software for the MacOSX operating system, standard on Apple computers. Similar software plays CDs on the Windows operating system (see Figure 2.2). Even if the iTunes GUI is not familiar, anyone who has ever used a CD player can look at it and figure out how it works.

We can successfully guess how the software works because the GUI shown in Figure 2.1 graphically presents a familiar "music player" metaphor. In addition to

Figure 2.1. Graphical user interface for the iTunes audio CD player on an Apple Macintosh.

the red (close), yellow (minimize), and green (maximize) buttons common to all MacOSX GUIs, it shows three white (plastic-looking) buttons with icons at the upper left that are meaningful to us in the context of playing recorded music: last track, pause, and next track. Below those buttons is a volume control. To the right an LCD window shows the name of the CD—The Beatles—with elapsed time and a diamond moving along a slot, which we can guess is a visual description of how much of the track has been played. In the main window is the playlist titled "Song Name" giving the usual information. Notice the icon by the track that is playing. At the bottom are other buttons with icons, some of which are familiar, e.g., shuffle, repeat, and eject. We also see the number of songs, total time, and memory size (MB is megabytes). On the left is a list of "Sources." The highlighted item is "Revolver"—the Beatles album we're playing. The other items, we can guess, are places where other recorded music is stored.

Because we know from experience that one "pushes" a button on a computer by clicking it with the mouse, anyone who has played recorded music can intuitively learn to control the iTunes GUI. We don't need instruction because the software designers present a metaphor that we immediately understand. We apply what we know about the metaphor; therefore, we can use the software without reading the user's manual.

That's the idea behind all personal computing software: When you have a task, e.g., playing music, expect the software's GUI to present a familiar metaphor, e.g., a physical CD player. Apply your knowledge about the metaphor as a guide for using the software.

Figure 2.2. Graphical user interface for playing audio CDs with Windows Media Player.

Understanding the Designer's Intent

The designers of the iTunes player invested plenty of effort to make the GUI familiar. For example, the volume control looks like the volume control on a physical CD player. Its operation is identical to the blue slider bar at the bottom, but the designers didn't use that kind of standard slider. They took the trouble to customize the iTunes volume control to resemble one found on physical CD players, including the "soft" and "loud" icons. They designed the buttons in the same way. The buttons didn't have to be special or look plastic. Instead of the icon, the word "pause" could have been printed on the large button. The oval LCD display, common on physical CD players, was created purposely to match the look and feel of a physical CD player. There are easier and fancier ways to display the information—so why do software designers go to so much trouble?

Everyone who invents a new tool, including software designers, has to teach users how to operate their inventions. Developers do write manuals explaining the software's slick features, but it's much faster and easier if users can figure out the software without studying the manual. So software designers, like CD player designers, try to pick easy-to-understand user interfaces. Instead of creating a GUI that requires explanation, the designers guessed that the metaphor of the familiar physical CD player would be intuitive. And they guessed right. By analogy, the basic features of the software are obvious. The audio CD software for the Windows operating system uses a similar interface, as shown in Figure 2.2.

To summarize, software designers want to make the GUI intuitive so that users can figure it out. We should expect that we can "brain out" how it works. We use this idea every time we use new software.

CONSISTENT INTERFACES

Because computers can do many things, GUIs use many different metaphors. GUIs are built using simple metaphors, such as buttons. Software designers use these metaphors similarly; they make them look and work alike (for their operating system). The result is a **consistent interface**. The consistent interface is one of the secrets of the digerati: Whenever they see an icon or metaphor they have seen before, they know immediately how it works, which explains why they always seem to know what to do even if they have never used the software before. You will do the same thing!

Although the iTunes GUI contains many custom features to make it more intuitive, it also uses many standard metaphors found in all GUIs. We'll take a moment to look more closely at some of them.

Command Buttons

As we have seen command buttons take a variety of forms such as a 3D rectangle, an oval or a circle. They are highlighted as explained in Chapter 1 with an icon or text centered on the button. This label says what the command does. To **invoke** the command—that is, to tell the software to perform the operation shown on the label—we "press" the button by clicking it with the mouse. We receive feedback telling us that the button has been clicked, usually by means of a color change, shadow, highlight, text/icon change, or audible click. Some people think audible clicks are obsessive attempts at realism by developers, but some form of feedback is essential for effective computer use, as explained below.

*fit*TIP

A Click Is Enough. When clicking on a button, it is not a good idea to press down on the mouse button slowly or for a long time, because the computer may interpret a too-long click as a different action.

Slider Control

The volume control shown in Figure 2.3(a) is a slider control. A **slider control** sets a value from a "continuous" range, such as volume. To move the slider, place the mouse pointer on the slider, hold down the (left) mouse button, and move in the direction of change. The most common examples of sliders are the scroll bars in a window display, usually shown at the right and bottom of the window, as shown in Figure 2.3(b). When the window is not large enough to display all of the information in the horizontal or vertical direction, a scroll bar is shown for each direction in which information has been clipped. For example, the complete information of the playlist is not shown, so the horizontal scroll bar has been placed at the bottom of the window. The range is the size of the information in the direction that's hidden. Often the size of the slider is scaled to show what proportion of information is displayed. Thus, if the slider takes up half of the length of the "slot," about half of the information is displayed. There are usually directional triangles ◄ ► at one or both ends of the scroll bar; clicking on them moves the slider one "unit" in the chosen direction.

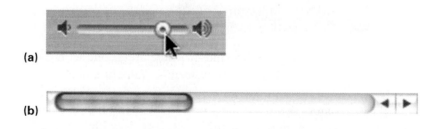

(a)

(b)

Figure 2.3. Slider controls. (a) A volume control. (b) A scroll bar.

Triangle Pointers

To reduce clutter, GUIs hide information until the user needs or wants to see it. A triangle pointer indicates the presence of hidden information or an alternative form of the information. Clicking on the triangle reveals that information. So, at the end of slider bar, the triangles ◄ ► allow you to shift the contents of the

window. You can see other triangles in Figure 2.1. There is a triangle shown in the LCD display  ; clicking on it reveals the familiar sound levels display, as shown in Figure 2.4. A triangle in an iTunes column header indicates the order in which the songs are displayed. In Figure 2.1, for example, the songs are displayed in ascending numeric order as they occur on the CD. Clicking on the triangle reorders the listed songs in reverse order.

Figure 2.4. *The iTunes GUI displaying the hidden sound level information.*

We have discussed a few examples to illustrate the metaphor concept. There are many others, and beginning users should get to know them quickly. The point is to emphasize that computer applications have many operations in common, and software designers purposely use them consistently so that they can take advantage of the user's knowledge and experience. Experienced users look for familiar metaphors, and when they recognize a new one they add it to their repertoire.

*fit***BYTE**   **Mac or PC?** Is the PC better than the Macintosh, or vice versa? The question usually sets off a pointless argument. Listening to the battle, many wrongly guess that the other system must be very different and difficult to use. In fact, the two systems are much more alike than they are different, sharing the concepts we discuss in this chapter and much, much more. Any competent user of one system can quickly and easily learn to use the other. And every Fluent user should.

ANATOMY OF AN INTERFACE

In addition to the window where users conduct most of their interactions by typing or clicking, there are menus. A **menu** is a list of operations that the software can perform. Menus are grouped by the similarity of their operations and listed across the top of the screen in the **menu bar**, as shown in Figure 2.5. All operations performed by the software are listed in a menu.

Menu Operation

Menus listed in the menu bar across the top of a window are called **pull-down** or **drop-down** menus. All of the operations available with the software are listed "under" the menus, even if they are also available by clicking on an icon elsewhere in the window. In some situations, menus are also displayed at the spot where the mouse is pointing when the mouse button is clicked; these are called **pop-up** menus. Both menu types work the same way.

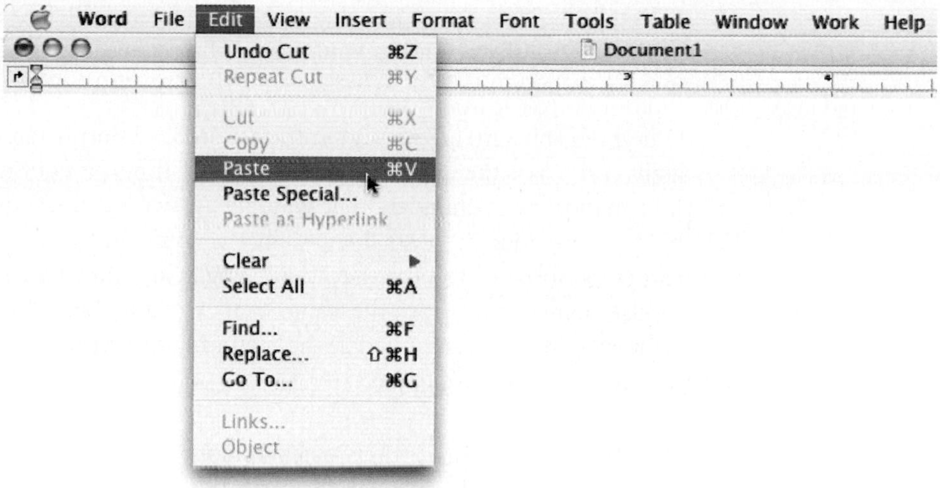

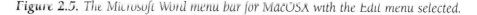

| | Word | File | **Edit** | View | Insert | Format | Font | Tools | Table | Window | Work | Help |

Undo Cut ⌘Z
Repeat Cut ⌘Y

Cut ⌘X
Copy ⌘C
Paste ⌘V
Paste Special...
Paste as Hyperlink

Clear ▶
Select All ⌘A

Find... ⌘F
Replace... ⇧⌘H
Go To... ⌘G

Links...
Object

Document1

Figure 2.5. The Microsoft Word menu bar for MacOSX with the Edit menu selected.

To pull down or pop up a menu requires a mouse click, which reveals a list of operations. Sliding the mouse pointer down the list highlights the items as it passes over them. That is, they reverse color like the **Paste** command shown in Figure 2.5. Clicking or releasing the mouse button on the highlighted (selected) menu item causes the computer to perform the listed operation.

Reading a Menu

Menus give more information than just a list of items. They tell you whether an operation is available or not, they indicate when more user input is needed, and sometimes they give you shortcuts. Refer to Figure 2.5 as you read these descriptions.

Which Operations Are Available?
Unlike restaurant menus that are printed once and reused, GUI menus are created each time they are opened. So they specify exactly which operations are available. An operation may not apply in every context. For example, **Copy** is not available if nothing has been selected to be copied. Operations that can be applied immediately are shown in solid color and operations that are not available at the moment are shown in a lighter color or "grayed out," as shown for the **Copy** operation in Figure 2.5. Unavailable items are not highlighted as the cursor passes over them, and of course, they cannot be selected.

Is More Input Needed?
Some operations need further specification or more input from the user. Menu items that need further specification have a triangle pointer ▶ at the right end of the entry (see Clear in Figure 2.5). Selecting such an item pops up a menu with the additional choices. Making the selection causes the operation to be performed unless it still needs more specification. Menu items show that they need more input with an ellipsis ⋯ after their name.

Selecting the item opens a dialog box for specifying the extra input. For example, in Figure 2.5, the operation **Find** has an ellipsis because it needs the user to specify what to look for.

When the software has enough information, it performs the operation immediately and closes the menu(s) and window(s). If not, it continues to ask for more information by opening another window. Answering these questions may lead to more information requests. Eventually the command will be fully specified and can be performed. You can stop the dialog at any time by simply moving your mouse pointer away from the menu or by clicking **Cancel**. Clicking **Cancel** is the same as never having looked at the menu in the first place, no matter how much information you have entered.

Is There a Shortcut? Sometimes it's more convenient to type a keyboard letter than to pull down a window with the mouse and slide the cursor down the list. So some menu items have shortcuts. A **shortcut** is a combination of keyboard characters, shown next to the menu item, that have the same effect. The shortcut is specified by a combination of a special key and a letter. In Figure 2.5, the shortcut for **Cut** is ⌘-**X**, shown to the right of the operation in the menu entry; the shortcut for **Copy** is ⌘-**C**.

The special character for the Mac is Command ⌘, sometimes referred to as a clover. The special character for the Windows operating system is Control Ctrl (see Figure 2.6). To use the shortcut it is not necessary to pull down the menu. It is enough to hold down the special key—Command ⌘ or Control Ctrl depending on which operating system you are using—and type the letter. Even though the letter is shown as a capital, it is not correct to hold down the Shift key while performing this action.

The important thing to notice about the shortcuts is that the same letter command is used for both operating systems. Compare Figures 2.5 and 2.6. That is, once you have learned the shortcuts for an application running on one operating system, you can easily switch to another operating system because the vendors keep the shortcuts—and nearly everything else—consistent. In fact, basic operations like **Copy**, **Paste**, **Print**, **Find**, etc. that are used in most applications use these same letters. This is another way in which the interface is kept consistent.

Shortcuts are not very important for a casual user, but they are extremely handy for people who use a single application intensively.

fit **BYTE**

A Win for Users. The Microsoft Windows operating system includes most of the GUI metaphors developed for the Apple Macintosh, so in 1988 Apple sued Microsoft for patent infringement. Apple claimed Microsoft illegally used the "look and feel" of its Mac. The legal issues were complex, but the judge ruled that Microsoft could freely use the metaphors Apple had developed. This might not seem fair to Apple, but it was a great win for users, because it meant that GUIs could work pretty much the same on the Mac and the PC.

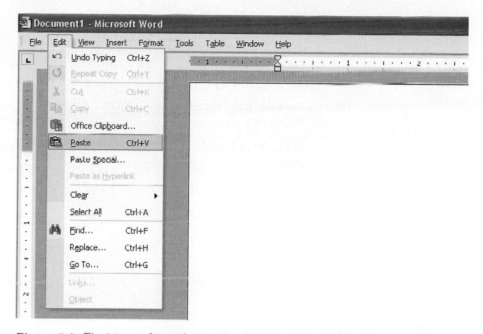

Figure 2.6. *The Microsoft Word menu bar for Windows with the Edit menu selected.*

STANDARD GUI FUNCTIONALITY

There are some operations that almost all personal computer applications should be expected to perform simply because they process information. That is, whether the information is text, spreadsheets, circuit diagrams, or digitized photographs, the fact that it is information stored in a computer means that certain operations will be available in the software. We call these operations the **standard functionality**. For example, it should be possible to **Save** the information to a file, **Open** a file containing the saved information, **Print** the file, and so on. You should expect to find these functions in almost every software application.

File Operations

To help users, the standard operations are grouped—usually with other operations specific to the application—into two menus labeled **File** and **Edit**. Generally, the operations under the **File** menu apply to whole instances of the information being processed by an application. An **instance** is one of whatever kind of information the application processes. For example, for word processors, an instance is a document; for MP3 players, an instance is a song; for photo editors, an instance is a picture. The **File** menu items treat a whole document. The operations you can expect to see under the **File** menu and their meanings are as follows:

> **New** Create a "blank" instance of the information.

> **Open** Locate a file on the disk containing an instance of the information and read it in.

> **Close** Stop processing the current instance of the information, close the window, but keep the program available to process other instances.

> **Save** Write the current instance to the hard disk or a floppy disk, using the previous name and location.

> **Save As** Write the current instance to the hard disk or a floppy disk with a new name or location.

> **Page Setup** Specify how the printed document should appear on paper; changes to the setup are rare.

> **Print** Print a copy of the current instance of the information.

> **Print Preview** Show the information as it will appear when printed.

> **Exit** or **Quit** End the entire application.

There are usually other operations unique to the application.

New Instance

Notice that **New** under the **File** menu creates a "blank" **instance**. What is "blank information"?

To understand this fundamental idea, notice that all information is grouped into types, based on its properties. Photographs (digital images) are a type of information; among the properties of every image is its height and width in pixels. Monthly calendars are a type of information with properties such as the number of days, day of the week on which the first day falls, and year. Text documents are another type of information and the length of a document in characters is one property. Any specific piece of information—an image, month, or document—is an **instance** of its type. Your term paper is an instance of the document type of information; June, 2005 is an instance of calendar type information.

To store or process information of a given type, the computer sets up a structure to record all of the properties and store its content. A "new" or "blank" instance is simply the structure without any properties or content filled in. For example, imagine an empty form for contact information in an electronic address book, as shown in Figure 2.7. That's a **New** contact, ready to receive its content.

Edit Operations

The **Edit** operations let you make changes within an instance. They often involve selection and cursor placement. The operations are performed in a standard sequence: select, cut/copy, indicate, paste, and revise. Selection identifies the information to be moved or copied. Selection is usually done by moving the cursor to a particular position in the instance and, while holding down either the (left) mouse button or keyboard keys, moving the cursor to a new position. All information between the two positions is selected. Highlighting, usually color reversal, identifies the selection. If the information is to be recorded and deleted

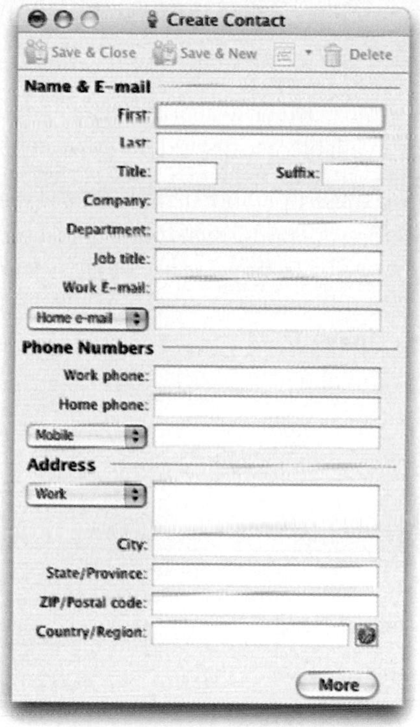

*Figure 2.7. A **New** contact (i.e., a "blank" instance) in an electronic address book.*

from its current position, the **Cut** command is used. The **Copy** command records but does not delete the information. Then, the new location for the information is indicated in preparation for pasting it into position, although in many applications the indicate step is skipped and the text is pasted into a standard place. The **Paste** command copies the information recorded in memory into the indicated position. Because a copy is made in memory, the information can be pasted again and again. Often, revisions or repositioning are required to complete the editing operation.

The operations under the **Edit** menu and their meanings are as follows:

> **Undo** Cancel the most recent editing change, returning the instance to its previous form.

> **Repeat** Apply the most recent editing change again.

> **Cut** Remove the selected information and save it in temporary storage, ready for pasting.

> **Copy** Store a copy of the selected information in temporary storage, ready for pasting.

> **Paste** Insert into the instance the information saved in the temporary storage by **Cut** or **Copy**; the information is placed either at the cursor position or at a standard position, depending on the application.

> **Clear** Delete the selected information.

> **Select All** Make the selection be the entire instance.

Undo is not always available because not all operations are reversible. **Redo** may not be available because some operations cannot be repeated.

Because these operations are standard—available for most applications and consistent across operating systems—it is a good idea to learn their shortcuts, as shown in Table 2.1. (To prevent accidents, **Clear** often does not have a shortcut.) In addition, "double-click"—two (rapid) clicks with the (left) mouse button—often means **Open**.

Table 2.1. Standard Shortcuts. These common shortcut letters for standard software operations combine with "Control" ⟨Ctrl⟩ for Windows or "Command" ⟨⌘⟩ for MacOSX.

File Functions		Edit Functions	
New	N	**Cut**	X
Open	O	**Copy**	C
Save	S	**Paste**	V
Print	P	**Select All**	A
Quit	Q	**Undo**	Z
Redo	Y	**Find**	F

*fit*TIP   **Command and Control.** Sometimes it is necessary to refer to an operation like **Copy** by its shortcut without being specific about which operating system is used. In such cases we write ^C to indicate that the operation takes either Command ⟨⌘⟩ or Control ⟨Ctrl⟩, depending on the OS.

Expecting Feedback

A computer is our assistant, ready to do whatever we tell it to do. It is natural that when any assistant performs an operation, he, she, or it must report back to the person who made the request, describing the progress. This is especially true when the assistant is a computer, because the user needs to know that the task was done and when to give the next command. So a user interface will always give the user feedback about "what's happenin'."

In a GUI, **feedback** is any indication that the computer is still working, or has completed the request. Feedback takes many forms, depending on what operation a user has commanded. If the operation can be performed instantaneously—that is, so fast that a user does not have to wait for it to complete—the GUI simply indicates that the operation is complete. When the operation is an editing change, for example, the proof that it is done is that the revision is visible. When the effect of the command is not discernable—say, when one clicks a button—then there is some other indication provided; for example, highlighting, shading, graying, underlining, changing color, or an audible click.

The most common form of feedback is the indication that the computer is continuing to perform a time-consuming operation. As the operation is carried out, the cursor is replaced with an icon such as an hourglass ⧗ (on Windows systems) or a rainbow spinner 🌀 (on Macintosh systems). Applications can also give the user custom feedback. A common indicator is the busy spinner ◔, a revolving circle divided into quarters, two white and two black. The file transfer application Fetch turns the cursor into a running dog 🐕. When the completion time can be predicted, applications show a meter that "fills" as the operation progresses. Often these displays give a time estimate for 100 percent completion. Finally, when an operation is processing a series of inputs, the "completion count" gives the tally of the completed instances, or equivalently, the number remaining.

---

*fit*TIP

Be Selective. New users can get confused when an operation they want to use is not available (that is, it is "grayed out"). This happens because the operation needs the user to select something and nothing is selected. For example, the computer cannot perform **Copy** until you have selected what you want to copy.

● "CLICKING AROUND"

When the digerati encounter new software, they expect a consistent interface. They expect to see the basic metaphors, find standard operations, and receive feedback while the application is working. Digerati automatically look for these interface features and begin to explore. The purpose of their exploration is to learn what the software can do.

We call the act of exploring a user interface **clicking around**. It involves noting the basic features presented by the GUI and checking each menu to see what operations are available. For example, when experienced users see a slider bar, they slide it to see what happens. When we slide the volume slider in iTunes we notice a change in volume, and in accordance with the feedback principle, we see in Figure 2.3 that the circle in the middle of the slider is colored blue ◉ while we drag it.

When the digerati see a button, they hover their cursor over the button—not clicking it, yet—until the 'balloon help' explanation tells them what the button does. For example, in the iTunes GUI, as shown in Figure 2.1, there are several buttons at the bottom that we don't immediately understand. Hovering over them reveals the explanation, as seen in Figure 2.8. Then, like the digerati, if our curiosity isn't satisfied, we click the button to see what happens. Perhaps we don't know what "Visual Effects" means, but noting that it is an "off and on" type of control, we click it (see Figure 2.9).

*fit*TIP

A Fast Start. When you're using software for the first time, practice "clicking around":

> Take a minute to study the GUI graphics.
> Open each window to see what operations are available.
> Determine the purpose of icons and controls.
> Hover the cursor over unknown buttons or GUI features for a short explanation of their purpose.

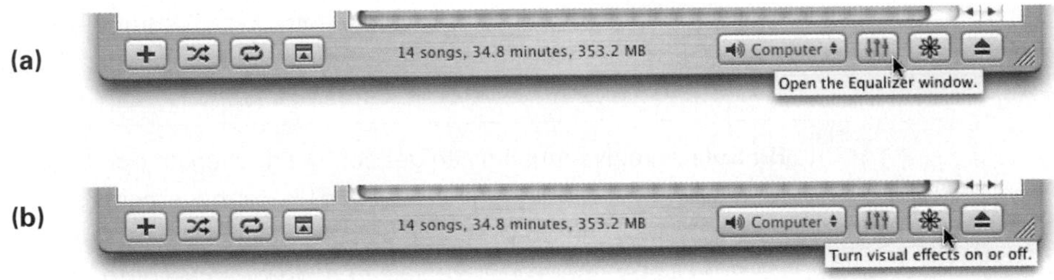

(a)
14 songs, 34.8 minutes, 353.2 MB
Computer
Open the Equalizer window.
(b)
14 songs, 34.8 minutes, 353.2 MB
Computer
Turn visual effects on or off.

Figure 2.8. *Hovering the cursor over unknown buttons shows the help description: (a) Equalizer window, (b) visual effects.*

iTunes
Search
Options
Computer
Turn visual effects on or off.

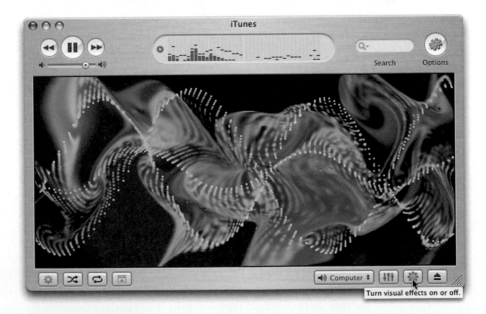

Figure 2.9. *Clicking on the Visual effects button in iTunes.*

"Clicking around" can help us figure out what operations are available without having to be taught or to read the manual. Software manuals are notoriously dull reading and hard to use. But "clicking around" does not make them obsolete. Manuals—mostly online **Help** resources—are still necessary and useful. "Clicking around" works because (a) we come to the new software with technological experience and (b) software designers try to build on what we know by using metaphors and consistent interfaces. When new software works like the last software did, we already "know" how to use it. The manual is usually needed only to understand advanced features or subtleties of operation. Ironically then, manuals are most useful for experienced users, not beginners.

Returning to the iTunes GUI shown in Figure 2.1, we previously explored the triangle by the "Song Name," and when we clicked on it, the playlist was shown in descending numerical order. But why is the box containing the triangle colored blue? On closer inspection, its shading somewhat resembles a button. Is it a button? Hovering over it doesn't give a short description, so it isn't an 'official' button. But since we're exploring by clicking around, we should try to figure out what the color means. What happens if we click in the box containing the words "Song Name"? When we click in the box, it changes color; it has an up-pointing triangle; the playlist is alphabetized by title; and the square next to it is no longer blue nor has a triangle pointer (see Figure 2.10). We then click on the up-pointing triangle in the "Song Name" box to see what happens and the list is rearranged in reverse alphabetical order. From our clicking around we figure out that these are the controls provided for organizing our playlist. We can order the songs by ascending or descending number, by increasing or decreasing time, alphabetically by title (a-to-z or z-to-a), alphabetically by artist, etc. To choose how we want to organize our

Figure 2.10. *iTunes GUI with the playlist organized by song title.*

playlist, we click on the box above the column, and possibly on the triangle itself. This is intuitive; no one has to teach us how to use these controls.

"Clicking around" is exploration and may not reveal all of the software features. We may need to experiment, test repeatedly, and try again. But this clicking around technique usually gives useful information quickly. If it doesn't, the software design has undoubtedly failed to some extent.

Following Protocol. Our normal interactive use of computers alternates between our commanding the computer to do something and the computer's doing it. If the computer can't finish immediately, it gives feedback showing the operation is in progress. If the computer is finished, we can see the effects of the command. Be attuned to this alternating protocol. If nothing seems to be happening, the computer is waiting for you to give a command.

"BLAZING AWAY"

After getting to know a software application by "clicking around," the next step is to try it. We will call this **blazing away**. The term suggests a user's trying an application assertively—exploring features even without a clear idea of what they will do. "Blazing away" is sometimes intimidating for beginning users because they're afraid they'll break something if they make a mistake. A basic rule of information processing is: *Nothing will break!* If you make a mistake, the software is not going to screech and grind to a halt, and plop on the floor with a clunk. When you make a mistake, the software may "crash" or "hang," but nothing actually breaks. Most of the time nothing happens. The software catches the mistake before doing something wrong and displays an error message. By paying attention to these messages, you can quickly learn what's legal and what isn't. Therefore, "blazing away" is an effective way to learn about the application even if you make mistakes.

Of course, saying that nothing will break is not the same as saying that it's impossible to get into a terrible mess by "blazing away." Creating a mess is often very easy. Beginners and experts do it all the time. The difference between the two is that the experts know another basic rule of information technology: *When stuck, start over.* That may mean exiting the program. It may mean rebooting the computer. It may simply mean "undoing" a series of edits and repeating them. The simple point is that the mess has no value. It does not have to be straightened out or fixed, because it didn't cost anything but your time to create in the first place. Because this time is chalked up to "experience" or "user training," there's no harm in throwing the mess out. Therefore, an experienced user who is "blazing away" on a new software system will probably exit the software and restart the application over and over, without saving anything.

Usually, we are working with new software because we have something specific we want to do, so it pays to focus on getting that task done. This means that we should "blaze away" on those operations that will contribute to completing the task; we don't have to become experts. It's common for Fluent users to know only the most basic functions of the software systems they use infrequently. And, because they are not regular users of these programs, they usually forget how the applications work and have to "click around" and "blaze away" each time.

 fitBYTE

> **Getting Out and Getting Back In.** Starting over is so common for computer users—it's called, *getting out and getting back in*—that it's become the subject of some geek humor. A mechanical engineer, an electrical engineer, and a computer engineer are camped at Mt. Rainier. In the morning, they pack up to leave and get into their car, but it doesn't start. The ME says, "The starter motor is broken, but I can fix it," and he gets out of the car. The EE says, "No way. It's the battery, but I know what to do," and she gets out of the car. The CE says while getting out of the car, "Now, let's get back in."

Obviously, if you are "blazing away" and starting over when you get into trouble, you shouldn't spend too much time creating complicated inputs. For example, if the software asks for text input and gives you space for several paragraphs, just enter `Test text` and continue to explore. Once you understand how to do the task, you can focus on using the software productively.

WATCHING OTHERS

"Clicking around" and "blazing away" are the first steps when learning new software because you are likely to succeed using your own observation and reasoning skills. And, if you need to know something very specific about the software, you can always read the manual or online help. However, these two extremes may not cover all of the possibilities. Complicated software systems usually have some features that are not obvious, too advanced, or too specialized to learn on our own. They include GUI features that most of us do not think to look for and they provide capabilities that we may not even know we need.

The Shift-Select Operation

An example of a not-so-obvious feature is the ⟨Shift⟩ key in selection operations. Suppose we want to select only the red and green circles of the stoplight in Figure 2.11(a). Clicking on the red circle selects it (Figure 2.11(b)), as shown by the small boxes around the circle. Clicking on the green circle selects it and deselects the red circle (Figure 2.11(c)). Dragging the cursor vertically from the red circle to the green circle selects all the circles (Figure 2.11(d)). So how do we select just red and green without the yellow? The problem is that when we select something (e.g., the green circle), anything that is already selected (e.g., the red circle) becomes deselected automatically. We need some way to bypass that automatic protocol.

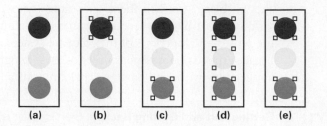

Figure 2.11. Examples of selection.

The solution is to select the first item (e.g., click on the red circle) and then hold down the ⌗Shift⌗ key while selecting the second item (e.g., clicking on the green circle). Using the ⌗Shift⌗ key during a selection means to "continue selecting everything that is already selected." Because the red circle is already selected when the green circle is shift-selected, both become selected, completing the task.

Learning from Others

The **shift-select** operation, meaning "continue to select the item(s) already selected," is a common feature in commercial software. Without knowing about shift-select, however, we probably wouldn't discover it by "clicking around" or "blazing away." We would not think to try it. We might not even know that we need the feature in the first place. So how do we learn about this kind of feature?

We can take a course on the specific software or read the user's manual, but an alternative is to observe others as they use a program we are familiar with. As we watch, we should be able to follow what they are doing, though it might seem very fast. If we see an operation that we do not understand, we ask about it. Most people are eager to share their expertise. Many an obscure feature, trick, or shortcut is learned while looking over the shoulder of an experienced user, so it pays to pay attention.

*fit***TIP** | **Toggling shift-select.** Generally when you use shift-select, one or more additional items is selected, because you usually click on an unselected item. But what happens when you use shift-select on an item that is already selected? It deselects that item only, leaving all other items selected. This property of changing to the opposite state—selecting if not selected, deselecting if selected—is called **toggling**. It's a handy feature in many situations.

● PRINCIPLE: FORM FOLLOWS FUNCTION

A theme of this chapter is that computer systems are very similar because software designers want us to figure out how to use them based on our previous experience with other software. So, they use consistent interfaces and metaphors. When features of a new system work like the same features in a familiar system, we already know how to use parts of the new system. But there is a much deeper principle at work to explain the similarity among software systems. We state this principle as Form Follows Function.

The **Form Follows Function** principle states that the fundamental operations of a software system and the way they work are determined by the task being solved. This doesn't mean that two software systems for the same task look alike; it means that they will have the same basic operations and those operations will work similarly. Of course, their GUIs can be very different with fancier icons and glitzier buttons, but those differences are superficial. At the core, the application defines the operations and how they work. Performing the task requires that the information is processed in a specific way.

Similar Applications Have Similar Features

To illustrate the principle, text processing applications such as Word, Word Perfect, BBEdit, Simple Text, Apple Works, NotePad, and a dozen others use a cursor to mark your place in text. They all have operations for typing text, deleting text, selecting text, copying text, searching text, replacing text, etc. The software vendors did not invent these operations; they are fundamental in text processing. Furthermore, the operations work in much the same way in every system. For example, the [Backspace] (or [Delete]) key removes the character to the left of the cursor's present position and it is impossible to select disconnected blocks of text. These are the natural and sensible meanings of those operations in the context of text, which is why they share many features.

If vendors cannot make better software by changing the fundamental operations, how can they compete? Easy, they add other non-fundamental features that make their systems more convenient, friendlier, faster, less error prone, etc. For example, in some, but not all text processing systems, it's possible to select text and drag it to a new position. This is not a fundamental text processing operation, since it can be achieved with a select, cut, reposition-the cursor, and paste sequence of operations. But text dragging is convenient, and so it has been added to many systems. Software vendors also try to attract new customers by making their software more appealing by adding cool icons or animated "helpers" like paperclips.

Take Advantage of Similarities

Form Follows Function in browser software, spreadsheet software, drawing software, photo-editing software, and so on. Because it's a general principle, when we learn an application from one software maker, we learn the core operations for that task as well as the handy features and annoying quirks of that vendor's product. Then when we use software from a different vendor, we should look for and expect to recognize the basic operations. The features and quirks may or may not be present. The basic operations will have a different look and feel, but they will still be there and work roughly the same way.

The Form Follows Function principle is important to our everyday use of computers for three reasons:

> When a new version of familiar software is released, we should expect to learn it very quickly because it shares the core functions and many of the features and quirks of the earlier version.

> When we must perform a familiar task using unfamiliar software, we should expect to use its basic features immediately because we're already familiar and experienced with them.

> When we are frustrated with one vendor's software, we should try another's. Because of our experience with the first system, we will learn the new system quickly. (And "voting" by purchasing better software helps to improve overall software quality.)

In summary, because the function determines how a system must work, different software implementations for a task must share basic characteristics. You don't need to feel tied to a particular software system that you learned years ago. You should experiment with new systems because you already know the basic functional behavior of the program.

---

*fit***TIP**

Mixed Messages. Software is notorious for confusing error messages. It's a difficult problem to fix: Finding errors is easy, but diagnosing the cause is difficult. And programmers explain errors in programming jargon. The result is an incomprehensible error message. But, don't ignore it entirely; a hint of the cause may be buried in the message. For example, this error message

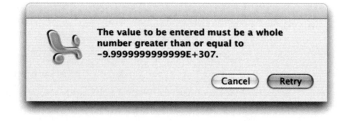

resulted from typing a letter rather than a number. Why doesn't it say, "Enter a number!"? In fact, it does, but in a very complicated way. The conclusion: Spend a moment trying to understand the error message; a useful hint may be hidden there.

SEARCHING TEXT USING FIND

The principle that form follows function has another advantage: It lets us learn how certain computer operations work without referring to any specific software system. Of course, we must focus only on the basic processing behavior rather than on the "bells and whistles" of the GUI, but learning in this way lets us apply our knowledge to any vendor's software. We illustrate this idea with text searching.

Many applications let us search text. Text searching, often called **Find**, is used by word processors, browsers (to look through the text of the current page), email readers, operating systems, and so on. **Find** is typically available under the **Edit** menu, because locating text is the first step in editing it. In cases where editing doesn't make sense—for example, when looking through a file structure in an operating system—**Find** may be listed under the File menu or as a "top level" application. The shortcut for Find—`Ctrl`-**F** for Windows and `⌘`-**F** for MacOSX—is standard with most applications.

Things to be searched are called **tokens**. Most often, tokens are simply the letters, numbers, and special symbols like @ and & from the keyboard, which are also called **characters**. However, sometimes we search for composite items, such as dates that we want to treat as a whole. In such cases, the date is the token, not its letters and digits. For the purposes of searching, tokens form a sequence, called the **search text**, and the tokens to be found are called the **search string**. One property of the search string is that it can contain any tokens that may be in the text. In other words, if the text contains unprintable characters like tabs, the search string is allowed to contain those characters.

How to Search

To illustrate searching, suppose the search string is `content` and the text is a sentence from Martin Luther King's "I Have a Dream" speech:

```
I have a dream that my four little children will one day live
in a nation where they will not be judged by the color of their
skin, but by the content of their character.
```

Searching begins at the beginning or at the current cursor position. Although computers use many clever ways to search text, the easiest one to understand is to think of "sliding" the search string along the text. At each position, compare to see if there is a token match. This simply means looking at corresponding token pairs to see if they are the same:

```
I have a dream ...
↑↑↑↑↑↑↑↑
↓↓↓↓↓↓↓↓
content
```

(Notice that spaces are characters too.) If there is a match, then the process stops and you see the found instance. But if there is no match, you slide the search string one position along and repeat:

```
... by the content of ...
    ↑↑↑↑↑↑↑↑↑↑↑↑↑↑
    ↓↓↓↓↓↓↓↓↓↓↓↓↓↓
... ccccccccontent
```

If the search string is not found when the end of the text is reached, the search stops and is unsuccessful. (Search facilities typically give you the option to continue searching from the beginning of the text if the search did not start there.) The search ends where it began when the search string is not found.

Search Complications

Character searching is easy, but to be completely successful, you should be operationally attuned. There are four things to keep in mind when you are searching: case sensitivity, hidden text, substrings, and multiword strings.

Case Sensitivity.

One complication is that the characters stored in a computer are case sensitive, meaning that the uppercase letters, such as `R`, and lowercase letters, such as `r`, are different. So a match occurs only when the letters *and* the case are identical. A case-sensitive search for `unalienable rights` fails on Jefferson's most famous sentence from the *Declaration of Independence*:

```
We hold these truths to be self-evident, that all men are
created equal, that they are endowed by their Creator with
certain unalienable Rights, that among these are Life, Liberty
and the pursuit of Happiness.
```

To find `unalienable rights` in a text that uses the original capitalization, we would have to ignore the case. Search tools are case sensitive if case is important to the application. For example, word processors are usually case sensitive, but operating systems are not. If the search has case sensitive capabilities, the user has the option to ignore them.

Hidden Text.

Characters are stored in the computer as one continuous sequence. There are two types of characters: keyboard characters that we type and formatting information added by the software application using tags. Because every system uses a different method for the formatting information and because it is usually not important to the search anyhow, we will show the formatting information using our own invented tags.

Tags are abbreviations in paired angle brackets, such as `<Ital>` that describe additional information about the characters (in this case that they should be in italics). Tags generally come in pairs so that they can enclose text like parentheses. The second of the pair is the same as the first, except with a slash (/) or backslash (\) in it. (Tags are used often in our Fluency study, so backslash (\) is used here for the invented tags of our generic application to distinguish them from later uses in HTML and the OED digitization, which use slash.) For example, to show that the word "Enter" should appear in italics, a software application might represent it as `<Ital>Enter<\Ital>`. These formatting tags are invisible to the reader.

For example, the balcony scene from *Romeo and Juliet* appears in a book of Shakespeare's plays as:

SCENE II.   *Capulet's orchard.*

                              Enter Romeo.

Romeo.   He jests at scars that never felt a wound.
                                        [*Juliet appears above at a window.*
But, soft ! what light through yonder window breaks?
It is the east, and Juliet is the sun.

But, this scene might be stored in the computer as follows:

```
SCENE·II.·♦<Ital>Capulet's·orchard.<\Ital>↵↵<Center><Ital>Ente
r<\Ital>Romeo.<\Center>↵<Ital>Romeo.<\Ital>♦He·jests·at·scars
·that·never·felt·a·wound.↵<Right>[<Ital>Juliet·appears·above·a
t·a·window.<\Ital><\Right>↵But,··soft·!·what·light·through·yon
der·window·breaks?·↵It·is·the·east,·and·Juliet·is·the·sun.↵
```

The word processor's tags surround the italic text (`<Ital>`, `<\Ital>`), and the text to be centered (`<Center>`, `<\Center>`) or right-justified (`<Right>`, `<\Right>`). The user typed the other characters and they are the ones we are interested in now. These characters include the text we see as well as formatting characters we can't see: **spaces** (·), **tabs** (♦), and **new lines** (↵). Because these characters control formatting and have no printable form, there is no standard for how they are displayed; for example, the new line character is the **paragraph symbol** (¶) in some systems. Users can ask that all the characters they type be displayed:

```
SCENE·II.·♦   Capulet's·orchard.↵
↵
                    Enter·Romeo.↵
↵
Romeo.♦       He·jests·at·scars·that·never·felt·a·wound.↵
                        [Juliet·appears·above·at·a·window.
↵
But,··soft·!·what·light·through·yonder·window·breaks?↵
It·is·the·east,·and·Juliet·is·the·sun.↵
```

Because the effects of the formatting are shown, it is easy to see where the non-printed formatting characters are. During a search, the software's formatting tags are generally ignored, but all of the characters typed by the user are considered.

Some systems allow tags to be searched by giving you a way to search for formatted text such as italic.

Substrings.   It gets more complicated when we think of search strings as having a meaning more complex than tokens. For example, we often look for words, although the tokens are characters. The problem is that the software may be searching for token sequences, not the more complicated objects that we may have in mind. So searches for the search string **you** in President John Kennedy's inaugural address turn up five hits:

```
And so, my fellow Americans: ask not what
your country can do for you-ask what you
can do for your country.
My fellow citizens of the world: ask not
what America will do for you, but what
together we can do for the freedom of man.
```

Of the five hits, only three are the actual word we're looking for; the other two hits *contain* the search string. To avoid finding **your**, we can search for **·you·** because words in text are usually surrounded by spaces. However, that search discovers *no* hits in this quote because **you** doesn't appear with spaces on both sides. The five hits for **you** are followed by **r**, a dash, a new line, an **r**, and a comma, respectively. The **you** at the end of the second line probably should have had a space between it and the new line, but the typist left it out.

Because looking only for the word **you** and avoiding **your** means checking for all of the possible starting and ending punctuation characters and blanks, it's probably better to relinquish finding the exact word matches and simply ignore the cases where the search string is part of another word. If the search is part of a system such as a word processor, where words are a basic element, the ability to search for words is available. Such cases amount to changing the tokens from characters to words.

Multiword Strings.   A similar problem occurs with multiword search strings. The words of a multiword string are separated by spaces, but if the number of spaces in the search string is different from the number in the text being searched, no match is found. For example, the search string

```
That's·one·small·step·for·man
```

Neil Armstrong's words on first stepping on the moon, will not be found in the quote

```
That's·one·small·step·for··man,·one·giant·leap·for·mankind.
```

because there are two spaces between **for** and **man** in the text.

One Small Step. It is a good idea to look for single words in your search instead of longer phrases. For example, looking for `leap` or `mankind` might work because they are probably not used again in the moon walk transcript.

In summary, searching is the process of locating a sequence of tokens, the search string, in a longer sequence of tokens, the text. Character searches are usually limited to the characters typed, even though other characters may be present. Typed characters can include nonprinting formatting characters such as new line characters. Searches look for token sequences and the tokens (for example, characters) are often more basic than what we can build from them (for example, words). To be successful, we must create search strings so that we find all the matches we're interested in.

EDITING TEXT USING SUBSTITUTION

Search-and-replace, also known as **substitution**, is a combination of searching and editing documents to make corrections. The string that replaces the search string is called the **replacement string**. Although substitution can apply to a single occurrence of the search string in the text if necessary, there is little advantage to using a search-and-replace facility over simply searching and editing the single occurrence directly. The real power of substitution comes from applying it to all occurrences of the search string. For example, if you typed "west coast" in your term paper but then realized that regions are usually capitalized, it is simple to search for all occurrences of `west coast` and replace them with `West Coast`.

Because substitution is a powerful tool that we want to study closely, we will express it in this book using a left-pointing arrow (←) between the search string and the replacement string. The capitalization example is shown as

`west coast` ← `West Coast`

Such an expression can be read "`west coast` *is replaced by* `West Coast`" or "`West Coast` *substitutes for* `west coast`." Another example is

`Norma Jeane Mortensen` ← `Marilyn Monroe`

describing her 1946 name change when she signed her first movie contract.

We emphasize that the arrow is only a *notation* that helps us discuss substitutions in this book; it doesn't appear within the application. When using an application, a GUI is used to specify the replacement (see Figure 2.12). For example the two text fields of the GUI correspond to the information on each side of the arrow. **Find** is the left side of the arrow and **Replace** is the right side. We don't type the arrow in applications. It is only for our use here.

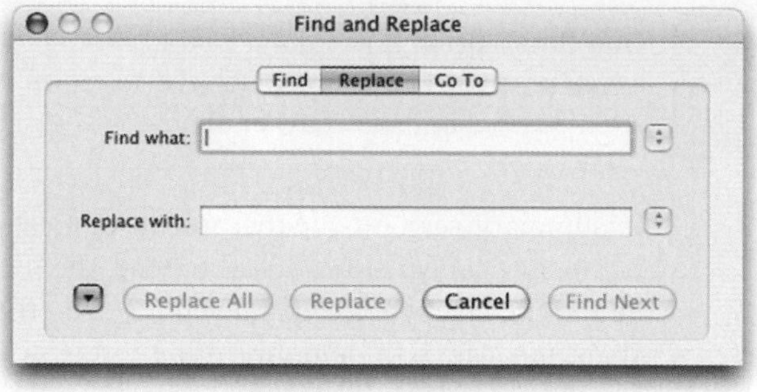

Figure 2.12. *A Find and Replace GUI.*

Unwanted Spaces

In the last section, we noted that multiple spaces separating words in a text complicates searching for multiword strings. Substitution can fix the "multiple spaces in a document" problem: Simply collapse double spaces to single spaces. That is, if the search string is ·· and the replacement string is ·, a search-and-replace of the whole document results in all double spaces becoming single spaces. Expressed using the arrow notation, the "two spaces are replaced by one" substitution is

·· ← ·

Changing from smart quotes to simple quotes is easy enough by writing

" ← "

" ← "

Can we change simple quotes to smart quotes? We can't write

" ← "

because that changes all of the simple quotes to opening smart quotes, including the closing quotes. But we can use the context around the quotes: Opening quotes are preceded by a space, and after changing them, we replace the remaining quotes with close quotes. So we write

·" ← ·"

" ← "

solving the problem.

Formatting Text

One situation where substitution is particularly handy is when text is imported into a document from another source and the formatting becomes messed up. For example, suppose you find the Articles from the UN's Universal Declaration of Human Rights on the Web:

Article 1 All human beings are born free and equal in dignity and rights. They are endowed with reason and conscience and should act towards one another in a spirit of brotherhood.

Article 2 Everyone is entitled to all the rights and freedoms set forth in this Declaration, without distinction of any kind, such as race, color, sex, language, religion, political, or other opinion, national or social origin, property, birth or other status.

Furthermore, no distinction shall be made on the basis of political, jurisdictional or international status of the country or territory to which a person belongs, whether it be independent, trust, non-self-governing, or under any other limitation of sovereignty.

Article 3 Everyone has the right to life, liberty and security of person.

But when you copy the first three articles and paste them into your document, they come out looking like this:

Article 1 All human beings are born free and equal in dignity and rights. They are endowed with reason and conscience and should act towards one another in a spirit of brotherhood.

Article 2 Everyone is entitled to all the rights and freedoms set forth in this Declaration, without distinction of any kind, such as race, color, sex, language, religion, political or other opinion, national or social origin, property, birth or other status.

Furthermore, no distinction shall be made on the basis of political, jurisdictional or international status of the country or territory to which a person belongs, whether it be independent, trust, non-self-governing, or under any other limitation of sovereignty.

Article 3 Everyone has the right to life, liberty and security of person.

The formatting is a mess. Displaying the text with the formatting characters reveals:

```
········Article·1··All·human·beings·are·born·free·and·equal·in·dignity·and·↵
rights.·They·are·endowed·with·reason·and·↵
········conscience·and·should·act·towards·one·another·in·a·spirit·↵
of·brotherhood.··↵
↵
········Article·2··Everyone·is·entitled·to·all·the·rights·and·freedoms·set·forth↵
·in·this·Declaration,·without·distinction·of·any↵
········kind,·such·as·race,·color,·sex,·language,·religion,·political·↵
or·other·opinion,·national·or·social·origin,·↵
········property,·birth·or·other·status.··↵
↵
········Furthermore,·no·distinction·shall·be·made·on·the·basis·of·↵
political,·jurisdictional·or·international·status·of·↵
········the·country·or·territory·to·which·a·person·belongs,·whether·↵
it·be·independent,·trust,·non-self-governing,·↵
········or·under·any·other·limitation·of·sovereignty.··↵
↵
········Article·3··Everyone·has·the·right·to·life,·liberty·and·security·of·person.··↵
```

We see that extra leading spaces and new lines have been inserted when we imported the text into the document.

Clearly, removing the groups of eight spaces at the beginning of lines is simple: we replace them with nothing. When writing the substitution expression, we express "nothing" with the Greek letter epsilon, which is called the empty string; that is, the string with no letters. (Notice that epsilon is used only for writing out substitution expressions for ourselves. In the Find-and-Replace facility of an application, we simply leave the replacement string empty.)

········ ← ε

Removing these leading spaces is easy because they appear only at the beginning of the lines. Correcting the new line characters is more difficult.

We want to get rid of the new line characters that have been inserted within a paragraph but we want to keep the double new lines that separate the paragraphs. But getting rid of the single new line

⏎ ← ε

will get rid of *all* the new lines! How can we keep the double new lines but remove the singles?

The Placeholder Technique

An easy strategy, called the **placeholder technique**, solves our problem. It begins by substituting a placeholder character for the strings we want to keep; that is, the new line pairs in the example. We pick # as the placeholder because it doesn't appear anywhere else in the document, but any unused character or character string will work. The substitution expression is

⏎⏎ ← #

Our text without the leading blanks and double new lines now looks like this:

```
Article·1··All·human·beings·are·born·free·and·equal·in·dignity·and·⏎
rights.·They·are·endowed·with·reason·and·⏎
conscience·and·should·act·towards·one·another·in·a·spirit·⏎
of·brotherhood.#Article·2··Everyone·is·entitled·to·all·the·rights·and·freedoms·set·forth·⏎
in·this·Declaration,·without·distinction·of·any⏎
kind,·such·as·race,·color,·sex,·language,·religion,·political·⏎
or·other·opinion,·national·or·social·origin,·⏎
property,·birth·or·other·status.#Furthermore,·no·distinction·shall·be·made·on·the·basis·of·⏎
political,·jurisdictional·or·international·status·of·⏎
the·country·or·territory·to·which·a·person·belongs,·whether·⏎
it·be·independent,·trust,·non-self-governing,·⏎
or·under·any·other·limitation·of·sovereignty.#Article·3··Everyone·has·the·right·to·life,·liberty·and·security·of·person.
```

The new lines that remain are the ones to be removed, so we need to replace them with nothing

⏎ ← ε

The resulting text has no new line characters left:

> Article·1··All·human·beings·are·born·free·and·equal·in·dignity·and·rights.·They·are·endowed·
> with·reason·and·conscience·and·should·act·towards·one·another·in·a·spirit·of·brotherhood·#
> Article·2··Everyone·is·entitled·to·all·the·rights·and·freedoms·set·forth·in·this·Declaration,·
> without·distinction·of·any·kind,·such·as·race,·color,·sex,·language,·religion,·political·or·
> other·opinion,·national·or·social·origin,·property,·birth·or·other·status.#Furthermore,·no·
> distinction·shall·be·made·on·the·basis·of·political,·jurisdictional·or·international·status·of·the·
> country·or·territory·to·which·a·person·belongs,·whether·it·be·independent,·trust,·non-self-
> governing,·or·under·any·other·limitation·of·sovereignty.#Article·3··Everyone·has·the·right·to·
> life,·liberty·and·security·of·person.

Finally, replace the placeholder with the desired character string

← ↵↵

which gives us

> Article·1··All·human·beings·are·born·free·and·equal·in·dignity·and·rights.·They·are·endowed·
> with·reason·and·conscience·and·should·act·towards·one·another·in·a·spirit·of·brotherhood.
>
> Article·2··Everyone·is·entitled·to·all·the·rights·and·freedoms·set·forth·in·this·Declaration,·
> without·distinction·of·any·kind,·such·as·race,·color,·sex,·language,·religion,·political·or·
> other·opinion,·national·or·social·origin,·property,·birth·or·other·status.
>
> Furthermore,·no·distinction·shall·be·made·on·the·basis·of·political,·jurisdictional·or·
> international·status·of·the·country·or·territory·to·which·a·person·belongs,·whether·it·be·
> independent,·trust,·non-self-governing,·or·under·any·other·limitation·of·sovereignty.
>
> Article·3··Everyone·has·the·right·to·life,·liberty·and·security·of·person.

Except for the bold font for the Article titles and numbers, the resulting file looks like the original document showing the double new lines as appropriate. The final replacements:

Article 1 ← **Article 1**

Article 2 ← **Article 2**

Article 3 ← **Article 3**

complete the task. You may also change the titles to bold directly by editing.

To summarize, the placeholder technique is used to remove short search strings that are part of longer strings that we want to keep. If we were to remove the short strings directly, we would trash the longer strings. The idea is to convert the longer strings into the placeholder temporarily. Of course, a single placeholder character can replace the long strings because all we're keeping track of is the position of the longer string. With the longer strings replaced by the placeholder, it is safe to remove the short strings. Once they are gone, the longer string can replace the placeholder. The substitution expressions

$$LongStringsContainingInstance(s)OfAShortString \leftarrow Placeholder$$

$$ShortString \leftarrow \varepsilon$$

$$Placeholder \leftarrow LongStringsContainingInstance(s)OfAShortString$$

summarize the idea.

⬤ TECHNOLOGY: TAKE IT PERSONALLY

We have revealed some secrets known to expert computer users. Now, it's not miraculous that the digerati appear to know how to use software they have never seen before. They expect consistent interfaces and suggestive icons that allow them to apply their previously learned knowledge intuitively. Now we can exploit that strategy, too.

The important thing about our discussion of learning to use technology is how we figured it all out. We thought about technology as it relates to us. We thought, "We need to learn how to use this technology," so we asked, "How did the inventors of this technology expect us to learn it?" We thought about tool inventors who want people to use their inventions. Inventors can write manuals and we can read them, but they will have more users and users will have more success if the inventions are intuitive, allowing people to "brain out" how to use them. We concluded that we should expect intuitive interfaces. This approach of thinking about technology as it relates to us personally and analyzing the situation in that context is essential for any technology use.

 **There is a series of similar questions that we should ask** ourselves when we need to use new technology, especially software:

- ☑ *What do I have to learn about this software to do my task?*
- ☑ *What does the designer of this software expect me to know?*
- ☑ *What does the designer expect me to do?*
- ☑ *What metaphor is the software showing me?*
- ☑ *What additional information does the software need to do its task?*
- ☑ *Have I seen these operations in other software?*

When we think about information technology in terms of our personal or workplace needs, we may also ask questions such as:

- ☑ *Is there information technology that I am not now using that could help me with my task?*
- ☑ *Am I more or less productive using this technological solution for my task?*

☑ *Can I customize the technology I'm using to make myself more productive?*

☑ *Have I assessed my uses of information technology recently?*

These and similar questions can help you use technology more effectively. Information technology, as a means rather than an end, should be continually assessed to ensure that it is fulfilling your needs as the technology changes and evolves.

SUMMARY

This chapter began by exploring how we learn to use technology. We concluded that:

> People are either taught technology or they figure it out on their own.

> We can figure out software because designers use consistent interfaces, suggestive metaphors, and standard functionality.

> We apply our previous experience to learn new applications.

> Features of the iTunes GUI are familiar, even if we have never seen it before.

> In computer software, if we make a mistake, nothing breaks.

> We should explore a new application by "clicking around" and "blazing away."

> We should watch other users and ask questions.

> Form follows function.

> Searching and substituting, which are available with many applications, work consistently, demonstrating the idea behind form follows function.

> We should think personally about technology and apply general principles and ideas to become more expert users.

EXERCISES

Multiple Choice

1. Experienced computer users are known as
   A. digerati
   B. literati
   C. mazzerati
   D. culturati

2. What is a GUI?
   A. graphical update identification
   B. general user identification
   C. graphical user interface
   D. general update interface

3. Software designers use analogies to help a user understand software because doing so
   A. makes it easier for the user to learn and use the software
   B. makes the software more popular
   C. is required by law
   D. more than one of the above

4. An example of a metaphor is
   A. The player played with the heart of a lion.
   B. The silence was deafening.
   C. The computer played chess as well as the best humans.
   D. all of the above

5. Which of the following is not a common computer metaphor?
   A. buttons
   B. door handles
   C. menus
   D. sliders

6. A slider control is used for selecting
   A. one of several options
   B. one or more of several options
   C. within a continuous range of options
   D. one or more items from a list

7. In Windows, closing a subwindow
   A. is not allowed
   B. leaves the application running
   C. exits the application
   D. automatically saves your file

8. A dialog will open when a menu has a(n) _____ in it.
   A. shortcut
   B. ellipsis
   C. check mark
   D. separator

9. Menu options that are unavailable
   A. have a check mark by them
   B. are gray
   C. have a line through them
   D. are hidden

10. Which of the following is not an instance?
    A. an image
    B. a song file
    C. a word processing document
    D. a menu

11. The Greek letter epsilon ε can be used to represent "nothing." In a find and replace, you would have to use
    A. _
    B. null
    C. nothing (empty)
    D. ∅

Short Answer

1. _____ is the word used to describe people who understand digital technology.

2. GUI stands for _____.

3. Software designers help users understand their software through the use of _____.

4. A(n) _____ is a figure of speech where one object is compared to another.

5. _____ are used to indicate that there is hidden information available.

6. **Open**, **New**, **Close**, and **Save** can usually be found in the _____ menu.

7. To avoid cluttering the screen with commands, software designers put most of their commands in _____.

8. **Undo**, **Cut**, **Copy**, and **Paste** are usually found in the _____ menu.

9. The online manual is usually found in the _____ menu.

10. Menus that can show up anywhere on the screen are called _____.

11. Another name for a pull-down menu is a(n) _____.

12. When the computer needs more information from the user before it completes an action, it gets the information via a(n) _____.

13. Menus that are unavailable are generally colored _____.

14. Menu options that open a dialog display are identified because they contain a(n) _____.

15. The clover-shaped shortcut key on a Macintosh is called the _____ key.

16. Menus are grouped by similarity of operation and listed across the top of the screen in the _____.

Exercises

1. Explain the desktop metaphor.

2. Discuss the advantages of a consistent interface. Look at it from the consumer's view and from the developer's view.

3. List the technology tools you can typically use without reading the owner's manual.

4. What are the two keys to success with information technology?

5. Match the buttons on the two CD interfaces in Figures 2.1 and 2.2. Label the commands. Speculate on how the features found on only one are implemented on the other.

6. What happens when we apply the ** ← * replacement to *****? Try this out with your text editor. How many times did it find and replace? How many were left? Explain how this process worked.

7. Describe the similarities and differences between the Windows CD Player and the Windows Media Player. If you have a Mac, use the CD Player and the QuickTime Player.

8. Using Lincoln's Gettysburg Address, what appears more often, "that" or "here"?

9. How many times does the word "the" appear in Lincoln's Gettysburg Address? How many times do the letters "t·h·e" appear together?

chapter

3

MAKING THE CONNECTION
The Basics of Networking

learning objectives

> Describe changes that networked computers have brought to society

> Tell whether a communication technology (Internet, radio, LAN, etc.) is synchronous or asynchronous, broadcast or point-to-point

> Explain the roles of Internet addresses, domain names, and DNS servers in networking

> Distinguish between types of protocols (TCP/IP and Ethernet)

> Describe how computers are interconnected by an ISP and by a LAN

> Distinguish between the Internet and the World Wide Web

chapter 3

MAKING THE CONNECTION
The Basics of Networking

The open society, the unrestricted access to knowledge, the unplanned and uninhibited association of men for its furtherance—these are what make a vast, complex, ever growing, ever changing, ever more specialized and expert technological world nevertheless a world of human community.

—J ROBERT OPPENHEIMER, 1953

The presence of humans in a system containing high-speed electronic computers and high-speed accurate communications is quite inhibiting [to the system].

—STUART LUMAN SEATON, 1958

COMPUTERS alone are useful. Computers connected together are even more useful. Dramatic proof of this occurred in the mid-1990s when the Internet, long available to researchers, became generally available to the public. The **Internet** is the totality of all wires, fibers, switches, routers, satellite links, and other hardware for transporting information between addressed computers, as shown in Figure 3.1. For the first time, people could conveniently and inexpensively connect their computers to the Internet and thereby connect to all other computers attached to the Internet. They could send email and surf the Web from home. This convenient access to volumes of information, eCommerce, chat rooms, and other capabilities greatly expanded the benefits people derived from computers.

We begin this chapter by considering how connecting computers with the Internet has changed the world. We identify five of the most significant effects of the Internet—not all of them clearly beneficial. After we discuss the impact of the Internet, we define some communication terms. These will help you compare the Internet with other forms of communication. Some topics are designed to give you a sense of how the Internet works without the technical details: naming computers, packets, the TCP/IP and Ethernet protocols, and connecting your computer to the Internet. Next, the World Wide Web and file structures are explained in preparation for our discussion of HTML in Chapter 4.

NETWORKED COMPUTERS CHANGE OUR LIVES

A skeptic might wonder whether all of the excitement and frenzy surrounding the Internet is anything more than hype. After all, for a hundred years, average citizens in developed countries have had access to great repositories of information in libraries, have been able to communicate with each other via telephones or traditional mail (snail mail), and have enjoyed the benefits of retail commerce. Since early in the last century wire services have routinely brought the news from distant locales, and broadcast media such as newspapers, radio, and television conveyed that news widely. Has anything actually changed? Very definitely.

The interconnection of computers—networking—has brought us the Information Age and with it profound changes. For example, now:

> Nowhere is remote.

> People are more interconnected.

> Social relationships are changing.

> English is becoming a universal language.

> Freedom of speech and of assembly have expanded.

We'll consider each change in detail.

Nowhere Is Remote

In the past, centers of commerce, learning, and government justly claimed an advantage over geographically remote places in the world based on their ready access to information. Today, thanks to networking, nowhere is remote. Places like Unalakleet, Alaska are now nearly equivalent to world capitals like New York City. From finding up-to-date maps of Prague's subway system for vacation planning, to finding NASDAQ share prices for investing, to listening to online sports radio for keeping up with "them Mets," the Internet is a complete information resource no matter where you are.

Differences remain because not all information is online. Most pre-1985 information found in the New York Public Library is not yet online, but almost all currently produced information is. And it's available simultaneously to all. Readers of the *Sydney Morning Herald* in Sydney, New South Wales and Sydney, Nova Scotia can enjoy the paper at the same time despite being on opposite sides of the planet. Also, our homes are not remote from work. "Information workers" routinely telecommute, allowing them to live in rural picturesque locations distant from their offices.

People Are More Interconnected

People tend to stay in closer, more frequent contact with friends and family across the country or internationally via the Internet than by telephone or snail mail.

Email is cheaper, faster, and not subject to "time zone" conflicts. And the Internet gives everyone the choice of treating email like traditional mail by reading it later, or like a phone conversation by answering it online immediately.

The World Wide Web lets us meet people passively. When you create a Web page describing your interests and other information, you publish a personal "advertisement" that's available all over the world. Most importantly, your page can be found by Web search engines, which allows others with similar interests to find you. If your Web page describes how you grow bonsai trees from *Sequoia sempervirens*, someone else who is interested in Sequoia bonsai can locate your page with a Web search engine (see Chapter 5). That person can contact you, and a friendship or collaboration based on your shared interest may blossom. In this way, people interested in very specialized topics, topics that may be too obscure to support an organization or society, can become acquainted. And associations can form rapidly—a whole interest group can develop around an unfolding event, such as a typhoon or election.

Social Interactions Are Changing

Not all aspects of information technology are beneficial. One possible downside is that time spent online displaces other activities. It's called the **displacement effect**. It contends that if people spend time surfing the Web, playing games, or engaging in other activities that displace in-person social interaction, the outcome may be less than desirable. Recent studies from Carnegie-Mellon and Stanford Universities indicate a decline in social interactions after people become intensive computer users. Claims were even made for an "increase in depression." The topic is complicated and requires further study.

As an example of the complications, consider that a person's time online might be spent participating in chat rooms or sending email to friends and family. Isn't this simply a modern form of in-person social interaction? Possibly, but maybe not. We might know our electronic acquaintances only superficially compared to our in-the-flesh friends. On the other hand, maybe we "open up" and speak more candidly to someone we know only anonymously. Also, the chance to keep in close electronic contact with family or to meet others passively who have similar interests may be more rewarding than our face-to-face acquaintances, which are limited to people physically nearby. The Internet is changing people's social interactions, but we don't fully understand how.

English Is Becoming a Universal Language

Since the end of World War II, there have been growing indications that English may become a universal language. Among the reasons are the influences of American movies and pop culture and the dominance of science and technology in English-speaking countries. English is not yet universal, but it is the leading candidate and IT gives English a huge advantage.

Although Microsoft Windows is available in German and Japanese editions, much software is available only in English; non-English software options are limited to a few major languages. Still, the driving force behind the desire to read and understand English is not only software, but also the Web. Most Web pages are in English, and when they are multilingual, English is usually an option. English is also widely used on eCommerce sites. People fluent in English have greater access to the Web's benefits, reinforcing the prospect of English as a universal language. Of course, computer translation can convert English to another language, but these translations are not usually very faithful, and they are available only for a few widely spoken languages. Most of the world's languages will likely never be translated electronically.

Interestingly, if English becomes the universal IT language, it will probably have little effect on other languages. In non-English-speaking countries, English would be taught as a second language and the population would be bilingual. This is already true in many countries. There is little threat to the native language because it's used for most other aspects of daily life.

Freedom of Speech and of Assembly Have Expanded

Creating a Web page is a means of identifying ourselves. We can state who we are (or think we are) and what we believe in. Web pages can be viewed from anywhere and located by a search engine. Most important, in most countries, Internet use is **unmediated** (not subject to any editorial oversight or significant restrictions). Such an unfettered, worldwide communication medium presents an unprecedented degree of freedom of speech, previously available only to those who owned broadcast channels or printing presses. It allows political and artistic expression (within the limits of the medium), and all forms of promotion (including shameless self-promotion). It enables Web logs, or **blogs**, to record personal thoughts for public viewing. As with freedoms generally, free speech on the Web can be abused, leading to hate propaganda or detailed instructions on how to build bombs. The opportunity for *unmediated* expression, however, seems to be a new benefit of the Internet.

Along with free speech, the Internet also promotes freer association. Like-minded people can find each other by searching the Web. Once connected, they can communicate by email or form chat rooms and newsgroups. Unlike ham radio, which relies on broadcast to connect a group, email and Web browsing are private. Though criminals and terrorists can exploit the privacy, everyone benefits. For example, information on sensitive topics like abortion, contraception, or sexually transmitted diseases can be accessed privately using the Web.

*fit*BYTE | **Internet.** The present-day Internet is the commercial descendant of the ARPANET, developed for the U.S. Department of Defense Advanced Research Projects Agency (DARPA). The ARPANET sent its first messages in 1969.

COMPARING COMMUNICATION TYPES

To understand the Internet, it's necessary to explain some basic communication vocabulary.

General Communication

Communication between two entities, whether they are people or computers, can be separated into two broad classes: synchronous and asynchronous. **Synchronous communication** requires that both the sender and the receiver are active at the same time. A telephone conversation is an example of synchronous communication because both people in the conversation must perform one of the two parts of the communication—sending (talking) or receiving (listening)—simultaneously. In **asynchronous communication**, the sending and receiving occur at different times. A postcard is an example of asynchronous communication because it is written at one time and read later. Answering machines and voice mail make synchronous telephones asynchronous because the caller leaves a message that the receiver listens to later. Email is asynchronous, but applications like instant messaging make it essentially synchronous.

> *fit*BYTE
>
> **Spamming.** Spam is unsolicited email. It is an annoying aspect of email, although spam filters—software that intercepts spam and moves it out of your inbox—can help. The term is widely believed to derive from a *Monty Python* skit in which the word "spam" was chanted by Vikings to drown out restaurant conversation, humorously showing that unwanted input impedes legitimate communication.

Another property of communication concerns the number of receivers. **Broadcast communication** involves a single sender and many receivers. Radio and television are examples of broadcast communication. The term **multicast** is used when there are many receivers, but the intended recipients are not the whole population. Magazines, often covering specialized topics, are an example of multicast communication. The opposite of broadcasting and multicasting is **point-to-point communication**. Telephone communication is point-to-point. The property of broadcast *versus* point-to-point communication is separate from the property of synchronous *versus* asynchronous communication.

The Internet's Communication Properties

A fundamental feature of the Internet is that it provides a general communication "fabric" linking all computers connected to it (see Figure 3.1). That is, the computers and the network become a single medium that can be applied in many ways to produce alternatives to established forms of communication. For example, the Internet's point-to-point asynchronous communication functions like the postal system, but at electronic speed. In fact, the Internet is fast enough to mimic synchronous communication, enabling instant messaging (IM): Two or more people can have a conversation by the rapid exchange of asynchronous messages. So the Internet can be used like a phone. (With special software, an Internet-connected computer can *be* a phone, too.) Also, multicasting is possible, enabling small- to modest-size groups to communicate via chat rooms. Finally, because it is possible to post a Web page that can be accessed by anyone, the Internet offers a form of broadcasting that compares with radio or television. The Internet is truly a universal communications medium.

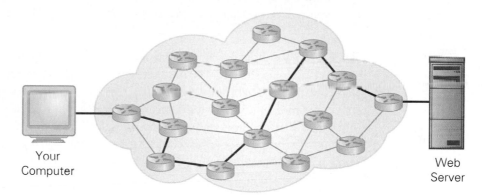

Figure 3.1. A diagram of the Internet.

The Internet also becomes more effective with each additional computer added to it. That is, if *x* computers are already attached to the Internet, adding one more computer results in *x* potential new connections—that computer with each of the original machines.

The Client/Server Structure

Most interactions over the Internet use a protocol known as **client/server interaction**. This simple idea is illustrated by following what happens when you browse the Web.

A Brief Encounter. When you click on a link, your computer begins the process of accessing the page for you. At that moment, your computer enters into a client/server interaction. Yours is the client computer and the computer on which the Web page is stored is the server computer, which is why it's called a **Web server** (see Figure 3.2). The term "client" refers to any situation where one computer, the *client*, gets services from another computer, the *server*. As a result of your client request, the server sends the page back over the Internet, fulfilling the request. That completes the operation started with your click on the link, and it ends that client/server relationship.

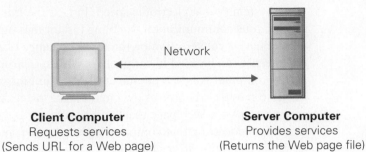

Client Computer
Requests services
(Sends URL for a Web page)

Server Computer
Provides services
(Returns the Web page file)

Figure 3.2. *The basic client/server interaction, as illustrated by the browser (client) requesting Web pages provided by the Web server.*

The client/server structure is fundamental to Internet interactions. A key aspect of the idea is that, as shown in Figure 3.2, only a single service request and response are involved. It is a very brief relationship, lasting from the moment the request is sent, to the moment the service is received. Unlike a telephone call, in which a connection is made and *held* for as long as the call lasts, and during which there are many alternating exchanges, the client/server relationship is very short. It only entails the client's single request for a service and the server's reply in response.

Many Brief Relationships. An important advantage of this approach is that the server can handle many clients at a time. Typically between two consecutive client requests from your browser—between getting a Web page and asking for the next Web page from the same site—that server could have serviced hundreds or perhaps thousands of other clients. This is a very efficient system, because the server is busy with you only for as long as it takes to perform your request. Once it's fulfilled, the relationship is over from the server's viewpoint. But the relationship is over from your viewpoint, too. Your next click could be on a link for a different server. Between that click and the next time you visit the site, if ever, you and your browser could be clients to hundreds or perhaps thousands of other Web servers. So, Figure 3.3 shows the client/server relationship over an interval of time.

fit **BYTE**

Staying Connected. With conventional telephones, callers stay connected even if no one is talking. In a client/server interaction, there is no connection. There is a client-to-server transmission for requests and a server-to-client transmission for replies. But doesn't your computer stay connected to the Internet? Yes, but only to your ISP—that is, to the Internet—not to a Web server.

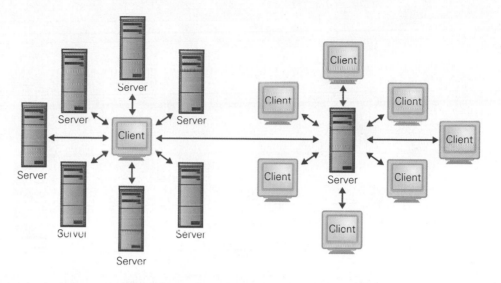

Figure 3.3. Client/server relationships as they might evolve over time.

THE MEDIUM OF THE MESSAGE

How does the Internet transmit information such as Web pages and email messages? Complex and sophisticated technologies are used to make today's Internet
work, but the basic idea is extremely simple.

The Name Game of Computer Addresses

To begin, remember that the Internet uses point-to-point communication. When
anything is sent point-to-point—a phone conversation, a letter, or furniture—the
destination address is required.

IP Addresses. Each computer connected to the Internet is given a unique
address called its **IP address**, short for **Internet Protocol Address**. An IP address
is a series of four numbers separated by dots, as shown in Figure 3.4. For example, the IP address of the computer on which I am typing this sentence is
`128.95.1.207`, and the machine to which my email is usually sent is
`128.95.1.4`. Although the range of each of these numbers (0–255) allows for
billions of Internet addresses, IP addresses are actually in short supply.

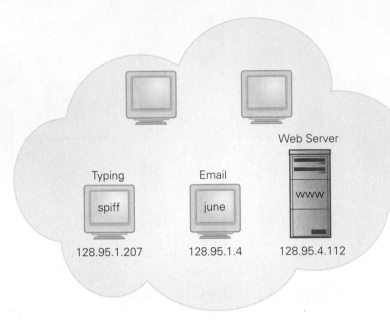

Figure 3.4. Computers connected to the Internet are given IP addresses.

*fit***BYTE**

Change of Address. Since the 1970s we have used Internet Protocol Version 4 (IPv4). It is IPv4 that specifies that IP addresses are four numbers long. Four was plenty for the days when only about 200 computers were networked. Now about 200 million computers are networked, motivating the development of Internet Protocol Version 6 (IPv6). IPv6 specifies IP addresses will be sixteen numbers long in the future, solving the IP address problem for good.

Domain Names. If we needed to know the four numbers of the IP addresses of our friends' computers to send them email, the process would be very annoying and uncivilized. Instead, the Internet uses human-readable symbolic names for computers that are based on a hierarchy of *domains*. A **domain** is a related group of networked computers. For example, the name of my computer is `spiff.cs.washington.edu`, which reveals its domain membership by its structure. Pulling apart the name, my computer (`spiff`) is a member of the Computer Science and Engineering Department domain (`cs`), which is part of the University of Washington domain (`washington`), which is part of the educational domain (`edu`), as shown in Figure 3.5(a) and (b). This is a hierarchy of domains because each is a member of the next larger domain. Another of my computers, `tracer.cs.washington.edu`, has a name with a similar structure, so it is apparently a member of the same domain. Other departments at the University of Washington, such as Astronomy (`astro.washington.edu`), have names that are peers of `cs` (on the same level) within the `washington` domain, and other schools (for example, `princeton.edu`) have names that are peers with `washington` within the `edu` domain. These names are symbolic and meaningful, making them easier to read than numbers, and arranged in a hierarchy that makes them easier to remember.

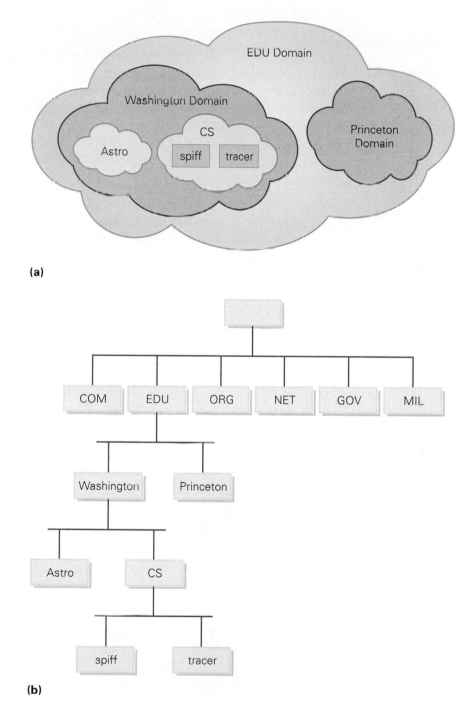

(a)

(b)

Figure 3.5. *Two ways to think of the Internet domain hierarchy.*

DNS Servers. How do the convenient domain names like `spiff.cs` `.washington.edu` get converted into the IP addresses like `128.95.1.207` that computers need? The **Domain Name System (DNS)** translates the hierarchical, human-readable names into the four-number IP addresses, as shown in Figure 3.6. This allows both people and computers to use their preferred scheme.

Every Internet host (a computer connected to the Internet) knows the IP address of its nearest **Domain Name System server**, a computer that keeps a list of the human-readable symbolic names and the corresponding IP addresses. Whenever you use the hierarchical symbolic name to send information to some destination, your computer asks the DNS server to look up the corresponding IP address. It then uses that IP address to send the information. Notice that when your computer asks a DNS server to translate a name to the IP address, it is in another client/server relationship.

Usually the DNS server knows the translation for the symbolic name to the IP address and replies immediately. But if it doesn't know the address it asks one of 13 **Root** name servers. These computers, scattered around the world, keep the master list of all of the name-to-address translations. If they don't know, they try to find out by asking the Authoritative name server. Each domain has a server that keeps a record of the name-to-address translations for its domain, and it replies to the Root name server, which passes the name back on to your DNS and then to your computer (see Figure 3.6).

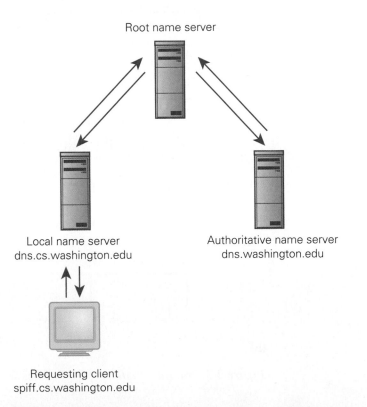

Root name server

Local name server
dns.cs.washington.edu

Authoritative name server
dns.washington.edu

Requesting client
spiff.cs.washington.edu

Figure 3.6. *Hosts like spiff make requests to a local DNS server.*

Notice that computers change their client and server roles all the time. When your local DNS server asks the Root server for help, it changes from being a server, which it was to your (client) computer, to being a client of the Root server.

---

try it

Does the Root name server ever become a client and if so, when?

Answer: Yes, when it requests a translation from the Authoritative name server.

Top-level Domains. The `.edu` domain for educational institutions is one of several **top-level domain** names. In addition to `.edu` the top-level domains include:

- `.com` for commercial enterprises

- `.org` for organizations

- `.net` for networks

- `.mil` for the military

- `.gov` for government agencies

These original domains all apply to organizations in the United States. The set of top-level domains has recently been expanded. There is also a set of mnemonic two-letter country designators, such as `.ca` (Canada), `.uk` (United Kingdom), `.fr` (France), `.de` (Germany, as in Deutschland), `.es` (Spain, as in España), `.us` (United States), and so on. (See Table 3.1 for a complete list.) These allow domain names to be grouped by their country of origin. The period, always pronounced *dot*, simply separates the levels of the domains, and was chosen to be easy to type and say.

---

*fit***BYTE**

Where It's @. Email addresses, like domain names, have a structure. For example: `president@whitehouse.gov`. The portion to the right of the @ sign is the **destination address**, so it has domain structure. It is processed by the sending computer(s). The information to the left of the @ sign is the **user ID**, and it is processed by the receiving computer.

Following Protocol

Having figured out how a computer addresses other computers to send them information, we still need to describe how the information is actually sent. The sending process uses **Transmission Control Protocol/Internet Protocol** or **TCP/IP**. It sounds technical, and is. But the concept is easy to understand.

TCP/IP Postcard Analogy. To explain how TCP/IP works, we repeat an analogy used by Vincent Cerf, one of the pioneers of IP: Sending information over the Internet is like sending your novel from your home in Tahiti to your publisher

Table 3.1. *Top-level Country Domain Abbreviations*

AF	Afghanistan	EG	Egypt	LT	Lithuania	SN	Senegal
AL	Albania	SV	El Salvador	LU	Luxembourg	SC	Seychelles
DZ	Algeria	GQ	Equatorial Guinea	MO	Macau	SL	Sierra Leone
AS	American Samoa	ER	Eritrea	MK	Macedonia, the for-	SG	Singapore
AD	Andorra	EE	Estonia		mer Yugoslav	SK	Slovakia (Slovak
AO	Angola	ET	Ethiopia		Republic of		Republic)
AI	Anguilla	FK	Falkland Islands	MG	Madagascar	SI	Slovenia
AQ	Antarctica		(Malvinas)	MW	Malawi	SB	Solomon Islands
AG	Antigua & Barbuda	FO	Faeroe Islands	MY	Malaysia	SO	Somalia
AR	Argentina	FJ	Fiji	MV	Maldives	ZA	South Africa
AM	Armenia	FI	Finland	ML	Mali	GS	South Georgia &
AW	Aruba	FR	France	MT	Malta		South Sandwiches
AU	Australia	FX	France, Metropolitan	MH	Marshall Islands	ES	Spain
AT	Austria	GF	French Guiana	MQ	Martinique	LK	Sri Lanka
AZ	Azerbaijan	PF	French Polynesia	MR	Mauritania	SH	St. Helena
BS	Bahamas	TF	French Southern	MU	Mauritius	PM	St. Pierre &
BH	Bahrain		Territories	YT	Mayotte		Miquelon
BD	Bangladesh	GA	Gabon	MX	Mexico	SD	Sudan
BB	Barbados	GM	Gambia	FM	Micronesia	SR	Suriname
BY	Belarus	GE	Georgia	MD	Moldova,	SJ	Svalbard & Jan
BE	Belgium	DE	Germany		Republic of		Mayen Islands
BZ	Belize	GH	Ghana	MC	Monaco	SZ	Swaziland
BJ	Benin	GI	Gibraltar	MN	Mongolia	SE	Sweden
BM	Bermuda	GR	Greece	MS	Montserrat	CH	Switzerland
BT	Bhutan	GL	Greenland	MA	Morocco	SY	Syrian Arab Republic
BO	Bolivia	GD	Grenada	MZ	Mozambique	TW	Taiwan, Province of
BA	Bosnia &	GP	Guadeloupe	MM	Myanmar		China
	Herzegovina	GU	Guam	NA	Namibia	TJ	Tajikistan
BW	Botswana	GT	Guatemala	NR	Nauru	TZ	Tanzania, United
BV	Bouvet Island	GN	Guinea	NP	Nepal		Republic of
BR	Brazil	GW	Guinea-Bissau	NL	Netherlands	TH	Thailand
IO	British Indian Ocean	GY	Guyana	NC	New Caledonia	TG	Togo
	Territory	HT	Haiti	NZ	New Zealand	TK	Tokelau
BN	Brunei Darussalam	HM	Heard & McDonald	NI	Nicaragua	TO	Tonga
BG	Bulgaria		Islands	NE	Niger	TT	Trinidad & Tobago
BF	Burkina Faso	HN	Honduras	NG	Nigeria	TN	Tunisia
BI	Burundi	HK	Hong Kong	NU	Niue	TR	Turkey
KH	Cambodia	HU	Hungary	NF	Norfolk Island	TM	Turkmenistan
CM	Cameroon	IS	Iceland	MP	Northern Mariana	TC	Turks & Caicos
CA	Canada	IN	India		Islands		Islands
CV	Cape Verde	ID	Indonesia	NO	Norway	TV	Tuvalu
KY	Cayman Islands	IR	Iran (Islamic	OM	Oman	UG	Uganda
CF	Central African		Republic of)	PK	Pakistan	UA	Ukraine
	Republic	IQ	Iraq	PW	Palau	AE	United Arab
TD	Chad	IE	Ireland	PA	Panama		Emirates
CL	Chile	IL	Israel	PG	Papua New Guinea	GB	United Kingdom
CN	China	IT	Italy	PY	Paraguay	US	United States
CX	Christmas Island	JM	Jamaica	PE	Peru	UM	United States Minor
CC	Cocos (Keeling)	JP	Japan	PH	Philippines		Outlying Islands
	Islands	JO	Jordan	PN	Pitcairn	UY	Uruguay
CO	Colombia	KZ	Kazakhstan	PL	Poland	UZ	Uzbekistan
KM	Comoros	KE	Kenya	PT	Portugal	VU	Vanuatu
CG	Congo	KI	Kiribati	PR	Puerto Rico	VA	Vatican City State
CK	Cook Islands	KP	Korea, Democratic	QA	Qatar	VE	Venezuela
CR	Costa Rica		People's Republic of	RE	Reunion	VN	Vietnam
CI	Cote d'Ivoire	KR	Korea, Republic of	RO	Romania	VG	Virgin Islands
HR	Croatia (local name:	KW	Kuwait	RU	Russian Federation	VI	Virgin Islands (US)
	Hrvatska)	KG	Kyrgyzstan	RW	Rwanda	WF	Wallis & Futuna
CU	Cuba	LA	Lao People's	KN	Saint Kitts & Nevis		Islands
CY	Cyprus		Democratic Republic	LC	Saint Lucia	EH	Western Sahara
CZ	Czech Republic	LV	Latvia	VC	Saint Vincent & the	YE	Yemen
DK	Denmark	LB	Lebanon		Grenadines	YU	Yugoslavia
DJ	Djibouti	LS	Lesotho	WS	Samoa	ZR	Zaire
DM	Dominica	LR	Liberia	SM	San Marino	ZM	Zambia
DO	Dominican Republic	LY	Libyan Arab	ST	Sao Tome &	ZW	Zimbabwe
TP	East Timor		Jamahiriya		Principe		
EC	Ecuador	LI	Liechtenstein	SA	Saudi Arabia		

#1
Chapter 1:
It was a dark
and stormy night.
Rain pelted the
glass as Sir
Bulwer-Lytton
dozed restlessly.

Great Books
1830 1st Ave
New York, NY
USA

in New York City using only postcards. How could you do that? You would begin by breaking up the novel into small units, only a few sentences long, so that each unit fits on a postcard. Then number each postcard to indicate where in the sequence of your novel the sentences belong, and write the publisher's address on each. As you complete the postcards, drop them into a mailbox. The postal service in Tahiti sends them to the publisher (eventually), but the cards are not kept together, nor do they all take the same route. Some postcards may go west, via Hong Kong; others may go east, via Los Angeles. From Hong Kong and Los Angeles, there are multiple routes to New York City. Eventually the postcards arrive at the publisher, who uses the numbers to put the postcards in order and reconstruct the novel, as shown in Figure 3.7.

Cerf's postcard analogy makes the concept of TCP/IP clear. Sending any amount of information, including a whole novel, is possible by breaking it into a sequence of small fixed-size units. An **IP packet**, like the postcard, has space for the unit, a destination IP address, and a sequence number. IP packets are filled in order and assigned sequence numbers. The packets are sent over the Internet one at a time using whatever route is available, as shown in Figure 3.8. At the destination, they are reordered by sequence number to assemble the information.

Figure 3.7. The TCP/IP postcard analogy.

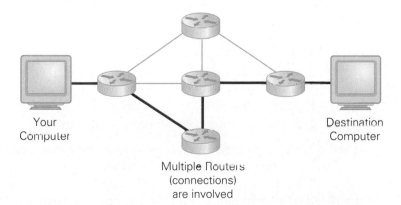

Your
Computer

Multiple Routers
(connections)
are involved

Destination
Computer

Figure 3.8. The Internet makes use of whatever routes are available to deliver packets.

Packets Are Independent. Consider the advantages of TCP/IP. For example, it is natural to assume that IP packets would take a single path to their destinations, like conventional telephone calls, but they do not. Because each packet can take a different route, congestion and service interruptions do not delay transmissions. If sending the first postcard via Hong Kong meant that all following postcards had to be sent via Hong Kong, then a typhoon preventing aircraft from flying between Tahiti and Hong Kong would delay the novel's transmission. But if the postcards can take any available route, the transmission can continue via Los Angeles. As a result, all of the novel might be delivered via LA before airline service is restored between Tahiti and Hong Kong. This concept motivated engineers to decide to make TCP/IP packets independent.

Moving Packets: Wires and More. Although Cerf's analogy uses postcards and airplanes, the Internet uses electrical, electronic, and optical communication means. The original ARPANet used long-distance telephone lines and the Internet continues to rely on telephone carriers for long-distance connections. However, as the Internet has grown and as new technologies such as fiber optics have matured, the Internet now uses separate dedicated lines as well. Because the TCP/IP protocol describes exactly how IP packets are structured and handled, the technology used to move the packets only concerns the carrier. The computers at each end of the communication do not know or care what medium is used because they simply send and receive IP packets. Indeed, transmissions often rely on multiple technologies as the packets move across the Internet.

Ironically, with the growth of Internet capacity, telephone companies are also sending telephone conversations over the Internet. Speech is digitized, stuffed into IP packets at the speaker's end, sent over the Internet, unpacked at the listener's end, and converted to the analog form acceptable to a phone set. This suggests that the Internet is fast becoming the universal information carrier.

Far and Near: WAN and LAN

The Internet is a collection of **wide area networks** (**WAN**), meaning networks designed to send information between two locations widely separated and not directly connected. In our postcard analogy, Tahiti and New York City are not directly connected; that is, there is no single airline flight between Tahiti and the Big Apple. So each postcard takes a sequence of connecting flights to reach New York City. In the same way, the Internet is a collection of point-to-point channels, and packets must visit a sequence of computers to reach their destination. In networking terms, packets take several **hops** to be delivered. The trace in Figure 3.9 shows that a ping—a "please reply" message—from my machine `spiff` to `eth.ch`, the Swiss Federal Technical University, takes 18 hops on its route from Seattle to Zürich.

When computers are close enough to be linked by a single cable or pair of wires, the interconnection is referred to as a **local area network** (**LAN**). Ethernet is the main technology for local area networks, and is appropriate for connecting all the computers in a lab or building. An Ethernet network uses a radically different approach than the Internet, but it's equally easy to understand.

Ethernet Party Analogy. Depending on the technology, the physical setup for an Ethernet network is a wire, wire pair, or optical fiber, called the **channel**, that winds past a set of computers. (Robert Metcalfe, the inventor described the channel as the "The Ether," giving the technology its name, see Figure 3.10.) Engineers "tap" the channel to connect a computer, allowing it to send a signal (that is, drive an electronic pulse or light flash onto the channel). All computers connected to the channel can detect the signal, including the sender. Thus the channel supports broadcast communication.

VisualRoute 7.1d Trial Version							
File Edit Options Tools Help							
Address `eth.ch`				IP Addresses `129.132.1.15`			☑ Advanced mo

Report for eth.ch [129.132.1.15]

Analysis: 'eth.ch' [weasel-rz.ethz.ch] was found in 18 hops (TTL=238).

Hop	IP Address	Node Name	Location	Tzone	ms	Graph	Network
0	128.95.1.207	spiff.cseresearch.cs.washington.edu				172	University of Washington WASH
1	128.95.1.199		...		0		University of Washington WASH
2	140.142.153.23	uwbr1-CE2-0.cac.washington.edu	...		0		University of Washington UW-SI
3	198.107.151.12	hnsp2-wes-ge-1-0-1-0.pnw.gigapop.net	...		0		Verio, Inc. VRIO-198-106
4	198.107.144.2	abilene-pnw.pnw-gigapop.net	...		1		Verio, Inc. VRIO-198-106
5	198.32.8.50	dnvrng-sttng.abilene.ucaid.edu	...		25		Exchange Point Blocks NET-EP
6	198.32.8.14	kscyng-dnvrng.abilene.ucaid.edu	...		36		Exchange Point Blocks NET-EP
7	198.32.8.80	iplsng-kscyng.abilene.ucaid.edu	...		52		Exchange Point Blocks NET-EP
8	198.32.8.76	chinng-iplsng.abilene.ucaid.edu	...		62		Exchange Point Blocks NET-EP
9	198.32.8.83	nycmng-chinng.abilene.ucaid.edu	...		76		Exchange Point Blocks NET-EP
10	62.40.103.25	abilene.uk1.uk.geant.net	(United Kingdom)	*	140		IP allocation for GEANT network
11	62.40.96.89	uk.fr1.fr.geant.net	(United Kingdom)	*	146		IP allocation for GEANT network
12	62.40.96.29	fr.ch1.ch.geant.net	(United Kingdom)	*	156		IP allocation for GEANT network
13	62.40.103.18	swiCE2-P6-1.switch.ch	(United Kingdom)	*	156		IP allocation for GEANT network
14	130.59.36.22	swiEZ2-G1-1.switch.ch	(Switzerland)	+01:00	156		SWITCH Teleinformatics Servic
15	192.33.92.1	rou-rz-gw-giga-to-switch.ethz.ch	(Switzerland)	+01:00	158		Swiss Federal Institute of Techr
16	192.33.92.130	rou-ethz-access-intern.ethz.ch	(Switzerland)	+01:00	156		Swiss Federal Institute of Techr
17	129.132.99.65	rou-rz-mega-transit ethz.ch	(Switzerland)	+01:00	163		Swiss Federal Institute of Techr
18	**129.132.1.15**	eth.ch	(Switzerland)	+01:00	156		Swiss Federal Institute of Techr

Roundtrip time to eth.ch, average = 156ms, min = 156ms, max = 172ms - 30-Apr-03 4:49:50 PM

Figure 3.9. *A ping from the author's machine to* `eth.ch`*.*

*fit***BYTE** **Getting Ether.** Robert Metcalfe described the Ethernet (in 1973) as a "multipoint data communication channel with collision detection." His first implementation connected the 100-node *Alto Aloha Network* at Xerox's Palo Alto Research Center.

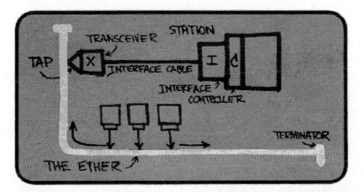

Figure 3.10. *Robert Metcalfe's original drawing of the Ethernet design; the unlabeled boxes (computers), "tap" onto the wire that Metcalfe labeled "The Ether."*

To understand how an Ethernet network works, consider another analogy. A group of friends is standing around at a party telling stories. While someone is telling a story, everyone is listening. The speaker is broadcasting to the group. When the story is over, how do the friends decide who tells the next story? There may be a momentary pause while the friends wait for someone to speak. Since there is no plan or agreement as to who should speak next, someone typically just begins talking. If no one else begins talking, that speaker continues telling the story to completion. At the end of the story, the same situation arises. There is a pause, and then someone else starts talking. If two or more people begin talking after the pause, they will notice that someone else is speaking and immediately stop. There is a pause while everyone waits for someone to go ahead. Assuming speakers tend to wait a random length of time, someone will begin talking. It's possible that two or more speakers will again start at the same time, notice the situation, stop, and wait a random length of time. Eventually one person will begin telling another story.

In this analogy we have assumed all the friends are equal; that is, there is no difference in status, nor does anyone have an especially loud or soft voice. Even so, the system isn't fair, because it favors the person who waits the shortest length of time at the end of a story. Of course, we all know such people!

Ethernet communication works like the party protocol. When the channel is in use, as when someone is telling a story, all of the computers listen to it. (Unlike storytelling, however, only one computer typically keeps the transmitted information; that is, this broadcast medium is being used for point-to-point communication.) A pause indicates the end of the transmission when no computer is sending signals and the channel is quiet. A computer wanting to transmit starts sending signals and, at the same time, starts listening to the channel to detect what is being transmitted. If it is exactly the information the computer sent, the computer knows it's the only one sending, and it completes its transmission. If the computer's signals are mixed in with signals from one or more other computers, it notices the garbled message and stops transmitting immediately. The other computer(s) stop too. Each machine pauses for a random length of time. The computer that waits the shortest length of time begins sending, and if there are no conflicting computers, it continues. If not, the colliders repeat the process.

*fit*BYTE   **Many versus One.** There is an important difference between the way the Internet works and the way an Ethernet works. The Internet uses a point-to-point network to implement point-to-point communication. An Ethernet uses a broadcast network for point-to-point communication. The difference is that with the Internet multiple communications can take place at once over different wires, but with the Ethernet only one communication can take place at a time. This limitation is usually not a problem, because Ethernets usually carry much less traffic.

Notice that the Ethernet scheme is completely decentralized, and requires no schedule or plan. Each computer listens to the channel, and if it's quiet, it's free.

The computer transmits unless some other computer starts at the same moment. When that happens, both computers back off for a brief (random) amount of time and then try again.

Connecting a Computer to the Internet

How are computers actually connected to the Internet? Today there are two basic methods:

> > By an Internet service provider (ISP)

> > By a campus or enterprise network

Most of us use both kinds of connections daily, depending on where we study or work. Let's look at each approach.

Connections by ISP. As the name implies, Internet service providers sell connections to the Internet. Examples of ISPs are `AOL.com` and `Earthlink.net`, but there are thousands of providers. Most home users connect to the Internet by ISPs. Here's how an ISP connection usually works.

Users plug their computer into the telephone system just as they would connect an extension telephone. (The plug, called an RJ-11, is universal in North America, but an adapter may be needed elsewhere.) Then the computer's modem, which is generally built into modern personal computers, can dial up the ISP and establish a connection. This operation is similar to a fax machine dialing another fax machine. (An alternative to a dial-up line is a dedicated connection to the ISP, such as a **digital subscriber line (DSL)**. The modems—one at each end of the telephone connection—enable the home computer to talk to the ISP's computer so that they can send and receive information. The ISP's computer is connected to the Internet, so it relays information for its customers. For example, when you surf the Web and click on a remote link (that is, a page stored on a distant computer), the request for the page is sent from your computer to the ISP's computer, across the Internet to the remote computer, which then sends the Web page back across the Internet to the computer at the ISP. From there, the page is sent over the phone line to your computer and displayed on your screen.

Enterprise Network Connections (LAN). The other way to connect to the Internet is as a user of a larger networked organization such as a school, business, or governmental unit. In this case, the organization's system administrators connect the computers and form a local area network (LAN). The Ethernet technology mentioned earlier is an example of a local area network. These local networks, known as **intranets**, support communication within the organization, but they also connect to the Internet by a gateway. Information from a distant Web computer is sent across the Internet, through the gateway to the organization's intranet, and across the LAN to the user's computer.

With either method, ISP or LAN, you usually send and receive information across the Internet transparently—that is, without knowing or caring which method is used.

Wireless Networks.   The two preceding examples cover the usual cases for fixed location computers, that is, those tethered by the phone or network cables (and power cables, too). Laptops, notebooks, and other mobile computers can also be connected to network cables, but they are most convenient when they use **wireless** communication. Wireless networking is a variation on the LAN connection. A computer, called the **hub**, is physically connected to the Internet and is capable of broadcasting and receiving signals, usually radio frequency (rf) signals, which the mobile computers can also send and receive. The hub and any computers within signal range (with their wireless communication turned on) participate in a network based on the Ethernet principles described above. The hub relays Internet requests for the participating computers.

*fit*BYTE   **Should I know my computer's IP address?** No. If you are dialing into the Internet via an ISP, your computer is assigned a temporary IP address when you log in and you use it until you log out. If you access the Internet via an intranet, one of two cases applies. Your network administrator may have assigned your computer an IP address when it was set up. Alternatively, no permanent address was assigned, and through the Dynamic Host Computer Protocol (DHCP), your computer is assigned an address each time you turn it on. Wireless uses DCHP, too. In any case, the IP address is nothing you have to worry about.

THE WORLD WIDE WEB

Some of the computers connected to the Internet are **Web servers**. That is, they are computers programmed to send files to browsers running on other computers connected to the Internet. Together these Web servers and their files comprise the **World Wide Web** (**WWW**). The files are Web pages, but Web servers store and send many other kinds of files, too. These files are often used to create the Web page (for example, images or animations) or to help with other Web services (for example, software used to play audio).

When described in these terms, the Web doesn't seem like much. And technically, it's not. What makes the World Wide Web significant is the information contained in the files and the ability of the client and server computers to process it.

*fit*BYTE   **No Confusion.** The World Wide Web and the Internet are different. The Internet is all of the wires and routers connecting named computers. The World Wide Web is a subset of those computers (Web servers) and their files.

Requesting a Web Page

As noted above, Web requests are processed in a client/server interaction. When you request a Web page, such as my university Web page (`http://www.cs.washington.edu/homes/snyder/index.html`), your browser is a client asking for a file from a Web server computer. The request, called a **Universal Resource Locator**, or **URL**, has three main parts:

Protocol. The `http://` part, which stands for **Hypertext Transfer Protocol**, tells the computers how to handle the file. There are other ways to send files, such as `ftp`, File Transfer Protocol.

Server computer's name. The name is the server's IP address given by the domain hierarchy, `www.cs.washington.edu`. Your computer uses the name to send a request to the server computer for the page.

Page's pathname. The pathname is the sequence following the IP address: `/homes/snyder/index.html`. The pathname tells the server which file (page) is requested and where to find it.

All URLs have this structure, although you may not think so, because in some cases you can leave parts out and the software fills in the missing part. (This is further explained in the next section.) It is never a mistake to use the full form.

Summarizing, Web browsers and Web servers both "speak" http. When you specify a URL in your browser's location window, you say where the information is to be found (server's name), what information you want (pathname), and what protocol the two computers will use to exchange the information (http).

---

fit **BYTE** | **Universal Language.** Most people are amazed at the Web's ability to provide access to information around the world. Few have observed, however, that it is the universal http language that makes this communication possible. Every computer, regardless of who manufactured it, how it's configured, its operating system type and version, the applications it runs, the (native) language of its user, etc., can communicate because the computers "know" this common language. Imagine the benefits if every person on the planet spoke a common language!

Describing a Web Page

As you know, servers do not store Web pages in the form seen on our screens. Instead, the pages are stored as a *description* of how they should appear on the screen. When the Web browser receives the description file (**source** file), it creates the Web page image that we see. There are two advantages to storing and sending the source rather than the image itself:

> A description file usually requires less information.

> The browser can adapt the source image to your computer more easily than a literal pixel-by-pixel description.

For example, it's easier to shrink or expand the page from its description than to use the image itself. Though browsers show the image, they always give you the option of seeing the description, too. Next time you are online, look under **View** and find **Source** or **Page Source** in your browser. Figure 3.11 shows a simple Web page and its source.

Hypertext

To describe how a Web page should look, we usually use **Hypertext Markup Language** (**HTML**). Markup languages, traditionally used in publishing and graphic design, describe the layout of a document, including margin width, font, text style, image placement, and so on. Hypertext began as an experiment to break away from the straight sequence of normal text: first paragraph, second paragraph, etc. With hypertext, it's possible to jump from one point in the text to somewhere else in the text or to some other document, and then return. This feature, which breaks a document's linear sequence, gives it a more complex structure. The (usually blue) highlighted words of Web pages are called *hyperlinks*, the points from which we can (optionally) jump and return. The term *hypertext* was coined in the late 1960s by Theodore Nelson, although in his *Literary Machines,* he credits the original idea to computer pioneer Vannevar Bush. Combining the two ideas—markup languages and hypertext—lets us build nonlinear documents, ideal for the dynamic and highly interconnected Internet. The World Wide Web was born.

In Chapter 4 we study HTML to learn how Web pages are created and processed. In Chapters 5 and 6, we explore the content of the WWW.

*fit*BYTE **Accelerating Ideas.** In 1990, while working at CERN, the European Laboratory for Particle Physics, Tim Berners-Lee invented HTML, a markup language that includes hypertext.

THE INTERNET AND THE WEB

Some Web servers have www as part of their domain name, some don't. Some Web servers, like www.cs.washington.edu, seem to add on the www if you leave it out, and some, like New York City's Museum of Modern Art (MoMA), work either way; both www.moma.org and moma.org display the same Web site. When is the www required and when is it optional?

First remember that names like www.cs.washington.edu are simply names. That is, like spiff, www is the name of a computer, the Web server, in the cs.washington.edu domain. And, like all computers connected to the Internet, Web servers have IP addresses. To refer to a Web server, you *must* give its name exactly, because your computer will ask the DNS server for the Web server's IP

**Alto,
A Computer of Note**

The Alto was the first networked personal computer. It was invented at the Xerox Palo Alto Research Center (PARC) by the team of Ed McCreight, Chuck Thacker, Butler Lampson, Bob Sproull and Dave Boggs to explore office automation. Altos were the first production computers to have a bit-mapped display, windows and a mouse. Ethernet technology, also invented at PARC, was first used to connect Altos.

Though Xerox was unable to market the Alto -- they cost $32,000 in 1979 -- the computer impressed many others who did push the technologies. For example, Apple Computer co-founder Steve Jobs was so impressed when he saw the Alto, he created the revolutionary Apple Macintosh in its image.

```html
<html>
<head> <title> Alto Computer </title> </head>
<body bgcolor="white"><font face="Helvetica">
    <img align="right" src="alto.jpg">
    <h1>Alto, <br>A Computer of Note</h1>

        <p>The Alto was the first networked personal computer.
        It was invented at the Xerox Palo Alto Research Center
        (PARC) by the team of Ed McCreight, Chuck Thacker,
        Butler Lampson, Bob Sproull and Dave Boggs to explore
        office automation. Altos were the first production
        computers to have a bit-mapped display, windows and a
        mouse. Ethernet technology, also invented at PARC, was
        first used to connect Altos. </p>

        <p>Though Xerox was unable to market the Alto — they cost
        $32,000 in 1979 — the computer impressed many others who
        did push the technologies. For  example, Apple Computer
        co-founder Steve Jobs was so impressed when he saw the
        Alto, he created the revolutionary Apple Macintosh in
        its image.</p>

</body>
</html>
```

Figure 3.11. *A Web page and the HTML source that produced it. Notice that an additional image file,* alto.jpg, *is also required to display the page.*

address using that name. If the name is wrong, either you will access the wrong IP address, or more typically, the DNS lookup will fail. Your browser will give you an error message saying that it cannot locate the server and will direct you to check the address. So, there is no option: You must give the name exactly.

No organization taking the trouble to put a Web server on the Internet wants visitors to fail to reach them, so their Web administrators try to save users from mistakes. For example, if you try to access my Web page but forget the `www`, your request `http://cs.washington.edu/…` will reach the wrong computer. However, that computer has been programmed to notice `http://` requests and to return the reply, "You probably meant `www.cs.washington.edu`." This is called a **redirection**.

Browsers are designed to try again with the recommended address. So, if when you type `http://cs.washington.edu/homes/snyder`, your location window quickly changes to `http://www.cs.washington.edu/homes/snyder`, making it seem that the `www` has been added. What you see is your browser trying the redirection address. The redirection could have been `http://www.aw.com/snyder/`, the URL for this book. In that case, the redirection looks like a replacement, which is what it really is. Redirection is used extensively at Web sites to avoid telling users that they made a mistake and to get them to where they want to be.

Rather than using redirection, some organizations, like the Museum of Modern Art simply make several names work. That is, MoMA has registered both `moma.org` and `www.moma.org` to the IP address `4.43.114.168`, saving us from making a mistake no matter which choice we make and avoiding redirection. Both names produce the same result because they connect to the same computer.

Web servers don't have to be named `www`. It's just what people usually name their Web servers. Web servers are named `www` because as the Web got started, many domains added a separate computer as their Web server. The server needed a name that people could remember, because redirection was not yet widely used. Because the first groups named their servers `www`, later groups did too. Now it seems like a requirement, but it is only a tradition.

*fit***BYTE**   **Punctuating the Internet.** Notice the structure of email addresses and URLs, and their punctuation:

Email addresses: `receiver@domain.address`

URLs: `http://domain.address/pathname`

The `domain.address` has one or more dots, no @, and no slashes. Email addresses have an @, but URLs do not. The `receiver` can have dots, dashes (-), and underscores (_). Spaces are not allowed in either email addresses or URLs.

FILE STRUCTURE

To use networks well, we need to understand file structures, although the topic is not technically part of networking. Recall from your experience using a personal computer that a **directory**—also known as a **folder**—is a named collection of files or other directories or both.

Directory Hierarchy

Because directories can contain directories, which can contain files and other directories, and on and on, the whole scheme—called the **file structure** of the computer—forms the **directory hierarchy**. Think of any hierarchy as a tree; in the case of the file structures, directories are the branch points and files are the leaves. Hierarchy trees are often drawn in odd ways, such as sideways or upside down, but in all cases two terms are standard:

> *Down or lower* in the hierarchy means into subdirectories; that is, toward the leaves.

> *Up or higher* in the hierarchy means into enclosing directories; that is, toward the root.

To illustrate these terms, Figure 3.12 shows part of the hierarchy of this book formed from its parts, chapters, and sections; the "tree" of Figure 3.12 is drawn on its side with the root, Fluency, to the left. The path from the root (the whole book) to the leaf (this section) is highlighted. We move *up* or *higher* in the hierarchy when we move, say, from Chapter 3 to Part 1, since it is more inclusive; we move *down* or *lower* in the hierarchy when we move, say, from Chapter 3 to the Directory Hierarchy section, since it is more specific.

Learning the "directionality" of hierarchical references makes navigating the Web simpler.

*fit***TIP** **Pulling Rank**. An easy way to remember the directionality of "higher" and "lower" is to think of the military hierarchy: general, colonel, major, captain, lieutenant, sergeant, corporal, private. Moving up or down in the hierarchy corresponds to moving up or down the chain of command, or to higher or lower rank.

Part of the directory hierarchy is shown in the pathnames of URLs. For example, the URL `http://www.nasm.si.edu/galleries/gal100/pioneer.html` gives a National Air and Space Museum's site describing Pioneer 10, the first man-made object to leave the solar system. The page is given by a pathname, `/galleries/gal100/pioneer.html`, that tells the computer how to navigate through the Air and Space Museum's directory hierarchy to the file, as shown in

▼ Fluency
  ▼   Part 1
      ▶   Chapter 1
      ▶   Chapter 2
      ▼   Chapter 3
          ▶   Communication Types
          ▼   File Structure
              ▼   Directory Hierarchy
                    Figure 3.12
                    Figure 3.13
              ▶   Organizing the Directory
          ▶   Networked Computers
          ▶   The Medium of the Message
          ▶   The World Wide Web
      ▶   Chapter 4
      ▶   Chapter 5
      ▶   Chapter 6
    ▶   Part 2
    ▶   Part 3
    ▶   Part 4

Figure 3.12. *The hierarchy of this book highlighting the path to this figure.*

Figure 3.13. Each time we pass a slash (/), reading the pathname from left to right, we move into a subdirectory or to the file. That is, we go lower in the hierarchy. We start at a top-level directory called `galleries`. (The NASM has 23 exhibit rooms called galleries, and we might assume that this directory contains information about each of them.) Within the `galleries` directory, there is a subdirectory called `gal100`, which we might assume refers to Gallery 100, the room containing famous "firsts" in air and space exploration. And in the `gal100` directory, there is a file called `pioneer.html`, the Web page we want.

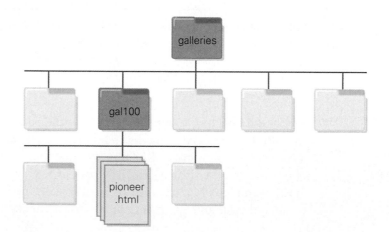

Figure 3.13. *The pathname hierarchy ending in* `pioneer.html`*.*

In general, the path in a URL tells the server computer where to find the requested file in the server's file structure. The server computer follows down the hierarchical structure just as we did in the NASM example.

---

fit **TIP**

Case In Point. Remember that case sensitivity means computers treat uppercase and lowercase letters as different characters. In URLs, domain names are not case sensitive, because they are standardized for DNS lookup. Pathnames can be case sensitive, because they tell how to navigate through the Web server's file structure, which may be case sensitive. Be careful when typing pathnames, and when in doubt, try lowercase first.

Organizing the Directory

A common way to organize the information in a directory is to list or index the files that are in the directory. The information about NASM's Gallery 100 is organized this way. There is a file in the `gal100` directory, `gal100.html`, that lists the links to Web pages about exhibits in the gallery. Because an index linking to the files in a directory is common, browsers know to look for it. When a URL ends in a slash (which means the last item on the path is a directory rather than a filename), the browser automatically looks for a file called `index.html` in that directory. So, a request for the URL

`http://www.cs.washington.edu/homes/snyder/index.html`

to my university Web page is the same as

`http://www.cs.washington.edu/homes/snyder/`

because a browser that finds the directory named `snyder` will automatically look for a file called `index.html` in it. Of course, the `index.html` file will exist only if the person who set up the Web pages and built the file hierarchy decided to organize it as such and provide the index pages. Some people do and some people don't, but the browser will look for `index.html` when necessary.

Why build a hierarchy at all? Why not lump all the files into one huge directory and save typing? Most people build hierarchies to organize their own thinking and work. For example, the gallery exhibit organization is clear and simple. Because directories cost nothing, there is no reason not to use them, and it is highly recommended. (In this book, when we create a Web page, for example, we will always use a subdirectory for organizing the pictures on the page.)

---

fit **BYTE**

Netting a Prize. Vint Cerf and Bob Kahn received the 2005 Turing Award from the Association of Computing Machinery, computing's Nobel Prize, for the development of the Internet.

SUMMARY

The chapter opened with a discussion of five fundamental ways networked computers have changed the world and our lives. We went on to discuss:

> Basic types of communication: point-to-point, multicast, broadcast, synchronous, and asynchronous.

> Networking that included: IP addresses, domains, IP packets, IP-protocol, WANS and LANS, Ethernet protocol, ISPs, and enterprise networks.

> The difference between the Internet and the World Wide Web.

> The history of HTML and we reviewed file hierarchies in preparation for our further study of HTML.

EXERCISES

Multiple Choice

1. Passive interaction via the Internet allows interaction of individuals
   A. separated by distance
   B. separated by time
   C. with a shared interest
   D. all of the above

2. English is becoming the universal language as a result of all of the following except
   A. American pop culture
   B. the dominance of science and technology in English-speaking countries
   C. IT's predominant use of English
   D. the Alto Project

3. Overall, the ability of individuals to create and publish Web pages
   A. presents an enormous security risk
   B. extends human expression
   C. has led to a proliferation of hate pages and pornographic sites
   D. has unduly diverted huge sums from other IT projects

4. Spamming is like
   A. telemarketing
   B. junk mail
   C. advertising inserts
   D. all of the above

5. If the Internet consisted of four computers, there would be six possible connections. If it consisted of five computers, there would be ten possible connections. How many connections are possible with ten computers?
   A. 10
   B. 30
   C. 45
   D. infinite

6. What is the potential number of IP addresses available?
   A. 65,536
   B. 16,777,216
   C. 4,294,967,296
   D. limitless

7. The part of an email address to the right of the @ is most like a
   A. mailbox
   B. post office
   C. letter
   D. return address

8. DNS stands for
   A. Determined Name of Sender
   B. Determined Not Spam
   C. Domain Name System
   D. Domain Number Sequence

9. The origins of the Internet can be traced to
   A. news services sending wire stories to local newspapers
   B. phone companies creating the long distance system
   C. government, big business, and educational institutions conducting Cold War research
   D. the United States and USSR creating a hotline

10. As an aspiring TV exec, the ideal country to locate the top-level domain for your new quiz show "What's My IP?" would be
    A. Papua New Guinea
    B. Cocos Islands
    C. Tuvalu
    D. Nauru

11. Between client requests from a specific IP address, a Web server
    A. cannot handle requests from another client
    B. can handle requests up to the number of clients specified by the administrator
    C. can handle up to 255 other requests
    D. might handle hundreds or even thousands of requests

12. The displacement effect is
    A. when computer time displaces other activities
    B. when personal information is mistakenly replaced
    C. when files are inadvertently replaced by other files
    D. information and productivity that is lost by computer network downtime

13. Unmediated access to the Internet is available in
    A. only the United States
    B. only in western countries
    C. most countries
    D. worldwide

14. Root name servers
    A. maintain a list of all computer users
    B. manage all emails sent
    C. maintain the relationship between IP addresses and symbolic computer names
    D. maintain a list of all Web pages

15. To connect to the Internet with a wireless connection you'd need to communicate through a device that is physically connected to a network. This device is called a
    A. port
    B. Ethernet
    C. switch
    D. hub

Short Answer

1. eCommerce is the shortened term for _____.
2. The interconnection of computers has led to an era called the _____.
3. A communication that goes out to many people within a specific target audience is called a(n) _____.
4. A hierarchy of related computers on a network is called a(n) _____.
5. Computers on the same level of a domain are known as _____.
6. A "please reply" message sent over the Internet is called a(n) _____.
7. Computers on an Ethernet network "tap into" a cable called a(n) _____.
8. A company that supplies connections to the Internet is called a(n) _____.
9. Intranets connect to the Internet via _____.
10. Local networks that support communications wholly within an organization are called _____.
11. Special computers that send files to Web browsers elsewhere on the Internet are known as _____.
12. The `http://` in a Web address is the _____.
13. Files are often sent over the Internet via a process known by the acronym _____.
14. The source file for a Web page contains the _____ of the page, not the actual image of the page.
15. HTML stands for _____.
16. In a client/server structure, the customer's computer is the _____ and the business's computer is the _____.
17. A personal log posted on the Web for public viewing is called a(n) _____.
18. All IP addresses are maintained and managed by 13 _____ servers scattered around the world.

Exercises

1. How have networked computers made your life different from the life of your parents?

2. Discuss five changes the Information Age has brought.

3. There's an adage, "Guns don't kill people. People kill people." How does this relate to human nature and the Internet?

4. Label the following with either an S to indicate synchronous communication or an A to indicate asynchronous communication.

    _____ movie   _____ book
    _____ chat session   _____ concert
    _____ email   _____ text messaging
    _____ video conference   _____ Web board
    _____ Web page

5. Go to `www.mids.org/mapsale/world/index.html` and check out the Internet maps of the world. Where is most of the traffic? Plot the course of a packet from Tahiti to New York. What routes are available and where are the bottlenecks?

6. Try the Web address above without the file name. What do you get?

7. Describe how the Internet is like a bus route, a subway route, UPS, or Federal Express. How is it different from these? Go to `www.mta.nyc.ny.us/nyct /maps/submap.htm` to see a map of the NYC subway system. How does it compare? Compare the Internet to the Prague subway map by going to `www.odyssey.on.ca/~europrail/prague.htm`.

8. What industries have prospered and which ones might have suffered because of the growth of the Internet? Why?

9. Are there more client computers or more server computers on the Internet?

chapter

4

MARKING UP WITH HTML
A Hypertext Markup Language Primer

learning objectives > Know the meaning of and use hypertext terms

> Use HTML tags to structure a document

> Use the basics of HTML tag attributes

> Use HTML tags to link to other files

> Explain the differences between absolute and relative pathnames

> Use HTML to encode lists and tables

MARKING UP WITH HTML
A Hypertext Markup Language Primer

*Most of the fundamental ideas of science are essentially simple and may as a
rule be expressed in a language comprehensible to everyone.*

—ALBERT EINSTEIN

WEB PAGES are created, stored, and sent in encoded form; a browser converts
them to the image we see on the screen. The Hypertext Markup Language (HTML)
is the main language used to define how a Web page should look. Features like
background color, font, and layout are all specified in HTML. Learning to "speak"
HTML is easy. So easy, in fact, that most Web pages are not created by writing
HTML directly, but by using Web authoring software; that is, by using programs
that write the HTML automatically. Learning basic HTML helps us to understand
the World Wide Web, gives us experience directing a computer to do tasks for us,
and prepares us for other Fluency study topics. When we are finished, we will
speak a new "foreign" language!

This chapter begins by reviewing the concept of tags, which we discussed in
Chapter 2, and we introduce the dozen most basic HTML tags. Next comes document structuring, including details such as headings and alignment. After discussing special characters, we create an example of a text-only Web page. We
decide that the page should have an image and hyperlinks, so we learn about
placing images and links and how to connect them. With this knowledge we
improve our example page. Finally, we introduce the basics of lists, tables, and
colors, which give us more control over the "look and feel" of our Web pages.

● MARKING UP WITH HTML

HTML is straightforward. The words on a Web page are simply structured by hidden formatting tags that describe how they should look.

Formatting with Tags

Remember from Chapter 2 that tags are words or abbreviations enclosed in angle brackets, `<` and `>`, like `<title>`, and that tags come in pairs, the second with a slash (/), like `</title>`. The tag pair surrounds the text to be formatted like parentheses. So a title, which every HTML Web page has, is written as

`<title>Tiger Woods, Masters Champion</title>`

These two tags can be read as "beginning of title text" and "end of title text." The title appears on the title bar of the browser (the very top of the window where the close button is) when the page is displayed. In HTML, the tags are not case sensitive, but the actual text is. So, in this example, we could have used `<TITLE>`, `<Title>`, `<tITle>`, or any other mix of lowercase and uppercase letters. We will follow tradition and use only lowercase letters in our tags.

Tags for Bold and Italic

HTML has tags for bold text, `<b>` and `</b>`; for italic text, `<i>` and `</i>`; and for paragraphs, `<p>` and `</p>`. You can use more than one kind of formatting at a time, such as bold italic text, by "nesting" the tags, as in

`<p><b><i>Veni, Vidi, Vici!</i></b></p>`

which produces

Veni, Vidi, Vici!

It doesn't matter in which order you put the tags. You get the same result if you put the italic before the bold:

`<p><i><b>Veni, Vidi, Vici!</b></i></p>`

The key is to make sure the tags are nested correctly. All the tags between a starting tag and its ending tag should be matched. So, in the *Veni, Vidi, Vici* example, between the starting `<p>` tag and its ending `</p>` tag, all other starting tags are properly nested with their matching ending tags.

---

*fit***TIP**   **Easy Going.** HTML is relaxed about some coding rules, but when and how is often complicated. So in this book we ignore any relaxed rules to avoid complication because they don't make a difference in the pages you can create.

A few tags are not paired and so do not have a / ending form. One example is the horizontal rule `<hr>` tag, which displays a horizontal line. Another example is the break `<br>` tag, which continues the text on the next line and is useful for ending each line of an address. These tags do not apply to multiple characters, so they don't surround anything.

An HTML Web page file begins with the `<html>` tag, ends with the `</html>` tag, and has the following structure:

```
<html>
    <head>
        preliminary material goes here
    </head>
    <body>
        the main content of the page goes here
    </body>
</html>
```

The section surrounded by `<head>` and `</head>` contains the beginning material like the title. The section surrounded by `<body>` and `</body>` contains the content of the page. *This form must always be followed, and all of these tags are required.*

There's not very much to HTML. By the end of the next section, we will have created a respectable Web page—our first!

---

fit **CAUTION**

Use Simple Text Editors. While we are giving ignore-at-your-own-peril rules about a Web page's form, we should offer a caution about text editors. HTML must be written using basic ASCII characters. We discuss these in Chapter 8, but for now, think of ASCII as the characters from the keyboard. As we learned in Chapter 2, standard word processors (e.g., WordPerfect, Word, and Claris Works) produce files with ASCII characters, but they also include special formatting information that browsers do not like. For that reason, you *must* write HTML using a basic text editor such as NotePad (Windows), TextEdit (Mac), BBEdit (UNIX), or the like. And always make sure that you save your file using Text format. This way the HTML file will make sense to Web browsers. Also, be sure that your file name ends with the `.html` extension so that the browser knows it is reading an HTML document.

STRUCTURING DOCUMENTS

The point of a markup language is to describe how a document's parts fit together. Because those parts are mostly paragraphs, headings, and text styles like italic and bold, the tags of this section are the most common and most useful.

Headings in HTML

Because documents have headings, subheadings, and so on, HTML gives us several levels of *heading* tags to choose from, from level one (the highest) headings,

<h1> and </h1>, to level two, <h2> and </h2>, all the way to level eight, <h8> and </h8>. The headings display the material in large font on a new line. For example,

```
<h1>Pope</h1>  <h2>Cardinal</h2>  <h3>Archbishop</h3>
```

appears as

Pope

Cardinal

Archbishop

You should use the heading levels in numerical order without skipping a level, although you don't have to start at level one. Notice that the headings are bold and get less "strong" (smaller and perhaps less bold) as the level number increases.

HTML Format versus Display Format

Notice that although the HTML text was run together on one line, it was displayed formatted on separate lines. This illustrates the important point that the HTML source tells the browser how to produce the formatted image based on the *meanings* of the tags, not on how the source instructions look. Though the source's form is unimportant, we usually write HTML in a structured way to make it easier for people to understand. There is no agreed upon form, but the example might have been written with indenting to emphasize the levels:

```
<h1>Pope</h1>
    <h2>Cardinal</h2>
        <h3>Archbishop</h3>
```

White Space

The two HTML forms give us the same result. Computer experts call space that has been inserted for readability **white space**. We create white space with spaces, tabs, and new lines. HTML ignores white space. The browser turns any sequence of white space characters into a single space before it begins processing the HTML. The only exception is **preformatted** information contained within <pre> and </pre> tags, which is displayed as it appears.

The fact that white space is ignored is important when the browser formats paragraphs. All text within paragraph tags, <p> and </p>, is treated as a paragraph, and any sequence of white space characters is converted to a single space. So

```
<p> <b>Xeno's Paradox: </b>
Achilles and a turtle were to run a race. Achilles could
run twice as fast as the turtle. The turtle,
being a slower runner,
got a 10 meter head start, whereupon
Achilles started and ran the 10 meter distance. At that
moment the turtle was 5 meters farther. When Achilles had run
that distance the turtle had gone another 2.5 meters,
and so forth. Paradoxically, the turtle always remained
ahead. </p>
```

appears as

Xeno's Paradox: Achilles and a turtle were to run a race. Achilles could run twice as fast as the turtle. The turtle, being a slower runner, got a 10 meter head start, whereupon Achilles started and ran the 10 meter distance. At that moment the turtle was 5 meters farther. When Achilles had run that distance the turtle had gone another 2.5 meters, and so forth. Paradoxically, the turtle always remained ahead.

The width of the line is determined by the width of the browser window. Of course, a narrower or wider browser window makes the lines break in different places, which is why HTML ignores white space and changes the paragraph's formatting to fit the space available. Table 4.1 summarizes the basic HTML tags.

Table 4.1. Basic HTML Tags

Start Tag	End Tag	Meaning	Required
`<html>`	`</html>`	HTML document; first and last tags in an HTML file	✔
`<title>`	`</title>`	Title bar text; describes page	✔
`<head>`	`</head>`	Preliminary material; e.g., title, at start of page	✔
`<body>`	`</body>`	The main part of the page	✔
`<p>`	`</p>`	Paragraph, can use `align` attribute	
`<hr>`		Line (horizontal rule), can use `width` and `size` attributes	
`<h1>...<h8>`	`</h1>...</h8>`	Headings, eight levels, use in order, can use `align` attribute	
`<b>`	`</b>`	Bold	
`<i>`	`</i>`	Italic	
`<a href="fn">`	`</a>`	Anchor reference, *fn* must be a pathname to an HTML file	
`<img src="fn">`		Image source reference, *fn* must be a pathname to `.jpg` or `.gif` file	
` `		Break, continue text on a new line	

Brackets in HTML: The Escape Symbol

Notice that there would be a problem if our Web page had to show a math relationship such as $0 < p > r$, because the browser might misinterpret $< p >$ as a paragraph tag and not display it. So to show angle brackets, we use an **escape symbol**—the ampersand (&) —followed by an abbreviation, followed by a semicolon. For example:

> `&lt;` displays as <

> `&gt;` displays as >

> `&amp;` displays as &

Notice that the escape symbol, the ampersand, needs an escape, too! So, our math problem would be solved in HTML by

`<i>0 &lt; p &gt; r</i>`

Accent Marks in HTML

Letters with accent marks also use the escape symbol. The general form is an ampersand followed by the letter (and whether it is uppercase or lowercase makes a difference) followed by the name of the accent mark followed by a semicolon. So, for example, `&eacute;` displays as é, `&Egrave;` displays as È, `&ntilde;` displays as ñ, and `&ouml;` displays as ö. Table 4.2 lists a few useful special symbols for some Western European languages. You can find a complete list at

www.w3.org/MarkUp/html13/latin1.html

Table 4.2. Special Symbols for Western European Language Accent Marks

Symbol	HTML	Symbol	HTML	Symbol	HTML	Symbol	HTML
à	`&agrave;`	á	`&aacute;`	â	`&acirc;`	ã	`&atilde;`
ä	`&auml;`	å	`&aring;`	ç	`&ccedil;`	è	`&egrave;`
é	`&eacute;`	ê	`&ecirc;`	ë	`&euml;`	ì	`&igrave;`
í	`&iacute;`	î	`&icirc;`	ï	`&iuml;`	ñ	`&ntilde;`
ò	`&ograve;`	ó	`&oacute;`	ô	`&ocirc;`	õ	`&otilde;`
ö	`&ouml;`	ø	`&oslash;`	ù	`&ugrave;`	ú	`&uacute;`
û	`&ucirc;`	ü	`&uuml;`				

Note: For an accent mark on an uppercase letter, make the letter following the & uppercase.

Attributes in HTML

Though most text properties are a single key term or abbreviation, some properties, such as how to align text, require more information. For example, we can't just say we want text justified; we have to specify that we want it left justified, centered, or right justified. We do this by using the tag's **attributes**. Attributes, which are generally optional, appear inside the angle brackets.

`Align, Justify.` For example, paragraphs and headings have an align attribute specifying whether the text should be left justified, centered, or right justified. The attribute follows the tag word, separated by a space, and is separated from its value (in double quotes) by an equal sign. So

```
<p align = "center"> <b>Thought for Today:</b> </p>
<p> As I would not be a <i>slave</i>, so I would not be a
<i>master</i>. This expresses my idea of democracy. Whatever
differs from this, to the extent of the difference, is no
democracy.</p>
<p align = "right"> — Abraham Lincoln</p>
```

displays as

> **Thought for Today:**
>
> As I would not be a *slave*, so I would not be a *master*. This expresses my idea of democracy. Whatever differs from this, to the extent of the difference, is no democracy.
>
> — Abraham Lincoln

Notice that when we don't specify the alignment attribute, as in the second line, the default is left justified.

`Horizontal Rule Attribute.` The horizontal rule tag `<hr>`, mentioned earlier, also has attributes. One attribute, `width`, specifies how wide the line should be as a percentage of the browser window's width; another attribute, `size`, says how thick the line should be. So `<hr width="50%" size=1>` displays a horizontal line that takes up half of the horizontal width and is the minimum thickness, as in

The default size is 2. Experiment to find the size that works best for your application. Notice that the width, `50%`, is enclosed in quotation marks, but the size specification, 1, is not. This has been done for illustration purposes. HTML does not need the quotes *if a browser can figure out what is intended*. But don't take chances—put quotes around anything that follows the equal sign.

fit **CAUTION**

Misquotes. Quotation marks are the cause of many HTML errors. Of course, quotes must match, and it is easy to forget one of the pair. But, there are also different kinds of quotes: The simple quotes (" and ') are the kind HTML likes; the fancy, curved quotes, called "smart quotes"— “ ” —are the kind HTML doesn't like. Check *carefully* for messed-up quotes if your HTML produces an incorrect result.

Though we have introduced only a few HTML tags so far, we can already create Web pages, as shown in Figure 4.1. Study the HTML and notice the following points:

> The title is shown on the title bar of the browser window.

> The alignment attribute has been used in the level one heading to center the heading.

> The level two headings are left justified because that is the default.

> The statement of Russell's Paradox is in bold.

> The HTML source paragraphs are indented more than the `<h2>` heading lines to make them more readable.

> The line between the two paragraphs is three quarters the width of the browser window.

> Acute accents are used in Magritte's first name.

> The French phrase from the painting is in italics.

> The word *picture* is in italics for emphasis.

It's a simple page and it was simple to produce.

*fit*TIP | **Compose and Check.** It's a good idea to write the text first and then format it in HTML. A productive way to work is with two windows open: your text editor and your browser. After writing a few HTML formatting tags in the editor, *save* your file and then check the result in the browser by *reloading* the source.

MARKING LINKS WITH ANCHOR TAGS

The example shown in Figure 4.1 may be an interesting Web page, but it doesn't use hypertext at all. It would be more informative, perhaps, if it linked to biographies of Russell and Magritte. Also, it would be easier to understand if it showed Magritte's painting or linked to it.

Two Sides of a Link

In this section we learn how to make hyperlinks. When a user clicks on a hyperlink, the browser loads a new Web page. This means there must be two parts to a hyperlink: the text in the current document that is highlighted, called the **anchor text**, and the address of the other Web page, called the **hyperlink reference**.

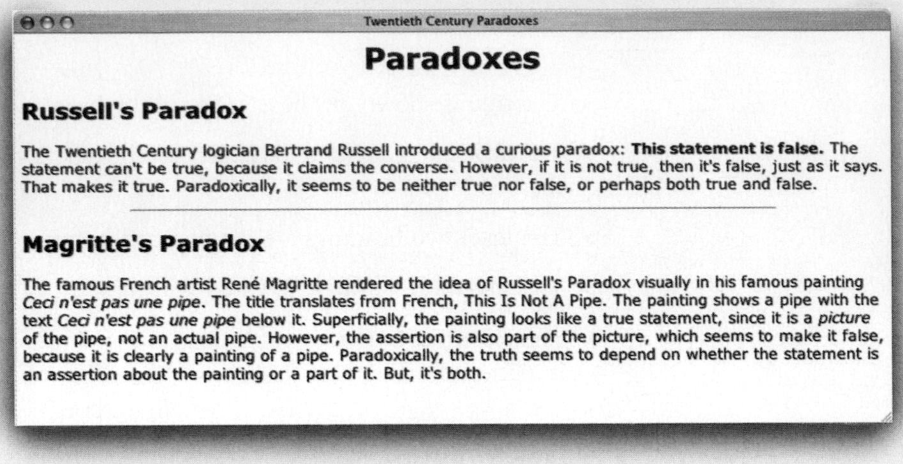

```html
<html>
    <head>
        <title>Twentieth Century Paradoxes</title>
    </head>
    <body>
        <h1 align="center">Paradoxes</h1>
        <h2>Russell's Paradox</h2>
            <p> The Twentieth Century logician Bertrand Russell
            introduced a curious paradox: <b>This statement is
            false.</b> The statement can't be true, because it
            claims the converse. However, if it is not true, then
            it's false, just as it says. That makes it true.
            Paradoxically, it seems to be neither true nor false,
            or perhaps both true and false.</p>
            <hr width="75%">
        <h2> Magritte's Paradox</h2>
            <p> The famous French artist Ren&eacute; Magritte
            rendered the idea of Russell's Paradox visually in
            his famous painting <i>Ceci n'est pas une pipe</i>.
            The title translates from French, This Is Not A Pipe.
            The painting shows a pipe with the text <i>Ceci n'est
            pas une pipe</i> below it. Superficially, the painting
            looks like a true statement, since it is a
            <i>picture</i> of the pipe, not an actual pipe.
            However, the assertion is also part of the picture,
            which seems to make it false, because it is
            clearly a painting of a pipe. Paradoxically, the truth
            seems to depend on whether the statement is an
            assertion about the painting or a part of it. But,
            it's both.</p>
    </body>
</html>
```

Figure 4.1. HTML source of `paradoxes.html` *and the corresponding Web page resulting from its interpretation by a browser.*

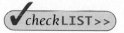   Both parts of the hyperlink are specified in the **anchor tag**, constructed as follows:

  ☑ *Begin with <a making sure there's a space after the a. The a is for anchor.*

  ☑ *Give the hyperlink reference using* `href="filename"`, *making sure to include the double quotes.*

  ☑ *Close the anchor tag with the > symbol.*

  ☑ *Specify the anchor text, which will be highlighted when it is displayed by the browser.*

  ☑ *End the hyperlink with the* `</a>` *tag.*

For example, suppose `http://www.bioz.com/bios/sci/russell.html` were the URL for a Web biography of Bertrand Russell; we would anchor it to his last name on our Web page with the anchor tag

```
Bertrand <a href="http://www.bioz.com/bios/sci/russell.html">Russell</a>
```
normal text   hyperlink reference   anchor

This hyperlink would be displayed with Russell's last name highlighted as

Bertrand <u>Russell</u>

When the browser displays the page and the user clicks on Russell, the browser downloads the bio page given in the `href`. As another example, if Magritte's biography were at the same site, the text

```
<a href="http://www.bioz.com/bios/art/magritte.html">Magritte</a>
```

would give the reference and anchor for his hyperlink.

Absolute Pathnames (URLs)

In these anchor tag examples, the hyperlink reference is an entire URL because the Web browser needs to know how to find the page. Remember from Chapter 3 that the URL is made from a protocol specification, `http://`, a domain or IP address, `www.bioz.com`, and a path to the file, `/bios/sci/russell.html`. The files are two levels down in the directory (folder) hierarchy of the site.

From the Russell and Magritte examples, we guess that at the Bioz Company site, the biographies have been grouped together in a top-level directory (see Chapter 3) called `bios`. Probably the scientists, like Russell, are grouped together in the subdirectory called `sci`, and the artists are grouped together under the subdirectory called `art`. Within these directories are the individual biography files: `russell.html` and `magritte.html`. The slash (/) separates levels in the directory hierarchy, and "crossing a slash" moves us lower in the hierarchy into a subfolder. Such complete URLs are called **absolute pathnames**; they are the right way to reference pages at other Web sites.

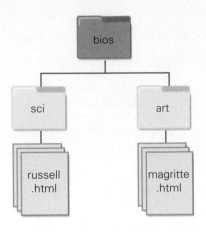

Relative Pathnames

Often a link refers to other Web pages on the same site. Because these pages will all be stored in the same or nearby directories, their anchor tags use **relative pathnames**. A relative pathname describes how to find the referenced file *relative* to the file in which the anchor tag appears. So, for example, if the anchor tag is in an HTML file that is in directory X, and the anchor references another file also in directory X, only the name of the file is given, not its whole absolute path.

Suppose that we have written our own biographies for Russell and Magritte for our `paradoxes.html` page. If the files are named `russellbio.html` and `magrittebio.html`, and they are in the same directory as `paradoxes.html`, the anchor tags of the Paradoxes page can use relative references:

`<a href="russellbio.html">Russell</a>`

and

`<a href="magrittebio.html">Magritte</a>`

This saves us typing the protocol part, the domain part, and the path to the folder part, but that's not why we like relative pathnames. Relative pathnames are more flexible because they let us move Web files around as a group without having to change the references. This flexibility is important as you begin to manage your own Web page.

Going "Deeper" in a Directory.   Relative pathnames are very simple when the file containing the anchor and the referenced file are in the same directory—we just give the file name. When the referenced file is "deeper" in the directory hierarchy, perhaps in a folder or in a folder inside another folder, we simply give the path from the current directory down to the file. For example, in the directory containing `paradoxes.html` we create a subdirectory, `biographies`, which contains the two profiles. Then the anchor for the Russell bio becomes

`<a href="biographies/russellbio.html">Russell</a>`

because we must say how to navigate to the file from the Paradoxes page's location. Of course, using relative pathnames means that the files for the pages must be kept together in a fixed structure, but that's the easiest solution anyway.

Going "Higher" in a Hierarchy. The only problem left is how to refer to directories higher up in the hierarchy. The technique for doing this (which comes from the UNIX operating system) is to refer to the next outer level of the hierarchy—that is, the containing directory—as `..` (pronounced "*dot dot*"). So if we imagine that the directory structure has the form

```
mypages
    biographies
        russellbio.html
        magrittebio.html
    coolstuff
        paradoxes.html
```

then, in `paradoxes.html`, the Russell biography anchor would be

```
<a href="../biographies/russellbio.html">Russell</a>
```

because the biography can't be reached by going down from the directory (`coolstuff`) containing `paradoxes.html`. Instead we have to go up to the next higher level to `mypages`. From there, we can navigate down to the bios through the `biographies` directory. We can use a sequence of dots and slashes (`../../`), so that each pair of dots moves the reference up one level higher in the hierarchy. For example, another page with the reference

```
<a href="../../humorpages/dumbjokes/knockknock4.html">
```

moves up to the directory containing the directory containing the page, then down through the `humorpages` and `dumbjokes` directories to the actual `knockknock4` HTML page.

Summarizing, hyperlinks are specified using anchor tags. The path to the file is given as the `href` attribute of the anchor tag, and the text to be highlighted (the anchor), is given between the anchor tag and its closing `</a>`. Paths can be absolute paths—that is, standard URLs—for offsite pages. Relative pathnames should be used for all onsite pages. The relative path can be just a name if the referenced file is in the same directory as the page that links to it; it can specify a path deeper, through descendant directories; or it can use the `..` notation to move higher in the directory structure. These path rules apply to images as well as hyperlinks.

INCLUDING PICTURES WITH IMAGE TAGS

Pictures are worth a thousand words, as the saying goes, so we include them in an HTML document to enhance our page. To link to a picture, that is, to enable the reader to click on a link to see a picture, we use the anchor tags as just explained. To display the picture, that is, to show it on the page, we use an image tag.

Image Tag Format

An image tag, which is analogous to an anchor tag, specifies a file containing an image. The image tag format is

`<img src="`*filename*`">`

where `src` stands for "source" and the *filename* uses the same rules for absolute and relative pathnames as anchor tags. So, for example, if the image of Magritte's painting is stored in a file `pipe.jpg`, in the same directory as the Paradoxes page, we can include the image with a relative pathname

`<img src="pipe.jpg">`

which finds the image and places it in the document.

GIF and JPEG Images

Images can come in several formats, but two of them are important for Web pages: **GIF** (pronounced either with a hard or soft *g*) and **JPEG** (pronounced JAY·peg.) GIFs (Graphics Interchange Format), are best suited for cartoons and simple drawings. JPEGs, named for the Joint Photographic Experts Group, are appropriate for high-resolution photographs and complex artwork. To tell the browser which format the image is in, the file name should have the extension `.gif`, `.jpg`, or `.jpeg`.

Positioning the Image in the Document

Where does the image go on the Web page? To understand how images are placed, notice that HTML lays out text in the browser window from *left to right*, and from *top to bottom*, the same way English is written. If the image is the same size or smaller than the letters, it is placed in line just like a letter at the point where the image tag occurs in the HTML. For example, when we insert a small image ▢ in the text, it is simply drawn in place. This is convenient for icons or smiley faces in the text. If the image is larger than the letters ▢, it appears in the text in the same way, but the line spacing is increased to separate it from the neighboring lines. The HTML default rule is: *Images are inserted in the page at the point where the tag is specified in the HTML, and the text lines up with the bottom of the image.*

We can use the `align` attribute in the image tag to line up the top of the image with the top of the text (`align="top"`) or to center the text on the image (`align="middle"`) in the image. In all cases, the `bottom` (default), `middle`, and `top` alignments apply only to the line of text in which the image has been inserted.

Another common and visually pleasing way to place images in text is to flow the text around them, either by having the image on the left with the text to its right, or vice versa. To make the text flow around the image, we use the `align` attribute in the image tag with the value `"left"` or `"right"`. This forces the image to the left or right of the browser window. The text will continue from left to right, and from top to bottom, in the remaining space, flowing around the image.

Finally, to display an image by itself without any text around it, simply enclose the image tag within paragraph tags. That will separate it from the paragraphs above and below. You can even center the paragraph to center the image:

*fit*TIP

Clearer Directions. Notice that there are two sets of tags for alignment attributes. For horizontal alignment, such as paragraph justification, use `left`, `center`, `right`. For vertical alignment, such as placing images relative to a line of text, use `top`, `middle`, `bottom`.

So how do we put the image of Magritte's painting in the Paradoxes page? Perhaps the most pleasing solution is to right-justify it and let the paragraph flow around it. We can do this by writing

```
<img src="pipe.jpg" align="right">
```

as long as the picture doesn't take up all or most of the window, which would prevent the text from flowing naturally.

To specify how large the picture should be, use the `height` and `width` attributes in the image tag. Give the size in pixels. Thus,

```
<img src="pipe.jpg" align="right" height="130" width="192">
```

specifies an image that will be about one eighth of the width of a thousand-pixel screen. If the natural size of the image is different from the `height/width` specifications, the browser shrinks or stretches it to fit in the allotted space. (The natural size of an image is the best size to use, if possible. However, in our example the natural size is too large, so we divide the dimensions by 3 and round to the nearest whole number.)

*fit*TIP

Image Size. You can determine the size of an image by checking **File > Properties** (Windows) or **File > Get Info** (Mac) of the image file.

We can also use images to fill in a background by **tiling**, copying a small image over and over to make a background pattern. Use bland, low-contrast, evenly colored images for background tiling, so they are not distracting. Collections of pictures and graphics to use as backgrounds are widely available, including ones that make your pages look like fine textured linen paper. The image is specified as the background attribute of the body tag, as in

```
<body background="filename">
```

where the *filename* has the same path properties as hyperlink references for anchor tags.

● HANDLING COLOR

Color can improve a Web page dramatically and can be used for both the background and text. The `bgcolor` attribute of the body tag gives you a solid color for the background. You can specify the color either by number, as explained later, or by using a small set of predefined color terms, as in

```
<body bgcolor="silver">
```

The color choices are shown in Table 4.3. The body tag attribute `text` is used to give the entire document's text a specific color. The example

```
<body text="aqua" link="fuchsia">
```

illustrates how to control the link colors, too. You can change the text in specific places by using the font tag with the color attribute. So, to make Russell's Paradox red, write

```
<b><font color="red">This statement is false.</font></b>
```

The predefined colors are handy, but you may want to access more than 16 colors; that's where the numeric colors come in.

Table 4.3. *Predefined HTML Colors*

black	silver	white	gray
red	fuchsia	maroon	purple
blue	navy	aqua	teal
lime	green	yellow	olive

Color by Number

As we mentioned briefly in Chapter 1, computer colors are usually described by their amounts of red, green, and blue light. The intensity of each color is specified by a number from 0 through 255. So, for example, a zero amount of all three colors (0,0,0) produces the color black. If all three colors are at full intensity (255, 255, 255), the color is white because white is a mix of the three colors of light. Though it makes no difference for black and white, the order is always red, green, blue—so we call it **RGB color specification**. Thus, if there is full intensity of one color and none of the other two, as in

> `(255, 0, 0)` Intense Red
>
> `(0, 255, 0)` Intense Green
>
> `(0, 0, 255)` Intense Blue

we get the three pure colors.

You can select custom colors for backgrounds and fonts in HTML by giving the three RGB intensity values. The only catch is that you do not specify them as whole numbers between 0 and 255, but as pairs of hex digits between 00 and FF. A **hexadeximal (hex) digit** is one of the symbols {0, 1, 2, 3, 4, 5, 6, 7, 8, 9, A, B, C, D, E, F} from the base-16 or hexadecimal numbering system, which we will discuss in Chapter 11. But we can use them now without understanding hex. Because the smallest value is 00, which is the same as a normal 0, and the largest value is FF, which is the same as a normal 255, the three pure colors are expressed in HTML as

#FF0000 Intense Red

#00FF00 Intense Green

#0000FF Intense Blue

The number sign (#) means that what follows is a hexadecimal number. The easiest way to find the values for a custom color, say (255, 142, 42), which is the color of a carrot, is to look up the numbers in Table 4.4 to find their two hex digits. First find the intensity for each color in the table, and then read the first hex digit from the left end of the row and the second hex digit from the top of the column. Thus the carrot color is

#FF8E2A Carrot Orange

because 255 is FF, 142 is 8E, and 42 is 2A.

Even though numeric colors need two levels of translation—first the translation of the color into the three RGB intensities, and then the translation of those values into hex digit pairs—they give us much more flexibility in Web page design, so most HTML programmers prefer them.

There is another way to find the numeric specification for a color, and it is the easiest. In Appendix A, Table A.1 shows a standard set of HTML colors and their hex specification. (These colors give best results on most monitors.) Find the color in the table, and read the hex digits.

With the information you have learned in the last three sections, it's possible to enhance the Web page shown in Figure 4.1. The result is shown in Figure 4.2. Notice the local pathnames to our own biographical profiles of Russell and Magritte, the background and text colors, the change of color for the font and for the headings, and, of course, the added image.

Table 4.4. *Hexadecimal Digit Equivalents*

Hex	0	1	2	3	4	5	6	7	8	9	A	B	C	D	E	F
0	0	1	2	3	4	5	6	7	8	9	10	11	12	13	14	15
1	16	17	18	19	20	21	22	23	24	25	26	27	28	29	30	31
2	32	33	34	35	36	37	38	39	40	41	42	43	44	45	46	47
3	48	49	50	51	52	53	54	55	56	57	58	59	60	61	62	63
4	64	65	66	67	68	69	70	71	72	73	74	75	76	77	78	79
5	80	81	82	83	84	85	86	87	88	89	90	91	92	93	94	95
6	96	97	98	99	100	101	102	103	104	105	106	107	108	109	110	111
7	112	113	114	115	116	117	118	119	120	121	122	123	124	125	126	127
8	128	129	130	131	132	133	134	135	136	137	138	139	140	141	142	143
9	144	145	146	147	148	149	150	151	152	153	154	155	156	157	158	159
A	160	161	162	163	164	165	166	167	168	169	170	171	172	173	174	175
B	176	177	178	179	180	181	182	183	184	185	186	187	188	189	190	191
C	192	193	194	195	196	197	198	199	200	201	202	203	204	205	206	207
D	208	209	210	211	212	213	214	215	216	217	218	219	220	221	222	223
E	224	225	226	227	228	229	230	231	232	233	234	235	236	237	238	239
F	240	241	242	243	244	245	246	247	248	249	250	251	252	253	254	255

Note: Find the decimal number in the table and then combine the entries in the left column and the top row symbols to form the hexadecimal equivalent. Thus decimal 180 is hexadecimal B4.

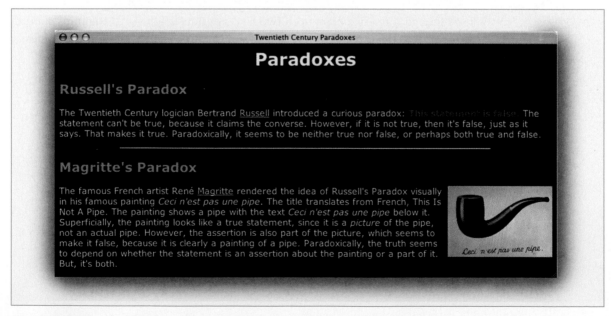

Figure 4.2. *Completed Web page and the HTML source (continues next page).*

```
<html>
   <head>
     <title>Twentieth Century Paradoxes</title>
   </head>
   <body bgcolor="#000000" text="#DDDDDD" link="#FFCC66">
     <h1 align="center"><font COLOR="yellow">Paradoxes</FONT></h1>
     <h2><font color="#FF8E2A">Russell's Paradox</font></h2>
         <p>The Twentieth Century logician Bertrand
         <a href="Russellbio.html">Russell</a> introduced a curious paradox:
         <b><font color="red">This statement is false.</font></b> The
         statement can't be true, because it claims the converse. However,
         if it is not true, then it's false, just as it says. That makes it
         true. Paradoxically, it seems to be neither true nor false, or
         perhaps both true and false.</p>

     <hr width="75%">

     <h2><font color="#FF8E2A">Magritte's Paradox</font></h2>
         <p> <img src="pipe.jpg" height="130" width="192" align="right">
         The famous French artist Ren&eacute;
         <a href="Magrittebio.html">Magritte</a> rendered the idea of
         Russell's Paradox visually in his famous painting <i>Ceci n'est pas
         une pipe</i>. The title translates from French, This Is Not A Pipe.
         The painting shows a pipe with the text <i>Ceci n'est pas une pipe</i>
         below it. Superficially, the painting looks like a true statement,
         since it is a <i>picture</i> of the pipe, not an actual pipe.
         However, the assertion is also part of the picture, which seems to
         make it false, because it is clearly a painting of a pipe.
         Paradoxically, the truth seems to depend on whether the statement
         is an assertion about the painting or a part of it. But, it's both.
         </p>
   </body>
</html>
```

Figure 4.2 (*continued*). *Completed Web page and the HTML source.*

HANDLING LISTS

There are many kinds of lists in HTML, the easiest being an unnumbered list. The unnumbered list tags `<ul>` and `</ul>` surround the items of the list, which are themselves enclosed in list item tags, `<li>` and `</li>`. The browser formats the list with each item bulleted, indented, and starting on its own line. As usual, though the form of the HTML doesn't matter to the browser, we write the HTML list instructions in list form. So, for example, the HTML for a movie list is

```
<ul>
   <li>Luxo Jr.</li>
   <li>Toy Story</li>
   <li>Monsters Inc.</li>
</ul>
```

which looks like

- Luxo Jr.
- Toy Story
- Monsters Inc.

Another kind of list is an ordered list, which uses the tags `<ol>` and `</ol>` and replaces the bullets with numbers. Otherwise, the ordered list behaves just like an unnumbered list. Thus, the HTML for the start of the list of chemical elements is

```
<ol>
   <li> Hydrogen, H, 1.008, 1 </li>
   <li> Helium, He, 4.003, 2</li>
   <li> Lithium, Li, 6.941, 2 1 </li>
   <li> Beryllium, Be, 9.012, 2 2 </li>
</ol>
```

which looks like

1. Hydrogen, H, 1.008, 1
2. Helium, He, 4.003, 2
3. Lithium, Li, 6.941, 2 1
4. Beryllium, Be, 9.012, 2 2

We can also have a list within a list, simply by making the sublists items of the main list. Applying this idea in HTML

```
<ul>
   <li>Pear</li>
   <li>Apple</li>
      <ul>
         <li>Granny Smith</li>
         <li>Fuji </li>
      </ul>
   <li>Cherry</li>
</ul>
```

looks like

- Pear
- Apple
  - Granny Smith
  - Fuji
- Cherry

Finally, there is a handy list form called the **definitional list**, indicated by the tags `<dl>` and `</dl>`. A definitional list is usually made up of a sequence of definitional terms, surrounded by the tags `<dt>` and `</dt>`, and definitional data, surrounded by the tags `<dd>` and `</dd>`. So, for example, a definitional list is expressed in HTML as

```
<dl>
   <dt> Man </dt>
   <dd> <i>Homo sapiens</i>, the greatest achievement
      of evolution. </dd>
   <dt> Woman </dt>
   <dd> <i>Homo sapiens</i>, a greater achievement of
      evolution, and clever enough not to mention it to man.
   </dd>
</dl>
```

and would be formatted by browsers as

Man
> *Homo sapiens*, the greatest achievement of evolution.

Woman
> *Homo sapiens*, a greater achievement of evolution, and clever enough not to mention it to man.

For especially short terms, a more compact form of the definitional list gives the definition on the same line as the term. Include the `compact` attribute in the `<dl>` tag for this type of list. For example, a definitional list of molecular biology abbreviations is

```
<dl compact>
   <dt>A</dt>
   <dd>Adenine </dd>
   <dt>C</dt>
   <dd>Cytosine </dd>
   <dt>C</dt>
   <dd>Guanine </dd>
   <dt>T</dt>
   <dd>Thymine </dd>
</dl>
```

which is displayed by browsers as

A   Adenine

C   Cytosine

G   Guanine

T   Thymine

Of course, other formatting commands such as italics and bold can be used within any line items.

HANDLING TABLES

A table is a good way to present certain types of information. Creating a table in HTML is straightforward. It is like defining a list of lists, where each of the main list items, called *rows*, has one or more items, called *cells*. The browser aligns cells to form columns.

Table Tags

The table is enclosed in table tags, **<table>** and **</table>**. If you want the table to have a border around it, use the attribute **border** inside the table tag. Each row is enclosed in table row tags, **<tr>** and **</tr>**. The cells of each row are surrounded by table data tags, **<td>** and **</td>**. So a table with two rows, each with three cells of the form

Canada	Ottawa	English/French
Iceland	Reykjavik	Icelandic

is defined by

```
<table border>
  <tr>
     <td>Canada</td>
     <td>Ottawa</td>
     <td>English/French</td>
  </tr>
  <tr>
     <td>Iceland</td>
     <td>Reykjavik</td>
     <td>Icelandic</td>
  </tr>
</table>
```

You can give tables captions and column headings. The caption tags are `<caption>` and `</caption>`. You place them within the table tags around the table's caption. The caption is shown centered at the top of the table in bold. You place the column headings as the first row of the table. In the heading row, you replace the table data tags with table heading tags, `<th>` and `</th>`, which also display in bold. The table row tags are `<tr>` and `</tr>` as usual. Thus we can change our example table to give it a caption and column headings:

```
<table border>
    <caption>Country Data</caption>
    <tr>
        <th>Country</th>
        <th>Capital</th>
        <th>Language(s)</th>
    </tr>
    <tr>
        <td>Canada</td>
        <td>Ottawa</td>
        <td>English/French</td>
    </tr>
    <tr>
        <td>Iceland</td>
        <td>Reykjavik</td>
        <td>Icelandic</td>
    </tr>
    <tr>
        <td>Norway</td>
        <td>Oslo</td>
        <td>Norwegian</td>
    </tr>
</table>
```

which will look like this

Notice that the first row uses the `<th>` tag rather than the `<td>` tag to specify the headings.

Controlling Text with Tables

Tables are a handy way to control the arrangement of information on the page. An example where this control might be desirable is when we have a series of links listed across the top of a page. The links only form a one-row table, but the table helps keep the links together. Figures 4.3 and 4.4 show two different HTML sources, one simply listing the links in sequence and the other placing the links into a table. When there is enough window space, the two solutions look the same.

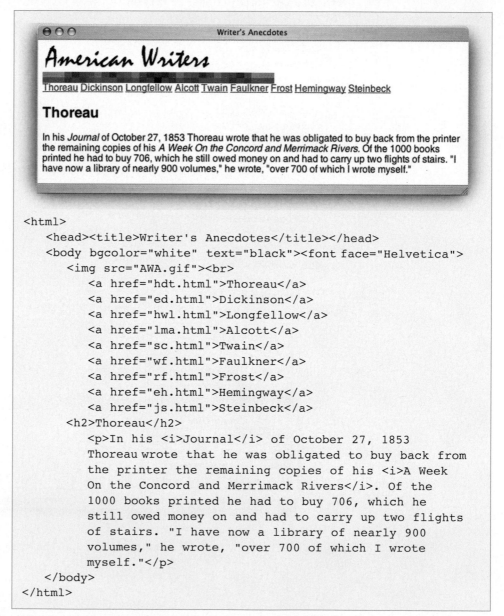

```
<html>
   <head><title>Writer's Anecdotes</title></head>
   <body bgcolor="white" text="black"><font face="Helvetica">
      <img src="AWA.gif"><br>
         <a href="hdt.html">Thoreau</a>
         <a href="ed.html">Dickinson</a>
         <a href="hwl.html">Longfellow</a>
         <a href="lma.html">Alcott</a>
         <a href="sc.html">Twain</a>
         <a href="wf.html">Faulkner</a>
         <a href="rf.html">Frost</a>
         <a href="eh.html">Hemingway</a>
         <a href="js.html">Steinbeck</a>
      <h2>Thoreau</h2>
         <p>In his <i>Journal</i> of October 27, 1853
         Thoreau wrote that he was obligated to buy back from
         the printer the remaining copies of his <i>A Week
         On the Concord and Merrimack Rivers</i>. Of the
         1000 books printed he had to buy 706, which he
         still owed money on and had to carry up two flights
         of stairs. "I have now a library of nearly 900
         volumes," he wrote, "over 700 of which I wrote
         myself."</p>
   </body>
</html>
```

Figure 4.3. *A page and its HTML for a simple listing of links.*

The difference is apparent when there is only a small amount of window space (see Figure 4.5). When there is not enough space for the full sequence of links, the browser **wraps** (continues on the next line) the links just as it wraps normal paragraph text. But the table keeps the links together in a row; scroll bars are added and the links are hidden. Some people prefer the row to the wrap. Some people don't. Keeping the links in a row is an example of when you would use an HTML table even if the situation does not necessarily require one.

```
<html>
    <head><title>Writer's Anecdotes</title></head>
    <body bgcolor="white" text="black"><fontface="Helvetica">
        <img src="AWA.gif">
            <table>
                <tr>
                    <td><a href="hdt.html">Thoreau</a></td>
                    <td><a href="ed.html">Dickinson</a></td>
                    <td><a href="hwl.html">Longfellow</a></td>
                    <td><a href="lma.html">Alcott</a></td>
                    <td><a href="sc.html">Twain</a></td>
                    <td><a href="wf.html">Faulkner</a></td>
                    <td><a href="rf.html">Frost</a></td>
                    <td><a href="eh.html">Hemingway</a></td>
                    <td><a href="js.html">Steinbeck</a></td>
                </tr>
            </table>
        <h2>Steinbeck</h2>
            <p>Steinbeck traveled to Russia several times, but
            never mastered the language. Traveling with
            photographer Robert Capa in 1947 he wrote, "...I admit
            our Russian is limited, but we can say hello, come in,
            you are beautiful, oh no you don't, and one which
            charms us but seems to have an application rarely
            needed, 'The thumb is second cousin to the left foot.'
            We don't use that one much."</p>
    </body>
</html>
```

Figure 4.4. *A page and its HTML for listing links in a table.*

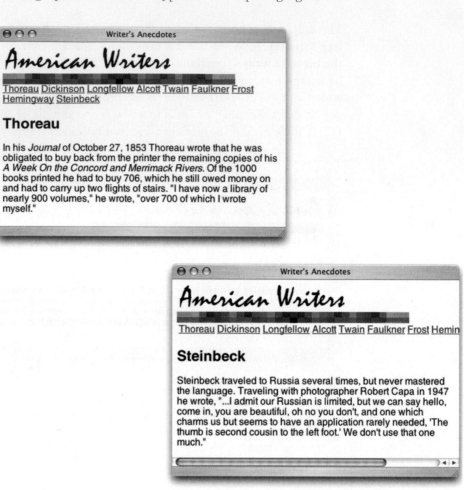

Figure 4.5. *The display of the two pages from Figures 4.3 and 4.4 in a small window showing that the table keeps the links in a single row (bottom) rather than wrapping them (top).*

*fit*BYTE

Spam Buster. Analogous to `<a href ...>`, HTML has `<mailto: ...>` to link to an emailer, so users can easily reply to Web content. Although originally popular, it's not now used because crawlers look for this tag when harvesting email addresses for spam. They look for ats (`@`) and dots (`.`), too. To include your email address on your Web page, make a `.gif` of your address. It's not as convenient as `mailto`, but it's safer.

HTML WRAP-UP

In learning HTML, we have seen how a Web page is encoded. Though HTML has a few more exotic features beyond those presented here, and the other Web languages have even more powerful features, they are all variations on the same theme: Tags surround all objects that appear on the page, the context is set by specifying global properties of the page (e.g., `<body bgcolor="white">`), and each feature of the format is specified in detail, `<i>isn't it?!</i>`. It's so easy, even a computer can do it!

Indeed, that's what happens most of the time. Web authors usually don't write HTML directly; they use Web authoring tools, such as Macromedia Dreamweaver, standard text editors like Microsoft Word, or the Composer feature of Mozilla. They build the page as it should look on the screen using a WYSIWYG Web authoring program, and then the computer generates the HTML to implement it.

> *fit*BYTE
>
> **Uploading.** Pages are created and tested on a personal computer. To be accessed from other computers on the Internet, the HTML files, the image files, and the directory structure created for them must be uploaded (transmitted) to a Web server, a process known as **publishing**

SUMMARY

We learned that Web pages are stored and transmitted in an encoded form before a browser turns them into images and that HTML is the most widely used encoding form. The chapter opened by recalling the idea of using tags for formatting and went on to introduce us to:

> A working set of HTML tags, giving us the ability to create our first page.

> An explanation of how links are marked with anchor tags.

> Absolute and relative pathnames. Relative pathnames refer to files deeper and higher in the directory hierarchy.

> The two most popular image formatting schemes—JPG and GIF—and how we place them in a page.

> Numeric colors, lists, and tables.

> WYSIWYG Web authoring tools—programs that automatically create the HTML when our page design is complete.

EXERCISES

Multiple Choice

1. HTML commands are called
   A. hops
   B. brackets
   C. tags
   D. tokens

2. HTML tags are words enclosed in
   A. `( )`
   B. `// \\`
   C. `{ }`
   D. `< >`

3. Which of the following would put "Sheryl Crow — In Concert" in the title bar of a Web page?
   A. `<title>Sheryl Crow — In Concert</title>`
   B. `</title> Sheryl Crow — In Concert<title>`
   C. `<title> Sheryl Crow — In Concert<title/>`
   D. `<TITLE/> Sheryl Crow — In Concert</TITLE>`

4. Which of the following tags is not paired?
   A. `<hr>`
   B. `<i>`
   C. `<p>`
   D. `<html>`

5. The `<p> </p>` tags indicate the beginning and end of a
   A. table
   B. picture
   C. paragraph
   D. preformatted text section

6. The `<a. . .>` tag is called an
   A. anchor
   B. address
   C. add
   D. append

7. The attribute specifying a blue background is
   A. `bgcolor = #000000`
   B. `background = "blue"`
   C. `<color = blue>`
   D. `bgcolor = blue`

8. The .. notation in a relative path of hypertext reference means to
   A. open a folder and go down a directory
   B. close a folder and open the parent folder
   C. search a folder
   D. create a folder

9. To get an image to sit on the right side of the window with the text filling the area to the left of the image, your tag would need to look like
   A. `<img src = "mountains.jpg" align = "right">`
   B. `<img src align = "mountains.jpg" "right">`
   C. `<img = "mountains.jpg" src align = "right">`
   D. `<img "mountains.jpg" align src = "right">`

10. The dimensions for an image on a Web page
    A. are set using the `x` and `y` attributes
    B. are set using the `width` and `height` attributes
    C. must be set to the actual size of the image
    D. are automatically adjusted by the browser to fit in the space allotted

Short Answer

1. Today most Web pages are created using _____.

2. To improve readability of HTML text, the computer experts suggest adding _____ to the source instructions.

3. The _____ tag is a way to get more than one consecutive space in a line of a Web page.

4. _____ tags are tags between other tags.

5. Special commands inside a tag are called _____.

6. _____ are usually used to link to pages on the same site.

7. A .. in a hypertext reference indicates a ____ path.

8. The `src` in an image tag stands for _____.

9. GIF stands for _____.

10. JPEG stands for _____.

11. To get the RGB color black using hexadecimal numbers, you would write _____.

12. To put the ten greatest inventions of all time, in order, on a Web page, you should use a(n) _____.

Exercises

1. Why learn HTML at all if authoring tools will do the work for you? Give other examples of where you are expected to learn something when there are tools available that will do the work.

2. Use HTML to properly display the following.

General
Colonel
Major
Captain
Lieutenant
Sergeant

Corporal

Private

3. Explain why a page needs to be reloaded in a browser to see the results of editing changes made in the text editor of an HTML document.

4. Indicate the hyperlink reference and the anchor text in this anchor tag. Then break down the hyperlink reference into the protocol, domain, path, and file name.

   ```
   <a href="http://www.nasm.si.edu/nasm/museum/museum.htm">
   National Air and Space Museum</a>
   ```

5. Treat your birthday (mm/dd/yy) as hexadecimal and then determine what color it is.

6. Experiment with hexadecimal colors until you find the seven combinations that will give you the colors of the rainbow.

7. Create a calendar for the current month using a table. Put the month in a caption at the top. Change the color of the text for Sunday and holidays. Make note of any special days during the month. Add an appropriate graphic to one of the blank cells at the end of the calendar.

8. Create a page with links to your favorite friends. Use one column for their names, another for their homepages, and a third column for their email addresses. Link to their homepages.

9. View and then print the source for the author's homepage. It's at

   ```
   www.cs.washington.edu/homes/snyder/index.html
   ```

   What is the title of the page? Indicate the heading and the body for the page. Find the table. Find the list. Find the email links. Find the absolute hyperlinks and the relative hyperlinks. How many graphics are on this page?

chapter 5

SEARCHING FOR TRUTH

Locating Information on the WWW

learning objectives

> Explain the benefits of searching in obvious places and in libraries

> Analyze how Web site information is organized

> Explain how a Web search engine works

> Find information by using a search engine

> Decide whether Web information is truth or fiction

SEARCHING FOR TRUTH
Locating Information on the WWW

The art of reading between the lines is as old as manipulated information.
                                        —SERGE SCHMEMANN

A WELL-KNOWN JOKE tells of a man out for an evening walk. He meets a
drunk who is on his hands and knees under a streetlight. "What are you doing?"
asks the man. "Looking for my car key," replies the drunk. "You lost it here?" asks
the man in conversation as he begins to help look. "No, I dropped it by the tav-
ern." "Then why are you looking over here?" "The light's better," the drunk replies.
The joke lampoons a principle—the best place to look for something is where it's
likely to be found—that is key to finding information.

     In this chapter we discuss searching for information and evaluating its accura-
cy. To find anything, we have to look where it's likely to be found. Historically,
libraries have housed well-organized archives, collections, and other information
resources that are good places to look. Now many of those resources are available
online, so we can update the "visit the library" advice: Log in to the library. To find
what we're looking for we must also understand the hierarchical organization of
information. Hierarchy speeds searching, and recognizing hierarchies when we see
them helps us find information faster. Of course, using a computer to search greatly extends our reach, so we also need to understand how search engines work,
how they organize the information they store, and how to interpret search results.
If we are going to use search engines effectively, we need to ask the right questions, which is as important as looking in the right place. But finding information
and finding truthful, accurate, insightful information are two different things. So
we must be aware that deceptive information lurks on the Internet, and learn to
recognize accurate sources. Finally, we test our understanding by deciding whether
information on a Web page is true or false.

SEARCHING IN ALL THE RIGHT PLACES

Ask a reference librarian where to find a *Scientific American*–type article on black holes and the reply will always be "*Scientific American.*" Yet many of us ask questions like that because we don't think about where to look for the information we want. Reference librarians do think about it, and we can learn from them and become better information gatherers. That's important because on the Web we don't have a librarian's help. The key to finding information is to think logically and creatively.

The Obvious and Familiar

If we're going to "look in the right place," we need to know where the information we want can be found. Like *Scientific American*, many sources are obvious and familiar if we think about it:

> To find tax information, ask the federal (IRS) or state tax office.

> To find the direction to Dover from London, look at a map of the United Kingdom.

> To find out how many shares of IBM stock are outstanding, check the company's annual report.

Many of the answers we want to find have an obvious source, so we can simply guess the online address: **www.irs.gov**, **www.mapquest.com**, and **www.ibm.com**, respectively.

Libraries Online

One advantage that research librarians have over most of us is that they know about many more information sources than we do. Their advantage can be our advantage if we use libraries. Libraries remain substantial information resources despite the growth of the Internet. Most college libraries and many large public libraries let you access not only the online catalog of their own collections, but also many other information resources. These libraries are just a "click away."

For example, the University of Washington's Libraries site, **www.lib.washington.edu**, opens with an inviting page presenting a series of links to online information resources (see Figure 5.1a). You can search in the UW catalog or the Library of Congress' collection. By clicking on the Research Databases link, you're transported to a new page linking to hundreds of databases (see Figure 5.1b). Many of these resources are commercial databases that UW subscribes to, so only UW students and faculty can use them. However, your library probably gives you access to similar collections. Checking these sources is a quick and easy way to find information.

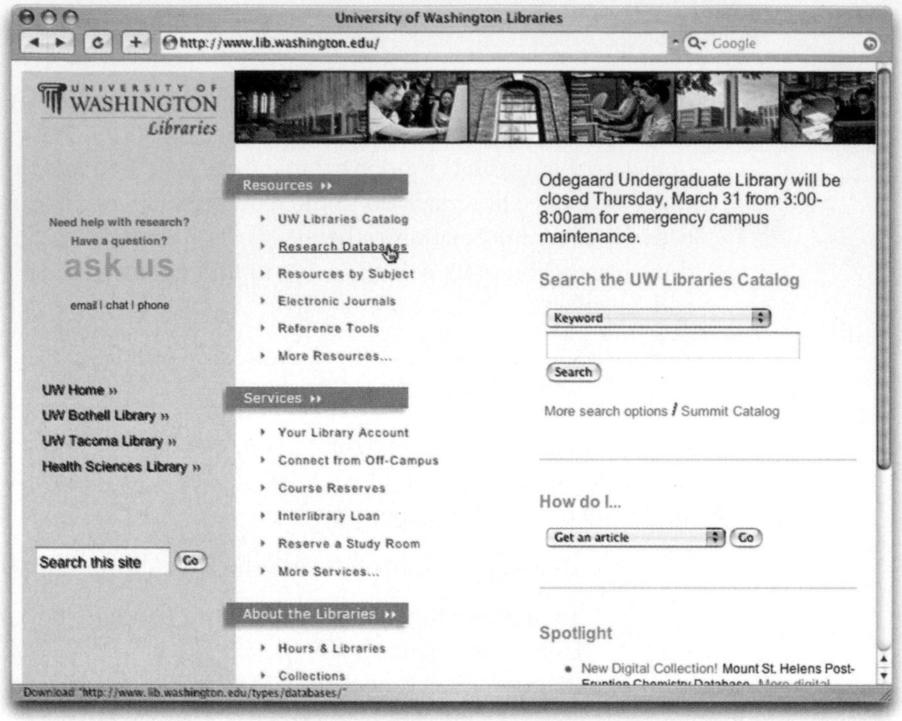

(a)

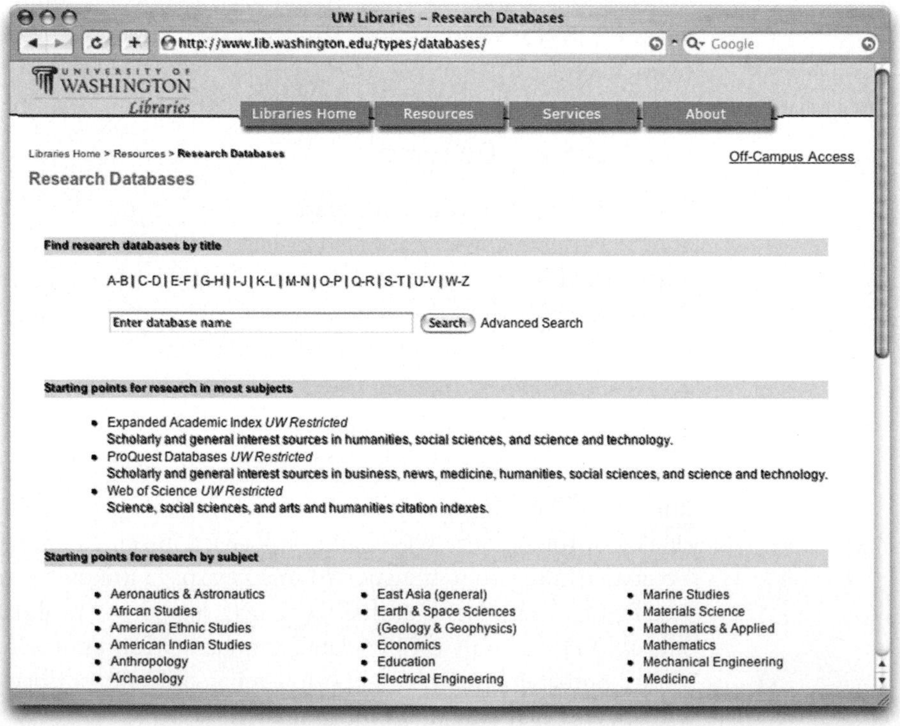

(b)

Figure 5.1. *The (a) UW Libraries homepage and the (b) Research Databases page (continues next page).*

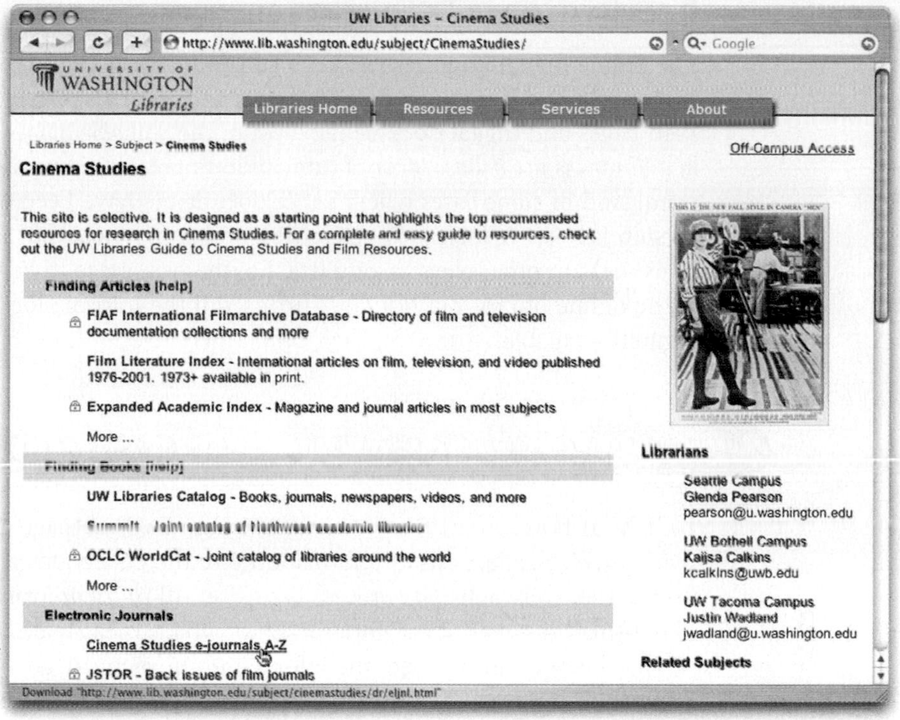

(c)

Figure 5.1 (continued). *(c) Cinema Studies page.*

In addition to linking to these huge database resources, UW's librarians have helped us even more. At the bottom of the Research Databases page (Figure 5.1b) is "Starting points for research by subject." These are topic-specific pages that the librarians have set up. They bring together many of the library's resources on specific topics. Clicking on Cinema Studies, we see a page devoted specifically to that topic (see Figure 5.1c). And at the bottom of this page is the link for "Cinema Studies e-journals, A–Z." In three clicks we can begin to poke around the archives on the exact topic of interest to us.

The point is not that UW's librarians have done an especially nice job, though I think they have, but that libraries in general provide many online facilities that are well organized and trustworthy. For example, the Chicago Public Library, `www.chipublib.org`, lists similar resources on its Selected Internet Resources page, and the Library of Congress, `www.loc.gov/library/`, has huge online collections and services for Internet users. These resources are free and open to everyone. So, to find out information, go (electronically) to the library.

Pre-Digital Information

The online digital library is not yet a substitute for going to the physical library and checking out traditional paper books and journals. Despite the billions of Web pages and digital documents, most of the *valuable information typically found in a library is not online*. Most of humankind's pre-1985 knowledge is not yet digitized. And in some cases where paper documents have been digitized, the online version is missing footnotes, references, and appendices, has unreadable equations, or is in other ways incomplete. So, the best place to begin your research is at the online library, but don't be surprised if the information you need is not yet digitally available.

HOW IS INFORMATION ORGANIZED?

To help us find information, librarians, archivists, Web-page designers, and others who organize collections of information give the collections a structure to make them easier to search. The process is simple: All of the information is grouped into a small number of categories, each of which is easily described. This is the top-level *classification*. Then, the information in each category is also divided into a few subcategories, each with a simple description. These are the second-level classifications (see Figure 5.2). Those subcategories are also divided into still smaller categories with brief descriptions, the third-level classifications. And on and on. Eventually, the classifications become small enough that it's possible to look through the whole category to find the information you need.

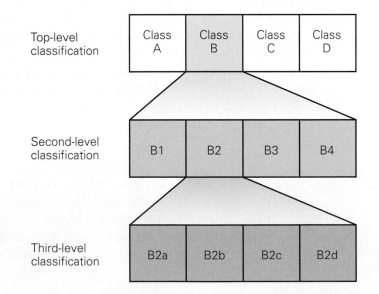

Figure 5.2. *Top-level, second-level, and third-level classifications of a collection.*

For example, a source of information about radio stations in the US that carry National Public Radio might use their *geographical region* as its top-level classification, making the top-level categories:

Northeast, Mid Atlantic, Southeast, North Central, South Central, Mountain, Pacific

Within each region, the second-level classification might use the state, making the Pacific category's subcategories:

Alaska, California, Hawaii, Oregon, Washington

The third-level categories could be large cities with multiple public radio stations in populous states like California and Texas. When the final classification is small enough—Hawaii has only four NPR stations—no finer classification is needed.

There are several important properties of classifications.

> The descriptive terms must cover all of the information in the category and be easy for a searcher to apply. Region of the country, state, city, etc., have this property.

> The subcategories do not all have to use the same classification. So, the Pacific category could be categorized by states and the Northeast could be categorized by cities.

> The information in the category defines how best to classify it.

There is no single way to classify information.

This structure is called a *hierarchy*. As with the directory hierarchy we discussed in Chapter 3, it is a natural way to organize information. Remember that hierarchies are often drawn as trees. One very famous hierarchy is the "tree of life," the biological taxonomy of organisms. It is too large to display as a tree, but Table 5.1 shows the layers of classification for human beings, from the top level (highest) classification—kingdom—to the last (lowest)—species. Because hierarchies are a logical way to organize information, we find them everywhere. And because they are so intuitive, we don't often consciously notice them. Our goal for the rest of this section is to recognize hierarchies when we see them because being aware of them speeds up our information discovery.

*fit*BYTE | **Choose to Exclude.** Hierarchies work well not because of what we choose, but what we don't choose. For example, suppose a collection has a million items divided into ten (roughly) equal-size categories. Picking a category eliminates from consideration the 900,000 items in the other categories. If the chosen category is also classified into ten categories, the next choice eliminates another 90,000 items. With two choices we eliminated 990,000 items!

Table 5.1. *The Biological Classification of Human Beings,* Homo sapiens

Taxonomic Level	Name of Classification
Kingdom	Animalia
Phylum	Chordata
Subphylum	Vertebrata
Class	Mammalia
Order	Primates
Family	Hominoidea
Genus	*Homo*
Species	*sapiens*

For example, consider the National Public Radio Web site, `www.npr.org`, shown in Figure 5.3. We might visit this site to find audio information about current news. The site uses hierarchical organization in several ways.

Studying the NPR page, as shown in Figure 5.3, we first notice that the information is divided into two categories: **navigation information** at the top and left sides, and **browsing information** in the remainder. This is a standard format. The navigation links are provided for people checking the page for specific information, while the browsing information is for casual visitors who want to read the latest stories NPR is covering. The browsing information has been further clustered into groups such as Top News Stories and Editor's Picks, but generally, the items are individual stories. The navigation information is different.

Recognizing a Hierarchy

Notice the ten gray links on the left side below the **find** button. Clicking on any of these links causes it to expand into another short list of links on subtopics of the main topic. For example, clicking on **News** displays four subclassifications: Nation, World, Middle East, and Iraq. Clicking on **Business** displays four subclassifications: Economy, Your Money, Technology, and Media (see Figure 5.4a).

These gray navigation links are the first levels of a hierarchy, which we call the Story Hierarchy that connects to all of NPR's current stories. The links that display when we click on a first-level link are the second levels of the hierarchy. If we want to see NPR's stories related to the media, we can reach them with two clicks: > Business > Media. A page showing all of the stories is displayed. Figure 5.5 illustrates the Story Hierarchy structure drawn as a tree. We discuss this hierarchy further below.

There are other hierarchical structures present as well, mostly listed across the top of the NPR homepage. For example, **Archives** is the root of a huge hierarchy of past programs organized at the top level by time interval and within that by program (see Figure 5.4b). **Discussions**, which links to listener comments, has more than a dozen top-level classifications in its hierarchical structure.

Figure 5.3. *The National Public Radio (NPR) homepage* www.npr.org

(a)   **(b)**

Figure 5.4. *NPR hierarchies: Navigation links after clicking on (a) Business and (b) Archives (with the time-frame drop-down menu displayed).*

Design of Hierarchies

Figure 5.5 shows the Story Hierarchy drawn as a **tree**. The tree is drawn on its side with the **root** (All Stories) to the left and the **leaves** (Individual Stories, not shown) to the right. Hierarchy trees are often drawn sideways because it's more convenient to write (English) text that way. It is also common to draw trees upside down, with the root at the top. Either way, the important point is not the orientation, but the branching metaphor.

Hierarchies use a general set of rules for their design and terminology:

> > Because hierarchy trees are often drawn with the root at the top, we say, "going up in the hierarchy" and "going down in the hierarchy." (Similar language—higher and deeper—was used with directory hierarchies in Chapter 3.) The terms are relative to the root being drawn at the top. So

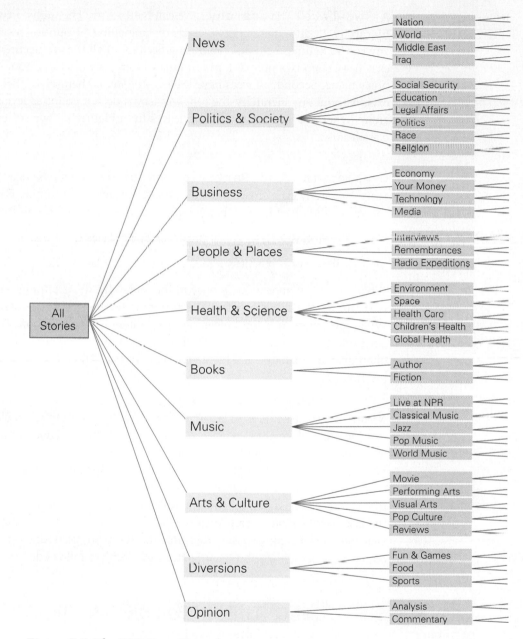

Figure 5.5. The NPR Story Hierarchy tree.

"going up" means the classifications become more inclusive; they are closer to the root. "Going down" means the classifications become more specific; they are farther from the root.

> The greater-than symbol (>) is a common way to show going down in a hierarchy through levels of classification:

All Stories > News > Nation > Disney Replaces CEO Eisner

A Two-Level Hierarchy. We call NPR's Story Hierarchy a **two-level hierarchy** because there are two levels of "branching." Counting levels of a hierarchy can sometimes be a little confusing because of all the connecting lines, but it's easy if we keep two points in mind. First, the tree always has a root—the collection's name. Second, all trees have leaves—the items themselves. Because they exist without any hierarchy, the root and leaves do not count as levels of the hierarchy. When we ignore the root and leaves from Figure 5.5, we see two levels of classification.

Overlapping and Partitioning of Levels. Notice that in the Story Hierarchy each story can be listed as a leaf more than once. For example, the story of Michael Eisner's being replaced can be reached by multiple paths:

All Stories > News > Nation > Disney Replaces CEO Eisner

All Stories > Business > Media > Disney Replaces CEO Eisner

When every leaf appears only once in the hierarchy, the groupings are called **partitionings**. The tree of life is a partitioning because every species is listed once. When groupings "overlap," meaning that an item is listed in more than one category, the leaves are repeated. Classifications that are convenient for the searcher often overlap, making such hierarchies easy to use. There is no best way to classify information.

Number of Levels May Differ. Finally, the number of classifications of a hierarchy does not need to be the same for all items. That is, the number of levels between a leaf and the root does not need to be the same for every leaf. Some groupings might require more levels of classification to reduce the group to a manageable size. For example, the **Archives** hierarchy in Figure 5.4(b) shows that stories are classified into several different time intervals. We expect that for the last classification, "heard since 1996." there will be a classification layer by year that doesn't apply to the other time intervals. So, yesterday's story is reached by a longer path when the "heard since 1996" link is followed.

SEARCHING THE WEB FOR INFORMATION

A **search engine** is a collection of computer programs that helps us find information on the Web. Though programs for text searching existed long before the Web, the explosion of Web-based digital information and its distribution across the planet made the invention of search engines necessary. No one organizes the information posted on the Web, so these programs look around to find out what's out there and organize what they find. It's a big task. How do search engines do it?

How a Search Engine Works

A search engine has two basic parts: a **crawler** and a **query processor**. The crawler visits sites on the Internet, discovering Web pages, and building an **index** to the Web's content. The query processor looks up user-submitted keywords in the index and reports back which Web pages the crawler has found containing those words. Popular search engines include Google, Yahoo!, Alta Vista, Excite, and InfoSeek. We will use the Google search engine as our example (see Figure 5.6).

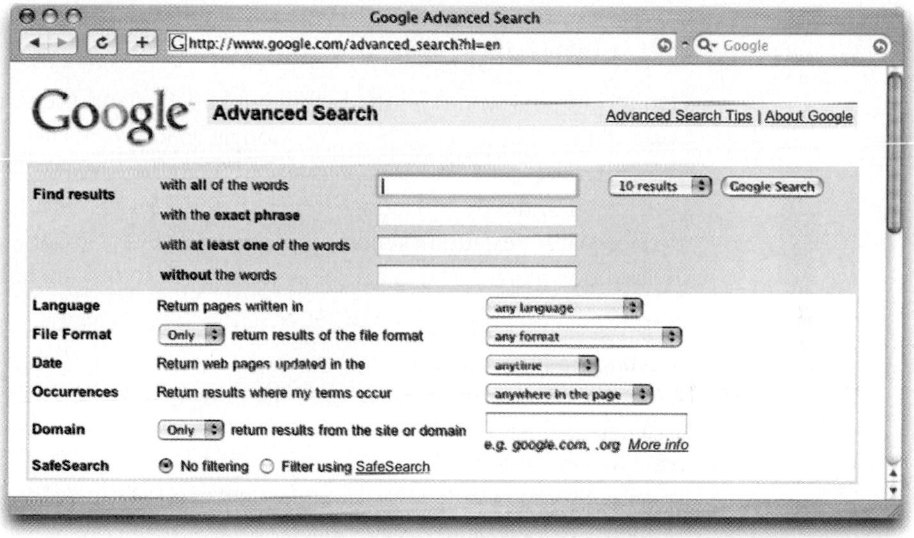

Figure 5.6. *The Google search engine's advanced search view.*

*fit***BYTE**

A Big Name in Searching. "Google" is a variant spelling of googol, a term coined by American mathematician Edward Kasner's nine-year-old nephew Milton Sirotta for the number 10^{100}; that is, 1 followed by one hundred zeros.

Crawlers. When a crawler visits a Web page, it first identifies all the links to other Web pages on that page. It checks its records to see if it has visited those other pages recently. If not, it adds them to its "to do" list of pages that must be crawled. Thus crawlers find pages to visit by saving links to pages not yet visited from pages they've already seen. (Google also lets Web page authors submit their pages to be crawled.)

The crawler also records in an index the keywords used on a page. The words can appear in either the title or body of the page. For example, the HTML homepage for the Hot Dang! Thai restaurant (`www.hotdang.com`) might have the title block

```
<title> Hot Dang! Restaurant, Cuisine of Siam </title>
```

so, in the index, the crawler would associate the keywords "hot," "dang," "restaurant," "cuisine," and "siam" with the `www.hotdang.com` URL. Small, unspecific words like "of" are ignored. Crawlers also ignore case.

Google pioneered the idea of including keywords from the *anchor* (that highlighted text associated with a link) in the index. That is, the words of the highlighted text of a link *to a page* are included among the descriptive terms for that page. For example, if your Web page referenced the Hot Dang! restaurant with the text

```
. . . my favorite <a href="http://www.hotdang.com">
Thai restaurants </a> . . .
```

<u>Thai restaurants</u> would be the highlighted anchor and the terms "Thai" and "restaurants" would be included by Google as keywords associated with `www.hotdang.com`. Anchors help a search engine find relevant pages because the anchors often describe the page better than the page's own content. For example, the Hot Dang! restaurant's motto is "Cuisine of Siam," so the page may not actually say anywhere that it is a Thai restaurant. But your anchor does.

---

fit **BYTE**

Shortsightedness. Search engines crawl only a fraction (substantially less than half) of the Web. Because it is growing so fast, there are always new pages to be visited. Librarians call the pages not crawled, the "Invisible Web." There are other reasons that crawlers miss pages:

> No page points to it, so it never gets on the "to do" list
> The page is synthetic—that is, created on-the-fly for each user by software
> The page has only images (no text))
> The format is one the crawler does not recognize

Query Processors.   The query processor of a search engine gets keywords from a user and looks them up in the index to find the URLs of pages associated with those keywords. So, for example, when a user asks for "Thai restaurants," all of the URLs associated with those words are reported back. If Google had crawled your page, the query processor will return `www.hotdang.com` among its responses to the "Thai restaurants" query because your anchor connected "Thai" and "restaurants" with the Hot Dang! site. Notice that in this case the Google crawler might not have crawled the Hot Dang! restaurant's site yet; that site might still be on the "to do" list. But it will still know that the site is connected with the terms "Thai" and "restaurants" because of the anchor on your page. If Google had crawled the Hot Dang! site, the query processor would also return `www.hotdang.com` among the responses to the "Thai cuisine" query because "Thai" is in your anchor and "cuisine" is in the restaurant's title.

It is important to give the query processor the right terms to look up. In the next sections, we explain how to create good queries. But even when you choose exactly the right terms, you can get hundreds or thousands of relevant URLs, or **hits**. For example, suppose someone in your hometown of Dallas queries "Thai restaurants in Dallas Texas." There could be a huge list of hits, including (presumably) the homepages for all Thai restaurants, but also your homepage because it uses those words, too. But your page has nothing to do with Thai restaurants, except for your comment about liking Hot Dang! If the search engine returns an unordered list of all hits, the user would have to click through the whole list, looking at pages that could be completely irrelevant. We need more help from the search engine!

Page Ranking. Google pioneered another idea called PageRank that it uses to order the hits by their relevance to the user. (Of course, it cannot have any clue, really, as to what you are looking for.) PageRank is Google's guess about how relevant a page is. It computes the PageRank by counting the links to a page. The more links there are *to* a page, the more relevant it must be. As the Google inventors describe it, if page A links to page B, consider the link as a vote by A for B. So, for example, because your page links to `www.hotdang.com`, it "votes" for the restaurant. If many sites vote, it must be of greater interest, so the search engine lists the pages with higher PageRank first. Google also looks at whether the page doing the "voting" is itself highly ranked.

Page Ranking's Limitations. In the previous example, if a restaurant reviewer has a page that many people link to, and the reviewer's page links to Hot Dang!, Google treats that link as a more significant vote than yours, assuming fewer pages link to your homepage. Thus Google would probably list `www.hotdang.com` before your page in the list of hits resulting from the query. Page ranking is highly successful in identifying the pages of greater interest, but, of course, fame isn't everything.

PageRank's idea of one page voting for another exactly captures your purpose of citing Hot Dang! as one of your favorite Thai restaurants. But, if your link had been part of a complaint about food poisoning with the purpose of discouraging others from going to Hot Dang!, Google would still count it as a vote for the restaurant's page. Yea or nay, it's still a vote.

Asking the Right Question

After "Look where the information is to be found," the best advice to someone looking for information is "Ask the right question." The question or **query** we are asking a search engine is, "What pages are associated with the following terms . . . ?" To get the right answer back means not only choosing the right terms but also knowing how the search engine will use them. In this section, we learn how to make effective queries. (All searching facilities have slight syntactic variations.)

fit **TIP**

> **Search Engine Rules.** Most search engines explain their specific rules in a link (located near the search window) called "Advanced" or "Hints" or some similar term. If the query rules you learn in this section don't produce the results you want, check the search engine's specific rules.

Words or Phrases?

The first point to understand is that text-searching facilities, including search engines, generally consider each word separately. Though most English speakers think of "Thai restaurants" as a single noun phrase, most search engines treat it as two words. We can ask the search facility to look for the exact phrase by placing quotation marks around it, as in

```
"Thai restaurants"
```

which has the effect of binding the words together.

But the problem with using the exact-phrase quotes is that the match must be perfect, ignoring spaces and case. Exact matching means information in other forms will be missed. For example, these phrases:

```
Thai restaurant
restaurants featuring Thai cuisine
Thai and Asian restaurants
```

would *not* match the quoted string. For this reason search facilities treat the words as separate and allow them to occur anywhere. It is best to limit the use of exact-phrase quotes to scenarios like titles,

```
"Crime and Punishment"
```

where the form is always the same. Notice that quoting part of a phrase, say `"Tale of Two Cities"`, is a safe solution when we cannot remember whether the title is *The Tale of Two Cities* or *A Tale of Two Cities*.

If the words are treated independently, should the search pick pages with both of the words "Thai" and "restaurants" or pages with just one of them? If it's just one of the words, pages referring to "Thai vacations" and pages referring to "steak restaurants" would also be hits. If we want both, but ask for either, we'll get an enormous number of useless hits.

Logical Operators.

So we need to spell out how the words should be processed. We do this by using **logical operators**. The three logical operators are AND, OR, and NOT. They are written using all capital letters to distinguish them from the keywords. Remember that search facilities usually ignore case, so we don't need to capitalize keywords. Capitalizing the logical operators makes them stand out for us. AND and OR are the most commonly used logical operators in queries, and they are **infix operators**, meaning that they are placed between keywords. AND means *both*. OR means *either* or *both*. So, for example, the phrase

```
Thai AND restaurants
```

finds pages with both words appearing in any position; that is, they may not be together in the given order. The query

```
Thai OR Siam
```

finds pages with either word, including pages where they both appear. Of course, we could write queries that include both operators, but we must be careful. For example, does

```
Thai OR Siam AND restaurants
```

mean either a page containing the words *Thai* and *restaurants,* or *Siam* and *restaurants,* or a page containing either the word *Thai* or the two words *Siam* and *restaurants*? We meant the first. The latter would hit on pages about Thai vacations. Because the query is *ambiguous* (it has more than one interpretation), there is no way to guess how the search engine will interpret it. So, to be unambiguous, we include parentheses the way we do when we write algebraic formulas:

```
(Thai OR Siam) AND restaurants
```

Now the search engine will look for pages that have *restaurants* and also either *Thai* or *Siam.*

We can use NOT to exclude pages with the given word. NOT is a prefix operator, meaning that it comes before the word to be excluded. So, to exclude restaurant review pages from the Thai restaurant search, we might write

```
Thai AND restaurants AND NOT review
```

Notice that we need the AND to show that three conditions must be met: matching *Thai*, matching *restaurants*, and not matching *review*. Most often we use NOT when we recognize a pattern of unintended interpretations.

So far, we have assumed the simplest case, where the search facility offers only a single window for giving the query. The Google Advanced Search page (recommended) gives us several windows to simplify creating queries with the logical operators. Figure 5.6 shows the GUI of the Advanced Search and each of its windows. There are separate windows for AND words, exact phrases, OR words, and NOT words. In this case, Google saves us from having to type the logical operators. (Though most of the searches illustrated in this book use Google, queries will always be written using the logical operators.) All we need to do is list the search words, separated by blanks, in the correct window. Notice that if more than one window is filled in, the search must fulfill the requirements of all windows together.

> **ƒⁱ𝘭 CAUTION**
>
> **Misspellings.** Correct spelling is obviously essential to effective searching. Search engines can recognize misspelled words, and ask if you meant to type another word. But it cannot guess that you've made a mistake if you mistype, for example, `trail` for `trial`. It pays to be careful.

Getting Close

An effective search requires you to pick meaningful and specific keywords. Choosing the right words is sometimes easy, as when you're looking for data on ibuprofen, because the term is unique. At other times, choosing the right words is very difficult, as when you're looking for information on the fuel economy of new cars, because the obvious terms—gas mileage and cars—are extremely common. In any event, thinking for a few moments about a search strategy pays off.

Five Tips for an Efficient Search

Here's a recommended process for creating a search:

1. *Be clear about what sort of page you seek.* Ask yourself whether you want a source page from a company or organization (for example, the Hot Dang! restaurant); or a reference page that points to a collection of similar pages (for example, the restaurant reviewer's page); or perhaps a resource page that compiles information on the topic (for example, a guide to Thai cooking). Thinking clearly about the kind of page you want helps to direct the search toward that page.

2. *Think about what type of organization might publish the page you want.* Is the information likely to come from a company, a government agency, a university, some special organization, or another country? You might be able to guess the Web address for a site you want, and avoid a search altogether. If you can guess a likely URL, for example, `www.hotdang.com`, then try it! Even if you can't guess the URL, you can limit the search by the domain suffix—that is, the "dot com" part of a domain name (see Figure 5.6).

3. *List terms that are likely to appear on the pages you are looking for.* You want to find a combination of words that will appear on the page you want and the fewest number of unwanted pages. You must include words that describe the category (for example, *Thai* and *restaurant*), and then use AND to limit unwanted words:

   > Location-specific words such as *Dallas* AND *Texas*

   > Time-specific words such as *Monday* because businesses often give the times they're open

   > Activity-specific words such as *entrées*

   > Specialty terms such as *phad* because every Thai restaurant probably serves phad Thai

   The pages we seek have many specific properties, each with their characteristic terms. With some thought, we can come up with those terms.

4. *Assess the results.* Before looking at each returned page, check the results to see how effective your search was. Look for the two errors of including too much and not including enough. One way to include too much is to get a type of match you didn't expect. For example, all the pages

about vacationing in Thailand probably describe the restaurants where tourists will eat. You can do another search with a NOT keyword (for example, **NOT vacation**) to eliminate these. The other error, not including enough, is possibly harder to recognize. For example, if we include "Monday" in our search, we eliminate all of the restaurants that are open Tuesday to Sunday. So, we must be alert to what we are not finding and consider whether we should drop some of our keywords.

5. *Consider a two-pass strategy.* Because it's hard to get the search terms just right, it is probably a good idea when using the Google search engine to use a "two-pass" strategy. First do a broad topic search, and then do one or more searches within your results. Google lets you narrow your search with additional keywords (see Figure 5.7). Searching "within results" lets us capture the pages within the category and then narrow our search until we find what we are looking for. If we limit the search too much, we can simply back up to the point where the hits are inclusive enough. Notice that the terms in the search-within-results window are more AND terms; that is, they are required on the page. We can force the absence of a term, say, vacation, by writing a minus sign before it like this: **–vacation**.

Figure 5.7. *Restricting the Thai restaurant "hits" by eliminating any page containing the word "vacation".*

> *fit* **TIP**
>
> **Finding the Needle.** Narrowing the search to the right page is the first task, but finding the information can mean more searching on the page itself. Remember that browsers have a word-search facility, **Find**, under the **Edit** menu. To search on a page, use **Find**.

Using the principles just outlined, imagine that you plan to go windsurfing and need a sailboard. You are thinking of going to Hood River, Oregon, where the Hood joins the Columbia, a famous windsurfing area. You're flying, so you will need to rent equipment when you arrive. Your queries yield:

sailboards	34,400 hits
sailboards AND oregon	967 hits
sailboards AND oregon AND "hood river"	914 hits
sailboards AND oregon AND "hood river" AND rental	110 hits

which includes the shops and tourist facilities pages you want.

In summary, successful searches result from well-thought-out queries based on specific terms. It is wiser to spend time thinking up exact queries, possibly querying several times, or searching through results to pinpoint the few pages of interest, than it is to read through many worthless pages that result from unspecific searches.

WEB INFORMATION: TRUTH OR FICTION?

In Chapter 3 we noted that an increased exercise of freedom of speech is a fundamental change brought about by the World Wide Web. It is possible in many countries of the world to publish anything on the Web, uncensored by companies or governments. This is a benefit, but, like all freedoms, this one carries with it some important responsibilities—not so much for the speaker, but for the reader or listener. Because anyone can publish anything on the Web, some of what gets published is false, misleading, deceptive, self-serving, slanderous, or simply disgusting. We have to be alert for this and always ask, "*Is this page legitimate, true, and correct?*" In this section we consider whether the pages we've found in our search provide reliable information.

Do Not Assume Too Much

The first thing to look for is who or what organization publishes the Web page. For example, health information from the Centers for Disease Control, the World Health Organization, or the American Medical Association is about the best you can access. These respected organizations try to publish current and correct information, so we can trust their Web pages. The published information is based on science; therefore, new discoveries might occasionally invalidate something. But we're not discussing the philosophical aspects of the *nature of truth* here. We can assume that respected organizations publish the best information available at the time, and we're unlikely to find better.

Checking the organization that publishes the information seems like overkill. After all, if the Web site's domain name is `ama-assn.org`, it claims to be the AMA page, and it's giving out medical information, it must be the American Medical Association, right? In fact, it is. But, just because a page seems to be from a certain organization and the domain name *seems* plausible, it isn't necessarily true. Domain names are not checked. Anyone could have reserved the domain name `ama-assn.org` and published bogus health information. You must be wary.

To illustrate that sites are not always what they appear to be, consider the hoax perpetrated by the site `www.gatt.org`. The domain name looks like it is related to the General Agreement on Tariffs and Trade (GATT), the free-trade agreement of the 1990s. The site looks like the official publication of the World Trade Organization (WTO), the free-trade group that followed on from the GATT treaty. The page shows photographs of WTO President Michael Moore, quotes him, and posts WTO-related free-trade news. However, the site is actually run by an *anti-free-trade* organization known as the Yes Men.

According to the January 7, 2001, *New York Times*, organizers of a meeting of international trade lawyers in Salzburg, Austria, sent mail to `www.gatt.org` inviting WTO President Moore to speak at their meeting. From `www.gatt.org` came an email reply declining on behalf of Mr. Moore, but offering (a fictitious) speaker, Dr. Andreas Bichlbauer, as a substitute. The meeting organizers accepted Dr. Bichlbauer who came to their October 2000 meeting and gave a very offensive speech critical of Italians and Americans. The perpetrators of the hoax even claimed that a WTO protestor threw a cream pie at Dr. Bichlbauer. They claimed that the pie contained a *bacillus*, that Bichlbauer had taken ill and was hospitalized, and that he had died. The whole hoax, which caused much embarrassment, began when someone assumed that `www.gatt.org` was a legitimate WTO site.

A Two-Step Check for the Site's Publisher

How can you find out if a site is legitimate? A two-step process can help:

1. The InterNIC site `www.internic.net/whois.html` lists the company that assigned the site's IP address (i.e., domain). Type in the domain name, such as `company.com`. In some instances you will receive the registration information for the domain directly. In most cases, however, the InterNIC information about the domain includes a site called a `WhoIs Server` maintained by the company that assigned the address. That site will tell you who owns the domain.

2. Go to the `WhoIs Server` site and type in the domain name or IP address again. The information returned is the owner's name and physical address.

When checking a Web site, remember to pull out the domain name from the URL.

Elaborate hoaxes like `gatt.org` are rare, although there have been others. A more likely situation is that information is unintentionally wrong or simply fictional. "Urban legends"—stories like alligators living in the New York City sewer system—that people pass along as true, although they don't have primary evidence or an authoritative basis for believing it, fall into the first category. Urban myths are usually harmless, but not always. Stories in the second category, fictional and humorous, are meant to entertain us. April Fools' pages, alien spaceships visiting Seattle's Space Needle, and reports of one-ton squirrels are common and fun. Still, it's best to approach Web pages with some skepticism.

Characteristics of Legitimate Sites

What cues can alert a reader to misinformation? In a recent survey, Internet users thought that a site was more believable if it had these features:

> **Physical existence.** The site provides a street address, telephone number, and legal email address.

> **Expertise.** The site includes references, citations or credentials, and links to related sites.

> **Clarity.** The site is well organized, easy to use, and provides site-searching facilities.

> **Currency.** The site was recently updated.

> **Professionalism.** The site's grammar, spelling, punctuation, and so forth are correct; all links work.

Of course, a site can have these characteristics and still not be legitimate. A site trying to fool people can appear to be legitimate. If you have doubts, check it out. The name and address should be in `www.whitepages.com`. If it's not listed, it may be suspicious. If it's a business, look for it in the yellow pages. If the author gives credentials, citations, or other links, check them out, too. By checking, you will feel confident that the information you are getting is reliable (or not).

Check Other Sources

Finally, if the information is important to you, check more than one source. After all, it is very easy to use the Internet to find information, and it's equally easy to use it to confirm information. Ask yourself, "If this information were true, what other source could directly or indirectly confirm it?" Of course, we must be equally skeptical about the supporting information. For example, we cannot count the number of sites referencing information as proof that it's true, because by that reasoning the alligators in the sewer urban legend would seem to be supported by the 10,600 hits on `alligator AND sewer`. A better approach is to find sites that speak directly to the urban legend topic, such as `www.snopes.com`.

THE BURMESE MOUNTAIN DOG PAGE

To test our ability to assess a site, suppose we have found `descy.50megs.com/akcj3/bmd.html`, a site describing the Burmese Mountain Dog (see Figure 5.8). The page looks authoritative. It has been posted by someone claiming DVM credentials, probably meaning doctor of veterinary medicine. There are photographs, links to the American Kennel Club, and so on. The page seems completely legitimate and meets most of the criteria that Internet users have listed as indicating authenticity. If we ask Google to find `Burmese AND mountain AND dog`, we get 12,500 hits. Many people would probably accept the page as truthful.

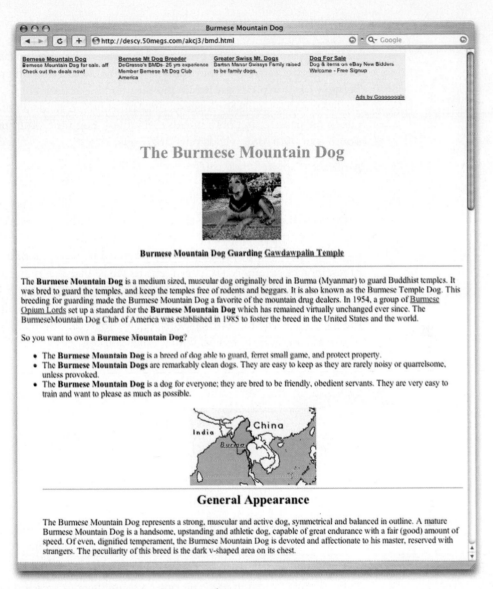

Figure 5.8. The Burmese mountain dog page.

Because the page has a link to the American Kennel Club, `akc.org`, which lists all breeds the club recognizes, it's possible to check out the Burmese Mountain Dog. In the AKC's list of breeds, we find that there is no Burmese Mountain Dog, but there is a Bernese Mountain Dog, named for Berne, Switzerland. What gives? First, we ask if `akc.org` is legitimate by using the `InterNIC WhoIs` service, and we find that it is. Next, we check `50megs.com` and find it is a free Web hosting site. This seems reasonable because if the Burmese Mountain Dog is not yet recognized by the AKC, perhaps an independent group of enthusiasts is behind the site. Accepting that the AKC is giving correct information about the Bernese Mountain Dog, we conclude that either the Burmese page is a fake or the Burmese Mountain Dog is not yet a recognized breed.

It is interesting that there are so many hits on Burmese Mountain Dog, but when we ask Google to look up `bernese AND mountain AND dog` we get 90,300 hits, so the Bernese seems to be even more popular. When we look at photos of the two dogs, we notice that they look very similar. The main difference is that the Bernese has a white chest, while the Burmese has a dark chest with a brown V. Such a striking similarity suggests that someone has made a comparison, so we check for pages citing both breeds. Searching `bernese AND burmese AND mountain AND dog` yields only 2820 hits.

A phrase displayed by Google,

*not **Burmese**, please, that's a cat*

suggests two points: Many of these pages must be listing both cats and dogs, and there is a Burmese cat. (Removing cat (`-cat`) yields 1350 hits.) The other possibility is that people may be mispronouncing and misspelling Bernese as Burmese. A quick look at several of the pages tells us we've guessed right. Some personal pages show a photo of what the AKC calls a Bernese Mountain Dog, but they erroneously call it a Burmese Mountain Dog. Another page makes a point of saying it's from Berne not Burma. So, we guess that the original page is fiction, and return to it to admire how skillful a hoax it is.

● SUMMARY

The secret to finding the information we're looking for is to look in the right place. This chapter taught us that:

> Libraries are excellent primary resource tools.

> Large public and university libraries have extensive online resources.

> Libraries not only provide information digitally, they also connect us with "pre-digital" archives—the millions of books, journals, and manuscripts that still exist only in paper form.

> We need software and our own intelligence to search the Internet effectively.

> We create queries using the logical operators AND, OR, and NOT, and specific terms to pinpoint the information we seek.

> Once we've found information, we must judge whether it is correct by investigating the organization that publishes the page, including checking the credentials of the people who write the copy.

> We must crosscheck the information with other sources, especially when the information is important.

EXERCISES

Multiple Choice

1. One of the downsides of unmediated expression on the Web is
   A. a need for verification of the accuracy of the content
   B. duplication of information
   C. that very little information is available
   D. all of the above

2. Information created in _____ is likely to be digitized.
   A. 1956
   B. 1976
   C. 1996
   D. more than one of the above

3. We visit a library electronically to
   A. find information
   B. use research tools
   C. not have to whisper
   D. more than one of the above

4. A hierarchy resembles a
   A subway map
   B. tree
   C. spoked wheel
   D. list

5. Someone searching with a search engine would use the
   A. crawler
   B. query processor
   C. index
   D. anchor

6. Most Web pages are not indexed because
   A. search engines have not crawled them
   B. pages are created on demand and those cannot be indexed
   C. other pages do not point to it
   D. all of the above

7. Google was the first search engine to get its keywords from
   A. InterNIC
   B. page titles
   C. anchors tags
   D. user submissions

8. The number of results from a search using AND will be _____ a search using OR.
   A. no more than
   B. the same as
   C. fewer than
   D. unrelated to

9. To omit a word from a search in Google, you would
   A. put the word MINUS in front of the word
   B. put the word in parentheses
   C. put a minus sign in front of the word
   D. put the word inside quotation marks

10. Which of the following is not an indication of the believability of a Web site?
    A. professionalism
    B. WWW Consortium approval
    C. expertise
    D. physical existence provided by the site

Short Answer

1. Historically, the _____ has been the repository of information.

2. On the computer, you would look for information using a(n) _____.

3. _____ provide connections to specialized pages.

4. _____ are computer programs that help people find information on the Web.

5. _____ uses the keywords in the anchor link of Web pages to index its pages.

6. Counting the number of pages linked to a page helps to determine that page's _____.

7. AND, OR, and NOT are called _____.

8. Operators placed between words in a query are called _____.

9. A(n) _____ is a method of organizing information by groups.

10. If a word or phrase is enclosed in quotes in a search, the search engine will search for a(n) _____.

11. Web pages found using a search engine are called _____.

12. The _____ operator is used to exclude a word or phrase from a search.

13. In a search, the plus (+) sign is the same as using the word _____.

14. In a search, the minus (–) sign is the same as using the word _____.

15. _____ is a company that tracks information on who owns a Web site.

Exercises

1. Write down the organization chart used by Yahoo! (`www.yahoo.com`) for its home page. What type of classification is it?

2. Go to InterNIC (`www.internic.net/whois.html`). Type in the name of a Web site and check its information. Do the same for other sites.

3. How would you find a search engine that specializes in European Web sites? Find one and use it. What do you find?

4. Create a classification scheme for clothing items. In your list, what items can be classified in more than one group?

5. Use Switchboard.com (`www.switchboard.com`) to look up your phone number.

6. Use MapQuest (`www.mapquest.com`) to look up your home address. Print the map.

7. What is the Web address for the New York Public Library?

8. Pick an issue. Find sites on both sides of the issue and analyze their content.

6

SEARCHING FOR GUINEA PIG B
Case Study in Online Research

learning objectives

> Explain the advantages and disadvantages of online research

> Explain the advantages and disadvantages of primary and secondary sources in research

> Apply the case study example (R. Buckminster Fuller)

- Expand and narrow an online search as needed
- Locate primary and secondary sources
- Assess the authority of sources
- Use online photos, video clips, and audio clips to enhance the research
- Resolve controversial questions online
- Follow up on interesting side questions

> Use the skills above to be able to do a curiosity-driven online research project

chapter 6

SEARCHING FOR GUINEA PIG B
Case Study in Online Research

Sometimes I think we are alone [in the universe]. Sometimes I think we are not. In either case, the thought is quite staggering.

—R BUCKMINSTER FULLER

WE'RE ALL CURIOUS, and the IT knowledge we have developed so far is enough to help us discover the answers to questions we wonder about. Usually these questions are simple: "Is the Colorado ski area Telluride named after the chemical element Tellurium?" With a few clicks we find the answer, perhaps mention it to a friend, and that's that. The Web allows us to find the answer without visiting the library. Now, with the speed and convenience of the Web, we can easily add to our store of useless facts and amaze our friends.

But information technology offers us more than a simple chance to answer a single question. It allows us to investigate substantial topics that interest us and probe deeply wherever our curiosity leads us. This is called **curiosity-driven research**. For centuries, inquisitive people who were curious about a topic would consult books, but now online research expands their opportunities.

Books do have certain advantages: They are generally authoritative, having been carefully researched, usually well written, and permanent. The disadvantages are that books contain only the information the author selects, so they give us only one point of view; they can take years to produce, so the information they offer may be dated; they are static; and despite so many titles, they cover only a limited number of topics. Books remain excellent sources of information. But the fact is, a book exists because someone was curious about a topic, researched it, and interpreted the findings. With the World Wide Web, we can choose a topic, conduct our own research, and interpret our findings. That is, our own curiosity drives the research.

In this chapter we learn to do curiosity-driven research on the Web, using the ideas introduced in earlier chapters. One goal is to explore the limits of the research that can be done on the Web, because not everything is in digital form, and not everything in digital form is worth reading. Another goal is to enjoy a tour through the life and mind of an amazing man, R. Buckminster Fuller, who described himself as both an engineer and a poet. The topic requires using different kinds of information resources. Finally, we learn to fill in the gaps in our knowledge. Although the case study covers many pages, it represents the search and research activity of a single interesting and enjoyable evening. The conclusion is that curiosity-driven research can be fun, and more interesting and rewarding than watching another rerun of *Friends*.

GETTING STARTED WITH ONLINE RESEARCH

Curiosity-driven research usually begins with a name or word we've heard or read. We wonder about it, but often at first, we have too little information to begin an informed search with a search engine. In this case, we wonder about R. Buckminster Fuller, a man with a unique name. Even so, performing a Google search on

`Buckminster AND Fuller`

produces at least 92,800 hits, way too many to consider. Limiting the search to biographies

`Buckminster AND Fuller AND biography`

reduces the hit count to 13,900, which is still too many. So, we must gather some identifying information from another source to guide an effective search-engine search. In this case, we make use of the fact that short biographies of famous people are online. Other topics will require different resources.

*fit*TIP **Student Aid.** Curiosity-driven research can be a random process, as different discoveries steer our search. It appears even more aimless when it's someone else's curiosity doing the driving. Though I explain why we choose the path we take, it is still possible for you to lose track of where we are. If that happens, you may want to check the summary provided at the end of the chapter in Table 6.1, which gives an overview of the research path we follow.

Narrowing the Search

After visiting a convenient online library, we find among its research links a list of sources for biographies, including

Biography.com	`www.biography.com/search/`
Info Please	`www.infoplease.com/people.html`
Lives, the Biography Resource	`amillionlives.com`

and we try the first one. We have no reason for selecting one resource over another; if you intend to use biographies repeatedly, it's wise to shop around because the completeness and quality of the entries vary. The response to the `Buckminster Fuller` search request is successful, as shown in Figure 6.1.

Expanding the View

Reading Fuller's biography, we learn his name is actually Richard Buckminster Fuller (RBF). The first line mentions that he is the great-nephew of Margaret Fuller. Who's she? Because we are at a biography site, we can look her up. A portion of her Biography.com entry is shown in Figure 6.2. Reading her biography,

> **Fuller, R(ichard) Buckminster (1895–1983)**
> Inventor, designer, and futurist, born in Milton, Massachusetts, USA. The great-nephew of Margaret Fuller, he left Harvard early and largely educated himself while working at industrial jobs and serving in the U.S. Navy during World War I. One of the century's most original minds, he free-lanced his talents, solving problems of human shelter, nutrition, transportation, environmental pollution, and decreasing world resources, developing over 2000 patents in the process. He wrote some 25 books, notably Utopia or Oblivion (1969) and Operating Manual for Spaceship Earth (1969). A professor at Southern Illinois University (from 1959), he became in his later decades a popular public lecturer, promoting a global strategy of seeking to do more with less through technology. His inventions include the Dymaxion House (1927), the Dymaxion Car (1933) and, foremost, the geodesic dome (1947). He has the distinction of having both his names used for a scientific entity, the fullerene (also known as a 'bucky-ball'), a form of carbon whose molecule resembles his geodesic dome.

Figure 6.1. Biography.com's biography of Buckminster Fuller.

we note that both Margaret and her nephew preferred to go by their middle names. More significant parallels in their lives also exist: They were both largely self-taught, they were both intellectually gifted, and they were both concerned about making the world a better place—she through her feminist writings and he through his inventions. Her tragic shipwreck death with her new husband and young child reminds us that Buckminster Fuller's profile doesn't mention if he was married or had children. So, we seek more biographical information. We could check the other two biography sites, but since we've already found the identifying information we need to guide a Google search, we do that.

In the first biography, the term *Dymaxion,* perhaps a term Fuller thought up, is mentioned as a name of both a house and a car that he invented. Surely any biography will mention these inventions, so we search on

```
Buckminster AND Fuller AND biography AND Dymaxion
```

which reduces the number of hits from more than 13,000, when only "biography" is included, to a manageable 543. Interestingly, "Buckminster" and "Dymaxion" are so unusual and so descriptive of this one person that his last name is almost unnecessary! Searching on `Buckminster AND Dymaxion AND biography` hits 544 times.

Early in the list of hits is another biography from IdeaFinder.com, as shown in Figure 6.3. Reading this biography reveals something researchers encounter all the time: Different sources differ. Whereas the first biography says Fuller had over 2000 patents, this one says he was awarded 25. Though we could track down which number is correct, we will leave it unresolved for now. He obviously didn't take himself too seriously, based on his self-description, *Guinea Pig B*.

Fuller, (Sarah) Margaret 1810–1850

Feminist, literary critic; born in Cambridgeport, Mass. Her father, Timothy Fuller, was a prominent Massachusetts lawyer-politician who, disappointed that his child was not a boy, educated her rigorously in the classical curriculum of the day. Not until age 14 did she get to attend a school for two years (1824–26) and then she returned to Cambridge and her course of reading. Her intellectual precociousness gained her the acquaintance of various Cambridge intellectuals but her assertive and intense manner put many people off.

From 1836 to 1837, after visiting Ralph Waldo Emerson in Concord, she taught for Bronson Alcott in Boston, and then at a school in Providence, R.I. All the while she continued to enlarge both her intellectual accomplishments and personal acquaintances. Moving to Jamaica Plain, a suburb of Boston, in 1840, she conducted her famous "Conversations" (1840–44), discussion groups that attracted many prominent people from all around Boston. In 1840, she also joined Emerson and others to found the *Dial*, a journal devoted to the transcendentalist views; she became a contributor from the first issue and its editor (1840–42). . . .

She went on to Italy in 1847 where she met Giovanni Angelo, the Marchese d'Ossoli, ten years younger and of liberal principles; they became lovers and married in 1849, but their son was born in 1848. Involved in the Roman revolution of 1848, she and her husband fled to Florence in 1849. They sailed for the U.S.A. in 1850 but the ship ran aground in a storm off Fire Island, N.Y., and Margaret's and her husband's bodies were never found.

Figure 6.2. *Excerpt from Biography.com's biography for Margaret Fuller, RBF's great aunt.*

The fifth paragraph emphasizes how he overcame his despair at the death of his daughter, turned his thoughts away from suicide—"his life belonged to the universe"—and went on to see what he could do on behalf of humanity. He actually worked on the problem of world hunger, a problem most people dismiss as not solvable. His philosophy of treating life as an experiment in "what the little, penniless, unknown individual might be able to do effectively on behalf of all humanity" is inspiring! We need to know more.

Searching for Images

Perhaps before going any further we should find out what Fuller looked like. To locate some photographs, we use Google's image search, `www.google.com/advanced_image_search`. Entering `Buckminster Fuller` yields more than 2800 `.jpg` and `.gif` images. They're not all of RBF—some people have named their cats Buckminster Fuller—but there is a wide range of interesting images of Fuller. Three images from later in life, as shown in Figure 6.4, show us an intense man who also seems grandfatherly, the sort of guy who might give you the keys to the Dymaxion car for the weekend.

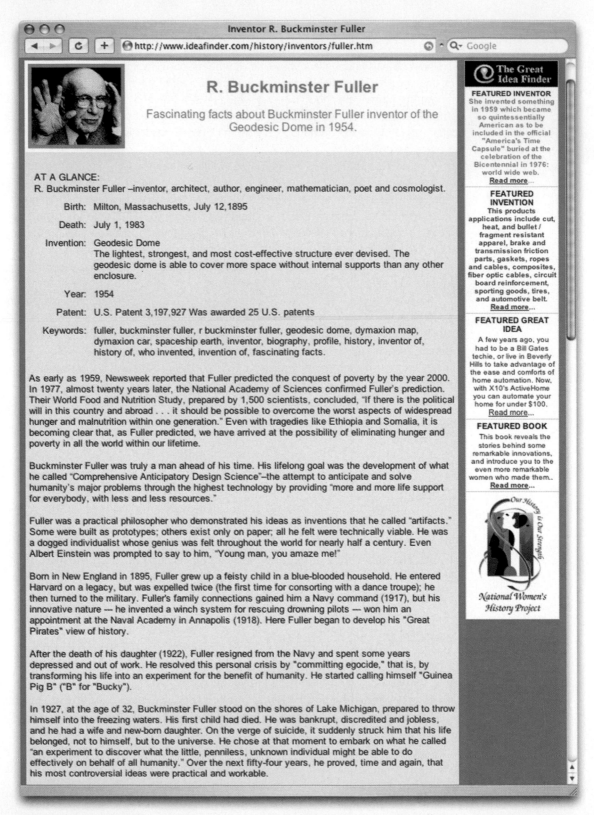

Figure 6.3. *Excerpts from* IdeaFinder.com's *biography of Buckminster Fuller.*

Figure 6.4. *Three photographs of R. Buckminster Fuller.*

Bookmarking Links

We won't take the time to look through all of the Fuller images, nor will we follow all of the links from the IdeaFinder.com biography site now. You might want to check them out later. And we have no idea how we will use the information, so we just bookmark the site. (For pictures it's easiest to *save* a copy on your computer rather than bookmarking the URL.)

---

fitTIP

Online Research Methodology. When using the Web for research, bookmark every site you visit (deleting bookmarks later is simple) and record your search keywords—both search engine and site searches—in a notebook file. With this information you can revisit the sites and reconstruct the search.

PRIMARY SOURCES

To find out more about Fuller's philosophy and personal life, we decide to do another search on the exact phrase `"Guinea Pig B"`—a name so distinctive there cannot be others. Recall that Google lets us search for an exact phrase; in this case the search gives 744 hits. When we change the search to `Buckminster AND "Guinea Pig B"` the count drops to 294. This list is a goldmine of specific information about Fuller, and we will return to it.

The first hit for the `Buckminster AND "Guinea Pig B"` search is a page from WNET, New York City's public television station, about a documentary they produced on Fuller's life titled "Buckminster Fuller: Thinking Out Loud." The Guinea Pig B page from this site is shown in Figure 6.5.

The WNET page shows us a new photograph of RBF, cites a recent book about him, and quotes a small excerpt. This is all useful, but the links to four essays at the bottom of the page, are perhaps most valuable:

Who Was R. Buckminster Fuller? by E. J. Applewhite, author and Fuller collaborator.

Experience and Experiencing by Allegra Fuller Snyder, Bucky's daughter.

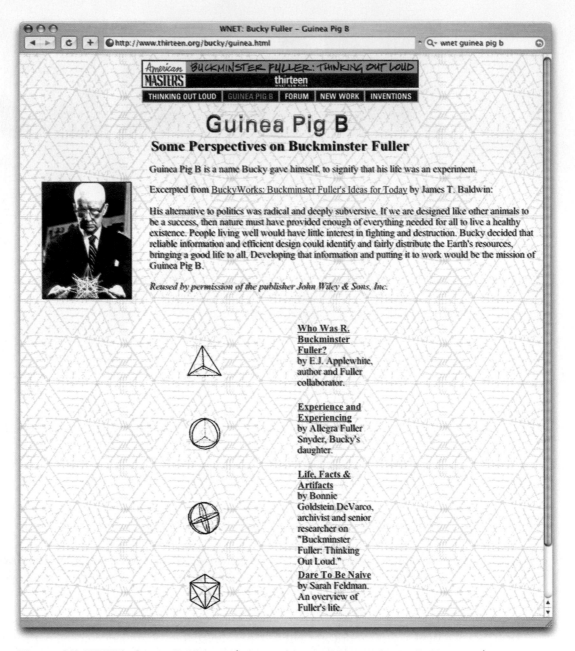

Figure 6.5. WNET's Guinea Pig B page (`www.thirteen.org/bucky/guinea.html`).

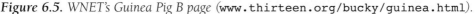

Life, Facts and Artifacts by Bonnie Goldstein DeVarco, archivist and senior researcher on "Buckminster Fuller: Thinking Out Loud."

Dare To Be Naïve by Sarah Feldman. An overview of Fuller's life.

From the list we note that Fuller had a daughter, Allegra, who apparently married someone named Snyder. (No relation to the author of this text.)

Assessing the Authenticity of Sources

These essays are important because they are extremely reliable sources of information. Applewhite, as a collaborator, and Snyder, as Fuller's daughter, write from direct personal experience. We call them **primary sources**. We prefer information from primary sources for several reasons. First, the information is actual experience and personal impressions. Therefore, the information is unbiased, except to the degree that anything a person gathers from experience is subject to that person's ability to perceive it, motivation to be objective, and expressiveness. Primary sources are not subject to the distortion or omission that can happen when someone else reports information from a primary source. We call this "second-hand" reporting a **secondary source**. If someone reports from a secondary source, creating a tertiary source, more distortion and omission are possible. Using primary sources helps us perceive our own impression and point of view on the subject.

Source 1 – An RBF Collaborator. E. J. Applewhite, a collaborator, is considered a primary source (see Figure 6.6).

Who Was R. Buckminster Fuller?
by E. J. Applewhite

Buckminster Fuller had one of the most fascinating and original minds of his century. Born in 1895 in Milton, Massachusetts, he was the latest—if not the last—of the New England Transcendentalists. Like the transcendentalists, Fuller rejected the established religious and political notions of the past and adhered to an idealistic system of thought based on the essential unity of the natural world and the use of experiment and intuition as a means of understanding it. But, departing from the pattern of his New England predecessors, he proposed that only an understanding of technology in the deepest sense would afford humans a proper guide to individual conduct and the eventual salvation of society. Industrial and scientific technology, despite their disruption of established habits and values, was not a blight on the landscape, but in fact for Fuller they have a redeeming humanitarian role.

Fuller rejected the conventional disciplines of the universities by ignoring them. In their place he imposed his own self-discipline and his own novel way of thinking in a deliberate attempt—as poets and artists do—to change his generation's perception of the world. To this end he created the term Spaceship Earth to convince all his fellow passengers that they would have to work together as the crew of a ship. His was an earnest, even compulsive, program to convince his listeners that humans had a function in universe. Humans have a destiny to serve as "local problem solvers" converting their experience to the highest advantage of others.

Fuller was an architect, though he never got a degree and in fact didn't even get a license until he was awarded one as an honor when he was in his late 60s. This did

---

Figure 6.6. *Excerpt from the Applewhite essay at the WNET "Guinea Pig B" site (continues next page).*

not prevent him from designing the geodesic dome: the only kind of building that can be set on the ground as a complete structure—and with no limiting dimension. The strength of the frame actually increases in ratio to its size, enclosing the largest volume of space with the least area of surface. This was his virtuoso invention, and he said it illustrated his strategy of "starting with wholes" rather than parts.

He was also a poet, philosopher, inventor and mathematician, as documented amply in many other web sites on the net.

America has been in the middle of a love-hate affair with technology—and Fuller is right in the middle of it. He introduced not only a unique rationale for technology, but an esthetic of it. Likewise his synergetic geometry bears for Fuller an imperative with an ethical content for humans to reappraise their relationship to the physical universe. Manifest together as design science, they offer the prospect of a kind of secular salvation.

Figure 6.6 (continued). Excerpt from the Applewhite essay at the WNET "Guinea Pig B" site

Source 2 – RBF's Daughter. Buckminster Fuller's daughter, Allegra Fuller Snyder, is clearly a primary source (see Figure 6.7).

Experience and Experiencing
by Allegra Fuller Snyder

. . .

My father was a warm, concerned and sharing father. As focused as he was on his own work he nevertheless included me in his experiences and experiencing. I remember with great clarity when I was about four years old. I was sick in bed and he was taking care of me. He sat down on the bed beside me, with his pencil in hand, and told me, through wonderful free-hand drawings, a Goldilocks story. I was Goldilocks and with his pencil he transported me, not to the Bear's house, but to universe, to help me understand something of Einstein's Theory of Relativity. What he was telling me was neither remote nor abstract. I was in a newly perceived universe. I was experiencing my father's thoughts and he was experiencing his own thinking as he communicated with me. It was exciting. We were sharing something together and I felt very warm and close to him in that experience. Something of this episode was later remembered in a book called Tetrascroll.

. . .

Figure 6.7. Excerpt from the Allegra Fuller Snyder essay at the WNET "Guinea Pig B" site (continues next page).

He loved our island in Maine because it was a physically involving place. We have no fresh water, except cistern-caught rain and well water, which has to be drawn or pumped and then hauled; kerosene and candles for light, a fire in the hearth for heat. Each of these basic requirements involves physical action to produce the needed results. . . . And then, of course, there was sailing, which he loved, where the dialog between nature and human action is so dynamic.

At the heart of each one of these actions, was the sense of the "special case" that would lead to a generalized principle. Any experience would become a "special case," the doorway to larger comprehensivity. When you were around him you were aware how sensitive he was to the smallest experience. His focus could zero in on a pebble on the beach, a twig or flower along a path. Each became the stepping stone to the largest whole.

"The human brain apprehends and stores each sense reported bit of information regarding each special case experience. Only special case experiences are recallable from the memory bank."

. . .

Intuition, imagination, all relate to and are a part of experience. Let me turn for a moment to Bucky's own words on these matters. (What follows are drawn from E. J. Applewhite's wonderful Synergetics Dictionary.)

Intuition is practically physical, the kind of supersensitivity that a child has Imagination. Image-ination involves rearranging the "furniture" of remembered experience as retrieved from the brain bank.

Speaking with an audience he would say, "All that I can really give you I must always identify by experience." One of his great gifts as a speaker was the fact that he made you experience his ideas and carried you along with the connection between your experience and his experience. "Information is experience. Experience is information."

. . .

Where or how does experience continue to be a part of the picture when, as Bucky pointed out,

"At the dawning of the twentieth century, without warning to humanity, the physical technology of Earthians' affairs was shifted over from a brain-sensed reality into a reality apprehended only by instruments."

His response is that invisibility can be "understood and coped with only by experience-educated mind.

. . .

Figure 6.7 (continued). Excerpt from the Allegra Fuller Snyder essay at the WNET "Guinea Pig B" site.

Source 3 – An RBF Archivist. Bonnie Goldstein DeVarco presents a fascinating account of Fuller's archive—he saved everything! Much of the content concerns specifics of the archive that are somewhat tangential to our interest. But two paragraphs stand out in her section on Ephemeralization, quoted here (see Figure 6.8).

Life, Facts and Artifacts
by Bonnie Goldstein DeVarco

Ephemeralization
Although the tactile pleasures of sorting through the physical artifacts of Bucky's life brings a dimension all its own to the discovery of who he was and who he shared his life with, almost the same could be done with the same body of materials available on a computer screen—from drawings, letters and manuscripts to "ephemerabilia," at the touch of a fingertip. In hundreds of letters spanning well over half a century, the love story of Bucky and Anne is told. Anne's letters carry a lilting youthful quality that punctuates even the most fatuous groupings of correspondence to be found in the Chronfile* boxes. Her handwriting is like a beautiful victorian stenciled wallpaper and her ardent and boundless devotion gives life to the saying that behind every great man is a great woman. It is no wonder he personally deemed his most famous geodesic dome, at the 1967 Montreal Exposition, his "Taj Majal to Anne" in honor of their 50th anniversary.

The letters of sculptor Isamu Noguchi, Bucky's lifelong friend, span decades and flavor the correspondence files with Asian subtlety, each page an artwork in and of itself, all on sheer white rice paper written with a brown fountain pen, always poignant, always aesthetically disarming. And how affecting it is to see in a letter to his mother bound into the 1928 Chronfile volume, Fuller's youthful discovery of his Great Aunt Margaret Fuller's thought and its parallels to his own as he writes, "I have been reading much by Margaret Fuller lately. I was astonished to find that some things I have been writing myself are about identical to things I find in her writings. I am terribly interested and am astounded fully that I should have grown to this age and never have read anything of her or grandfather Fuller's."

. . .

*RBF kept his correspondence and other documents in a bound file organized in chronological order called the *Chronfile*.

Figure 6.8. *Excerpt from the DeVarco essay at the WNET "Guinea Pig B" site.*

DeVarco's essay is based on information from the archive of Fuller's papers and artifacts, which DeVarco described as "approximately 90,000 pounds of personal history." Fuller produced this information, so it is a primary source. We presume that DeVarco, an archivist and researcher, is accurate and reliable. Though her essay is not technically a primary source, we can trust it.

Source 4 – An Institute Developer and Writer. Sarah Feldman's essay has relied on the Fuller archive for its information, so it may be an excellent resource. As researchers, however, we wonder who she is. Her title or relationship to Fuller is not provided. For example, is she a scholar with academic credentials who we assume tried to be accurate, or does she write advertising copy for used car companies and perhaps embellishes the facts? We look her up in

Biography.com, but her bio is not available. We go to the WNET Web site and search the site for her name. We get a link to her bio, which reads

---

Sarah Feldman

Sarah Feldman is the National Project Director for the National Teacher Training Institute (NTTI) at Thirteen/WNET New York. She is also a content developer and writer for Thirteen's wNetStation and wNetSchool, and other online venues. She taught second grade in the South Bronx and Harlem.

As a director at a national teacher-training institute, content developer, and writer with access to the Fuller archive, Feldman sounds very reliable and so we are confident that her essay is also. See Figure 6.9 for an excerpt of her essay.

Dare to Be Naïve
by Sarah Feldman

Jobless, without savings or prospects, with a wife and newborn daughter to support, suicidal and drinking heavily, in 1927 Richard Buckminster Fuller had little reason to be optimistic about the future. R. Buckminster Fuller—or "Bucky," as he's affectionately known—transformed that low point in his life into a catalyst for transforming our planet's future as well as his own. A mathematical genius, environmentalist, architect, cartographer, poet, and an engineer of rare foresight and a philosopher of unique insight, Fuller was born in 1895 but can be truly considered a twenty-first-century man.

Renouncing personal success and financial gain, at age 32 Fuller set out to "search for the principles governing the universe and help advance the evolution of humanity in accordance with them." Central to his mission were the ideas that 1) he had to divest himself of false ideas and "unlearn" everything he could not verify through his own experience, and 2) human nature—and nature itself—could not be reformed and therefore it was the environment—and our response to it—that must be changed. Fuller entered into a two-year period of total seclusion, and began working on design solutions to what he inferred to be mankind's central problems.

With his goal of "finding ways of doing more with less to the end that all people—everywhere—can have more and more," Fuller began designing a series of revolutionary structures. The most famous of these was the pre-fabricated, pole-suspended single-unit dwelling Dymaxion House. (The term Dymaxion was derived from the words "dynamic," "maximum," and "ion.") . . . Fuller's designs tended to be based [on] a geometry that used triangles, circles and tetrahedrons more than the traditional planes and rectangles. His Dymaxion Air-Ocean Map, which projected a spherical world as a flat surface with no visible distortion, brought him to the attention of the scientific community in 1943, and his map was the first cartographic projection of the world to ever be granted a U.S. patent.

In 1947 and 1948, Fuller's study of geodesics, "the most economical momentary

---

Figure 6.9. Excerpt from the Feldman essay at the WNET "Guinea Pig B" site (continues on next page)

relationship among a plurality of points and events," led him to his most famous invention, the geodesic dome. A hemispherical structure composed of flat, triangular panels, the domes were inexpensive to produce, lightweight yet strong space-efficient buildings. . . . Today, Fuller's geodesic domes can be found in varying sizes in countries all over the world, from Casablanca to Baton Rouge. Recognized as a landmark achievement in design and architecture, Fuller's dome was described in 1964 by Time magazine as "a kind of benchmark of the universe, what seventeenth-century mystic Jakob Boehme might call 'a signature of God.'" In 1959 he joined the faculty of Southern Illinois University in Carbondale and used that as a base of operations for what Fuller called his "toings and froings." For the next two decades, Fuller globe-trotted and lectured and consulted on a variety of projects. During this period of upheaval and great change, Fuller's ideas and work in such areas as ecology, conservation, education and environmental design found an enthusiastic audience among young people all over the world. After a stint at the University Science Center in Philadelphia, in 1972 the non-profit Design Science Institute was formed in Washington, DC to perpetuate Fuller's ideas and designs.

A self-proclaimed "apolitical," Fuller maintained there was "no difference between [the] left and the right." Nevertheless, he admitted he struggled to "dare to be naïve," and retained an optimistic faith that "an omni-integrated, freely intercirculating, omni-literate world society" was within our grasp. A prolific writer, Fuller's magnum opus is undoubtedly "Synergetics: Explorations in the Geometry of Thinking," on which he collaborated with E. J. Applewhite in 1975. The work is considered a major intellectual achievement in its examinations of language, thought and the universe.

Though he only stood 5'2" tall, R. Buckminster Fuller looms large over the twentieth century. Though a man of incredible intellect and vision, many of "Bucky's" fans remain most impressed by the man's awe-inspiring humility—and his abiding love for his planet and his fellow human beings. "Above all," said Fuller, "I was motivated in 1927 and ever since by the most mysterious drive we ever experience—that of love. I don't think there's any influence upon my life that compares with . . . love."

R. Buckminster Fuller
July 12, 1895–July 1, 1983

Figure 6.9 (continued). *Excerpt from the Feldman essay at the WNET "Guinea Pig B" site.*

Assessing Our Progress

So far, we have found four essays (Figures 6.6 through 6.9) about RBF and assessed the quality of their information. They are either from primary sources or from researchers who used the Fuller archive. This is excellent information, and we will take the time to read it. Notice that we do not mean that you should not use secondary or tertiary sources—we just used two from Biography.com and an IdeaFinder.com profile. They were unsigned biographical sketches that probably relied on generally available information about Fuller. We assumed they are accurate, although we noted a difference in the count of his patents. The point is that the two biographies met our need for a quick introduction to the material. Now, because we want to find the most accurate information about Fuller's life and philosophy, we go to the source(s) ourselves.

Reading the essays gives us extraordinary insight into Buckminster Fuller; we can now describe him in our own words. He believed, according to Applewhite, that technology is not the "problem" but rather the "solution," and that deeply understanding technology is the key to individual behavior as well as to "saving" society. Snyder's essay emphasized how Fuller only trusted his direct experience as he tried to overcome the bias of conventional wisdom that he believed prevented effective thinking. He tried to do more with less. DeVarco quotes Fuller's description of the Montreal geodesic dome as the "Taj Majal to Anne" (his wife), and Feldman quotes Fuller as saying that he turned his life around in 1927, motivated by love, the greatest influence on his life. It is a personal story of a deep thinker. The geodesic dome was his "virtuoso invention" [Applewhite] and *Synergetics*, a "major intellectual achievement," was his greatest work [Feldman].

And our search answers questions that the short biographies cannot. Feldman, for example, explains that Dymaxion stands for "dynamic," "maximum," and "ion."

Finding Video Clips

While thinking about this complex man, we cruise the WNET site and discover a page with two short video clips under the heading Buckminster Fuller. This is also primary information. Take a few minutes to download the video clip `www.thirteen.org/bucky/qt/1985.qt`. It shows Fuller describing in his own words some of his most radical ideas. He says,

> This is the *real* news of the last century. It is highly feasible to take care of all of humanity at a higher standard of living than anybody has ever experienced or dreamt of, to do so without having anybody profit at the expense of another . . . so that everybody can enjoy the whole earth . . . and it can all be done by 1985.

In the video clip we not only hear the conviction in his voice, but we also see the emphasis of his gestures. His tone seems to say "not only *can* we raise humanity's standard of living, we *should*." In this regard, the spoken word is more powerful than the written word. This digitized information has given us valuable insight.

● CHRONFILE AND EVERYTHING I KNOW

Recall that the WNET page was the first item in our Google search results with the terms `Buckminster AND "Guinea Pig B"` Now that we have learned everything we can from that page, we go to the next item, which is a link to the Buckminster Fuller Institute (BFI). See Figure 6.10.

Figure 6.10. Buckminster Fuller Institute chronology of RBF's life.

The BFI timeline of Fuller's life is very interesting, ending with the amazing fact (not shown in the figure) that *Anne* (his wife) *and Bucky died within 36 hours of one another one week before their sixty-seventh wedding anniversary!* If this page is what it seems to be—a site associated with the Fuller estate—the information is surely authoritative. Keeping in mind that some sites are hoaxes, we check to see who owns the `bfi.org` domain. Remember that we explained the process of determining who owns a domain (which takes less than a minute), in Chapter 5. After a few clicks, we learn that the Buckminster Fuller Institute of Santa Barbara, California owns the site.

Audio Clips: Everything I Know

Clicking around the BFI site, we find a huge amount of authoritative information, including Chronfile information, copies of complete books by Fuller, and 42 hours' worth of recordings from 1975 titled *Everything I Know*. This huge archive of online information is divided into 12 parts, each of which is subdivided into paragraph-size units called clips. We listen to a few minutes to get familiar with *Everything I Know*. It's interesting, and we notice from its description that it includes deep, abstract ideas as well as personal stories. We're interested in both. What, we wonder, does he say about Allegra?

If the archive only included the 42 hours of audio clips, we would have to listen to them to find out, because audio information is not searchable. However, JoAnne Ishimine, a BFI volunteer, has transcribed the audio into text so the clips can be searched. We can search the site for Allegra. Among the resulting hits is one where Fuller mentions how Allegra loves to dance and then describes a conversation they had.

> And, when she was twelve, she said "Daddy," we were living in New York at that time, she said "Daddy, you were brought up in Boston with the custom that it is ill mannered for men to make gestures that the man who is properly cultivated is well in possession of his movements, and he just doesn't even move his head, he just talks and sits very motionless, beautifully disciplined to do that." And she said, "I'll tell you, I don't know if I really am a dancer, but whatever I am, my body wants to talk all the time." And she said, "Daddy, I like your ideas very, very much and I want them to prevail, but I think you are frustrating your ideas by your disciplining yourself to sit motionless. I think if you'd just let yourself go things would happen way better for you." She was used to my having a lot of hard luck, nobody was paying any attention to me in those days. And so she seemed so wise that I think I did everything I could to free myself up. . . . But she did make it perfectly clear, a child does move comfortably and uses his body, so I began to let myself do [*sic*] I am utterly unaware of the motions, I assure you, but I have had moving pictures taken of me I've seen myself when I've been giving a lecture and I'm practically going all over the stage like a ballet dancer.

We can see that he *is* an animated speaker in the lectures we watched from the WNET "Buckminster Fuller: Thinking Out Loud" program.

We bookmark the *Everything I Know* archive because it is a rich resource of Fuller information, in his own words. When his ideas pique our interest, we can return to the archives.

Surfing the BFI Site

Looking around the site, we quickly come across Fuller's Dymaxion Map—the surface of the globe projected onto an icosahedron that produces a minimal-distortion flat map. Thinking of an icosahedron inside the earth and imagining the earth's curved surface shrinking down onto the icosahedron's faces gives the idea of the projection. Unfolding the icosahedron, as shown in Figure 6.11, produces the flat map (www.bfi.org/map_animation.html). The animation by Chris Rywalt gives us a good idea of how the map is created. This minimal-distortion map shows the continents in realistic proportion to one another. The specific unfolding shows the continents as one essentially contiguous island in a single sea. It's Fuller's schematic diagram for Spaceship Earth.

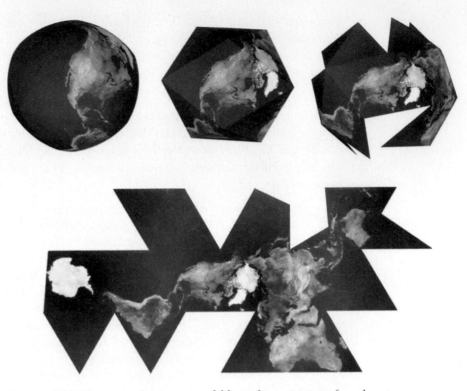

Figure 6.11. *Dymaxion Map—an unfolding of a projection of earth onto an icosahedron.*

RESOLVING QUESTIONS

There is something confusing here. We knew before we started surfing the site that Fuller invented the geodesic dome, as shown in Figure 6.12. It's his "virtuoso invention." And he invented the Dymaxion Map, as shown in Figure 6.11. The map page tells us that the map projects the globe onto an icosahedron. But the geodesic dome of the Montreal Expo '67 was smoother than an icosahedron (Figure 6.12). What's the difference? Are they the same idea? If not, how is a geodesic dome related to an icosahedron?

The local BFI site may be the best place to find information about geodesics and the map's projection. Or maybe we should try a Google search on `difference AND icosahedron AND geodesic`. If we think about the question before searching, we notice that answering it could be as easy as learning the two definitions. The best place to find definitions is in a dictionary, so we access an online dictionary. (Again, if we forget the site name for an online dictionary, we can go to our favorite library's research or reference page to find a link to one.) The two principles at work here are (1) determine what kind of information will answer the question, and (2) look where that type of information may be found. We might be able to answer the question simply by learning the meaning of the two words.

Figure 6.12. *Geodesic Dome—from the U.S. Pavilion at the Montreal Expo '67.*

The online dictionaries give the following definitions and drawing:

geodesic, *n*: The shortest line between two points on any mathematically defined surface.

icosahedron, *n*: A 20-sided polyhedron.

Obviously these are not the same. The icosahedron is a solid and a geodesic is a line. But, this doesn't really explain how a geodesic dome differs from an icosahedron, because the definition we found is for the noun "geodesic," and when we refer to the "geodesic dome," we use it as an adjective. Looking further in the dictionary we find

geodesic, *adj*: Made of light straight structural elements mostly in tension <a *geodesic* dome>.

geodesic dome, *n*: A domed or vaulted structure of lightweight straight elements that form interlocking polygons.

These definitions help. The icosahedron has just 20 triangular sides, and no matter how large it is—even the size of the earth—it must still have 20 sides (faces). The geodesic dome has any number of faces. From the picture of the Expo dome we can see, first, that the sides are also triangles and, second, that they form interlocking hexagons. That is, the triangles that form one hexagon can also be grouped to be parts of other adjacent hexagons. Looking at the icosahedron, we see that the triangles form interlocking pentagons. Because the geodesic definition requires only "straight elements that form interlocking *polygons*," we conclude that an icosahedron is a geodesic solid. It's no surprise that Fuller came up with both the map idea and the dome idea.

We could pursue more detailed questions on structures—it's possible to build a geodesic dome from straws and pipe cleaners—but we're more interested in the man than the engineering, so we continue to check the information from the `"Guinea Pig B"` search.

● SECONDARY SOURCES

So far, our search has been very successful. It has revealed a complex and productive man, "one of the most original thinkers of the twentieth century." He was rational, sensitive, and used "both sides of his brain." Our primary sources have been extensive and rich, including text, photographs, audio clips, video clips, and an animation. Indeed, the information is so extensive it overwhelms us—we've studied only a tiny fraction of it!

Now we have two problems. First, we need to know what is missing in our understanding of Fuller. Second, our thinking seems to have no organization. At the moment, we have only a collection of facts and impressions. One way to solve both problems is to check some secondary sources.

Completing the Picture

Though it's always best to gather information from primary sources, secondary sources are also valuable. Secondary sources can

> Give us a more thorough investigation of the topic—certainly more thorough than ours to this point—and help us fill in gaps.

> Help us organize the information.

> Provide other authors' interpretations, including insights we have not thought of.

As always, we need to check out the sources for authenticity.

From the results of the `Buckminster AND "Guinea Pig B"` search, we find a 3000-word biography by Kirby Urner, who maintains the Synergetics Web page. (From the homepage we learn that Urner is a writer and curriculum developer from Portland, Oregon.) The part of the biography shown in Figure 6.13 organizes some of the information that we've found and tells us more about Fuller's navy days. It discusses controversies regarding the independence of Fuller's ideas from those of Ken Snelson, Alexander Graham Bell, and Walter Bauersfield. These controversies are new to us.

A 20th-Century Philosopher
by Kirby Urner
Originally posted: May 11, 1998; Last updated: June 19, 2000

. . .

Although the family had a four-generation tradition of sending its sons to Harvard, Fuller was too much the wild romantic to settle in and was expelled for treating an entire New York dance troupe to champagne on his own tab. The family sentenced him to hard labor in a Canadian cotton mill, where he sobered up quite a bit, but he still didn't like Harvard upon giving it a second try and was again expelled. He later returned to Harvard as the Charles Eliot Norton Professor of Poetry (1962).

Given his nautical background as a boy messing about with boats around Bear Island, Fuller was attracted to the navy, and managed to achieve a command with family assistance (1917). His marriage to Anne Hewlett was in grand military style. His native genius as an inventive soul was recognized (he developed a winch for rescuing pilots downed over water) and this led to an appointment at the Annapolis Naval Academy (1918).

At Annapolis, under the tutelage of retired admirals, Fuller felt very much at home, and began to germinate his "Great Pirates" narrative, wherein the big picture thinking then offered to young officers was a culmination of a long tradition of "thinking globally, acting locally" on the part of high seas figures, many of them pirates, and many of them lost to history because operating invisibly, over the horizon from those who kept the historical accounts (mostly landlubbers).

A few years after his honorable discharge, Fuller attempted to make money using his father-in-law's invention, a morterless brick building system, but failed in this enterprise (1926). This failure, which led to joblessness in Chicago, coupled with the trauma of losing his first child Alexandra to prolonged illness in 1922, pushed Fuller to the brink in 1927. He considered suicide but, as he put it, resolved to commit "egocide" instead, and turn the rest of his life into an experiment about what kind of positive difference the "little individual" could make on the world stage. He called himself "Guinea Pig B" (B for Bucky) and resolved to do his own thinking, starting over from scratch. Hugh Kenner likens this to Descartes' resolve to shut himself in a room until he'd discerned God's truth— a kind of archetypal commitment to a solitary journey.

. . .

It was over this concept of "tensegrity" that early divisions over the issue of Fuller's character and integrity came to the foreground. Ken Snelson, a star pupil at Black Mountain College (1948), at first enchanted by Bucky's spell, became highly disillusioned when it appeared that Fuller planned to abscond with the "tensegrity" idea without properly crediting his student.

Fuller's reputation for egomania and improperly seizing upon others' ideas as his own may be traced to this Fuller-Snelson split, and led many to question whether the geodesic dome, widely credited to Fuller (who took out a number of patents around the idea) was another case in point. . . . Alexander Graham Bell had also made extensive use of the octet truss circa 1907, another one of Fuller's key concepts (also patented).

Fuller's own archives, maintained since his death in 1983 by the Buckminster Fuller Institute (BFI) and his estate (EBF), details his side of the story and he seems to have died with a clear conscience regarding these matters realizing they would remain bones of contention. . . .

Figure 6.13. Excerpt from Kirby Urner's biography of R. Buckminster Fuller,
`www.grunch.net/synergetics/bio.html`

Investigating Controversial Questions

The Snelson controversy concerns discoveries that Fuller called tensegrity, for *tension integrity*. Ken Snelson, a sculptor (`www.grunch.net/snelson/`), gives his version of its history in an email to the *International Journal of Space Structures* in answer to their request for information for a planned special publication on tensegrity (`www.grunch.net/snelson/rmoto.html`). The events happened at Black Mountain College in North Carolina in the summer of 1949. Snelson, who had met Fuller at Black Mountain the previous summer, had spent an aimless year building models (or artwork—he couldn't decide whether he was an engineer or an artist) that used geometrical ideas he learned from Fuller.

Snelson's email, which we were not permitted to reprint, tells of his first morning at Black Mountain when he showed Fuller his plywood X-Piece. Snelson had sent Fuller photos of the sculpture, but based on Fuller's reaction, he concluded that Fuller had not understood the design. But now, Fuller turned the sculpture over and over, studying it carefully. Finally, Fuller asked if he could keep it. Relieved that Fuller was not annoyed with him for having used Bucky's geometry for artwork, Snelson agreed, although he hadn't planned to give his work away. Later, according to Snelson, Bucky said that the sculpture had "disappeared" from his apartment.

At the core of Snelson's belief that he contributed to ideas Fuller took credit for, is Fuller's apparently slow comprehension of the X-Piece. Snelson offers a second example of proof that Fuller did not fully comprehend the implications of tensegrity. He says that on the next day, Fuller told him that the idea was clever, but that the configuration was wrong. Rather than using compression members in an X structure, they should be arranged in a tetrahedron. Snelson reports that he'd already used the tetrahedron in a mobile and had decided that the X structure was better than the tetrahedron because the X could grow along all three axes rather than the single axis of the tetrahedron. But Snelson was reluctant to challenge his teacher—students just didn't do that in 1949. Again, Snelson believes Bucky didn't fully comprehend the idea, and therefore didn't conceive it first.

Snelson says that the next day he built Bucky a model of the tetrahedral structure using adjustable metal curtain rods. He described himself as "wistful" as he watched Bucky being photographed with the model, but he didn't suspect Fuller's motives.

Fuller said in a letter to Snelson that he mentioned Snelson's role in speeches. But, according to Snelson, he never got credit in print. When in 1959, Fuller's tensegrity ideas were displayed at the Museum of Modern Art in New York City, Snelson forced Fuller publicly to admit the truth about the idea for the structure.

Searching at the Buckminster Fuller Institute for `Snelson`, we quickly find Fuller's version of the incident in *Everything I Know*, Vol. 8, though he incorrectly places it in 1958–1959:

Then in the second summer at Black Mountain, Ken showed me a sculpture that he had made, and, in an abstract world of sculpture, and what he had made was a–a tensegrity structure. And he had a structural member out here two structural members out here, that were not touching the base, and they were being held together held they were in tension. And I explained to Ken that this was a tensegrity. Man, I had found, had only developed tensegrity structure in wire wheels and in universal joints. . . . When Ken Snelson showed me this little extension thing he did it was really just an arbitrary form, he saw that you could do it [tension integrity], but he was just, as I say, an artistic form or something startling to look at. And I said, "Ken, that really is the tensegrity and it's what I'm looking for because what you've done I can see relates to the octahedron and this gives me a clue of how this goes together in all the energetic geometry."

So Ken opened up my eyes to the way to go into the geometry.

Fuller clearly sees Snelson as having contributed, in the form of his artwork, one more instance of tensegrity to the two that Fuller already knew. He seems not to be very defensive in his version.

He is also at peace with the fact that Alexander Graham Bell independently invented the octet truss—a key tensegrity structure. Fuller explains as he answers questions in an interview (`www.grunch.net/synergetics/docs/bellnote.html`):

Q. It seems to me that Bell's tetrahedron, which he developed while working on kites, is very like your geodesic structure.

A. Exactly the same.

Q. When you developed your structures, did you know about the work of Alexander Graham Bell?

A. I did not. I was astonished to learn about it later. It is the way nature behaves, so we both discovered nature. It isn't something you invent. You discover.

The Bell case seems to be a case of independent discovery. According to archivist DeVarco, on two different occasions, Bell's descendants gave Fuller octet truss models that Bell had made. So, they apparently harbor no disagreement with this view.

Overall, Snelson's criticism of Fuller mutes the rah-rah enthusiasm of the many sites we have found. Snelson makes a case for his contribution to tensegrity, but there's more to Fuller's work than that. RBF has a rock-solid reputation still, but even the finest diamonds have tiny imperfections.

● EXPLORING SIDE QUESTIONS

Finally, in terms of filling out our profile of Fuller, there is the repeated mention of buckminsterfullerenes. What are they? The biography (*Biography.com*) ends with the statement:

> He has the distinction of having both his names used for a scientific entity, the "fullerene" (also known as a "buckyball"), a form of carbon whose molecule resembles his geodesic dome.

It's a carbon molecule. To find more, we ask Google to search on `buckminsterfullerene` and we find many useful links. From a *Scientific American* link we find a page from the State University of New York at Stony Brook, `sbchem.sunysb.edu/msl/fullerene.html`, showing images of the molecule, and we see that the structure fulfills the "interlocking polygons" requirement of the geodesic dome definition (see Figure 6.14). The next link, `www.msu.edu/~hungerf9/bucky1.html`, is to Michigan State University's Nanotechnology Laboratory, which gives us a definition:

> **Buckminsterfullerene**, C_{60}, the third allotrope of Carbon, was discovered in 1985 by Robert Curl, Harold Kroto, and Richard Smalley. Using laser evaporation of graphite they found C_n clusters (where $n > 20$ and even) of which the most common were found to be C_{60} and C_{70}. For this discovery they were awarded the 1996 Nobel Prize in Chemistry.

Checking the online dictionary, we find that *allotrope* means "structural form of" (making buckyballs different from graphite and diamond forms of carbon). We now know that a fullerene is a stable molecule of carbon composed of 60 or 70 atoms in the shape of a geodesic sphere (see Figure 6.15). However, the discovery of fullerenes piques our curiosity, and we decide to go to the Nobel Prize site to learn more about the discovery.

Recalling that all countries have a country extension, and that Sweden is the home of the Nobel Prize, we guess that the site is `www.nobel.se`, which redirects us to the correct site, `nobelprize.org`. There we click `chemistry > laureates >1996` to find the page shown in Figure 6.15. From there we can read the "illustrated presentation" explaining the equipment and experiment that Curl, Kroto, and Smalley used to produce buckyballs and win the Nobel Prize. As it happens, C_{60} has the same structure as a soccer ball: 12 pentagons and 20 hexagons.

Of course, the mention of soccer gets us to wondering how the A. C. Milan team is doing, so we click up. . . .

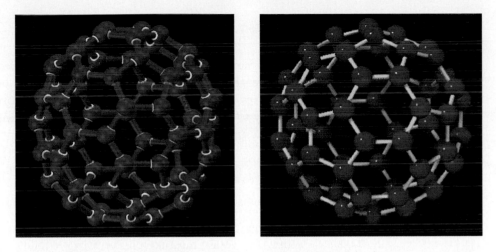

Figure 6.14. *Drawings of buckminsterfullerenes, C_{60} and C_{70} (also known as fullerenes or buckyballs).*

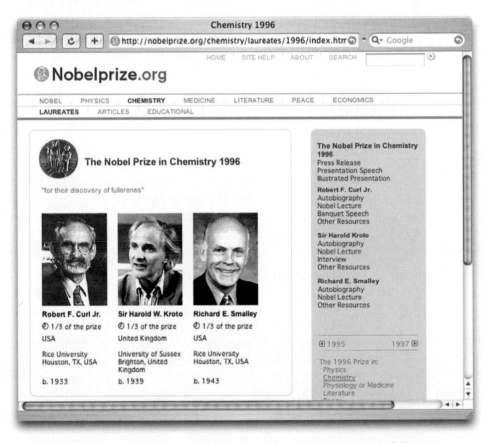

Figure 6.15. *The Nobel Prize site for the discovery of the buckminsterfullerene.*

CASE STUDY WRAP-UP

We explored Buckminster Fuller's life because he was an interesting person. We're finished, at least for the moment, so we can put the computer to sleep and get some sleep ourselves. But often the next step is to use the information for some other purpose, say, to write a report. In that case, before turning off the computer we should create a summary file containing:

> - Bookmarks from the sites we visited—they can be copied from the browser as a group

> - Notebook entries of the search terms used with the search engines

> - Brief notes on our impressions from the information we found—interesting discoveries, most useful sites, why we followed up on some topics and skipped others, and so forth

This information is our record of the research process, which we can refer to for writing our report. We should write down our impressions right away because they fade. The amazement of new discoveries wears off, we forget things, and time changes our attitude about the content. It is important to have time to digest what we've learned and to organize it in our minds, but the excitement of learning something new gives a fresh quality that we cannot reconstruct later.

THE PROCESS

The goal of this chapter was to illustrate curiosity-driven research using the Web, and we have been quite successful (see a summary of our efforts in Table 6.1). The two main themes of this tour through Buckminster Fuller's life were the process of finding the information and the methods of deciding whether the information was authoritative. We tried to use the "right" source for the type of information we wanted.

Searching for Guinea Pig B: The Buckminster Fuller Research Path

The entries in Table 6.1 describe the research path followed in this chapter. Most lines represent an access to a WWW document, image, audio or film clip, and so on. Indenting indicates subsidiary actions.

Table 6.1. *Record of the case study search (continues next page)*

Begin with a Google search because "Buckminster" is a distinctive name; fail—too many hits
Restart by checking online biography sites to find some characterizing term; succeed—find "Dymaxion"
Learn basic facts about RBF's life, including that he is related to Margaret Fuller
Check online biography of Margaret Fuller—nineteenth-century feminist thinker, died in shipwreck

Check Google for further biographical material using "Dymaxion"; select a highly ranked biography

    Find that he called himself "Guinea Pig B," a characterizing, personal term

    Discover his "little, penniless, and unknown individual" quote and his dream of helping humanity

Check Google for images to find out what he looked like

Check Google using "Guinea Pig B"

    Find WNET site and four essays: Applewhite, Snyder, DeVarco, and Feldman

        Assess sources—Applewhite and Snyder are primary, DeVarco is archivist

      Check on Feldman, first at biography site, then WNET personnel; writer with access to papers

        Read Applewhite's essay for professional assessment—great intellect, creative, influential

        Read Snyder's essay for RBF as father—warm, loving, deeply believed in primary experience

        Read DeVarco's essay—the "ephemera" of RBF's life; he called Expo dome Taj Majal to Anne

        Read Feldman's essay—threads RBF facts with personal aspects of success, tragedy, and family

      Summarize our impressions of essays

      View video clip; Fuller passionately argues world hunger/housing woes can be eliminated by 1985

Visit Buckminster Fuller Institute site

    Check BFI's authenticity

    Review Basic Chronology—married to Anne; two children, one died; many jobs, many awards

    Discover *Everything I Know*—42 hours of audio

    Listen to Fuller describe Allegra's asking him to become more animated

    Discover Dymaxion Map on icosahedron and watch animation

    View the Montreal Expo geodesic dome

      Wonder how icosahedron and geodesic dome relate

        Check dictionaries for definitions—unsatisfactory

        Check dictionaries further and interpret definitions relative to map and Expo dome

Assess how complete our knowledge of Fuller is—decide to read another biography

    Check the Kirby Urner biography found in the "Guinea Pig B" search

      Check out Urner

    Discover there is controversy over the originality of Fuller's ideas: Snelson, Bell

      Check Ken Snelson, the sculptor

      Check the *Journal of Space Structures* page giving Snelson's view of discovery

      Return to BFI's site and *Everything I Know* for Fuller's view; he acknowledges Snelson

      Check an interview with Fuller regarding independent discovery with Bell; he acknowledges it

    Conclude that our knowledge of Fuller is reasonably complete and balanced for a start

Wonder what a buckminsterfullerene is, and use Google to find citations

    Find through *Scientific American* graphic renderings of C_{60} and C_{70}—geodesic spheres, not domes

    Find a definition and the discoverers' names from SUNY Stonybrook

      Look up *allotrope* in the dictionary and infer the difference from graphite and diamond

    Wonder about the discoverers of buckyballs

      Navigate Nobel site and find short biographies of the discoverers

To make the search effective, we wanted to learn enough to ask the right questions. So, we started by checking a brief biography. We learned that Fuller had invented something called a Dymaxion house and car, so we decided to search for biographical information containing *Dymaxion*. This greatly reduced the hits. In the same way, searching on `"Guinea Pig B"` led to a rich set of links mostly of primary sources. Later on, "buckminsterfullerene," with its narrow technical meaning, led us to that information quickly. We didn't do a Web search each time we wanted information; instead we went directly to a likely source—dictionary, biography database, WNET personnel, the RBF Institute, the Nobel Prize page— based on the type of information we wanted. This saved us from "aimless wandering" around the Web.

When we found information, we were always concerned with its authoritativeness. In some cases, it didn't matter much, such as when we checked the short biography to find words like *Dymaxion*. In other cases, we looked for primary sources, knowing that they are the purest forms of information about a topic because they are based on direct experience. For secondary sources, we checked the author's credentials. Secondary sources were valuable because they could both fill in gaps in our knowledge and show us how others interpreted the same information. Our goal was to learn as much as possible from primary sources so that we could interpret the information ourselves, and then to read secondary sources for more viewpoints and information. This strategy helped us to differentiate other people's opinions from the facts.

SUMMARY

We began the chapter by noting that for research, the Web is better in many ways than reading a book. In a short time we found interesting and definitive information about our topic, Buckminster Fuller:

> We accessed primary data from Fuller, his colleagues, and his family.

> We read short biographies, looked at photographs and film clips, heard audio clips, consulted the dictionary, watched animations, and used many other types of reference material.

> Multimedia resources gave us the chance to form our own opinions based on more than printed words.

> Computer searches, including global Google searches, site searches, and page searches accelerated our discovery process.

> Information we gleaned from several authors' essays on Fuller connected us to additional sources.

> We discovered Buckminster Fuller based on our own curiosity.

EXERCISES

True/False and Multiple Choice

1. A tertiary source draws directly from personal experience.

2. Each step away from a primary source increases the likelihood of error and omissions.

3. Books have limited research value because they
   A. take a long time to produce
   B. contain only information the author selects
   C. contain only a single point of view
   D. all of the above

4. Advantages of the Web over a book include
   A. the Web can be easily updated
   B. easier access
   C. dissemination of information is faster and cheaper
   D. all of the above

5. A primary source is
   A. the only source on a topic
   B. a source with personal experience
   C. a source that has been verified
   D. all of the above

6. Secondary sources are valuable for all of the following reasons except
   A. refuting primary sources
   B. organizing information
   C. providing interpretation
   D. filling in gaps

7. Which of the following is not an advantage of online research?
   A. the ability to quickly scan multiple sources
   B. the ability to view multimedia contents such as photographs, audio and video
   C. the unerring reliability of information found online
   D. the speed with which a search can be conducted

8. What type of inconsistencies can be found in online information?
   A. misspellings
   B. gaps and inconsistencies
   C. bias and outright lies
   D. all of the above

NOW THAT we are more skilled with information technology, it's time to learn a few of the underlying concepts that make IT possible. Like black holes in astronomy or natural selection in ecology, the underlying IT phenomena are interesting to learn about. The difference is, IT concepts can have direct applicability to your daily IT use.

In Part 2 we learn how information is represented—from basic bits, through sound and video, to virtual reality. We also explain what a transistor is, and how a few million of them can process information. And we introduce the fundamental idea of an algorithm, though you've already encountered several in Part 1. At the end of Part 2 you will have an intuitive idea of what's happening inside a computer and how it stores information.

In your experience so far, you have known the frustration that comes when some aspect of IT does not work the way you want. So, you know that figuring out what's wrong is one of the most important capabilities a computer user can possess. We can't give you a guaranteed, works-every-time algorithm to debug your problems, but we can provide useful guidelines that will help you solve IT mysteries more quickly.

7

TO ERR IS HUMAN
An Introduction to Debugging

> Explain how ordinary precision differs from precision required in IT

> Describe the six-step strategy for debugging
> - Explain the purpose of each step
> - Give an example of each step

> Apply the six-step strategy for debugging the HTML code for a Web page
> - State what changes you made during debugging
> - State what changes were unnecessary

> Learn how to approach debugging when you don't understand the system

TO ERR IS HUMAN
An Introduction to Debugging

One item could not be deleted because it was missing.

—MAC OS SYSTEM 7.0 ERROR MESSAGE

You are not thinking. You are merely being logical.

—NEILS BOHR TO ALBERT EINSTEIN

A COMMON saying among computer users is "To err is human, but to really foul things up takes a computer." One characteristic that makes a computer so useful—and sometimes so frustrating—is that it does exactly what it is told to do, and nothing more. Because it follows each instruction "to the letter" and continually checks itself, it operates almost perfectly. So, in truth, the computer doesn't foul things up at all. We humans—those of us who write the software and those of us who use it—are not perfect, and that combination can really foul things up. So we have to learn how to troubleshoot what's wrong and to get ourselves out of trouble. Learning debugging techniques—the subject of this chapter—is perhaps the best way to deal successfully with mistakes and errors, and to avoid the foul-ups in the first place.

The first goal of this chapter is to recognize that the greatest, most common source of problems is our lack of precision. Computers don't understand what we *mean*, only what we *say*. So we must say exactly what we mean. The next objective is to understand what debugging is in modern IT systems. We introduce the debugging process using a student/parent scenario. This lets us analyze the process during the student/parent interaction. The next goal is to abstract the debugging principles from the story. These principles do not give a mechanical procedure guaranteeing success, but rather a reliable set of guidelines. We apply the principles to debugging a faulty Web page design. This detective work won't reveal *who*-dunit because we are the obvious "perps," but rather *what*dunit, our error. The final objective is to illustrate how to debug a system when we have no idea how the system works.

PRECISION: THE HIGH STANDARDS OF IT

When using information technology, we must be precise. The standard of accuracy in IT is extremely high, much higher than our everyday precision level.

Precision in Everyday Life

In normal conversation, for example, when giving telephone numbers, many North Americans will say "oh" rather than "zero," as in "five-five-five-oh-oh-one-two" for 555-0012. Of course, the listener knows that phone numbers are numeric, and simply makes the mental conversion. A computer does not know this unless it has been specifically programmed to know it and to make the conversion. To a computer, the "oh" and "zero" are different (bit sequences). So, if we type "oh" for "zero," a computer will simply accept the input, try to use it literally, and cause an error.

fit **BYTE**

> **Merrily Mistaken.** Sometimes we purposely and humorously exploit this confusion, as in Canada's alternating letter-numeral postal code for Santa Claus, H0H 0H0.

The "oh" for "zero" substitution is used by North Americans because it is easier to say, having only one syllable. (Other English speakers say *"naught"* for *"zero."*) It is probably not the sort of error we would make if we were asked to type a phone number into a database system or modem software. And, even if it were, the software might catch the error, because some software systems *have* been programmed to know that phone numbers are numeric. Rather than converting "oh" to "zero," however, they usually just object to receiving nonnumeric input. But there are many cases in which the computer cannot help us when we make an error.

EXACTLY HOW ACCURATE IS "PRECISE?"

New email or Web users often type in an incorrect email address or URL. A common error is to confuse "oh" and "zero," or "el" and "one," though there are many other similar mistakes new users make. If computers can catch mistakes like "oh" for "zero" in modem software or databases, why can't they catch them in email addresses and URLs? The reason is simple: Although "oh" and "el" are illegal in all phone numbers, they are not illegal in all email addresses and URLs. For example, `flo@exisp.com` and `fl0@exisp.com` are both legitimate email addresses. If the software made "zero" for "oh" and "one" for "el" substitutions, poor Flo would never get any email. So, computers must accept the letters or numbers as typed for email addresses and URLs. Users must be precise when entering the information.

fit **CAUTION**

> **Be Sensitive.** Be alert to case sensitivity—the difference between lowercase and uppercase—in email addresses and URLs. To computers, C and c are different, so we must type the case exactly. Sometimes computers are programmed to ignore case. For example, case does not matter in Internet domain names—`flo@exisp.com` and `flo@ExISP.COM` are the same—because case is normalized for DNS lookup. But frequently the "local" information in URLs—that is, the text after / symbols—is case sensitive because it is processed by the destination Web server. So, `www.exisp.com/flo/home/` and `www.exisp.com/FLO/HOME/` may be different. When in doubt, assume that case matters.

Lexical Structures

We call the kinds of inputs just discussed **field inputs** because they are the sorts of information that are entered into boxes on forms that are used for names, code numbers, user IDs, files, folder names, and so on. All field inputs are governed by some **lexical structure**, rules about the legal form for input fields. The lexical structure limits the symbols that can be used in specific positions; possibly how many symbols can be used (i.e., a length limit); and possibly which punctuation symbols can be used. Lexical constraints can be very restrictive. For example, the lexical structure for inputting course grades is limited to two symbols: the first symbol must be chosen from {A, B, C, D, F} and the second symbol must be chosen from {+, −, ɓ}. (The ɓ denotes *blank*.) So, A+ is acceptable, but C++ is wrong. Lexical constraints can be loose, too, allowing any sequence of symbols of any length. Computers check to see that the lexical constraints are met, preventing lexical errors. But if the lexical structure permits alternatives of a commonly confused symbol, no check can be made. Both alternatives are legal, as in the `flo` and `f1o` UserIDs. Precision is essential.

fit **TIP**

> **Spacing Out.** The ɓ represents blank or space. This solves the problem that spaces must be visible in some cases so that we know that they're there. "Multiplication dots," ·, are used by word processors (see Chapter 2), but when they are easily confused with other symbols, we use ɓ to represent blank.

Because we have to be accurate when supplying input to a computer, we can avoid considerable grief by being as exact as possible. It's faster and less frustrating to enter information exactly the first time, than to be sloppy, discover our mistake, and re-enter it correctly.

DEBUGGING: WHAT'S THE PROBLEM?

Debugging is the method of figuring out why a process or system doesn't work properly. Debugging is usually applied to computer or communication systems, especially software, but the techniques are the same whether the systems are mechanical, architectural, business, etc. Though debugging relies on logical reasoning and is usually "learned from experience," there are general debugging principles and effective strategies that we can learn. Knowing these techniques is important because in IT, a major part of using a system is knowing how to figure out why things are not working properly.

Debugging in Everyday Life

People debug or **troubleshoot** all the time. When their cars don't start, they figure out whether the battery is dead or whether the fuel tank is empty. Faults and failures in everyday life usually involve otherwise correct, working systems with a broken or worn-out part. That is, the system is properly designed and constructed, but some part failed. The car's dead battery keeps it from starting, for example. When the part is replaced, the system works.

Debugging in Information Technology

Debugging an information system is slightly different. In information systems, we might have entered wrong data or wrong configuration information in a working system. When it's corrected, the system works. Another possibility is that it might have a **logical design error.** An analogy in car design is when the backup lights, which should only work when the car is in reverse, also come on when we step on the brakes. This is a design or construction error. In software, such logical errors are quite possible even in commercial software, and users must be aware that they may not be using a correct, working system. Despite this fact, we will always begin by assuming a "correct, working system."

Whose Problem Is It?

When debugging an information system, remember that *we* are almost always part of the problem: We command the computer to do tasks and we input the information. When the computer is in an error state despite our thinking that everything should have worked perfectly, two of the three possible problems—wrong data, wrong command, or broken system—involve us. Furthermore, since the hardware and software have been tested thoroughly, the two possibilities that involve us are the two most likely possibilities. Our commands or data probably led to the problem, and so we'll have to fix them. Computers cannot debug themselves.

Because people don't knowingly make errors, we think that what we did is right, and that it's the computer's fault that something has gone wrong. It might be— both hardware and software errors do happen—but they are much, much rarer than human errors. If our checking doesn't quickly reveal a small typographical error or the like, then we usually assume that the problem is with the computer or software. But we should consider one more possibility: It may be that we think we did everything right because we misunderstand the system and how it works, and so maybe we really did make a mistake. It's hard to admit, sometimes, that we've made a mistake, but at least the computer can't change its opinion of us!

{GREAT *fit* MOMENTS}

Computer Pioneer Grace Hopper >>

Rear Admiral Grace Murray Hopper, a computer pioneer, coined the term *bug* for a glitch in a computer system while she was working on the Harvard Mark I in the 1940s. When the Mark II computer had a moth jammed in one of its relays (electro-mechanical switches), bringing the machine down, technicians taped the bug into the machine's logbook (see Figure 7.1).

Hopper was one of the inventors of a kind of software known as a compiler, which translates a programming language into machine instructions (see Chapter 9), and she greatly influenced the development of the programming language Cobol. Conscious of the physical limitations on computing, Hopper used a length of copper wire (approximately one foot long) to illustrate a "nanosecond" (1/1,000,000,000th of a second), because it is approximately the distance electricity can travel in that time.

A Navy ship was named in her honor.

*fit*BYTE

A Bug's Life. What insect was jokingly called the first bug? On a recent TV game show, answering this question correctly was worth $1 million. The answer? A moth, as shown in Figure 7.1 below.

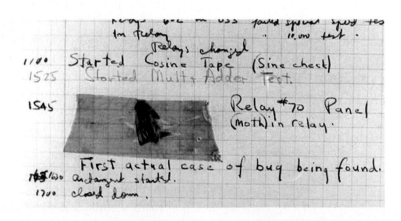

Figure 7.1. *The Harvard Mark II logbook noting "First actual case of bug being found."*

Using the Computer to Debug

Not only is the computer unable to debug itself, we can't debug it directly, either. That is, the error, even if it's our mistake, is internal to the computer, either in the stored data or the software logic. To get information about the error, we have to ask the computer to tell us what data it has stored, to run the faulty software, and so forth. We are one step removed from the failure and what's causing it, and we need the computer to help us find the problem.

Though there may be a bug in our software, most of it works correctly. A computer version of the 1960s slogan "If you're not part of the solution, you're part of the problem" is: "If it's not part of the solution, it can't be part of the problem." That is, if you can find a solution to your task that does not use a problem (faulty) part of the system, you've achieved your goal. Bypassing an error with an alternative approach is called a **workaround**. Workarounds are essential when we use commercial software. Bugs in commercial systems are usually not fixed until the updated version is released, so we have to work around them until then.

A DIALOG ABOUT DEBUGGING

Consider the following scenario:

You and your friends make a video spoofing college life. You show it to your cluster in the dorm and everyone thinks it's hilarious. You send a copy to your parents and anxiously await their praise of your cleverness, but you hear nothing. Eventually you phone them to ask if they received the tape, and they reply, "Yes. We tried it in the VCR, but something's wrong." Your impulse is to say, "Fix it!" but you ask brightly, "What's wrong?"

You are about to debug your parents' VCR. What you know is that they've tried the videotape in their VCR player—which you're very familiar with, having spent most of last vacation watching movies on it—and it didn't play the tape. That's all the information you have, and it's typical.

Debugging is solving a mystery. Just as we watch detectives solve mysteries in whodunits, we should watch ourselves solve mysteries when debugging. Why? Because this approach will probably reach a solution faster than if we aimlessly "try stuff." By purposely asking questions such as, "Do I need more clues (inputs)?"; "Are my clues reliable?"; and "What is a theory to explain the problem?" we focus better and will discover a solution faster.

The first step in debugging is to check that the error is reproducible. Computers are deterministic, which means that they will do exactly the same thing every time if given the same input. But there is a tiny possibility that a one-time transient glitch caused the problem. So, start by trying to reproduce the problem.

You ask your folks,

> "Can you try the tape again?"

And, as the scenario unfolds, your parents report that there is nothing showing on the TV.

The next step is to be sure that you know exactly what the problem is. Mystery novels usually have a dead body, making the problem clear. The mystery is who murdered the person, not why the dead person failed to show up for work the next morning. But in IT, the computer may perform a sequence of operations *after* an error, and they must be eliminated first as the focal point of the debugging. For example, the reason there are no mailing labels coming out of your printer may be due to a printer problem, but it could be due to a problem with the word processor or database that is sending the labels to the printer, or it could be that the file containing the addresses is empty; that is, there are no addresses to print. We don't want to debug the printer when the problem is an empty file. Determining what exactly *is* the problem is critical.

Your parents should be a little more specific about the problem. You patiently ask,

> "What's on the screen?"
>
> "Nothing."
>
> "Is it black nothing, blue nothing, or snow nothing?"
>
> "Snow."

A standard next step is to check all of the "obvious" error sources. Of course, if the error were all that obvious, you wouldn't be debugging—you'd have already fixed the problem. What kinds of errors are obvious depends on the problem, naturally, but checking inputs, connections, links, and so on is standard.

Ask your parents to check all of the obvious causes:

> "Is there power to the VCR?" (The TV obviously has power.)
>
> "Yes."
>
> "Is the tape in the machine?" (It couldn't be upside down because the drive mechanism doesn't allow that.)

"Yes."

"Is the tape rewound?"

"Yes."

"Have you clicked Play?"

"Yes."

"Is the tape advancing?"

"Sounds like it."

"What happens?"

"Snow reigns."

Clearly the VCR is pretty much as you left it. Except it isn't playing your hilarious tape.

It's now time to apply a basic strategy of debugging: Isolate the problem by dividing the operation into those parts that are working and those that are not. This means theorizing about where the problem is located, and possibly gathering more information. At this point you should take nothing for granted. Limit the number of untested assumptions you make. The error could be anywhere. The goal is to eliminate as many possibilities as you can, or to focus on the failing part.

In the case of your parents' VCR, the system has two basic units, the TV and the VCR player. The data, which is on the tape, is read by the player and sent to the TV for display. You ask yourself, can either of them be eliminated from consideration? If the VCR is operating and the TV is faulty, then the TV probably wouldn't show regular programs. You ask your parents:

"Do you get normal TV programs?"

"Define normal."

"You know what I mean . . . ABC?"

"Yes."

So, if the TV is okay, the VCR must be broken, although it seems from your earlier conversation that it is working mechanically; that is, the videotape is running through it. So, if the VCR is okay, what other parts are there? There's the cable connecting the VCR to the TV.

"Are the TV and VCR connected?"

"Didn't look, but it's the way it's always been."

So, they're connected as you left them when you left for college. And there are no other parts.

Everything seems to check out. This is a common situation when debugging. You analyze the problem, perhaps getting more data, and conclude that everything is okay. Except it's not. There's a bug somewhere. It's natural to become frustrated, but the best response is to review your analysis. You've made some assumptions, gathered data, made some tests, interpreted the results, and made some deductions. Ask yourself: "Is there a wrong assumption?" "Did I misunderstand the data?" "Did I make a wrong deduction?" It's important at this point to think objectively about the process. *A good approach is to step through the process from beginning to end, comparing what should be happening with what is happening.*

So, starting from the beginning, you ask your parents to put in a different tape.

"OK, we put in the tape of your sister's wedding, but it's the same thing. Snow."

You know that tape works. You had to sit through the whole two tedious hours of it last summer.

"Is it rewound?"

"Yes. Just did it."

"When you clicked on Rewind, was the screen blue and were the letters R-E-W displayed?"

This is a prediction you make about how the TV/VCR system is supposed to operate based on your knowledge or experience with it.

"No, it's still snow."

At this point you have a prediction that doesn't match the facts. That's what you're looking for. Why is the VCR not telling the TV that it is rewinding the tape? Maybe because they're not connected.

"Can you check if the VCR cable is plugged into the back of the TV?"

And now you know the problem. As you're waiting for your parents to verify that the cable is not connected to the back of the TV, you recall last summer when the Women's Olympic Soccer final was on and how a bunch of your friends came over to watch the game and you carried the TV out to the patio. Everyone sat around eating pizza and cheering. It was late when you carried the TV back into the house, and you postponed plugging in the VCR cable until morning. And you forgot. When you left for college they were still unconnected.

"Nope, the cable wasn't plugged into the TV. It's working now. How'd you figure that out?"

"Got lucky, I guess. Hope you like the video."

DEBUGGING RECAP

The key point of the debugging illustration is not that debugging occasionally reveals embarrassing errors, but rather that there is a semi-organized process to follow to find out what's wrong. The key points are:

> > Make sure that you can reproduce the error.

> > Determine exactly what the problem is.

> > Eliminate the "obvious" causes.

> > Divide the process, separating out the parts that work from the part that doesn't.

> > When you reach a dead end, reassess your information, asking where you may be making wrong assumptions or conclusions; then step through the process again.

> > As you work through the process from start to finish, make predictions about what should happen and verify that your predictions are fulfilled.

This is not a recipe, but it is a useful set of guidelines. Debugging requires tough, logical reasoning to figure out what's wrong. But, it's possible to do, and though it is not as entertaining as deducing whodunit from the clues in a mystery novel, there is a certain satisfaction to figuring it out.

*fit*BYTE

Closer Examination. Watching yourself debug as if you were a mystery detective is important. It helps you be more objective—is the debugger (you) chasing the wrong lead?—and it helps you separate yourself from the process, reducing frustration. Thinking about what you are doing is a good idea generally, of course. After all, Socrates said, "The unexamined life is not worth leading."

BUTTERFLIES AND BUGS: A CASE STUDY

To illustrate the debugging principles in action, we imagine we've developed a simple page in HTML. Our goal page is shown in Figure 7.2, but the results we're getting are shown in Figures 7.3–7.5. Obviously, there is an error somewhere. The HTML code we've written is shown in Figure 7.6. We can study the HTML very, very closely and "brain out" where the error is, or we can use the debugging strategy. You can follow along online with our debugging process at
`www.aw.com/snyder/`

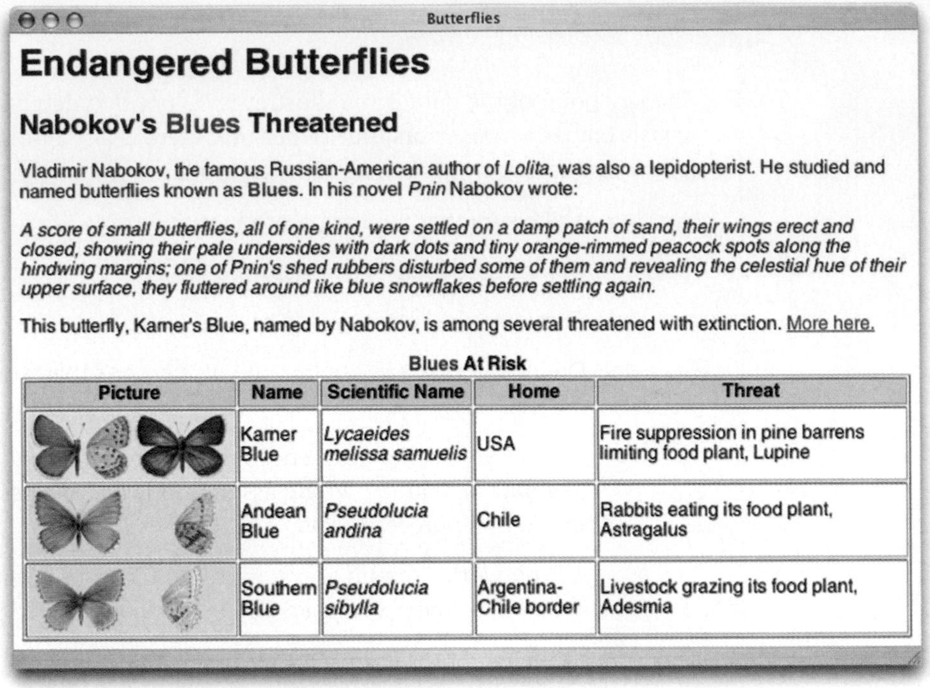

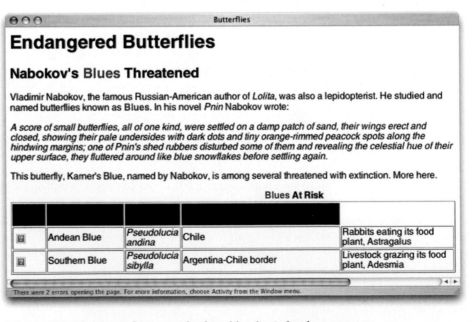

Figure 7.2. *The intended Web page.*

Figure 7.3. *The Butterflies page displayed by the Safari browser.*

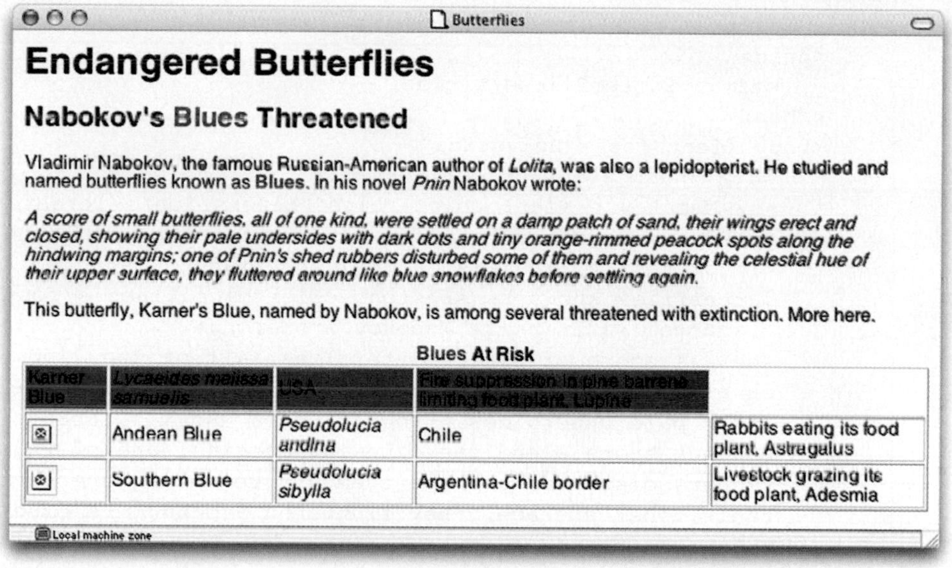

Figure 7.4. *The Butterflies page displayed by the Internet Explorer browser.*

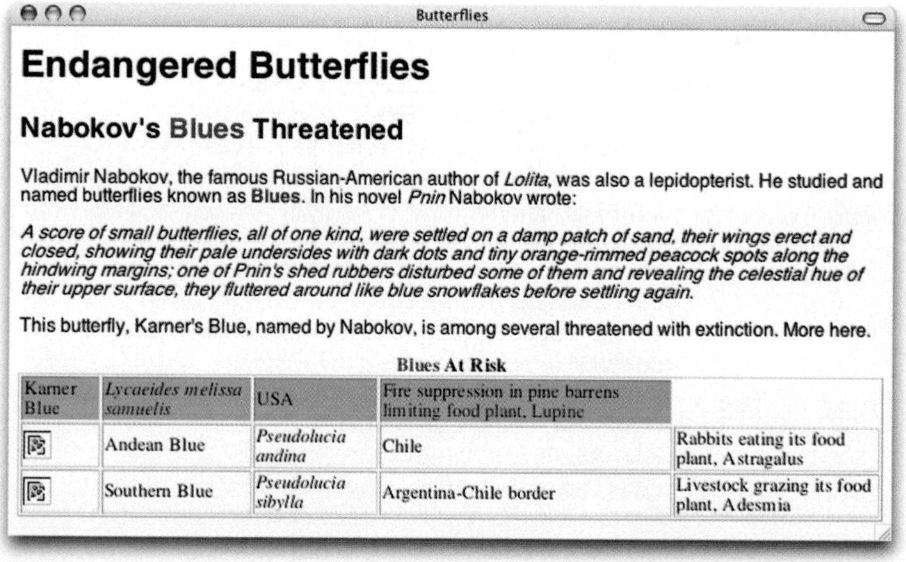

Figure 7.5. *The Butterflies page displayed by the Mozilla browser.*

```
<html>
   <head>
      <title>Butterflies</title>
   </head>
   <body><font face="Helvetica">
      <h1> Endangered Butterflies</h1>
      <h2>Nabokov's <font color="blue">Blues</font> Threatened</h2>
      <p>Vladimir Nabokov, the famous Russian-American author of
      <i>Lolita</i>, was also a lepidopterist. He studied and named
      butterflies known as <b><font color=blue>Blues </font></b>. In
      his novel <i>Pnin</i> Nabokov wrote:</p>
      <p><i>A score of small butterflies, all of one kind, were settled
      on a damp patch of sand, their wings erect and closed, showing
      their pale undersides with dark dots and tiny orange-rimmed
      peacock spots along the hindwing margins; one of Pnin's shed
      rubbers disturbed some of them and revealing the celestial hue of
      their upper surface, they fluttered around like blue snowflakes
      before settling again. </i></p>
      <p>This butterfly, Karner's Blue, named by Nabokov, is among
      several threatened with extinction.
      <ahref="http://www.libraries.psu.edu/nabokov/endan2.htm"> More
      here.</a></p>
      <table border>
         <caption><b><font color=blue">Blues</font> At Risk </b>
         </caption>
         <tr bgcolor="silver">
            <th>Picture</th>
            <th>Name</th>
            <th>Scientific Name</td>
            <th>Home</th>
            <th>Threat</th></tr>
         <tr><td><img src="lmeli.jpg"></td>
            <td> Karner Blue</td>
            <td><i>Lycaeides melissa samuelis</i></td>
            <td>USA</td>
            <td>Fire suppression in pine barrens limiting food plant,
            Lupine</td></tr>
         <tr><td><img src="pandi.jpg"></td>
            <td> Andean Blue</td>
            <td><i>Pseudolucia andina</i></td>
            <td>Chile</td>
            <td>Rabbits eating its food plant, Astragalus</td></tr>
         <tr><td><img src="psiby.jpg"></td>
            <td> Southern Blue</td>
            <td><i>Pseudolucia sibylla</i></td>
            <td>Argentina-Chile border</td>
            <td>Livestock grazing its food plant, Adesmia</td></tr>
      </table>
   </body>
</html>
```

Figure 7.6. Faulty HTML text for the Butterflies page.

As we begin, watching ourselves debugging the HTML, we recall that the first step is to be sure we can reproduce the error.

Reproduce the Error. So, we close our browser and reopen our file using a "fresh" copy. Unfortunately the results are the same. In fact, the Internet Explorer (Figure 7.4) and Mozilla (Figure 7.5) browsers produce different, but equally incorrect results. There is definitely a problem with our HTML.

> *fit***BYTE** **Some of these things are kind of different.** Notice the differences and similarities between the three browsers applied to the Butterflies page. Each browser's designers followed the rules for displaying HTML, but there is room for different interpretations resulting in slightly different looking pages. Though annoying when we are planning a page, the differences can sometimes help when debugging.

Determine the Problem Exactly. The next step is to determine the problem exactly. In the case of debugging HTML, identifying the problem is simple: just look at the displayed page. We see we have a faulty table with no pictures and a stripe filling in most of the first row; the word *blue* in the caption is actually red, which is weird. As we look closer, we also notice that the "More here." link is not highlighted, as it should be. Since these errors seem to be related to different parts of the page, we can assume they are caused by different mistakes in the HTML. It is common when debugging to be looking for more than one bug, but usually we don't know it. Here at least, we suspect multiple bugs.

Eliminate the Obvious. Once we know what the problem is, we look for the "obvious" errors. The most obvious HTML error is to forget to close a tag; that is, to forget the matching "slash-tag." Checking the HTML, however, we see that every tag is matched. So that simple tactic fails.

Looking at the faulty pages, the most obvious problem is that the word "Blues" is colored red. The obvious reason for this is that we specified the color incorrectly. So we look at the color specification for the caption

```
<caption><b><font color=blue">Blues</font>
```

and the error is obvious. We did specify `blue`, but we didn't match the quotes properly. When we insert a quote before `blue"`, "Blues" becomes blue. Why did a missing quote result in the browser coloring the word "Blues" red? We'll never know. When browsers are given broken HTML they work in mysterious ways.

With one bug swatted, we focus on another obvious error: Why is the "More here." link not highlighted? Again, the obvious answer is that we messed up the anchor tag, perhaps giving the wrong URL. Looking at the anchor tag

```
<ahref="http://www.libraries.psu.edu/nabokov/endan2.htm">More
here.</a></p>
```

we see immediately what's wrong: The anchor tag is given by the single letter `a`, and `href` is an attribute; therefore a space should follow the `a`. As we expect, when we insert the space, the link is highlighted.

Two bugs down and one to go. Turning to that one, why is the table messed up? The colored bar in the first row is peculiar. No "obvious" cause for it comes to mind, unless it is related to the fact that the figures are not displaying. There is an obvious possible cause for this: A mistake in the `<img src= >` specification. We check the names of the three image files: `lmeli.jpg`, `pandi.jpg`, and `psiby.jpg` against the three files (see Figure 7.7), and we notice that there is a difference. The file names in the HTML are lowercase, but the file names themselves are uppercase. Sometimes this matters and sometimes it doesn't. Not remembering whether it's important for our computer, we capitalize the names in the HTML file, but there is no change. That "obvious" idea fails. So, we move on to the next step.

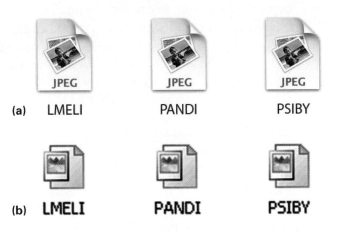

Figure 7.7. The image files for (a) MacOSX and (b) Windows.

`Divide Up the Process.` The next step is to separate those parts of the system that work from the part that does not. This is not always possible to do perfectly, but we should try. In the present case most of the page is fine, so we focus on the first row of the table. When we carefully compare the intended solution with the faulty solution, we immediately notice that there is a whole row missing: The table is supposed to have a top row, shown in silver, with the column headings. Perhaps whatever is messing up the headings is messing up the first row, too. So, we focus on the heading row and the first data row of the table.

When we look back at Figure 7.6, both rows look perfect. What can the problem be? We can pour over the HTML closely looking for errors, but we need some help. It would be great if the browser software could tell us how it is interpreting our HTML. Then, maybe we can spot where it's getting into trouble. Browsers and debugging systems for HTML *can* give us a color-code version of the HTML showing how it's being interpreted. Figure 7.8 shows the first two rows of the table source as displayed by the Mozilla browser, found from **View > Page Source**.

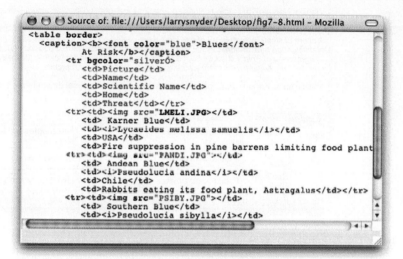

Figure 7.8. *The Source View displayed by the Mozilla browser for the start of the table.*

The color-coding of the browser shows the text colored in black, the tags in violet, and the user-supplied attribute data in blue. But the coloring is very unusual: The entire heading line of the table is colored blue, indicating that the browser is interpreting it as part of a single attribute. That's incorrect. When we look closely at the row tag for the heading,

```
<tr bgcolor="silveró>
```

we notice an unusual character following the word silver. It's supposed to be a quote to match the quote at the beginning of silver. When we re-check Figure 7.6, we notice that the line reads

```
<tr bgcolor="silver">
```

and that we have used a fancy closing quote, which browsers do not understand. So, the browser, mistaking our closed quote for an "accented o" keeps looking for a closing quote. It eventually finds one in the image tag at the beginning of the next table row. So, the browser considers the background color to be everything from the beginning of the word silver up to the start of the file name `LMELI.JPG`, as it shows us in blue. Obviously, this isn't a color, and it explains what happened to the heading row—it was misinterpreted as part of the color specification. Replacing the fancy (smart) closed quote with the plain quote, preferred by all browsers, gives us a table with a heading row and three data rows, as shown in Figure 7.9. Narrowing the focus of our search to the first part of the table works.

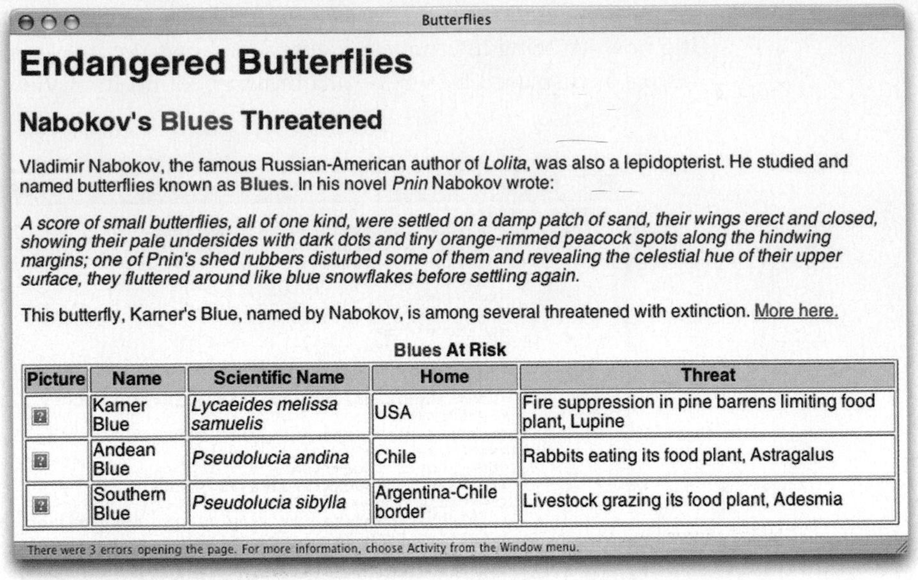

Figure 7.9. The Butterflies page after correcting the heading color.

Unfortunately, our debugging effort is not complete, because the pictures do not display. We now focus our attention on the image tags in each row. We checked them earlier, and corrected them to be uppercase like the file names,

```
<tr><td><img src="LMELI.JPG"></td>
```

but that didn't help. Nothing else seems wrong with the image tags. What do we do next? Again, it is a good tactic to check the browser's color-coded **Source View**, but as we see in Figure 7.8, the image tags, for example for the `PANDI.JPG` file, are being interpreted correctly by the browser.

Reassess. We seem to be stuck. We've narrowed the problem to the image tags, checked them, and determined that they are well structured. We have made the names uppercase to match the file names and we've verified that the browser is interpreting the text properly. Everything looks correct. Frustration seems like the next step.

More constructively, we acknowledge that the HTML can look perfect *to us* and still not work. What we *think* is true leads us to the wrong conclusion. So, we reassess to figure out what mistake we're making in our understanding of the HTML. In this process we ask ourselves such questions as "What wrong assumptions am I making?" "What wrong conclusions am I drawing?" Eventually, we may have to consider the possibility that the software we are using is broken, but that's usually the last possibility. Finding the answers to these questions usually locates the bug, but it will take some hard thinking and some experimentation.

In the present case we say, "I think the images are okay, but are they really?" To check, we insert one image into another document, and discover that it looks fine.

So, the answer is "yes," the images are okay. Next, we say, "Is there something wrong with the JPEG specification?" So we make a little GIF file named `butterfly.gif` and change the first row figure to

```
<tr><td><img src="butterfly.gif"></td>
```

but it displays fine, as shown in Figure 7.10.

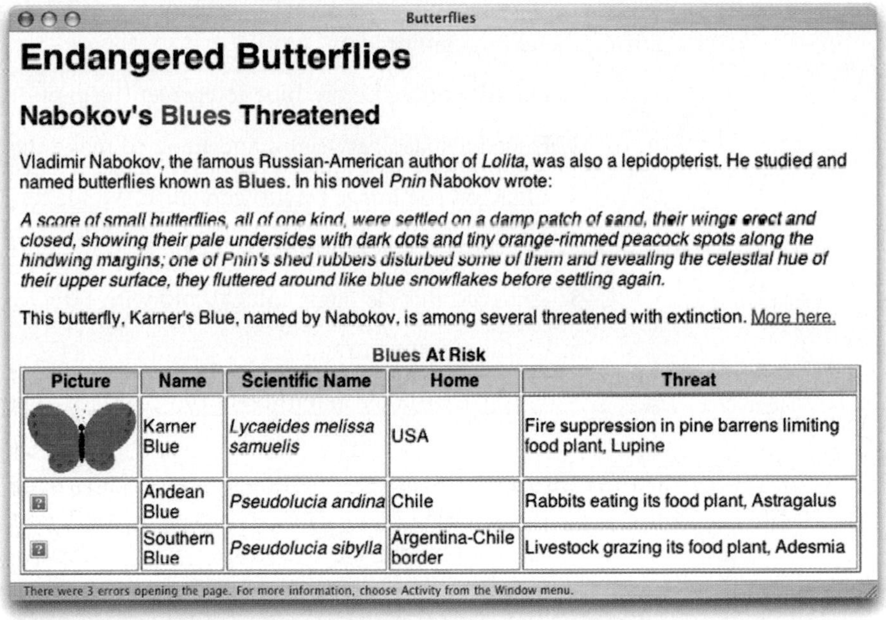

Figure 7.10. The table from the Butterflies page after revising with a new file.

This is an important development because it proves that the browser is displaying our pictures. It's just not displaying the JPEG figures we want. Maybe there's another odd character in the image tag that we didn't notice. We type in the file name `LMELI.JPG` again, and it still doesn't display. So, the problem isn't a bad character in the original image tag. It must be a problem with the file name because that is all we changed when we displayed the GIF. What have we assumed that isn't true? To check the name, we open the LMELI file with the browser, since it shows the complete file name in the Location Window. The window shows

```
/Desktop/Webfile/Endangered/LMELI.JPEG
```

indicating that the file's extension is `.JPEG`, not `.JPG` as we have been using in the image tags. (We recall from Chapter 4 that browsers understand both `.JPEG` and `.JPG` as image files, but the operating system still must have the exact name for the file.) We can fix this by correcting the image tags or changing the names of the files. When we revise the image tags as in

```
<tr><td><img src="LMELI.JPEG"></td>
```

the result is identical to Figure 7.2. We've solved it!

Butterflies and Bugs, A Postmortem

We have found the bugs in the HTML of the Butterflies page. In the process of tracking them down we made a series of conjectures, tried different changes to the program, ran a couple of experiments, and drew conclusions. How did we do? Certainly, the result turned out fine.

Changes Made. For the record, we made the following changes to the HTML during the debugging process:

1. Placed a quote before blue to correct the caption.

2. Placed a space between `a` and `href` to make the link active.

3. Changed the image tags to capitalize the file names.

4. Fixed the quote following `silver`.

5. Replaced the file name `LMELI.JPG` with `butterfly.gif`.

6. Restored `LMELI.JPG`.

7. Corrected the file extensions from `.JPG` to `.JPEG`.

Unnecessary Changes. Of these seven changes, only 1, 2, 4, and 7 were necessary to fix the problem. The other changes were unnecessary: change 3 was not necessary because the file names are not case sensitive on the computers we used; change 5 was an experiment to force the browser to display a figure; and change 6 reversed change 5, repeating the "`JPG` error." The unnecessary changes were introduced when we made wrong conjectures about the cause of the error or were experimenting. Making changes that are unnecessary is quite typical, because making incorrect conjectures is also quite typical. Luckily these changes didn't make the situation worse, but it is possible to introduce new errors when following the wrong logical path or experimenting.

Hiding Other Errors. When we first described the errors, we thought we had three: a bad caption, a bad link, and a broken table. Because there were two things wrong with the table—messed up heading line and wrong file names specified—we actually had four errors.

The table errors were complicated to analyze because with one of the figures missing, we couldn't be sure whether the two problems were independent, as they turned out to be. Perhaps the missing figure was causing both errors—the missing heading line and the missing images. It is common for one error to hide another, so we always have to suspect that there is more than one error.

Viewing the Source. Notice that the most effective technique in our debugging exercise—after thinking logically—was to use the browser's **Source View** feature. Seeing the color- and font-coded HTML source told us how the browser interpreted our page. This revealed an error directly. In general, one of the most powerful debugging techniques is to find ways for the computer to tell us the meaning of the information it stores or the effects of the commands it executes. Having the computer stipulate how it's interpreting our instructions can separate the case in which we give the right command, but mess up expressing it, with giving the wrong command. This is an important difference for finding a bug.

Little Errors, Big Problems. Finally, the errors in the HTML code were quite tiny: a missing quotation mark, a missing space, a wrong quote, and three missing *e* characters in the file extensions. Of the 1014 non-content characters in the original file, the six wrong characters represent about half of 1 percent of the HTML programming. The conclusion: We must be extremely precise.

NO PRINTER OUTPUT: A CLASSIC SCENARIO

Debugging HTML is possible because we know and write HTML, but we don't create most computer systems, and they are extremely complex, way beyond our understanding. A standard personal computer and its software are more complex than the space shuttle in several ways. As users, we have little idea how something so complex works; how is it possible to troubleshoot a system we don't understand?

Of course, we cannot debug software and information systems at the detailed level used by programmers or engineers. If there is a basic, conceptual error in the system, we probably won't find it. But we don't have to. Before we come in contact with a system, it is tested extensively. This testing doesn't eliminate all errors, but it probably means that the "standard operations" used by "average" users are run through their paces many times. Systems should be bug-free, and we should be able to depend on the software.

---

*fit***BYTE**

Putting It to the Test. As noted in Chapter 2, "getting out and getting back in" often works when an application is not operating correctly. The reason this method works is related to how software is tested. Beginning with a fresh configuration, the testing proceeds "forward" into the application, with the common operations getting the most attention. So the most stable part of a system is the part that is reachable from an initial configuration—the part you first meet when you're "getting back in."

To illustrate debugging a system without understanding it, consider a classic debugging scenario: You try to print a document and nothing comes out of the printer. This problem happens often to all users. In many ways this situation is like our videotape example. Like the TV/VCR system, a cable connects the computer/printer system, part of the system is mechanical, the flow of information is from one device to the other, and the system has worked in the past.

Applying the Debugging Strategy

The printing problem is solved just as the videotape problem was solved: *reproduce the error, understand the problem, and check the obvious causes.* These steps include checking the printer's control panel, the paper, the cartridges, the cable connections, the file to be printed, the installation of the printer driver (the correct printer dialog box comes up when the print command is issued), whether others can print if this is a shared printer, and whether you can print a different document. If these steps do not solve the problem, you may think it's time to ask for help. You've already gone further than most users, so it's not embarrassing, but you can do more.

Pressing On

Take the next step in the debugging strategy: *Try to isolate the problem.* This is daunting because you don't really understand how printing works. Not to worry. It's still possible to make progress.

Because you have printed before, you know your computer is configured correctly. You try to print a simple document like a text file, but it's the same story: The printer driver's dialog box comes up, asks how many copies you want, and so forth—you reply 1, click **Print**, and the machine appears to compute for a moment. But when you check the printer, nothing's there. What is happening to your output?

Thinking through what you imagine to be the process, you guess that when you click **Print**, the printer driver must convert the file into the form suitable for the printer. Because the computer runs briefly after you click **Print**, it's a safe bet that it's doing something like a conversion. Then your computer must send the converted file to the printer. Does it go? Surely, if the computer tried to send the file to the printer and the printer didn't acknowledge getting it, the computer would tell you to plug in the printer. Or would it? Suppose you unplugged the printer from the computer and tried again to print. You run this experiment and the same thing happens! The printer can't even receive the converted file, and there are no complaints. What's happening? Where is the file?

Perhaps the computer is saving the converted file. Why? Shouldn't it print if it's told to print? This is a little odd, because it's not asking you to plug in the printer. Could the other files you tried to print be waiting too, even though the printer was plugged in earlier? So, you start looking around for the stranded file(s). You locate the printer driver's printing monitor (**Start > Settings > Printers** on the PC; among the active programs on the Mac). When you open this monitor, you find a list of all the files you've tried to print recently. They're not printing—they're just listed (see Figure 7.11).

The Print Queue

You have discovered the "print queue" for your machine. You didn't even know that computers *have* print queues, but apparently they do. It's obvious that your file is stalled in the printing queue. As described in Chapter 2 under "Clicking Around," you explore the monitor application, discovering that the queue is "turned off" or possibly "wedged." (The actual description for "turned off" varies from system to system; for the PC it is **Use Printer Offline**, which is set under **File**; for Macs the Print Queue button is configured to **Start Print Queue**; shared printers are different still.) Though machines are different, the situation is the same: The computer's settings tell it to queue your converted files rather than print them immediately. How it got into this state you may never know. The best approach is to cancel or trash all of the jobs in the queue, because there are probably many duplicates, and restart the queue. That is, configure it so that it tries to print your files immediately rather than queuing them. Your printing problem may be solved! Or have you forgotten to re-cable your printer?

*fit***BYTE** | **Sleep on It**. Professionals know that when they can't find a bug, it's time to take a break. Whether our minds continue to work on the problem subconsciously or that returning refreshed to the problem clears our thinking, briefly getting away from the problem helps.

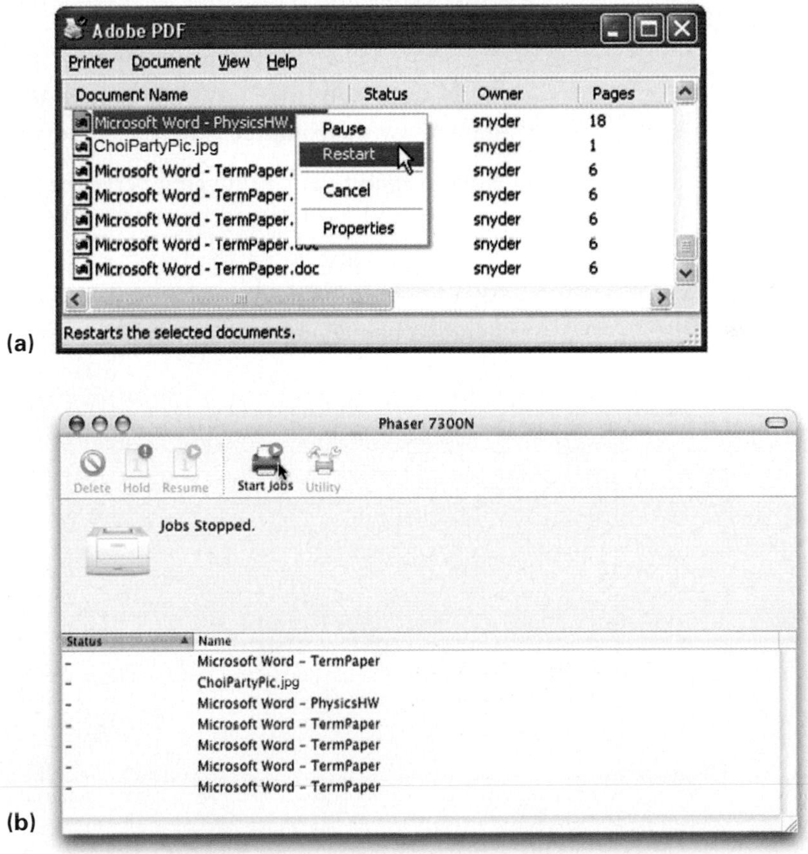

(a)

(b)

Figure 7.11. Printer queues for (a) Windows and (b) Mac operating systems.

Calling Tech Support?

Summarizing the situation, you debugged the printing operation in spite of the fact that it's complicated and you know almost nothing about how computers print. You aptly assumed that the software is okay. You discovered that computers use a print queue, though it's a mystery why. The queue can stop or stall, but by using the print monitor you can restart it. Locating the problem involved the standard debugging strategy applied with courage and common sense, and the results were successful. Obviously, there are many problems that are not solved using this approach—those that actually require some technical knowledge—but you should always assume that the standard debugging strategy will work. Only when you've applied it without success, is it time to call Tech Support.

SUMMARY

The chapter began by emphasizing why being precise is important when using computers. The standard of precision is higher than in most other situations, so being careful and exact makes using computers easier. We learned:

> What debugging is and why we need to know how to do it.

> Basic debugging strategy, including the whys and hows of debugging.

> To debug a Web page, using the **Source View** of the document that shows how the computer interprets the HTML.

> How to analyze our debugging performance, noting that debugging involves both correct and incorrect conjectures.

> That it's possible to debug a sophisticated system like a computer printer with little more than a vague idea of how it works, by using our standard debugging strategy applied with common sense and courage.

EXERCISES

Multiple Choice

1. An example of an understanding error is a
   A. memory error
   B. data entry error
   C. design error
   D. none of the above

2. The best way to solve an understanding error is to
   A. restart the system
   B. change software
   C. try again
   D. all of the above

3. The first step in debugging is to
   A. check for obvious errors
   B. try to reproduce the problem
   C. isolate the problem
   D. find exactly what the problem is

4. The debugging process can be described as a
   A. recipe
   B. road map
   C. set of guidelines
   D. list

5. The last step in the debugging process is to
   A. look again to identify the mistake
   B. reproduce the problem
   C. divide up the process
   D. determine the exact problem

Short Answer

1. _____ are information that is entered into boxes on a form.

2. A _____ is a set of rules that determines what is legal for field input.

3. Use a _____ to represent a space on the computer.

4. _____ and debugging mean essentially the same thing.

5. A glitch in a computer system is called a(n) _____.

6. A(n) _____ is an error in the way a system was developed.

7. An alternative approach to get around a problem is called a(n) _____.

Exercises

1. You walk into a room and flip the light switch. Nothing happens. Describe the debugging process you use to solve the problem.

2. What advantages does an organized approach have over a trial and error approach?

3. Draw a schematic of the debugging process. Apply this to the debugging process for question 1.

4. How would you say "Room 309"? Did you say "zero" or "oh"? How about a zip code? Try 90210.

5. What is the lexical structure for entering dates into the computer? Use the standard American format for a two-digit month, a separator, a two-digit day, a separator, and a four-digit year.

6. Devise a lexical structure for entering a phone number into the computer. What characters are allowed and when? Do the same thing for zip codes.

7. Think "outside the box" to solve a problem. You have a quiz in an hour and you're stranded. You must contact the professor before the quiz or you won't pass the course. How do you contact the professor? List multiple alternatives.

8. You've been doing debugging since you learned how to check your math back in grade school. Check the math on this problem.

$$N = -((12 + 6) - 7 \times 4 + ((9 - 2) \times 3) / 7)$$
$$N = 18 - 7 \times 4 + 7 \times 3 / 7$$
$$N = 11 \times 4 + 21 / 7$$
$$N = 44 + 25 / 7$$
$$N = 49 / 7$$
$$N = 7$$

9. Design several workarounds for the computer printing error. Pretend it's your term paper and it has to be printed. How would you get around the problem that that computer and the printer aren't printing?

10. Here is the HTML for a simple Web page. Find the errors in it and get the page to display properly. Test the page to be sure it works properly.

```
<html>
   <head>
      <title>My Favorites</title>
   </head>
   <body>
      <ol>
         <li>Movies</li>
      </ol>
      <ul>
         <li><i>Grease</i></li>
         <li><i>Road to Perdition</i></li>
         <li><i>Titanic</i></li>
      </ul>
```

```
        <ol>
            <li>Shows</li>
            <li><i>Survivor</i></li>
            <li><i>American Idol</i></li>
            <li><i>Everybody Loves Raymond</i></li>
            <li>Stars</li>
        </ol>
        <ol>
            <li>Matt Damon</li>
            <li>Kate Hudson></li>
            <li>Lucy Lui</li>
        </ol>
    </body>
</html>
```

BITS AND THE "WHY" OF BYTES

Representing Information Digitally

learning objectives

> Explain the link between patterns, symbols, and information

> Compare two different encoding methods

> Determine possible PandA encodings using a physical phenomenon

> Give a bit sequence code for ASCII; decode

> Explain how structure tags (metadata) encode the *OED*

BITS AND THE "WHY" OF BYTES
Representing Information Digitally

Ancora imparo "I am still learning."

—MICHELANGELO, MOTTO

MOST PEOPLE know that computers and networks record and transmit information in *bits* and *bytes*. From basic English, you can guess that bits probably represent little pieces of information. But what are bytes? And why is "byte" spelled with a *y*? In this chapter we confirm that bits do represent little pieces of information, we define bytes, and, by the end, we explain the mysterious *y*. But the chapter is much more fundamental than these basic concepts. It describes how bits and bytes—the atoms and molecules of information—combine to form our virtual world of computation, information, and communication. (Multimedia is covered in Chapter 11.) We even explain how information exists when there is nothing, as when Sherlock Holmes solves the mystery using the information that "the dog didn't bark in the night."

The first goal of this chapter is to establish that digitizing doesn't require digits—any set of symbols will do. We explore encoding information using dice, learn how pattern sequences can create symbols, and discover that symbols can represent information. Our next goal is to learn the fundamental patterns on which all information technology is built: the presence and absence of a phenomenon. Called PandA encoding here, this meeting of the physical and logical worlds forms the foundation of information technology. We then define bits, bytes, and ASCII. Finally, we describe the digitization of the *Oxford English Dictionary (OED)* to show how metadata is added to content so computers can help us use it.

DIGITIZING DISCRETE INFORMATION

The dictionary definition of *digitize* is to represent information with digits. In normal conversation, *digit* means the ten Arabic numerals 0 through 9. Thus digitizing uses whole numbers to stand for things. This familiar process represents Americans by Social Security numbers, telephone accounts by phone numbers, and books by ISBN numbers. Such digital representations have probably been used since numerals were invented. But this sense of *digitize* is much too narrow for the digital world of IT.

> *fit* **BYTE**
>
> **Digital Man.** The first person to apply the term digital to computers was George Stibitz, a Bell Labs mathematician. While consulting for the U.S. military, he observed that "pulsed" computing devices would be better described as digital because they represent information in discrete (that is, separate) units.

Limitation of Digits

A limitation of the dictionary definition of *digitize* is that it calls for the use of the ten digits, which produces a whole number. But in most cases the property of being numeric is unimportant and of little use. Numbers quantify things and let us do arithmetic, but Social Security numbers, phone numbers, and ISBN numbers are not quantities. You are not better than someone else is if you have a larger telephone number. So, when we don't need numbers, we don't need to use digits. But what else can we use to digitize?

Alternative Representations

Digitizing in IT can use almost any symbols. For example, the North American telephone number 888 555 1212 could be represented as *** %%% !@!@. This encoding, rather than using {1, 2, 3, 4, 5, 6, 7, 8, 9, 0}, uses the symbol set {!, @, #, $, %, ^, &, *, (,)}. These symbols are simply the uppercase digit characters on a keyboard. If we use the symbol set { ▶ , ▼ , ◀ , ▶▶ , ■ , ◀◀ , ▶▶| , ▲ , |◀◀ , || } the phone number is represented as: ▲ ▲ ▲   ■ ■ ■   ▶ ▼ ▶ ▼ . This could be called **player encoding** because it uses the standard symbols from tape and CD players. These symbols work just as well as the digits as long as the telephone keypad is relabeled, as shown in Figure 8.1. The reason the encoding works is that a phone number's digits simply tell us which sequence of keys to press. Any ten distinct symbols will work as long as the keypad is labeled properly.

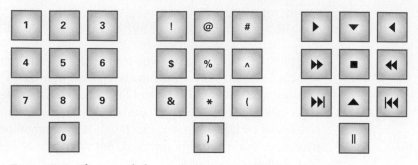

Figure 8.1. Three symbol assignments for a telephone keypad.

Symbols, Briefly

One practical advantage of digits over other less familiar symbols is that digits have short names. Imagine speaking your phone number as "asterisk asterisk exclamation point closing parenthesis exclamation point. . . ." In fact, as IT has adopted these symbols, the names are getting shorter. For example, computer professionals often say exclamation point as *bang* and asterisk as *star*. Instead of saying "eight eight eight five five five one two one two" we could say "star star star per per per bang at bang at," which is just as brief. So, the advantage of brevity is not limited to digits.

Ordering Symbols

One other advantage of digits for encoding information like telephone numbers is that the items can be listed in numerical order. This feature is rarely used for the kinds of information discussed here; for example, telephone books are ordered by the name of the person rather than by the number. But sometimes ordering items is useful.

To place information in order by using symbols (other than digits), we need to agree on an ordering for the basic symbols. This is called a **collating sequence**. In the same way that the digits are ordered

0 < 1 < 2 < 3 < 4 < 5 < 6 < 7 < 8 < 9

the player symbols could be ordered

❙❙ < ▶ < ▼ < ◀ < ▶▶ < ■ < ◀◀ < ▶❙ < ▲ < ❙◀◀

Then, two coded phone numbers can be ordered based on which has the smaller first symbol, or if the first symbol matches, then on which has the smaller second symbol, or if the first two symbols match, which has the smaller third symbol, and so on. For example,

▲ ❙❙ ❙❙ ■ ■ ■ ▶ ▼ ▶ ▼ < ▲ ▲ ▲ ■ ■ ■ ▶ ▼ ▶ ▼

Today, digitizing means *representing information by symbols*—not just the ten digit symbols. But which symbols would be best? Before answering that question, we should consider how the choice of symbols interacts with the things being encoded.

ENCODING WITH DICE

Because information can be digitized using any symbols, consider a representation based on dice. A single die has six sides, and the patterns on the sides of the dice can be used for this digital representation. (The patterns can be interpreted as numbers, of course, but for the moment we ignore that property.)

Consider representing the Roman alphabet with dice.

There are 26 letters in the Roman alphabet, but only six different patterns on a die; therefore there are more letters to represent than there are patterns available. This is a typical encoding problem. So we use multiple patterns to represent each letter. How many are required? Two dice patterns together produce $6 \times 6 = 36$ different pattern sequences because each of the six patterns of one die can be paired with each of the six different patterns of the other die (see Figure 8.2). Three dice can define $6 \times 6 \times 6 = 216$ different pattern sequences because there are six choices for the first position, six for the second position, and six for the last. More generally, n dice together can produce 6^n different pattern sequences. If instead of six there is some other number, p, of basic patterns, a sequence of n of them produces p^n different pattern sequences. (Recall that p^n means $p \times p \times \ldots \times p$; that is, n copies of p multiplied together.)

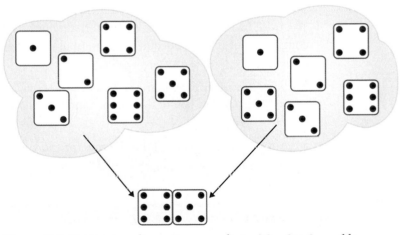

Figure 8.2. *Pairing two dice patterns results in 36 = 6 × 6 possible pattern sequences.*

Returning to the problem of digitizing the alphabet, let's call each of the pattern sequences produced by pairing two dice a symbol. Then we can associate these dice-pair symbols with the letters simply by listing them.

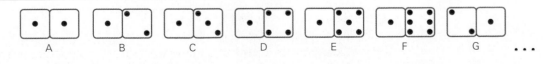

It helps to be systematic when associating the letters with the symbols to make the encoding easier to remember. In fact, because two dice form the symbols, the simplest way to present the association between the symbols and the values they encode (letters) is a table, as illustrated in Figure 8.3.

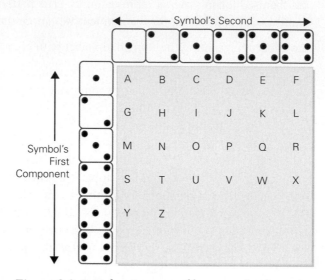

Figure 8.3. Initial assignment of letters to the dice-pair symbols.

The table is organized so that the pattern along the left side of the table is the first component of the symbol and the pattern along the top is the second. This makes the digitizing process easy.

> > *Encode a letter.* Find the letter in the table and use the pattern of the row as the left half of the symbol and the pattern of the column as the right half.

> > *Decode a symbol.* Find the row for the left half of the symbol and the column for the right half; the letter is at the intersection of the row and column.

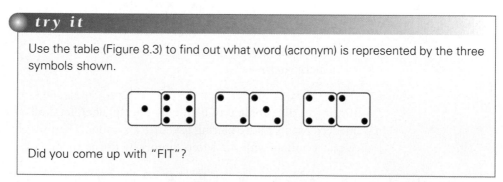

try it

Use the table (Figure 8.3) to find out what word (acronym) is represented by the three symbols shown.

Did you come up with "FIT"?

Extending the Encoding

The representation has associated 26 of the symbols with the Roman letters, leaving ten positions unassigned. If the information to be digitized only uses letters, we're done, because a symbol is associated with each letter. But this rarely happens. A more common situation is that the information uses letters and numerals; many automobile license plates use those 36 characters. In such cases, associating the Arabic numerals with the unassigned symbols of Figure 8.3 would then complete the digitization, as shown in Figure 8.4(a).

But usually the textual information to be digitized includes more than letters and numerals; it also includes punctuation. Including punctuation complicates the dice-pair representation because we need more symbols than we have pairs of dice. Anyone inventing a digitization faces the problem of deciding which items are the most important to represent.

Perhaps the most important character is the space character, because we use it to *delimit* letter sequences, that is, separate words. We cannot use spacing in the digitization (that is, separations in our arrangement of dice-pairs) to indicate word separations in the text because we have no control over how the digital form will be used. For example, using the Figure 8.4(a) digitization, two people could communicate in a noisy environment with a single pair of dice by spelling out words one letter at a time. But with only one pair of dice, there is no way to "separate the pairs" to indicate the end of a word. The point is that the digitization must encode all the information and the spaces separating words are part of the information. So space must be assigned to some symbol. After that the nine remaining symbols are not enough to represent the digits, so we'll use them for more punctuation. A representation of this type is shown in Figure 8.4(b).

Figure 8.4(b) has the advantage of representing space and other punctuation, but it doesn't represent the numerals. In some cases, this might not be a serious problem because we can find other ways to represent these characters. For example, the two people communicating in a noisy environment with a pair of dice might simply spell out each numeral. There would be no single symbol for zero, for example, but it could be presented as

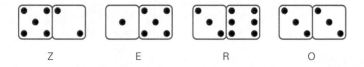

But spelling out numerals limits how this digital representation can be used, and we want to avoid limitations if we possibly can. Though it appears that we need to use dice triples, there is an alternative.

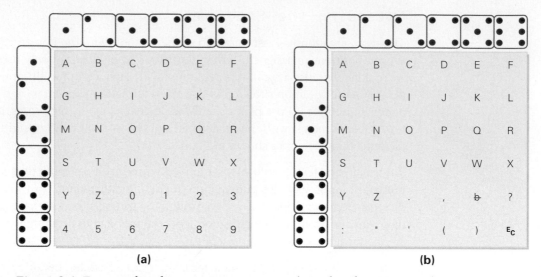

Figure 8.4. *Two complete dice-pair representations. (Note: ᵬ indicates a space.)*

The Escape: Creating More Symbols

In Figure 8.4(b) the "boxcars" symbol (double sixes) is associated with an unfamiliar character, ᴱc. This character, which is not a letter, numeral, or punctuation character, will be called *escape*. It has been included to illustrate how to extend a representation. Because escape does not match any legal character, we will never need it in the normal process of digitizing text. So we can use it to indicate that the digitization is "escaping from the basic representation" and applying a secondary representation. In this way, more symbols can be represented because pairing escape with another symbol doubles the number of representations, although the new symbols are twice as long.

To illustrate the idea, let's encode the numerals by pairing the escape symbol with each of the first ten symbols of the encoding, that is, those assigned to A through J. Each symbol pair, that is, four dice, is assigned to a numeral in order. Thus the symbol pair,

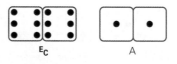

which is escape-A, represents 0. Escape-B represents 1, and so on. Notice that the escape symbol precedes the letter. So, 10 is represented as

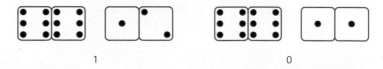

There can be no "group discount" here: We can't place escape before the first of a whole string of digits because the decoder would not know when the string ends

and the base encoding (non-escape characters) resumes. So, a ten-digit number needs 20 symbols in this dice-pair encoding extended by escape.

*fit***BYTE**

Shifty. The escape technique is familiar. The (Shift) keys are used to "escape" from lowercase on the keyboard; they double the encoding, providing uppercase characters. The (Ctrl) key works this way, too.

Double Escape

Using this escape gives only 35 basic symbol assignments because the ^{E}c takes up the boxcars symbol. But, escape gives an equal number of two-symbol assignments. These secondary assignments should probably be associated with the less frequently used values because the encoding is less efficient. Of course, the idea can be continued because we could use ^{E}c ^{E}c as another escape for yet another alternate set of symbols. But there are other, more sophisticated ways to use the escape symbol. The point is that in digitizing information, do not associate all symbols with legal information, as was done in Figure 8.4(a), but rather reserve one symbol as an escape, as shown in Figure 8.4(b). The escape gives flexibility to a representation.

Notice that when the 36 symbols created from two dice weren't enough for the letters, numerals, and punctuation, we could have used three dice pattern sequences. That would have given $6^3 = 216$ symbols. The advantage is that numerals would have been encoded with three dice rather than four. The disadvantage is that the letters and punctuation would have been encoded with three dice rather than two. If numerals make up less than half of the characters we wish to encode, our "two plus escape" uses fewer dice than the "triples" solution.

To summarize, digitizing involves associating symbols with values, which in the case of text are the keyboard characters. The method of constructing symbols—combining base patterns—creates a fixed-size set of symbols. The symbol set must be large enough to represent each value. Saving one symbol for escape allows the encoding to be extended.

FUNDAMENTAL INFORMATION REPRESENTATION

The six base patterns of a die are familiar, but not fundamental. The fundamental patterns used in IT come when the physical world meets the logical world. In the physical world, the most fundamental form of information is the presence or absence of a physical phenomenon:

> Does matter occupy a particular place in space and time, or not?

> Is light detected at a particular place and time, or not?

> Is magnetism sensed at a particular place and time, or not?

The same goes for pressure, charge, flow, and so on. In many cases, the phenomena have a continuous range of values. For example, light and color have a smooth range of intensities

while others like clicking and drumming are discrete

(The continuous case is discussed in Chapter 11.) From a digital information point of view, the amount of a phenomenon is not important as long as it is reliably detected—whether there is some information or none; whether it is present or absent.

In the logical world, which is the world of thinking and reasoning, the concepts of *true* and *false* are important. Propositions such as "Rain implies wet streets" can be expressed and combined with other propositions such as "The streets are not wet" to draw conclusions such as "It is not raining." Logic is the foundation of reasoning, and it is also the foundation of computing. *By associating true with the presence of a phenomenon and false with its absence, we can use the physical world to implement the logical world. This produces information technology.* We make this association in this section.

The PandA Representation

PandA is the name we use for the two fundamental patterns of digital information based on the presence and absence of a phenomenon. PandA is the mnemonic for "presence and absence." A key property of the PandA representation is that it is black and white; that is, the phenomenon is either present or it is not; the logic is either *true* or *false*. Such a formulation is said to be *discrete*, meaning "distinct" or "separable"; it is not possible to transform one value into the other by continuous gradations. There is no gray.

A Binary System. The PandA encoding has just two patterns—Present and Absent—making it a **binary system**. The names Present and Absent are not essential to our use in digitization, so we often associate other words with them that suggest the discrete, black-and-white nature of the two patterns (see Table 8.1). The assignment of these names to the two patterns is also arbitrary. There is no law that says that in all cases *On* means "Present" and *Off* means "Absent." We could agree to assign the names the other way around; engineers deep into a circuit design often do. As long as all of the information encoders and decoders agree, any assignment works. The associations given in the table seem reasonable, however, and they are probably the most common. But the entries are only names for the two fundamental patterns.

Table 8.1. *Possible interpretations of the two PandA patterns*

Present	Absent
True	False
1	0
On	Off
Yes	No
+	−
Black	White
For	Against
Yang	Yin
Lisa	Bart
...	...

Bits Form Symbols. The unit that can assume the different patterns can vary. In the dice representation, the unit was the top of a single die. This unit could be set to any of six patterns to encode letters. In the same way, in the PandA representation the unit is a specific place (in space and time), where the presence or absence of the phenomenon can be set and detected. The PandA unit is known as a *bit*, which can assume either of the two PandA patterns, Present or Absent. *Bit* is a contraction for "binary digit." (The term *bit* was originally adopted because early computer designers interpreted the two patterns as 1 and 0, the digits of the binary number system; they are more economical to write than "present" and "absent," so we continue to use them.) Though bit sequences can be interpreted as binary numbers, the key idea is that bits form *symbols*. Encoding numbers is a particularly useful application of symbols, but the idea is more general.

*fit*BYTE

Coincidence? Though *bit* means "small piece" in English, the term actually derives from a contraction of *binary* and *digit*. Of course, bits represent small pieces of information, suggesting the choice may not have been a coincidence.

{ *fit* BYTE }

Encoding Bits on a CD ROM >>

The compact disc read-only memory (CD-ROM) is the technology of the familiar audio CD applied to storing programs and data. Developed jointly by the Phillips and Sony Corporations, the CD was originally intended only for recorded audio and video. But the two companies engineered the technology so cleverly that CDs are almost error free, making them perfect for storing data and software. Here's how CDs work.

CDs are made of clear plastic that is forced into a round mold, something like a round waffle iron, having a smooth bottom and a bumpy top. When the plastic hardens and is removed from the mold, the topside bumpy pattern is covered with aluminum to make it shiny. A protective layer is put over the aluminum and the "label" is printed on the top.

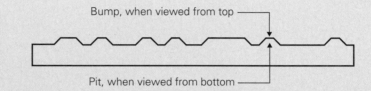

Bump, when viewed from top

Pit, when viewed from bottom

The bumps encode the information. Because they are read from the bottom of the CD, the bumps are called *pits*. The region between the pits is called the *land*. A laser beam is focused up through the CD onto the pitted surface. The beam reflects off of the aluminum and back to a sensor that detects whether the beam is striking a pit, a land, or a diagonal in between.

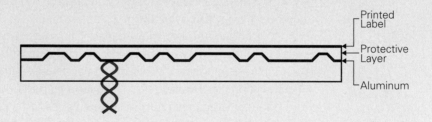

Printed Label

Protective Layer

Aluminum

The pits are arranged in a line that begins at the *inner* edge of the CD and spirals out to the *outer* edge. (Notice that inside-out is the opposite of vinyl records.) The first part of the spiral is used for calibrating the laser reading device; then comes an index (track list) for locating specific positions on the CD; and finally the actual information (music or software) is stored in binary.

In addition to CD ROMs, which are manufactured with the information already stored on them—it's a pattern in the mold—there are CD Recordable (CD-R) discs and CD Rewriteable (CD-RW) discs. Both types are blank to begin with and use somewhat different materials. CD-R disks can be written to once and only read thereafter; CD-RW disks can be written to and rewritten to.

Positive Presence. The use of physical phenomena to represent information sometimes poses problems because there might be more than two alternatives. For example, a magnetic material might not be magnetized at all, or it can have positive polarity or negative polarity; that is, there are three possibilities. In such situations, engineers adopt one state such as positive polarity to mean "present" and all other states to mean "absent."

Bits in Computer Memory

Memory is arranged inside a computer in a very long sequence of bits. That is, places where a phenomenon can be set and detected.

Analogy: Sidewalk Memory. To illustrate how memory works, imagine a sidewalk made of a strip of concrete with lines (expansion joints) across it forming squares, and suppose it has been swept clean. We agree that a stone on a sidewalk square corresponds to 1 and the absence of a stone corresponds to 0. This makes the sidewalk a sequence of bits (see Figure 8.5.) Sidewalk memory can encode information just like computer memory. It's just not as economical with space!

Figure 8.5. Sidewalk sections as a sequence of bits (1010 0010).

The bits can be set to write information into the memory, and they can be sensed to read the information out of the memory. To write a 1, the phenomenon must be made to be present; for example, put a stone on a sidewalk square. To write a 0, the phenomenon must be made to be absent; for example, sweep the sidewalk square clean. To determine what information is stored at a specific position, check whether the phenomenon is present or absent. So, if a stone is on a square, the phenomenon is present (1); otherwise, it is absent (0).

Alternative PandA Encodings.   There is no limit to the number of ways to encode two states using physical phenomena, of course. Remaining in the world of sidewalks, we can use stones on all squares, but use white stones and black stones for the two states. We can choose black as present and not black as absent. Or, we can use multiple stones of two colors per square, saying that more white stones than black means 1 and more black stones than white means 0. (We must take care that the total number of stones on each sidewalk square is always odd.) Or we can place a stone in the center of the square for one state and off center for the other state. And so forth. These are all PandA encodings, provided the "phenomenon" is chosen properly: presence of black, presence of majority of white, and presence of a centered stone.

fit **BYTE**   **No Barking.** Sherlock Holmes uses one bit of information to solve the disappearance of a prize racehorse in the story "Silver Blaze." In the vicinity of the stable during the night (place and time), the phenomenon (barking watchdog) was not detected (absent), implying to Holmes the dog knew the thief, who had to be Simpson, the owner. Holmes reasons that barking "present" implies the thief is not known to the household; barking "absent" implies the opposite. There is information present even though the phenomenon is absent.

Combining Bit Patterns.   Like the sides of a die, the two bit patterns alone give us a limited resource for digitizing information. That is, we can represent things with only two values: votes (*aye, nay*), personality types (*A, B*), baseball games (*won, loss*). Usually the two patterns must be combined into sequences to create enough symbols to encode the intended information. As we learned in the last section, if there are $p = 2$ patterns, as in the PandA representation, arranged into n-length sequences, we can create 2^n symbols. Table 8.2 relates the length of the bit sequence to the number of possible symbols.

Table 8.2. Number of symbols when the number
of possible patterns is two

n	2^n	Symbols
1	2^1	2
2	2^2	4
3	2^3	8
4	2^4	16
5	2^5	32
6	2^6	64
7	2^7	128
8	2^8	256
9	2^9	512
10	2^{10}	1024

The 16 symbols of $n = 4$ length bit sequences are shown in Table 8.3.

The PandA encoding is the fundamental representation of information. By grouping bits together, we can produce enough symbols to represent any number of values. By creating symbols using the two PandA patterns, we can record and transform information using resources from the physical world. Information and computation are abstract concepts without physical form, but with the miracle of IT they can become real. Our lives are simplified when machines and networks do the work.

Table 8.3. Sixteen symbols of the 4-bit PandA representation

Symbol	Binary	Physical Bits	Hex	Symbol	Binary	Physical Bits	Hex
AAAA	0000		0	PAAA	1000		8
AAAP	0001		1	PAAP	1001		9
AAPA	0010		2	PAPA	1010		A
AAPP	0011		3	PAPP	1011		B
APAA	0100		4	PPAA	1100		C
APAP	0101		5	PPAP	1101		D
APPA	0110		6	PPPA	1110		E
APPP	0111		7	PPPP	1111		F

HEX EXPLAINED

Before using PandA to represent text, let's solve a mystery from Chapter 4. Recall that when we specified custom colors in HTML—`<font color="#FF8E2A">`, as shown in Figure 4.2—we used **hex digits**, short for hexadecimal digits, or base-16. We didn't explain hex at the time, but we presented Table 4.4 so we could convert back and forth between decimal and hexadecimal.

The reason for using hexadecimal is as follows. When we specify an RGB color or other encoding using bits, we must give the bits in order. The bit sequence might be given in 0's and 1's,

`<font color="#111111110011000111000101010">` *Illegal HTML tag*

but writing so many 0's and 1's is tedious and error prone. Computer professionals long ago realized that they needed a better way to write bit sequences, so they began to use hexadecimal digits.

The 16 Hex Digits

The digits of hex are 0, 1, . . . , 9, A, B, C, D, E, F. Because there are 16 digits—maybe we should call them hexits—they can be represented perfectly by the 16 symbols of 4-bit sequences. In Table 8.3, the binary and hex are given for each value. So bit sequence 0000 is hex 0, bit sequence 0001 is hex 1, and so forth, up to the bit sequence 1111, which is hex F. (This is simply a numeric interpretation of the bits, which will be explained in Chapter 11.)

Changing Hex Digits to Bits and Back Again

Because each hex digit corresponds to a 4-bit sequence, and vice versa, we can translate between hex and binary easily: given hex, write the associated groups of 4 bits. Given a sequence of bits, group them into sequences of four, and write the corresponding hex digit. Thus,

`0010 1011 1010 1101 = 2BAD`

and

`FAB4 = 1111 1010 1011 0100`

So, in HTML when we specify the color white as `"#FFFFFF"`, we effectively set each bit of the RGB specification bits to 1.

---

try it

What is ABE8 BEEF as a bit sequence? To find the answer, check out Table 8.3. Find each letter in the hex column, and write the corresponding 4-bit sequence from the binary column. For example, A is in the second column and corresponds to the bits: 1010.

Answer: 1010 1011 1110 1000 1011 1110 1110 1111

DIGITIZING TEXT

The two earliest uses of the PandA representation—or binary representation when 1 and 0 are numeric—were to encode numbers and keyboard characters. These two applications are still extremely important, but now representations for sound, images, video, and other types of information are almost as important. In this section we talk about how text is encoded; we'll discuss how the other forms of information are encoded in Chapter 11.

Remember that the number of bits determines the number of symbols available for representing values: n bits in sequence yield 2^n symbols. And, as we've learned, the more characters we want encoded, the more symbols we need. Roman letters, Arabic numerals, and about a dozen punctuation characters are about the minimum needed to digitize English text. We would also like to have uppercase and lowercase letters, and the basic arithmetic symbols like +, −, *, /, and =. But, where should the line be drawn? Should characters not required for English but useful in other languages like German (ö), French (é), Spanish (ñ), and Norwegian (ø) be included? What about Czech, Greek, Arabic, Thai, or Cantonese? Should other languages' punctuation be included, like French (« ») and Spanish (¿)? Should arithmetic symbols include degrees (°), pi (π), relational symbols ($\leq$), equivalence ($\equiv$), and for all ($\forall$)? What about business symbols: ¢, £, ¥, ©, and ®? What about unprintable characters like backspace and new line? Should there be a symbol for smiley faces (☺)? Some of these questions are easier to answer than others. We want to keep the list small so that we use fewer bits, but not being able to represent critical characters would be a mistake.

Assigning Symbols

The 26 uppercase and 26 lowercase Roman letters, the 10 Arabic numerals, a basic set of 20 punctuation characters (including blank), 10 useful arithmetic characters, and 3 nonprintable characters (new line, tab, backspace) can be represented with 95 symbols. Such a set is enough for English and is accessible using the keys on a basic computer keyboard. To represent 95 distinct symbols, we need 7 bits because 6 bits gives only $2^6 - 64$ symbols. Seven bits give $2^7 = 128$ symbols, which is more than we need for the 95 different characters. Some special control characters must also be represented. These control characters are used for data transmission and other engineering purposes. They are assigned to the remaining 33 of the 7-bit symbols.

An early and still widely used 7-bit code for the characters is **ASCII**, pronounced AS·key. ASCII stands for American Standard Code for Information Interchange. The advantages of a "standard" are many: computer parts built by different manufacturers can be connected, programs can create data and store it so that different programs can process it later, and so forth. In all cases, there must be an agreement as to which character is associated with which symbol (bit sequence).

Extended ASCII: An 8-bit Code

As the name implies, ASCII was developed in the United States. By the mid-1960s, it became clear that 7-bit ASCII was not enough because it could not fully represent text from languages other than English. So IBM, the dominant computer manufacturer at the time, decided to use the next larger set of symbols, the 8-bit symbols, as the standard for character representation. Eight bits produce $2^8 = 256$

symbols, enough to encode English and the Western European languages, their punctuation characters, and a large set of other useful characters. The larger, improved encoding was called **Extended ASCII**, as shown in Figure 8.6. The original ASCII is the "first half" of Extended ASCII; that is, 7-bit ASCII is the 8-bit ASCII representation with the leftmost bit set to 0. Though Extended ASCII does not handle all natural languages, it does handle many languages that derived from the Latin alphabet. Handling other languages is solved in two ways: recoding the second half of Extended ASCII for the language's other characters, and using the 16-bit Unicode representation.

IBM's move to 8 bits was bold because it added the extra bit at a time when computer memory and storage were extremely expensive. IBM gave 8-bit sequences a

ASCII	0000	0001	0010	0011	0100	0101	0110	0111	1000	1001	1010	1011	1100	1101	1110	1111
0000	Nu	Sh	Sx	Ex	Et	Eq	Ak	Bl	Bs	Ht	Lf	Yt	Ff	Cr	So	Si
0001	Dl	D1	D2	D3	D4	Nk	Sy	EΣ	Cn	Em	Sb	Ec	Fs	Gs	Rs	Us
0010		!	"	#	$	%	&	'	(	)	*	+	,	-	.	/
0011	0	1	2	3	4	5	6	7	8	9	:	;	<	=	>	?
0100	@	A	B	C	D	E	F	G	H	I	J	K	L	M	N	O
0101	P	Q	R	S	T	U	V	W	X	Y	Z	[	\	]	^	_
0110	`	a	b	c	d	e	f	g	h	i	j	k	l	m	n	o
0111	p	q	r	s	t	u	v	w	x	y	z	{	|	}	~	Dt
1000	80	81	82	83	In	Nl	Ss	Es	Hs	Hj	Ys	Pd	Pv	Ri	S2	S3
1001	Dc	P1	Pz	Se	Cc	Mm	Sp	Ep	Q8	Qq	Qa	Cs	St	Os	Pm	Ap
1010	Ao	¡	¢	£		¥	¦	§	¨	©	♀	«	¬		®	¯
1011	°	±	²	³	´	µ	¶	·	¸	¹	♂	»	¼	½	¾	¿
1100	À	Á	Â	Ã	Ä	Å	Æ	Ç	È	É	Ê	Ë	Ì	Í	Î	Ï
1101	Ð	Ñ	Ò	Ó	Ô	Õ	Ö	×	Ø	Ù	Ú	Û	Ü	Ý	Þ	ß
1110	à	á	â	ã	ä	å	æ	ç	è	é	ê	ë	ì	í	î	ï
1111	ð	ñ	ò	ó	ô	õ	ö	÷	ø	ù	ú	û	ü	ý	þ	ÿ

Figure 8.6. ASCII, The American Standard Code for Information Interchange.

Note: The original 7-bit ASCII is the top half of the table; the whole table is known as Extended ASCII (ISO/IEC8859-1). The 8-bit symbol for a letter is the four row bits followed by the four column bits (e.g., female (♀) = 10101010, while male (♂) = 10111010). Characters shown as two small letters are control symbols used to encode nonprintable information (e.g., **Bs** = 00001000 is backspace). The bottom half of the table represents characters needed by Western European languages, such as Icelandic's eth (ð) and thorn (Þ).

special name, **byte**, and adopted it as a standard unit for computer memory. Bytes are still the standard unit of memory, and their "8-ness" is noticeable in many places. For example, recent computers are "32-bit machines"—not 30-bit or 35-bit—so their data paths (the part that processes most instructions) can handle 4 bytes at a time.

*fit***BYTE** | **The Ultimate.** Though ASCII and its variations are widely used, the more complete solution is a 16-bit representation, called *Unicode*. With 65,536 symbols, Unicode can handle *all* languages.

ASCII Coding of Phone Numbers

Let's return to the phone number, 888 555 1212, whose representation concerned us at the start of the chapter. How would a computer represent this phone number in its memory? Remember, this is not really a number, but rather, it is a keying sequence for a telephone's keypad represented by numerals; it is not necessary, or even desirable, to represent the phone number as a numerical quantity. Because each of the numerals has a representation in Extended ASCII, we can express the phone number by encoding each digit with a byte. The encoding is easy: Find each numeral in Figure 8.7, and write down the bit sequence from its row, followed by the bit sequence from its column. So the phone number 888 555 1212 in ASCII is

```
0011 1000 0011 1000 0011 1000
0011 0101 0011 0101 0011 0101
0011 0001 0011 0010 0011 0001 0011 0010
```

You can use Figure 8.7 to check this encoding. This is exactly how computers represent phone numbers. The encoding seems somewhat redundant because each byte has the same left half: 0011. The left halves are repeated because all of the numerals are located on the 0011 row of the ASCII table. If only phone numbers had to be represented, fewer bits could be used, of course. But there is little reason to be so economical, so we adopt the standard ASCII.

*fit***BYTE** | **Two bits, four bits . . .** The term *byte* has motivated some people to call 4 bits—that is, half a byte—a *nibble*.

Notice that we have run all of the digits of the phone number together, even though when we write them for ourselves we usually put spaces between the area code and exchange code, and between the exchange code and the number. The computer doesn't care, but it might matter to users. It's easy to add these spaces and other punctuation.

> **try it**
>
> Encode the phone number (888) 555-1212 in Extended ASCII, that is, insert the punctuation. (Notice that there is a space before the first 5.)
>
> To find the answer, locate each character in Figure 8.7 and write the four bits at the left of the row and the four bits at the top of the column. For example, the open parenthesis (is in the third row and corresponds to 0010 1000.
>
> *Answer:*
>
> 0010 1000 0011 1000 0011 1000 0011 1000 0010 1001
> 0010 0000 0011 0101 0011 0101 0011 0101 0010 1101
> 0011 0001 0011 0010 0011 0001 0011 0010

NATO Broadcast Alphabet

Finally, although we usually try to be efficient (use shortest symbol sequences) to minimize the amount of memory needed to store and transmit information, not all letter representations should be short. The code for the letters used in radio communication is purposely inefficient in this sense, so they are distinctive when spoken amid noise. The NATO broadcast alphabet, shown in Table 8.4, encodes letters as words; that is, the words are the symbols, replacing the standard spoken names for the letters. For example, *Mike* and *November* replace "em" and "en," which can be hard to tell apart. This longer encoding improves the chances letters will be recognized when spoken under less-than-ideal conditions. The digits keep their usual names, except nine, which is frequently replaced by *niner*.

Table 8.4. NATO broadcast alphabet designed not to be minimal

A	Alpha	H	Hotel	O	Oscar	V	Victor
B	Bravo	I	India	P	Papa	W	Whiskey
C	Charlie	J	Juliet	Q	Quebec	X	X-ray
D	Delta	K	Kilo	R	Romeo	Y	Yankee
E	Echo	L	Lima	S	Sierra	Z	Zulu
F	Foxtrot	M	Mike	T	Tango		
G	Golf	N	November	U	Uniform		

*fit*BYTE

It's Greek to Me. There are dozens of phonetic alphabets for English and many other languages. The NATO alphabet, used for air traffic control, begins with "alpha," raising the question, "What is the first letter of the Greek phonetic alphabet?" Alexandros.

THE *OXFORD ENGLISH DICTIONARY*

Representations like Extended ASCII encode text directly, 8 bits per letter, with more characters available by using the escape technique. But most documents have more than just text. For example, one might need to format information, such as font, font size, justification, etc. We could add formatting characters to ASCII—for example, Escape A might represent the Times Roman font—but this is a poor idea for several reasons. The most serious problem is that it mixes the content (i.e., the text) with the description of its form. The descriptive information (**metadata**) specifies the content's formatting or structure, and should be kept separate from the text. So, we specify metadata by using tags, as we have seen in the searching discussion (see Chapter 2) and HTML (see Chapter 4). Tags use the same character representation as the content itself, which simplifies the encoding, and they are much more versatile. In this section, we illustrate how tags encode the structure of a document, by describing the digitization of the *Oxford English Dictionary*.

Using Tags to Encode

The *Oxford English Dictionary* is the definitive reference for every English word's meaning, etymology, and usage. Because it is comprehensive, the *OED* is truly monumental. The printed version is 20 volumes, weighs 150 pounds, and fills 4 feet of shelf space. In 1857, the Philological Society of London established the goal of producing a complete list of all English words. They expected that the completed dictionary would comprise 6400 pages in four volumes. By 1884, with the list completed only up to *ant*, it became clear to James Murray, the lexicographer in charge, that the effort was much more ambitious than they originally thought. The first edition, completed in 1928, long after Murray's death, filled 15,490 pages and contained 252,200 entries. In 1984, the conversion of the *OED* to digital form began.

Now imagine that you have typed in the entire *OED* as a long sequence of ASCII characters from A through the end of the definition for *Zyxt*, the last word in English. That task would take one person about 120 years. The result would be a digitized dictionary, but in the form of a very long sequence of ASCII characters. Would a computer be able to help us use it?

Suppose we want to find the definition for the verb *set*, which is notable for having the longest entry in the *OED*. The searching software—as described in Chapter 2—would look for *s-e-t* and find it thousands of times. This is because *set* is part of many words, like clo*set*, hor*set*ail, and *set*tle, and *set* is used in many definitions, for example, "*match-point* in tennis is the final score ending the present game, *set,* and match."

We can solve the first problem—avoiding *s-e-t* within words—by ignoring all occurrences that do not have a punctuation character or space before and after the *s-e-t*. The software can do that. But how does it find the definition for *set* among the thousands of true occurrences of the word *set* in other definitions? The software processing the text file, unable to understand the dictionary's contents, would have no clue which one it is.

People use a number of cues to find information in the dictionary, such as alphabetic order and the fact that a new definition begins on a new line, and the defined word is printed in bold. Though we could insert HTML-like tags for new lines or boldface type, a better solution is to use the tags to describe the *structure* of the dictionary's content. That is, incorporate meta-data.

Structure Tags

A special set of tags was developed to specify the *OED*'s **structure**. For example, `<hw>` is the *OED*'s tag for a *headword*, the word being defined. As usual, because tags surround the text like parentheses, there is a closing *headword* tag, `</hw>`. Thus, the place in the *OED* where the verb *set* is defined appears in the tagged text file of the dictionary as

`<hw>set</hw>`

Other tags label the pronunciation `<pr>`, the phonetic notations `<ph>`, the parts of speech `<ps>`, the homonym number `<hm>` for headwords that sound the same, and so forth. There are also tags to group items, such as `<e>` to surround an entire entry and `<hg>` to surround a head group (that is, all of the information at the start of a definition). In the *OED* the first entry for the verb set begins

set (sɛt), *v.*[1]

giving the word being defined, the pronunciation, the part of speech (verb), and the homonym number (1). We expect it must be tagged as

`<e><hg><hw>set</hw>  <pr><ph>s&epsilont</ph></pr>,  <ps>v</ps>.`
`<hm>1</hm></hg>`

Notice the use of the escape code (`&epsilon`) for the epsilon character in the pronunciation. Also, the `</e>` is not shown because it must be at the very end of the entry.

With the structure tags in the dictionary, software can find the definition of the verb *set* easily: Search for occurrences of `<hw>set</hw>`, which indicate a definition for set, check within its head group for `<ps>v</ps>`, which indicates that it is a verb form of set being defined, and then print out (formatted) all of the text within the `<e>`, `</e>` tags.

Of course, the tags do not print. They are included only to specify the structure, so the computer knows what part of the dictionary it is looking at. But in fact, structure tags are very useful for formatting. For example, the boldface type used for headwords can be automatically applied when the dictionary is printed based on the `<hw>` tag. In a similar way, the italics typeface can be applied in the part of speech. The parentheses surrounding the pronunciation and the superscript for the homonym number are also generated automatically. Thus, knowing the structure makes it possible to generate the formatting information.

The opposite is not true. That is, formatting tags do not usually tell us enough about a document to allow us to know its structure. In the *OED* example, though boldface is used for headwords, it is also used for other purposes, meaning that just because a word is boldface does not mean it is a headword. In fact, because some formatting information, like italics, has both structural and nonstructural occurrences, the *OED* digitization includes some formatting information with the structural information. The structure is more important, but most complex documents use both types of tags.

Sample *OED* Entry

Figure 8.7 shows the entry for *byte*, together with its representation, as it actually appears in the file of the online *OED*. At first the form looks very cluttered, but if you compare it with the printed form, you can make sense of the tags. The tags specify the role of each word of the dictionary. So, for example, to find the first

---

byte (baIt). *Computers*. [Arbitrary, prob. influenced by <u>bit</u> sb.[1] and <u>bite</u> sb.] A group of eight consecutive bits operated on as a unit in a computer.

1964 *Blaauw* & *Brooks* in *IBM Systems Jrnl.* III. 122 An 8-bit unit of information is fundamental to most of the formats [of the System/360]. A consecutive group of *n* such units constitutes a field of length *n*. Fixed-length fields of length one, two, four, and eight are termed bytes, halfwords, words, and double words respectively. **1964** *IBM Jrnl. Res. & Developm.* VIII. 97/1 When a byte of data appears from an I/O device, the CPU is seized, dumped, used and restored. **1967 *P. A. Stark*** *Digital Computer Programming* xix. 351 The normal operations in fixed point are done on four bytes at a time. **1968** *Dataweek* 24 Jan. 1/1 Tape reading and writing is at from 34,160 to 192,000 bytes per second.

```
<e><hg><hw>byte</hw> <pr><ph>baIt</ph></pr></hg>. <la> Computers</la>. <etym>
Arbitrary, prob. influenced by <xr><x>bit</x></xr> <ps>n.<hm>4</hm></ps>and
<xr><x>bite</x> <ps>n.</ps></xr></etym> <s4>A group of eight consecutive bits
operated on as a unit in a computer.</s4><qp><q><qd>1964</qd><a>Blaauw</a>
&amp. <a>Brooks</a><bib>in</bib> <w>IBM Systems Jrnl.</w> <lc>III.122</lc>
<qt>An 8-bit unit of information is fundamental to most of the formats <ed>of
the System/360</ed>.&es.A consecutive group of <i>n</i> such units
constitutes a field of length <i>n</i>.&es.Fixed-length fields of length one,
two, four, and eight are termed bytes, halfwords, words, and double words
respectively. </qt></q><q><qd>1964</qd> <w>IBM Jrnl. Res. &amp. Developm.
</w> <lc>VIII. 97/1</lc> <qt>When a byte of data appears from an I/O device,
the CPU is seized, dumped, used and restored.</qt></q><q><qd>1967</qd> <a>P.
A. Stark</a> <w>Digital Computer Programming</w> <lc>xix. 351</lc> <qt>The
normal operations in fixed point are done on four bytes at a time.</qt></q>
<q><qd> 1968</qd> <w> Dataweek</w> <lc>24 Jan. 1/1</lc> <qt>Tape reading and
writing is at from 34,160 to 192,000 bytes per second.</qt></q></qp></e>
```

Figure 8.7. *The OED entry for the word* byte, *together with the representation of the entry in its digitized form with tags.*

time the word byte was used in print, the software searches for `<hw>byte</hw>`, then looks for the quote date tags, `<qd>,</qd>`, to find that the first use of the word was in 1964. Structure tags help the software help the user.

Because the tag characters are included with the content characters, they increase the size of the file compared with plain text. The entry for *byte* is 841 characters, but the tagged code is 1204 characters, almost a 50 percent increase.

Why "Byte"?

As informative as the *OED* definition is, it doesn't answer that nagging question: Why is *byte* spelled with a *y*? To understand the charming nature of the answer, we need to know that computer memory is subject to errors (a zero changing to a one, or a one to a zero), caused by such things as cosmic rays. Really. It doesn't happen often, but often enough to worry computer engineers, who build special circuitry to detect and correct memory errors. They often add extra bits to the memory to help detect errors—for example, a ninth bit per byte can detect errors using parity.

Parity refers to whether a number is even or odd. To encode bytes using **even parity**, we use the normal byte encoding, e.g., *1010 0010*, and then count the number of 1's in the byte. If there is an even number of 1's, we set the ninth bit to 0; if there is an odd number, we set the ninth bit to 1, e.g., *1010 0010 1*. The result is that all 9-bit groups have even parity, either because they were even to begin with and the 0 didn't change that, or they were odd to begin with, but the 1 made them even. Any single bit error in a group causes its parity to become odd, allowing the hardware to detect that an error has occurred, although it can't detect which bit is wrong.

So, why is *byte* spelled with a *y*? The answer comes from Werner Buchholz, the inventor of the word and the concept. In the late 1950s, Buchholz was the project manager and architect for the IBM supercomputer, called Stretch. For that machine, he explained to me, "We needed a word for a quantity of memory between a bit and a word." (A "word" of computer memory is typically the amount required to represent computer instructions; on modern computers, a word is 32 bits.) Buchholz continued, "It seemed that after 'bit' comes 'bite.' But we changed the 'i' to a 'y' so that a typist couldn't accidentally change 'byte' into 'bit' by the single error of dropping the 'e'." No single letter change to *byte* can create *bit*, and vice versa. Buchholz and his engineers were so concerned with memory errors that he invented an error-detecting *name* for the memory unit!

SUMMARY

We began the chapter by learning that digitizing doesn't require digits—any symbols will do. We explored:

> Problems of encoding keyboard characters and solved them by using sequences of dice, assigning a special escape symbol, and deciding not to encode certain characters.

> PandA encoding, which is based on the Presence and Absence of a physical phenomenon. Their patterns are discrete; they form the basic unit of a bit. Their names (most often 1 and 0) can be any pair of opposite terms.

> 7-bit ASCII, an early assignment of bit sequences (symbols) to keyboard characters. Extended or 8-bit ASCII is now the standard.

> How documents like the *Oxford English Dictionary* are digitized. We learned that tags associate meta-data with every part of the *OED*. Using that data, a computer can easily help us find words and other information.

> The mystery of the y in *byte*.

EXERCISES

Multiple Choice

1. Without an escape sequence, a pair of dice can encode _____ symbols and three dice can encode _____ symbols.
   A. 36, 72
   B. 36, 256
   C. 36, 216
   D. 72, 216

2. How many characters could be represented by two eight-sided dice?
   A. 16
   B. 36
   C. 64
   D. 256

3. Which of the following is not an example of an escape key?
   A. Ctrl
   B. Alt
   C. Shift
   D. Tab

4. Using just the letter keys and the Shift, Alt, and Ctrl modifier keys, how many possible combinations are there?
   A. 29
   B. 78
   C. 104
   D. 256

5. Which of these is not digital?
   A. a clock with hands
   B. a calendar
   C. a checkbook balance
   D. a television channel

6. PandA is a combination of
   A. true and false
   B. on and off
   C. yes and no
   D. all of the above

7. Finish this: I like cats. Fluffy is a cat. Therefore
   A. Fluffy is not a dog.
   B. I don't like dogs.
   C. Cats don't like dogs.
   D. I like Fluffy.

8. A binary system
   A. consists of only two possible items
   B. uses discrete data
   C. can be represented by PandA
   D. all of the above

9. The medium used for storing data on a CD is made from
   A. iron
   B. plastic
   C. magnetism
   D. light

10. On the computer, the word PandA is represented by
    A. 1 and 0
    B. 0 and 1
    C. bytes
    D. off and on

Short Answer

1. If bits are to atoms, bytes are to _____.

2. To _____ is to represent information with digits.

3. PandA is short for _____.

4. When data are _____, they are separate and distinct and cannot be transformed into another value by gradations.

5. A(n) _____ is an agreed upon order for basic symbols.

6. A(n) _____ is another name for a separator.

7. A(n) _____ is a character that is not a letter, numeral, or punctuation character.

8. All the values in a PandA formulation are _____.

9. _____ is short for binary digit.

10. The _____ of a bit is its storage pattern in the physical world.

11. _____ is short for hexadecimal.

12. Base-16 is also called _____.

13. Letters, numbers, and symbols are represented on the computer using the _____.

14. All computer systems share a _____ set of symbols used to represent characters.

Exercises

1. Make a list of the numbers you use that are not treated as numbers. (For example, you do not perform math on them.)

2. What is a bit and how was the word created?

3. What does PandA stand for and what does PandA name?

4. Come up with a list of ten different PandA items.

5. What North American telephone number is: ▲ ‖ ‖ ◀ ◀ ■ ▲ ◖◀ ‖ ‖ ?

6. Encode (888) 555-1212 in Extended ASCII, including punctuation.

7. You bought a mosaic coffee table in Santorini, Greece, last summer called "Animals of Atlantis." While listening to a boring story about your friend's visit home, you notice the table is eight tiles across, which could be the bits of a byte. What ASCII message did the Greeks encode, using the obvious PandA encoding?

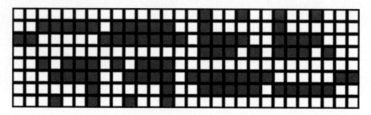

8. The Hawaiian alphabet has 18 symbols. Discuss the symbols you would use for their character set and how many bits would be needed for it.

9. Translate the following hexadecimal into binary and then into English.

   68   65   78   61   64   65   63   69   6D   61   6C

10. Change the letters of the sentence "THE APPLE LOGO HAS A BYTE MISSING" into NATO broadcast code (ignore spaces in all cases) and then represent the result with ASCII. How many bytes are required for each?

9

FOLLOWING INSTRUCTIONS

Principles of Computer Operation

learning objectives

> Describe how the Fetch/Execute Cycle works, listing the five steps

> Explain the function of the memory, control unit, ALU, input unit and output unit, and program counter

> Explain why integration and photolithography are important in integrated circuits

> Discuss the purpose of an operating system

> Describe how large tasks are performed with simple instructions

FOLLOWING INSTRUCTIONS
Principles of Computer Operation

chapter 9

> *Where . . . ENIAC is equipped with 18,000 vacuum tubes and weighs 30 tons, computers in the future may have 1,000 vacuum tubes and perhaps weigh just one-half ton.*
>
> —POPULAR MECHANICS, 1949

> *There is no reason why anyone would want to have a computer in their home.*
>
> —KEN OLSEN, PRESIDENT OF DIGITAL EQUIPMENT CORPORATION, 1977

THIS CHAPTER introduces two key inventions in information technology that rank among the top technological achievements of all time: computers and integrated circuits (ICs). They are both complex and sophisticated topics, so specialized in fact, that a Ph.D. degree is not sufficient training to understand current technologies fully. Making today's computers and chips requires large teams of specialists. If an individual expert can't completely understand computers and integrated circuits, is there hope for the rest of us?

Both topics are based on easy-to-understand ideas. Pushing the basic ideas to their limit makes the technology complex and sophisticated, and that is definitely beyond our needs. But we should learn the main ideas, because the same basic instruction execution processes used by computers pop up in information technology. Web browsers process Web pages using instruction execution that is just like a computer's operation. Spreadsheets use the same ideas. You operate as an instruction executer when you prepare your income taxes. This idea is fundamental to processing information and a key concept of IT.

First, we discuss the Fetch/Execute Cycle. Second, we describe the parts of a computer, how they're connected, and briefly, what each does. Then we outline how these parts execute instructions. We give a detailed example that shows that computers operate straightforwardly. Next, we discuss software and operating systems to explain how a computer's primitive abilities can achieve impressive results. Finally, we explain the "big ideas" behind integrated circuits and how semiconductor technology works.

INSTRUCTION EXECUTION ENGINES

Before dissecting a computer, consider what a computer actually does. The obvious answer, "It computes," doesn't say very much, because "computing" mostly involves software, not hardware.

What Computers Can Do

Computers deterministically perform or execute instructions to process information. We can describe a computer as an "instruction execution engine." The most important aspect of this definition is that a computer does what it is told—it follows instructions—so someone or something else must decide what those instructions are. Programmers do that, of course. If the instructions don't work, it's not the computer's fault because the computer simply follows the programmed instructions.

What Computers Can't Do

A key feature of the definition is the term *deterministically*. When it's time for the computer to determine which instruction to execute next, it's required by its construction to execute a specific instruction based only on the program and the data it's been given. It has no options. As compared to people, computers are very methodical:

> Computers have no imagination or creativity.

> Computers have no intuition.

> Computers are literal, with no sense of irony, subtlety, proportion, or decorum.

> Computers don't joke or have a sense of humor.

> Computers are not vindictive or cruel. (Some frustrated users will find these assertions far-fetched.)

> Computers are not purposeful.

> Computers have no free will.

Computers only execute instructions. Deterministically. Consequently, rerunning a program with the same data produces exactly the same result every time.

*fit*BYTE

World Domination. During the 1950s and 1960s, as computers were leaving the lab and entering business, there was concern in the popular press about "computers taking over the world." People worried because computers could do some tasks amazingly well, for example, they could add 100,000 numbers in one second. There were grim stories of tyrannical computers enslaving people. But when it finally happened—when life as most people knew it *depended* on computers—no one apparently noticed.

{GREAT *fit* MOMENTS}

No. 1 Computer >>

Credit for inventing the first electronic computer is in dispute, but most people give the credit to J. Presper Eckert and John Mauchley of the University of Pennsylvania. Named **ENIAC** for Electronic Numerical Integrator And Calculator, the Eckert/Mauchley machine was built for the U.S. Army in 1946. ENIAC is in many ways the intellectual antecedent of current computers. Another academic, John V. Atanasoff of Iowa State University, developed ideas used by Eckert and Mauchley, and at about the same time, built the Atanasoff Berry Computer **(ABC)**, with graduate student Clifford E. Berry. In an epic patent infringement lawsuit, Judge Earl Larson decided on October 19, 1973 that Atanasoff's prior invention invalidated the Eckert/Mauchley patent.

Clockwise from top left: J. Presper Eckert and John Mauchley, John V. Atanasoff, Clifford E. Berry, the ENIAC with operators.

● THE FETCH/EXECUTE CYCLE

Calling a computer an "instruction execution engine" suggests the idea of a machine cycling through a series of operations, performing an instruction on each round. And that's pretty much the idea. Computers implement in hardware a process called the **Fetch/Execute Cycle**. The Fetch/Execute Cycle consists of getting the instruction, figuring out what to do, gathering the data needed to do it, doing it, saving the result, and repeating. It's a simple process, but repeating it billions of times a second accomplishes a lot.

A Five-Step Cycle

The five steps of the Fetch/Execute Cycle have standard names, and because these operations are repeated in a never ending sequence, they are often written with an arrow from the last step to the first showing the cycle (see Figure 9.1). The step names suggest the operations described in the previous paragraph. But the Fetch/Execute Cycle is a little more complicated than that. What is an instruction like? How is the next instruction located? When instructions and data are fetched, where are they fetched from, and where do they go?

```
Instruction Fetch (IF)
Instruction Decode (ID)
Data Fetch (DF)
Instruction Execution (EX)
Result Return (RR)
```

Figure 9.1. The Fetch/Execute Cycle.

● ANATOMY OF A COMPUTER

To understand how the Fetch/Execute Cycle works, we must understand how a computer's parts are arranged to fetch and execute instructions. All computers, regardless of their implementing technology, have five basic parts or subsystems: memory, control unit, arithmetic/logic unit (ALU), input unit, and output unit. These are arranged as shown in Figure 9.2. *Note:* It is just a coincidence that there are five steps to the Fetch/Execute Cycle and five subsystems to a computer—they're related, of course, but not one-to-one.

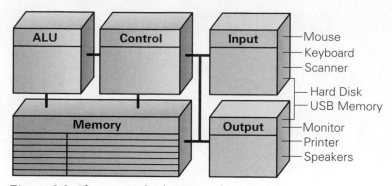

Figure 9.2. The principal subsystems of a computer.

The five subsystems of a computer have the following characteristics.

Memory

Memory stores both the program while it is running and the data on which the program operates. Memory has the following properties:

> **Discrete locations.** Memory is organized as a sequence of discrete locations, like apartment building mailboxes. In modern memory, each location is composed of 1 byte (that is, a sequence of 8 bits).

> **Addresses.** Every memory location has an address, like a mailbox, although computer memory addresses are whole numbers starting at 0.

> **Values.** Memory locations record or store values, like a mailbox holds a letter.

> **Finite capacity.** Memory locations have finite capacity (limited size). So programmers must keep in mind that the data may not "fit" in the memory location.

Byte-Size Memory Location.   These features motivate a commonly used diagram of computer memory (see Figure 9.3). The discrete locations are represented as boxes. The address of each location is displayed above the box. The value or contents of the memory locations are shown in the boxes.

0	1	2	3	4	5	6	7	8	9	10	11	
100	T	h	a	N	K	$	*	4	ƀ	d	a	...

Figure 9.3. Diagram of computer memory illustrating its key properties.

The 1-byte size of a memory location is enough to store one ASCII character (letter, numeral, or punctuation symbol), or a number less than 256. Therefore, a single computer memory location has very limited capacity. To overcome this limitation, programmers simply use a sequence of memory locations, and ignore the fact that they all have separate addresses; that is, programmers treat the address of the first location as if it were the address of the whole block of memory. For example, blocks of 4 bytes are used as a unit so frequently that they are called memory **words**.

Random Access Memory. Computer memory is called **random access memory** (RAM). The modifier "random access" is out-of-date and simply means that the computer can refer to the memory locations in any order. RAM is most often measured in megabytes (MB). A large memory is preferable to a small memory because there is more space for programs and data.

fit BYTE

> **Free Memory.** *Mega-* is the prefix for "million," so a megabyte should be 1,000,000 bytes of memory. In fact, a megabyte is 1,048,576 bytes. Why such a weird number? Computers need to associate 1 byte of memory with every address. A million addresses require 20 bits. But with 20 bits, $2^{20} = 1,048,576$ addresses are possible with binary counting. So, to ensure that every 20-bit address is allocated 1 byte of memory, the extra 48,576 bytes are included "free."

In summary, memory is like a sequence of labeled containers known as locations: The address is the location's number in sequence; the value or the information stored at the location is the container's contents; and only so much can fit in each container.

Control Unit

The **control unit** of a computer is the hardware implementation of the Fetch/Execute Cycle. Its circuitry fetches an instruction from memory and performs the other operations of the Fetch/Execute Cycle on it.

Computer instructions are much more primitive than the commands we give computers from GUIs. A typical machine instruction has the form

```
ADD 4000, 2000, 2080
```

which appears to command that three numbers, 2000, 2080, and 4000, are added together, *but it does not*. Instead, the instruction asks that the two numbers stored in the memory locations 2000 and 2080 are added together, and that the result is stored in the memory location 4000. So the Data Fetch step of the Fetch/Execute Cycle must get the two values at memory locations 2000 and 2080, and after they are added, the Result Return step stores the answer in memory location 4000.

We must emphasize a fundamental property of computer instructions. The instruction

```
ADD 4000, 2000, 2080
```

does not command the computer to add the numbers 2000 and 2080—the answer is 4080 and it is pointless to program a computer to do a task that we know the answer to. Rather, the instruction commands the computer to add the numbers *stored in memory locations* 2000 and 2080, whatever those numbers are. Because different values are in those memory locations each time the computer executes the instruction, a different result is computed each time. The concept is that computer instructions encode the memory addresses of the numbers to be added (or subtracted or whatever), not the numbers themselves, and so they refer to the values *indirectly*. The indirection means that a single instruction can combine any two numbers simply by placing them in the referenced memory locations (see Figure 9.4). Referring to a value by referring to the address in memory where it is stored is fundamental to a computer's versatility.

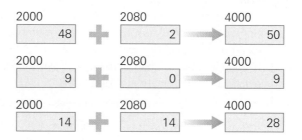

Figure 9.4. *Illustration of a single ADD instruction producing different results depending on the contents of the memory locations referenced in the instruction.*

Arithmetic/Logic Unit (ALU)

As its name suggests, the **arithmetic/logic unit (ALU)** performs the "math." The ALU is the part of the computer that generally does the work during the Instruction Execute step of the Fetch/Execute Cycle. So, for the example instruction

```
ADD 4000, 2000, 2080
```

the ALU does the actual addition. A circuit in the ALU can add two numbers—an amazing capability when you think about it. There are also circuits for multiplying two numbers, circuits for comparing two numbers, and so on. You can think of an ALU as carrying out each machine instruction with a separate circuit, although modern computers are so sophisticated that they can combine several operations into one circuit.

Most computer instructions perform some kind of math, that is, most instructions transform data. But information processing also includes moving data, that is, some instructions transfer data. Instructions for data transfer don't usually use the ALU. Computers have instructions for both transforming and transferring information.

For instructions that use the ALU, it is clear what the Data Fetch and Result Return steps of the Fetch/Execute Cycle must do. Data Fetch gets the values from memory that the ALU needs to perform operations like ADD and MULTIPLY. These values are called **operands**. The instruction includes the addresses where the data is to be found. The Data Fetch step delivers these values to the ALU. When the ALU completes the operation, producing a sum or product or other value, the Result Return step moves that answer from the ALU to the memory at the address specified in the instruction.

Input Unit and Output Unit

These two components, which are inverses of each other, and therefore easily discussed together, are the wires and circuits through which information moves into and out of a computer. A computer without input or output—that is, the memory, control, and ALU sealed in a box—is useless. Indeed, from a philosophical perspective, we might question whether we can say it "computes."

The Peripherals.

As shown in Figure 9.2, many kinds of devices—called **peripherals**—connect to the computer **input/output (I/O)** ports, providing it with input or receiving its output. The peripherals are not considered part of the computer; they are specialized gadgets that encode or decode information between the computer and the physical world. The keyboard encodes our keystrokes into binary form for the computer. The monitor decodes information from the computer's memory and displays it on a lighted, color screen. In general, the peripherals handle the physical part of the operation, sending or receiving the binary information the computer uses.

The cable from the peripheral to the computer connects to the input unit or the output unit. These units handle the communication protocol with the peripherals. As a general rule, think of the input unit as moving information from the peripheral into the memory, and the output unit as moving information from the memory and delivering it to the outside world.

Portable Disks and Hard Drives.

Some peripherals, such as USB memory and hard disks, are used by computers for both input and output. They are storage devices, places where the computer files away information when it is not needed (an output operation) and where it gets information when it needs it again (an input operation). The hard disk is the *alpha-peripheral*, being the most aggressively engineered and tightly linked device to the computer. The hard disk is essential because although programs and their data must reside in the computer's memory when programs run, they reside on the hard disk the rest of the time because the hard disk provides more permanent space. In that sense, the hard disk is an extension of the computer's memory even though typically it is a hundred times larger and several thousand times slower.

A Device Driver for Every Peripheral. Most peripheral devices are "dumb" because they provide only basic physical translation to or from binary signals. They rely on the computer for further processing, which is almost always required to make the peripheral operate in an "intelligent way." So, as I type the letters of this sentence, signals are sent from the keyboard to the computer indicating which keys my fingers press. When the computer receives information that I've pressed the *w* and the (Shift) key simultaneously, the computer—not the keyboard—converts the *w* keystroke to an uppercase *W*. Similarly, keys like (Ctrl) and (Backspace) are just keys to the keyboard. Added processing by a piece of software called a **device driver** gives the keyboard its standard meaning and behavior. Every device needs a device driver to provide this added processing. Because the peripheral device has unique characteristics, a device driver is specialized to one device only.

fit **TIP**   **New Toys.** Many users are excited about purchasing a new peripheral such as a printer, scanner, or CD-ROM drive. They plug it into their computer, but forget that it needs a device driver to run. Computers often come loaded with standardized or popular device drivers, so users don't know, or forget, that peripherals require them. Peripherals should come with device driver(s); if not, they can be downloaded from the manufacturer's Web site.

THE PROGRAM COUNTER: THE PC'S PC

The final question is how a computer determines which instruction to execute next.

Address of the Next Instruction

Recall that when the Fetch/Execute Cycle executes a program, the instructions are stored in the memory. That means every instruction has an address, which is the address of the memory location of the first byte of the instruction. (Instructions of current computers use 4 bytes, or one word.) Computers keep track of which instruction to execute next by its address. This address, stored in the control part of the computer, should probably be called the *next instruction address*, but for historic reasons it is actually known by the curious term, **program counter**, abbreviated PC. (*For the rest of the chapter* PC *refers to program counter, not personal computer.*)

The Instruction Fetch step of the Fetch/Execute Cycle transfers the instruction from memory at the address specified by the program counter to the decoder part of the control unit. Once the instruction is fetched, and while it is being processed by the remaining steps of the cycle, the computer prepares to process the next instruction. It assumes that the next instruction is the next one in sequence. Because instructions use 4 bytes of memory, the next instruction must be at the memory address PC + 4, that is, 4 bytes further along in sequence. Therefore, the computer adds 4 to the PC, so that when the F/E Cycle gets around to the Instruction Fetch step again, the PC is "pointing at" the new instruction.

Branch and Jump Instructions

This scheme of executing instructions in sequence seems flawed: Won't the Fetch/Execute Cycle blaze through the memory executing all the instructions, get to the last instruction in memory, and "fall off the end of memory," having used up all of the instructions? This won't happen unless the program has a bug because computers come with instructions called *branch* and *jump* that change the PC. After the control unit prepares for the next instruction in sequence by adding 4 to the PC, the Instruction Execute step of the current (branch or jump) instruction resets the PC to a new value. This overrides the selection of the next instruction in sequence and makes the PC address some other instruction in memory. The next instruction is fetched from that memory location on the next round of the Fetch/Execute Cycle.

INSTRUCTION INTERPRETATION

The process of executing a program is also called **instruction interpretation**. The term derives from the idea that the computer interprets our commands, but in its own language.

To illustrate the idea of interpreting instructions, let's follow the execution of a typical ADD instruction. Figure 9.5 shows the situation before the Fetch/Execute Cycle starts the next instruction. Notice that some of the memory locations and the program counter (PC) are visible in the control unit.

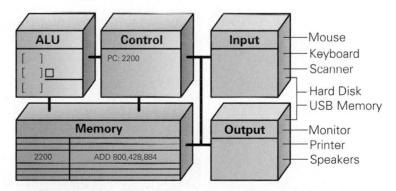

Figure 9.5. *Computer before executing an ADD instruction.*

Instruction execution begins by moving the instruction at the address given by the PC from the memory unit to the control unit. (See Figure 9.6, where the instruction address is 2200 and the example instruction is ADD 800, 428, 884 .)

The bits of the instruction are placed into the decoder circuit of the control unit. Once the instruction is fetched, the PC can be readied for fetching the next instruction. For today's computers whose instructions are 4 bytes long, 4 is added to the PC. (The updated PC value is visible in the Data Fetch configuration, as shown in Figure 9.8 and those that follow.)

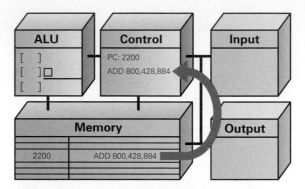

Figure 9.6. *Instruction Fetch: Move instruction from memory to the control unit.*

Figure 9.7 shows the Instruction Decode step, in which the ALU is set up for the operation in the Instruction Execute step. Among the bits of the instruction, the decoder finds the memory addresses of the instruction's data, the *source operands*. Like ADD, most instructions operate on two data values stored in memory, so most instructions have addresses for two source operands. These two addresses (428, 884) are passed to the circuit that will fetch the operand values from memory during the next (Data Fetch) step. Simultaneously, the decoder finds the *destination address*, the place in memory where the answer will be sent during the Result Return step. That address (800) is placed in the RR circuit. Finally, the decoder figures out what operation the ALU should perform on the data values (ADD) and sets up the ALU appropriately for that operation.

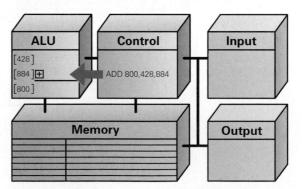

Figure 9.7. *Instruction Decode: Pull apart the instruction, set up the operation in the ALU, and compute the source and destination operand addresses.*

Figure 9.8 shows the Data Fetch step. The data values for the two source operands are moved from the memory into the ALU. These values (12, 42) are the data that the instruction will work on in the next (Execute) step.

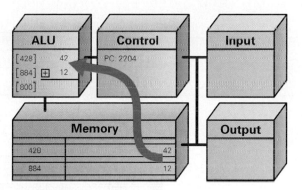

Figure 9.8. *Data Fetch: Move the operands from memory to the ALU.*

Instruction Execution is illustrated in Figure 9.9. The operation—set up during the Instruction Decode step—performs the computation. In the present case, the addition circuit adds the two source operand values to produce their sum (54). This is the actual computation.

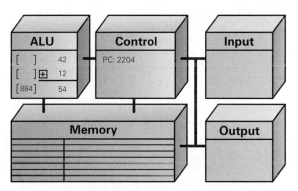

Figure 9.9. *Instruction Execute: Compute the result of the operation in the ALU.*

---

*fit***BYTE** **Micro Computer.** In our presentation, Instruction Execution—the "compute" part of the Fetch/Execute Cycle—accounts for only 20 percent of the time spent executing an instruction; it averages even less on real computers. Measured by silicon area, the ALU—the circuitry that does the computing—takes up less than 5 percent of a typical processor chip.

Finally, the Result Return step, shown in Figure 9.10, returns the result of Instruction Execution (`54`) to the memory location specified by the destination address (`800`) and set up during Instruction Decode. Once the result is returned, the cycle begins again.

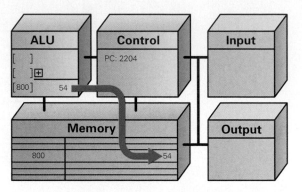

Figure 9.10. *Result Return: Store the result from the ALU into the memory at the destination address.*

Many, Many Simple Operations

Computers "know" very few instructions. That is, the decoder hardware in the controller recognizes, and the ALU performs, only about 100 or so different instructions. And there is a lot of duplication. For example, different instructions are used for different kinds of data: one instruction adds bytes, a different instruction adds whole words (4 bytes), a third adds "decimal" numbers, and so on. So, there are only about 20 different kinds of operations. *Everything* that computers do must be reduced to some combination of these primitive, hardwired instructions. They can't do anything else.

The **ADD** instruction has average complexity, and **MULT** (multiply) and **DIV** (divide) instructions are at the screaming limit of complexity. Examples of other instructions include:

> Shift the bits of a word (4 bytes) to the left or right, filling the emptied places with zeros and throwing away the bits that fall off the end.

> Compute the logical **AND**, which tests if pairs of bits are both true, and the logical **OR**, which tests if at least one of two bits is true.

> Test if a bit is zero or nonzero, and jump to a new set of instructions based on the outcome.

> Move information around in memory.

> Sense the signals from input/output devices.

Computer instructions are very primitive. There is no DRAW_A_BUTTON or SPELL_CHECK.

*fit***BYTE**   **Stop!** If the Fetch/Execute Cycle is an infinite loop, how does a computer stop? Early computers actually had Start and Stop buttons, but modern computers simply execute an "idle loop" when there's nothing to do. The instructions keep checking to see if there's anything to do, like process a mouse click or keystroke.

CYCLING THE F/E CYCLE

Using ADD, we have illustrated how a computer is able to execute instructions. ADD is representative of the complexity of computer instructions—some are slightly simpler, some slightly more complex. There are no instructions like

```
Check_spelling_of_the_document_beginning_at_memory_location 884
```

With such primitive instructions, it is surprising that computers can do anything at all. But they achieve success with speed. Computers manifest their impressive capabilities by executing many simple instructions per second.

The Computer Clock

Computers are instruction execution engines. We have just studied in detail how the Fetch/Execute Cycle carries out one ADD instruction. Since the computer does one instruction per cycle, the speed of a computer—the number of instructions executed per second—depends on the number of Fetch/Execute Cycles it performs per second. The rate of the Fetch/Execute Cycle is determined by the computer's **clock**, and it is measured in **megahertz**, or millions (mega) of cycles per second (hertz). Computer clock speeds have increased dramatically in recent years, resulting in speeds of 1000 MHz or more. A 1000 MHz clock ticks a billion (in American English) times per second, which is one gigahertz (1 GHz) in any language. (See Figure 9.11 for terms; "giga" is pronounced with hard g's.) Clock speeds are a common feature of computer advertisements, but how important are they?

1000^1	kilo-	$1024^1 = 2^{10} = 1,024$	milli-	1000^{-1}
1000^2	mega-	$1024^2 = 2^{20} = 1,048,576$	micro-	1000^{-2}
1000^3	giga-	$1024^3 = 2^{30} = 1,073,741,824$	nano-	1000^{-3}
1000^4	tera-	$1024^4 = 2^{40} = 1,099,511,627,776$	pico-	1000^{-4}
1000^5	peta-	$1024^5 = 2^{50} = 1,125,899,906,842,624$	fcmto-	1000^{-5}
1000^6	exa-	$1024^6 = 2^{60} = 1,152,921,504,606,876,976$	atto-	1000^{-6}
1000^7	zetta-	$1024^7 = 2^{70} = 1,180,591,620,717,411,303,424$	zepto-	1000^{-7}
1000^8	yotta-	$1024^8 = 2^{80} = 1,208,925,819,614,629,174,706,176$	yocto-	1000^{-8}

Figure 9.11. *Standard prefixes from the Système International (SI) convention on scientific measurements. Generally a prefix refers to a power of 1000, except when the quantity (for example, memory) is counted in binary; for binary quantities the prefix refers to a power of 1024, which is 2^{10}.*

> *fit* **TIP**
>
> **Beauty of Prefixes.** Prefixes "change the units" so that very large or small quantities can be expressed with numbers of a reasonable size. A well-known humorous example concerns Helen of Troy from Greek mythology "whose face launched 1000 ships." The beauty needed to launch one ship is one-thousandth of Helen's, that is, 0.001 Helen, or 1 MilliHelen.

One Cycle per Clock Tick

A computer with a 1 GHz clock has one billionth of a second—one nanosecond—between clock ticks to run the Fetch/Execute Cycle. In that short time, light travels about one foot (30 cm). Is it really possible to add or multiply that fast? No. In truth, modern computers try to *start* an instruction on each clock tick. They pass off completing the instruction to other circuitry, like a worker on an assembly line. This process, called *pipelining*, frees the fetch unit to start the next instruction before the last one is done. As shown in Figure 9.12, if the five steps of the Fetch/Execute Cycle take a nanosecond *each*—which is still extremely fast—it's possible to finish one instruction on each clock tick as long as there is enough circuitry for five instructions to be "in process" at the same time. That way the computer finishes instructions at the starting rate of one per tick. Of course, to execute 1000 instructions in a five-stage pipeline takes 1004 clock cycles—1000 to start each instruction, and four more for the last four steps of the last instruction. So it is not quite true that 1000 instructions are executed in 1000 ticks. But it's probably close enough.

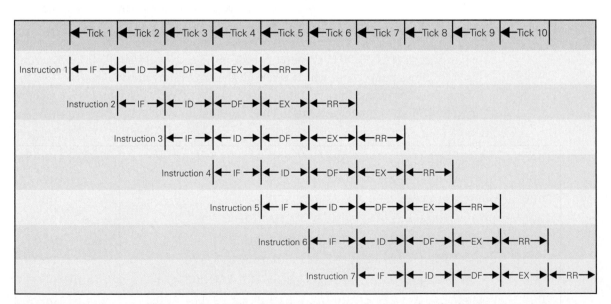

Figure 9.12. *Schematic diagram of a pipelined Fetch/Execute Cycle. On each tick, the IF circuit starts a new instruction, and then passes it along to the ID (Instruction Decode) unit; the ID unit works on the instruction it receives, and when it finishes, it passes it along to the DF (Data Fetch) circuit, and so on. When the pipeline is filled, five instructions are in progress at once, and one instruction is finished on each clock tick, making the computer appear to be running at one instruction per tick.*

A Billion Instructions per Second?

So, does a computer with a 1 GHz clock execute a billion instructions per second? Computer salespeople would like you to believe it's true, but it's not. We said that computers *try* to start an instruction on each clock tick, but there is a long list of reasons why it's not always possible. If the computer cannot start instructions on each clock tick, its execution rate falls *below* 1 billion instructions per second. But the situation is even more complicated. Computer engineers have figured out how to start more than one instruction at a time, even though instructions are supposed to be finished before the next one starts. If several instructions can be started at the same time often enough, they can make up for not starting instructions at other times. Thus the rate can be *more than* 1 billion per second. It is extremely difficult—even for experts—to figure out how fast a modern computer runs. As a result, the one-instruction-per-cycle guideline—which was once dependable—is no longer correct.

SOFTWARE

We have studied what computer hardware can do, and what we learned is "not very much." That is, computers are very fast but the operations they can perform at each step are extremely simple. How can all of the amazing things computers do—video games, PhotoShop, grammar checks, Google searches, and on and on—be done with such primitive instructions? The answer, of course, is *software*.

A Computer's View of Software

In Chapter 1 we defined software as a collective term for programs. We'll learn about algorithms and how they are specialized into programs in Chapter 10, but for now consider software more generically.

When a computer "sees" software, that is, when it's told to install the snazzy new application you just bought, it finds an extremely long sequence of 4-byte groups (words) of bits, the binary instructions as described in the last section, on the installation CD. For example, a sequence of instructions for a contemporary computer has the binary form:

```
10001111 10010100 00000011 01110100
10001111 10011000 00000001 10101100
00000010 10011000 10100000 00100000  ↔  ADD 20, 20, 24
10101111 10010100 00000001 10010000
```

This sequence, the **binary object** file, or simply the **binary**—can be hundreds of thousands to millions of words long. Once installed on the hard disk, the computer runs the software by copying the binary instructions into the RAM and interpreting them using the Fetch/Execute Cycle. It does whatever the instructions tell it to do.

Assembly Language

Although the binary object file is the only form in which a computer can be given software, it is anything but user-friendly. It's not really human readable. Humans can decode it, of course, but it's so difficult that understanding even a handful of words can take hours, motivating people to do anything to avoid it. And humans don't want to produce it either. In fact, people are so error prone that it's essentially impossible for us to produce more than a few words of correct binary manually. Binary object code is a form of software only a computer can love.

Luckily, computers can be programmed to translate software expressed in other forms into the binary form they like. The process, shown in Figure 9.13, has two steps; we'll focus first on the second step: *Assembling*.

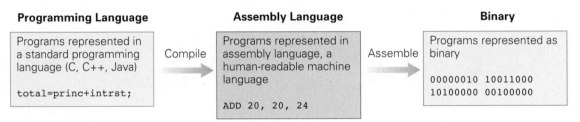

Figure 9.13. *The three primary forms of encoding software: programming language, assembly language, and binary machine language.*

Assembly language is simply an alternative form of machine language expressed using letters and normal numbers so people can understand it. It was invented almost immediately after the invention of computers, because working with binary is so brutal. The translation process to binary is straightforward: The computer scans the program written in assembly code, and as it encounters words like **ADD**, it looks them up in a table to find how to encode them in binary; it converts all numbers to binary, and then *assembles* the binary pieces into an instruction. Assembly language is the "lowest" software level—meaning, the most primitive—that humans work with, and then only rarely. Mostly, assembly language is the output of the more complex process of *compiling*.

Programming Languages

Virtually all software today is written in a **high-level programming language**, where the "high-level" phrase differentiates the language from assembly language and binary, which are technically also programming languages—notations used to express computation. Programs written in a high-level language are compiled, that is, translated, into assembly language programs, which are then assembled into binary. A program, therefore, is a computation that is represented in three different forms.

Because 99.9 percent of today's software is written using such programming languages—C, C++, Java, and a dozen others—we drop the "high-level phrase" label;

it adds little. These languages are preferred because unlike assembly language, they have special statement forms that help programmers describe the complicated tasks they want computers to do. For example, computations frequently test whether or not some situation exists; so programming languages have `if` statements to help to create the test. An `if` statement has three parts

> a yes/no question (the test)

> instructions the computer should perform if the test is true

> instructions the computer should perform if the test is false

Figure 9.14 shows a fragment of program text; lines 7–10 illustrate the programmer's use of an `if` statement. Lines 4–6 illustrate a `for`-statement, a specialized statement form that causes instructions to be repeated. Programming languages have many other specialized capabilities to help programmers. When the programming language statements are compiled and assembled into binary, a few lines of program usually result in many, many machine instructions.

```
1  var j, frame = -1, duration = 150, timeout_id = null;
2  var images = new Array(20);
3  function advance() {
4    for (j = 0; j < 19; j++) {
5      document.images[j].src = document.images[j+1].src;
6    }
7    if (frame == -1)                                        test
8      document.images[19].src = pics[randNum(8)].src;       true instructions
9    else
10     document.images[19].src = pics[frame].src;            false instructions
11   timeout_id = setTimeout("animate()", duration);
12 }
```

Figure 9.14. *A fragment of program text written in a high-level language.*

Operating Systems

Computers are capable of doing so few things independently, that without software, they can't even start up. The start-up process (booting) is one of a long list of basic operations that are necessary to effectively use a computer, but which are not built into the hardware. The programs for these basic tasks are collectively the **operating system (OS)**. The three most widely used operating systems are Microsoft's Windows, Apple's MacOSX, and Unix, which has variations including Linux. None is best—each has its triumphs and tragedies. They all fill the gap between the limited capabilities of the hardware and the needs of a useful working environment.

In addition to booting, operating systems perform memory management. Examples include keeping track of where programs are stored on the hard disk and copying them into the RAM when you (click on the icon to) run them. The OS doesn't copy the whole program into RAM initially, because you might not need every feature. As you use more features, the memory manager finds and loads the software for them without your awareness. Operating systems manage all of the I/O devices such as the keyboard, mouse, screen, hard drive, printer, etc. They also manage the computer's Internet connection, but the browser is not part of the OS. In general, operating systems perform tasks needed by all other software, making computers much more useful than they are as raw hardware.

User applications draw on OS facilities. For example, the OS provides the file system, so when you save your work in an application, the software asking you to specify the file name and the directory into which it should be stored is a facility provided by the OS.

{GREAT *fit* MOMENTS}

Programming Pioneers >>

Programming Pioneers. The first programmers, who wrote and ran the programs on the ENIAC, were women: Kathleen McNulty Mauchley Antonelli, Jean Jennings Bartik, Frances Snyder Holberton, Marlyn Wescoff Meltzer, Frances Bilas Spence, and Ruth Lichterman Teitelbaum. They were recruited from the ranks of "computers," humans who used mechanical calculators to solve complex mathematical problems before the invention of electronic computers.

On left from top: Kathleen McNulty Mauchley Antonelli, Jean Jennings Bartik, Frances Snyder Holberton

On right from top: Marlyn Wescoff Meltzer, Frances Bilas Spence (also pictured on right in photo of ENIAC above), Ruth Lichterman Teitelbaum

Programming

In addition to using powerful languages, programmers use another technique that makes their difficult job easier: They build on previously developed software. Consider the analogy with house building. Strictly speaking, a house "begins" with trees, sand, rock, etc., but no one actually starts construction at such a low level; we build with nails, lumber, and glass, materials that have been transformed from their original natural form to simplify construction. These materials are further transformed into more complex components, such as ceiling trusses, windows, cabinets, etc. before carpenters put them together into a house. Software works the same way: The basic operations and facilities from the OS are used to construct useful, but primitive functions. These are combined to make more complex operations, which are further combined to create still more sophisticated facilities, etc.

For example, all of the software for a GUI—the frame around the window, the slider bars, buttons, triangle pointers, menus, etc. are packaged for programmers and provided with the operating system. This is why GUIs for an OS are so similar. (In Chapter 2 we implied that programmers use consistent interfaces to help users learn their software quickly—and it's true—but it's also true that it's easy for programmers to make use of the library of standard GUI parts.) For example, the `setTimeout` operation in line 11 of Figure 9.14 applies software someone else wrote; and it was almost certainly written by a programmer who applied other software from the operating system that someone else wrote, etc. The ability to create software by combining other software is known as **functional composition**, and is discussed more completely in Chapter 20.

There is an important point about powerful programming language and its easy ability to build on other programmers' work: Programmers can easily create extremely complex systems providing tremendously useful capabilities to many users. The situation is different from the "construction analogy" in a significant way. To own a house, you must pay for the know-how to build it *and* the materials that go into it; to own software, you only need to pay for the know-how to build it, because no (significant) materials or time are needed to replicate software. Creating software is expensive; copying it is (essentially) free. This means that many benefit from the expertise and hard work of others. True, programming is difficult and programmers are well paid, but because there are almost no "replication costs," using their work is easy. One of the best characteristics of computers is that it is so easy to apply and benefit from other people's intellect.

INTEGRATED CIRCUITS

Integrated circuits (ICs) are important because the technology allows extremely complex devices to be made cheaply and reliably. Two characteristics of ICs make this possible: integration and photolithography. Oh, yes. Integrated circuits are also very small.

Miniaturization

Modern computer clocks can run at GHz rates because their processor chips are so tiny. The farthest electrical signals can travel in a nanosecond is about one foot, and in a computer much more has to happen to the signals than simple transmission. Early computers, which filled whole rooms, could never have run as fast as modern computers because their components were farther apart than one foot. Making everything smaller has made computers faster by allowing for faster clock rates.

Integration

But the real achievement of microchip technology is not miniaturization, but **integration**. It is impossible to overstate its significance. T. R. Reid, in his book *The Chip* called the invention "a seminal event of postwar science: one of those rare demonstrations that changes everything."

To appreciate how profound the invention of integrated circuitry is, understand that before integration, computers were made from separate parts (discrete components) wired together by hand. The three wires coming out of each transistor, the two wires from each resistor, the two wires from each capacitor, and so on, had to be connected to the wires of some other transistor, resistor, or capacitor. It was very tedious work. Even for printed circuit boards in which the "wiring" is printed metallic strips, a person or machine had to "populate" the board with the discrete components one at a time. A serious computer system would have hundreds of thousands or millions of these parts and at least twice as many connections, which were expensive and time consuming to produce, error prone, and unreliable. If computers were still built this way, they would still be rare.

The "big idea" behind integrated circuits is really two ideas working together. The first idea is that the active components—transistors, capacitors, and so forth—and the wires that connect them, are manufactured with similar materials by a single (multistep) process. So, rather than making two transistors and later connecting them by soldering a pair of their wires together, IC technology places them side by side in the silicon, and at some stage in the fabrication process—perhaps while some of the transistor's internal parts are still being built—a wire connecting the two is placed in position. The crux of integration is that the active and connective parts of a circuit are built together. Integration saves space (promoting speed), but its greatest advantage is that it produces a single monolithic part for the whole system all at once without hand wiring. The resulting "block" of electronics is extremely reliable.

Photolithography

The second idea behind integrated circuits is that they are made with **photolithography**, a printing process. Here's how it works. Making a chip is like making a sandwich. Start with a layer of silicon and add layers of materials to build up

{GREAT *fit* MOMENTS}

IC Man >>

Jack Kilby shared the 2000 Nobel Prize in Physics for inventing the integrated circuit. Kilby worked for the electronics firm Texas Instruments. New to the staff, Kilby hadn't accrued summer vacation time, so while the other employees were away on their holidays, he invented integrated circuits.

Using borrowed and improvised equipment, he conceived of and built the first electronic circuit in which all of the components, both active and connective, were fabricated in a single piece of semiconductor material. On September 12, 1958, he successfully demonstrated the first simple microchip, which was about half the size of a paper clip. Kilby went on to pioneer applications of microchip technology. He later co-invented both the hand-held calculator and a thermal printer used in portable data terminals.

For perspective, the worldwide integrated circuit market in 2000 had sales of $177 billion.

---

the transistors, capacitors, wires, and other features of a chip. For example, wires might be made of a layer of aluminum. But the aluminum cannot be smeared over the chip like mayonnaise covers a sandwich; the wires must be electrically separated from each other and connected to specific places. This is where photolithography comes in.

Transistors and other features of a chip are created in a series of steps that begin by depositing a layer of material on the silicon, see Figure 9.15. That layer is covered by a light-sensitive material called **photoresist**, and a mask is placed over it. The mask (like a photographic negative) has a pattern corresponding to the features being constructed. Exposure to (ultraviolet) light causes open areas to harden; unexposed areas do not and can be washed away leaving the pattern. Hot gases etch the original layer, and when the remaining photoresist is removed, the pattern from the mask—and the new features—remain.

The key aspect of photolithography is that regardless of how complicated the wiring is, the cost and amount of work involved are the same. Like a page of a newspaper, which costs the same to print whether it has 5 or 5000 words, the cost of making integrated circuits is not related to how complicated they are. Thanks to the photolithographic process, computers and other electronics can be as complicated as necessary.

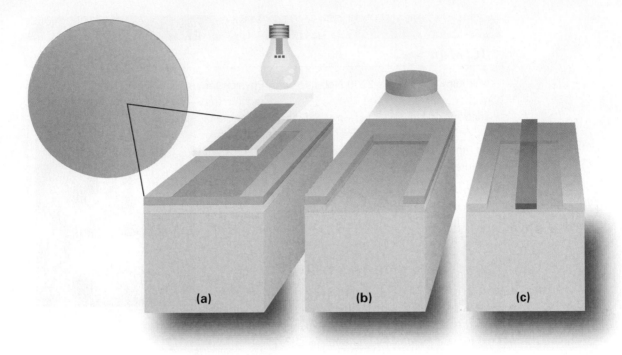

Figure 9.15. *Early steps in the fabrication process. (a) A layer of photoresist (light blue) is exposed to UV light through a pattern mask, hardening the exposed areas; (b) after washing away the unexposed photoresist, hot gases etch away (nearly all of) the exposed layer; (c) the remaining resist is washed away and other layers are created by repeating the patterning and etching processes. In later stages of the fabrication process, (d) "Impurities"*

● HOW SEMICONDUCTOR TECHNOLOGY WORKS

Silicon is a **semiconductor**, meaning just what its name implies—it sometimes conducts electricity and sometimes does not. The ability to control when semiconductors do and don't conduct electricity is the main process used in computer construction. To understand this point, consider an example.

In Chapter 5 we used the **AND** operation when we searched for Thai restaurants. We wanted to find Web pages that included both keywords. During our search Google tested to see if "Thai" was on a given page and tested to see if "restaurants" was on the same page. When the results of those two tests were known, an instruction in the Google computer **AND**ed them together. How can that be done with electricity?

The On-Again, Off-Again Behavior of Silicon

Imagine that we have a wire with two gaps in it. We fill each gap with specially treated semiconducting material (see Figure 9.16). We send an electrical signal along the wire, which we will interpret as yes, both "Thai" and "restaurants" appear on the page. At the other end of the wire we detect whether the "yes" is

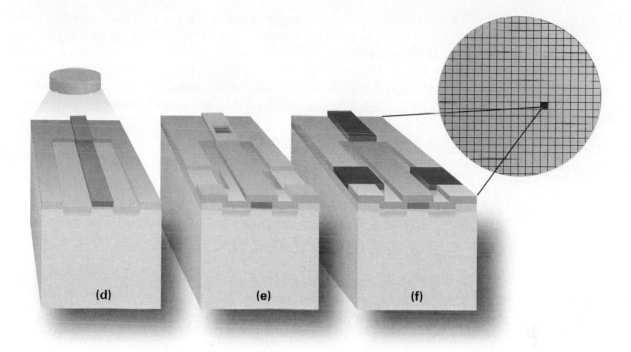

(green) such as boron are diffused into the silicon surface in a process called doping, which improves the availability of electrons in this region of the silicon; (e) after additional layering, etching exposes contact points for metal wires; (f) a metal (dark blue) such as aluminum is deposited creating "wires" to connect to other transistors; millions of such transistors form a computer chip occupying a small square on the final fabricated wafer.

present or absent, an application of the PandA encoding from Chapter 8. In between we control the conductivity of the semiconducting material using the outcomes of the two tests. We make the material in the first gap conduct if "Thai" is found, and the material in the second gap conduct if "restaurants" is found. If the material conducts electricity, the signal can pass to the other end of the wire. So, if "yes" is detected at the output end, both gaps must be conducting; that is, both outcomes are true. If "yes" is not detected, then one or the other (or possibly both) of the two semiconducting points must not be conducting, which means "Thai" and "restaurants" are not both found.

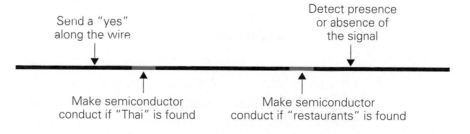

Figure 9.16. Computing `Thai AND restaurants` *using a semiconducting material.*

This simple principle—the setting up of a situation in which the conductivity of a wire is controlled to create the logical conclusion needed—is the basis of all the instructions and operations of a computer. In the hardware of the computer where this test is done, the two semiconducting points of the AND circuit are not limited to the specific question of whether "Thai" AND "restaurants" is true; instead the circuit computes *x* AND *y* for any logical values *x* and *y*. Such a circuit is part of the ALU of Google's computer (and yours), and it performs the Execute step of all the AND instructions.

The Field Effect

So how do we control the conductivity of a semiconductor? We use the **field effect**. As we all know from combing our hair with a nylon comb on a dry day, objects can be charged positively or negatively. The comb strips off electrons from our hair, leaving the comb with too many electrons and our hair with too few. Because like-charges repel, our hair "stands on end" as each hair pushes away from its neighbors; but opposites attract, so the comb pulls the hair toward it. This effect that charged objects have on each other without actually touching is called the field effect. We can use the field effect to control a semiconductor.

The ends of the two wires is specially treated (doped) to improve their conducting and nonconducting properties, that is, when they conduct they conduct better than pure silicon. The part between the ends is called a *channel,* because it creates a path for electricity to travel on. An insulator such as glass, silicon dioxide, covers the channel. Passing over the insulator (at right angles) is a third wire called the *gate*. The gate is separated from the semiconductor by the insulator, so it does not make contact with the two wires or the channel. Thus, electricity cannot be conducted between the two wires unless the channel is conducting. But how does the channel conduct?

The silicon in the channel can conduct electricity when it is in a charged field. The conductivity is the result of electrons being attracted or repelled in the silicon material, depending on the type of treatment on the ends (see Figure 9.17). So, by charging the gate positively we create a field over the channel; electrons are attracted from the silicon material into the channel causing it to conduct electricity between the two wires. If the field is removed, the electrons disperse into the silicon, the channel doesn't conduct, and the two wires are isolated. Of course, the gate is simply another wire, which is or is not conducting (charged) under the control of other gates, and so on.

Transistors

Our example illustrates a **field effect transistor**. A **transistor** is simply a connector between two wires that can be controlled to allow charge to flow between the wires (conduct) or not. The transistor described is an **MOS** transistor (**metal, oxide, semiconductor**). These three terms refer to the materials in the cross-

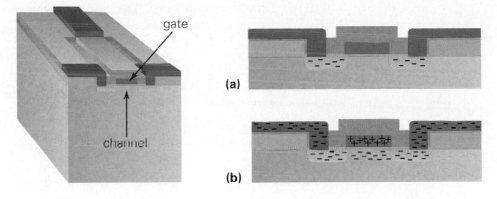

Figure 9.17. *Operation of a field effect transistor. (a) the gate (red) is neutral and the channel, the region in the silicon below the gate, does not conduct, isolating the wires (blue); (b) charging the gate causes the channel to conduct, connecting the wires.*

section of the transistor from top to bottom: the gate is metal, the glass insulator is oxide, and the channel is the semiconductor. Modern computers are developed with **CMOS** technology, which stands for "complementary MOS" and means two different, but complementary, treatments for the channels.

COMBINING THE IDEAS

Let's put these ideas together. We start with an information-processing task. The task is performed by an application implemented as a large program written by a programmer in a programming language like C or Java. The program performs the specific operations of the application, but for standard operations like **Print** or **Save**, the application program uses the OS. The program's commands, written in the programming language, are compiled into many simple assembly language instructions. The assembly instructions are then translated into a more primitive binary form (the machine instructions), that the computer understands directly.

The application program's binary instructions are stored on the hard disk. When we click on the application's icon, the OS copies the first part of the program's instructions into the computer's RAM and tells the computer to begin to execute them. When more instructions are needed, the OS brings them in.

The Fetch/Execute Cycle, a hardwired sequence of five steps that are repeated over and over, executes the instructions:

1. (IF) Fetch the instruction stored at the memory location specified by the PC and place it in the control part of the computer. The PC is advanced to reference the next instruction after the fetch.

2. (ID) Decode the instruction. That is, decide what the operation is, where the data values (operands) are, and where the result should go.

3. (DF) Fetch the data from memory while the arithmetic/logic unit is set up to perform the operation.

4. (EX) Execute; the ALU performs the operation on the data values.

5. (RR) Store the result back in memory.

The cycle is repeated endlessly.

All of the computer's instructions are performed by the ALU circuits. The AND instruction, for example, is implemented with MOS technology by breaking a wire in two places and filling the gaps with the semiconducting material of a field effect transistor forming channels connecting the wires. An oxide insulator and a metal gate cover each semiconductor channel. If, for example, the instruction is

```
AND 4040, 4280, 2020
```

then the data value fetched from memory location 4280 would control the gate on the first MOS transistor, and the data value fetched from memory location 2020 would control the gate on the second MOS transistor. A true operand value creates a field, causing the channel to conduct, and a false operand value is neutral, preventing the channel from conducting. An electrical signal interpreted as "yes" is sent down the wire. If the "yes" is detected at the output end of the wire, both transistors are conducting, and the result is true; otherwise the result is false. Either way, the result is returned to memory location 4040.

That's it, from applications to electrons. It is a sequence of interesting and straightforward ideas working together to create computation. No single idea is *the* key idea. They all contribute. The power comes from applying the ideas in quantity: Application programs and operating systems are composed of millions of machine instructions, the control unit executes billions of cycles per second, memories contain billions of bits, processors have hundreds of millions of MOS transistors, and so on in an impressive process.

Ours has been a simple, but accurate description of a computer. This description mirrors the design and operation of many early computers built in the days before silicon technology advanced to the microprocessor stage; that is, before everything in Figure 9.2 fit on a chip. Once silicon technology matured to that stage, computer architects—the engineers who design computers—became very aggressive. By applying integrated circuitry to its fullest, they optimized the Fetch/Execute Cycle and the simple structure of Figure 9.2 almost beyond recognition. To achieve their impressive speeds, today's computers are dramatically more complex than explained here. But the abstraction—the logical idea of how a computer is organized and operates—is as presented.

SUMMARY

The chapter began by describing the Fetch/Execute Cycle, the instruction interpretation engine of a computer system. We continued on to learn that:

> The repeating process fetches each instruction (indicated by the PC), decodes the operation, retrieves the data, performs the operation, and stores the result back into the memory.

> This process is hardwired into the control subsystem, one of the five components of a processor.

> The memory, a very long sequence of bytes, each with an address, stores the program and data while the program is running.

> The ALU does the actual computing.

> The input and output units are the interfaces for the peripheral devices attached to the computer.

> Machine instructions do not refer to the data (operands) directly, but rather indirectly. Thus, different computations can be done with an instruction, just by changing the data in the referenced memory locations each time the instruction is executed.

> Programmers must create complex computations by software layers, building up simple operations from the base instructions, more complex operations from the simple ones, and so forth.

> Programmers use sophisticated programming languages to create operating systems as well as complex applications software.

> The basic ideas of integrated circuits—integrating active and connective components, fabrication by photolithography, and controlling conductivity through the field effect.

EXERCISES

Multiple Choice

1. Which of the following is a characteristic of a computer?
   A. literal
   B. free will
   C. creativity
   D. intuition

2. There are _____ steps in the Fetch/Execute Cycle.
   A. 3
   B. 4
   C. 5
   D. 6

3. The Fetch/Execute Cycle operates
   A. once a second
   B. thousands of times a second
   C. hundreds of thousands of times a second
   D. hundreds of millions of times a second

4. One byte of memory can store
   A. any number
   B. one word
   C. one character
   D. one block

5. The ALU is used in the
   A. Instruction Fetch
   B. Instruction Execution
   C. Result Return
   D. Instruction Decode

6. Which of the following is used for input and output?
   A. keyboard
   B. hard disk
   C. mouse
   D. printer

7. The program counter is changed by instructions called
   A. Fetch and Execute
   B. Branch and Jump
   C. Input and Output
   D. Now and Next

8. When there are no instructions for the Fetch/Execute Cycle, the computer
   A. crashes
   B. executes an idle loop
   C. sends an empty instruction to processing
   D. always has instructions to execute

9. From smallest to largest, the correct order is
   A. giga, kilo, mega, tera
   B. kilo, mega, giga, tera
   C. tera, kilo, mega, giga
   D. kilo, mega, tera, giga

10. Modern computers know
   A. only a handful of instructions
   B. a couple of dozen instructions
   C. about a hundred instructions
   D. thousands of instructions

11. Which of the following is not a high-level programming language?
   A. Java
   B. C
   C. Assembly
   D. Visual Basic

Short Answer

1. _____ deterministically execute instructions to process information.

2. Computers operate under a set of operations called the _____.

3. _____ is an acronym for the name of the location where computer programs run and data is stored.

4. The _____ part of the computer is the hardware part of the Fetch/Execute Cycle.

5. Computers operate _____, that is, they follow instructions exactly based on the program and data they have been given.

6. The math in the computer is done by the _____.

7. Transferring and transforming information is called _____.

8. _____ are the devices that connect to the computer.

9. The _____ encodes keystrokes into binary form for the computer.

10. The computer's clock is measured in _____.

11. _____ is the task of creating complex instructions for the computer to follow from a set of simple instructions.

12. Computers keep track of the next instruction to execute by its _____.

13. _____ is the technical term for the process of executing a program.

14. A(n) _____ sometimes conducts electricity and sometimes doesn't.

15. The flow of electricity in a channel in a semiconductor is controlled by a(n) _____.

16. _____ is a long list of words, more accurately, a long series of 0's and 1's that make up a computer program.

17. Today, most software is written using a _____ programming language.

Exercises

1. Break the process of brushing your teeth into separate steps. Be as specific as possible.

2. How many bits in a kilobyte? megabyte? terabyte?

3. Find out how much memory your computer has. Calculate exactly how many bytes it has.

4. If a 1 GHz computer can start four instructions per cycle and can start a new instruction on 80 percent of its cycles, how many instructions can it complete in a second? in a minute?

5. If the mouse cable is five feet long, how long does it take the current generated by a mouse click to travel from the mouse to the computer?

6. If the cable connecting the hard disk to the computer is six inches long, what effect would it have on performance if the length was reduced by half? doubled?

7. Explain why the keyboard and the mouse are input devices and the monitor is an output device.

8. Explain how a complicated process like driving can be accomplished as a series of simple steps.

9. Explain how a system that can do only a limited number of very simple tasks can accomplish an almost unlimited number of complicated tasks.

10. Do an online search to find an explanation of how computer circuits are made.

11. Locate a computer circuit and take a close look at it. Describe what it looks like.

12. Using the Fetch/Execute Cycle, describe how you'd answer a true/false question.

13. Most of the cost of a new drug is tied up in research and testing. The actual production and distribution of the medication is only a small part of the cost. Explain how this parallels software development.

chapter 10

WHAT'S THE PLAN?
Algorithmic Thinking

learning objectives

> List the five essential properties of an algorithm

> Explain the difference between an algorithm and a program

> Use the *Alphabetize CDs* algorithm to illustrate algorithmic thinking:
  - Follow the flow of the instruction execution
  - Follow an analysis to pinpoint assumptions
  - Explain the function of loops and tests

> Demonstrate algorithmic thinking by being able to:
  - Explain what the *Beta* sweep abstraction does
  - Explain what the *Alpha* sweep abstraction does

WHAT'S THE PLAN?
Algorithmic Thinking

The most beautiful thing we can experience is the mysterious. It is the source of all true art and science.

—ALBERT EINSTEIN, 1930

The process of preparing programs for a digital computer is especially attractive, not only because it can be economically and scientifically rewarding, but also because it can be an aesthetic experience much like composing poetry or music.

—DONALD E KNUTH, 1970

AN ALGORITHM is a precise, systematic method for producing a specified result. We know algorithms as recipes, assembly instructions, driving directions, business processes, nominating procedures, and so on. Algorithms are key to processing information, of course, and we've already met several in this book. There are three main reasons to learn more about algorithms. First, we must create algorithms so that other people or computers can help us achieve our goals. To be successful, our algorithms must "work." This chapter explains how to create effective algorithms. Second, we will follow algorithms created by others. If we know the "dos" and "don'ts" of algorithm design, we can pay better attention to the details and be alert to errors in other people's instructions. Finally, learning about algorithms completes the study we began in Chapter 8 of how computers solve problems. Understanding this process makes us better computer users, better debuggers, and better problem solvers—that is, more Fluent.

The goals of this chapter are to understand what algorithms are and to learn to think algorithmically. We begin by looking at everyday algorithms. Next, we introduce and illustrate the five fundamental properties of algorithms. We explain the role of *language* in specifying algorithms and the value of a formal language. Then, we discuss the relationship between algorithms and programs. Guidelines—useful when writing out driving directions—help us understand the role of context in executing algorithms. We create an algorithm for alphabetizing our audio CD collection, which helps us discover how and why algorithms are structured the way they are. We execute the algorithm; that is, we sort a five-slot rack of our favorite CDs, watching the progress of the algorithm. Then, perhaps most important, we analyze the algorithm to extract key concepts in algorithmic thinking.

ALGORITHM: A FAMILIAR IDEA

In Chapter 1 we defined an algorithm as a precise and systematic method for producing a specified result. Algorithms are familiar—we've already seen several of them in this book.

> **Recognition of a button click.** In Chapter 1, after describing how computers draw buttons on the screen (an algorithm itself), we explained how the button is "clicked." The systematic method described how, when the mouse is clicked, the computer can look through the list of buttons it has drawn on the screen, and for each button, check to see if the cursor is inside the square defining the button.

> **Placeholder technique.** In Chapter 2 we described a three-step process to eliminate short letter sequences (for example, new lines), which can also be parts of longer strings (for example, double new lines), without also eliminating them in the longer strings.

> **Hex to bits.** In Chapter 8 we used algorithms to convert back and forth between hexadecimal digits and bits.

> *fit*BYTE

Weird Word. *Algorithm* seems to be an anagram of logarithm, but it comes from the name of a famous Arabic textbook author, Abu Ja'far Mohammed ibn Mûsâ al-Khowârizmî, who lived about A.D. 825. The end of his name, al-Khowârizmî, means *native of Khowârism* (today Khiva, Uzbekistan). It has been corrupted over the centuries into *algorithm*.

We use algorithms every day. The arithmetic operations—addition, subtraction, multiplication, division—we learned in elementary school are algorithms. Making change is an algorithm, as are looking up a number in a telephone book, sending a greeting card, and balancing a checkbook. Changing a tire is algorithmic, too, because it is a systematic method to solve a problem (replace a flat tire). Usually, though, *algorithm* means a precise method used in information processing.

Algorithms in Everyday Life

Most of the algorithms that we know, like arithmetic, we learned from a patient teacher or we figured out for ourselves, like how to look up a phone number. Because we are the ones performing the operations, we don't think much about algorithms as an explicit sequence of instructions. We simply *know* what to do. Other algorithms—recipes, bicycle assembly instructions, driving directions to a party, or income tax filing rules—are written out for us. Written algorithms interest us because we want to be able to think up an algorithm, write it out, and have some other agent—person or computer—perform its instructions successfully.

The specification of an algorithm must be "precise." The algorithms mentioned from the earlier chapters, though possibly clear enough for a person to follow, are not precise enough for a computer. Computers, as we saw in Chapters 7 and 9, are so clueless and literal that every part of a task they perform must be spelled out in detail. To write a precise algorithm, we need to pay attention to three points:

> **Capability.** Make sure that the computer knows what and how to do the operations.

> **Language.** Ensure that the description is unambiguous—that is, it can be read and understood one way only.

> **Context.** Make few assumptions about the input or execution setting.

These issues are not only crucial when algorithms are written for computers; but also important when they're written for people. We expect people to use their heads and compensate for weaknesses in our descriptions, but sometimes humans are clueless and literal, too, especially when dealing with unfamiliar situations. So, it's always in our best interest to make our instructions precise, avoid ambiguity, be sure users know what to do, and minimize assumptions, no matter what or who performs the algorithm.

Five Essential Properties of Algorithms

To write an algorithm that is specified well enough for a computer to follow, it must have five essential properties:

> Input specified

> Output specified

> Definiteness

> Effectiveness

> Finiteness

Input Specified. The **input** is the data to be transformed during the computation to produce the output. We must specify the type of data, the amount of data, and the form that the data will take. Suppose the algorithm is a recipe. We must list the ingredients (type of input), their quantities (amount of input), and their preparation, if any (form of input), as in, "1/4 cup onion, minced."

Output Specified. The **output** is the data resulting from the computation, the intended result. Often the description is given in the name of the algorithm, as in "Algorithm to compute a batting average." As with input, we must specify the type, amount, and any form of the output. A possible output for some computations is a statement that there is no output—that is, there is no possible solution. Recipes specify their output too, giving the type, quantity, and form of food, as in, "3 dozen 3-inch chocolate chip cookies."

Definiteness. Algorithms must specify every step. **Definiteness** means specifying the sequence of operations for transforming the input into the output. Details of each step must be spelled out, including how to handle errors. Definiteness ensures that if the algorithm is performed at different times or by different agents (people or computers) using the same data, the output is the same. Similarly, recipes should be definite, but because they often rely on the judgment, practicality, and experience of the cook, they can be much less definite than computer algorithms and still be successful. And where they are not definite—"salt and pepper to taste"—it's usually a good thing.

Effectiveness. It must be possible for the agent to execute the algorithm mechanically without any further input, special talent, clairvoyance, creativity, help from Superman, and so on. Whereas definiteness specifies which operations to do and when, **effectiveness** means that they are doable. Examples of ineffective instructions abound: "Enter the income you would have received this year if you had worked twice as hard," "Print Alexander the Great's blood type," and "Say whether the coin toss at the next Super Bowl is heads?"

Finiteness. An algorithm must have **finiteness**; it must eventually stop, either with the right output or with a statement that no solution is possible. If no answer comes back, we can't tell whether the agent is still working on an answer or is just plain "stuck." Finiteness is not usually an issue for noncomputer algorithms because they typically don't repeat instructions. But, as we shall see, computer algorithms often repeat instructions with different data. Finiteness becomes an issue because if the algorithm doesn't specify when to stop the repetition, the computer continues to repeat the instructions indefinitely.

A process with these five properties is called an algorithm.

---

*fit***BYTE**

Work without End. "Long" division is an algorithm in which finiteness is important. For example, divide 3 into 10. As we add each new digit (3) to the quotient, the computation returns to the same situation. When should the algorithm stop?

```
       3.33
   3)10.00
       9
       1.0
        9
       10
        ...
```

Language in Algorithms

Because algorithms are developed by people, but executed by another agent, they must be written in a language that is understood by both. The person who creates the instructions and the agent that performs them must interpret the instructions the same way.

Natural Language. If the agent is a person, we use a natural language, such as English. We assume that all speakers understand every sentence of a language similarly, but it's not true. In fact, it's probable that no two people understand a language exactly the same way. An instruction may mean one thing to the writer and something else to the agent. Ambiguity is very common in natural languages, but alternate interpretations are not to blame as much as the fact that natural languages are not very precise. For example, although recipe writers choose specific words like *fold in* or *beat* rather than *stir,* most of us mix the ingredients differently. Generally, a natural language is an extremely difficult medium in which to express algorithms.

Programming Language. Since natural languages don't work well, we use programming languages when the executing agents are computers. Programming languages are **formal languages**, designed to express algorithms. They are precisely defined. Programming languages are rarely ambiguous; their precise definition ensures that the programmer and the computer agree on what each instruction means. Programmers know that what they tell the computer to do is exactly what it will do. Of course, programmers make mistakes, but at least they are sure that if the computer does something wrong, the problem is with the algorithmic design, not with the computer's interpretation.

The Context of a Program

A program can fulfill the five properties of an algorithm (input specified, output specified, definiteness, effectiveness, and finiteness), be unambiguous, and still not work right because it is executed in the wrong **context** (the assumptions of the program are not fulfilled). For example, a form that asks you for your *Last Name* may mean your family name or surname, as is the case for Western names. The request produces the right result in the United States, but perhaps not in countries like China where the family name is given first. Good algorithm designers reduce the dependence on context by asking for *Family Name* rather than *Last Name* and *Given Name* rather than *First Name*.

Context Matters: Driving Instructions. Consider driving directions, another example where context matters. For example, the instruction

From the Limmat River go to Bahnhof Strasse and turn right

seems reliable, but it may not be. The "turn right" instruction assumes that you are traveling in a specific direction. If you are traveling east, the instruction works, because you are in the context the instruction writer assumed (see Figure 10.1). But if you are traveling west, the instruction doesn't work because you need to turn left on *Bahnhof Strasse*. You are following the instructions in a context the writer didn't expect. Turning right will send you north if you approach from one direction and send you south if you approach from the other direction.

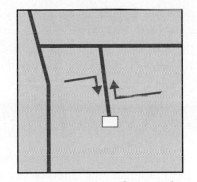

Figure 10.1. *Diagram of approaching a street (Bahnhof Strasse) from different directions, giving the "turn right" instruction different meanings.*

You must consider the context in which to apply the algorithm—in this case, the point of departure. You can write such conditions as input conditions or you can simply avoid them. The best solution is not to use words like *right* that depend on orientation until you've established it. Terms like *north*, which are orientation independent, are better.

✓ check LIST >>   **Travel Directions:** To give better travel directions, follow these rules to reduce the dependence on context.

- ☑ *Give the starting point, "From Place de la Concorde. . . ."*
- ☑ *State the direction of travel, "Going west on Route 66. . . ."*
- ☑ *Give landmarks, especially when turning, "Turn left; you'll see a temple (Todai-ji) on your right. . . ."*
- ☑ *Give measured distances (2.3 miles) instead of blocks, cross streets, or traffic lights, which can be ambiguous.*
- ☑ *Include an "overshot" test, "If you cross Via Giuseppi Verdi, you've gone too far."*

Program versus Algorithm

A program is an algorithm that has been customized to solve a specific task under a specific set of circumstances in a specific language. Making change—subtracting an amount of money, *x*, from a larger amount paid, *y*, and returning the result as coins and currency—is an *algorithm*, but making change in US dollars is a *program*. The program uses the "making change" algorithm specialized to the denominations of coins (1¢, 5¢, 10¢, 25¢, 50¢, $1) and paper currency ($1, $2, $5, $10, . . .) of the United States. Making change in New Zealand dollars is a different program; it also uses the making change algorithm but with the New Zealand coins (5¢, 10¢, 20¢, 50¢, $1, $2) and paper currency ($5, $10 $20, . . .). From our point of view, whether the method is general (algorithm) or specialized (program) makes no difference. They're both algorithms and the issues are the same.

AN ALGORITHM: *ALPHABETIZE CDS*

It's time for an example algorithm. Though most of the algorithms in later chapters use a programming language to ensure precision, our first algorithms are written in English.

Imagine that your CD collection, which fills a large, slotted rack, is completely disorganized. You've decided it's time to get organized, so you want to alphabetize your CDs by the name of the group, the performing musician, or perhaps the composer. How would you go about solving this problem?

Here is an algorithm for alphabetizing your CDs:

ALPHABETIZE CDS

Input: An unordered sequence of CDs filling a slotted rack
Output: The same CDs in the rack in alphabetical order
Instructions:

1. Use the term *Artist_Of* to refer to the name of the group, musician, or composer on a CD.

2. Decide which end of the rack is the beginning of the alphabetic sequence and call the slot at that end the *Alpha* slot.

3. Call the slot next to the *Alpha* slot the *Beta* slot.

4. If the *Artist_Of* the CD in the *Alpha* slot comes later in the alphabet than the *Artist_Of* the CD in the *Beta* slot, swap the CDs; otherwise, continue.

5. If there is a slot following the *Beta* slot, begin calling it the *Beta* slot and go to Instruction 4; otherwise, continue.

6. If there are two or more slots following the *Alpha* slot, begin calling the slot following the *Alpha* slot *Alpha* and begin calling the slot following it the *Beta* slot, and go to Instruction 4; otherwise, stop.

In the next sections, we'll check to see that the properties of definitiveness, effectiveness, and finiteness hold true; in other words, we'll check that we truly have an algorithm.

How does this algorithm work? Follow Figure 10.2 as we go through the process.

Instruction 1.   *Use the term* Artist_Of *to refer to the name of the group, musician, or composer.* This instruction gives a name to the operation of locating the name used for alphabetizing. (*Artist_Of* is shorthand for extracting the name of the performer, simplifying Instruction 4; it could be eliminated at the expense of a wordier Instruction 4.)

Instruction 2. *Decide which end of the rack is the beginning of the alphabetic sequence and call the slot at that end the* Alpha *slot.* The purpose of this instruction is to give the process a starting point. It also gives the initial meaning to the word *Alpha.* In the algorithm, *Alpha* refers to slots in the rack. At the start, *Alpha* refers to the first slot in the alphabetic sequence. As the algorithm progresses, it refers to successive slots in the rack.

Instruction 3. *Call the slot next to the* Alpha *slot the* Beta *slot.* This instruction gives the word *Beta* its initial meaning. The names *Alpha* and *Beta* have no inherent meaning; the programmer needs to name slots in the rack and chose these words.

Instruction 4. *If the* Artist_Of *the CD in the* Alpha *slot comes later in the alphabet than the* Artist_Of *the CD in the* Beta *slot, swap the CDs; otherwise, continue.* This is the workhorse instruction of the algorithm. It compares the names of the recording artists of the CDs in the slots *Alpha* and *Beta* and, if necessary, exchanges them so that they are in the proper order. It may not be necessary to swap if the CDs are already positioned properly. But either way, when this instruction is done, the alphabetically earlier CD is in the *Alpha* slot.

Instruction 5. *If there is a slot following the* Beta *slot, begin calling it the* Beta *slot and go to Instruction 4; otherwise, continue.* This instruction gives a new definition for the *Beta* slot so that it refers to the next slot in the sequence, if there is one. With this new definition of *Beta,* Instruction 4 can be executed again, comparing a different pair of CDs. One of the pair, the CD in the *Alpha* slot, was compared the last time Instruction 4 was executed, but because *Beta* refers to a new slot, the pair of CDs is "new." If all slots have been considered—that is, there is no next slot for *Beta* to refer to—the algorithm continues to Instruction 6 instead of returning to Instruction 4.

Instruction 6. *If there are two or more slots following the* Alpha *slot, begin calling the slot following the* Alpha *slot* Alpha *and the slot following it the* Beta *slot, and go to Instruction 4; otherwise, stop.* By the time we get to this instruction, the alphabetically earliest CD is in the *Alpha* slot, thanks to the combination of Instructions 4 and 5. The idea is to advance *Alpha* to the next slot and to sweep through the last of the rack, again locating the alphabetically earliest CD with the Instruction 4–5 combination, and now it's the alphabetically next-earliest. Then *Alpha* moves again, the Instruction 4–5 combination is repeated again, and so on. Each time, the CDs in slots up to and including *Alpha* are alphabetized. When there are no longer enough slots to call a new one *Alpha* and the next one *Beta,* the whole rack is alphabetized and the algorithm stops.

The *Alphabetize CDs* approach is better than dumping the CDs on the floor, and trying to return them to the rack in order. Keeping the CDs in the rack while it

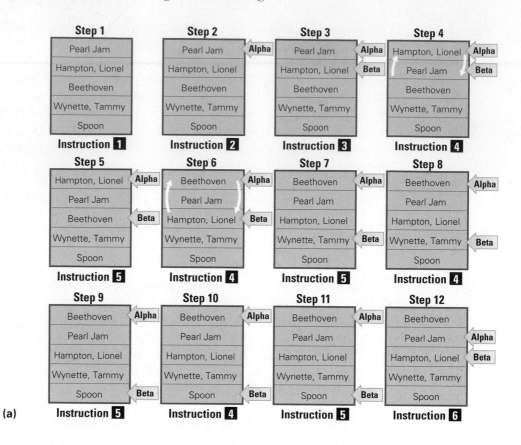

Figure 10.2. *The steps of* Alphabetize CDs *algorithm. A snapshot of the CD rack is shown at the completion of each instruction. Notice how* Beta *sweeps through all of the slots following* Alpha. *After the first 11 steps, the alphabetically earliest CD,* Beethoven, *is in the* Alpha *slot.*

orders them is not the property that makes *Alphabetize CDs* an algorithm. It could be rewritten to work with the CDs spread out on the floor. Rather, it is the fact that *Alphabetize CDs* uses a method to find the alphabetically first CD, then the next, then the next after that, and so forth until the alphabetically last CD is found. That is, *Alphabetize CDs* is systematic.

ANALYZING *ALPHABETIZE CDS* ALGORITHM

The *Alphabetize CDs* example illustrates the five basic properties of algorithms. The input and output are specified. Each instruction is described precisely—or as precisely as English allows—fulfilling the definiteness requirement. The operations

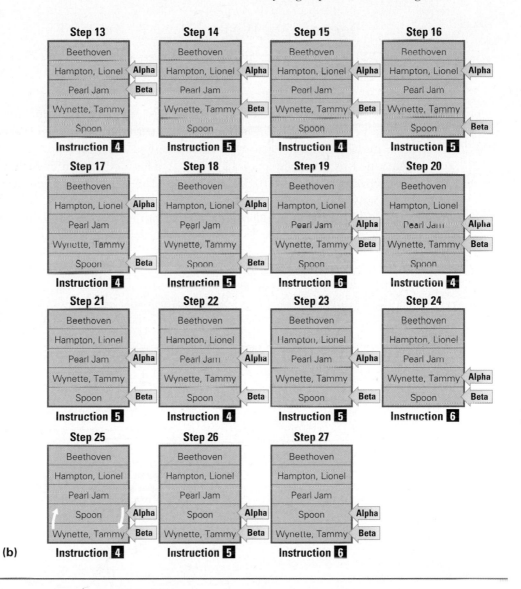

of the algorithm are effective because actions like selecting the next slot and counting to see if there are at least two slots left are simple and mechanically doable. The most complicated operation, deciding which of two artists' names is earlier in the alphabet, is also a completely mechanical process. We only need to compare the first two letters of the names; the one closer to A is the earlier. If those two letters are the same, we compare the second letters, and so forth. So, our algorithm has the effectiveness property. Finally, the algorithm is finite. Because Instructions 4, 5, and 6 are repeated, this property is not so obvious. However, notice that each time Instruction 4 is repeated, *Alpha* and *Beta* refer to a different pair of slots that has not previously been considered. Because slots can be paired in a rack in a finite number of *different* ways, Instruction 4 cannot be repeated forever. Instructions 5 and 6 cannot be repeated forever without repeating Instruction 4 forever. Hence, the program satisfies the finiteness property.

A Deeper Analysis

We have shown that *Alphabetize CDs* meets the requirements of an algorithm, but there are other, more interesting aspects to discover.

Structural Features.   The algorithm has two instructions, 5 and 6, in which the agent is directed to repeat instructions. Such instructions create **loops** in the algorithm. Loops are instruction sequences that repeat; they are more obvious when the instructions are given in a form other than English. Consider the flowchart in Figure 10.3. Loops are fundamental to algorithms because they cause parts of the computation to be performed as many times as there are data items. So, the loops in the *Alphabetize CDs* algorithm repeat instructions as many times as there are slots, or CDs.

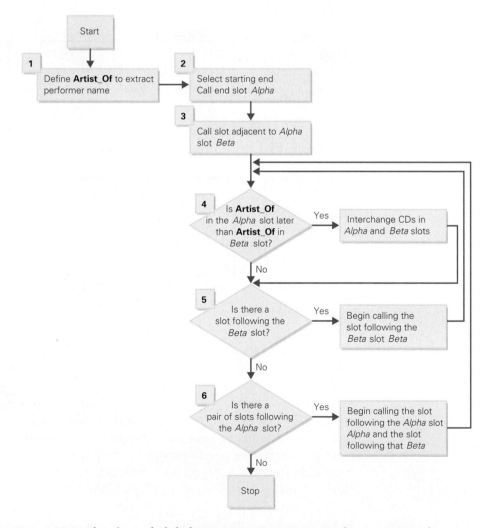

Figure 10.3. *Flowchart of* Alphabetize CDs. *Operations are shown in rectangles; decisions are shown in diamonds. Arrows indicate the sequencing of the operations.*

Loops and Tests. A loop must include a **test** to determine if the instructions should be repeated one more time. As Figure 10.3 shows, *Alphabetize CDs* has two loops. Instruction 5 tests whether there are slots following the *Beta* slot; if so, Instruction 4 is repeated; if not, that repetition of the inner loop ends. Instruction 6 tests whether there is at least a pair of slots after the *Alpha* slot. If so, Instructions 1 and 5 are repeated; if not, the outer loop ends. These tests cause the loop to complete and ensure the finiteness property.

*fit***BYTE**

Failed Test. Requiring a test to determine when to stop repeating instructions may seem obvious, but some shampoo directions read: "Wet hair, massage in shampoo, rinse, repeat," failing the finiteness test. What runs out first—the shampoo or the hot water?

Notice that for the loop to continue at Instruction 5, *Beta* must move to the next slot. Similarly, Instruction 6 moves *Alpha* to the next slot and resets *Beta* to follow it. These moves ensure that on the next test *Beta* and *Alpha* refer to different slots. If there are no changes between the two consecutive tests, the outcome is the same and the loop never stops.

Assumptions. Assumptions are made in specifying *Alphabetize CDs*. First, we assume (and state in the Input specification) that the CD rack is full. This matters because the instructions do not handle the case of empty slots. (For example, if *Beta* were an empty slot, how would Instruction 4 operate?) The algorithm requires that the *Artist_Of* two CDs are compared, but if one or both of the slots are empty, the agent might not know what to do. The specification is correct because it states that it expects a full CD rack as input. A better solution would explain what to do if the rack is not full. Then the "full" requirement could be dropped.

"Following" an Assumption. When the *Beta* slot is first set in Instruction 3, only one slot is next to *Alpha* because in Instruction 2 *Alpha* is chosen to be an end slot. This ensures that there is a unique slot *following Alpha* for *Beta* to refer to, and so the specification is effective. There is an assumption in the use of the term *following* in Instructions 5 and 6. Instruction 5 refers to a slot "following" *Beta,* which means a slot further from the end chosen in Instruction 2. Similarly, Instruction 6 refers to a pair of slots "following" *Alpha,* meaning the slots further from the end chosen in Instruction 2. But, nowhere is the term *following* defined. This makes the orientation of the term *following* an assumption. The orientation can be defined—and would have to be for a computer to execute the algorithm—but people know what "following" means.

The Exchange Sort Algorithm

The *Alphabetize CDs* example illustrates a standard algorithm called **Exchange Sort**. In the *Alphabetize CDs* example, we used the Exchange Sort algorithm to alphabetize CDs based on the names of the musicians. The Exchange Sort algorithm compares pairs of items chosen in a particular way, exchanges them if they are out of order, and continues to sweep through the items to locate the next minimal item.

A different program based on the Exchange Sort algorithm might alphabetize CDs based on their titles, and another might alphabetize CDs based on their recording company's label. The Exchange Sort algorithm can be specialized into programs for alphabetizing books by their authors, sequencing books by their ISBNs, ordering canceled checks by date, and so on. When we choose the kind of item (e.g., CDs), the criterion for "order" (e.g., alphabetically ordered by musician's name), and specific names for keeping track of the items (e.g., *Alpha* and *Beta)*, we create a program based on the algorithm. The algorithm is a systematic process, and the program is that process formulated for a particular situation. An algorithm continues to be an algorithm even when it is specialized into a program.

Are there other ways to alphabetize CDs? Of course. There are dozens of sorting algorithms; most of them can be the basis of programs for alphabetizing CDs. Why one algorithm is better than another is the sort of question computer scientists worry about. We don't have to be concerned.

{GREAT *fit* MOMENTS}

Impossible Dream >>

At the start of the twentieth century, German mathematician David Hilbert listed several great problems worthy of study in the new century. His tenth problem was to develop an algorithm to decide whether logical propositions were true or false. Algorithmically testing truth seemed like a great goal. Logicians Bertrand Russell and Alfred North Whitehead began setting down axioms and logic rules for mathematics in their three volume *Principia Mathematica*. But in 1931, Slovak-American logician Kurt Gödel astonished everyone by proving that mathematical truth testing wasn't possible. Soon American logician Alonzo Church and English mathematician Alan M. Turing extended Gödel's work, proving there can be no algorithm to decide truth and laying the foundation for theoretical computer science.

ABSTRACTION IN ALGORITHMIC THINKING

The *Alphabetize CDs* example seems very complicated when described in so much detail, but it's easier to understand than it first appears because we can think of parts of the algorithm's behavior as whole units rather than as individual instructions. This is abstraction, as defined in Chapter 1.

The idea of treating parts of the algorithm's behavior as a unit—not the instructions themselves, but the behavior the instructions define—is key to algorithmic thinking. We want to discipline ourselves to think about algorithms this way.

Know the Score. Try the Alphabetize CDs algorithm on five or six of your favorite CDs. Doing so simplifies the ideas in this section.

Beta Sweep Abstraction

Instructions 4 and 5 illustrate the idea of an abstract computational unit. We call it *Beta* Sweep. It's the operation of considering in order all CDs following a specific *Alpha*. The sweep tick-tick-ticks through those slots, comparing artists, and swapping them when necessary. More precisely,

> **Beta** Sweep: While *Alpha* points to a fixed slot, *Beta* visits each slot following *Alpha*, in sequence, comparing its CD with the CD in the *Alpha* slot, and swapping them when necessary.

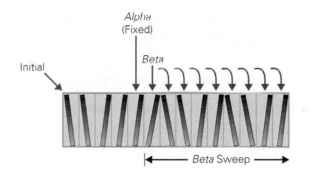

By thinking of *Beta* sweeping through the CDs as a single computational unit, we recognize that it has the effect of finding the next CD in order and moving it to the *Alpha* slot.

Properties of *Beta* Sweep Abstraction. When we think of the *Beta* sweep abstraction, we recognize some of its important properties. The *Beta* sweep is

1. **Exhaustive.** It considers all CDs from the *Alpha* slot to the end of the rack, making sure that none is left out.

2. **Nonredundant.** It considers each slot following *Alpha* only once. It never considers the same pair of CDs twice, which ensures that the sweep will stop.

3. **Progressive.** At any given time, the alphabetically earliest CD seen so far in this sweep is in the *Alpha* slot.

4. **Goal-achieving.** After the sweep completes, the alphabetically earliest CD among all CDs considered in this sweep (including *Alpha*) is in *Alpha*.

These are not general properties of all algorithms. These are only specific properties of the *Beta* sweep abstraction of the *Alphabetize CDs* program. (They are also properties of the "inner loop sweep" of the Exchange Sort algorithm if we make them general, not referring to "CDs," "slots," "*Alpha*," "*Beta*," etc.).

Where did the four properties of the *Beta* sweep abstraction come from? We noticed them when we analyzed how the *Alphabetize CDs* algorithm works, (see "Analyzing Alphabetize CDs Algorithm" section.) They are examples of features we should notice about the behavior of an algorithm when we study how it operates. Why? Because these properties (together with the *Alpha* sweep properties below) will convince us that the algorithm actually works, that it achieves its goal of alphabetizing.

To see how the properties of the *Beta* sweep can convince us that the algorithm works, first note that properties 1 through 3 imply property 4. That is, the *Beta* sweep considers all CDs once and keeps the alphabetically earliest in *Alpha* at all times. That behavior after processing all CDs in a sweep ensures that the alphabetically earliest CD is in *Alpha*, which is part of the answer.

Alpha Sweep Abstraction

For the rest of the answer, consider the **Alpha Sweep** abstraction.

> **Alpha Sweep:** *Alpha* sweeps from the slot where the alphabetization begins through all slots (except the last) performing the *Beta* sweep instructions each time.

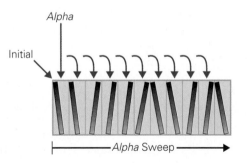

Properties of *Alpha* Sweep Abstraction. We can list properties that we notice about the *Alpha* sweep abstraction. The *Alpha* sweep is

1. **Exhaustive.** It considers all CDs from the first to (but not including) the last.

2. **Nonredundant.** No slot is assigned to *Alpha* more than once, so the process stops if the *Beta* sweep stops, and it does, by property 2 of the *Beta* sweep abstraction.

3. **Progressive.** At the end of each *Beta* sweep, the alphabetically next earliest CD is in *Alpha*.

4. **Complete**. When the last *Beta* sweep is completed, the CD in the last slot is later in the alphabet than the CD in the next-to-last slot because the last *Beta* sweep involved these last two slots and it is property 3 of the *Beta* sweep (Refer to Figure 10.2, Step 25.)

5. **Goal-achieving**. The alphabetically earliest CD is in the first slot at the end of the first *Beta* sweep, by its property 4 and the fact that all CDs are considered; thereafter, in every new position for *Alpha*, the *Beta* sweep assigns the next earliest CD. The program alphabetizes.

Property 5 of the *Alpha* sweep says this program works. We stated that it did originally, but by noticing these properties of the two abstractions—*Beta* sweep and *Alpha* sweep—we can see *why* it works. When we create computer solutions, knowing why our solution works is the only way to be sure the solution does work, achieving our IT goal. Algorithmic thinking involves inventing algorithms that achieve our goals and understanding why they work.

Abstracting for Other Algorithms and Programs

We must emphasize that the *Alpha* sweep and *Beta* sweep abstractions are *specific* to the Exchange Sort algorithm and to programs like *Alphabetize CDs* derived from it. Other algorithms and programs exhibit different behaviors and require different abstractions based on the way they solve their problems. Those abstractions will have properties different from (but analogous to) the four properties of the *Beta* sweep and the five properties of the *Alpha* sweep. Every situation is different, but the approach—abstracting the behavior and understanding the properties—is always the same.

Looking to the Future

This chapter introduced several new ideas. The reward for the reader who has reached this point with an understanding of these concepts is the satisfaction of having seen nearly all of the basic ideas underlying algorithms and programming. With perhaps two exceptions, every programming idea covered in the book appears in this chapter. So, there is not that much to algorithms and programming—all that's left is elaborating on these ideas and mastering them. That's plenty, of course, but it doesn't require many more ideas.

Because we have spent a lot of time understanding these ideas, it is worth it to spend a moment naming them, especially since we will run into them again in later chapters:

> **Variables**. *Alpha* and *Beta* are variables in the *Alphabetize CDs* program.

> **Locations**. The slots in the CD rack are like a computer's memory locations.

> **Values**. The CDs are the values stored in the locations.

> **Function**. *Artist_Of* is a function for locating the name of the group or performer on a CD (a value).

> **Initialization.** Instructions 2 and 3 initialize the variables *Alpha* and *Beta*, respectively.

> **Loops.** The Instructions 4 and 5 form a loop; the Instructions 4 through 6 also form a loop.

> **Array.** The rack is a (linear) array.

We will study these terms more completely in upcoming chapters.

SUMMARY

In this chapter we introduced algorithms, one of the most fundamental forms of thinking. We now understand that:

> Everyday algorithms (e.g., recipes), can be ineffective because we write them in an imprecise natural language.

> Algorithms have five fundamental properties.

> Alphabetizing CDs in a filled rack is an algorithm. The six-instruction program named two slots, *Alpha* and *Beta,* and made repeated sweeps over the remaining CDs.

> *Alphabetize CDs* is a program built using the Exchange Sort algorithm.

> Processing *Alphabetize CDs* involves two interacting behaviors: the *Beta* sweep and the *Alpha* sweep. These abstractions have several properties, which explain why the algorithm produces an alphabetized sequence.

> Abstractions and their properties are the essence of algorithmic thinking. Algorithmic thinking can become second nature, making us effective problem solvers.

EXERCISES

Multiple Choice

1. An algorithm has _____ basic requirements
   A. three
   B. four
   C. five
   D. seven

2. An algorithm must be
   A. precise
   B. approximate
   C. concise
   D. general

3. Which of the following does not fit?
   A. natural language
   B. formal language
   C. synthetic language
   D. programming language

4. A computer program must
   A. complete a specific task
   B. work in a specific set of circumstances
   C. be written in a specific language
   D. all of the above

5. Which instructions are repeated in the *Alphabetizing CDs* algorithm on pages 284–285?
   A. all of them
   B. 4 and 5
   C. 4 to 6
   D. 3 to 5

6. If you saw a monitor, keyboard, mouse, printer, and CPU, you would assume these parts formed a computer. This is an example of
   A. abstraction
   B. encapsulation
   C. utilization
   D. algorithm

7. You notice that the only item in alphabetical order after the first *Beta* sweep of *Alphabetize CDs* is the first item. This is an example of
   A. abstraction
   B. encapsulation
   C. utilization
   D. algorithm

8. In the *Alphabetize CDs*
   A. the *Alpha* sweep points to every slot except the last
   B. the *Beta* sweep points to every slot on every sweep
   C. the *Alpha* points to the first slot of the sweep and the *Beta* points to the rest
   D. the *Alpha* points to the first slot and the *Beta* points to the last slot

9. Following an *Alpha* sweep, how many items are you sure are in the correct order?
   A. 0
   B. 1
   C. 2
   D. all of them

Short Answer

1. An explicit set of instructions is a(n) _____.

2. A programming language is a(n) _____ language because it is precisely defined.

3. A(n) _____ is a generalized method while a(n) _____ is a specialized solution.

4. The _____ of an algorithm defines the setting for its use.

5. A(n) _____ finds the item in a list that is next in order to the *Alpha* item.

6. In a *Beta* sweep, the _____ property makes sure every item in the list is considered.

7. In a *Beta* sweep, the _____ property makes sure the sweep is finite.

8. The *Alpha* and the *Beta* in the *Alphabetize CDs* program are called _____.

9. A(n) _____ is the computer term of a set of instructions that repeat.

10. The memory locations of a computer store items, but the contents of these locations contain the _____ of the items.

Exercises

1. Describe the process for subtracting a four-digit number from a five-digit number.

2. Why aren't natural languages such as English good for programming?

3. Using the *Alphabetize CDs* algorithm, illustrate the five properties of an algorithm.

4. Does the instruction "go downhill" have the same problems as "go right"? Explain.

5. What is the purpose of the *Artist_Of*, step 1, of the *Alphabetize CDs* algorithm?

6. Given the following artists, write down the instructions and steps to put these in order.

Newton-John, Olivia
Hill, Faith
Incubus
Chapman, Steven Curtis
Mendelssohn, Felix

7. What would you need to do to arrange the CDs in reverse order instead of alphabetical order? What would you need to do to arrange them in order by copyright?

8. Discuss what you would need to add to the *Alphabetize CDs* algorithm to alphabetize the CDs of Juice Newton, Wayne Newton, and Olivia Newton-John.

9. Explain why *Alpha* doesn't have to reference the last slot.

10. Write a version of the Exchange Sort algorithm to alphabetize CDs in a slotted rack, from last to first order; that is, that has the same result as *Alphabetize CDs*, but from the back end forward.

chapter

11

LIGHT, SOUND, MAGIC
Representing Multimedia Digitally

learning objectives

> Explain how RGB color is represented in bytes

> Change an RGB color by binary addition

> Explain the meaning of "computing on a representation"

> Explain concepts related to digitizing sound waves

> Explain the meaning of the Bias-Free Universal Medium Principle

> Explain the difference between "bits" and "binary numbers"

chapter 11

LIGHT, SOUND, MAGIC
Representing Multimedia Digitally

Blue color is everlastingly appointed by the Deity to be a source of delight.

—JOHN RUSKIN, 1853

Science will never be able to reduce the value of a sunset to arithmetic.

—DR LOUIS ORR, 1960

A TYPICAL DAY at college involves so many forms of digital information that few of us notice: There's sending email, with an attached photo, to your folks, downloading MP3 tunes from the Web, having the required EKG to try out for the swim team, admiring your roommate's new DVD player, using the smart ID card from your work, and researching with the ever-popular database called the Library Online Catalog. Though these examples seem to be much more complicated than the digital representations we've seen so far—well, maybe not the catalog—they are not. As we'll see in this chapter, all these common multimedia build on the basic ideas we've already learned.

From our earlier discussions we learned that discrete things—things that can be separated from each other—can be represented by bits. We begin this chapter by looking closer at RGB color, which we've mentioned several times before. We learn how a color is encoded in bits, and how we can make the colors darker or lighter. This process—a basic part of digital photo software—is little more than arithmetic on binary numbers. Changing the color of an image and performing other modifications illustrates these concepts. Next, we discuss JPEG and MPEG and the need for compression techniques for images and video. We go on to discuss optical character recognition to emphasize the advantages of encoding information in digital form. The discussion of virtual reality that follows helps to clarify how well computers can create synthetic worlds. And finally, the whole topic of digital representation is summarized in one fundamental principle.

DIGITIZING COLOR

In Chapter 8 we discussed the binary encoding of keyboard characters to create the ASCII representation, but we (and the creators) didn't pay much attention to which bit patterns are associated with which characters. It's true that in ASCII the numerals are encoded in numeric order, and the letter sets are roughly in alphabetical order, but the assignment is largely arbitrary. The specifics of the keyboard character encoding don't matter much (as long as everyone agrees on them) because the bytes are used as units. We rarely manipulate the individual bits that make up the pattern for the characters. For other encodings, however, manipulating the individual bits is essential.

RGB Colors: Binary Representation

Recall that giving the intensities for the three constituent colors—red, green, and blue (RGB)—specifies a color on the monitor. Each of the RGB colors is assigned a byte (8 bits) to record the intensity of that color. But the color intensities are not assigned arbitrarily, like the letter characters in ASCII. Instead, color intensity is represented as a quantity, ranging from 0 (none) through 255 (most intense); the higher the number, the more intense the color. When we want to change the intensity, we just add to or subtract from the values, implying that the encoding should make it simple to perform arithmetic on the intensities. So, RGB intensities are encoded as binary numbers.

Binary Numbers Compared with Decimal Numbers. Binary numbers are different from decimal numbers because they are limited to two digits, 0 and 1, rather than the customary ten digits, 0 through 9. The number of digits is the **base** of the numbering system. But that is really the only difference. The other features distinguishing binary from decimal relate to that one difference.

For example, in decimal numbers, we use a **place value** representation, where each "place" represents the next higher power of 10, starting from the right. In binary, it's the same idea, but with higher powers of 2.

Place Value in a Decimal Number. Recall that to find the quantity expressed by a decimal number, the digit in a place is multiplied by the place value and the results are added. So, in Table 11.1, for example, the result is one thousand ten, found by adding from right to left: the digit in the 1's place (0) multiplied by its place value (1), plus the digit in the 10's place (1) multiplied by its place value (10), and so on: $0 \times 1 + 1 \times 10 + 0 \times 100 + 1 \times 1000$.

Table 11.1. *The decimal number 1010 representing one thousand ten = 1000 + 10.*

10^3	10^2	10^1	10^0	Decimal Place Values
1	0	1	0	Digits of Decimal Number
1×10^3	0×10^2	1×10^1	0×10^0	Multiply place digit by place value
1000	0	10	0	and add to get a decimal 1010

Place Value in a Binary Number. Binary works in exactly the same way except that the base of the power is not 10 but 2, because there are only two digits, not ten. Therefore, instead of the decimal place values, 1, 10, 100, 1000, . . . , resulting from the successive powers of 10, the binary place values are 1, 2, 4, 8, 16, . . . , resulting from the successive powers of 2:

Power	Decimal	Binary
0	$1 = 10^0$	$1 = 2^0$
1	$10 = 10^1$	$2 = 2^1$
2	$100 = 10^2$	$4 = 2^2$
3	$1,000 = 10^3$	$8 = 2^3$
4	$10,000 = 10^4$	$16 = 2^4$
...	...	...

Thus, if we are given a binary representation, we can find the (decimal equivalent) value if we multiply the digit times the place value and add the results. See Table 11.2, which shows that 1010 in binary has the value ten in decimal: $0 \times 1 + 1 \times 2 + 0 \times 4 + 1 \times 8$.

Table 11.2. *The binary number 1010, representing the decimal number ten = 8 + 2.*

2^3	2^2	2^1	2^0	Binary Place Values
1	0	1	0	Bits of Binary Number
1×2^3	0×2^2	1×2^1	0×2^0	Multiply place bit by place value
8	0	2	0	and add to get a decimal 10

*fit***BYTE** | **2nd Base.** The "base" of a numbering system, 10 for decimal and 2 for binary, is also called its **radix**.

Because powers of 2 don't increase as fast as powers of 10, binary numbers need more places than decimal numbers to represent the same amount. So, for example, representing one thousand ten as a binary number requires ten bits, as shown in Table 11.3. Compare Table 11.3 with Table 11.1.

Table 11.3. *Binary representation of the decimal number one thousand ten = 11 1111 0010*

2^9	2^8	2^7	2^6	2^5	2^4	2^3	2^2	2^1	2^0	Binary Place Values
1	1	1	1	1	1	0	0	1	0	Bits of Binary Number
$1×2^9$	$1×2^8$	$1×2^7$	$1×2^6$	$1×2^5$	$1×2^4$	$0×2^3$	$0×2^2$	$1×2^1$	$0×2^0$	Multiply place bit by place value
512	256	128	64	32	16	0	0	2	0	and add to get decimal 1010

Converting a Binary Number to a Decimal Number. Because the bit is either 0 or 1, the "multiply the digit times the place value" rule is especially easy in binary—a 1 means include the place value and a 0 means "forget it." So, to convert a binary number to its decimal equivalent, just add the place values for the places with 1's. Thus, in Figure 11.3, if we start with the highest place value, we have $512 + 256 + 128 + 64 + 32 + 16 + 2 = 1010$.

---

fit **TIP**

Spacing Out. When writing long decimal numbers, North Americans usually separate groups of three digits with a comma for readability. Binary numbers, which are usually even longer, are grouped in four-digit units, separated by a space.

Black and White Colors

Returning to the representation of color, the fact that a byte—8 bits—is allocated to each of the RGB intensities means that the smallest intensity is 0000 0000, which is 0, of course, and the largest value is 1111 1111. To figure out what decimal number this is, we add up the place values for the 1's,

$$1111\ 1111 \quad = 2^7 + 2^6 + 2^5 + 2^4 + 2^3 + 2^2 + 2^1 + 2^0$$
$$= 128 + 64 + 32 + 16 + 8 + 4 + 2 + 1$$
$$= 255$$

which explains why the range of values is 0 through 255 for each color.

As we learned in Chapter 4, black is no color,

0000 0000 0000 0000 0000 0000   *RGB bit assignment for black*
   red   green   blue
   byte   byte   byte

whereas white

1111 1111 1111 1111 1111 1111   *RGB bit assignment for white*
   red   green   blue
   byte   byte   byte

has full intensity for each color. Between these extremes is a whole range of intensity.

Changing a Decimal Number to a Binary Number

As we've seen, to convert a binary number to decimal representation we add up the powers of 2 corresponding to 1 bits. Converting a decimal number into a binary representation is only slightly harder, and is essentially the opposite process. We proceed by filling in the following table, which works for numbers less than 1000:

Number being converted										
Place value	512	256	128	64	32	16	8	4	2	1
Subtract										
Binary Number										

Start by placing the number to be converted, say 200, in the first cell.

Number being converted	200									
Place value	512	256	128	64	32	16	8	4	2	1
Subtract										
Binary Number										

Then we work across the table performing one of the following operations in each column depending on how large the number being converted is compared to the place value:

> **Smaller:** If the number being converted is smaller than the place value below it, copy the number into the next cell to its right; enter a 0 as the binary digit.
>
> **Equal or Larger:** If the number being converted is equal to or larger than the place value below it, subtract the place value from the number and copy the result into the first cell of the next column; enter a 1 as the binary digit.

Thus, the first step in converting 200 to binary is

Number being converted	200	200								
Place value	512	256	128	64	32	16	8	4	2	1
Subtract										
Binary Number	0									

and the completed table

Number being converted	200	200	200	72	8	8	8	0	0	0
Place value	512	256	128	64	32	16	8	4	2	1
Subtract			72	8			0			
Binary Number	0	0	1	1	0	0	1	0	0	0

indicates that the result is 1100 1000. Like decimal representation, we can drop any leading zeros.

Lighten Up: Changing Color by Addition

Returning to our discussion of color representation, the extreme colors of black and white are easy, but what color does the following represent?

1100 1000 **1100 1000** **1100 1000**
   red   green   blue
   byte   byte   . byte

First we notice that each byte contains the decimal value 200, which we recognize from the conversion just explained. So our mystery color is the color produced by the specification `RGB (200, 200, 200)`. In HTML we write this in hexadecimal as `#C8C8C8`. Like black and white, our mystery color has equal amounts of red, green, and blue, and it is closer to white than black. In fact, it is a medium gray ▪. All colors with equal amounts of RGB are gray if they are not black or white. It's just a question of whether they're closer to black or white.

To Increase Intensity: Add in Binary

To make a *lighter* color of gray, we obviously change the common value to be closer to white. Suppose we do this by increasing each of the RGB values by 16—that is, by adding 16 to each byte—as shown in Figure 11.1.

1100 1000	binary representing decimal number	200
+ 1 0000	binary representing decimal number	16
1101 1000	binary representing decimal number	216

Figure 11.1. *Adding 16 to an RGB value.*

The result in Figure 11.1 is found by simply setting the 16's place value—that is, changing it from 0 to 1. When the increase is applied to each color, the result is

1101 1000 **1101 1000** **1101 1000**
red   green   blue
byte   byte   byte

is a lighter shade of gray ■.

Lighter Still: Adding with Carry Digits

Imagine that we want the color lighter still by another 16 units of intensity for each RGB byte. Adding another 16 isn't quite as easy this time. The 16's position in the binary representation 1101 1000 of decimal 216 is already filled with a 1. So we "carry" to the next higher place. Thus,

1	carry digit	
1101 1000	binary representing decimal number	216
+ 1 0000	binary representing decimal number	16
1110 1000	binary representing decimal number	232

So our color intensities are

1110 1000 **1110 1000** **1110 1000**
red   green   blue
byte   byte   byte

Notice that if we'd simply added 32 to 200 originally, we'd have ended up with the same result—the gray with each intensity set at 232 ■.

We just illustrated the binary addition process. As with other aspects of binary, binary addition is similar to decimal addition. We work from right to left, adding corresponding digits in each place position and writing the sum below. Like decimal addition, there are two cases. Sometimes, we can add the two numbers and the result is expressed as a single digit. That was the case the first time we added 16 to the RGB byte: we added 1 + 0 in the place and the result was 1. Other times, when we add two digits their sum is larger than can be expressed by a single digit, so we must carry to the next higher place. That was the case the second time we added 16 to the RGB byte: we added 1 + 1 in the place, which is 10 in binary, and wrote a 0 in the place and carried a 1 to the next higher digit. Because there may be a carry involved, it is best to think of adding as involving three digits in each place: the two digits being added plus (possibly) a carry.

The rules for binary addition can be learned using an example for each case.

The first example—called the "no carry-in" case—adds A + B when A is the binary number 1100, which is 12 in decimal, and B is 1010, which is 10 in decimal.

⊔⊔⊔⊔	Illustrates the "no carry-in" cases
1 0000	← Carry, shown explicitly
1100	← A
+ 1010	← B
1 0110	← Sum

The four no carry cases of adding binary digits—all combinations of 0 and 1—are illustrated. In each case there is no *carry-in*—that is, no carry from the previous place. The only interesting case is 1 + 1. Of course, in decimal 1 + 1 = 2. But in binary, there is no 2 digit, only 0 and 1, so the result of 1 + 1 cannot be expressed by a single digit. The decimal number 2 is 10 in binary, so we put down the 0 in the place and carry the 1 to the next higher position. The carry to the next higher digit is called a *carry-out*, and we notice that the carry-out of one place becomes the carry-in of the next higher place. (Verify that the sum is the binary representation of 22 = 12 + 10.)

The second example, the "carry-in" case, adds A + B when A is 1011, which is 11 in decimal, and 111, which is 7 in decimal. Leading 0's are shown to complete the picture, and the rightmost place adds 1 + 1 to get the "carrying process" started.

```
   ↓  ↓↓↓        Illustrates the "carry-in" cases
   1  1110    ←  Carry, shown explicitly
   0  1011    ←  A
 + 0  0111    ←  B
 ─────────
   1  0010    ←  Sum
```

The four cases illustrate adding binary digits with a carry-in. Three of the four have the property that the sum of the two digits and the carry are too large to be expressed by a single binary digit, so there is a carry-out to the next higher place. Only the leftmost case, 0 + 0 with a carry-in, can be expressed by a single digit, 1. The new case is the second from right position, which adds 1 + 1 with a carry-in yielding the decimal 3 or binary 11. We write down the 1 in the place and carry a 1 to the next higher position. (Verify that the sum is the binary representation of 18 = 11 + 7.)

The rules from the examples are summarized in Table 11.4 We can now apply the rules to add the binary numbers 110 1001 and 110 0011. (What decimal numbers are these?) This time, we follow the usual procedure of showing only the nonzero carries.

```
    11     11     ←  Carry
      110  1001   ←  A
  +   110  0011   ←  B
  ──────────────
     1100  1100   ←  Sum
```

Binary addition is so easy, even computers can do it.

---

*fit***BYTE**

One and one. Sometimes we rhetorically ask if a clueless person knows that 1 + 1 = 2.

How clueless are computers?

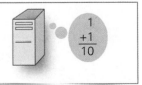

Table 11.4. *Summary of the rules for binary addition. The carry-in is added to the two operands, A and B, to give the place digit and the carry-out.*

Carry-in	0	0	0	0	1	1	1	1
A	0	1	0	1	0	1	0	1
B	0	0	1	1	0	0	1	1
Place digit	0	1	1	0	1	0	0	1
Carry-out	0	0	0	1	0	1	1	1

Overflow

Because computers use fixed-size bit sequences (for example, a byte is 8 bits long), an interesting question is what happens when there is a carry-out of the most significant bit—that is, the leftmost bit. For example, 255 + 5 in binary is

```
   1111  1111
 + 0000  0101
 1 0000  0100
```

But 260 needs 9 bits, one bit too many to fit into a byte. Such situations are called *overflow exceptions*. Computers report them when the computation they're told to perform overflows; it's up to programmers to recover from the error. Usually programmers try to avoid the situation by choosing large bit fields.

COMPUTING ON REPRESENTATIONS

Though we have focused on binary representation, conversions between decimal and binary, and binary addition, the previous sections have also introduced another fundamental concept of digital representation—the idea of *computing on representations*. When we made gray lighter, we showed how digital information—for example, the RGB settings of a pixel—can be changed through computation. For a better understanding of the idea, consider the more involved example that follows.

Changing the Colors of a Moon Photo

Imagine that you have scanned a black-and-white photo of the moon into your computer, similar to Figure 11.2(a). Unfortunately, when you took the photo, you only had black-and-white film loaded, so you missed the gorgeous orange of the close-to-the-horizon moon. In the computer, the pixels of your photo form a long sequence of RGB triples. What values do they have?

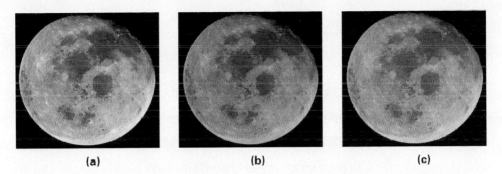

(a)   **(b)**   **(c)**

Figure 11.2. *Moon photos. (a) The original black-and-white picture, (b) tinted version of original, (c) with boosted highlights.*

Because they are all black, white, or gray, it's easy to guess. There is the (0,0,0) of the black night sky, the (255,255,255) of the brightest part of the moon, some light gray values very close to white—for example, (234,234,234)—of the craters and *marae* of the moon, and some dark gray values in the corner very close to black—for example, (28,28,28)—from a smudge left on the glass of your scanner. You want to email a colorized version of your photo (similar to Figure 11.2(c)), to your friends.

Removing the Smudge. To create the picture, you must remove the smudge and transform the pixels of the black-and-white image into the colors that you remember. The first task is easy because any value "close" to black can be changed to true black by replacing it with (0,0,0). But what does *close* mean? The example dark gray value (28,28,28) is represented in binary as

$$\boxed{0001\ 1100}\ 0001\ 1100\ 0001\ 1100$$

Though other dark gray values may be somewhat larger or smaller, it is a safe guess that any dark gray pixel will have the most significant (leftmost) 2 bits of each of its RGB bytes set to 00. That's because, from the binary representation, a byte whose most significant two bits are 00 is less than 64—that is, less than one quarter of full intensity—and any pixel, all of whose colors are less than a quarter magnitude, must be a darker color.

To change the smudge to pure black, we go through the image looking at each pixel and testing to see if the first 2 bits of each of its bytes are 00. If they are, we set each byte to 0. Recalling our substitution arrow from Chapter 2, we describe this operation as

$$\boxed{00xx\ xxxx}\ 00xx\ xxxx\ 00xx\ xxxx\ \leftarrow\ \boxed{0000\ 0000}\ 0000\ 0000\ 0000\ 0000$$

where *x* is a standard symbol for "don't care" or "wildcard"—that is, a symbol matching either 0 or 1. So the substitution statement says "Any three RGB bytes, each of whose first 2 bits are 00, are replaced with all zeros." Making that substitution throughout the image removes the digitized smudge. (Notice that this is an algorithm.)

Making the Moon Orange. Similarly, shifting the color of the moon to orange involves changing the white pixels (255,255,255). You decide that the orange of the moon ( ) must be about the color represented by (255,213,132). Changing all of the white pixels to this orange color requires the substitution

255 255 255 ← 255 213 132

or, in binary,

1111 1111 1111 1111 1111 1111 ← 1111 1111 1101 0101 1000 0100

to produce an orange moon. But it will not change the gray of the craters because they are not pure white and therefore won't be modified by this replacement. If, like changing the dark gray to black, the very light gray were changed to this orange too, all of the beautiful detail of the craters would be lost. How do we change the white to orange and change the gray to the appropriate orange-tinted gray?

Light Gray into Orange Tint. There are many very sophisticated ways to adjust color; we'll change light gray into orange in three steps:

> Red byte—leave unchanged

> Green byte—subtract 42 from the green value; that is, reduce the green slightly

> Blue byte—subtract 123 from the blue value; that is, reduce the blue quite a bit

Thus, the light gray color (234,234,234) is changed into (234,192,111), and the slightly darker light gray (228,228,228) is changed into (228,186,105), a slightly grayer orange. These numbers are computed by noting how white (255,255,255) changed into the chosen orange (255,213,132): the red byte was unchanged, the green byte was reduced by 42, and the blue byte was reduced by 123. If all pixels having the most significant bit of each RGB byte equal 1 (that is, the white pixels and all the light gray pixels) are changed by this three-step process, the white areas would become orange and the gray parts would become grayish orange.

You have cleaned up the smudge and colorized the moon, as shown in Figure 11.2(b).

Boosting the Red. Now you inspect your work and decide that the gray parts of the moon are really not as luminous as you remembered. So, you decide to boost the red. If the red in all of the orange pixels is shifted to 255, the moon's craters look too red and "unnatural." But a compromise is to "split the difference." That is, if the current value of the red byte in an orange tint is 234, say, half the difference between it and pure red—(255 − 234)/2 = 10.5—could be added to get 244. (You need whole numbers, so drop the "point 5.") Thus, the two example tints (234,192,111) and (228,186,105) become (244,192,111) and (241,186,105), respectively. This process brightens the craters, as demonstrated in Figure 11.2(c), without making them appear unnatural. The resulting image looks great, and you can attach it to your email to your friends.

Image Processing Summary

We have computed on a digital representation. We scanned a real photograph into the computer and created an artificial image. First, we improved it by removing the smudge from the scanning process. Then, we colorized it by changing white and light gray into orange and corresponding shades of orange-gray. Finally, we boosted the red in the orange-gray tints to make it a little brighter. We discussed these changes as if you were programming them, which you could do, but image processing software like Photoshop accomplishes these modifications through menu choices like changing Saturation, Brightness, Hue, and so forth. Such software manipulates the pixels with transformations like those described here, as well as in much more sophisticated ways. The result is not the photograph you would have taken had there been color film in the camera, but rather a different image, a synthetic image closer to what you remember or prefer. It is definitely not reality . . . because we can just as easily make "the man in the moon" smile.

DIGITIZING SOUND

In this section we learn about digitizing, though this time we focus on digitizing sound rather than images because it is slightly easier and equally interesting. The principles are the same when digitizing any "continuous" information.

An object—think of a cymbal—creates sound by vibrating in a medium such as air. The vibrations push the air, causing pressure waves to emanate from the object, which in turn vibrate our eardrums. The vibrations are transmitted by three tiny bones to the fine hairs of our cochlea, stimulating nerves that allow us to sense the waves and "hear" them as sound. The force, or intensity of the push, determines the volume, and the **frequency** (the number of waves per second) of the pushes is the pitch. Figure 11.3 shows a graph of a sound wave. The horizontal axis shows time and the vertical axis shows the amount of positive or negative sound pressure.

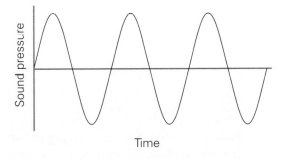

Figure 11.3. Sound wave. The horizontal axis is time; the vertical axis is sound pressure.

From a digitization point of view, the key is that the object vibrates *continuously,* producing a continuously changing wave. As the wave moves past, say, a microphone, the measured pressure changes smoothly. When this pressure variation is recorded directly, as it was originally by Edison with a scratch on a wax cylinder, and then later with vinyl records, we have a continuous (**analog**) representation of the wave. In principle, all of the continuous variation of the wave is recorded. Digital representations work differently.

Analog to Digital

To digitize continuous information, we must convert to bits. For a sound wave, we can record with a binary number the amount by which the wave is above or below the 0 line at a given point on our graph, that is, the amount of positive or negative sound pressure. But at what point do we measure? There are infinitely many points along the line, too many to record every position of the wave.

Sampling.   So, we **sample**, which means we take measurements at regular intervals. The number of samples in a second is called the **sampling rate**, and the faster the rate, the more accurately the wave is recorded (see Figure 11.4).

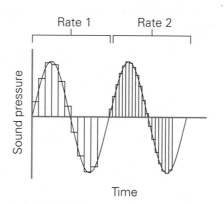

Figure 11.4. *Two sampling rates; the rate on the right is twice as fast as that on the left.*

How Fast a Sampling Rate?   To get a good recording of the wave, we need a sampling rate that is related to the wave's frequency. For example, if a sampling were too slow, sound waves could "fit between" the samples and we'd miss important segments of the sound.

Fortunately, we have guidelines for the sampling rates. In electrical engineering, the Nyquist Rule says that a sampling rate must be at least twice as fast as the fastest frequency. And what is the fastest frequency we can expect? Because human perception can hear sound up to roughly 20,000 Hz, a 40,000 Hz sampling rate fulfills the Nyquist Rule for digital audio recording. For technical reasons, however, a somewhat faster-than-two-times sampling rate was chosen for digital audio, 44,100 Hz.

ADC, DAC. The digitizing process works as follows: Sound is picked up by a microphone (called a transducer because it converts the sound wave into an electrical wave). This electrical signal is fed into an **analog-to-digital converter** (ADC), which takes the continuous wave and samples it at regular intervals, outputting for each sample, binary numbers to be written to memory.

The process is reversed to play the sound: The numbers are read from memory into a **digital-to-analog converter** (DAC), which creates an electrical wave by interpolation between the digital values—that is, filling in or smoothly moving from one value to another. The electrical signal is then input to a speaker, which converts it into a sound wave, as shown in Figure 11.5.

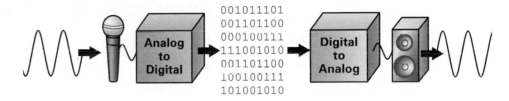

Figure 11.5. *Schematic for analog-to-digital and digital-to-analog conversion.*

How Many Bits per Sample? The problem of digitizing is solved except for describing how accurate the samples must be. To make the samples perfectly accurate, we would need an unlimited number of bits for each sample, which is impossible. But to start, we know that the bits must represent both positive and negative values, because the wave has both positive and negative sound pressure. Second, the more bits there are, the more accurate the measurement is. For example, with only 3 bits, one of which is used to indicate whether the sign is + or −, we can encode one of four positions in either direction (they align at 0). With so few bits, we can only get an approximate measurement, as shown in Figure 11.6(a). If we used another bit, the sample would be twice as accurate. (In Figure 11.6(b), each interval is half as wide, making the illustrated crossing in the "upper" half of the interval.)

Using more bits yields a more accurate digitization. The digital representation of audio CDs uses 16 bits, meaning that $2^{16} = 65,536$ levels are recorded, $2^{15} = 32,768$ for positive values and 32,768 for negative values.

---

*fit*BYTE

Unforgiving Minute. How many bits does it take to record a minute of digital audio? There are 60 seconds of 44,100 samples of 16 bits each, times 2 for stereo. That's 84,672,000 bits, or 10,584,000 bytes, more than 10.5 megabytes. An hour is 635 MB!

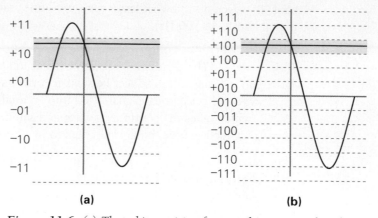

Figure 11.6. (a) *Three-bit precision for samples requires that the indicated reading is approximated as +10. (b) Adding another bit makes the sample twice as accurate.*

Advantages of Digital Sound

A key advantage of digital information (as demonstrated in the last section) is that we can compute on the representation.

MP3 Compression.   One computation of value is to *compress* the digital audio; that is, reduce the number of bits needed to represent the information. For example, an orchestra produces many sounds that the human ear can't hear—some too high and some too low. Our ADC still encodes these frequencies—not to annoy our dog, but simply as part of the encoding process. By computing special functions on the digital audio representation, it's possible to remove these waves without harming the way the audio sounds to us. This is the sort of compression used for MP3. In MP3 we typically get a **compression ratio** of more than 10:1, which means that the number of bits is reduced to less than one-tenth of what it was. So a minute of MP3 music typically takes less than a megabyte to represent. This makes MP3 popular for Internet transmission, because it has lower bandwidth requirements. We discuss bandwidth—the rate at which bits are transmitted—shortly.

We can "fix" a recording in the same way we "fixed" our moon picture. If someone coughs during a quiet moment of Verdi's *Requiem*, we can remove the offending noise from the recording. Performances can be sped up or slowed down without affecting pitch, volume, and so on.

*fit*BYTE   **MP3.** The "sound track" of a digital video in the MPEG representation is known as MPEG level 3, or MP3.

Reproducing the Sound Recording. Another key advantage of digital representations over analog is that they can be reproduced exactly. We can copy the file of bits that make up an audio performance, without losing a single bit of information. When the original and the copy are played by the same system, they sound exactly the same. With analog representation, the copy is never as exact as the original, and because of wear, a second (or third or hundredth) playing of the same version is never as good as the first. Digital recordings never have these problems as long as the bits remain stable.

---

*fit***BYTE**

Word Search. Searching digital audio for a segment of sound, though possible in principle, is impossible in practice because we have to specify the search string. Thus, in Chapter 6, we searched Fuller's *Everything I Know* recordings not by searching the audio, but by searching the textual transcript of the audio, which is in ASCII.

DIGITAL IMAGES AND VIDEO

Recall from our discussion of the moon picture that an image is a long sequence of RGB pixels. Of course, the picture is two-dimensional, but we think of the pixels stretched out one row after another in memory, which is one-dimensional. How many pixels are there? For an 8 × 10 image scanned at 300 pixels per inch, there are 80 square inches, each requiring 300 × 300 = 90,000 pixels for a grand total of 7.2 megapixels. At 3 bytes per pixel, it takes 21.6 MB of memory to store one 8 × 10 color image. Until recently, that's more memory than personal computers came equipped with. Sending such a picture across a standard 56 Kb/s modem—that's kilo*bits* per second—would take at least 21,600,000 × 8 / 56,000 = 3085 seconds, or more than 51 minutes (longer than the average college class). So, how can we see screen-size pictures in seconds when we're surfing the Web?

JPEG Compression

First, a typical computer screen has fewer than 100 pixels per inch, not 300, so storing the picture digitized at 100 ppi is a factor of 9 savings in memory. But this isn't quite the simplification we need, first because a picture that size still takes more than five and a half minutes to send, and second because once received, we might want to print the picture, requiring the resolution again. Luckily, electrical engineers invented the **JPEG** compression scheme. JPEG stands for "Joint Photographic Experts Group," a nickname for an International Standards Organization (ISO) team that guides the development of digital representation of still photographs.

Compression means to change the representation in order to use fewer bits to store or transmit information. For example, faxes are usually long sequences of 0's and 1's that encode where the page is white or black. Rather than sending all the

0's and 1's, we can use run-length encoding to take advantage of the fact that there are long sequences of 0's and 1's. **Run-length encoding** uses binary numbers to specify how long the first sequence (run) of 0's is, then how long the following sequence of 1's is, then how long the following sequence of 0's is, and so on. This works best for long, not short, sequences of 0's and 1's, and most of the time run-length compression is a big win. Run-length encoding is a **lossless compression** scheme, meaning that the original representation of 0's and 1's can be perfectly reconstructed from the compressed version. The opposite of lossless compression is **lossy compression**, meaning that the original representation cannot be exactly reconstructed from the compressed form. MP3 is lossy because the high notes cannot be recovered—but it doesn't matter since we can't hear them anyway.

JPEG compression is used for still images. Our eyes are not very sensitive to small changes in hue (chrominance), but we are quite sensitive to small changes in brightness (luminance). This means we can store a less accurate description of the hue of a picture (fewer bits) and, although this compression technique is lossy, our eyes won't notice the difference. With JPEG compression we can get a 20:1 compression ratio compared to an uncompressed still image, without being able to see a difference. For example, the digital image in Figure 11.7(a) originally required several megabytes, but a 14:1 JPEG compression produced the image shown, maintaining subtle color details.

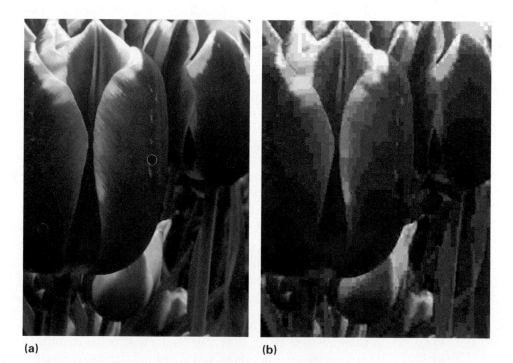

(a)   **(b)**

Figure 11.7. *Detail from an image compressed using JPEG.*
(a) 14:1 compression (b) 140:1. Check images at `www.aw.com/snyder`

The idea behind JPEG compression is visible in Figure 11.7(b), which has purposely been excessively compressed (140:1). Large areas of similar hues are "lumped together" as the same hue, so a whole area can be colored with a single set of RGB values. If the differences are slight, compression is not noticeable, but if the differences are large, the quality of the image degrades. For example, notice the large color difference between the stalk of the tulip on the right and the leaf behind it, and then notice the effect of coloring them the same green.

The repeated values can be run-length compressed to reduce the memory required even further. The handy feature of JPEG compression is that we can control the amount of compression: Image compression software gives us a control—a slider or dial, say—so we can choose the amount of compression we want. Fiddling with the control allows us to determine visually how much more compression can be applied without seriously affecting the look of the image.

MPEG Compression Scheme

MPEG, the compression scheme of the Motion Picture Experts Group of the ISO, is the same idea applied to motion pictures. On the one hand, it seems like an easier task because each image—each frame—is not seen for very long, so we should be able to get away with even greater levels of single-image compression. On the other hand, the problem seems more difficult because it takes many stills to make a movie. In MPEG compression, JPEG-type compression is applied to each frame, but then "interframe coherency" is used. Because two consecutive video images are usually very similar, MPEG compression only has to record and transmit the "differences" between frames. This results in huge amounts of compression, so MPEG only needs moderate amounts of bandwidth.

OPTICAL CHARACTER RECOGNITION

On toll roads, computers watch cars pass, read their license plates, find the "car's" account in a database, and deduct the toll from its account. It sure beats stopping every few miles to pay another toll! The interesting aspect of this technology is that there is no bar code or electronic transponder; a computer simply recognizes the letters of the license plate. Reading license plates is very easy for humans, but it's a big deal for computers.

Consider some of the difficulties. First, the computer must capture an image of the license plate, but the camera points at the highway and picks up many images that are not license plates—the scene, parts of cars, trailers, litter, road-kill before it is road-kill, and so on. An electronic device called a **frame grabber** recognizes when to "snap" the image and send it to the computer for processing. Assuming a frame with a license plate in it has been snapped, the computer must figure out where in the image it is, because there is no standard location for a license plate on a vehicle, and even if there were, the vehicle could be changing lanes. Looking for letters and numbers doesn't work, because some vehicles display bumper stickers or advertising. Once the license plate is found, recognizing its characters is the most significant challenge, because they're not yet characters, but thousands of pixels.

License plate colors are chosen because of their high contrast (for example, dark letters on a light background). The computer scans groups of pixels looking for edges where the color changes and it forms these into features. A *feature* is a part of a character to be recognized. For example, a *P* might be described by the features of a "vertical stroke" and a "hole" at the top of the stroke, because lines and holes are patterns that can be recognized by noting where color changes. Given the features, a **classifier** matches the features to the alphabet to determine which are close, perhaps finding a strong correlation with *P,* a weaker one with *9,* and an even weaker one with *D.* Finally, after picking the most likely characters, an optical character recognizer checks the context, trying to decide if the combination makes sense; for example, if a license exists with that combination of letters. Finding the number in the database, the computer determines that it has read the plate correctly, and debits the owner's account.

{GREAT *fit* MINDS}

Text-to-speech technology >>

Perhaps the most significant application of optical character recognition is Raymond Kurzweil's text-to-speech reading machines developed for the blind and partially sighted. First produced in 1976, the reading machine uses a flatbed scanner—a technology originally developed by Kurzweil—to scan reading material, recognize it as text, and then speak it using a voice synthesizer. Scanning, font-independent optical character recognition, large-vocabulary dictionaries, and speech synthesis, which Kurzweil had to create for his devices, are now standard technologies. For the disabled, the reader and its inverse, the speech-to-text machine, have dramatically improved personal lives and career opportunities. Says the blind musician Stevie Wonder, who credits the reader with changing his life, "It gave blind people the one life goal that everyone treasures, and that is independence."

Raymond Kurzweil received the National Medal of Technology and the Lemelson-MIT Award for Innovation, which is like a Nobel Prize for inventors.

(See the interview following this chapter for observations by Ray Kurzweil.)

Ray Kurzweil with the Kurzweil Personal Reader, a 1988 version of his invention.

Today's Kurzweil readers utilize flatbed scanners and software running on a personal computer.

Beginning Reader. In 1954, J. Rainbow demonstrated an optical character reader that could recognize uppercase typewritten characters at the rate of one letter per minute.

OCR Technology

Optical character recognition (OCR) is a very sophisticated technology that enables a computer to "read" printed characters. OCR's business applications are sorting mail and banking. The US Postal Service uses a system that locates the address block on an envelope or card, reads it in any of 400 fonts, identifies its zip code, generates a nine-digit bar code, sprays the bars on the envelope, sorts it, and, with only a 2 percent error rate, processes up to 45,000 pieces of mail per hour. In banking, the magnetic numbers at the bottom of the check have been read by computers since the 1950s; now OCR is used to read the *handwritten* digits of the numeric check amount to verify that a data entry person has interpreted the amount correctly. That is, the computer checks the person.

VIRTUAL REALITY: FOOLING THE SENSES

The ultimate form of digital representation is to create an entire digital world. The idea has become known as virtual reality (VR). So far, VR has less to do with representing the world and more to do with fooling our senses into perceiving something that doesn't exist.

Rapidly displaying still images is a standard way to fool our eyes and brain into seeing motion. Virtual reality applies that idea to our other senses and tries to eliminate the cues that keep us grounded in reality. For example, when we see a TV scene of a train coming toward us, we know by various cues, such as peripheral vision, that we're watching a TV; we see the motion but we're not fooled. However, if we're wearing a helmet with a TV in front of each eye that shows the train in a complete scene, gives us three-dimensional vision, and fills in our peripheral vision as well, so that when we move our head we can look at other parts of the scene, the cues are reduced or eliminated. Add high-quality audio in each ear and a treadmill so that we seem to be walking or running through the scene, and it's easy to imagine how a computer can effectively fool us into thinking the train is chasing us.

Haptic Devices

Certain deceptions are more useful. **Haptic devices** are input/output technology for interacting with our sense of touch and feel. For example, a haptic glove enables a computer to detect where our fingers are and to apply force against them. When we bring our fingers close enough together, the glove stops their movement, and leaves us with the feeling of holding something. With haptic gloves and the VR helmet, a computer can depict Legos in space, which, when we grab them, gives us the sensation of holding them and makes us think we are assembling them. When the glove pulls down on our fingers, we think the Legos are heavy, perhaps made of metal. The world is virtual, but credible. Such technology is used to train surgeons for complex operations.

fit **BYTE**   **Virtual Meaning.** The term *virtual* is used often in IT—for example, virtual memory—because the computer produces a believable illusion of something that doesn't exist. *Virtual* means "not actually but just as if."

The Challenge of Latency

The challenge with virtual reality and other sophisticated output devices like video, is for the system to operate fast enough and precisely enough to appear natural. When still images are presented too slowly in an animation, the illusion of motion is lost. When that happens in a VR system—when we turn our head but the scene doesn't smoothly change—we can get dizzy, maybe even sick. Our sensation of touch and feel actually operates faster than the 30 Hz standard for visual perception, closer to 1000 Hz. Therefore, for the illusion to work, when we "see" our virtual hand going to pick up a virtual Lego, we must "feel" that we've touched it before we "see" that we've touched it.

This phenomenon is called **latency**—the time it takes for information to be delivered. We are familiar with long latencies, such as when Web pages are not delivered instantly, but the phenomenon arises wherever information is generated or transmitted. In most cases, as with Web pages, long latencies just make us wait, but in video, VR, voice communication, and so on, long latency can ruin the medium. Reducing latency is a common engineering goal, but there is an absolute limit to how fast information can be transmitted—the speed of light. Eventually, the virtual world is constrained by the physical world.

The Challenge of Bandwidth

Closely related to latency is **bandwidth**—a measure of how much information is transmitted per unit time. Bandwidth is related to latency in that a given amount of information (for example, 100 KB) transmitted with a given bandwidth (for example, 50 KB/s) determines the (best) latency by dividing the amount by the bandwidth; in this case, 100 / 50 = 2, or 2 seconds of latency. Other delays can extend the latency beyond this theoretical best. Higher bandwidth usually means lower latency. (The rule eventually fails for speed-of-light and switching-delay reasons.) So, faster modems mean that Web pages load faster.

VR is a developing technology. It is still challenged by both latency and bandwidth limitations—it takes many, many bytes to represent a synthetic world. Creating them and delivering them to our senses is a difficult technical problem. Nevertheless, it is an exciting future application of IT.

BITS ARE IT

Looking back over this and previous chapters, we have seen that 4 bytes can represent many kinds of information, from four ASCII keyboard characters to numbers between zero and about 4 billion. This is not an accident, but rather a fundamental property of information, which we summarize in this principle:

Bias-Free Universal Medium Principle: Bits can represent all discrete information; bits have no inherent meaning.

Bits: The Universal Medium

The first half of the principle—all discrete information can be represented by bits—is the universality aspect. Discrete things—things that can be separated from each other—can be represented by bits. At the very least, we can assign numbers to each one and represent those numbers in binary. But, as we saw with color, it's possible to be much smarter. We assigned the RGB colors so the intensity could be increased or decreased using binary arithmetic. This representation of color is much more organized than simply saying, "Black will be 0, purple will be 1, yellow will be 2," and so on. As a result of organizing the representation in a sensible way, we can *easily* compute on it, making changes like brightening the image. Of course, if the information is continuous—that is, if it is analog information like sound—it must first be made discrete by an analog-to-digital conversion. But once digitized, this information, too, can be represented by bits.

Bits: Bias-Free

The second half of the principle—bits have no inherent meaning—is the bias-free aspect. Given a bit sequence

```
0000 0000 1111 0001 0000 1000 0010 0000
```

there is no way to know what information it represents. The meaning of the bits comes entirely from the *interpretation* placed on them by us or by the computer through our programs. For example, the 4 bytes could be a zero byte followed by the RGB intensities (241,8,32) ■. Or, the 4 bytes could be an instruction to add two binary numbers. As a binary number, the bits work out to 15,796,256.

So, bits are bits. What they mean depends on how the software interprets them, which means they work for any kind of information. Storage media needs to store one pair of patterns only: 0 and 1. The principle explains why, for example, a single transmission medium—the TCP/IP packet—is all that's needed to deliver any kind of digital information across the Internet to your computer: text, photos, or MP3 tunes. It delivers bits and that's enough.

Bits Are Not Necessarily Binary Numbers

Since the public first became aware of computers, it's been "common knowledge" that computers represent information as binary *numbers*. Experts reinforce this view, but it's not quite right. Computers represent information as bits. Bits can be *interpreted* as binary numbers, as we've seen, which is why the experts are not wrong. But the bits do not always represent binary numbers. They can be interpreted as ASCII characters, RGB colors, or an unlimited list of other things (see Figure 11.8). Programs often perform arithmetic on the bits, as we saw when we modified the moon image; but often they do not, because it doesn't make sense with the intended interpretation of the information. Computers represent information with bits. They are an amazing medium.

```
0000 0000 1111 0001 0000 1000 0010 0000 = 15,796,256 interpreted as a binary number
                                        = ■ interpreted as an RGB(241,8,32) color (last 3 bytes)
                                        = ADD 1,7,17 interpreted as a MIPS machine instruction
                                        = N U B s ñ b interpreted as 8-bit ASCII—null, backspace,
                                            n-tilde, blank
                                        = L: +241, R: +280 interpreted as sound samples
                                        = 0.241.8.32 interpreted as an
                                          IP address
                                        = 00 F1 08 20 interpreted as a
                                          hexadecimal number
```

Figure 11.8. *Illustration of the principle that "bits are bits." The same 4 bytes shown can be interpreted differently.*

SUMMARY

In this chapter we considered how different forms of information are represented in the computer. We learned that:

> With RGB color, each intensity is a 1-byte numeric quantity represented as a binary number.

> Binary representation and binary arithmetic are like decimal numbers, but they are limited to two digits.

> The decimal equivalent of binary numbers is determined by adding their powers of 2 corresponding to 1's.

> We can use arithmetic on the intensities to "compute on the representation," for example, making gray lighter and colorizing a black-and-white picture of the moon.

> When digitizing sound, sampling rate and measurement precision determine how accurate the digital form is; uncompressed audio requires more than 80 million bits per minute.

> Compression makes large files manageable: MP3 for audio, JPEG for still pictures, and MPEG for video. These compact representations work because they remove unnecessary information.

> Optical character recognition is a technology that improves our world.

> Virtual reality illustrates the complexities of conveying information to all of our senses simultaneously.

> The Bias-Free Universal Medium Principle embodies the magic of computers through universal bit representations and unbiased encoding.

EXERCISES

Multiple Choice

1. Each RGB color intensity ranges from
   A. 0–15
   B. 0–255
   C. 1–16
   D. 1–256

2. The RGB setting for blue is (0 is off, 1 is on)
   A. 0000 0000 0000 0000 0000 0000
   B. 1111 1111 0000 0000 0000 0000
   C. 0000 0000 1111 1111 0000 0000
   D. 0000 0000 0000 0000 1111 1111

3. Analog information is
   A. discrete
   B. continuous
   C. random
   D. digital

4. According to the Nyquist Rule, the sampling rate of sound is roughly
   A. half of what humans can hear
   B. the same as what humans can hear
   C. twice what humans can hear
   D. three times what humans can hear

5. The accuracy of a digitized sound is determined by
   A. the sampling rate
   B. the precision of the sample
   C. the size of the digitized file
   D. all of the above

6. A digital-to-analog converter
   A. changes digital information to analog waves
   B. converts continuous sound to digital sound
   C. converts sound to an electrical signal
   D. sets approximated values

7. MP3 is the sound information of
   A. MPEG movies
   B. all digital movies
   C. all computer sound
   D. all digital computer sound

8. Jessica Simpson's "A Little Bit" is 3 minutes 47 seconds long. How many bits is that?
   A. 1,411,200
   B. 40,012,800
   C. 84,672,000
   D. 320,342,400

9. OCR is used in all of the following areas except
   A. text-to-speech recognition
   B. ZIP code recognition
   C. supermarket checkout
   D. bank account recognition

10. Raymond Kurzweil is known as the inventor of
    A. OCR
    B. text-to-speech recognition
    C. image compression
    D. virtual reality

Short Answer

1. When all the RGB color settings are set to 0, the color displayed is _____.

2. The first digit of a binary number is always _____.

3. _____ is the term used when digital values are converted to create an analog sound.

4. _____ sound removes the highest and lowest samplings as part of its compression algorithm.

5. A(n) _____ is used to convert analog sound to digital values.

6. _____ is a compression scheme for digital video while _____ is the scheme for digital images.

7. _____ is the group that oversees the development of digital media standards.

8. On the computer, _____ means to store or transmit information with fewer bits.

9. A process that allows the computer to "read" printed characters is called _____.

10. Conversion of the written word to speech is called _____.

11. The creation of a digital representation of the world is called _____.

12. JPEG is to still images what _____ is to motion pictures.

13. _____ are used with computers to control a person's sense of touch.

14. _____ is the time it takes information to be delivered.

15. The _____ states that bits can represent all discrete information even though the bits have no meaning of their own.

Exercises

1. Write the algorithm for converting from decimal to binary.

2. Write the algorithm for converting from binary to decimal.

3. Add 1492 and 1776 in binary and display the answer in binary.

4. In binary, add 1011, 1001, 110, and 1100.

5. Convert RGB 200, 200, 200 to hex C8C8C8 by converting it to binary and then to hex.

6. Add 168 and 123 in binary. How many bytes does it take to represent each number? How many bytes are needed for the answer? What happens if there aren't enough bytes to store the answer?

7. Software is now in use that can let you "try on" a dress virtually. What process would be used to change that bright red, taffeta dress into a soft pink? What would be needed to change it to sea foam (light green)? What would it take to turn it into a color to match your eyes?

8. Explain how a picture at 300 pixels per inch could be converted to a picture with 100 pixels per inch.

9. Most music is now sold on CD-ROM. Explain how a singer's voice in the recording studio goes to the earphones on your computer? Why are both processes needed for this to succeed?

10. Digitally, what would need to be done to raise (or lower) a singer's voice an octave?

11. Why are JPEG, MPEG, and MP3 considered algorithms?

12. To the computer, bits are bits. To a page, letters are letters. Use this to explain the meaning of the Bias-Free Universal Medium Principle.

RAY KURZWEIL was the principal developer of the first omni font optical character recognition, the first print-to-speech reading machine for the blind, the first CCD flat-bed scanner, the first text-to-speech synthesizer, the first music synthesizer capable of re-creating the grand piano and other orchestral instruments, and the first commercially marketed large-vocabulary speech recognition. Ray has successfully founded and developed nine businesses in OCR, music synthesis, speech recognition, reading technology, virtual reality, financial investment, medical simulation, and cybernetic art. In addition to scores of other national and international awards, Ray was inducted into the National Inventors Hall of Fame and received the 1999 National Medal of Technology, the nation's highest honor in technology, from President Clinton. Ray's Web site, KurzweilAI.net, is a leading resource on artificial intelligence.

Do you have a "favorite story" to tell about one of your inventions?

We announced the Kurzweil Reading Machine, which was the first print to speech reading machine for the blind, on January 13, 1976. I remember this date because Walter Cronkite, the famous news anchor for CBS News, used it to read his signature sign-off that evening "And that's the way it was, January 13, 1976." It was the first time that he did not read this famous phrase himself.

I was subsequently invited to demonstrate this new reading machine on the *Today Show*. We only had one working model and we were nervous about demonstrating it on live television since there was always the possibility of technical glitches. They responded that it was live or nothing.

We arrived at the *Today Show* studio very early in the morning and set up the reading machine. Sure enough, it stopped working a couple of hours before show time. We tried various easy fixes that failed to rectify the problem. So our chief engineer frantically took the machine apart. With electrical pieces scattered across the studio floor, Frank Field, who was to interview me, walked by, and asked if there was a problem. We said that we were just making a few last minute adjustments.

Our chief engineer put the machine back together, and it still was not working. Then, in a time-honored tradition of repairing delicate technical equipment, he picked up the machine and slammed it into the table. It worked perfectly from that moment on, and the live demonstration and interview went without a hitch.

Stevie Wonder happened to catch me on the broadcast, and called our office wanting to stop by and pick up his own reading machine. Our receptionist did not believe it was really the legendary musical artist, but she put him through anyway. We were just finishing up our first production unit, so we rushed that to completion. Stevie stopped by, stayed several hours to learn how to use it, and went off with his new Kurzweil Reading Machine in a taxi. That was the beginning of a nearly thirty-year friendship that continues to this day. A few years later, Stevie was instrumental in my launching Kurzweil Music Systems, Inc.

Your inventions range from the Kurzweil 250 to a nutritional program that cured you of type 2 Diabetes. Is there a tie that binds your many inventions?

My original, and still primary, area of technology interest and expertise is a field called "pattern recognition," which is the science and art of teaching computers to recognize patterns. It turns out that the bulk of human intelligence is based on our remarkable ability to recognize patterns such as faces, visual objects, speech, and music. Most of my technology projects are related to recognizing patterns, for example character recognition and speech recognition. Even my work in music synthesis was influenced by pattern recognition. We had to answer the question as to what patterns cause humans to recognize sounds as coming from a particular type of instrument, such as a grand piano.

I quickly realized that timing was important for my inventions, and began to develop mathematical models of how technology develops over time. This endeavor took on a life of its own. By using these models, I was able to make predictions about technologies ten to thirty years into the future, and beyond. From these efforts, I realized that the twenty-first century was going to be an extraordinary time in advancing human civilization. This insight has been a major motivation for me to find the means to live long enough, and in good health, to experience this remarkable century.

I also realized that one of the areas of technology that is accelerating is health and medical technology. Therefore the tools we will have to keep ourselves healthy will grow in power and sophistication in the years ahead. It is important, therefore, to keep ourselves healthy using today's knowledge so that we are in good shape to take advantage of the full flowering of the biotechnology revolution, which is now in its early stages.

Many of your past predictions about the future of technology have "come true." How is it that you are able to make such specific and accurate predictions?

Most futurists simply make predictions without a well-thought-out framework or methodology. I have been studying technology trends for at least a quarter century, and have been developing detailed mathematical models of how technology in different fields evolves. I have a team of people gathering data to measure the key features and capabilities of technologies in a wide array of fields, including computation, communications, biological technologies, and brain reverse engineering. From this work, it has become clear that technologies, particularly those that deal with information, are growing at a double exponential rate (that is the rate of exponential growth is itself growing exponentially). Typically, an information-based technology at least doubles its capability for the same unit cost every year.

The other important issue is that very few people realize that the pace of technical change, what I call the paradigm shift rate, is itself accelerating. We are doubling the pace of technical change every decade. I spoke recently at a conference celebrating the fiftieth anniversary of the discovery of the structure of DNA. We were all asked what changes we foresaw for the next fifty years. With very few exceptions, the other speakers used the amount of change in the last fifty years as a guide to the amount of change we will see in the next fifty years. But this is a faulty assumption. Because the rate of change is accelerating, we will see about thirty times as much change in the next fifty years, as we saw in the last half century.

In your book *The Age of Spiritual Machines*, you foresee a future where computers have exceeded human intelligence. How and when do you expect this to come about?

We can separate this question into two questions: When will computers have the computational capacity (the "hardware" capability) of the human brain? Secondly, when will we have the content and methods (the "software") of human intelligence?

In my book, *The Age of Spiritual Machines*, which came out in 1999, I said we would achieve the computational capacity of the human brain for about $1,000 by 2019. I estimate this capacity to be about 100 billion neurons, times about 1,000 interneuronal connections per neuron, times 200 calculations per second per connection, or about 20 million billions calculations per second. This was considered a controversial projection in 1999, but there has been a sea of change in perspective on this issue since that time. Today, it is a relatively mainstream expectation that we will have sufficient computational resources by 2019. Computers are at least doubling their speed and memory capacity every year, and even that rate is accelerating.

The more challenging issue is the software of intelligence. A primary source of what I call the "templates" of human intelligence is the human brain itself. We are already well along the path of reverse engineering the brain to understand its principles of operation. Here also we see exponential advance. Brain scanning technologies are doubling their resolution, bandwidth, and price-performance every year.

Knowledge about the human brain, including models of neurons and neural clusters, is doubling every year. We already have detailed mathematical models of several dozen of the several hundred regions that comprise the human brain. I believe it is a conservative projection to say that we will have detailed models of all the regions of the brain by the mid-2020s.

By 2029, we will be able to combine the subtle powers of pattern recognition that the human brain excels in, with several attributes in which machine intelligence already exceeds human capabilities. These include speed, memory capacity, and the ability to instantly share knowledge. Computers circa 2029, possessing human levels of language understanding, will be able to go out on the Web and read and absorb all of the available literature and knowledge.

Will these computers of the future have human emotions?

Indeed, they will. Emotional intelligence is not a side issue to human intelligence. It is actually the most complex and subtle thing we do. It is the cutting edge of human intelligence. If a human had no understanding of human emotions, we would not consider that person to be operating at a normal human level. The same will be true for machines. Already, there is significant interest in teaching computers about human emotions: how to detect them in humans and how to respond to them appropriately. This is important for the next generation of human-machine interfaces. As we reverse engineer the human brain, and understand how the different regions process information, we will gain an understanding of what our emotions mean. A very important benefit of this endeavor will be greater insight into ourselves.

What drawbacks do you foresee for the future you envision?

Technology is inherently a double-edged sword. All of the destruction of the twentieth century (for example, two world wars) was amplified by technology. At the same time, we are immeasurably better off as a result of technology. Human life expectancy was 37 years in 1800 and 50 years in 1900. Human life was filled with poverty, hard labor, and disease up until fairly recently.

We are now in the early stages of the biotechnology revolution. We are learning the information processes underlying life and disease, and are close to developing new treatments that will overcome age-old diseases, such as cancer, heart disease, and diabetes. This same knowledge, however, can also empower a terrorist to create a bioengineered pathogen. There is no easy way to separate the promise from the peril, as both stem from the same technology. We will see similar dilemmas with nanotechnology (technology in which the key features are less than 100 nanometers) and with artificial intelligence.

The answer, I believe, is to substantially increase our investment in developing specific defensive technologies to protect society from these downsides. We can see a similar battle between promise and peril in the area of software viruses. Although we continue to be concerned about software viruses, the defensive technologies have been largely successful. Hopefully we will be able to do as well with biotechnology and other future technologies.

Could you offer some advice to students with regard to keeping pace with information technology and perhaps with regard to inventing it?

This is a very exciting time to be embarking on a career in science and technology. The pace of change and the expansion of new knowledge is greater than at any time in history, and will continue to accelerate. The impact of science and technology goes substantially beyond these subjects themselves. Ultimately, new technological advances will transform every facet of human life and society.

I would advise students to:

1. Obtain a strong background in math, as this is the language of science and technology. Math also represents a way of thinking that leads to discovery and understanding.

2. Become an ardent student of technology and technology trends. Build your inventions for the world of the future, not the world you see in front of you today.

3. Focus on a particular area of science or technology that particularly fascinates you. The days when one person could master all of science and technology are long gone. However, as you focus, don't put on the blinders to what is going on in fields around you.

4. Follow your passion.

part 3

DATA AND INFORMATION

OUR UNDERSTANDING of information technology deepens as we become more versatile users. With greater knowledge and wider experience, it's wise to consider the bigger picture, noticing how IT can be used and abused. In Part 3 we discuss topics such as netiquette (etiquette for network users), viruses, and passwords.

We will focus on databases—how they store, structure, and deliver information that interests us. Knowing how to create our own databases helps us organize our own information, but it also makes us more effective at accessing other databases.

Two important topics covered in Part 3 are especially active in the "public debate" about IT: privacy and security. We present the technical description of each topic, as well as both sides of the debate. Every IT user is personally interested in privacy and security. It is important to be informed.

chapter 12

COMPUTERS IN POLITE SOCIETY
Social Implications of IT

learning objectives

> Describe several tips associated with netiquette and explain the benefits of following them

> Explain the phrase "expect the unexpected" and how that advice helped in handling an email bug

> List some ways your computer can become infected with malicious software

> Name three permitted/not permitted uses of licensed software

> Explain what rights are granted to material that is copyrighted

> Discuss some issues related to safety-critical applications

COMPUTERS IN POLITE SOCIETY
Social Implications of IT

*While modern technology has given people powerful new communications tools,
it apparently can do nothing to alter the fact that many people have nothing
useful to say.*

—LEE GOMES, SAN JOSE MERCURY NEWS

WHEN COMPUTERS moved out of the lab and onto our desks, laps, and
palms, they became part of our social interactions. Usually they are passive tools, a
means of communication and an aid to our work. But a tool can be used crudely
or skillfully. By using it skillfully, we smooth our social interactions and make life
more pleasant for one another. In this chapter, we break from our usual theme of
becoming better computer users to become more considerate computer users.

The chapter begins with three sections on email. Our first goal is to understand the limitations of email, so that we can use it in the right situations and
express ourselves well. Next, we look at a set of guidelines called *netiquette,* etiquette for the Internet. Then we introduce an important problem in applying IT—
the problem of expecting the unexpected. Unexpected things can happen in any
situation, of course, but email is so familiar that it gives us a good context for discussing the issue. The next three topics concern familiar situations in our everyday
use of computers and information: passwords, viruses, and copyright law. The
"Creating Good Passwords" section helps us think up and manage passwords. The
"Viruses and Worms" section explains how viruses and worms work, and how you
can protect your information. We also talk about phishing, which are disguised
email scams. The "Copyright: Protecting Intellectual Property" section helps you
decide when you can and cannot legally copy programs and information. The final
section discusses how completely we can trust computer systems, especially their
software, in safety-critical applications. How can we be sure that there are no bugs
in the program of a computer-run life-support system?

IMPROVING THE EFFECTIVENESS OF EMAIL

For many of us, email is as routine as telephone communication. In fact, email often replaces telephone calls or face-to-face conversations. Is this progress? Certainly the fact that email is asynchronous—the other person doesn't have to receive the communication at the time that it's created and sent—makes it very convenient. And its multicast property—you can send many people a message as easily as you can send it to one recipient—has its value. So, we use email for factual communication, like "The next meeting has been postponed until Tuesday at 1:30." But should we use it for everything, like "Your brother died at 4:00 this morning"?

When is email appropriate and when isn't it? There's no algorithm to help us decide, so we'll approach the subject by identifying some email weaknesses.

Problems with Email

We will consider five problems:

> Conveying emotion

> Emphasis

> Conversational pace

> Ambiguity

> Flame-a-thons

Keep these weaknesses in mind as you decide when and how to use email.

Conveying Emotion. It is difficult to convey sympathy, grief, and other subtle emotions using email. The problem is not the writing—sympathy cards convey emotional content as text (and graphics), for example. Rather, it seems that email is too informal, too impersonal, and often too casually written. Even simple feelings like happiness or sadness often don't come across in email because it is treated as a chatty conversation. We type words that in conversation would come with cues such as tone of voice, inflection, stress, pacing, intensity, volume, pauses, and other sounds such as chuckling, and though the words may have those cues in our minds, they don't on the screen. Without the cues, the reader might interpret the words in a way we do not intend. This is why **emoticons**—for example, characters forming smiley faces **:)**—are popular in email. The emoticon tags a sentence indicating the emotion we mean to communicate. In general, expressing sympathy, grief, and so on with email is so difficult that it is inappropriate in almost all cases. In regular email we should be aware of emotional content; sometimes we need to rewrite to make our feelings clear.

Emphasis. At an even more primitive level, the simple act of typing for emphasis can convey the wrong message. Readers could interpret text in all capitals as yelling. For example, "Do you know you forgot my birthday?" has a different sense than "DO YOU KNOW YOU FORGOT MY BIRTHDAY?" Generally, stress must be used with care because email is still largely ASCII-text-based and often does not make the standard indicators of emphasis like italics or underlining available. A common way to express emphasis is with special symbols like *asterisks* or _underscores_ on both sides of the word. So you can write, "Do you _know_ you forgot my birthday?" to give some emphasis. Certain email reading programs convert to *bold* and _italics_, but others do not. Because you probably don't know what email reader your correspondent uses, typing the asterisks and underscores is wise. And it's best to avoid uppercase letters unless you intend to yell.

Conversational Pace. It's difficult to have a dialog (a rapidly alternating communication) asynchronously. This is one reason why chat room "conversations" are often so inane. If the purpose of the communication is interactive, say, a negotiation, the telephone is preferable because it replaces the asynchronous compose/send/wait/receive cycle of email with synchronous conversation that switches quickly. The ability to alternate rapidly not only speeds up the pace of the communication, but it helps us recognize confusion or misunderstanding through audio cues, such as the feedback of long pauses (cluelessness) rather than periodic "uh huhs" (understanding). Of course, email is useful for setting the time for a phone conversation and exchanging phone numbers.

Ambiguity. Expressing ourselves is difficult, but it's even worse when our text is interpreted in a way that we did not intend. Ambiguity is a problem with natural language generally, and therefore with all writing that is not programming or mathematics. But ambiguity seems to happen even more in email, because email is more casual than most other writing. Some people apparently don't proofread what they write, much less take time to consider carefully how their writing might be misinterpreted. If you write, "I cannot recommend saffron rice too highly," you might mean that the dish is so good that you cannot overstate your praise, but your reader may interpret the sentence as saying that there is little that you can say that is good about saffron rice. If there are no other cues, your reader may get the wrong idea. It is always a good idea to proofread your emails carefully and to look for ambiguities.

> **fit CAUTION**
>
> **Universal Mistake.** It is nearly impossible to be sarcastic in email and not offend some readers. Many writers try to be funny by being sarcastic, but it rarely works unless you know the recipient well. A good rule: Do not use sarcasm in email you are sending to multiple recipients.

Flames. Perhaps the worst abuse of email after spam is the phenomenon known as a **flame-a-thon** or **flame war**, an email battle named after the computer slang **flame** for "inflammatory email." It's hard to generalize on how flame-a-thons begin, but they continue for the same reason conflicts continue in some parts of the world: Neither side wants to quit without getting revenge for the most recent attack. The main reason that flame-a-thons occur and continue seems to be email's immediacy. Email written in anger and sent immediately gives the sender no time for reflection. Including a cc list, of course, makes it worse. If, like snail mail, email had to be addressed to a single person and then carried to the post office or a mailbox, most of us would probably cool down before we dropped the envelope through the slot. No one wins a flame-a-thon. Clearly the best response when you are angered by email is to delay answering it until you've cooled down, and consider a different form of communication with the other person.

Generally, email is a very handy medium. It is most effective when we are sensitive to its weaknesses.

Netiquette

There are a few rules, popularly known as **netiquette**, that promote civilized email usage. The world won't end any sooner if you don't follow them, but if you do follow them, at least people won't think you're a boor.

Ask about One Topic at a Time. An email message that requires a response from the receiver should treat only one topic. For example, don't ask your parents for money in the same email that you ask if you left your brown sweater at home. Because most of us handle one matter at a time, the reader of a one-topic message can respond to the matter, and then delete or archive the mail. With multiple topics, it is likely that one or more will be dropped or ignored. For example, you'll find out you did forget the sweater, but your money request might be ignored. The subject line of the email can describe that one topic. Email is cheap; it costs no more to send two messages than one. But managing one-topic messages is much easier for everyone.

Include Context. An all too common email reply, unfortunately, is "Yes." We all like to get positive email, of course; the unfortunate part is we've forgotten the question. The subject line is no help; it reads, `Re: Question`.

Any email-reading software worth two bits gives you a way to include the original message in a reply. Including the question with the reply is a courtesy. It provides the context for your answer, so you can give a short reply without leaving the receiver clueless. A problem with always including the message in a reply is that an email conversation can become lengthy. If every word is typed by one of the two correspondents, however, there is little chance that the email history will become gigantic. But it's courteous to limit the context to the most recent message or to the most relevant point.

Use an Automated Reply. When you are unable to answer your email for a long time, it is polite to set up an **automated reply** saying you are away, and perhaps indicating when you expect to read your email again. The automated reply, called a "vacation message" in the earliest mailers, is generally available from your mail server. The benefit of using the vacation message is that readers know why you're not responding. Otherwise, they may think they are being ignored or snubbed.

> **fitTIP**
>
> **Nor Rain, Nor Heat, Nor Gloom of Night.** Email does get lost occasionally, but it is generally quite reliable. If an Internet destination is *not responding* for a given time, typically four hours, you are usually notified. Attempts to deliver the message continue for three days, but if they fail, the sender is notified. So "I never got the message" is a questionable excuse.

Answer a Backlog of Emails in Reverse Order. When we keep up with reading our email, we usually answer messages in the order they're received. But if we haven't answered our email for a while and our inbox is brimming, it's best to answer email in *reverse* order of its arrival. The reason for this is simple. Many of the oldest messages will have, in computer jargon, "timed-out." That is, we may not have to answer a message because a more recent follow-up message supercedes it. Or we may receive a "forget it" message sent by someone who received our vacation message, and realized they couldn't wait for a reply. Not answering such email saves us time and saves our correspondent aggravation. For example, when your boss sends a message asking for everyone's availability for a future meeting, it is unnecessary and somewhat embarrassing to reply when a later message sets the time for the meeting. Answering email in reverse time-order allows us to read these resolution messages before we read the original. There's only one caution: Avoid the temptation to quit and never finish reading the backlog. After all, one of those unread messages may be the announcement that you have won a new car in a raffle you entered.

Get the Sender's Permission before Forwarding Email. As a general rule, most people assume that when they send email, it is private. It is impolite and inconsiderate to forward email without getting the sender's permission. Asking permission to forward email gives the sender a chance to review the message to decide if there is something in it that should not be passed along. The sender's opinion is important because although the mail may look innocent to you, other readers may react differently and the sender may know that. It is the original sender who should decide who should read his or her email. Notice that most email in the United States is *not* a private conversation. Companies, colleges, or other organizations can (under most circumstances) review emails sent or *received* by the members of their organization; that is, *your* personal email account might be private, but your readers' may not be (see Chapter 17).

Use Targeted Distribution Lists. There are many good reasons, such as changing your address, for sending the same email message to many recipients. But keeping a single list of all people you've ever exchanged email with and then forwarding the latest lame Internet joke is just a bad idea. Not only is it an abuse of one of the benefits of email—that a group of people can be informed simultaneously—but they've probably already seen it. It doesn't take long for the recipients of such mass mailings and forwards to start deleting all messages from the sender *unread*. Your correspondents will appreciate it if you only send email targeted to them. So, having short lists like *Brothers* and *Moms_Family* is better than a list like *Relatives*. Not everything you'd send your brother will interest every member of your family. Smaller, more specific lists mean more effective communication.

✓ check LIST >>   By observing the following rules and general courtesies, your email can be more pleasant and effective.

> ☑ *Ask about one topic at a time.*
>
> ☑ *Include context*
>
> ☑ *Use an automated reply.*
>
> ☑ *Answer a backlog of email in reverse order.*
>
> ☑ *Get the sender's permission before forwarding email.*
>
> ☑ *Use targeted distribution lists.*

EXPECT THE UNEXPECTED

Expecting the unexpected is a valuable survival skill in life and in IT. When something unexpected happens, we should not only notice it, but also we should ask ourselves "Why did that happen?" or "What's going on?" By wondering about the unexpected event and analyzing what might have caused it, we may discover an advantage, avoid harm, learn something new, or, perhaps most important, save ourselves from looking like total dummies! Because it is difficult to discuss "the unexpected" in general terms, consider a specific situation in which analyzing the unexpected is beneficial.

A Mailing List Handler Has a Bug

Occasionally—meaning every year or two in my experience—a mailing list application for a large (1000 names or more) mailing list fails. (Another name for a mailing list application is a **list-server**.) The problem could be a bug in the mailing list software, or the list's **moderator**—the person responsible for deciding what is sent out to the mailing list—could have misconfigured it. Whatever the cause, there is a more-or-less typical sequence of messages to everyone on that mailing list that reveals that some people don't expect the unexpected.

The event begins innocuously enough with a message such as

```
From:  "Sue Marie Acker" <smacker@thermalmail.com>
Subject:  Re: Topic of most recent mailing to this list
To:  Mondo_list

Remove me from this list, please.
```

A few similar messages of this sort follow. This is an unexpected event. Mailing lists are for sending information from one source, say, an organization, to many receivers. This kind of mail looks like communication from a receiver back to the source, and then back to all receivers. Unexpected.

Though there are many systems for managing mailing lists, and we probably don't understand how they work, no software for handling mailing lists should send requests for removal from the list to the entire list. They should probably be sent to the moderator or intercepted by someone else managing the list. Something is wrong here. It could be in the protocol for removing from the list, or it could be something else. *Everyone* on the mailing list should have noticed this and given it some thought. The moderator, especially, should have noticed, fixed it, and sent a short apology.

But because he or she didn't fix it, the next message is

```
From:  "A. S. King" <new2net@coolmail.com>
Subject:  Re: Re: Topic of most recent mailing to this list
To:  Mondo_list

Why am I getting these messages??

> From: "Sue Marie Acker" <smacker@thermalmail.com>
> Subject: Re: Topic of most recent mailing to this list
> To: Mondo_list
>
> Remove me from this list, please.
```

From this mail we can conclude that the problem is not simply with the "unsub-scribe" feature, the facility that removes people from a mailing list. (The fault might have been limited to "unsubscribe" because all previous mail concerned that issue.) Now it is clear that the mailing list handler is reflecting all of the mail it receives. If we send anything to this list, everyone will get it. The moderator is not intercepting replies to the list. So, until someone fixes the problem, the only way to avoid getting more email is if everyone stops sending to this list.

At this point everyone should have figured out the situation, and there should be no further traffic. That is what would happen if everyone were expecting the unexpected. (It would be good if a civic-minded individual sent a private email to the moderator pointing out the problem.) Nevertheless, there follow several more messages of the form

```
From: "Jackie S. Low" <dipsy_fan@tepidmail.com>
Subject: Re: Re: Topic of most recent mailing to this list
To: Mondo_list


Yeah, why am I getting this mail? I don't even know why I'm on this list.
Remove me too.


> From: "A. S. King" <new2net@coolmail.com>
> Subject: Re: Re: Topic of most recent mailing to this list
> To: Mondo_list
>
> Why am I getting these messages??
>
> > From: "Sue Marie Acker" <smacker@termalmail.com>
> > Subject: Re: Topic of most recent mailing to this list
> > To: Mondo_list
> >
> > Remove me from this list, please.
```

After a dozen of these "Yeah, what's up with this?" types of messages, someone gets completely frustrated with those who don't seem to be figuring out that continuing to send email to the list prolongs everyone's agony. That person—actually there are usually several—writes

```
From: "M. St. Eamed" <code_ranger@infernomail.net>
Subject: Busted Mailing List Handler
To: Mondo_list


Hey, dummies, the list handler's broken. Don't send anything more to it.
```

This will be immediately followed by a message of the form

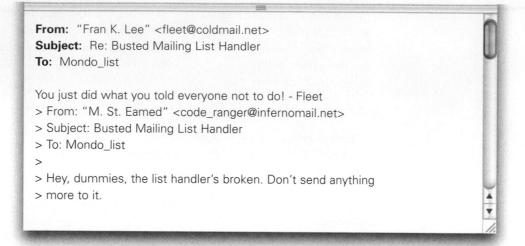

Or perhaps the message will read, "I find it offensive getting messages calling me a dummy." Then other frustrated people will jump in with comments pointing out that any person who sends email to a broken email list claiming to be offended at being called a dummy probably is a dummy, and so on. This can go on for dozens of messages before the person responsible for the mailing list finally gets it fixed. Keep in mind that the people sending these messages are on the mailing list because they have something in common, which means that they probably know each other. How embarrassing!

The point about this email history is that it should have been obvious very quickly (with A. S. King's message) that something unusual was happening. With a moment's thought, people should have realized how to act in a rational manner even though they had no way of knowing exactly what was wrong. Clearly most of the people involved in the event did so; otherwise there would have been *much more* such email.

fit **CAUTION**   **Unexpectedly Flaky.** Occasionally a familiar application will do something strange, such as slowing down, "forgetting" changes, or failing in other ways. Such behaviors are unexpected, and often immediately precede a crash. When you notice your software "acting strange," act immediately: save *to a new file name*, exit, and restart. The problem is usually just with the software, but it could be with the instance; a new file name avoids overwriting your previously saved version.

The lesson to be learned is not simply to be alert to mailing list handler bugs, but to be alert to unusual events of any kind at any time. Then, think about them. At the very least, it could save you some embarrassment.

CREATING GOOD PASSWORDS

One day electronic hardware may reliably detect who we are when we come in contact with a computer, and there will be no need for **passwords**. Meanwhile, passwords are a key part of our daily interaction with computers. This section considers selecting, changing, and managing passwords as well as password principles that can make your daily computer usage easier. Chapter 17 deals with the related topic of computer security.

The Role of Passwords

The point of a password is to limit computer or software system access to only those who know a not-likely-to-be-guessed sequence of keyboard characters. So, obviously, it is necessary to select such a sequence. We'll discuss how to choose an effective password momentarily.

Breaking into a Computer without a Password. But couldn't one computer break into another if we program it to try all passwords algorithmically until it finds the true password? Computers are surely fast enough, but they're not that dumb. Or, rather, the software running on them won't let potential users (other computers) try zillions of passwords. The software for the login protocol may include a delay when notifying the user that the password is wrong. The delay is not particularly noticeable to a human user, but it slows down the login protocol to the point that it is too slow to try zillions of passwords. Alternatively, software may notice long sequences of failed attempts to type the correct password and take some action. Of course, humans sometimes produce a sequence of failed attempts because they are agitated or groggy or try to log in using a pencil held in their teeth while holding a coffee cup in one hand and a Danish pastry in the other. So, login protocols allow several password failures before deciding that someone is trying to break in.

Forgetting a Password. Another curiosity about passwords is that if we forget ours and ask the system's administrator to find out what it is, he or she can't usually tell us. How can that be? Don't they have complete access—known as **superuser** or **administrator** status—to all of the computers, and so aren't they able to look up passwords? Yes, but the actual password is not stored on the computer.

When a new password is created, it is scrambled or encrypted and then stored in that form. The new password is thrown away. Then, at login, the password is scrambled using the same algorithm used originally when the new password was set. The two scrambled sequences are then compared. If they are the same, the right password must have been given. If not, the password must have been wrong. This technique is used so that passwords are not stored as "clear text" that some-one can steal. How the scrambling is done is explained in Chapter 17. When you ask for your forgotten password, the superuser creates a new password and forces its scrambled form to replace the old one. You then use the new password.

Guidelines for Selecting a Password

When we receive a new computer account, we are usually given an automatically generated password that is a scramble of letters and digits and possibly special characters: `rU4Uw2?gR8`. And we are told to change it so that we'll select some-thing we can remember. Changing it to our girlfriend's name wouldn't be a good idea because that's too easily guessed, at least by our friends. But what is a good choice?

Passwords are better if they are longer, at least six characters, and if they contain a mix of uppercase and lowercase letters, numbers, and, if allowed, punctuation characters. It's better to pick a sequence that is not found in dictionaries and has no "obvious" personal association, such as your name. And passwords are better if they are easy to remember. These may seem like difficult constraints to fulfill, but it's still pretty easy to think of a good password in only a few minutes.

✓ *check* **LIST** >>   Here are a few **heuristics**—guidelines to help solve a problem, which are not algorithmic—that should give good results:

- ☑ *Select a personally interesting topic, such as a parent, favorite movie, or best travel destination, and* always *select passwords related to that topic. Because you will use many passwords, selecting from one topic helps you to remember them.*

- ☑ *Develop a password from a phrase rather than a single word. The phrase must be memorable to you. It will be compressed according to the next rule.*

- ☑ *Encode the password phrase, trying to make it short (6–12 characters) by abbreviating, and by replacing letters or syllables with alternative characters, spellings, or encodings that include numbers and uppercase letters.*

The goal is to create letter strings (consisting of a mixture of numbers and letters) that are not in dictionaries.

For example, if you are using your father as the topic and your chosen phrase is his alma mater, Oxford University, then:

Oxford University → `OxfordU`   Shorten standard abbreviation
　　　　　　　　→ `Ox4dU`   Replace *for* with "4"
　　　　　　　　→ `Ohx4dU`   Replace *O* with "Oh"

The result doesn't make much sense to someone who hasn't seen the construction process, but it wouldn't be difficult for you to remember.

If your topic is your favorite movie, *Gone With the Wind,* you might use the following process to construct a password:

Gone With The Wind	→ `GWTW`	Shorten, standard abbreviation
	→ `G2uTW`	Replace *W* with "2u"
	→ `G2uT2U`	Replace *W* with "2U"
	→ `G2uTdosU`	Replace *2* with Spanish "dos"

The last replacement is not really needed because the password is already pretty obscure, but the use of Spanish emphasizes that passwords can build on any part of your knowledge, heritage, or background.

Finally, if you are using your vacation to Australia as your topic, and your phrase is Surfing in Australia, you might come up with this:

Surfing In Australia	→ `SurfingInOz`	Australia is often abbreviated Oz
	→ `SurfinInOz`	Drop *g* as in slang
	→ `Surf2inOz`	Replace *in/n* with "2in"
	→ `sirf2inOz`	Replace *Sur* with "sir"
	→ `sirF2inOz`	Introduce a capital for variety

It is possible to be too clever, so it's smart to stop the process before your password gets too obscure. After all, you must be able to remember it!

> *fit* **TIP**
>
> **Total Recall.** It might seem that remembering such obscure passwords is difficult, but it usually is not. If you type them daily, they come to mind quickly. It's almost as if your "fingers memorize them." If you use them, say, only monthly for your credit card account, following these heuristics will help you remember how you made them.

Notice the importance of the topic. The topic provides context to narrow the possibilities for us personally, serving as a memory aid. If we're changing from having used `G2uT2U` for a year, a password based on phrases like "Frankly, my dear" or "Rhett and Scarlet," suitably transformed, should be easy to remember. And even if (foolishly) we tell someone our password, and (more foolishly) explain what it means, and (most foolishly) describe the topic from which we select passwords, the topic is probably rich enough that we can still use it. There are probably enough phrases and enough variations that we can still create obscure passwords.

This process is intended to produce an obscure password (not in a dictionary) that should be easy to recall without having to write it down. But should it be written down anyway? It's a personal choice. Some people are not comfortable unless their password is written down somewhere. Others are sure they'll remember it under any circumstances, even after an all-night party at a brewery.

Changing Passwords

Passwords should be changed periodically. Organizations often have a policy as to how often a password must be changed, and sometimes there are security intrusions that cause administrators to ask that passwords be changed. Whether you should change your password depends on how likely it is that the password has become known and how important it is to keep the information secure. If you haven't changed your password in a year, it may be time to consider changing it.

Every system that uses passwords has software to change them, though we usually don't notice it when we don't need it. Check the GUI where you enter your password for the option to change it. If that doesn't work, do a search for "password" with the online **Help** facility. These systems typically ask for your current password, your new password, and a second copy of your new password. The second copy is simply a way of checking for a typing error. If they match, the password is changed.

Managing Passwords

People who make extensive use of computers may have to present passwords in dozens of situations. Obviously, if each password is different, it can become a serious challenge to remember them all. But using a single password might create a different headache. If some of them must change often, there is the hassle of having to visit all accounts frequently to update to a new password. One strategy is to have two current passwords, only one of which you change often. Then you only have to try three or four times to get the right password: the slowly changing one, the quickly changing one, and perhaps the last version of each one in case you hadn't yet gotten around to updating it.

Finally, it is possible to recycle passwords in two ways. First, if you have a good, easy-to-remember password, change it slightly using the process described above to create a new one. So, if you've been using the *Gone With the Wind* password, `G2uT2U`, and need to change it, go for the Spanish version, `G2uTdosU`. This works well for routine changes, but if there is a security concern related to your password, you should pick a totally new one from your topic area. Second, if you have several good passwords, it is probably safe to reuse them over time, especially if they are not variants of each another. Security experts do not like this idea, but most of us don't have top-secret files on our computers. Just use good judgment when choosing and managing your passwords.

*fit*TIP   **Risk Assessment.** Use judgment when choosing passwords. For a personal computer kept at home that only you use, even a single-letter password is probably too much. For your online bank account, a password of the type discussed here is a good idea. Assess the risk in each case. Even your boyfriend's name can work in some instances.

VIRUSES AND WORMS

In the 1950s, shortly after computers were invented, scientists created programs that could make exact copies of themselves. Though these programs motivated philosophical discussions about the nature of life, computability, evolution, and so forth, they mostly remained curiosities. Then on November 2, 1988, Robert Tappan Morris, Jr., a computer science graduate student, apparently lost control of a program he wrote, and the general public learned for the first time that programs could replicate themselves.

Morris' program was supposed to embed in a computer once and then send copies of itself to other machines. It propagated itself to 6000 machines (about 10 percent of the Internet at the time). It was not designed to do any harm, but it had an unfortunate bug that caused it to continue to replicate itself on each machine it infected. This quickly filled each machine's memory and hard disk, crashing the machines. The machines had to be manually "cleaned up" at the cost of millions of dollars in wages and downtime. As a result, new security organizations were created to monitor and quickly react to such malicious programs.

*fit*BYTE **Crime and Punishment.** Morris was prosecuted and convicted under the US Computer Fraud and Abuse Act of 1986, sentenced to three years' probation and 400 hours of community service, and fined $10,000. A similar conviction today would doubtless draw a much stiffer punishment.

It's a Zoo Out There

A **virus** is a program that "infects" another program by embedding a (possibly evolved) copy of itself so that when the infected program runs, the virus makes copies of itself, infecting other programs. A virus is transmitted when an infected program is transferred to another computer.

A closely related phenomenon is a **worm**, which is an independent program that makes copies of itself from machine to machine across network connections. Morris's program was a worm. The difference—a virus hides in another program and travels with it, while a worm moves across the network on its own—is not so important from a user's point of view. What's important is that they can both cause irreparable harm to your computer, such as erasing your files and trashing your software installation.

A **Trojan program**, which takes its name from the Trojan Horse of Greek legend, is a program that hides inside another useful program, performing operations unbeknownst to the user. It's technically a virus. For example, Trojans can record keystrokes allowing them to get passwords, they can record other sensitive data, and they can load other malicious software. The frequency of Trojans has increased dramatically in recent years. Indeed, as shown in Table 12.1, Trojans accounted for four of the top 10 most frequent virus incidents in 2004.

Table 12.1. Panda Software's top 10 viruses and their frequency of occurrence. The list, which includes four Trojans and five worms, accounts for just over 52 percent of all incidents.

Trj/Downloader.GK	14.0%
W32/Netsky.P.worm	6.92%
W32/Sasser.ftp	4.97%
W32/Gaobot.gen.worm	4.31%
Exploit/Mhtredir.gen	4.22%
W32/Netsky.D.worm	3.98%
Trj/Downloader.L	3.56%
Trj/Qhost.gen	3.48%
W32/Netsky.B.worm	3.45%
Trj/StartPage.FH	3.34%

In computer security terminology, an **exploit** is a program that takes advantage of a vulnerability or security hole in software such as an operating system or communication protocol. A related concept is a **backdoor access**, which is a program that enters a computer and configures it so it can be controlled remotely without the user's awareness.

All of these unsavory software systems are included in the convenient term malicious software, or "malware."

The catch-22 that complicates protecting yourself from viruses and worms is that there are also virus **hoaxes**. These are email messages warning of a virus, advising some action, and asking that you forward the email notice to others. The recommended action may be to uninstall software or to make other serious changes to your computer. Obviously, you should ignore any recommendation to reconfigure your computer until you know for certain who is suggesting it and why.

How to "Catch" a Virus

Most viruses infect a computer as a result of some action by the user. The best way to avoid problems is to know the vectors of transmission.

Email Attachments.   The best-known means of transmitting a virus or worm is by **email attachments**, the files that are sent along with email messages.

Viruses exploit people's willingness to check attachments by embedding themselves in files of widely used software like word processing programs. When an unthinking email recipient opens such a document, the software "runs" the virus commands enabling it to do its work. A common behavior for the virus is to locate the user's email address book and to send email to people on the list, along with an attachment into which it has embedded itself. When the next person opens the attachment, the virus infects their computer and can continue its spread. The **Melissa virus** used this process; see "Looking at Melissa."

> *fit* **CAUTION**
>
> **Extension Service.** Always suspect unanticipated attachments; files with `.exe` and `.zip` extensions are especially worrisome on Windows systems.

Obviously, the process doesn't work if no one opens the attachments, but attachments are very useful, and it's easy to be fooled into opening them. Would you be tempted to open the attachment on this email message?

The sender is likely spoofed—at least, I don't recognize the address—and the message is a typical trick to induce the recipient to open the zipped file. In fact, the message is the `W32/Lovegate.x@MM!zip` worm. Since a dozen similar emails arrived on the same day as this one, it is certain that some people took the bait and clicked on the attachment.

The most effective deterrent is an attentive user who is not "trigger happy" about opening attachments and who reads email with a slight skepticism:

> > Is this email from someone I know?
>
> > Is the message a sensible follow-up to the last message from the sender?
>
> > Is the content of the message something the sender would say to me?
>
> > Is there a reason for the sender to include an attachment?

When in doubt, be cautious. Do not open attachments casually. You can send return email telling the sender you didn't understand his or her last email and asking for clarification. If you believe the email is infected—new worms and viruses are usually reported in the media with much fanfare—simply **Trash** it. You don't need to delete infected email permanently; viruses are generally harmless as long as the software does not open the file.

> *fit* **CAUTION**
>
> **It's a Jungle Out There.** Viruses and worms may not be highly reported in the news at any particular time, but they circulate on the Internet regularly. At `www.wildlist.org` you'll find a list of the currently active viruses, worms, and other malicious programs that are still "in the wild." The Melissa virus was still at large after three years, though it has not been reported recently.

Copying Software. Viruses embed in software, so the common way to infect a computer is to copy software from an infected computer. Thus, if a friend's computer is infected, and you copy software from that machine onto your machine—either by using a portable medium like a USB memory or by a direct transfer—the virus may come with the software. Once you run that software, the virus infects your machine. For example, suppose you download your friend's very cool, but infected, screen saver. Then, when the screen saver runs, the virus infects your computer.

Peer-to-Peer Exchange. Downloading files, for example music, from unreliable sources is a common way to import a virus accidentally. Usually, it's not the MP3 music that is infected, but the virus "rides in" on the download. Trojans and backdoors can enter this way. Avoiding infection from viruses is one more reason to download tunes legally.

New Software. Notice that any software distribution from **freeware** (software available on the Web at no cost) to **shareware** (software available on the Web that you pay for on the honor system) to standard commercial applications (software you can pay a bundle for) is a *potential* source of virus-infected code. However, the people who distribute software are *extremely* aware of the risks and take precautions to ensure that the software they publish is clean. Because computers are pretty useless without software, we must take a tiny risk when loading new software from these sources. A little care and skepticism is really all that's needed.

Virus-Checking Software

Because viruses, worms, and other unsavory critters are at large, every computer must have up-to-date **virus-checking software** loaded and running. McAfee, Norton, and Sophos, Inc., are three of the many companies that sell antivirus software. These programs check for the known viruses, worms, and so on, but like biological organisms, new creatures are created all the time. So, it's necessary to get updates periodically. Typically, owning software from a vendor entitles one to updates that keep the diagnostics current. The task of keeping your computer free of malicious software is yours and it's never-ending.

Also, if you need honest information about viruses, worms, etc., check the companies that sell virus-checking software. Their Web sites always have up-to-the-minute information about viruses.

Phishing

Malicious software is written by hackers who want to compromise a computer or the information stored on it. But, there is no need to write software if users can be convinced to voluntarily turn over information or perform some other action simply by sending them email. This new kind of attack is called by the curious name **phishing**, short for password harvesting fishing.

{ *fit*BYTE }

Looking at Melissa >>

The Melissa virus—it's actually a worm, but widely known as the "Melissa virus"—is a classic example of malicious software. Known in security circles as W97M/Melissa, the worm burst onto the Internet on Friday March 26, 1999, embedded in Microsoft Word documents attached to email messages. The original Melissa email message had the form shown below.

Melissa was so virulent that many companies, including Microsoft, had to shut down their email servers to limit the spread of the virus. Would this look like a suspicious email if it came from someone you know?

Viruses mutate—hackers who get a copy change them and start them up again. For example, later versions of Melissa had a different attachment file name than LIST.DOC. Also, a variation, known as `W97M/Melissa.I`, used a random number generator to pick among different subject lines and email bodies, trying to fool people who were alert for the first form of the virus. The eight variations are shown in Table 12.2.

The outcome? David L. Smith—who was caught in less than a week—pleaded guilty to creating and propagating the Melissa virus. He was sentenced to 20 months in federal prison and fined $5000.

From: <Name of infected user>
Subject: Important Message From <name of infected user>
To: <50 names from infected user's email address book>

Here is that document you asked for ... don't show anyone else ;-)
Attachment: LIST.DOC

Table 12.2. *Variations of the Melissa virus email*

Subject Line	Email Body
Question for you ...	It's fairly complicated so I've attached it.
Check this!!	This is some wicked stuff!
Cool Web Sites	Check out the Attached Document for a list of some of the best Sites on the Web.
80mb Free Web Space	Check out the Attached Document for details on how to obtain the free space. It's cool, I've now got heaps of room.
Cheap Software	The attached document contains a list of web sites where you can obtain Cheap Software.
Cheap Hardware	I've attached a list of web sites where you can obtain Cheap Hardware.
Free Music	Here is a list of places where you can obtain Free Music.
* Free Downloads	Here is a list of sites where you can obtain Free Downloads.

* A randomly selected digit

In a phishing scam users—the fish—are sent spam email messages asking for credit card numbers, passwords, bank account numbers, or other private information. No one would reply to a random request for such information. So, to lower the user's skepticism, the email is disguised to appear to be from an organization such as a bank or business, and it often claims to be sent in response to some security problem (see Figure 12.1). Phishers spoof—that is, substitute misleading information for—the sender's address, the return address, and response links; when unsuspecting users click on them, they link to legitimate-looking, but bogus sites set up to steal the information. Further, these scammers use official .gif logos from the organization, and may even give authentic 800-numbers to the helpline. The messages and pop-up windows are extremely believable, especially when the targeted company is one you do business with. Many people have been duped, and phishing is a nightmare for the legitimate businesses.

```
┌──────────────────────────────────────────────────────────────────────────┐
│ ✉ U.S. Bank, 1/19/2004 02:23 PM -0400, Your account at U.S. Bank has been suspended.  _ □ X │
├──────────────────────────────────────────────────────────────────────────┤
│ ✂ 🖅 📋 🖉  ◇ ▾  Subject: Your account at U.S. Bank has been suspended.        │
├──────────────────────────────────────────────────────────────────────────┤
│ From: "U.S. Bank" <Carolina_Sika@1-base.com>                            ▲  │
│ To: <████████@███bs.com>                                                   │
│ Subject: Your account at U.S. Bank has been suspended.                     │
│ Date: Mon, 19 Jan 2004 14:23:38 -0400 (EST)                                │
│ X-Mailer: Microsoft Outlook Express 6.00.2720.3000                         │
│                                                                            │
│                                                                            │
│ Dear U.S. Bank account holder,                                             │
│                                                                            │
│ We regret to inform you, that we had to block your U.S. Bank account       │
│ because we have been notified that your account may have been compromised by │
│ outside parties.                                                           │
│                                                                            │
│ Our terms and conditions you agreed to state that your account must always be │
│ under your control or those you designate at all times.                    │
│ We have noticed some activity related to your account that indicates that other │
│ parties may have access and or control of your information in your account. │
│                                                                            │
│ These parties have in the past been involved with money laundering, illegal │
│ drugs, terrorism and various Federal Title 18 violations.                  │
│ In order that you may access your account we must verify your identity by  │
│ clicking on the link below.                                                │
│                                                                            │
│ Please be aware that until we can verify your identity no further access to │
│ your account will be allowed and we will have no other liability for your  │
│ account or any transactions that may have occurred as a result of your failure │
│ to reactivate your account as instructed below.                            │
│                                                                            │
│ Thank you for your time and consideration in this matter.                  │
│                                                                            │
│ https://www.usbank.com/account_verify/cgi/index.htm                     ▼  │
└──────────────────────────────────────────────────────────────────────────┘
```

Figure 12.1. *A typical phish story.*

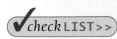 What can be done about phishing? Microsoft has published five very useful suggestions to protect us from phishing scams (`www.microsoft.com/hk/athome/security/spam/phishing.mspx`).

> ☑ *Never respond to requests for personal information like passwords via email; legitimate businesses do not request such information this way.*

☑ *Visit Web sites of companies with which you have business by typing the URL into your address window; do not click on links or accept pre-filled addresses because they can be spoofed.*

☑ *Check to make sure the Web site is using encryption; a small, closed padlock will appear near—but not in—the address window; click on it to read the security information and verify that the "Issued to" matches the business you're trying to reach.*

☑ *Routinely review your credit card and bank statements for unusual activity.*

☑ *Report suspected abuses of your personal information to the proper authorities.*

If you suspect you may have been a victim of a phishing scam, contact the business immediately. (But don't click on the links!) Also, contact the FBI at the Internet Fraud Complaint Center (**www.ifccfbi.gov/index.asp**). Finally, if you believe your personal information has been stolen, contact the FTC identity theft Web site (**www.consumer.gov/idtheft/**) as well. (Identity theft is discussed in Chapter 17.)

● PROTECTING INTELLECTUAL PROPERTY

Like land or Rover or a Land Rover, information is something that can be owned. Information, including photographs, music, textbooks, and cartoons, is the result of the creative process. The act of creation gives the creator ownership of the result in the United States and most of the world. Sometimes there are multiple forms of ownership. If on her new CD Norah Jones sings a song written by Paul Simon, he owns the words and music, and she owns the performance. If a person creates something while working for a company, the company generally owns the information. All such human creations are called **intellectual property** to distinguish them from real estate, pets, cars, and other stuff that can be owned.

The two forms of intellectual property that we are interested in here are software and copyright on the Web. Each affects how you can use information technology.

Licensing of Software

When you buy software, you load it onto your machine without giving much attention to the legal mumbo jumbo that you agree to by opening the package or downloading the file. (Sure, lawyers probably read the fine print, but the rest of us don't.) If you were to read it, you'd discover a remarkable fact: You didn't buy the software—you actually leased it. That is, **software licenses** tend to give you the use of the software, but the ownership remains with the company that is marketing it. (Of course, every license is different, forcing us to discuss the topic generally. To be sure about your particular agreement, check your software license.) We are not interested in why this is the case; rather, we want to know how such agreements constrain our behavior.

`Use of the Software.` If the agreement allows us to use the software, we can use it on all of the computers we own. The fact that we use it personally generally means that we use one instance at a time. Installing several instances for convenience should be okay. An analogous situation exists in companies. If a company has several engineers who need a certain specialized software package, they might buy x "site licenses" for that software. The site licenses authorize x engineers to use the software at the same time. The point is not how many hard disks contain a copy of the software, but rather how many people can use the software at once.

`Don't Sell It or Give It Away.` Because you don't *own* commercial software, you cannot give it to your friend. If you do, you would violate the terms of the contract that you agreed to when you opened the software package. But even if you simply bought software from a friendly programmer you met in the computer lab, you probably still can't give it away. The programmer created the software—it's his or her intellectual property—and the programmer has full copyright protection. Like a photographer who creates a stunning picture, the programmer's ownership of the software allows copies to be made and sold to people like you. You buy a photograph to frame and enjoy; you buy software to run and enjoy. Unless the programmer gives you the explicit right to copy and distribute the software, you cannot sell it or even give it away.

`Try before You Buy.` Finally, there is shareware, which is software that is usually distributed over the Internet. You can download a copy for free, and you can copy it and give it to your friends. The idea of shareware is that you can try out the software, and if you like it and use it, you pay the person who created it. (The price is listed.) It's a great system because it gives craftsman programmers a chance to distribute their often well-built and effective software and because you can try it before you purchase. But it is an honor system. If you use the software, you should pay for it. It is unethical to download software on the implied promise of paying for it if you use it, and then to use it without paying. Prices are generally very modest, and the software is often exceptionally good.

Copyright on the Web

When a person writes a term paper, builds a Web page, or creates a sculpture, he or she automatically owns the **copyright** on that "work" in the United States and most nations of the world. The creator typically owns the copyright, unless the creation is "work for hire," in which case the owner is the person who paid the creator, usually a company. For example, if you create a personal Web page, you own the copyright, but if you build a Web page as part of your job, the company owns it. Posting information on the Web is a form of publishing, and though Internet copyright and other law is not fully developed yet, it is a good assumption that information on the WWW is owned by someone.

*fit*BYTE

No © 'em. At one time, to claim copyright, you had to include the phrase "© Copyright *dates* by *author/owner* All Rights Reserved." That's no longer necessary for works produced after March 1, 1989. However, the copyright notice is still used as a reminder and reference.

What rights are included in a copyright? Obviously the right to copy it, but surprisingly, there are others. Copyright protects the owner's right to

> Make a copy of the work

> Use a work as the basis for a new work, called creating a derivative work

> Distribute or publish the work, including electronically

> Publicly perform the work, as in music, poetry, drama, or to play a video or audio recording or CD-ROM

> Publicly display the work, as in to display an image on a computer screen

It is the very act of creating the intellectual property that creates these rights. No application or approval is required. The work doesn't require the © symbol. It's copyrighted the moment it's finished.

Notice the second item in the list, using the work to create a derivative work. This is an important aspect of copyright because it prevents someone from, for example, changing each of the *Simpsons* characters in some small way —aging, perhaps—and then claiming to have created a new dysfunctional cartoon family. Only their creator, Matt Groening, has the right to change the characters. You might be tempted to bypass copyright law by restating a work in your own words, but if your creation is too much like the original, you've produced a derivative work rather than new intellectual property. Thus, for example, if someone restates this book in different words, I can sue them—and I might.

Free Personal Use.   Of course, just because someone else owns a work doesn't mean that you can't use and enjoy it. Obviously, the fact that they've published it on the Web means that you are free to read, view, or listen to it as you wish. Printing it so that you can read it on the bus is okay, as is filing away a copy on your computer for future *personal* enjoyment. You can mail the URL to your friends, notifying them of the information. Such applications are why the information was published on the Web in the first place.

When Is Permission Needed? Many sites have a written copyright policy. Often the information is placed in the **public domain**, meaning that it is free
for anyone to use, in any form. This is convenient because it means that you can
treat the information as your own. You can even sell it if you have a buyer.
Sometimes owners state that the information can be republished or used in other
forms, as long as you cite the source. They retain ownership, but you get to use it.
All you have to do is follow their guidelines. And, of course, some sites—those
that don't state otherwise—retain all rights to the Web-published information
under the applicable copyright laws. Generally, this means that if you want to use
works from such a site in one of the five ways listed earlier, you must get permission from the owners of the information. Using such copyrighted property without permission is illegal, of course. But the fact that a site retains the rights to its
information should not keep you from asking for permission. Many sites routinely
give permission; their purpose in requiring you to ask for it is to control the distribution of their works. It takes only a little effort to ask.

The Concept of Fair Use. Between the free personal use and the need
to get permission is a gray area in which limited use of copyrighted materials is
allowed without getting permission. This is known as the concept of "fair use."
Fair use is recognized in copyright law to allow the use of copyrighted material
for educational or scholarly purposes, to allow limited quotation of copyrighted
works for review or criticism, to permit parody, and a few other uses. For example, I can quote Stanley Kubrick's *2001, A Space Odyssey* in the following way

*One of the most widely known computer instructions is David Bowman's command,
"Open the pod bay doors, HAL."*

without getting the permission of the present owner (Warner Brothers), because I am
using the quotation for the educational purpose of instructing you about fair use. This
is true even though this book is a commercial application of the quoted material. And
you would be allowed to use similar brief quotations in class assignments. Indeed, fair
use provides many opportunities for using copyrighted material for socially beneficial
purposes. The problem is that it can be very unclear just when fair use applies.

When Is It Fair Use? The following four questions are applied to determine whether a given use of copyrighted information constitutes fair use.

> What is the planned use?

> What is the nature of the work in which the material is to be used?

> How much of the work will be used?

> What effect would this use have on the market for the work if the use
  were widespread?

What constitutes fair use is complex and subject to disagreements by fair-minded
Web users, lawyers, and even judges. Indeed, a recent two-year Conference on

fit TIP

No Harm in Asking. When asking for copyright permission, state what works you are interested in, such as "the photograph on your page . . . /greatpix/elvis/"; how you would like to use the works, such as "put copies on my personal Web page at . . . "; and any other relevant information, such as "I want to colorize his suede shoes so they are actually blue."

To:

Date:

I am writing to you to request permission to use the material described below. This material will be posted on a Web site that receives approximately _____ hits per month. The URL is _____

The material will be posted on <u>July 1</u> and will remain on the Web site for an <u>indefinite period</u>. I am asking permission for the nonexclusive, worldwide right to publish this material.

Description: <u>Include the title and author of the work, the source (if from a book, give the ISBN; if from a Web site, give the complete URL), and a copy of the work if possible (the text or art you want to use)</u>.

Full credit will be given to the source. A release form appears below, along with space for indicating your desired credit line

If you do not control these rights in their entirety, please let me know to whom else I must write. Thank you.

Sincerely,

<u>Your name</u>

<u>Your contact information</u>

I warrant that I have the right to grant the permission to republish the material specified above.

Permission is granted by: _____

Title: _____

Address: _____

Date: _____

Preferred acknowledgment: _____

Fair Use (CONFU) struggled mightily with the interpretations and failed to clarify the matter fully. It is beyond the scope of this section to delve into the nuances of deciding fair use. But the University of Texas publishes a very useful guideline: `www3.utsystem.edu/ogc/IntellectualProperty/copypol2.htm`

Violating the Copyright Law

Many people say that it is all right to use copyrighted material for noncommercial purposes, but that's false. You break the law whether you sell the material or not, though commercial use usually results in larger fines or damages when you're sued. Because the penalties for copyright infringement are substantial—up to $100,000 per act—it pays to be careful. By far the best approach is to think up your own material—that is, create intellectual property with your own intellect. You're not required to ask for anyone else's permission, and you enjoy copyright protection too!

fit **TIP** **Uncopyrightable Fact.** Facts cannot be copyrighted. For example, "*Uncopyrightable* is the longest English word without repeated letters" is a fact, and so is uncopyrightable.

ENSURING THE RELIABILITY OF SOFTWARE

Anyone who uses information technology regularly knows that software contains bugs, that errors occur routinely, and that even catastrophic errors—crashes—are frustratingly frequent. Most of these errors are just an annoyance. But computers control life-support systems and other medical apparatus, airplanes, nuclear power plants, weapons systems, and so on. Errors in these systems are potentially much more serious—"crash" is not a metaphor. How do we know the software running safety-critical systems is perfect? We don't! It's a sobering thought.

Safety-Critical Applications

Any system, whether mechanical or electronic, that supports life or controls hazardous devices or materials should work flawlessly. Accepting anything less seems reckless. But it is easier to say that we want perfection than it is to achieve it.

Hardware Failures. To understand the issues, distinguish first between hardware failures and software failures. In general, hardware failures can be resolved using techniques such as **redundancy**. For example, three computers can perform all the computations of a safety-critical system and make decisions based on majority vote. If a failure in one computer causes it to come up with a different answer, the other two overrule it. The chance that the identical error would happen in each computer simultaneously is infinitesimally small. Another technique, dubbed **burn in**, exploits the so-called "infant mortality" property of computer hardware failures caused by manufacturing problems: Most errors show up after only a few hours of operation. A computer that has a record of successful operation is likely to continue to operate successfully. Overall, such techniques give us confidence that the Fetch/Execute cycle and other hardware will work properly.

Software Failures. Software is another matter. Compared with mechanical and electronic systems, software is amazingly complex. The number of possible configurations that a typical program can define grows exponentially and quickly becomes unimaginably large even for small programs. All states that the software can get into, known as **reachable configurations**, cannot be examined for their correctness. This reality poses a serious problem for programmers and software engineers: How can they be sure their programs work correctly?

Like all engineers, programmers begin with a **specification**—a precise description of the input, how the system should behave, and how the output should be produced. The specification doesn't say how the behavior is to be achieved necessarily, just what it should be. Using various design methods, programmers produce the program. The program can be tested with sample inputs, and the outputs can be checked against the specification. If they do not match, there is a bug and the program must be fixed. *A program is said to be correct if its behavior exactly matches its specification.*

Though we have a tidy definition for correctness, there are two problems to achieving it, and both are showstoppers. First, it is not possible to know if the specification is perfect. Second, even if it were, it is not possible to establish correctness by testing. These two facts mean that we cannot *know* whether a program is correct, even if it is. Programmers and software engineers have developed many ingenious tools and technologies, including testing, to locate bugs and improve software. These can and do give us confidence that the program closely approximates its specification. But confidence, not certainty, is the best we can do.

---

*fit***BYTE** | **Hard Fact of Software.** Programming pioneer Edsger Dijkstra first stated this fundamental fact: Program testing reveals only the presence of bugs, never their absence.

The Challenge. What can we do about the fact that we can't prove that the software we use is correct? There are two aspects to consider:

> We must accept that software may contain bugs despite Herculean efforts of programmers and software engineers to get it right. So, we must monitor our software usage, be alert to unusual behavior that can indicate bugs, and be prepared to limit the harm that they can do.

> Because programmers and software engineers are aware of the challenge to produce correct software, poorly tested software is simply unprofessional; users should demand high quality software, refuse buggy software, and be prepared to change to better software.

Thus we must be cautious and informed users and take our business to those who produce the best product.

Fail-Soft and Fail-Safe Software

Returning to the problem of software that controls safety-critical systems, what should the standard of quality be? The software may be perfectly correct, but we can't be sure. But we can limit the harm that may result from using imperfect software. If we know that software is safe—that the life-support system does not cause patients to die, and the nuclear power plant software will not cause a meltdown—then perhaps we are less concerned about bugs. The idea of **safe software** changes the focus from worry about program correctness to concern about the consequences of errors in the software.

Testing and other techniques can give us confidence that software works "under normal circumstances," so safety focuses on what happens in unusual circumstances. It is difficult to test software under unusual circumstances, as when an earthquake damages a nuclear power plant. So, there are two design strategies: fail-soft and fail-safe. **Fail-soft** means that the program continues to operate, providing a possibly degraded level of functionality. **Fail-safe** means that the system stops functioning to avoid causing harm. The basic strategy, therefore, is to continue to operate as long as productive service is safely provided, but when that isn't possible, to avoid negative outcomes by stopping entirely.

Perfectly safe software is just as impossible as correct software, since the only way for the software to avoid all harm is not to do anything at all—not even start the nuclear power plant. Using software to control potentially dangerous systems means taking a risk, just like crossing a bridge or riding an elevator.

SUMMARY

The chapter began with a discussion of the weaknesses of email and the importance of netiquette. We learned that thoughtful email users limit messages requiring an answer to one topic, include context, and do not forward private messages or broadcast email indiscriminately. We continued our discussion about:

> "Expecting the unexpected" as a useful survival skill. The challenge is to think about the unexpected event and correctly determine whether and how to respond.

> Creating an easy-to-remember password. The approach emphasized selecting passwords that are connected to a common topic. It is smart to choose simple passwords when little security is needed and to choose more obscure passwords when there is greater risk.

9. Copyrighted material may be used
    A. only in non-profit instances
    B. only when written permission is granted
    C. if proper credit is given to the owner
    D. without permission in limited circumstances

10. Most software
    A. contains bugs
    B. is bug-free
    C. contains no known bugs
    D. works exactly as it should in every circumstance

Short Answer

1. _____ is etiquette for the Internet.

2. Email has a _____ property, that is, the ability to send the same message to many people at the same time.

3. Communication with email is _____ while _____ are synchronous.

4. A(n) _____ is a programmed response to your email that's sent when you are away.

5. A(n) _____ is the person who controls a list-server.

6. The individual who controls access to a computer system, including logins and passwords, is called a(n) _____.

7. A(n) _____ is a program that embeds itself in another program, copies itself, and spreads to other computers.

8. A(n) _____ is a program that copies itself from one machine to another across a network.

9. _____ is non-material, human creations that people can claim ownership to.

10. New work created from an existing work is called a(n) _____.

11. Information in the _____ is free for anyone to use.

12. All the possible states in which a piece of software can exist are its _____.

13. A(n) _____ program continues to operate when there is a problem, although its efficiency may be degraded.

14. A(n) _____ program shuts down to avoid causing problems.

15. _____ is the illegal use of email to scam users into surrendering their personal information, usually items like Social Security numbers, bank account numbers, and credit card numbers.

Exercises

1. What is this password: BH9oH2won0? (Hint: It was a popular '90s TV show.)

2. Devise a year's worth of passwords based on a common theme.

> The damage caused by viruses and worms. We can reduce the chance of infection by installing and running antivirus software. We must be aware of hoaxes and phishing scams. Copyright infringement poses a legal risk, so we shouldn't share software or pirate copyrighted material from the Web.

> The reliability of computers and software. It is practically impossible to have bug-free software, but this doesn't mean that we must quit using computers or accept bugs. We must watch for unusual behavior that might indicate bugs and take precautions to limit the harm that they can cause.

EXERCISES

Multiple Choice

1. Which of the following is not a weakness of email?
   A. conveying emotion
   B. multicasting
   C. emphasis
   D. ambiguity

2. Using ALL CAPS for an email message conveys
   A. sarcasm
   B. urgency
   C. anger
   D. humor

3. The best way to end a flame war is to
   A. cc all parties
   B. cool down before you reply
   C. use humor or sarcasm
   D. proofread your message

4. Email
   A. never fails to be delivered
   B. is usually delivered in four hours or less
   C. notifies you only if your message isn't delivered in three days
   D. is only about 90 percent reliable

5. A list moderator does all of the following except
   A. configures the list-server for its members
   B. edits all messages sent to the list
   C. maintains a list of members subscribed to the list-server
   D. handles errors and problems for the list-server

6. When you forget your password
   A. you must apply for a new one
   B. the system administrator looks up your password
   C. the system administrator unscrambles your password and gives it to you
   D. the system administrator assigns a new password for you to use

7. Computer viruses and worms have been around since
   A. the early days of computers
   B. the early days of the Internet
   C. the late 1980s
   D. the late 1990s

8. Computer viruses are typically spread by
   A. copying software from an infected computer
   B. receiving email from an infected computer
   C. opening email from an infected computer
   D. sending email to an infected computer

3. Go to **www.wildlist.org**. Check the current list to see how many viruses are currently considered "in the wild."

4. For each of the following, determine whether the practice is legal, illegal, or iffy. Defend your answer.
   a. You sell a copy of a computer game to your friend.
   b. You exchange computer games with your friend.
   c. You sell your old PC with the software still on it, but you keep the original copies of the software.
   d. You download a piece of shareware but don't pay for it.
   e. You frequently use a piece of shareware but don't pay for it.
   f. You install your company's software on your home computer.
   g. You frequently play a freeware game.
   h. You install software on your computer and the laptop of your college-bound child.
   i. You make a backup CD of a set of originals.
   j. You buy one license but install it throughout a lab.

5. For each of the following, determine whether the practice is legal or illegal.
   a. You create a comical, big-eared cartoon rodent.
   b. You publish a Web page without using the copyright notice.
   c. You write a sequel to *Titanic*.
   d. You include a link to a Web page in your term paper.
   e. You include a paragraph from the *Fluency* text in your term paper.
   f. You put your favorite band's picture on your Web site.
   g. You scan the autographed picture of your favorite band and put it on your Web site.
   h. You put a sound bite from a movie on your answering machine.
   i. You put a sound bite from a movie into your class presentation.
   j. You use parts of your friend's term paper from last semester in your term paper.

6. How many possible eight-character passwords can be created using only uppercase letters and numbers?

7. Use the Web to find rules on netiquette. From these, develop your own list of rules.

8. Describe how computer viruses and worms are like the living kind of viruses. In these same terms, describe how to protect your computer from these synthetic viruses.

9. Describe fail-soft and fail-safe systems on your computer and with your software. Approach the problem from a nontechnical, user standpoint. What safeguards are in place to keep you from damaging or destroying your system, programs, and data?

10. Take a major system such as a commercial airliner or a hydroelectric power plant and describe the fail-soft and fail-safe system they might have.

11. Describe five ways to protect yourself and your personal information from phishing.

13

FILL-IN-THE-BLANK COMPUTING
The Basics of Spreadsheets

learning objectives

> Explain how data is organized in spreadsheet software

> Describe how to refer to spreadsheet rows, columns, and cell ranges

> Explain relative and absolute references

> Apply concepts of relative and absolute references when filling a formula

> Explain the concept of tab-delimited input and output

FILL-IN-THE-BLANK COMPUTING
The Basics of Spreadsheets

There are 10 kinds of people in the world: Those who know binary and those who don't.

—ANONYMOUS

FROM THE VERY BEGINNING of mankind's use of symbols and writing, we have arranged information to make it more useful. Organized information is easier to understand, easier to remember, and easier to navigate. With the invention of information technology, there is a further reason to organize information: Computers can process it for us. This is a bonus we gain for very little effort, especially when we use spreadsheets.

In this chapter we introduce the basic ideas of spreadsheets. Because they make computer users so effective, especially in business, spreadsheets have become very sophisticated. This chapter introduces you to the basic ideas, making them personally useful. If you need more power, you'll have a great foundation for learning more; if not, you'll be acquainted with a very versatile tool.

We begin by introducing the basics of spreadsheet use, including constructing lists, sorting them, naming cells, and controlling the format of the entries. Next we add numeric information to the spreadsheet and learn how to manipulate it, which teaches us about formulas, relative and absolute references, and functions. Computing new numbers from numbers already in the table is what spreadsheets do best, and happily, it is extremely easy to learn and use. After learning these basic concepts, we practice them on "everyday" problems; that is, tasks of personal interest: We build a 1-minute calendar for our weekly schedule, set up a transportation schedule so we don't miss the bus so often, make a "cheat sheet" for computing discounts at the music store, and develop data for helping decide how much to borrow for a "big ticket" purchase like a car or stereo. None of these tasks is so difficult as to require a computer, but since we're using a computer anyway, we can solve them quickly to our personal satisfaction. Finally, we use the Best Movie list to practice manipulating data in a spreadsheet.

ARRANGING INFORMATION

Commonly, textual information is organized into lists, as we know from making shopping lists, invitation lists, "to do" lists, class lists, and many others. As a running example, we'll use a list of migratory birds:

```
Short-tailed shearwater
Swainson's hawk
Wheatear
Arctic tern
Willow warbler
Long-tailed skua
```

Looking at the list, you see that it contains six bird names even though you may not be too familiar with birds. You probably figured it out because you know that hawks and warblers are birds and the items appear on separate lines. The names themselves are quite diverse as text: single word names, double word names, hyphenated names, and even a possessive. Since the computer doesn't have your knowledge, it needs to be told the extent of each entry, that is, how much text there is in each entry. The separate line cue helps, but if the entries were very long, they would spill to another line, and that cue wouldn't work.

fit **TIP**

Kinda the Same. Spreadsheet software is available from many sources. The content of this chapter applies generally to Microsoft Excel, OpenOffice, AppleWorks, Lotus 123, etc. Every system is different, however, because menus and defaults are particular to each system. With a moment's exploration you should be able to perform the operation on your system.

An Array of Cells

To help us create a list, spreadsheets give us an array of **cells** that we fill in to set up our list.

The lines are part of the graphic user interface; they help us and the computer agree on what an item is and how the positions of items are related to each other.

Notice that four of the six items in the list do not fit within the lines provided. Even though it takes more space to display the entry than the computer provides, entries do not straddle cells. Each occupies only the cell into which it is typed, as is shown when we enter test data in the cells to their right.

The test data, which blocks the long entries from spilling to the empty cells on the right, indicates that entries that are too long are clipped. (Items only spill when the cells to their right are unused.) We can either let the entries be clipped, or make the cells wider, as explained in Table 13.1 on page 372. We choose the latter.

Sorting the Data

A common operation on any list, especially when it gets long, is to alphabetize or sort it. Spreadsheet software makes sorting easy. We must say what items to sort, so naturally, we must select the list. We select the list by dragging the cursor across the cells; the resulting selection is indicated with highlighting.

All of the items inside the blue box are selected, including the white item, which is a different color only because it was the first cell selected, that is, it's the place where the dragging began. The **Sort ...** operation is found among the menu items. It allows us to choose ascending or descending order. The software uses an algorithm like the one we discussed in Chapter 10 to sort the items. Sorting our list of birds in ascending order produces the following result.

Notice that the sorting software orders the list alphabetically on the first letter of the entry, not on the type of bird, for example, "hawk." This is consistent with the spreadsheet view that the cell entries are "atomic" or "monolithic" from the computer's point of view, meaning that the computer does not consider any of their constituent parts. If the list contained both Swainson's hawk and Swainson's warbler, they would appear together in sorted order. But if we wanted those birds to be grouped with the hawks and the warblers respectively, then it would be necessary to sort on the second part of the name. That would require the type of the bird (e.g., "hawk" or "warbler") to be in a separate cell—in its own column.

Adding More Data to the List

Our list is not so complete. We will leave the common names in a single column, but we'll add the scientific names using two columns, one for genus and one for species.

As we know, scientific names are usually written in italics. Spreadsheets give us the ability to format cell entries with the kinds of formatting facilities found in word processors, such as italics, bold, font styles, font sizes, justification, colored text and backgrounds, etc. Naturally, the formatting facilities are found under the **Format** menu. We italicize the scientific names and right justify the genus name so it looks like it is paired with the species name.

Naming Rows and Columns. Now suppose we want to alphabetize on the second column, the genus. We begin by selecting the whole list because that is the information we want to reorder. With three columns selected, how do we specify that the second column is the one to sort on rather than the first column?

Spreadsheet programs automatically provide a naming scheme for referring to specific cells. The columns are labeled with letters and the rows are labeled with numbers. This allows us to refer to a whole column, as in column **C**, or to a whole row, as in row **4**, or to a single cell by specifying both the column letter and the row number, as in **B2**. Thus, when we request to sort the entries, the sorting software displays this **Sort** GUI.

We choose to sort the selected rows based on entries in column **C** (which contains our *genus* entries) by clicking on the directional arrows. This produces the following result.

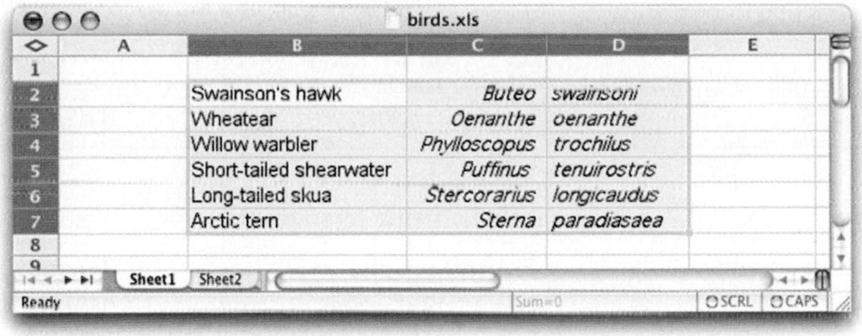

Notice that the naming scheme allows us to refer to a group of cells, by naming the first cell and the last cell and placing a colon (**:**) in between, as in "the cells **B2:D7** are highlighted in the figure." This kind of reference is called a **cell range**.

---

try it

Q: What is the cell range for the scientific names of the birds whose common name ends with "-tailed"?

A: C5:D6 because the two birds with "-tailed" in their names are in rows 5 and 6, and the scientific names span Columns C and D.

Headings. Though the software provides names for referring to cells, it is convenient for us to name the rows and columns with more meaningful names. For example, we can label the columns with the type of information entered.

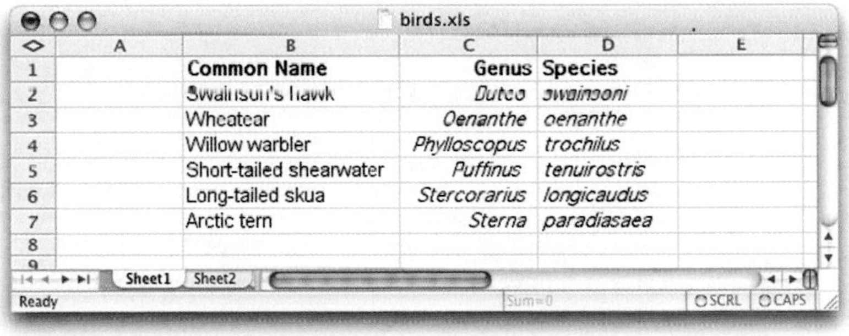

Summarizing, spreadsheets are made up of cells that are displayed to the user as rectangles in a grid. Information is entered in a cell and treated as an elemental piece of data no matter how long it is or if it contains spaces or other punctuation symbols. Generally, we build a list of items that can be sorted simply by selecting them, and requesting the sorting operation. If multiple columns must be sorted, we select all of the information to be reordered, request **Sort**, and specify the column to sort on when the GUI asks for it. Spreadsheets automatically provide a labeling for specifying the column/row position of any element in the grid, but it is also convenient to add our own, more significant names. Table 13.1 gives other common operations useful for lists.

Table 13.1. *Common spreadsheet operations*

Operation	Using Excel ...	Using Open Office ...
Change column width manually	Place cursor at right side of column name, then drag	Place cursor at right side of column name, then drag
Change column width automatically	**Format > Column > Autofit Selection**	**Format > Column > Optimal Width...**
Cut, copy, paste contents	Standard: ^x, ^c, ^v	Standard: ^x, ^c, ^v
Fancy formatting	**Format > Cells...**	**Format > Cells...**
Clear cells	**Edit > Clear > All**	**Edit > Delete Contents...**
Delete columns, rows	**Edit > Delete**	**Edit > Delete Cells ...**
Hide a column or row	**Format > Column > Hide**	**Format > Column > Hide**

All spreadsheet applications provide these common operations; explore your system.

COMPUTING WITH SPREADSHEETS

Though spreadsheets don't have to contain a single number to be useful, their most common application is to process numerical data. Numerical data is usually associated with textual information, too, so most spreadsheets have both. For example, suppose our migratory bird spreadsheet has been further filled out, as shown in Figure 13.1.

	B	C	D	E	F	G
1	Common Name	Genus	Species	Migration	Disance (km)	Body Len (m)
2	Swainson's hawk	Buteo	swainsoni	USA-Argentina	13500	0.52
3	Wheatear	Oenanthe	oenanthe	Alaska-E Africa	13500	0.16
4	Willow warbler	Phylloscopus	trochilus	Chukotka-S Africa	15500	0.11
5	Short-tailed shearwater	Puffinus	tenuirostris	Tasmania-Bering Straight	12500	0.43
6	Long-tailed skua	Stercorarius	longicaudus	N Greenland-Southern Ocean	16000	0.51
7	Arctic tern	Sterna	paradiasaea	Greenland-Antarctic	19000	0.35
8						

Figure 13.1. *Bird migration spreadsheet.*

The `Migration` column gives the end points of the bird's semiannual migration route, the `Distance` column gives the approximate length of that flight in kilometers, and `Body Len` gives the size of the bird (length) in meters. In the following discussion the `Genus`, `Species`, and `Migration` columns will be hidden.

Writing a Formula

Suppose we want to find out how far Swainson's Hawk flies in miles rather than kilometers. Because one kilometer is 0.621 miles, we must multiply the value in cell **F2** by 0.621 to find out. We can perform this specific computation with a calculator, but we will probably want to know the distances in miles for all of the migration flights. So, we decide to create a new column for the distance in miles, and instruct the spreadsheet how to compute it.

	B	F	G	H	I	J	K
1	Common Name	Distance (km)	Body Len (m)	Distance (Mi)			
2	Swainson's hawk	13500	0.52				
3	Wheatear	13500	0.16				
4	Willow warbler	15500	0.11				
5	Short-tailed shearwater	12500	0.43				
6	Long-tailed skua	16000	0.51				
7	Arctic tern	19000	0.35				
8							

What entry do we want in position **H2**? We'd like it to be equal to **F2** × 0.621, so we type

```
=F2*0.621
```

which appears in the **H2** window and the **Edit Formula** window on the edit bar above.

=F2*0.621

	B	F	G	H	I	J	K
1	Common Name	Distance (km)	Body Len (m)	Distance (Mi)			
2	Swainson's hawk	13500	0.52	=F2*0.621			
3	Wheatear	13500	0.16				
4	Willow warbler	15500	0.11				
5	Short-tailed shearwater	12500	0.43				
6	Long-tailed skua	10000	0.51				
7	Arctic tern	19000	0.35				
8							

Notice that we use an asterisk (*) for the multiplication symbol rather than a cross or dot. When we type return, the value in **H2** is the result of the computation, that is, 8383.5 miles.

We have just instructed the spreadsheet software to compute the value in cell H2 by telling it what the cell should equal. We did this by typing a formula into the cell. Formulas, which begin with an equal sign (=), define the value for the entry based on the values of other entries. We used numbers (0.621), cell references (F2), and standard arithmetic operations (*) as found on a calculator. If we ever change our estimate of the distance Swainson's Hawk migrates, that is, change the value in F2, then the spreadsheet software will *automatically change* the value in H2 to reflect the revision.

*fit*TIP   **Equal Opportunity.** When we type characters into a cell, the spreadsheet software needs to know if we are giving it data that should be stored, or if we are giving it a formula saying how to compute information for that cell. The equal sign (=) is the indicator: It's a formula if it starts with =; otherwise it's data.

Consider the formula a bit more. We entered the formula =F2*0.621 into cell H2. The cell contains this formula, not 8383.5. We can prove this by temporarily changing the value in F2 from 13,500 to, say, 14,000, and noting that H2 automatically increases to 8694.

By specifying this formula, we have defined an equation

$$H2 = F2 \times 0.621$$

just as we would in algebra. Recall that such an equation means that both sides of the equal sign refer to the same value. So, entering the formula into H2 means that we want the cell to have the value of F2 * 0.621 now and forever. Because F2 presently contains the data 13,500, cell H2 displays as 8383.5. When we change the value of F2, the value of H2 must change, because the equality must be preserved. Thus, when we put a formula into a cell (the right side of the equation), the computer does the math and displays its value (the left side of the equation).

Repeating a Formula

We can specify a similar computation for cell H3 and the other cells in that column by entering them in the same way.

Copy/Paste. Thinking about it, however, we might guess that **Copy/Paste** will work to replicate the equation to other cells. So, we select cell H2, which, in Excel, is indicated by an animated highlight (the dashes revolve around the box). Other spreadsheet software simply shows a solid box around the item.

| | =F2*0.621 | | | | | |

	B	F	G	H	I	J	K
				birds.xls			
1	Common Name	Distance (km)	Body Len (m)	Distance (Mi)			
2	Swainson's hawk	13500	0.52	8383.5			
3	Wheatear	13500	0.16				
4	Willow warbler	15500	0.11				
5	Short-tailed shearwater	12500	0.43				
6	Long-tailed skua	16000	0.51				
7	Arctic tern	19000	0.35				
8							

Sheet1 Sheet2 Sheet3   Select destination and press ENTER or choose Paste   Sum=8383.5   SCRL CAPS NUM

The cell's contents are shown in the **Edit Formula** window. We **Copy** this cell (^C), select the remaining cells in the column by dragging the mouse across them, and **Paste** (^V). The result shows all of the distance values computed. This is quite a bit of computation for very little effort on our part.

| | =F3*0.621 | | | | | |

	B	F	G	H	I	J	K
				birds.xls			
1	Common Name	Distance (km)	Body Len (m)	Distance (Mi)			
2	Swainson's hawk	13500	0.52	8383.5			
3	Wheatear	13500	0.16	8383.5			
4	Willow warbler	15500	0.11	9625.5			
5	Short-tailed shearwater	12500	0.43	7762.5			
6	Long-tailed skua	16000	0.51	9936			
7	Arctic tern	19000	0.35	11799			
8							

Sheet1 Sheet2 Sheet3   Select destination and press ENTER or choose Paste   Sum=47506.5   SCRL CAPS NUM

Notice that in the **Edit Formula** window the equation shows as F3*0.621. This corresponds to the computation for the cell H3, the first of the highlighted cells (white) into which we pasted the formula. And we notice a curious thing: Whereas the formula we pasted was F2*0.621, the formula was transformed into F3*0.621 when it was pasted into H3; it was transformed into F4*0.621 for H4, etc. This is exactly what we want for this column, namely that the value in column H is based on the corresponding values in column F. The software makes this transformation for us automatically. (This is explained in Transforming Formulas.)

Filling. It's possible for these computations to be performed even more easily! Let's go back and redo them from the point where we had just entered the formula for the Swainson's Hawk,

Notice in the image that the highlighted cell **H2** is outlined in color, but there is also a small box or tab beyond the cell's lower right corner (near the cursor). This is called its *fill handle*. We can grab this handle with the cursor and "pull" it down the column, applying the operation we just performed on **H2** to those cells.

This process is known as *filling*. It's automated copying and pasting! Filling is a shortcut that allows us to replicate, that is, **Copy/Paste**, the contents of the cell with the fill handle, saving us from explicitly setting each cell in the column or manually using the **Copy/Paste** operations. Whenever the fill handle is visible on a highlighted cell, the contents can be replicated by filling.

try it

Q: Suppose we would also like to see the birds' body lengths measured in inches. Using the fact that a meter is 39 inches, what steps do we perform to add this information to the spreadsheet?

A: *Step 1.* The recommended first step is to label the next column, **I**, with an appropriate heading, though it is not actually required.

Step 2. Enter the formula =G2*39 in cell **I2**, which computes the length of Swainson's Hawk in inches; it's 20.28 inches.

Step 3. Click once on cell **I2** to select it, and drag the fill handle down the column to fill in the lengths of the other birds.

=G2*39

	B	F	G	H	I	J	K
					birds.xls		
1	Common Name	Distance (km)	Body Len (m)	Distance (Mi)	Length (In)		
2	Swainson's hawk	13500	0.52	8383.5	20.28		
3	Wheatear	13500	0.16	8383.5	6.24		
4	Willow warbler	15500	0.11	9625.5	4.29		
5	Short-tailed shearwater	12500	0.43	7762.5	16.77		
6	Long-tailed skua	16000	0.51	9936	19.89		
7	Arctic tern	19000	0.35	11799	13.65		
8							

Sheet1 Sheet2 Sheet3

Ready   Sum=81.12   SCRL CAPS NUM

Transforming Formulas: Relative versus Absolute

The software automatically transforms the formulas as it pastes them or fills them into a cell because we used a relative cell reference when we wrote **F2** and **G2**. Spreadsheets allow two kinds of cell references—relative and absolute—and we must be careful which we use. The absolute forms for these cells are **F2** and **G2**; they tell the software never to change the reference when filling or pasting. Here's what's happening.

Relative means "relative position from a cell." When we pasted the formula **=F2*0.621** into **H2**, the software noticed that cell **F2** is two cells to the left of **H2**. That is, the formula refers to a cell in the same row, but two cells to the left.

=F2*0.621

	B	F	G	H	I	J	K
					birds.xls		
1	Common Name	Distance (km)	Body Len (m)	Distance (Mi)			
2	Swainson's hawk	13500	0.52	=F2*0.621			
3	Wheatear	13500	0.16				
4	Willow warbler	15500	0.11				
5	Short-tailed shearwater	12500	0.43				
6	Long-tailed skua	16000	0.51				
7	Arctic tern	19000	0.35				
8							

Sheet1 Sheet2 Sheet3

Edit   Sum=8383.5   SCRL CAPS NUM

Since this is a relative reference, the software preserves the relationship of "two cells to the left in the same row" between the position of the referenced cell and the cell where the formula is pasted. So, when we **Paste** or fill this same formula into **H3**, the software transforms the formula so it still refers to the cell two cells to the left in the same row; that is, the formula is changed to **=F3*0.621**. And similarly whenever a relative formula is pasted or filled.

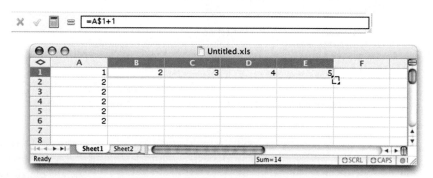

	B	F	G	H	I	J	K
1	**Common Name**	**Distance (km)**	**Body Len (m)**	**Distance (Mi)**			
2	Swainson's hawk	13500	0.52	=F2*0.621			
3	Wheatear	13500	0.16	=F3*0.621			
4	Willow warbler	15500	0.11	=F4*0.621			
5	Short-tailed shearwater	12500	0.43	=F5*0.621			
6	Long-tailed skua	16000	0.51	=F6*0.621			
7	Arctic tern	19000	0.35	=F7*0.621			
8							

An absolute reference always refers to the fixed position—the software never adjusts it.

Because there are two dimensions in spreadsheets—columns and rows—there are actually two ways a formula can be relative. This makes four cases:

F2—column and row are both relative

$F2—absolute column, but relative row

F$2—relative column, but absolute row

F2—column and row are both absolute

For example, assume cell A1 contains 1. When the formula =A$1+1 is filled from A2 down column A into new rows, the formula is untransformed and 2's are computed, because the cell's row reference ($1) is absolute and the column reference, though relative, didn't change as we filled down the column into new rows. All cells refer to the same cell, A1. But when that formula is filled from B1 across row 1 into new columns, the relative column reference (A) is transformed, =B$1+1, =C$1+1, =D$1+1, etc., and the numbers 2, 3, 4, . . . are computed.

The spreadsheet software preserves the relative position in whichever dimension(s) you specify, and leaves absolute references unchanged.

Cell Formats

Although it is amazing that the migratory birds fly so far twice a year, it is perhaps even more impressive that the smaller birds do it. One analysis that a biologist might make to take both distance and size into consideration is to divide the bird's size into the distance flown. This *flying score* measures each bird in a way that allows a more equal comparison.

We will use the distance in kilometers (column F) and length in meters (column G) so that the "meters" cancel out giving a "unitless" score. As before, we define a new column, and enter the equation into the first cell. After finding the hawk's score, we fill the column with the formula and compute the results.

The scores are somewhat difficult to read because they have too many digits, or as a mathematician might say, more digits than are significant. For the numbers to be useful, we need to format them, say, by making them whole numbers.

All spreadsheet software provides control over the format of the information displayed. For example, Excel displays this GUI for formatting cells.

This GUI gives us control over the types of information in the fields (**Category**); control over the number of decimal digits for the **Number** category chosen; control over setting the "1000s" separators (commas for North America); and control over the display of negative numbers.

When we reduce the number of decimal digits to 0, that is, specify whole numbers only, we get this result.

	B	F	G	J	K	L	M
1	Common Name	Disance (km)	Body Len (m)	Flying Score			
2	Swainson's hawk	13500	0.52	25962			
3	Wheatear	13500	0.16	84375			
4	Willow warbler	15500	0.11	140909			
5	Short-tailed shearwater	12500	0.43	29070			
6	Long-tailed skua	16000	0.51	31373			
7	Arctic tern	19000	0.35	54286			
8							

birds.xls — Sheet1 / Sheet2 / Sheet3 — Ready — Sum=365974 — SCRL CAPS NUM

This confirms our intuition that smaller birds score higher even if their distances flown are not the largest.

FUNCTIONS

Picking the Willow warbler as the most amazing flier is based on its being the maximum value in the `Flying Score` column. Visually finding the maximum for this column is easy to do, but it's somewhat harder to do for the other columns because the entries have the same number of digits; also the list can be much longer. So we set up the spreadsheet to compute the maximum.

Finding the Maximum

Spreadsheet software provides **functions** for computing common summary operations such as totals (`sum`), averages, maximums (`max`), and many others. To use these functions, we give the function name and specify the cell range to be summarized in parentheses after it. So, for example, we write

```
=max(J2:J7)
```

in a cell at the bottom of column `J`, and label that row with the "`Maximum:`" caption.

| MAX ▼ ✗ ✓ ▦ ≣ | =max(J2:J7) |

birds.xls

	B	F	G	J	K	L	M	N
1	**Common Name**	**Disance (km)**	**Body Len (m)**	**Flying Score**				
2	Swainson's hawk	13500	0.52	25962				
3	Wheatear	13500	0.16	84375				
4	Willow warbler	15500	0.11	140909				
5	Short-tailed shearwater	12500	0.43	29070				
6	Long-tailed skua	16000	0.51	31373				
7	Arctic tern	19000	0.35	54286				
8								
9	Maximum:			=max(J2:J7)				
10								
11								

Sheet1 / Sheet2 / Sheet3   Sum=140909   ○SCRL ○CAPS ●NUM

Edit

The formula directs the software to find the largest value in the cell range `J2:J7`, that is, the `Flying Score` column. Notice that there is a triangle pointer by the function **MAX** in the upper left corner of the image. We'll find a list of the available functions here. When we don't remember the function names, we can check this list; or check the list under **Edit > Insert Function** . . . .

fit **TIP**

> **The Easy Case.** Functions and column letters are not case sensitive in spreadsheets, so we can type them however we wish. The software stores the result as uppercase, which is how it's displayed after its initial entry.

Having computed the maximum for `Flying Score`, we can figure the maximum of the other columns as before, by filling. That is, we grab the `J9` cell by its fill handle and pull it left to column `F`. The result is curious.

| ✗ ✓ ▦ ≣ | =MAX(J2:J7) |

birds.xls

	B	F	G	J	K	L	M	N
1	**Common Name**	**Disance (km)**	**Body Len (m)**	**Flying Score**				
2	Swainson's hawk	13500	0.52	25962				
3	Wheatear	13500	0.16	04075				
4	Willow warbler	15500	0.11	140909				
5	Short-tailed shearwater	12500	0.43	29070				
6	Long-tailed skua	16000	0.51	31373				
7	Arctic tern	19000	0.35	54286				
8								
9	Maximum:	✛ 19000	1	140909				
10								
11								

Sheet1 / Sheet2 / Sheet3   Sum=171729   ○SCRL ○CAPS ●NUM

Ready

The "1" in the `Body Len` column is a whole number rather than 0.52, the largest of the two-decimal-digit fractions in column `G`. Why? Because the maximum value computation in the `Flying Score` column inherits the whole number setting from before. When we drag it across to the other columns, it brings its formatting with it. So, the software looks for the largest value in `Body Len`, finds that it is 0.52, and then rounds it to a whole number, i.e., 1. Formatting this cell so that it displays numbers with two decimal digits fixes the problem.

For completeness, let's also compute the average for each column using the average function. The result requires some additional formatting in the last two columns.

	B	F	G	J	K	L	M	N
				=AVERAGE(J2:J7)				
1	Common Name	Disance (km)	Body Len (m)	Flying Score				
2	Swainson's hawk	13500	0.52	25962				
3	Wheatear	13500	0.16	84375				
4	Willow warbler	15500	0.11	140909				
5	Short-tailed shearwater	12500	0.43	29070				
6	Long-tailed skua	16000	0.51	31373				
7	Arctic tern	19000	0.35	54286				
8								
9	Maximum:	19000	0.52	140909				
10	Average:	15000	0.35	60996				
11								

birds.xls — Sheet1 Sheet2 Sheet3 — Ready — Sum=85324.47669 — SCRL CAPS NUM

Filling Hidden Columns

Perhaps unexpectedly, we have computed more than is visible in this image. Notice that we have two hidden columns between `G` and `J`, the columns that we used earlier for converting from metric to English units. When we "unhide" these columns we see that by dragging the cell definitions across the rows, we have computed the maximum and average of the previously hidden columns, too.

	B	F	G	H	I	J	K	L
1	Common Name	Disance (km)	Body Len (m)	Distance (Mi)	Length (In)	Flying Score		
2	Swainson's hawk	13500	0.52	8383.5	20.28	25962		
3	Wheatear	13500	0.16	8383.5	6.24	84375		
4	Willow warbler	15500	0.11	9625.5	4.29	140909		
5	Short-tailed shearwater	12500	0.43	7762.5	16.77	29070		
6	Long-tailed skua	16000	0.51	9936	19.89	31373		
7	Arctic tern	19000	0.35	11799	13.65	54286		
8								
9	Maximum:	19000	0.52	11799	20.28	140909		
10	Average:	15000	0.35	9315	13.52	60996		
11								
12								

birds.xls — Sheet1 Sheet2 Sheet3 — Ready — Sum=0 — SCRL CAPS NUM

This makes sense because these columns are part of our spreadsheet; they just were not displayed previously. Of course, if we no longer wanted the English conversion columns, we could delete them. The final spreadsheet, slightly adjusted in formatting, is shown in Figure 13.2.

	B	C	D	E	F	G	H	I	J
1	**Common Name**	**Genus**	**Species**	**Migration**	**Disance (km)**	**Body Len (m)**	**Distance (Mi)**	**Length (In)**	**Flying Score**
2	Swainson's hawk	*Buteo*	*swainsoni*	USA-Argentina	13500	0.52	8383.5	20.28	25962
3	Wheatear	*Oenanthe*	*oenanthe*	Alaska-E Africa	13500	0.16	8383.5	6.24	84375
4	Willow warbler	*Phylloscopus*	*trochilus*	Chukotka-S Africa	15500	0.11	9625.5	4.29	140909
5	Short-tailed shearwater	*Puffinus*	*tenuirostris*	Tasmania-Bering Straight	12500	0.43	7762.5	16.77	29070
6	Long-tailed skua	*Stercorarius*	*longicaudus*	N Greenland-Southern Ocean	16000	0.51	9936	19.89	31373
7	Arcto tern	*Sterna*	*paradisaea*	Greenland-Antarctic	19000	0.35	11799	13.65	54286
8									
9				**Maximum:**	19000	0.52	11799	20.28	140909
10				**Average:**	15000	0.35	9315	13.52	60996
11									

Figure 13.2. *Final spreadsheet for the migratory birds.*

DAILY SPREADSHEETS

Some people use computers all day and never use a spreadsheet; others use spreadsheets constantly. The rest of us are somewhere in between: Spreadsheets are convenient and versatile tools that simplify computing. In this section we look at a few personal applications as a way to gain a bit more experience with using spreadsheets.

Many opportunities exist to use spreadsheets to organize one's personal information. We can

> track our performance in our personal exercise program—distances, time, reps

> set up an expense budget for the next term

> keep a list of the books and CDs we've lent to others

> follow our favorite team's successes by importing the season schedule and annotating it with wins and losses and our own comments about the games

> record flight hours or dives after each flying or scuba lesson

> document expenses such as travel, or income such as tips for income tax purposes

> save records generated while online banking

Spreadsheets can even serve as an address book or recipe file.

Here are more ways to apply spreadsheets in personally relevant ways.

Calendar

Calendars are everywhere, and computers come with calendar software, so making a calendar with a spreadsheet hardly seems like an important application. But you would be surprised. Some people find calendar software clumsy, some people want to restructure their week, beginning, say on Wednesday, some people want a mix of larger/smaller appointment timeslots, workers with "2-on-1-off" jobs want double week calendars, etc. At a meeting, one might set up a schedule for room or equipment usage or for a team's practices; it's often convenient to present information as a calendar, say espresso sales by hour and day. Making a custom calendar solves these problems, and it only takes a minute. Really!

To begin we enter a day of the week into a cell in the spreadsheet, say `Sunday`, and format it as we like it, perhaps with bold letters and a background color. Depending on which software we are using, we either drag the fill handle across the next six columns to fill in the successive days of the week, or we request such a fill operation using the menus.

The result should be enhanced by the day of the month. So, we enter a date, say `January 2`, in the row below, format it, and fill it across.

That result is ready for the times of day. We enter `8:00 AM` into cell `A5`, format it to taste, including bold and color . We want half hour appointment slots, but normally the time fill increments by hours rather than half hours. We could figure out how to change the increment, but instead we enter `8:30 AM` in cell `A6`.

Using this pair of cells we fill down the column to `8:00 PM`. This achieves the desired half hour appointment times.

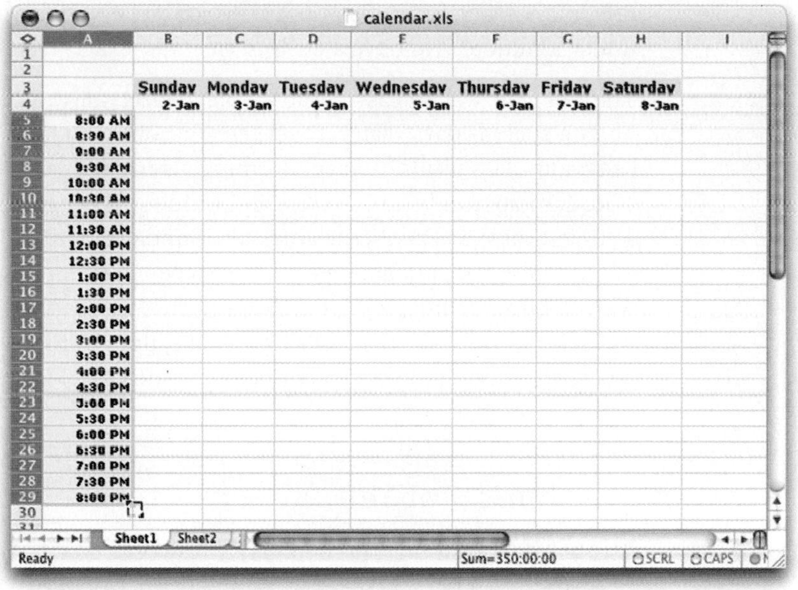

This double-cell fill is an easy way to cause the spreadsheet software to count by a specific amount. Note that entering `8:00` without the "`AM`" results in an international or military time fill.

The result is shown in Figure 13.3 with example contents.

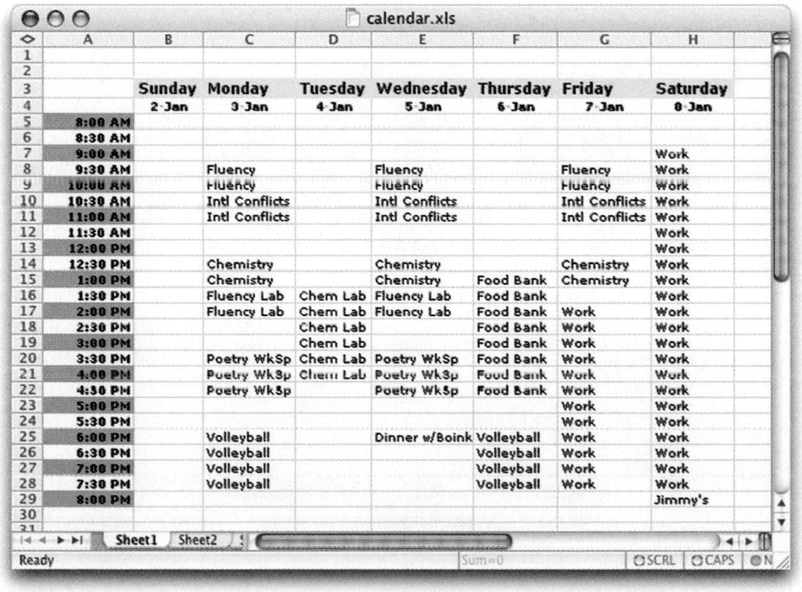

Figure 13.3. Calendar spreadsheet with entries added.

The point is not that we've created a spectacular appointment calendar, but that the spreadsheet software makes it easy to create one. We did almost no typing: We entered `Sunday` and filled; we entered `January 2` and filled; we entered `8:00 AM` and `8:30 AM` and filled the pair. We were done! It's possible to do this in under a minute. We have a custom calendar exactly matching our needs.

The calendar was so easy because spreadsheet software, when it fills certain types of data such as days, dates, times, etc., automatically increments, that is, automatically adds 1 as it fills each cell forming a **series**. The software knows that "adding 1" to Sunday results in Monday, and "adding 1" to January 31 results in February 1. It assumes, when it sees values like Sunday, that it's not ASCII data, but rather one of these special data types. If you type in `Sunday` and you want to copy the word *Sunday*, that is, you don't want to treat it as a special type of data, then don't use series fill. Simply **Copy/Paste**. Finally, double-cell fill also indicates a series, where the amount of increment between successive items is the difference between the pair.

Discount Table

Because downloading music for MP3 players is so popular, music stores that sell CDs try to compete by offering "store credit" discounts, that is, discounts on future purchases at the store. One store offers

> > $1.00 store credit for each $10.00 spent plus

> > $3.00 store credit for every two CDs purchased. (One CD earns only $1.00 credit.)

To help you to figure your credits, you can construct a table, which you can print out and take to the store, showing the various discounts. This is another very easy spreadsheet application.

To begin, we decide on the axes of the table: The left column is the "dollars spent" column, showing $10.00 increments, and the top row is the "CDs purchased" row, showing 1 CD increments. These are both number series, but the spreadsheet software doesn't automatically provide series fill for numbers. So we must choose it, or fill in the series using formulas, which is also possible, of course. For the top row, we fill the first and second cells with 1 and 2 and then fill across.

For the left column, we enter the first two items, `$10.00` and `$20.00`, select the pair, and fill down.

The software figures out that we want to increment by $10.00. All that remains is to specify the table entries. For that, we write a formula.

For each $10.00 spent the store gives a $1.00 credit. So, part of the formula is to divide the item in column **B** by 10. For example

```
=$B3/10
```

To ensure that the number we are dividing is always in column **B**, we make the column reference absolute. The row reference should be relative because we want the calculation to apply to whatever row the formula is in.

The store also gives $3.00 credit for every two CDs purchased. The easiest way to apply this rule is to multiply the CD axis entry (in row 2) by 3/2.

```
=(3/2)*C$2
```

which is the right answer when the number of CDs is even, but for an odd number of CDs it is too much by half. For example, **1*3/2** is 1.5, that is, $1.50, but the store only gives $1.00 credit. The solution is to throw away any fractional digits, that is, to truncate the number. Spreadsheets have a function, **trunc**, for this purpose,

```
=trunc((3/2)*C$2)
```

As with the first rule, we use an absolute reference and a relative reference. Row 2 is absolute so that all entries refer to it, but the column should be relative, so that the computation applies to the column that the formula is in.

The combined formula for both discount rules is

```
=$B3/10 + trunc((3/2)*C$2)
```

which we enter into cell **C3**. This yields the right answer, $2.00 ($1.00 for the amount paid plus $1.00 for the single CD).

`=$B3/10+TRUNC(3*C$2/2)`

Filling the formula down the column and then across the rows produces the final table.

`=$B3/10+TRUNC(3*C$2/2)`

We can print out the table and take it with us to the store to help strategize our purchases to get the biggest discount. For example, we might trade CD purchases with a friend to get a larger combined discount, which we then share.

The table was easy to construct. We used two series, one for the dollars and one for the CDs, to create the axes. The table entries used a single formula that referenced the axis entries with one absolute and one relative coordinate so that the entry for the column/row position was computed correctly. This technique works whenever we have two axes.

Paying Off a Loan

Suppose you are considering a large purchase, which may or may not have woofers. Your uncle has agreed to lend you the money, but ever the businessman, he's charging you 5 percent interest. To decide how much to spend, you want to create a table of the monthly payments required for different amounts borrowed for different times. The table set-up follows the strategy of the last section: Fill a row across the top with different numbers of payments, and fill a column with different amounts.

Among the functions available with spreadsheets is the "payment" computation, PMT. When we click on it under the **Insert > Functions** . . . menu, a GUI is displayed for PMT.

The inputs to the function are the interest Rate, the number of payments (Nper), and the present value, or the amount of the loan (Pv). As with the discount table above, the inputs mix absolute and relative references to refer to the row and column entries. The formula result, shown at the bottom of the GUI, is the amount required to repay $1000 in six payments. Notice that the result is negative, because the payment is a cost to you.

Filling the formula down the column and across the rows results in a table with red, parenthesized values, which is the default display form for negative numbers.

If we don't like the parentheses, we can reformat the entries, say leaving them red.

Perhaps, because the table is intended to help us decide how much to borrow, the best way to display the entries is to display them in two colors: Green for those within our budget and red for those over our budget. Deciding that a payment of $250 per month is a comfortable limit, we click on **Format > Conditional Formatting** . . . and get this GUI.

We specify that cells greater than or equal to −250 should be formatted green. (Remember, the numbers tell how much we *pay*, so a number closer to 0 means less.) The green font is specified by clicking on the **Format** . . . button and picking a color. The final result makes it visually easy to decide how much to borrow.

Importing Data

Much of the data we are interested in comes from some other source, that is, we didn't produce it. This probably means it has already been organized, and so may already exist in a spreadsheet or in a table in another application. Call this **foreign data**—data from another application that we want to import into a spreadsheet. Though importing previously formatted data into a spreadsheet can be tricky, there are some guidelines to make it easier.

As a rule spreadsheets prefer to import foreign data as **tab-delimited text**. "Text" means ASCII text, that is, files with `.txt` extensions. Because they are text files, numbers like *100* are represented as three numeral characters rather than as a single binary number. This allows the spreadsheet software to convert the ASCII form into whatever internal number representation it prefers. "Tab-delimited" means that each cell's entry is delimited (ends with) a tab in the file, and each row is delimited with a carriage return (the symbol that results from pressing Return or Enter on the keyboard). Other delimiters are recognized, too, such as spaces and commas. Spreadsheets can output their lists as tab-delimited text. Copying and pasting tab-delimited text is a simple way to import foreign data.

Lists with some other form can often be converted into the preferred tab-delimited form by copying the foreign data into a text editor or word processor and editing it using **Search/Replace**, possibly using the Placeholder Technique (Chapter 2). The goal is to substitute a tab or other preferred delimiter for a delimiter in the file that the spreadsheet software doesn't understand. Writing the result to a text file eliminates any formatting characters from the word processor.

Another important source of data is the World Wide Web. The information is already in text form, and often is formatted with HTML table tags, as described in Chapter 4. It seems it should be possible to **Copy** a table from HTML and **Paste** it into a spreadsheet. For some browser-spreadsheet combinations it works, and for others it doesn't. It all depends on how the browser delimits "copies" taken from the screen. If you try to **Copy/Paste** table data from the Web and it doesn't work, try another browser before beginning the tedious task of reformatting the foreign data by other means. You'll probably get lucky.

✓ checkLIST>> Guidelines for importing foreign data:

    ☑ *When possible, save foreign data as tab-delimited ASCII text in a file with a* `.txt` *extension.*

    ☑ *When foreign data comes from the Web, select a browser that supports* **Copy/Paste** *of tagged tables.*

    ☑ *When the foreign data format is messed up, use a text editor with* **Search/Replace**, *apply the Placeholder Technique, and write the revised data with a* `.txt` *extension. Import.*

For example, suppose you want to print out a custom bus schedule. Transportation schedules often include more data than we need, so if we grab a copy of the whole schedule from the Web, we can trim and edit it to match our needs in a spreadsheet. Visiting the city's Web page, we locate the bus schedule and **Copy/Paste** it into the spreadsheet, as shown in Figure 13.4.

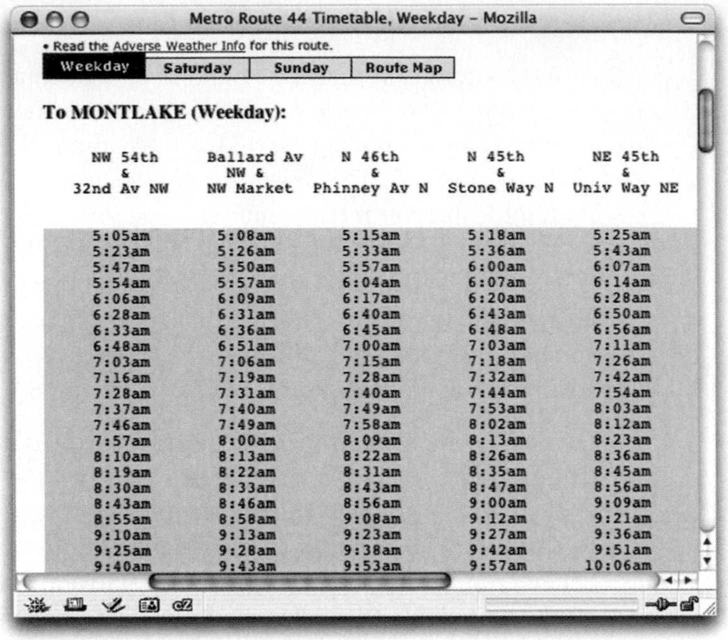

Figure 13.4. Bus schedule from the Web selected for copying.

We only want the departure time from our stop and the arrival time at campus. By deleting columns we can create a simple two-column schedule. Adding the two columns for the return trip produces a custom schedule, as shown in Figure 13.5, that can be printed and kept in a wallet or purse.

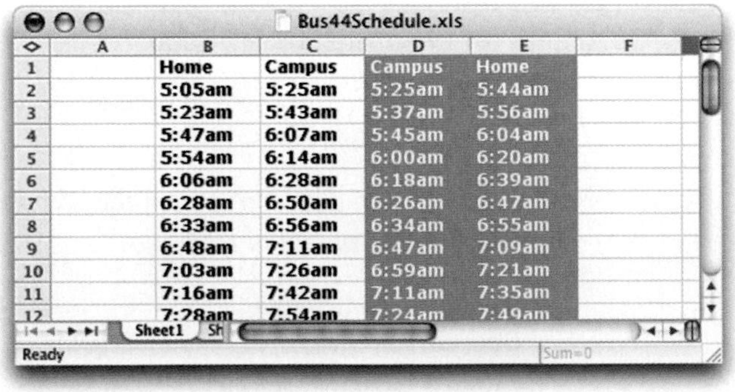

Figure 13.5. Customized schedule with "to campus" in white, "from campus" in blue.

Arranging Columns

Spreadsheets are designed to manipulate rows and columns of information easily. Most other applications are good with rows, but not columns. For example, it is common in word processing to present a list of information, one item per line, as in this 77-item list of Best Picture winners

Million Dollar Baby, 4 / 7, Clint Eastwood, 2004
Lord of the Rings: Return of the King, 11 / 11, Peter Jackson, 2003
Chicago, 6 / 13, Rob Marshall, 2002
A Beautiful Mind, 4 / 8, Ron Howard, 2001
Gladiator, 5 / 12, Ridley Scott, 2000
. . .

which includes Oscar *awards / nominations*, director, and year.

Though the lines may not be intended as a table, when each one contains the same information, we naturally align it into a table in our minds. Adding new rows is easy. Inserting or rearranging the columns is a headache. Spreadsheets can help.

To manipulate columns in an application not well suited to the task, we must create a consistently delimited text file of the data, and import it into a spreadsheet, as described above. (Most entries are delimited with commas, so only the "/" presents a problem.) We then manipulate the list, and write out the file as text. After being revised in the spreadsheet, the file can be returned to the application. We will illustrate the idea by rearranging the columns of the movie list above.

For example, suppose we want to reorder the columns so the year follows the movie, and change the *awards / nominations* data so it reads, for *Million Dollar Baby*, "4 of 7 Oscars."

To begin

> Make a file containing only the list

> Use **Search/Replace** to replace every space-slash-space (" / ") with a comma (","), so that the numbers get separate columns.

> Import the file into the spreadsheet

The result is shown in Figure 13.6.

	A	B	C	D	E	F	G
2							
3		Million Dollar Baby	4	7	Clint Eastwood	2004	
4		Lord of the Rings: Return of the King	11	11	Peter Jackson	2003	
5		Chicago	6	13	Rob Marshall	2002	
6		A Beautiful Mind	4	8	Ron Howard	2001	
7		Gladiator	5	12	Ridley Scott	2000	

Figure 13.6. The movie list imported into a spreadsheet.

Using **Cut** and **Paste** we move the last column to become the second column. We also create a new column that allows us to combine the awards and nominations into one phrase. The formula uses an operation called **concatenate**, which means to join pieces of text together, one after the other. We will join four pieces of text together—the number of awards, the text " of " (␣of␣), the number of nominations, and the text " Oscars" (␣Oscars).

awards " of " *nominations* " Oscars"

This is expressed by the formula

```
=concatenate(c3," of ",d3," Oscars")
```

For the movie *Million Dollar Baby*, the formula produces the phrase: `4 of 7 Oscars`. The function `concatenate` can join any number of text pieces, and is a handy tool for combining words and numbers.

The result, after filling into column `G`, is shown in Figure 13.7(a). This revised column converts two columns of data to a phrase that can replace them. We move the two numerical columns to the end of the table (we need to keep them or the `concatenate` formula won't work) and reorder the columns as we intend (see Figure 13.7b).

To complete the table, we want to **Cut** and **Paste** the Oscars column into column `E` and throw away the last two data columns. But if we do that, the data that the Oscars column depends on will be gone. What we must do is **Paste** the Oscars as *values*, that is as text, into column `E`. So, we use **Edit > Paste Special** . . . and select "values". This converts the Oscars column from formulas to text; it no longer depends on the data columns (see Figure 13.7c).

This completes our revisions, and we return the final spreadsheet to our document.

Million Dollar Baby, 2004, Clint Eastwood, 4 of 7 Oscars
Lord of the Rings: Return of the King, 2003, Peter Jackson, 11 of 11 Oscars
Chicago, 2002, Rob Marshall, 6 of 13 Oscars
A Beautiful Mind, 2001, Ron Howard, 4 of 8 Oscars
Gladiator, 2000, Ridley Scott, 5 of 12 Oscars

. . .

The result achieves our intended columnar modifications.

	A	B	C	D	E	F	G	H	I	J
2										
3		Million Dollar Baby	4	7	Clint Eastwood		2004	4 of 7 Oscars		
4		Lord of the Rings: Return of the King	11	11	Peter Jackson		2003	11 of 11 Oscars		
5		Chicago	6	13	Rob Marshall		2002	6 of 13 Oscars		
6		A Beautiful Mind	4	8	Ron Howard		2001	4 of 8 Oscars		
7		Gladiator	5	12	Ridley Scott		2000	5 of 12 Oscars		

(a)

	A	B	C	D	E	F	G	H	I	J	K
2											
3		Million Dollar Baby	2004	Clint Eastwood			4 of 7 Oscars	4	7		
4		Lord of the Rings: Return of the King	2003	Peter Jackson			11 of 11 Osca	11	11		
5		Chicago	2002	Rob Marshall			6 of 13 Oscar	6	13		
6		A Beautiful Mind	2001	Ron Howard			4 of 8 Oscars	4	8		
7		Gladiator	2000	Ridley Scott			5 of 12 Oscar	5	12		

(b)

	A	B	C	D	E	F	G	H
2								
3		Million Dollar Baby	2004	Clint Eastwood	4 of 7 Oscars			
4		Lord of the Rings: Return of the King	2003	Peter Jackson	11 of 11 Oscars			
5		Chicago	2002	Rob Marshall	6 of 13 Oscars			
6		A Beautiful Mind	2001	Ron Howard	4 of 8 Oscars			
7		Gladiator	2000	Ridley Scott	5 of 12 Oscars			

(c)

Figure 13.7. Revising the movie list. (a) constructing the phrase, (b) reordering the main columns, (c) the completed table.

SUMMARY

In this chapter we explored the basic ideas of spreadsheets. We found that:

> Spreadsheets present an array of cells each of which is capable of storing one data item, a number, a letter sequence, or a formula.

> Numbers and text can be formatted so that they display as we prefer — proper font, correct number of digits, etc.

> The power of spreadsheets comes from entering formulas that calculate new values based on the values in other cells.

> The formula is one side of an equation, which the computer solves for us, preserving the equality whenever the numbers that the formula depends on are changed and displaying the new value in the cell.

number of cells in the spreadsheet. Use one cell for the number of rows. Use another for the number of columns. Write the formula to display the answer in another cell.

5. Create a spreadsheet to display the classes in your plan of study. Use a column for each semester and enter the classes below it.

6. Modify the spreadsheet for Paying Off a Loan. Change it so you can enter the interest in a cell and have the cell in your formula. Test it to see how changes in the interest rate affect your ability to repay the loan.

7. Go to `http://www.dairki.org/tides/monthly.php`. Select a location and get the tide charts for that month. **Copy** the data and **Paste** it into a spreadsheet. Change the formatting of it to suit your tastes.

8. Create a spreadsheet to calculate the future value of an investment. Use the FV function for this. Future value is the value of a monthly investment at a certain rate over a period of time. You could use it for calculating your retirement nest egg. Enter the number of years in a row near the top. Start with 5 and go to 40 by fives. On the side enter the amount you're willing to invest each month. Start with $100 and fill it to $2,000. In the cell above the $100, enter the interest rate you expect to earn on the investment. In the first cell of the table (where the 5 and $100 intersect, enter your formula. Use FV. The first one is the interest rate. Enter that cell. The second one is the years. Enter that cell. The last one is the amount. Enter that cell. When you fill using this cell the formulas won't work. You'll need to modify them to always stay in the interest rate cell. You'll need a $ in front of the row and column. For the years, you'll need the $ in front of the column. For the amount, you'll need the $ in front of the row. You'll then be able to copy it. The numbers will be negative. To make them positive (after all it's money you're saving), use the absolute value function (**ABS**).

9. Create a personal budget. Put income in its own column. Total it. Put expenses in another column. Total it. The more accurate you are, the closer your budget will be. There should be at least a little money left over at the end of the month!

10. Create a GPA calculator. Enter your classes in one column. Next to it enter the number of credits. Next to that enter the grade points earned for that class. (Usually it's one point per credit for a D, two per credit for a C, three per credit for a B and four per credit for an A.) Total the credits and the grade points. The GPA is grade points divided by credits.

11. Create a spreadsheet of your expected annual income. Put the year into a column and fill it up until the year you expect to retire. Next to the first year, enter your expected annual income. In the next cell, enter a formula to add three percent to the first year's income. Fill this formula for the rest of the years. If you put the percentage increase in a cell of its own and then use that in the formula, you'll be able to change the annual salary increase to see how that affects your pay.

chapter 14

GETTING TO FIRST BASE
Introduction to Database Concepts

learning objectives

> Explain the differences between everyday tables, spreadsheets, and database tables

> Explain how the concepts of structure, entities, and attributes are used to design a database table

> Explain the use of name, attribute, data type, and primary key

> Use the six database operations: `Select`, `Project`, `Union`, `Difference`, `Product`, and `Join`

> Explain the way in which the `Join` (natural join) operation differs from the `Product` operation

GETTING TO FIRST BASE
Introduction to Database Concepts

*Now that we have all this useful information, it would be nice to do something
with it. (Actually, it can be emotionally fulfilling just to get the information. This
is usually only true, however, if you have the social life of a kumquat.)*
                                        —UNIX PROGRAMMER'S MANUAL

WE HAVE seen the benefits of using spreadsheets to organize lists of information. By arranging similar information into columns and using a separate row for
each new list item, we can easily sort data, use formulas to summarize values, get
help from the computer to set up series, and so forth. Spreadsheets are very powerful, but with databases it's possible to apply even greater degrees of organization
and receive even more help from the computer.

The key idea is to supply metadata describing the properties of the information in the list. Recall that **metadata** is simply information describing properties of
other information. We applied the idea of specifying metadata in Chapter 8, when
we used tags—the metadata—to describe the content of the *Oxford English
Dictionary*, enabling the computer to help us search for words and definitions. The
metadata for databases is different—for example, we don't use tags—but the same
principles apply. Specifying the properties of the data in our lists tells the computer what it needs to know to help us manipulate the data more easily.

In this chapter we explain how to set up the metadata for lists to create database tables. The principles are straightforward and intuitive. Then we explain the
five basic operations on databases. These are powerful enough to answer any
question that we might ask about data organized as a table. Then we add one
more operation—natural join—that simplifies asking questions of databases.

TABLES: SPECIAL KINDS OF LISTS

A database (DB) stores data; a relational database—the kind studied here—stores data in tables. Relational databases describe the relationships among the different kinds of data, allowing the software to answer our queries about the data.

Database tables differ from our informal idea of tables. Our informal concept of a table is mostly an orderly picture of information. Database tables are more like the lists encountered in spreadsheets, but with added constraints, which limit the kinds of data they can contain, and expand the operations they can perform.

∫ιιBYTE

> **A Bright Idea.** Though many people contributed to the creation of relational databases—the kind we discuss here—E. F. Codd of IBM is widely credited with the original concept. He received the Association of Computing Machinery's Turing Award, the field's Nobel Prize, for his idea.

Thinking about Tables

When we refer to tables informally, we think of a two-dimensional structure of rows and columns with a caption, column headings, and rows. For example, HTML tables have tags for all of these features, and spreadsheets have facilities for them too, as seen in Figure 14.1.

        (a)   **(b)**

Figure 14.1. (a) An HTML table (b) a spreadsheet table.

The problem with these tables is that we can enter almost anything into the table, including complete nonsense. For example, we can change the island data of Figure 14.1 to currency amounts, colors, exclamations, pictures, and many other kinds of inappropriate data, as shown in Figure 14.2.

The resulting table is meaningless. This is bad because we expect databases to contain correct data, and if nothing limits what can be entered, it's possible to create tables that are complete garbage.

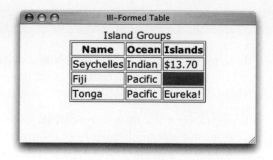

Figure 14.2. *A table with meaningless entries.*

Of course, we do not intend to trash a table, but even when our intentions are good, we can still create inconsistent tables. For example, Table B.3 in Appendix B, has entries as follows (we are only interested in the form of the table here, not the meaning of the entries).

Name	Symbol	# of Operands Data Type	Example	Result of Example
Addition	+	2 Numeric	4 + 5	9
. . .				
Equal	==	2 Numeric	4 == 4	true
		2 String	"a" == "A"	false
. . .				

Most of the table's rows are like the Addition row; they have one entry per cell. Some rows, however, like the Equal row, have two entries in some cells. The table makes sense to readers who need the information it contains, which is why it works as an informal table. But Table B.3 is not properly structured for a computer to help us use its information, that is, it is not sufficient as a database table.

Thus, database tables require us to specify the structure and the kind of data that can appear in every row and column. This allows the software to verify that appropriate data is always present and helps us use it.

Entities

What *do* we want in database tables? Entities. "Entity" is about as vague as "thing" or "stuff," but the inventors of databases didn't want to limit the kinds of information that can be stored. An **entity** is anything that can be identified by a fixed number of its characteristics, called **attributes**; the attributes have names and values, and the values are the data that's stored in the table.

For example, a whale is an entity with several characteristics, such as a common English name, a scientific name, a preferred food, a typical adult weight, etc.

Figure 14.3 shows five entities. The entities in the figure are described by the values of their named attributes. Notice that the attributes are unordered—they are simply entity characteristics.

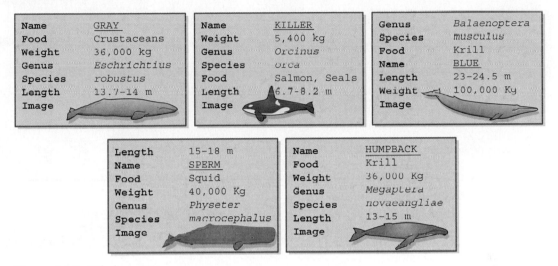

Figure 14.3. Whale entities.

To create a table, we must specify the entity's name (the table name), the names of the entity's attributes, and the kinds of values each attribute can have. When we've done that, we've created a table. For example, we can define the **Whales** table using the form shown in Figure 14.4. The name is given in bold followed by the attribute's name, type of data, and a helpful comment. Though they are written as rows in the metadata specification, they describe columns of the table. A data type like **Character, 15** means that the attribute's value is a sequence of 15 characters. Database software provides about a dozen different data types to describe legal values, but we permit any convenient description of the data's type here. (We'll explain Primary Key momentarily.) The result of placing the entities of Figure 14.3 into the table of Figure 14.4 is shown in Figure 14.5.

```
Whales
     name        Character, 15    The common English name
     genus       Character, 15    First part of scientific name
     species     Character, 15    Second part of scientific name
     food        Character, 25    Primary food source
     weight      Integer          Average adult weight
     length      Character, 20    Length range on typical adult
     image       GIF              Picture of adult
Primary Key: name
```

Figure 14.4. Specification of the **Whales** table.

Whales						
name	genus	species	food	weight	length	image
Gray	*Eschrichtius*	*robustus*	Crustaceans	36,000	13.7–14m	
Killer	*Orcinus*	*orca*	Salmon, Seals	5,400	6.7–8.2m	
Blue	*Bala enoptera*	*musculus*	Krill	100,000	23–24.5m	
Sperm	*Physeter*	*macrocephalus*	Squid	40,000	15–18m	
Humpback	*Megaptera*	*novaeangliae*	Krill	36,000	13–15m	

Figure 14.5. *An instance of the* `Whales` *table.*

If we want the tables shown in Figure 14.1 to be database tables, we create a definition like this.

```
Island_Groups
    Name      Character, 20    Political name of the island group
    Ocean     Character, 20    Name of the island's ocean or sea
    Islands   Integer          Count of islands in the archipelago
Primary Key: Name
```

The fact that the `Islands` attribute is defined to have a number as its data type prevents it from having the value of a currency, color, or exclamation. This solves the problem posed earlier.

*fit*BYTE

For the Record. Because databases are so important and long-studied, the concepts are known by several terms. The technical term for a row is a **tuple** (short u) from words like quintuple, sextuple, septuple, etc. Rows are often called **records**, a holdover from computing's punch-card days. Attributes are also known as **fields** and **columns**; an attribute's data type is sometimes referred to as its **format**. Tables are technically known as **relations**.

PROPERTIES OF ENTITIES

The concepts just introduced—entities, tables, attributes—require a little more explanation.

Table Instances

Once a database table is defined, as in Figure 14.4, it exists. The table is initially empty. That is, an **empty table** has a name and column headings (the attribute names), but no rows. Each table row represents an entity, and if there is nothing in the table, there are no rows. We will find that this curious concept is useful once we begin to manipulate tables.

An **instance** of a database table is the table with a specific set of rows. Thus, Figure 14.5 illustrates one instance of the `Whales` table. If we remove the gray whale row, we create a different instance. Obviously, the empty table is also an instance.

Structure, Content, and Metadata

The reason concepts like "empty table" and "table instance" make sense is because we have separated the structure of the information from the information itself. So, a definition like Figure 14.4 defines the structure of the table in which we will store information about whales. An empty table has no content, only structure. An instance like Figure 14.5 has both structure and content. And the entities themselves, that is, the whale species, exist and have many characteristics. We have chosen to represent whales by seven of these; we could have chosen more or fewer attributes.

The structure is (part of) the metadata describing whale information in our database.

To be explicit, a table's metadata includes its name, its attributes' names, the types of values that each attribute can have, and the primary key (see Keys section on page 408). This is a minimum; most database software allows us to describe the data even more completely. Moreover, in Chapter 15 we will learn about an additional kind of metadata that can relate entities, that is, it defines relationships between the tables.

There are some table properties that are not metadata. For example, the attributes are listed in a specific order in the definition (there is no other way to write things), but the order is not important. This is why attributes have names; so we may refer to them without reference to their position. Also, the order of the rows in any database instance is unimportant. Therefore, a random arrangement of rows and the sorted arrangement of the same rows are the same instance.

> *fit* **TIP**
>
> **Spreadsheets and Databases.** Notice that spreadsheets and databases are similar, but not the same. For example, both represent data in tabular form, but position matters in spreadsheets, but not in databases. It is common to move data back and forth between databases and spreadsheets, motivating us to apply the more stringent requirements of databases—always adding column headings, for example—to our spreadsheets.

Entities and Uniqueness

There are few limits on what an entity can be. Things that can be identified or distinguished from each other based on a fixed set of attributes qualify as entities, which covers most things. Amoebas are not entities, because they have no characteristics that allow us to tell them apart. (Perhaps amoebas can tell each other apart, and if we could figure out how, then the characteristics on which they differ could be their attributes and they could become entities.) Of course, one-celled animals are entities.

Entities don't have to exist in the physical world. The characters in Cervantes' fictional *Don Quixote* never existed in the physical world, but they can be rows in a database table using attributes such as their first and last names. Abstractions, philosophies, degrees of enlightenment, circles of Hell, theories, etc., can all be distinguished by their characteristics and therefore can be entities in a database.

Notice that it is not necessary for every attribute alone to separate the entities from each other. In Figure 14.5, two kinds of whales reach an adult weight of 36,000 Kg, so weight doesn't distinguish whales; their common name does, and their genus and species together do. It is sufficient for all attributes taken together to separate the entities. So, for example, there may be several Michael Jordans in a table of basketball players, but some other attributes, say their team, might make them distinct. If a team has two or more Michael Jordans, then, perhaps the date they joined the NBA could separate them. Entities with identical values for all attributes are the same, which is equivalent to saying, a database table doesn't have any duplicate rows.

Keys

The fact that no two rows in a database table are identical motivates us to ask which attributes distinguish them. In most cases, there will be several possibilities. Single attributes might be sufficient, like common `name`; or pairs of attributes like `genus` and `species` could be used; or three or more attributes taken together might make the rows unique. Any set of attributes for which all entities are different is called a *candidate key*. Because database tables usually have several candidate keys, we choose one and call it the **primary key**. For the `Whales` table, `name` is the primary key.

Notice that candidate keys qualify only if they distinguish among all entities forever, not just those that are in the table at the moment, that is, in a given instance. For example, all the whales in the Figure 14.5 instance have different length ranges, but we don't expect this to be true of whales generally—there may be other species with the same length ranges as these, so length is not a candidate key.

If no combination of attributes qualifies as a candidate key, then a unique ID must be assigned to each entity. That's why your school issues student IDs: Some other student *might* match you on all of the attributes that the school records in its database; since the school doesn't want to worry about the possibility, it issues an ID number to guarantee that one attribute distinguishes each student.

Atomic Data

Databases, in addition to requiring a description of each attribute's type of data, also require that the information is atomic, that is, not decomposable into any smaller parts. So, for example, an address value

`1234 Sesame Street`

is treated in a database table as a single sequence of ASCII characters; the street number and street name cannot be separated. This is why forms—both paper and Web—have separate fields for street, city, state, and zip code: Most uses of address information must manipulate the city, state, and postal code information independently, which means the data must be assigned to separate fields.

Notice that in the Table B.3 example, the *Operands and Data Types* column stores non-atomic data, which is a weakness of that table from a database perspective.

The "only atomic data" rule is usually relaxed for certain types of data such as dates, time, and currency. Strictly speaking, a date value of `01/01/1970` must be treated as a single unit; any use of the date that refers to the month alone would have to store the date as three attributes: day, month, and year. But database software usually bends the rules allowing us to specify the format of the date attribute, say `dd/mm/yyyy`, which allows the program to understand how the field decomposes. This format saves us the trouble of manipulating three attributes.

Database Tables Recap

Summarizing the important points of the last two sections, tables in databases are not simply an arrangement of text, but rather they have a structure that is specified by metadata. The structure of a database table is separate from its content. A table structures a set of entities—any things we can tell apart by their attributes—by naming the attributes and giving their data types. The entities of the table are represented as rows. We understand that rows and columns are unordered in databases. (Of course, when defining a table or displaying it, we must list them in some order.) Tables and fields should have names that describe their contents, the fields must be atomic (i.e., indivisible), and one or more attributes define the primary key (i.e., field(s) with the property of having a different value for every row in any table instance).

OPERATIONS ON TABLES

A database is a collection of database tables. The main use of a database is to look up information. Users specify what they want to know and the database software finds it. For example, imagine a database containing Olympic records. There might be a table of participants for each Olympics, including attributes of name, country, and event; there might be a table of the medal winners of each Olympics, including attributes for the medal, the winner's name, the winner's country, and perhaps the score, distance, time, or other measure of the achievement. The database has many tables, but if we want to know how many marathon medalists have come from African countries, there is no table to look in. The data is in the database, but it's not stored in a single table. What we need to do is describe the information we want in such a way that the computer can figure out how to find it for us.

Database operators allow us to ask questions of a database in a way that lets the software find the answer for us. For example, we will ask for the number of African marathon winners by saying:

> *Put together the medalists for all of the Olympic Games (the operation will be called* union*), find the rows of medalists who won in the marathon (the operation will be called* select*), and pick out those who come from African countries (the operation will be called* join*). Count the resulting rows, which is the answer we want.*

This example illustrates two important points. First, we can perform operations on tables to produce tables. It's analogous to familiar operations on numbers: Operations like addition combine two numbers and produce a new number; operations like union combine two tables and produce a new table. Second, the questions we ask of a database are answered with a whole table. If the question has a single answer—who won the marathon in 2000?—then the table instance answering the question will have only a single row. Generally there will be several answers forming the table. Of course, if there is no answer, the table will be empty.

In this section, we illustrate the idea of combining tables to produce new tables. For our running examples, we imagine a table of the countries of the world like one that might be used by a travel agency. Its structure and sample entries are shown in Figure 14.6. Using that table, `Nations`, we'll investigate the five fundamental operations that can be performed on tables: `Select`, `Project`, `Union`, `Difference`, and `Product`.

```
Nations
   Name        Character, 15    Common rather than official name
   Domain      Character, 2     Internet top-level domain name
   Capital     Character, 20    Nation's capital
   Latitude    Integer          Approx. latitude of capital
   N_S         Boolean          Latitude is N(orth) or S(outh)
   Longitude   Integer          Approx. longitude of capital
   E_W         Boolean          Longitude is E(ast) or W(est)
   Interest    Character, 50    Short description of the country
Primary Key: Name
```

Name	Dom	Capital	Lat	NS	Lon	EW	Interest
Ireland	IE	Dublin	52	N	7	W	History
Israel	IR	Jerusalem	32	N	35	E	History
Italy	IT	Rome	42	N	12	E	Art
Jamaica	JM	Kingston	18	N	77	W	Beach
Japan	JP	Tokyo	35	N	143	E	Kabuki

Figure 14.6. The `Nations` *table definition and sample entries.*

Select Operation

The **Select** operation takes rows from one table to create a new table. Generally we specify the **Select** operation by giving the (single) table from which rows are to be selected and the test for selection. We use the syntax:

Select *Test* **From** *Table*

The *Test* is applied to each row of the given table to decide if it should be included in the new result table. The *Test* is a short formula that tests attribute values. It is written using attribute names, constants like numbers or letter strings, and the relational operators <, ≤, =, ≠, ≥, and >. The relational operators test whether the attribute value has a particular relationship, for example, **Interest = 'Beach'** or **Latitude < 45**. If the *Test* is true, the row is included in the new table; otherwise, it is ignored. Notice that the information used to create the new table is a copy, so the original table is not changed by **Select** (or any of the other table-building operations discussed here).

To use the **Nations** table to create a table of countries with beaches, we write a select to remove all rows for countries that have **Beach** as their **Interest** attribute. The operation is

Select **Interest = 'Beach'** **From** Nations

This gives us a new table, shown in part in Figure 14.7. Notice that the information in the last column is constant because the *Test* required the word Beach for that field for all selected rows.

Name	Dom	Capital	Lat	NS	Lon	EW	Interest
Australia	AU	Canberra	37	S	148	E	Beach
Bahamas	BS	Nassau	25	N	78	W	Beach
Barbados	BB	Bridgetown	13	N	59	W	Beach
Belize	BZ	Belize	17	N	89	W	Beach
Bermuda	BM	Hamilton	32	N	64	W	Beach

Figure 14.7. *Part of the table created by selecting countries with a Test for Interest equal to Beach.*

The *Test* can be more than a test of a single value. For example, we can use the logical operations **AND** and **OR** in the way they were used to conduct searches in Chapters 5 and 6. So, for example, to find countries whose capitals are located at least 60° north latitude, we write

Select Latitude ≥ 60 AND N_S = 'N' **From** Nations

which should produce a four-row table created from the **Nations** table's rows for Greenland, Iceland, Norway, and Finland.

Project Operation

If we can pick out rows of a table (using `Select`), we should be able to pick out columns too. `Project` (pronounced pro·JECT) is the operation that builds a new table from the columns of an existing table. We only need to specify the name of the existing table and the columns (field names) to be included in the new table. The syntax is

Project *Field_List* **From** *Table*

For example, to create a new table from the `Nations` table without the `capital` and position information—that is, to keep the other three columns—we write

Project Name, Domain, Interest **From** Nations

The new table has as many rows as the `Nations` table, but just three columns. Figure 14.8 shows part of that table.

Name	Dom	Interest
Nauru	NR	Beach
Nepal	NP	Mountains
Netherlands	NL	Art
New Caledonia	NC	Beach
New Zealand	NZ	Adventure

Figure 14.8. *Sample entries for a* `Project` *operation on* `Nations`.

`Project` does not *always* result in a table with the same number of rows as the original table. When the new table includes a key from the old table (e.g., `Name`), the key makes each row distinct; the new table includes fields from all rows of the original table, so both tables have the same number of rows. But if some of the new table's rows are the same—which can't happen if key columns are included, but can if none are keys—they will be merged together into a single row. The rows have to be merged because of the rule that the rows of any table must always be distinct. If rows in one table are merged, the two tables will, of course, have different numbers of rows. So, for example, to list the interest descriptions that travel agents use to summarize countries, we create a new table of only the last column of `Nations`:

Project Interest **From** Nations

which produces a one-column table with a row for each descriptive word: `Beach` appears once, `Art` appears once, and so on. Thus the table has as many rows as unique words, but not as many rows as `Nations`.

We often use `Select` and `Project` operations together to "trim" base tables to keep only some of the rows and some of the columns. To illustrate, we define a table of the countries with northern capitals, called `Northern`, and define it with the command

Northern = (**Select** Latitude ≥ 60 AND N_S = 'N' **From** Nations)

which is the table we created earlier. To throw away everything except the name, domain, and latitude to produce Northland, we write

Northland = (**Project** Name, Domain, Latitude **From** Northern)

as shown in Figure 14.9.

Name	Dom	Lat
Finland	FI	64
Greenland	GL	72
Iceland	IS	65
Norway	NO	62

Figure 14.9. Northland, *the table of countries with northern capitals.*

Another way to achieve the same result is to combine the two operations:

Project Name, Domain, Latitude **From**
    (**Select** Latitude ≥ 60 AND N_S = 'N' **From** Nations)

First a temporary table is created with the four countries, just as before. Then the desired columns are removed. It might be a slightly more efficient solution if we don't need the Northern table for any other purpose, but generally either solution is fine.

Union Operation

Besides picking out rows and columns of a table, another operation on tables is to combine two tables. This only makes sense if they have the same set of attributes. The operation is known as Union, and is written as though it were addition:

Table1 + Table2

The plus sign (+) can be read "combined with." So, if the table of countries with capitals at least 45° south latitude are named Southern with the command

Southern = (**Select** Latitude ≥ 45 AND N_S = 'S' **From** Nations)

then places where the northern or southern lights should be visible—call it Aurora—would be

Aurora = Northern + Southern

The result is shown in Figure 14.10. This table could also have been created with a complex Select command.

Name	Dom	Capital	Lat	NS	Lon	EW	Interest
Falkland Is.	FK	Stanley	51	S	58	W	Nature
Finland	FI	Helsinki	64	N	26	E	Nature
Greenland	GL	Nuuk	72	N	40	W	Nature
Iceland	IS	Reykjavik	65	N	18	W	Geysers
Norway	NO	Oslo	62	N	10	E	Vikings

Figure 14.10. The Aurora *table created with* Union.

Union can be used to combine separate tables, say, Nations with Canada_Provinces. (Canada_Provinces gives the same data about the provinces as Nations does about countries, except the Domain field is CA for all rows.) For example, had the Northern table been defined by

Select Latitude ≥ 60 AND N_S = 'N'
   From (Nations + Canada_Provinces)

Then the Yukon would be included because its capital, Whitehorse, is north of 60°.

Difference Operation

The opposite of combining two tables with Union is to remove from one table the rows also listed in a second table. The operation is known as Difference and it is written with the syntax

*Table*1 − *Table*2

The operation can be read, "remove from *Table*1 any rows also in *Table*2." Like Union, Difference only makes sense when the table's fields are the same. For example,

Nations − Northern

produces a table without those countries with northern capitals—that is, without Finland, Greenland, Iceland, and Norway. Interestingly, this same command works just as well if Northern had included Canadian provinces like the Yukon. That is, in a Difference command, the items "subtracted away" do not have to exist in the original table.

Product Operation

Adding and subtracting tables is easy. What is multiplying tables like? The Product operation on tables, which is written as

*Table*1 × *Table*2

creates a super table. The table has all the fields from *both* tables. So, if the first table has five attributes and the second table has six attributes, the Product table has eleven attributes. The rows of the new table are created by **appending** or concatenating each row of the second table to each row of the first table—that is, by putting the rows together. The result is the "product" of the rows of each table. For example, if the first table is **Nations** with 230 rows, and the second table has 4 rows, there will be $230 \times 4 = 920$ rows because each row of the **Nations** table would be appended with each row of the second table to produce a row of the result.

For example, suppose you have a table of your traveling companions, as described in Figure 14.11(a), containing the information shown in Figure 14.11(b).

```
Travelers                                    Friend      Homeland
   Friend       Character, 20
   Homeland     Character, 15                 Isabella    Argentina
                                              Brian       South Africa
Primary Key: Friend                           Wen         China
                                              Clare       Canada

        (a)                                             (b)
```

Figure 14.11. (a) *The definition of the* **Travelers** *table and* (b) *its values.*

Then the **Product** operation

Super = Nations × Travelers

creates a new table with ten fields—eight fields from **Nations** and two fields from **Travelers**—and 920 rows. Some of the rows of the new table are shown in Figure 14.12. For each country, there is a row for each of your friends.

The **Product** operation may seem a little odd at first because its all-combinations approach combines information that may not "belong together." And it's true. But most often, **Product** is used to create a super table that contains both useful and useless rows; then it is "trimmed down" using **Select**, **Project**, and **Difference** to contain only the intended information. We'll see this powerful approach used many times in this and the next two chapters.

Name	Dom	Capital	Lat	NS	Log	EW	Word	Friend	Homeland
Cyprus	CY	Nicosia	35	N	32	E	History	Clare	Canada
Czech Rep.	CZ	Prague	51	N	15	E	Pilsner	Isabella	Argentina
Czech Rep.	CZ	Prague	51	N	15	E	Pilsner	Brian	South Africa
Czech Rep.	CZ	Prague	51	N	15	E	Pilsner	Wen	China
Czech Rep.	CZ	Prague	51	N	15	E	Pilsner	Clare	Canada
Denmark	DK	Copenhagen	55	N	12	E	History	Isabella	Argentina

Figure 14.12. Some rows from the **Super** table, the product of **Nations** and **Travelers**; for each row in **Nations** and each row in **Travelers**, there is a row in the product table that combines them.

To illustrate, suppose your traveling companions volunteer to tutor students preparing for the National Geographic Society's Geography Bee. Each friend agrees to tutor students "on their part of the world," that is, in the quarter of the planet from which they come. For example, Isabella, who comes from Argentina in the southern and western hemispheres, agrees to tutor students on the geography of that part of the world. Then you can produce a master list of who's responsible for each country. We'll call it the `Master` table. It is produced by these commands:

```
Super  = Nations × Travelers
Assign = (Select N_S = 'S' AND E_W = 'W'
            AND Friend = 'Isabella' From Super)
         +(Select N_S = 'S' AND E_W = 'E'
            AND Friend = 'Brian' From Super)
         +(Select N_S = 'N' AND E_W = 'E'
            AND Friend = 'Wen' From Super)
         +(Select N_S = 'N' AND E_W = 'W'
            AND Friend = 'Clare' From Super)
Master = Project Name, Friend From Assign
```

How do these commands work? The `Super` table is the product table discussed earlier with a row for each nation paired with each friend (see Figure 14.12). Then the `Assign` table is created by the `Union` operation (+) that combines four tables, each created by a `Select` operation from `Super`. The first `Select` keeps only those countries from `Super` that have Isabella's name and are in the southern and western hemispheres. The second `Select` keeps only those countries from `Super` that have Brian's name and are in the southern and eastern hemispheres. The same kind of operations are used for Wen and Clare. The resulting `Assign` table has 230 rows—the same as the original `Nations` table—with one of your friends' names assigned to each country.

We know that all of the countries are in the `Assign` table because every country is in one of the four hemisphere pairs and in `Super` there is a row for each country for each friend. When the right combination "comes up," the country is chosen by one of the four selects. In addition, `Assign` has the property that each person is given countries in "their" part of the world. (Wen is assigned the greatest amount of work!) Finally, we throw away all of the location information to create our `Master` list, keeping only the names of the countries and the friends responsible for tutoring students about that geography. Part of the result is shown in Figure 14.13.

Name	Friend
Chad	Wen
Chile	Isabella
China	Wen
Christmas Is.	Clare
Cocos Is.	Brian

Figure 14.13. A portion of the `Master` table of your friends' assignments.

We have introduced five basic operations on tables. They are straightforward and simple. It is surprising, therefore, that these five operations are the only ones needed to create tables in relational databases. In practice, we rarely use the operations directly because they are incorporated into database software. When we want to create tables from other tables—an idea that is now quite natural—we will hardly be aware that we're using these operations.

*fit***BYTE**

Quotient Intelligence. There *is* a `Divide` operation on tables, but it's complicated and rather bizarre. Because it doesn't give us any new capabilities, we will leave it to the experts.

Join OPERATION

Another powerful and useful operation for creating database tables is `Join`. Indeed, it is so useful that although `Join` can be defined from the five primitive database operations of the previous section, it is usually provided as a separate operator.

Join Defined

`Join` combines two tables, like the `Product` operation does, but it doesn't necessarily produce all pairings. If the two tables each have fields with a common data type, the new table produced by `Join` combines only the rows from the given tables that match *on the field*, not all pairings of rows, as does `Product`. We write the `Join` operation as follows:

Table1 $\bowtie$ *Table2* **On** *Match*

The unusual "bow tie" symbol suggests a special form of `Product` in which the two tables "match up." "Match" is a comparison test involving a field from each table, which when true for a row from each table produces a result row that is their concatenation. To refer to attributes in each table, we use the notation `Table.Field`, as in `Master.Name`.

To show how `Join` works, recall the `Northland` table (Figure 14.9) and the `Master` table of your friends' assignments (Figure 14.13). The `Join`

`Master` $\bowtie$ `Northland` **On** `Master.Name = Northland.Name`

pairs all rows where the country name matches a friend's homeland. Which rows are they? Beginning with the first rows of the `Master` table (shown here)

Name	Friend
Afghanistan	Wen
Albania	Wen
...	...

the Afghanistan row does not have the same `Name` field as any of the four countries of `Northland`, so it is not part of the result. Nor does the `Name` in the second row of Master (Albania) appear as a Name field in Northland. Indeed, only four rows of `Master` have the same `Name` field as rows in `Northland`: Finland, Greenland, Iceland, and Norway. We combine these four rows with their corresponding rows in `Northland` to produce the four-row result, as shown in Figure 14.14. As you see, `Join` associates the information from the rows of two tables in a sensible way. Thus, `Join` is used to create new associations of information in the database.

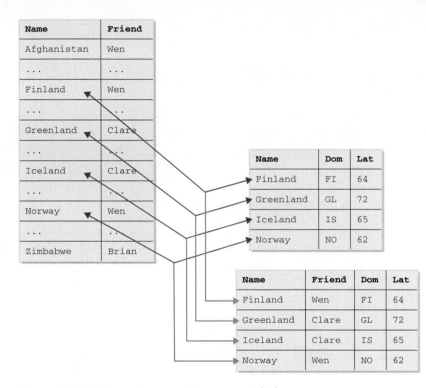

Figure 14.14. *The* `Join` *operation:* `Master` ⋈ `Northland`.

There are at least two ways to think about the `Join` operation. One way is to see it as a "lookup" operation on tables. That is, for each row in one table, locate a row (or rows) in the other table with the same value in the common field; if found, combine the two; if not, look up the next row. That's how we explained it in the last paragraph. Another way is to see it as a `Product` operation forming all pairs of the two tables and then eliminating all rows that don't match in the common fields. Both ideas accurately describe the result, and the computer probably uses still another approach to produce the `Join` table.

`Join`, as described, is called a natural join because the natural meaning of "to match" is for the fields to be equal. But as is typical of IT, it is also possible to join using any relational operator ($<, \leq, =, \neq, \geq, >$), not just = to compare the common field. Unnatural or not, a `Join` where `T1.fieldID < T2.fieldID` can be handy.

African Marathon Runners

To complete the task we discussed above, to find out how many African marathon winners there have been in the history of the Olympics, we assume there are tables `Medalists1896`, `Medalists1900`, ... `Medalists2004` and that there is a table, `Africa`, of African nation names, which includes colonial names like Rhodesia and modern names like Zimbabwe.

Assuming these tables, we write

```
All_Medalists = Medalists1896 + Medalists1900 +
                ... + Medalists2004
```

which is a lot of typing. The `All_Medalists` table contains the names, medal, event, and country of everyone who won in the Olympics. Next, we pick out the marathon winners with

```
Distance26 = Select medal='gold' AND event='marathon'
             From All_Medalists
```

The `Distance26` table contains all runners who received a gold medal in the Olympic marathon event. Next, we eliminate everyone but the African winners with

```
Africa_marathon = Distance26 ⋈ Africa
                  On Distance26.country = Africa.name
```

producing a table of African winners. Counting the rows produces the result. Most database systems provide a function for counting, which is applied in the present cases as

count(Africa_marathon)

Using the operators, we specified a set of tables that allowed us to find our solution. We will refine this skill in the next chapter.

SUMMARY

The chapter began by introducing the ideas and terminology for tables, and by comparing everyday tables with database tables. We learned that:

> Database tables have names and fields that describe the attributes of the entities contained in the table.

> The data that quantitatively records each property has a specific data type and is atomic.

> There are five fundamental operations on tables—`Select`, `Project`, `Union`, `Difference`, and `Product`. These operations are the only ones we need to create new tables from a database of tables.

> `Join` is an especially useful operation that associates information from separate tables in new ways, based on a common field.

EXERCISES

Multiple Choice

1. In database terminology, a set of entities refers to
   A. field
   B. column
   C. table
   D. information

2. The columns of data in a database are often known as
   A. fields
   B. records
   C. tables
   D. tuples

3. The definition of a database table includes all of the following except
   A. tuples
   B. name
   C. attributes
   D. primary key

4. The kind of information stored in a field in a database is described by the
   A. tuple
   B. field name
   C. data type
   D. record

5. In the field name, `Fall_Schedule.Room`, `Fall_Schedule` and `Room` represent, respectively
   A. *table_name*, *field_name*
   B. attribute, entity
   C. row, tuple
   D. *field_name*, *table_name*

6. A field name
   A. is identical to a column heading
   B. describes the entities in a table
   C. cannot be subdivided
   D. can only contain letters

7. Which of the following fields could not be a key field for a student?
   A. Social Security number
   B. student ID number
   C. phone number
   D. Web address

8. The *Test* in Select is used to
   A. add rows to an existing table
   B. remove rows from an existing table
   C. include rows in a new table
   D. describe rows in any table

9. The `Project` operation is used to
   A. create a new table from existing rows in a table
   B. create a new table from existing fields in a table
   C. exclude specific rows from a table
   D. remove existing fields from a table

10. Information from two tables can be combined using the
    A. `Test` operation
    B. `Combine` operation
    C. `Union` operation
    D. `Apply` operation

11. Using the `Product` operation on a table with 4 fields and 9 rows and a table with 7 fields and 6 rows will result in a table with
    A. 11 fields and 9 rows
    B. 11 fields and 54 rows
    C. 28 fields and 15 rows
    D. 26 fields and 15 rows

12. The `Join` operation can work with the relational operators
    A. =, ≠
    B. ≤, ≥
    C. <, >
    D. all of the above

Short Answer

1. A(n) _____ is an organized collection of information on a particular topic.

2. Databases are based on information organized in _____.

3. Normal tables show a _____ of the information while a database also shows the _____ of the information.

4. Column headings for a database table are called _____.

5. _____ are the values of an entity in a database.

6. When creating a database, you can _____ a field by specifying the attribute name and the data type.

7. A(n) _____ is a unique identifier for any row in a database table.

8. The _____ operation takes rows from a table to create a new table.

9. A _____ is used to see if a row should be included in a table.

10. The _____ operation is used to combine information from two tables.

11. Putting the rows of two tables together using the `Product` operation is known as _____.

12. The _____ operation combines two tables and removes the duplicate rows from the resulting table.

13. The `Join` operation works by combining tables based on a(n) _____.

14. The _____ operation is used to remove the contents of one table from another table.

15. A(n) _____ makes use of the multiple tables of related information.

Exercises

1. For the following, either indicate that the field is atomic or divide the field to make the result atomic.

Field	Contents
Phone	(212) 555-1212
Name	Maria Murray
Class	CSE 100
City	Seattle, WA
DOB	September 26, 1948

2. Define the attribute names, data types, and optional comments needed to create a table that could be used as a datebook.

3. Define the field names, data formats, and comments needed to create a table that could be used for your college coursework. Include such fields as college courses, credits, prerequisites, major, minor, and elective courses.

4. Write an operation to display the `Name` and `Interest` from the `Nations` table in Figure 14.5 for those countries with `Beach` and store it in a table called `Vacation`.

5. Write an operation using `Product` to combine the `Tropics` and `Tops` tables.

6. Write an operation to remove `Tops` from `Tropics`.

7. Write an operation to combine the `Vacation` and `Tops` tables into a table called `Sp_Break`.

8. Use the `Join` operation to combine the `Tropics` and `Tops` tables based on `Name`.

15

A TABLE WITH A VIEW
Database Queries

learning objectives

> Explain the idea of a "relationship" between two database entities

> Give some examples of relationships

> Explain the difference between a physical and a logical database

> Explain a view and how it is created by a database query

> Describe the structure of an SQL query

> Interpret and create an entity-relationship (ER) diagram

> Classify a relationship as one-to-one or many-to-one

chapter 15

A TABLE WITH A VIEW
Database Queries

Computers are useless. They only give answers.

—PABLO PICASSO

IN CHAPTER 14 we learned that a database is a collection of tables with properties specified by metadata. We also learned that databases separate the structure of the tables from the data (entities) they contain. By separating the structure from the contents, it's easy to see that the data can be restructured into different tables. For example, an Olympic records database might contain a table of medalists showing the name of the athlete, the medal, the event, the record, and the winning year. The same data might also be organized into a collection of tables, one for each event. Each table would have rows for each Olympics in which the event was held, in which the names of the gold, silver, and bronze winners and their records would be listed. It's the same data, but organized differently. Which is the better arrangement? It depends on what you want to look up. Do you want information about gold medalist Mark Spitz or are you interested in the 100 m butterfly?

The concept that tables can be structured in different ways to make it easier to find specific information raises an interesting question: What is the best way to organize a database in the first place? It seems like a tough question because if we choose one form—say, medalists—it will be difficult to find certain information even though the answer is in the data—for example, how often has the women's 100 m butterfly record been broken? If we choose the Event tables organization, finding the answer to such questions is easy.

Fortunately, the concept of separating the data from the structure also leads to an easy answer to the original question: Almost any *good* organization will do. If the structure isn't perfect for answering a question then we can easily restructure the data into a new set of tables that is better for answering the question. Being able to restructure the database easily simplifies the problem and motivates database designers to speak of the **physical database**—the tables actually stored on the disk drive—and the **logical database**—the restructured version of the data that is suitable for a specific user, called a *view*. This strategy of having one stored form (physical) and building the appropriate form for the user (logical) allows every user to have a customized perspective on the data. It's a perfect solution.

THE PHYSICAL DATABASE

The **physical** database refers to the tables stored on the disk drive. As we asserted, "almost any *good* organization will do" for a physical database. But what does "good" mean? Database designers have many ways to assess the goodness of a physical DB design, such as making restructuring data fast and easy; an important criterion for goodness is avoiding *redundancy*.

Redundancy Is Bad, Very, Very, Very Bad

Databases are usually formed from several tables. A basic rule of database design is: *Never duplicate information*. It is common sense that avoiding duplication, or **redundancy**, is good because storing multiple copies of the same information uses more resources (such as disk storage) than storing only a single copy. But disk space is so inexpensive that copies cost essentially nothing, so that's not the real reason we want to avoid redundancy.

The main reason to avoid redundancy is to avoid **inconsistency** among the copies. The same information, such as an address, stored in different rows or different tables of the database can be different in its different locations. We might change the information in one place and forget to change it in the others. For example, if one database table stores your home address as 4 Wheel Dr., and another table stores it as 1 Supreme Ct., the database is inconsistent. Which, if either, is correct?

Inconsistent data, known as **garbage**, is actually worse than having no data at all. With no value for the address, the row might be flagged, prompting someone to track down your correct address. Inconsistent data "looks good" in each place. Duplication creates the opportunity for inconsistency, which has the potential of converting perfectly good data into garbage. So we adopt the rule: *Never duplicate information*.

Keep Only One Copy of Information

When we design a database we strive to keep only one copy of the information. Avoiding duplication promotes internal consistency in the database, but how do we confirm that the one copy of information is correct? We do not. The goal of a database is to record and return to the user the information stored in it. If wrong information was originally stored, then wrong information is returned.

*fit*BYTE | **It's a Rule.** Database designers and administrators emphasize the importance of accurate input by the maxim *garbage in, garbage out* (GIGO).

The problem with keeping only one copy of the specific information in a database is that the information may be needed in several places. For example, think of the campus units that need your address:

> The administration needs to send your tuition bills.

> The library needs to send notices of your outstanding books.

> The dean needs to send congratulations on your outstanding grades.

> The sports center needs to send your Outstanding Athlete certificate.

And a dozen other campus organizations might need to know your address. These organizations—all logically part of a campus database system—can each store a copy of your address. But they don't (at least they shouldn't) because of redundancy. Instead, they record your student ID number, and when they need your address, they find it in a master list of student addresses keyed to student ID numbers.

Keep a Separate Table and a Key

This familiar idea, which illustrates a standard approach to avoiding database redundancy, can be abstracted as follows: Rather than repeating information in a database (e.g., addresses), keep a separate table of the information (e.g., master address list), keyed with a unique identifier (e.g., student ID). Then, store the unique identifier, called a **foreign key**, wherever the information would have been repeated. Whenever the information is needed, simply look it up in the master list using the foreign key.

By this indirect reference, we avoid redundancy—there is only one copy of the information—but we can link the information to other information in the database. This is an important enough idea that we use it in the next section to introduce other new database ideas.

THE DATABASE SCHEMA

The metadata of a database's tables is called its **database schema**, or **database scheme**. Interactive software can help us define a database schema, but, as we saw in Chapter 14, declaring an entity's structure is easy enough to do without software. The database schema is important because it describes the database design. When we want to analyze a database design, we look at its schema.

To illustrate our strategy for removing redundancy, imagine a college having at least two tables defined in its database schema, `Student` and `Home_Base`:

```
Student
    Student_ID          Integer              8 digits
    First_Name          Character, 25        Single name, starting
                                             with a capital
    Middle_Name         Character, 25        All other names
    Last_Name           Character, 25        Family name
    Birthdate           Date
    On_Probation        Boolean              0 = good standing;
                                             1 = academic trouble
Primary Key: Student_ID
```

```
Home_Base
    Student_ID          Integer              8 digits
    Street_Address      Character, 100       All address info before
                                             city
    City                Character, 25        No abbreviations like NYC
    State               Character, 25        Or province, canton,
                                             prefecture, etc.
    Country             Character, 25        Standard postal
                                             abbreviations OK
    Postal Code         Character, 10        Many including zip+4 are
                                             not numbers
Primary Key: Student_ID
```

Connecting Database Tables by Relationship

The **Student** entity records the information basic to the person's identity and associates a student with his or her **Student_ID**. This is the college's master record for each student. Part of each student's information is where he or she lives. We can put addresses in the **Student** table, but we decide not to. Other campus units need to access the address information, but they shouldn't have access to all of the information (especially the sensitive information) about each student. The addresses are stored in a different table, the **Home_Base** table. Though these two tables are separate, they are not independent. The **Student_ID** connects each row in **Student** with his or her address in **Home_Base**. There is a **relationship** between the two entities.

A **relationship** is a correspondence between rows of one table and the rows of another table. Relationships are part of the metadata of a database, and because they are critical to building the logical database from the physical database, we give them names and characterize their properties.

The relationship between **Student** and **Home_Base**—that for each row in **Student** there is a single row in **Home_Base** (found by the **Student_ID**)—will be called *Lives_At*. Setting up the tables in this way is largely equivalent to storing the address in `Student`, but not all relationships are so close. This one is especially close because it's based on the `Student_ID`, which is the key for both tables. (Recall that keys are unique, meaning no two rows can have the same value.) The *Lives_At* relationship is said to be one-to-one.

Because we used the key `Student_ID` in both tables we not only can find the address for each student, but we can also find the student for each address. That is, there is a second relationship in the opposite direction, which we can call *Home_Of*, meaning that the home base entry is the address of the student who has that ID. Like *Lives_At, Home_Of* is a one-to-one relationship, because each row in `Home_Base` corresponds to a single row in `Student`.

Familiar relationships that we encounter everyday illustrate that their description often ends with a preposition:

> > *Father_Of*, the relationship between a man and his child
>
> > *Daughter_Of*, the relationship between a girl and her parent
>
> > *Employed_By*, the relationships between people and companies
>
> > *Stars_In*, the relationships between actors and movies

Names of database relationships should be meaningful, to help people working with the database, but like all names in computing, the computer doesn't know whether the name makes sense or not.

Reconstruction Using Join

The relationships between the `Student` and `Home_Base` tables allow us to **construct** a single table, called the `Master_List` containing the combined information from both tables. We do this by using the natural `Join` operation described in Chapter 14. Recall that the natural `Join` creates a table out of two other tables by joining rows that match—it's an equality test—on specified fields. Thus, we write

```
Master_List = Student ⋈ Home_Base
   On Student.Student_ID = Home_Base.Student_ID
```

where the match is on the common field of `Student_ID`. Sample fields of the resulting table are shown in Figure 15.1. We don't lose anything by storing the basic student information in one table and the addresses in another, because with a simple command, we can create a table that recombines the information just as if it were stored in a single table.

The key idea here is that although we choose to store the information in two tables, we never lose the association of the information because we keep the `Student_ID` with the addresses. The relationship, *Lives_At*, lets us connect each student with his or her address by the `Student_ID`. The approach gives us the flexibility to arrange tables to avoid problems of redundancy—though we haven't demonstrated that benefit yet—while keeping track of important information, like a person's address. We will use this idea routinely in our database designs.

```
Student_ID
First_Name
Middle_Name
Last_Name
Birthdate
On_Probation
Street_Address
City
State
Country
Postal_Code
```

Figure 15.1. Fields of the `Master_List` *table.*

Designing a Database Schema

Consider other entities in the college's database schema that need address information, for example, the dean's office and the sports center. We define the tables, but we don't include the addresses:

```
Top_Scholar                    Good_Sport
   Student_ID                     Student_ID
   Nickname                       Locker_Number
   Major                          Deposit_Amt
   GPA                            Sport

Primary Key: Student_ID        Primary Key: Student_ID
```

(We don't bother to define the field information while we are designing the database schema.)

The `Top_Scholar` and `Good_Sport` tables each have a one-to-one relationship with the `Home_Base` table. These relationships are based on the `Student_ID` attribute, just as `Student` was: For each scholar, there is an address in `Home_Base`, as there is for each athlete. Therefore, there is a relationship between the `Top_Scholar` and the `Home_Base` tables, which we'll call *Resides_At*, and between the `Good_Sport` and the `Home_Base` tables, which we'll call *Trains_At*. So, both the dean's office and the sports center have access to student addresses, just as the administration does.

`Student_ID` also connects both `Top_Scholar` and `Good_Sport` to `Student`. This is lucky, because otherwise neither the dean nor the sports center knows the students' legal names, only their IDs. Thus, combined tables can be created for the dean's office or the sports center using one or more natural `Join` operations that associate information from `Student` and `Home_Base`. We implement these tables in the next section.

Including addresses in `Top_Scholar` and `Good_Sport` creates redundancy, but referencing the `Home_Base` table avoids duplication. It's a good design.

> *fit* **TIP**
>
> **Being Discreet.** It is not *necessary* to create a separate `Home_Base` table because addresses can be stored in `Student`. But `Student` contains sensitive information—academic probation status, for example—that should not be widely distributed. Defining a separate `Home_Base` table records the addresses without being bundled with sensitive information. It is a better design.

Physical versus Logical Database

We've defined a set of four tables that include the student's home address information, but we avoided redundancy. There is only one copy of the address (`Home_Base`); the others simply refer to it.

From these physical database tables we can create other tables, customized to different campus units. The customized tables are called the **logical database**. Because they are logical, or virtual, they do not physically exist. They are created fresh every time they are needed, using the current values in the physical database. Whenever the dean's office or the sports center needs to access its database, a fresh one is created specifically for that request. Then, when the application is closed—say, the dean moves on to the alumni database—the current version of the *Dean's View* vanishes. It is newly constructed the next time it's needed.

This approach of storing the database in one form but building a different form on demand may seem silly. It appears as if we could save work by storing the logical database on the disk, too. But the logical database is built from information in the physical database. So the logical database tables *contain duplicate information*. If we store them, we create redundancy—there would be a copy in the physical database and a copy in the logical database—violating our principle of no duplication. Suppose one copy were changed but not the other! So, logical databases can only exist in the virtual world of the user's screen. In this way, modern databases always deliver fresh, current data to users.

Separating the logical and physical structure of a database is smart for another reason, too. The logical tables people look at on their screens can be customized to their needs exactly. These personalized logical tables, **database views**, allow every user group to see the database in a different way. These various logical tables are created from the single physical database. Personal considerations guide the logical database design, while technical considerations (like avoiding redundancy) guide the physical database design. The idea of separating databases into logical and physical forms—they're all part of the one schema—was an intellectual milestone.

LOGICAL DATABASE: CREATING VIEWS

Views are the logical tables constructed by database operations from the physical tables. The operations that create views are called **database queries**. The "master student list" table created by combining `Student` and `Home_Base` using a natural `Join`, was created by a database query:

```
Master_List =
    Student ⋈ Home_Base
    On Student.Student_ID = Home_Base.Student_ID
```

The queries creating the views are part of the logical database of the database schema, making them part of the metadata. Thus, *every named table of the database is either a physical table, stored on the hard disk, or a logical table created by a query.* Let's consider other views and the queries that create them.

Creating a Dean's View

Imagine a table, known as the *Dean's View*, containing information specific to the dean's unique needs. For example, because the dean is not the person who sends letters to top students telling them they made the "Dean's List," the *Dean's View* doesn't need the students' full home addresses. (Someone else in the dean's office does.) Knowing the students' hometowns is enough information for the dean to make small talk at parties honoring the top students. So the *Dean's View* will include information selected from the physical tables, as shown in Figure 15.2.

Dean's View	Source Table	
Nickname	Top_Scholar	Used by the dean to seem "chummy" toward students
First_Name	Student	Name information required
Middle_Name	Student	because the dean forgets the
Last_Name	Student	person's actual name, being so chummy
Birthdate	Student	Needs to know if the student is of "drinking age"
City	Home_Base	Hometown (given by city, state) is important for small talk, but full address not needed by dean
Major	Top_Scholar	Indicates what the student's doing in college besides hanging out
GPA	Top_Scholar	Needs to know how the student is doing grade-wise

Figure 15.2. *The Dean's View; information from several tables.*

Join Three Tables into One. The first step to create a query for the *Dean's View* is to note that it contains information from three tables: `Top_Scholar`, the table actually storing the data the dean wants kept; `Student`, the college's permanent record of the student; and `Home_Base`, the college's current address list. The information for each student must be associated to create the `Dean's_View` table, and the `Join` operation is the key to doing it. The expression

```
Dean_Data_Collect =
    (Top_Scholar ⋈ (Student ⋈ Home_Base
        On Student.Student_ID = Home_Base.Student_ID)
    On Student.Student_ID = Top_Scholar.Student_ID)
```

makes a table that has a row for each student in the dean's `Top_Scholar` table, but it also has all of the information from all three tables for that student. The association of each student's row in each table is accomplished by matching on the `Student_ID` attribute.

Trim the Table. The resulting table contains too much information because it includes all columns from the three tables. The dean doesn't want to see so much information. So, the second step is to retrieve only the columns the dean wants to see. The `Project` operation retrieves columns:

```
Dean's_View =
    Project Nickname, First_Name, Middle_Name, Last_Name,
        Birthdate, City, State, Major, GPA
    From Dean_Data_Collect
```

Notice that the dean doesn't even want to see the `Student_ID`, so it is not shown. But it is essential to creating the table.

In English, the query says, "Save the `Nickname` column, `First_Name` column, and so forth, from the table, `Dean_Data_Collect`, that is formed by joining— that is, associating on `Student_ID`—the three tables `Top_Scholar`, `Student`, and `Home_Base`." This is precisely what the dean wants. The query defines the `Deans_View` table. Although the dean probably thinks the table exists physically, it's really created fresh every time it's needed.

The join-then-trim strategy used to create the `Dean's_View` table is a standard approach used to create logical tables: a super table is formed by joining several physical tables. These are then trimmed down to keep only the information that is of interest to the user. The `Dean's_View` query used `Project`, but `Select` is also frequently used to achieve similar results.

Creating a Sport's Center View

As another example, the sports center (SC) view would join its table `Good_Sport` with the administration's tables. The table of interest to the SC is defined in Figure 15.3. The table can be created by the query

```
SC_View =
    Project Student_ID, First_Name, Last_Name, Birthdate,
        Sport, Locker_Number, Deposit_Amt, Street_Address,
        City, State, Postal_Code
    From (Good_Sport ⋈ (Student ⋈ Home_Base
        On Student.Student_ID = Home_Base.Student_ID)
    On Student.Student_ID = Good_Sport.Student_ID)
```

SC_View		
Student_ID	Student	*The ID is in each table*
First_Name	Student	*The name is handy, but the*
Last_Name	Student	*middle name is not needed*
Birthdate	Student	
Sport	Good_Sport	
Locker_Number	Good_Sport	
Deposit_Amt	Good_Sport	
Street_Address	Home_Base	*Address information is*
City	Home_Base	*needed to return the locker*
State	Home_Base	*deposit*
Postal_Code	Home_Base	

Figure 15.3. The fields and sources for the sports center's view; information drawn from three physical tables.

And logical tables can be used just like physical tables. So if the sports center wants to create intramural water polo teams, it might use the query

```
Project Student_ID, First_Name, Last_Name, Birthdate
From (Select Sport="Water Polo" From SC_View)
```

In concept, the computer first creates the logical table **SC_View** and then uses it to build the water polo table. In reality, a database system would be much cleverer.

A QUERY LANGUAGE: SQL

The relational database concepts introduced so far are abstract and independent of any specific database system. They are written in **conceptual** form using a notation invented for teaching purposes. Although every database system implements these concepts, each system has its own way of specifying them. So, to have a real database, we must translate our conceptual form into the form used by a commercial software system. For that, we need to learn how to specify the conceptual form for the software.

SQL (Structured Query Language) is a widely used standard language. As the name suggests, SQL doesn't support arbitrary queries using the full power of the five fundamental relational database operators we learned about in Chapter 14. Instead, it provides a specific query structure that works well for techniques like join-then-trim. Database *users* don't usually need to know SQL, but nearly everyone else involved with databases does. We will learn enough basics of SQL to build simple databases.

Though vendors have their own dialects of SQL—and SQL is complicated to begin with—simple queries like ours are roughly the same no matter which version you use. SQL's query structure has the following syntax:

SELECT	*List of fields*
FROM	*Table(s)*
WHERE	*Constraints on the rows*

(Confusingly, **SELECT** in SQL means *select fields*, and therefore closely approximates **Project**, presented in Chapter 14. Unfortunately, these two standard terms conflict.)

SQL's query structure is perfect for the join-then-trim approach to creating tables. **FROM** gives the table(s) that the fields are to be taken from, **SELECT** says which fields those are, and **WHERE** specifies any additional conditions that must be met by individual rows. Typically, the **FROM** clause specifies a single super table formed using **Product** or **Join**. SQL has several kinds of **Join**s, but the **INNER JOIN** type corresponds to the **Join** operation discussed previously.

SQL ON Clause

Recall the **Dean's_View** table constructed earlier in the chapter using the conceptual query:

Project Nickname, First_Name, Middle_Name, Last_Name, Birthdate,
    City, State, Major, GPA
From Top_Scholar ⋈ (Student ⋈ Home_Base
    On Student.Student_ID = Home_Base.Student_ID)
    On Student.Student_ID = Top_Scholar.Student_ID

This can be expressed in SQL using the following query:

```
SELECT    Top_Scholar.Nickname,Student.First_Name,
          Student.Middle_Name,Student.Last_Name,
          Student.Birthdate,Home_Base.City,Home_Base.State,
          Top_Scholar.Major,Top_Scholar.GPA
FROM      Top_Scholar INNER JOIN (Student INNER JOIN Home_Base
          ON Student.Student_ID=Home_Base.Student_ID)
          ON Student.Student_ID=Top_Scholar.Student_ID
```

The table names have been color-coded blue and the field names fuchsia to make the query easier to read. Notice that following the **SELECT** is the list of fields that form the *Dean's View*. Then, the **FROM** field has two **Join**s that have been grouped together (as we did in the earlier conceptual form). First, `Student` and `Home_Base` are joined `ON` equal `Student_IDs`, and then `Top_Scholar` is joined with the result, again `ON` matching `Student_IDs`.

SQL WHERE Clause

There is no `WHERE` clause in the *Dean's View* because it doesn't require further limiting. However, if the dean wanted to view only students whose GPA is greater than 3.75, a `WHERE` clause can choose those rows:

```
SELECT   Top_Scholar.Nickname,Student.First_Name,
         Student.Middle_Name,Student.Last_Name,
         Student.Birthdate,Home_Base.City,Home_Base.State,
         Top_Scholar.Major,Top_Scholar.GPA
FROM     Top_Scholar INNER JOIN (Student INNER JOIN Home_Base
         ON Student.Student_ID=Home_Base.Student_ID)
         ON Student.Student_ID=Top_Scholar.Student_ID
WHERE    Top_Scholar.GPA > 3.75
```

Interestingly, the `WHERE` clause corresponds to our conceptual `Select` operator. Though the SQL query is longer because the table name must be specified with each field using the dot notation, the result matches the conceptual structure quite well.

Translating into SQL

As a final example, recall that the table in Figure 14.13, associating the northerly countries (`Northland`) with your friends' master tutoring list, had the conceptual form

`Master` ⋈ `Northland` **On** `Master.Name = Northland.Name`

which has the SQL form

```
SELECT   Master.Name, Travelers.Friend, Master.Domain,
         Master.Latitude
FROM     Master INNER JOIN Travelers
         ON Master.Name = Northland.Name
```

Again, this is a direct translation. The differences between the conceptual form we used in Chapter 14 and the SQL form are small—fields must be listed for SQL that are assumed in the conceptual query by default. And, computer software understands the SQL.

These SQL examples provide just a hint of the enormous capabilities of the query language. Many very handy extras can be included in SQL queries. Learning your system's dialect is necessary, but not particularly difficult, now that you understand the abstract ideas.

ENTITY RELATIONSHIP DIAGRAMS

To wrap up our discussion of views and queries, we return to the subject of relationships.

Creating new tables involves relationships. When we joined `Top_Scholar`, `Student`, and `Home_Base` to create the *Dean's View*, we used the `Student_ID`, which embodies associations from named relationships: The first `Join`, between `Student` and `Home_Base`, used the relationship *Lives_At*, and the second `Join`, between `Top_Scholar` and the result of the first `Join`, used the relationship *Resides_At*. This is not an accident. The point of identifying relationships in a database schema is to indicate how the information is interconnected and joins make these connections. If the potential for interconnections exists—that is, if there are relationships—then it is likely that they will be applied when building the logical database.

With many entities, attributes, keys, and relationships in a large database, the design can be confusing. So, database administrators and others who work daily with databases diagram the relationships to make the database's structure as clear as possible.

Such a diagram is known as an **entity-relationship diagram**, or an **ER diagram**. In an ER diagram, relationships are drawn as arrows between boxes, which represent entities. For example, in Figure 15.4 the arrow from `Student` to `Home_Base` (addresses) shows the relationship *Lives_At*. The other entities and relationships discussed earlier are expressed in the ER diagram of Figure 15.5 too. As we shall see, ER diagrams help us make sense out of the relationships among the entities.

Figure 15.4. *A diagram showing the Lives_At relationship.*

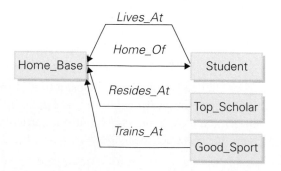

Figure 15.5. *ER diagram for the entities and relationships involving* `Home_Base`.

In its simplest form, the ER diagram uses arrows to represent the relationships between the boxes that represent the entities. But variations on this form can also be helpful. One form typical of database software shows the entity name outside the box and lists the attributes of the entity inside the box (see Figure 15.6).

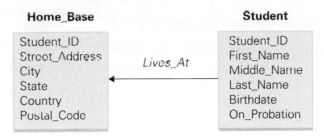

Figure 15.6. *Another form of an ER diagram typical of database software.*

One-to-One Relationships

One more piece of information is usually included in an ER diagram: the type of relationship. The type of a relationship says how the data in the two entities are associated. For example, a one-to-one relationship says that any row in the first entity is associated with at most one row in the other entity. The relationships in Figure 15.6 are all one-to-one because the relationships are all based on the `Student_ID` key.

Many-to-One Relationships

A more typical kind of relationship is based on entities that have different keys. When one entity refers to another entity by giving its key, the foreign key, there is generally a **many-to-one** relationship. That is, many of the rows of the first entity can be associated with a single row in the second entity. For example, imagine a `User_Acct` entity that lists all of the campus' student computer users. It has a many-to-one relationship to `Student`, called *Assigned_To*. The `User_Acct` has as its key the student's `User_ID`, and in each row the student's `Student_ID` is no doubt listed. However, since students can have many accounts, many rows in `User_Acct` may be associated by *Assigned_To* with one row in `Student`. For example, if Jean has a personal account as well as an account for his library job and an account for French, his major department, then *Assigned_To* associates those three rows with his row in `Student`. It is a many-to-one relationship.

In ER diagrams the type of the relationship can be shown in different ways. For example, a one-to-one relationship might be shown with one type of arrow, while a many-to-one relationship might use a different kind of arrow. In Chapter 16 we will see how the types of relationships are expressed in commercial database software.

SUMMARY

This chapter revealed the secret of modern databases: Many of the tables we see don't actually exist; they are logical tables constructed on-the-fly using the physical tables that do exist. Additionally:

> Relationships are the key to associating fields of the physical tables.

> The database administrator carefully designs the database's metadata, the underlying structure of tables and relationships.

> The design for the physically stored tables is optimized to avoid problems such as redundancy. If the physical tables are set up properly, it is easy, by using queries, to give users specific views of the data they want.

> A main tool for creating the views of the logical database is the join-then-trim method, which creates a super table by joining physical tables, and then keeps only the interesting information by trimming with the `Select` and `Project` operations.

> SQL, the query language of relational database software, is "structured" to support the join-then-trim technique.

> Despite different meanings for the word "select," SQL and the conceptual database form presented in Chapter 14 are very similar.

> ER diagrams give graphical form to a database design and help to organize its structure.

EXERCISES

Multiple Choice

1. SQL stands for
   A. Simple Query Language
   B. Simplified Question Line
   C. Structured Query Language
   D. Stored Question Logic

2. The main reason to avoid duplication in a database is
   A. the expense of maintaining the information
   B. the added size of the information
   C. inconsistency
   D. incompatibility

3. The intended connection between different parts of a database is controlled by
   A. entities
   B. relationships
   C. keys
   D. tables

4. Storing information in two tables rather than one
   A. greatly increases the size of the database
   B. unduly complicates the database design
   C. presents few problems and offers several advantages
   D. is not allowed

5. A one-to-one relationship between tables means
   A. each row has one field
   B. there is one row in each table
   C. the tables have corresponding rows
   D. the tables share the same fields

6. The design of a physical database is determined by
   A. security considerations
   B. the need for flexibility
   C. the need to avoid redundancy
   D. all of the above

7. _____ can be physical or logical.
   A. Queries
   B. Tables
   C. Views
   D. all of the above

8. A super table
   A. is created by joining two or more physical tables
   B. is created by joining two or more logical tables
   C. is a combination of logical and physical tables
   D. none of the above

9. SQL is designed to
   A. let any user create their own tables
   B. provide a specific query structure for relational databases
   C. eliminate the need for multiple tables
   D. eliminate the need for join-then-trim commands

10. The SQL `SELECT` clause is similar to the
    A. `Join` operation
    B. `Union` operation
    C. `Project` operation
    D. `Add` operation

Short Answer

1. The personalized content of a database is called a _____.

2. Connections among entities in a database are known as _____.

3. In a database, the existence of duplicate sets of information is known as _____.

4. Inconsistent data is known as _____.

5. GIGO is short for _____.

6. A(n) _____ is a set of tables that are actually stored on the computer.

7. A(n) _____ is created as needed from tables that are stored on the computer.

8. In SQL, you would choose fields for a query using the _____ clause.

9. To select a table in SQL, you need to use the _____ clause.

10. The _____ clause in SQL is used to find specific rows in a table.

11. The _____ clause in SQL is used to match key fields between tables.

12. A(n) _____ is used to graphically show relationships in a database.

13. A(n) _____ relationship exists when one row in a table is related to at most one row in another table.

14. When one field in a table is related to one or more fields in another table, a(n) _____ relationship exists.

Exercises

1. Why is a relationship needed to link the fields of two tables together?
2. Why is redundancy bad for databases when a backup is good for information?
3. Explain how the use of a foreign key avoids information redundancy.
4. Explain a many-to-one relationship using a company with multiple phone lines as an example.

The following information is used for questions 5–12.

The Digital Alliance of Technical Associates (DATA) has the following tables for its DATA file.

Personal

Last_Name	Character, 20	Employee Last Name
First_Name	Character, 15	Employee First Name
Emp_ID	Character, 10	Employee ID Number
Address	Character, 25	Permanent Address
City	Character, 20	City
State	Character, 2	State Abbreviation
Zip	Character, 5	Zip Code
Phone	Character, 15	Home Phone
Hire_Date	Date	Date of Hire

Payroll

Emp_ID	Character, 10	Employee ID Number
Pay_Rate	Integer	Hourly Pay Rate
Deductions	Integer	Number of IRS Deductions
Health	Y/N	Single Health Coverage
Life	Y/N	Company Life Policy

HR (Human Resources)

Emp_ID	Character, 10	Employee ID Number
Dept	Character, 15	Assigned Work Dept.
Hire_Date	Date	Date of Hire
Performance	Character, 255	Comments on Performance
Supervisor	Character, 20	Name of Boss
Projects	Character, 50	Current Projects Assigned

Softball

Emp_ID	Character, 10	Employee ID Number
Throws	Character, 1	Right or Left
Bats	Character, 1	Right or Left
Position	Character, 12	Playing Position

5. What key field connects all the tables in this database? Why is this field preferable to their name or their Social Security number?

6. Where is there redundancy in these tables? How could this be avoided?

7. What tables and fields should the company softball manager have access to? What relationship controls this association?

8. Where is there potential for a many-to-one relationship for the employee?

9. HR needs a list of all employees who are due for their annual review. The annual review is done during the month the employee was hired. What should the table that HR needs look like so they can complete their review?

10. Write the SQL for the logical table created in question 9.

11. The softball manager needs a list of players so they can be contacted about the upcoming season. What should the table look like?

12. Write the SQL for the logical table created in question 11.

16

HAI! ADVENTURE DATABASE
Case Study in Database Design

learning objectives

> Explain the purpose of a needs analysis

> Construct the tables of a physical database and avoid redundancy

> Analyze the relationships between several associated tables

> Determine the views of a database, given a design in progress

> Express simple conceptual queries for views using SQL

> Describe how and when the GUIs are created

HAI! ADVENTURE DATABASE
Case Study in Database Design

*Software is like Entropy; it's hard to grasp, weighs nothing, and obeys the
Second Law of Thermodynamics, i.e., it is always increasing.*

—NORMAN AUGUSTINE

THIS CHAPTER is about three entrepreneurial friends, Hon, Amanda, and
Ian. While discussing their "dream" jobs, they decide to start a business after college graduation. Their idea is to rent sports equipment to rich people at resorts in
ski areas, tropical islands, and in the mountains, including lessons and guided
activities, such as dives and climbs. What makes their business model different
from others is that the employees—they plan to call them *adventure specialists*—
will be well trained, knowledgeable, "up," and helpful, giving their customers
complete satisfaction so they return to the business again and again. To stay dedicated and positively motivated, the adventure specialists will rotate among several
resorts, in both the northern and southern hemispheres, working at different
rental shops. The entrepreneurial trio plan to call their business HAI! Adventure,
knowing that *hai* is Japanese for "yes." Whether HAI! Adventure is a realistic business idea or not is irrelevant—it presents great opportunities for a database (DB)
design.

The goal of this chapter is to illustrate a database design, using the ideas and
principles from Chapters 14 and 15. We start with a needs analysis, which exam-
ines the nature of the business. Then we follow the workflow of the enterprise,
asking at each step what specific information is required for that activity. A conceptual design emerges from our analysis. Next, we turn the conceptual design
into an operational database using standard database software. After we finish the
initial design, we consider how the design is prepared for other HAI! Adventure
business directions.

Finally, we extend the database design to handle business activities such as
lessons and guided tours. As before, we create a conceptual design for the database before we try to implement it. When we reach the lessons and guided tours
extension, we will discuss the pitfalls of alternative designs. The practical implementation follows. Our overall objective is to illustrate how a significant database
can be designed at a high conceptual level before all of the details of implementation are considered.

STRATEGY FOR BUILDING A DATABASE

Though this chapter focuses on the design for the HAI! Adventure database, the strategy can be applied to database design in general. Pay attention to the "big picture" of this example to learn how to create your own database. Like most design activities, however, it is not possible to give an algorithm for creating a database. The steps used here are only guidelines—heuristics—for other designs, because every case is different.

Follow this general pattern when constructing a database:

1. **Perform a needs analysis.** Understand how the database will be used, and list the kinds of data the users will input to the database as well as the kinds of information the database will output to the users. It is often helpful to study the information "flow" through the organization or business. A needs analysis helps us to understand the goals of the database design.

2. **Approximate and revise a physical design.** One approach to creating any design is to construct a rough solution and then to revise it. Once we have created a rough solution, we can assess it to see how well it fulfills the needs, and where it fails. Then, we can revise the solution. Because it is difficult to create the perfect design the first time, this iterative approach works well. The criteria for success include goals such as avoiding redundancy and meeting the users' needs. We create the design "on paper"—often using ER diagrams—making it easy to revise.

3. **Implement the physical design.** At some point, we stop making revisions and decide our design is "optimal," the best we can do up to that point. We will have defined the physical tables and established the relationships. If the process has been done thoughtfully, the physical database is finished and can be implemented. It is often a good idea to implement the physical tables using commercial database software and fill them with some sample values. The process reveals oversights or errors.

4. **Design the logical database.** Next we create the logical database. We consider who must interact with the database. Identifying the users helps us to decide how many views we need. We decide what data each user group will enter into the database, and what data they must see from the database. The view is generally the combination of these two types of information. Then, we create the queries using the join-then-trim approach we learned in Chapter 14, assess how the groups will be served by the views, and possibly revise the design.

5. **Implement the logical database.** With the views conceptually defined (and the physical tables and relationships already programmed), we implement the views in SQL. If the join-then-trim technique has been used, translating to SQL is usually very easy.

6. **Implement the GUIs.** Finally, it is time to complete the implementation. We create the GUIs the users will interact with. Though the process can be tedious and detail oriented, the software makes it easy.

7. **Evaluate the usefulness and (possibly) revise.** Like all designs, the database must be evaluated to be sure it fulfills the users' needs. Though the design process should produce a very useful database, it is almost always possible to think of improvements. The design can be revised to add more functionality.

THE HAI! ADVENTURE BUSINESSES

We're going to design the database for HAI! Adventure, a business founded by three college friends. The business, when it is fully up and running, will have shops at resort locations around the world. Each shop will offer equipment for a single activity such as skiing, wind surfing, scuba diving, mountain climbing, or kayaking. The shops will rent high-quality equipment, and the company plans to run organized activities such as lessons and guided tours. These activities—dives, climbs, bungee jumping, paragliding—will involve one or more customers and a guide, leader, or instructor. Though the business will have other data processing needs such as payroll, receivables, taxes, and equipment management, we won't include those in this design. We're only interested in the rentals and activities like lessons and tours.

The ideal HAI! Adventure employees—adventure specialists—will be active, outdoorsy people who like to travel. They will have some training in an active sport that qualifies them to advise customers renting equipment such as scuba gear, and to serve as instructors or guides. One employment perk is that the adventure specialists will change locations and activities from time to time. (Working for such a company is like being on a permanent vacation!)

All businesses need to start small, so the first HAI! Adventure business is The Snow Machine Ski Rental Shop (Snow Machine), a ski rental shop at a resort in the Canadian Rockies. The shop rents downhill skis and snowboards. The Snow Machine business has four rooms—a large Entry Room through which the customers enter and leave, a large Fitting Room in which the customers get their equipment, an Equipment Room behind the Fitting Room where the gear is stowed and maintained, and a small Staff Room. A typical customer proceeds through the following stages:

> **Selection.** The customer enters the store and is greeted by the receptionist. Available equipment and services and their prices are posted. Having decided to rent equipment, the customer gives the receptionist his or her name, address, and local contact information. The receptionist enters this information into the database.

> **Fitting.** The customer goes to the Fitting Room, where a specialist obtains the necessary information to set the ski bindings, for example, the customer's weight and ability. The equipment is selected and its

equipment identification numbers are recorded. The equipment is adjusted, the settings are recorded, and the gear is given to the customer.

> **Payment.** On the way out, the customer returns with the equipment to the Entry Room to sign the rental agreement—a legal contract stating personal data about the customer, what gear the person rented, the specialist's name who set the gear, and all of the legal mumbo-jumbo required to rent equipment for a life-threatening activity like skiing. The receptionist also collects payment from the customer.

Later, when the skis are returned, they are inspected by the specialist and stowed in the Equipment Room.

PERFORM A NEEDS ANALYSIS

We must decide how to organize the database to support HAI! Adventure's ski rental shop. Perhaps the best way to approach the matter is to consider what information is *created* and what information is *needed* to transact the business. The information created is the documentation on the customer (personal information) and the data on the equipment rented and adjustments set (technical information from the specialist). The information needed is the content of the rental agreement document, which the customer must sign before taking the equipment. The rental is the association of the customer's personal data with the technical data of the equipment, most of which must appear in the rental agreement.

The first idea might be to define a `Rentals` table, with a field for each kind of information needed for the contract. Each row of the table would represent one rental. This is a good place to begin the design, but the `Rentals` table as described may not be perfect. So, before adopting it, we must think about the design's usefulness.

Specifically, the contract needs to contain the customer's name, address, and phone number, implying that this information will be in the table. But if the HAI! Adventure business plan works out, customers will return repeatedly to the shop, which means that their names, addresses, and phone numbers will be repeated in the `Rentals` table several times. As we learned in Chapter 15, *redundancy*—having the same information stored in several places in a database—should be avoided. So we decide that we need a table of customers, `Clients`, so that their personal data is in the database only once.

There is a similar problem with the adventure specialists. For insurance reasons, the `Rentals` table needs to record which specialist adjusts the bindings. Because making binding adjustments requires training, the specialist's credentials for performing the operation should be available in the database. The credentials don't have to be in the contract—only the specialist's name does—so they shouldn't be stored in the `Rentals` table. There should be another table for the specialists' credentials, named the Adventure Specialist Team table, or `ASTeam` for short.

With the customers' and specialists' data moved to their own tables, referenced by keys, what remains in the `Rentals` table? Plenty. The table still records the date of the transaction, the equipment rented, adjustments, and a record of any special information that the specialist gave the customer.

The database so far includes three tables:

> > `Clients`—the table of customers' personal information

> > `ASTeam`—the table of adventure specialists, including their training records and certifications

> > `Rentals`—the table of rentals, listing the gear rented and the customer information such as level of skiing ability, weight, and settings

Relationships exist between the `Clients` and `Rentals` tables, and the `ASTeam` and `Rentals` tables, reflecting the fact that a customer and a specialist participate in the rental, but their specific information is stored in other tables.

APPROXIMATE/REVISE THE DB DESIGN

Next we specify the details for the tables required by the Snow Machine physical database. By being explicit about the design, we can work out additional details conceptually before trying to implement them.

Specify the Clients Table

The `Clients` table is straightforward. It includes customers' names, home and local addresses, and contact information. Although we expect repeat customers, we don't have to worry about the problems of frequent address changes, like colleges do. Customers will probably not change their permanent addresses while on vacation, so a single record will suffice for a single season. If the customer returns the following year, a new record will be created.

So, all of the personal information about a customer is stored in this table. We recognize the following fields, data types, and field sizes:

```
Clients
    Customer_ID    Integer          Unique identifier
    First          Character, 20    Given name
    Middle         Character, 15    Middle name
    Last           Character, 30    Family name
    Birthdate      Date             Date of birth
    Street         Character, 30    Home address
    City           Character, 20
    State          Character, 2     State/Province abbreviation
    ZIP            Character, 10    Postal code
```

```
        Country        Character, 10
        Home_Phone     Character, 20    Phone at residence
        Mobile_Phone   Character, 20
        Email          Character, 40
        Local_Contact  Character, 40    Where staying locally
                                        (hotel)
Primary Key: Customer_ID
```

The key for this relation is `Customer_ID`, a computer-produced unique number, since none of the other fields is guaranteed to give uniqueness to the rows of the table.

Specify the ASTeam Table

The full main `ASTeam` table will record employment information, such as Social Security number, and professional information, such as certification data; address information will be kept separately. All employees will use the same table, though some, like the receptionist, may not need the certification fields. The table contains the following fields:

```
ASTeam
        Nickname       Character, 10
        First          Character, 20
        Middle         Character, 15
        Last           Character, 30
        Birthdate      Date
        SS_Number      ddd-dd-dddd
        Mobil_Phone    Character, 20
        Email          Character, 40
        Certified      Y/N              Is the specialist certified?
        Cert_Expire    Date             When does certification
                                        expire?
        Cert_Detail    Character, 255   Description of certification
                                        type
Primary Key: Nickname
```

The HAI! Adventure team is an informal, tight-knit group, who know each other by nicknames like Sissy and Chip. They prefer to use these names rather than an employee ID number. So the database software will use the `Nickname` field as a key for `ASTeam`, even though the uniqueness requirement forces any two employees who go by the same name—say, Chip—to use different versions of that name—ChipR and ChipS. The Social Security number field also makes the entries unique, but by law Social Security numbers can be used for payroll and tax purposes only.

Because there are different kinds of certification, the `ASTeam` table has fields designating whether the person is certified, the certification expiration date, and the details of the certification, such as where, when, what type, and certifying organization. This information must be recorded, but it will probably not be used very often.

Unlike the clients, the employees of HAI! Adventure *do* move around, and they have both local addresses and permanent addresses. We will manage these addresses by setting up an employee contact schema. Recall that a **schema** is the abstract structure of an entity or entities.

```
Contact
    NickN           Character, 10       Unique Identifer
    Street          Character, 30
    City            Character, 20
    State           Character, 2        State/Province
                                        abbreviation
    ZIP             Character, 10       Postal code
    Country         Character, 10
    Phone           Character, 15       Phone at this address
Primary Key: NickN
```

The `NickN` field is the `Nickname` field of `ASTeam`. Its role, like `Student_ID` in Chapter 15 is to place the employees and their addresses into one-to-one correspondence.

The schema will be used to set up two tables, `AS_Home` and `AS_Local`, recording permanent and local address information, respectively. The tables are, therefore, two instances of the schema—that is, separate tables with the same structure.

The `Contact` schema can be used for the customers as well, but it's not necessary. The customers will not likely move in one season, and because we will probably archive and delete all of the `Clients` records at the close of each season, the addresses don't have to be carried across several years. The employee data must be kept over a longer period of time. Such differences in the characteristics of the data motivate keeping the employee addresses separate.

Specify the Rentals Table

The fields of the `Rentals` table are straightforward. They include both the customers' and the specialists' keys to refer to the `Clients` and `ASTeam` tables, and details about the gear rented. If the customer rents skis and therefore must have bindings set, the `Ski?` field is checked. If this field is checked, `Weight` must be filled in, `Ability` must be filled in, and the two settings fields must be filled in. The implementation will enforce these constraints.

The table that records a rental has the following fields:

```
Rental
    Rental_ID      Integer              Unique identifier
    Date           Date
    Customer       Integer              Clients.Client_ID
    ASTeamer       Character, 10        ASTeam.Nickname
    Boot_Serial    Character, 10        Serial number of boots
                                        rented
    Gear_Serial    Character, 10        Serial number applies to
                                        skis and boards
    Ski?           Y/N                  Yes, specifies skis and
                                        bindings
    Ability        Character, 12        Beginner/Intermediate/Expert
    Weight         Integer              Skier weight
    Binding_Set_L  Character, 5         Setting for left binding
    Binding_Set_R  Character, 5         Setting for right binding
    Poles          Character, 5         Mfr abbrev and length
    Out_Remarks    Character, 255       Cautions or directives to
                                        customer
Primary_Key: Rental_ID
```

The `Out_Remarks` field can be used for comments that the specialist thinks are important to the rental, such as cautions relayed to the skier or observations about the equipment. Notice that the `ASTeamer` field name is chosen to differentiate it from the table name `ASTeam`.

Summarizing, we have designed five database tables of the physical database to support the activity of the ski rental shop. Two of the entities—`Clients` and `ASTeam`—record information about people, and two other entities—`AS_Home` and `AS_Local`—record information about places. These tables record facts about physical phenomena. But the `Rentals` table records information about an event. The event occupies time in the same way the physical objects occupy space. Different types of entities are thus possible with a database.

Specify the Relationships

The `Rentals` table references the `Clients` and `ASTeam` tables. That is, `Rentals` has fields, `Customer` and `ASTeamer`, that contain keys for `Clients` and `ASTeam` tables. Additionally, the `ASTeam` key also references the `AS_Home` and `AS_Local` tables. These references establish relationships, and though they have been expressed clearly in our explanation, we must specify their characteristics for the implementation, too.

The relationships are all one-to-many relationships. That is, each relationship associates the key of one table (the "one" side) with rows in the other table (the "many" side). We name the relationships as follows:

> *Rents*, the `Clients:Rentals` relationship—In the `Rentals` table, customers are referred to by their key (`Customer_ID`) in the `Clients` table.

> *Serves*, the `ASTeam:Rentals` relationship—In the `Rentals` table, spe-
> cialists are referred to by their key (`Nickname`) in the `ASTeam` table.

> *Home_Of*, the `AS_Home:ASTeam` relationship—In the `ASTeam` table, the
> specialist's permanent address is referred to by its key (`NickN`) in the
> `AS_Home` table.

> *Sleeps_At*, the `AS_Local:ASTeam` relationship—In the `ASTeam` table, the
> specialist's local address is referred to by its key (`NickN`) in the
> `AS_Local` table.

By specifying these relationships, our intention is clear as to how the information
of the tables is interconnected.

At this point, the conceptual design of the Snow Machine database's physical components is done. The entities and relationships are defined. The design can be
implemented using any of the many database software systems, all of which support the relational database concepts used here. But before investing our time in
the detailed and time-consuming work of implementing the design, we should
assess it.

Revise the Physical Design?

As with any design, we assess this table organization to see how well it fulfills the
needs of the Snow Machine shop. We notice that there is little redundancy
because of the use of the `Clients`, `ASTeam`, `AS_Home`, and `AS_Local` tables. As a
result, the fields of the `Rentals` table concern only the details of a single ski
rental, plus links to the customer and specialist who participated in it. The design
is sound. Is this the best design?

From the point of view of the Snow Machine Ski Rental Shop, the design will
probably meet its needs well. But from the point of view of the HAI! Adventure
business, it might not. Why? The entrepreneurs who started HAI! Adventure
expect to grow, renting sports gear of many kinds at many sites. The ideas behind
the Snow Machine database design can apply to equipment rentals for scuba diving, wind surfing, kayaking, and mountain climbing equipment rentals, because
these sports have a similar set of requirements. But how would the five tables and
four relationships of the design translate to another business unit?

Table	Changes
`Clients` (Customer data)	None
`AS_Home` (Employee permanent address)	None
`AS_Local` (Employee local address)	None
`ASTeam` (Employee profile)	None, though the info entered in `Cert_detail` will differ
Rentals (Transaction)	Revise equipment detail for the specialized activity

Relationships	Changes
Rents (`Clients:Rentals`)	None
Serves (`ASTeam:Rentals`)	None
Home_Of (`AS_Home:ASTeam`)	None
Sleeps_At (`AS_Local:ASTeam`)	None

Though `Rentals` changes because a different kind of equipment is being rented, it's only the fields related to ski equipment that change.

Analyze the Tables. Imagine that another HAI! Adventure business unit, say Fat Daddy's Dive Shop on Grand Cayman Island, modifies the `Rentals` table for renting scuba diving gear. Only the first four fields would be the same, and possibly the last. All others change. This is not a hard technical task, but it means that the Fat Daddy's `Rentals` table and the Snow Machine `Rentals` table are different. The rentals of the scuba shop and rentals of the ski shop cannot be part of the same table because of these different fields. It's not a problem for the two shops—they're thousands of miles apart and they never interact. But from the point of view of the main company, HAI! Adventure, they're all rentals. The fact that different equipment is being rented is unimportant in many circumstances. It would be desirable to be able to treat all such transactions as *rentals*, each of a different kind of equipment. Is this possible? Of course, anything's possible.

What is the solution? In the same way that customer information has been recorded in a separate table, the details of the equipment rental can also be recorded in another table. Call it `Gear`. But `Gear` is different from `Clients` in one important way. Customers could rent several times, and the details of the equipment are different for each rental. That is, each `Rentals` row would be associated with exactly one `Gear` row, and vice versa. This is a one-to-one relationship like those we saw in Chapter 15 based on `Student_ID`, but we will not store it as such. We will use a separate key, `Equip_ID`, for the `Gear` table, and use it in `Rentals` as `Gear_facts`.

The `Gear` table for the Snow Machine's ski rentals has the following fields:

```
Gear
   Equip_ID      Integer         Key of rental (Rental_ID)
   Boot_Serial   Character, 10    Serial number of boots
                                  rented
   Gear_Serial   Character, 10    Serial number applies to
                                  skis and boards
   Ski?          Y/N              Yes, specifies skis and
                                  bindings
   Ability       Character, 12    Beginner/Intermediate/
                                  Expert
   Weight        Integer          Skier weight
```

```
    Binding_Set_L   Character, 5      Setting for left binding
    Binding_Set_R   Character, 5      Setting for right binding
    Poles           Character, 5      Mfr abbrev and length
    Out_Remarks     Character, 255    Customer/Specialist
                                      conversation
Primary Key: Equip_ID
```

These are simply the fields from the first version of `Rentals`.

The new `Rentals` table is simply the previous structure with the skiing details removed:

```
Rentals
    Shop_ID        Character, 10      Short name of the shop
    Rental_ID      Integer            Unique identifier
    Date           Date
    Customer       Integer            Clients.Client_ID
    ASTeamer       Character, 10      ASTeam.Nickname
    Gear_facts     Integer            Key for ski gear table
    Payment        Currency           Amount received for rental
Primary Key: Shop_ID, Rental_ID
```

Ensure Unique Fields. This structure can apply to any of HAI! Adventure's shops. Notice that we added a `Shop_ID` field to identify which shop made the rental. Entries in this field might be `SnoMachine` or `FatDaddys`, or we could use store numbers. This field creates unique records when the rentals of multiple stores are `Union`ed. (Recall from Chapter 14 that `Union` combines the rows of two tables that have the same fields.) That is, each store uses its own sequence of `Rental_ID` numbers, but to avoid disaster if two stores use the same number, we make the rows unique by using the store name as a prefix. Thus the primary key (from the point of view of the main company) is the composition of `Shop_ID` and `Rental_ID`. And we added a `Payment` field because HAI! Adventure's founders may be interested in that information, too.

Introduce New Relationship. By splitting up the original `Rentals` table into the core activity of renting (the new version of `Rentals`) and a table for the specific equipment rented (`Gear`), we introduce another relationship, the many-to-one relationship between the two tables:

> *Equips*, the `Gear:Rentals` relationship—In the `Rentals` table, the specific equipment in `Gear` is referred to by its key (`Equip_ID`).

This is a one-to-one relationship based on our planned use, but because we don't need to connect equipment with rentals, we use the easier many-to-one relationship.

Now it's possible for any HAI! Adventure shop to use the `Rentals` table unchanged, though different recreations will refer to different `Gear` tables. For example, Fat Daddy's rental will refer to a `Gear` table customized to scuba equipment. Of course, all shops renting the same kind of gear can use the same `Gear` table design.

IMPLEMENT THE PHYSICAL DB DESIGN

Having completed the approximate-and-revise process, we now have a physical database that meets our needs and we know the relationships among its tables. More revisions are possible, but further changes might not produce a better design. We need some experience with the design to see how well it works. So we stop the revision process and go with what we have—in other words, we "freeze" the design. We will implement it in a commercial database system and store some sample data. We will also specify the relationships in the database system. These physical tables will be the basis for the next design steps, and eventually will allow us to produce our first working system. Experience with the system may indicate that we need more changes to the physical database tables, so the revision process is not necessarily complete. But at this point we need some experience.

Define the Tables

All database systems support the concepts used in the design. For our example we'll use the Microsoft Access system.

The first step in the implementation is to define the tables. Defining tables is basically typing into the database system the information outlined above. It is tedious, but easy. We implement the tables at this stage to fill them with sample data in hopes of finding mistakes. Some of the Snow Machine tables are shown in Figure 16.1.

Define the Relationships

The next step is to define the relationships to connect the parts of the database. Again, the database systems give us easy-to-use software tools for defining the relationships. The specification of these relationships is shown in Figure 16.2.

Clients : Table

Field Name	Data Type	Description
Customer_ID	AutoNumber	Unique identifier
First	Text	First Name
Middle	Text	Middle Name
Last	Text	Last Name
Birthdate	Date/Time	Date of Birth
Street	Text	Street address
City	Text	City
State	Text	State/Province/Canton/Prefecture
ZIP	Text	Postal Code
Country	Text	Country of Residence
Home_Phone	Text	Phone at Residence
Mobile_Phone	Text	Cell
Email	Text	Email Address
Local_Contact	Text	Hotel or local phone number

ASTeam : Table

Field Name	Data Type	Description
Nickname	Text	Unique Identifier
First	Text	First Name
Middle	Text	Middle Name
Last	Text	Last Name
Birthdate	Date/Time	Date of Birth
SS_number	Text	ddd-dd-dddd
Mobile_Phone	Text	Cell
Email	Text	Email address
Certified	Yes/No	Any relevant certification?
Cert_Expire	Date/Time	Expiration date
Cert_Detail	Text	Details of when, where, etc.

Rentals : Table

Field Name	Data Type	Description
Store_ID	Text	Unique store name
Rental_ID	AutoNumber	Unique number for each rental
Date	Date/Time	Transaction Date
Customer	Number	Key into Clients
ASTeamer	Text	Key into ASTeam
Gear_facts	Number	Key into Ski_Gear or other
Payment	Currency	Amt received for rental

Ski_Gear : Table

Field Name	Data Type	Description
Equip_ID	AutoNumber	Unique Identifier
Boot_Serial	Text	Serial Number for boots
Gear_Serial	Text	Serial Number for skis or board
Ski?	Yes/No	Are bindings involved?
Ability	Text	Beginner/Intermediate/Exper
Weight	Number	Weight of skier
Binding_Set_L	Text	Binding setting, left
Binding_Set_R	Text	Binding setting, right
Poles	Text	Mfr Abbrev + length
Out_Remarks	Text	Comments about rental or to customer

Figure 16.1. Four of the six tables required for the revised Snow Machine physical database. The `AS_Home` and `AS_Local` tables are identical and are composed only of address fields, like fields 6–11 of `Clients`.

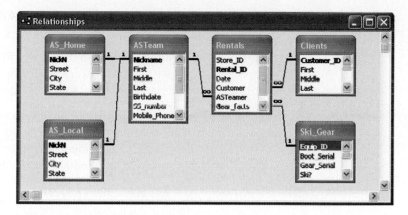

Figure 16.2. *The relationships of the Snow Machine database. The one-to-many relationships are shown with the "one" side (shown as the symbol "1") as a primary key to the relationship, and the many side (shown as a small infinity symbol "∞")as a position where the key is used as a reference.*

DESIGN THE LOGICAL DATABASE

Having defined the physical database, it is time to create the logical database. Though we have stored the information in a particular way (for example, to avoid redundancy), users will want to look at it differently. Different users require different views of the database customized to their needs, as discussed in Chapter 15.

Giving users views of the database is easy. We use a five-step approach:

1. Analyze the business activity to identify the information inputs and outputs—these are the needed views.

2. Determine what information the specialists need from each view and where it is stored in the tables.

3. Define a conceptual query for a new table as a join-then-trim process from existing tables.

4. Implement the conceptual query in SQL.

5. Define a GUI to display the information for the specialists.

To begin, we analyze the business activity. The adventure specialists interact with the Snow Machine database three times: at sign-in; at the fitting of gear; and at the signing of the rental agreement. Thus, there are three customer-related views:

> **Sign-in.** After the receptionist has greeted the customer and the customer has decided what to rent, the receptionist records the customer's personal information. That is, the receptionist establishes a new rental, and enters data about the customer into the **Clients** table. In addition,

the receptionist specifies whether ski or snowboarding gear is being rented.

> *Fitting.* The customer moves to the Fitting Room, where an adventure specialist helps with the selection and fitting of the gear. The specialist must enter information into the `Rentals` (his or her name) and `Gear` tables (equipment).

> *Agreement.* The customer takes the gear and stops at the receptionist station to sign the rental agreement and pay for the rental. The price is entered at this point. For the rental agreement contract, the information in the `Clients`, `Gear`, `ASTeam`, and `Rentals` tables must be combined into a contract and printed.

In addition to these three customer-related views, there is one employee-related view:

> *Hiring.* When new adventure specialists are hired, their information must be entered into the database. That is, information must be entered into three tables: `ASTeam`, `AS_Home`, and `AS_Local`.

Notice that Sign-in, Fitting, and Hiring are "input views" and Agreement is an "output view" in which database information is displayed.

Analyze the Tables for the Views

To present these four views of the database, we need to create the tables that correspond to them. These will not be stored tables, but rather logical tables computed by queries. The data in the new tables depends on what information the user must see. Analyze the four views:

> *Sign-in.* Begins a rental; requires fields `Rental_ID` and `Customer` from `Rentals`. It should also include the `ASTeamer` field so that the receptionist can send the customer to a particular specialist, if one is requested. All of the fields of `Clients` are required because the customer may be new to the store. Finally, the view must include the `Ski?` field from the `Gear` table.

> *Fitting.* Requires all the fields from `Gear`. It also requires the `Rental_ID` and `ASTeamer` fields from `Rentals`, so the specialist can sign in if no particular specialist is requested. In addition, so that the specialist can call the customer by name, the two fields `First` and `Last` from the `Clients` table are also required.

> *Agreement.* Requires all of the fields from `Rentals`, `Clients` (except `Email` and `Local_Contact`), and `Gear` and the name of the specialist from the `ASTeam` table.

> *Hiring.* Requires all of the fields from `ASTeam`, `AS_Home`, and `AS_Local` for signing in new specialists or updating their records.

This information is summarized in Table 16.1.

Table 16.1. Summary of the fields required for the Snow Machine database views

View	Clients	ASTeam	Gear	AS_Home	AS_Local	Rentals
Sign-In	*All*		Ski?			Rental_ID
						Customer
						ASTeamer
Fitting	First		*All*			Rental_ID
	Last					Customer
						ASTeamer
Agreement	*All—except*	First	*All*			*All*
	Email	Middle				
	Local_Contact	Last				
Hiring		*All*		*All*	*All*	

Create the View Queries

The views will be created using *queries*, commands formed from the basic table-manipulating operations using the join-then-trim approach described in Chapters 14 and 15. *Combine the base tables into a super table and then retrieve the items needed for the view.* Consider each query in turn.

Sign-in Query.   The *Sign-in* view begins a rental, so we should think of it as establishing a new `Rentals` row; specifically, the fields `Rental_ID` and `Customer.ASTeamer` from `Rentals` may also be defined if a customer asks for a specific adventure specialist. All of the fields from `Clients` are required, though they may have been entered on an earlier visit. Only `Ski?` is needed from `Gear`. The form for the query is

```
Sign_in =
    Project Customer_ID, First, Middle, Last, Birthdate,
        Street, City, State, ZIP, Country, Home_Phone,
        Mobile_Phone, Email, Local_Contact, Rental_ID,
        Customer, ASTeamer, Ski?
    From (Clients ⋈ Rentals
        On Clients.Customer_ID = Rentals.Customer) ⋈ Gear
        On Gear.Equip_ID = Rentals.Gear_facts
```

The first join relies on the *Rents* relationship between `Clients` and `Rentals`, matching whenever `Customer_ID` matches `Customer`, and the second join relies on the *Equips* relationship between `Gear` and `Rentals`, matching whenever `Equip_ID` matches `Gear_facts`.

Fitting Query.   The *Fitting* view needs data from three tables, `Rentals`, `Gear`, and `Clients`. From `Rentals`, only the `Rental_ID`, `ASTeamer`, and `Customer` fields are needed. The `Customer` field is needed to retrieve the customer's first and last name from `Clients`. All of the fields of `Gear` are needed. The query is

```
Fitting =
    Project Rental_ID, ASTeamer, Customer, First, Last,
        Equip_ID, Boot_Serial, Gear_Serial, Ski?, Ability,
        Weight, Binding_Set_L, Binding_Set_R, Poles, Out_Remarks
    From (Rentals ⋈ Clients
        On Clients.Customer_ID = Rentals.Customer) ⋈ Gear
        On Gear.Equip_ID = Rentals.Gear_facts
```

The super table is like the Sign-in view, relying on the *Rents* relationship and the *Equips* relationship.

Agreement Query. The contract, or agreement, will need information from the `Rentals`, `Clients`, `Gear`, and `ASTeam` tables. It needs all of the fields (except `Clients.Email` and `Clients.Local_Contact`) from the first three tables, and the name fields from `ASTeam`. Though straightforward, listing all of the fields for this *Agreement* view is rather lengthy:

```
Agreement =
    Project Shop_ID, Rental_ID, Date, Customer, ASTeamer,
        Payment, Customer_ID, Clients.First, Clients.Middle,
        Clients.Last, Birthdate, Street, City, State, ZIP,
        Country, Home_Phone, Mobile_Phone, Equip_ID,
        Boot_Serial, Gear_Serial, Ski?, Ability, Weight,
        Binding_Set_L, Binding_Set_R, Poles, Out_Remarks,
        NickName, ASTeamer.First, ASTeamer.Middle, ASTeamer.Last
    From (((Rentals ⋈ Clients On Clients.Customer_ID =
            Rentals.Customer) ⋈ Gear
        On Gear.Equip_ID = Rentals.Gear_facts) ⋈ ASTeam
        On Rentals.ASTeamer = ASTeam.Nickname)
```

The three relationships used for the joins are *Rents*, *Equips*, and *Serves*. We've seen the *Rents-* and *Equips*-based equality tests before. The join based on *Serves* creates rows whenever `ASTeamer = Nickname`.

Hiring Query. The *Hiring* view is more direct. It uses all of the fields from the three tables, `ASTeam`, `AS_Home`, and `AS_Local`. Because all of the fields are needed, no project operation (trimming) is required. The query is simply the three joins:

```
Hiring =
    (ASTeam ⋈ AS_Home
        On ASTteam.Nickname = AS_Home.NickN) ⋈ AS_Local
    On ASTeam.Nickname = AS_Local.NickN
```

The first join relies on the *Home_Of* relationship, combining rows whenever employee `ASTeam.Nickname = AS_Home.NickN`. The second join relies on the *Sleeps_At* relationship, forming rows whenever `ASTeam.Nickname = AS_Local.NickN`. All of the fields are kept.

Having defined the views that Snow Machine personnel will use to interact with the database, it's time to set up the interfaces to the views.

IMPLEMENT THE LOGICAL DATABASE DESIGN

Naturally the view queries can be implemented in database system software. With the tables and relationships already implemented, specifying the queries for the views is easy. We translate the conceptual queries directly into SQL. The best place to begin is with the *Hiring* query, because specialists must be added to the database before any customers can be processed.

Encode the Hiring Query

The *Hiring* query (**Hiring_Q**) is especially easy because it's simply the join of three tables:

(ASTeam ⋈ AS_Home) ⋈ AS_Local

The three key points to remember about the translation from our conceptual form of the query to SQL are:

> The conceptual natural join produces a table with all (unique) fields in it, but in SQL it is necessary to specify which fields should be included. Rather than picking out the fields with the operation **Project** . . . **From**, we use the command **SELECT** . . . **FROM**.

> Rather than the natural join operator, ⋈, we use the operator **INNER JOIN**.

> We must give the equality test that is the basis for the **INNER JOIN**.

> In addition, all references to fields use the *table name.field name* syntax.

Keeping those differences in mind, the translation of the *Hiring* query into SQL is

```
SELECT  ASTeam.Nickname, ASTeam.First, ASTeam.Middle,
        ASTeam.Last, ASTeam.Birthdate, ASTeam.SS_number,
        ASTeam.Home_Addr, ASTeam.Local_Addr, ASTeam.Mobile_Phone,
        ASTeam.Email, ASTeam.Certified, ASTeam.Cert_Expire,
        ASTeam.Cert_Detail, AS_Home.Street, AS_Home.City,
        AS_Home.State,AS_Home.ZIP, AS_Home.Country,
        AS_Home.Phone, AS_Local.Street, AS_Local.City,
        AS_Local.State, AS_Local.ZIP, AS_Local.Country,
        AS_Local.Phone
FROM    AS_Local INNER JOIN (AS_Home INNER JOIN ASTeam
            ON AS_Home.NickN = ASTeam.Nickname)
        ON AS_Local.NickN = ASTeam.Nickname;
```

It's an impressive command, but when it's decomposed into its components, it's far less remarkable. The command works as promised—the **SELECT** chooses all of the unique fields from the join of the three tables. Notice that although the order of the `INNER JOIN`'s operands is different from our conceptual form, the parentheses ensure that the operations are done in the same order; that is, `AS_Home INNER JOIN ASTeam` is first, though order doesn't matter when giving joins.

Encode the Sign-in Query

Next we translate the *Sign-in* query directly into SQL. Recall that the query is

```
Sign_in =
    Project Customer_ID, First, Middle, Last, Birthdate,
        Street, City, State, ZIP, Country, Home_Phone,
        Mobile_Phone, Email, Local_Contact, Rental_ID,
        Customer, ASTeamer, Ski?
    From (Clients ⋈ Rentals
            On Clients.Customer_ID = Rentals.Customer) ⋈ Gear
        On Gear.Equip_ID = Rentals.Gear_facts
```

Following the three guidelines listed above yields the `Sign-In_Q`:

```
SELECT    Clients.Customer_ID, Clients.First, Clients.Middle,
          Clients.Last, Clients.Birthdate, Clients.Street,
          Clients.City, Clients.State, Clients.ZIP,
          Clients.Country, Clients.Home_Phone,
          Clients.Mobile_Phone, Clients.Email,
          Clients.Local_Contact, Rentals.Rental_ID,
          Rentals.Customer, Rentals.ASTeamer, Gear.Ski?
FROM      (Clients INNER JOIN Rentals
              ON Clients.Customer_ID = Rentals.Customer)
          INNER JOIN Gear
          ON Rentals.Gear_facts = Gear.Equip_ID;
```

which is exactly the query required for the Sign-in view.

Encode the Fitting Query

The *Fitting* query is also an easy command to program directly in SQL. Recalling the conceptual form of the query

```
Fitting =
    Project Rental_ID, ASTeamer, Customer, First, Last,
        Equip_ID, Boot_Serial, Gear_Serial, Ski?, Ability,
        Weight, Binding_Set_L, Binding_Set_R, Poles, Out_Remarks
    From (Rentals ⋈ Clients
            On Clients.Customer_ID = Rentals.Customer) ⋈ Gear
        On Gear.Equip_ID = Rentals.Gear_facts
```

the `Fitting_Q` query is therefore

```
SELECT    Rentals.Rental_ID, Rentals.ASTeamer, Rentals.Customer,
          Clients.First, Clients.Last, Gear.Equip_ID,
          Gear.Boot_Serial, Gear.Gear_Serial, Gear.Ski?,
          Gear.Ability, Gear.Weight, Gear.Binding_Set_L,
          Gear.Binding_Set_R, Gear.Poles, Gear.Out_Remarks
```

```
FROM      (Clients INNER JOIN Rentals
              ON Clients.Customer_ID = Rentals.Customer)
          INNER JOIN Gear
          ON Rentals.Gear_facts = Gear.Equip_ID;
```

Encode the Agreement Query

Finally, the *Agreement* view query (**Agreement_Q**) for the rental agreement contract seems to be the most complicated because it involves four tables. But because it uses all of the fields (but two) of three tables, and only three fields of the other, it isn't conceptually difficult.

```
SELECT    Rentals.Store_ID, Rentals.Rental_ID, Rentals.Date,
          Rentals.Customer, Rentals.ASTeamer, Rentals.Payment,
          Clients.Customer_ID, Clients.First, Clients.Middle,
          Clients.Last, Clients.Birthdate, Clients.Street,
          Clients.City, Clients.State, Clients.ZIP,
          Clients.Country, Clients.Home_Phone,
          Clients.Mobile_Phone, Gear.Equip_ID, Gear.Boot_Serial,
          Gear.Gear_Serial, Gear.Ski, Gear.Ability, Gear.Weight,
          Gear.Binding_Set_L, Gear.Binding_Set_R, Gear.Poles,
          Gear.Out_Remarks, ASTeam.First, ASTeam.Middle,
          ASTeam.Last
FROM      Gear INNER JOIN
              (Clients INNER JOIN
                  (ASTeam INNER JOIN Rentals
                      ON ASTeam.Nickname = Rentals.ASTeamer)
                  ON Clients.Customer_ID = Rentals.Customer)
              ON Gear.Equip_ID = Rentals.Gear_facts;
```

In general, translating queries directly into SQL is about as complicated as these examples show. Because SQL is the standard language for database queries in production database systems, anyone expecting to build or be responsible for one (that is, anyone expecting to be a database administrator), should spend a few more minutes learning the details.

{ *ſiſ*BYTE }

Query-by-Example >>

Although translating from our conceptual form to SQL is not difficult, there is an even easier way to produce SQL: Query-by-Example (QBE). Developed at IBM in 1975, QBE is included in Microsoft Access as an alternative to programming SQL directly. The idea is that the user gives an example of the desired table by filling in the fields of a blank table. The software then generates an SQL query to create the example table. Let's see how it works for the Hiring view.

Figure 16.3 shows Access's Query-by-Example facility for defining the **Hiring_Q** query. Notice that there are two windows. The top window shows the entity-relationship diagram for the tables used in the query and the relationships used for the joins. These are displayed automatically when the user chooses the tables for the example.

The bottom window shows (part of) the display of the fields of the intended table. This is an "example" of how the table should look. Each position corresponds to a field of the intended table with the source table and source field indicated. It is possible to order the items of the table's column (`Sort`), include them, but not display them (`Show`), or put conditions on them (`Criteria, Or`). The software documentation gives more information.

The software translates the QBE queries into SQL automatically. It's possible (and informative) to look at the SQL generated by the software: **View > SQL View**. The SQL for `Hiring_Q` generated by the software is identical to the query we wrote.

Figure 16.4 shows the two windows of the QBE interface for the `Agreement_Q` query. Notice the tables/relationships and example table windows. The three relationships enable the query to assemble the necessary information. The query generated by SQL is again exactly the query we wrote.

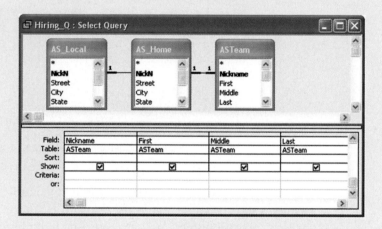

Figure 16.3. *Query-by-example display (from Microsoft Access) showing the tables with the relationships and the first four fields of the* `Hiring_Q` *query.*

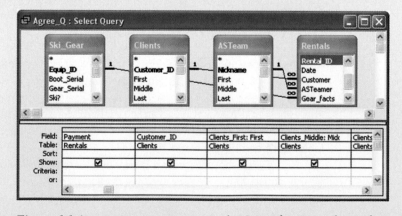

Figure 16.4. `Agreement_Q` *query in the Query-by-Example window.*

IMPLEMENT THE GUIS

Data can be entered directly into the "tabular sheet" form of the tables, but users expect a GUI to make data entry friendlier. Such GUIs are also known as *forms*. A GUI should be clear, convenient, and visually pleasing. Designing pleasing and effective GUIs is an art—a career for those who are talented at it—but we can offer some commonsense guidelines for the amateurs among us:

> **Arrange information sensibly.** Cluster the fields in a way that makes sense—names go together, address fields go together, and so on. Also, orient the fields the way the user expects to see them—perhaps arranging name information horizontally and address information vertically, to follow the most common orientation in which the information is written.

> **Avoid clutter.** Eliminate duplicate fields and avoid unnecessary text, lines, and visual effects. Many believe that sans serif fonts work best onscreen.

> **Preload fields.** Where possible, fill a field with a default value, or if there is a specific format expected, fill the field with the guidelines for its form, as in DD/MM/YYYY for dates.

Most people who use a data entry GUI probably stop noticing its pleasant or annoying features quickly. Still we should make the interface as fine as possible. Use your database system to build the GUIs.

Ta DAH! It's done. The Snow Machine Ski Rental Shop database has been designed and implemented (see Figure 16.5). HAI! Adventure is in business.

EXTENDING A DB: LESSONS AND TOURS

The Snow Machine database has been designed to handle new rental businesses of HAI! Adventure, such as renting scuba equipment and mountain climbing gear. It's a simple matter to develop new tables for the new equipment types.

Now we'll consider what changes are needed for the HAI! Adventure team to move into the lessons and tours business. How do we handle the fact that some of the adventure specialists will serve as instructors, guides, or leaders for activities related to the shop's sports specialty? Each of these activities includes a set of customers and a guide or instructor. The question is, "How should the present database be extended to handle these new activities?"

An Analogy

When thinking about how to design the tables to incorporate lessons and tours, it's natural to make analogies to familiar situations. We visualize a ski instructor and students, and think about organizing the table as a class list. Because the

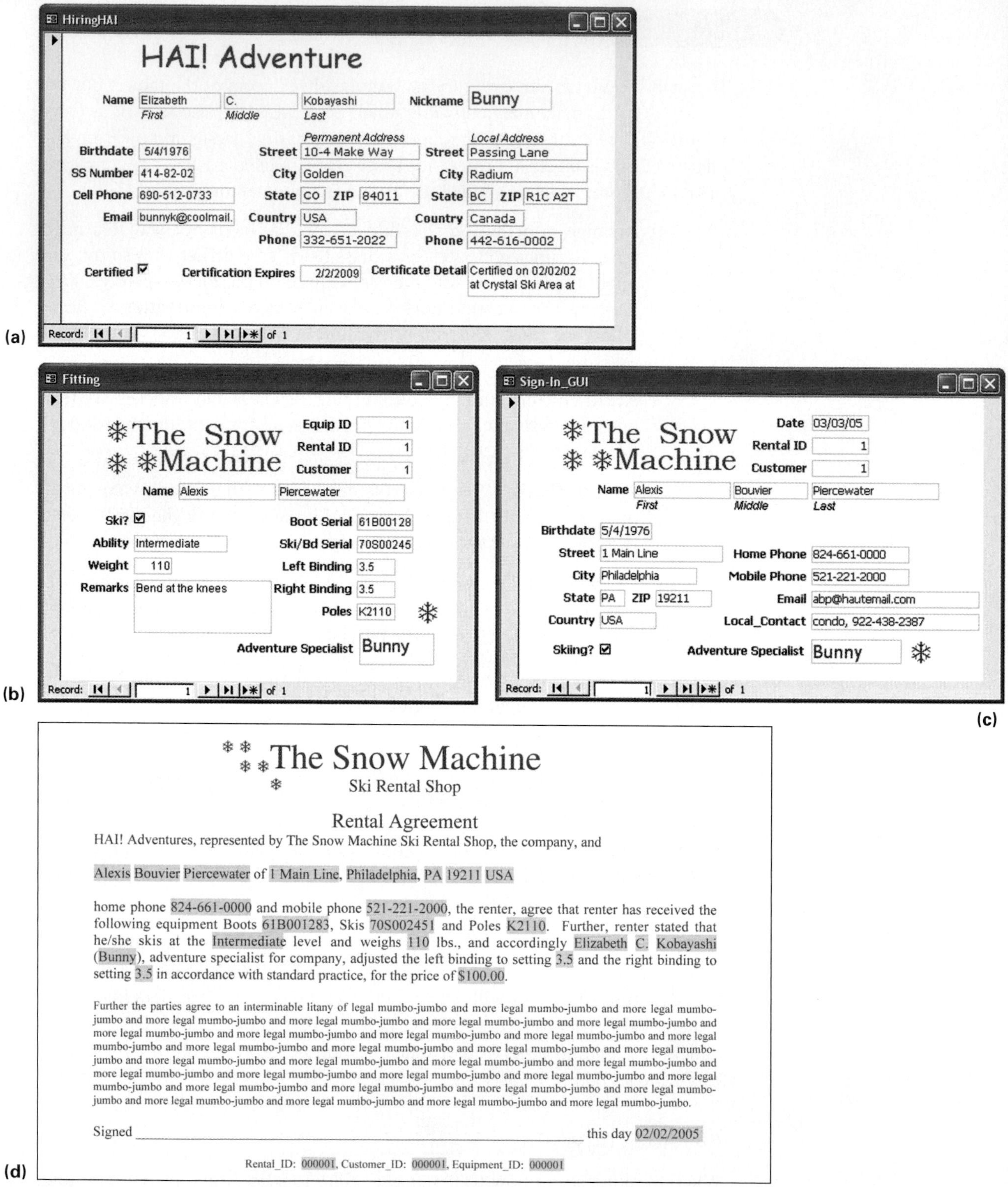

Figure 16.5. *Sample GUIs for the four Snow Machine views: (a) Hiring view, (b) Fitting view, (c) Sign-In view, and (d) Rental Agreement.*

number of students is limited, it seems that a `Class_List` table with the following schema should work:

```
Class_List                              CAUTION — NOT A GOOD DESIGN
    Class_ID        Number              Unique identifier
    Date            mm/dd/yyyy          Date of event or first
                                        lesson
    Type            Character, 50       Description of the lesson or
                                        tour
    Leader          Character, 10       ASTeam.Nickname value
    Participant1    Number              Clients.Customer_ID
    Participant2    Number              Clients.Customer_ID
    Participant3    Number              Clients.Customer_ID
    Participant4    Number              Clients.Customer_ID
    Participant5    Number              Clients.Customer_ID
Primary Key: Class_ID
```

The idea is that each group has a leader and a set of participants. By using the keys for the **Leader** and the **Participants**, we avoid redundancy. But we make a different mistake. This is *not* the way to extend the database to include lessons and tours, even though the analogy seems right.

The `Class_List` table idea has several problems, foremost, it binds data that should be *independent*. That is, participation in the class should not be ordered. But the `Class_List` definition implies, for example, that because we've assigned a numbered attribute to each student, being student number 2 is different from being student number 3. This structure implies that we are interested in rows in a table that are the same in all respects except that the participants are ordered differently, as shown in Table 16.2. But we don't want to recognize such distinctions. Students in a class should be unordered. This design is faulty.

Table 16.2. Possible rows based on the `Class_List` table definition

Class_ID	Date	Type	Leader	Partic 1	Partic 2	Partic 3	Partic 4	Partic 5
223	2/2/05	Beg'g Skiing	Thor	Jan	John	Jon	Ian	Juan
223	2/2/05	Beg'g Skiing	Thor	Juan	Jan	John	Jon	Ian
223	2/2/05	Beg'g Skiing	Thor	Ian	Juan	Jan	John	Jon

The Activities Table

An improved design is to create an entity that includes the common features and properties of the lessons and tours. The "thing" we're trying to describe is a scheduled activity—a lesson at a given time, a dive on a given morning, or a climb on a specific day—and a collection of such things forms a table of instances in which each would have the following fields:

```
Activities
   Activity_ID     Number              Unique identifier
   Date            Date                Date of activity
   Leader          Character, 10       ASTeam.NickName
   Description     Character, 50       Statement describing
                                       activity
   Limit           Number              Upper limit on participation
Primary Key: Activity_ID
```

HAI! Adventure plans to offer these activities. Basically this is the `Class_List` schema without the participants. This design not only avoids the problem of ordering the participants, but also regularizes lessons and tours for all sports because the nature of the activity is specified in the `Description` field. Having all lessons "look alike" in the database tables is as important to HAI! Adventure as making all `Rentals` look alike.

Thinking abstractly about the database design for a moment, how *will* we create a class list or tour-participants list? After all, even if it is unwise to implement the class list metaphor directly as a row in a table, it is nevertheless a useful document. Thinking about this guides us to a better solution.

The `Apply` Table

From our knowledge of the join-then-trim method, we expect to construct the class list by creating a query that combines some of the base tables, such as `ASTeam`, for the leader. From the resulting super table, we will remove the fields needed for the class list. That's what we did before when the logical database view didn't exactly match the tables of the physical database. What should we store so we can create the class list in this way? Obviously, we need a table of students. But we already have it—it's simply our `Clients` table.

Perhaps the activity the customer signs up for can be added to the `Clients` records. When thinking about how we might extend the `Clients` table to include "sign-up" information, however, we realize that the customer might register for several tours or lessons. And as we're imagining adding a series of fields to the `Clients` records—`Activity1`, `Activity2`, and `Activity3`, say—in which to store the `Activity_ID` keys of the lessons—we realize that we're about to make the same mistake as with the class list! The activities should be independent, too.

To solve these problems, think about how your school works. Colleges have students (like HAI! Adventure has `Clients`) and classes (like HAI! Adventure has `Activities`), but for a student to take a class, he or she must *register*. That is, the binding of `Clients` to `Activities` can be done using the concept of registration.

What form would the registration take? Because registration binds customers with activities, it will be like `Rentals`, but without the equipment table. It would likely have the following schema:

```
Apply
    Shop_ID        Character, 10    Short name of the shop
    Regist_ID      Number           Unique identifier
    Date           Date
    Activity       Number           Activities.Activity_ID
    Participant    Number           Clients.Customer_ID
    Skill          Character, 255    Skill level description
    Payment        Currency          Amount paid

Primary Key: Shop_ID, Regist_ID
```

The fields are self-explanatory except perhaps for `skill`, which is a text description of the participant's qualifications for the activity. The leader will evaluate this field. That is, registration is an *application* to participate, which is why we called the table `Apply`; the customer must have the right qualifications. Some activities, like skiing, require routine information, "Intermediate skier"; some activities, like mountain climbing, require detailed information, "Climbed the four highest peaks in the Bugaboos . . . "; and some activities, like bungee jumping, require little information, "Have mass." Like college, you have to have the prereqs.

Notice that everyone registered for an activity is in the `Apply` table; that is, the design works for participants of any class or tour. If a person is registered for more than one activity, he or she has more than one row in `Apply`, and the rows are independent (unordered). If two `Clients` are signed up for the same class, they are also unordered. If participants cancel their registration, they are given a refund and removed from the table, but they don't leave "holes" in the schedule, as they would have with the earlier `Class_List` design, because there is not yet any schedule. And, finally, a participants list or class list can be created by joining `Apply`, `Clients`, and `Activities`, as explained later in the chapter. The solution has every positive feature imaginable, except one: Even though there is a registration limit for each of the activities, this scheme doesn't automatically cap the enrollment at that number. Any number of people can register for a three-person trek to Aconcagua. But this problem is easily solved with database software systems, so we won't worry about it.

Establish Relationships between Tables

Creating the `Activities` and `Apply` tables for the physical database naturally defines some relationships:

> *Leads*, the `ASTeam:Activities` relationship—In the `Activities` table, specialists are referred to by their key (`Nickname`) in the `ASTeam` table.

> *Offers*, the `Activities:Apply` relationship—In the `Apply` table, lessons and tours are referred to by their key (`Activity_ID`) in the `Activities` table.

> *Registers_For*, the `Clients:Apply` relationship—In the `Apply` table, the participants are referred to by their key (`Customer_ID`) in the `Clients` table.

These are all one-to-many relationships. Figure 16.6 shows the relationships.

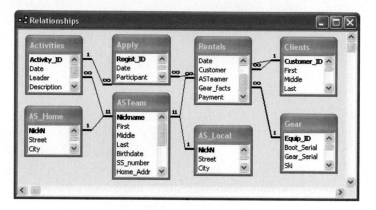

Figure 16.6. *The relationships of the Snow Machine database after adding the* `Activities` *and* `Apply` *tables, and their induced relationships.*

Creating the participants list or class list for a given activity is straightforward. The `Activities`, `Apply`, and `Customers` tables are joined, and the necessary fields are extracted. For the list, we want all fields from `Activities` and the participants' names from `Clients`. No information is actually needed from `Apply` because the instructor or leader will have already looked over the participants and decided who is qualified. (This requires another view, of course.) So our class list uses the registration table `Apply`, but only for associating `Activities` table entries to `Clients` table entries, as planned. The required `Class List` view is implemented by the table created by the `Attends_Q` query:

```
Attends_Q =
    Project Activity_ID, Date, Leader, Description, Limit,
        Activity, Participant, Customer_ID, First, Last
    From (Activities ⋈ Apply
        On Activities.Activity_ID = Apply.Activity) ⋈ Clients
        On Apply.Participant = Clients.Customer_ID
```

Converting this conceptual query to SQL is direct because it amounts to repeating the field list and testing equality on the fields of the *Offers* and *Registers_For* relationships. The result is

```
SELECT    Activities.Activity_ID, Activities.Date,
          Activities.Leader, Activities.Description,
          Activities.Limit, Apply.Participant, Clients.First,
          Clients.Last
FROM      Clients INNER JOIN
             (Activities INNER JOIN Apply
                ON Activities.Activity_ID = Apply.Activity)
             ON Apply.Participant = Clients.Customer_ID
```

A Class List Report

There's one more thing to do. `Attends_Q` will create a table of *all* the students signed up for *all* of the classes, which isn't quite what we want. What we actually need is the list for one class, or perhaps a list for one day, if there are few enough classes in a day. We can easily do this using `Activity_ID` or `Date` to select the necessary rows from the `Attends_Q` table. Using the conceptual `Select...From...` operation discussed in Chapter 15, we can revise the `Attends_Q` query to form the `Class_List_Q` query:

```
Class_List_Q =
   Select Date = current_date
   From (Project Activity_ID, Date, Leader, Description, Limit,
           Activity, Participant, Customer_ID, First, Last
      From (Activities ⋈ Apply
         On Activities.Activity_ID = Apply.Activity) ⋈ Clients
         On Apply.Participant = Clients.Customer_ID)
```

where `current_date` is a system-defined constant. `Select` keeps only those rows that satisfy its test, so that `Class_List_Q` produces the list of participants on a given day. To select on `Activity_ID`, the user asks for the name of the activity (by a GUI) and the returned value is matched in the `Select`.

To get the SQL `Class_List_Q` query, we only need to add a `WHERE` clause to the `Attends_Q` query that saves only those rows that meet the criterion. Therefore, the `Class_List_Q` query has the SQL form:

```
SELECT    Activities.Activity_ID, Activities.Date,
          Activities.Leader, Activities.Description,
          Activities.Limit, Apply.Participant, Clients.First,
          Clients.Last
FROM      Clients INNER JOIN
             (Activities INNER JOIN Apply
                ON Activities.Activity_ID = Apply.Activity)
             ON Clients.Customer_ID = Apply.Participant
WHERE     ((Activities.Date)="Date");
```

An example document produced by the `Class_List_Q` query is shown in Figure 16.7.

Participants List

Leader	Act ID	Date	Activity	Max	ID	First	Last
Bunny							
	2	3/3/2005	Heli Skiing 10am	3			
					5	Brittany	Rothshield
					4	Duane	Ho
					2	Franklin	Piercewater
Thor							
	1	3/3/2005	Heli Skiing 9am	3			
					3	Jackson	Lee
					1	Alexis	Piercewater

Figure 16.7. A participants list document displaying the results of the `Class_List_Q` *query.*

SUMMARY

Our design of the HAI! Adventure database is typical of most design efforts. It began with our best guess at a solution, followed by an analysis of how well the solution satisfied our needs. That led to revisions, which were followed by more analysis, and so on. The process of design-then-refine continued until we produced a quality solution. The end result, which was much different from our original concept, evolved from careful thought about how to improve the solution. Along the way we refined the design process by:

> Studying the structure and operation of the Snow Machine Ski Rental Shop. We used the physical structure of the shop to help us visualize its operation. The rental process and the allocation of employee tasks affected the database design.

> Understanding the rental process. The receptionist inputs the customer's information, the adventure specialist adds data, and the information is combined into a rental agreement.

> Developing a "mega" `Rentals` table in which all of the relevant information for each rental is stored in a single row. The arrangement introduced the dreaded problem of *redundancy*, so we created smaller tables that collected information in logically related units.

> Learning that there is no algorithm for formulating tables. It is simply a matter of thinking about the process and the types of information needed.

> Considering whether the Snow Machine database design could be used for other forms of equipment rental. It could not, so we revised the design before implementing the tables and relationships.

> Setting up the physical database after the tables and relationships were defined. To make it easy for users, we designed database views: *Sign-in*, *Fitting*, and *Agreement*.

> Joining a few tables, and then trimming as needed. Once the conceptual queries were created, it was a simple matter to encode those in SQL.

> Creating a GUI for the view to make the database convenient for the specialists.

> Looking at how HAI! Adventure could extend the rental version of its database to lessons and guided tours. Although reasoning by analogy is a very powerful design and problem-solving technique, it's not perfect; it's possible to use the wrong analogy or metaphor.

> Switching to a registration analogy, we created the `Activities` and `Apply` extensions. We created a `Class List` view within the `Activities`, `Apply` structure.

> Solving the database problems for HAI! Adventure and its Snow Machine shop uses ideas and approaches that can be applied in any database design. Understanding the details of the approach—(1) tables and relationships, (2) views, and (3) implementation—apply to most design situations. We were successful here simply by working through the process carefully. It's a powerful strategy.

EXERCISES

Multiple Choice

1. The first step in building a database is to
   A. design the logical database
   B. create the physical design
   C. determine the tables and their relationships
   D. perform a needs analysis

2. In building a database, the creation of ER diagrams would probably occur in the
   A. needs analysis phase
   B. approximate and revise a physical design phase
   C. implement the physical design phase
   D. implement the logical database phase

Questions 3–12 refer to the HAI! Adventure Database Case Study.

3. In the case study, customer personal information is stored in the
   A. `Rentals` table
   B. `Clients` table
   C. `ASTeam` table
   D. `Activities` table

4. The key field in the `Clients` table is
   A. `Birthdate`
   B. `Email`
   C. `Customer_ID`
   D. `Rental`

5. The Social Security number field cannot be used as a key field because
   A. it's not unique
   B. it's not long enough
   C. it's illegal to use it for anything but payroll and taxes
   D. fields cannot store the hyphens that are in a Social Security number

6. The `Clients` table contains information on clients. The `Rentals` table contains information on rentals to clients. The relationship of `Clients` to `Rentals` is
   A. one-to-many
   B. many-to-one
   C. one-to-one
   D. brother-to-sister

7. The key field for the `Clients` and `Rentals` relationship is the
   A. `Date`
   B. `Rental_ID`
   C. `Nickname`
   D. `Customer_ID`

8. In the case study, the relationship between `Clients` and `Rentals` is called
   A. *Rents*
   B. *Serves*
   C. *Home_Of*
   D. *Sleeps_At*

9. In the case study, the relationship between `ASTeam` and `AS_local` is
   A. one-to-one based on `Student_ID`
   B. one-to-one based on `Nickname`
   C. one-to-many based on `Rentals` and `AS_local`
   D. one-to-one based on `AS_local` and `AS_home`

10. The field that separates the `Rentals` table of one store from the `Rentals` table of another store is
    A. `Rental_ID`
    B. `Shop_ID`
    C. `Equip_ID`
    D. `Customer`

11. To combine the `Rentals` tables from each store into one table, you'd use the
    A. `Product` operation
    B. `Add` operation
    C. `Union` operation
    D. `Combine` operation

12. Using proper database naming conventions for `ASTeam.First`:
    A. `ASTeam` is the database and `First` is the table
    B. `ASTeam` is the table and `First` is the field
    C. `First` is the table and `ASTeam` is the field
    D. `ASTeam` is the field and `First` is the database

Short Answer

1. A(n) _____ analyzes the nature of a business, its workflow, and its information needs.

2. The _____ of information is the way information travels through a business or organization.

3. The relationship between `Rentals` and `Client` is a _____ relationship.

4. You _____ a design, that is, you stop making changes to a design, to test it to see how well it works.

5. The _____ is used to depict the many side of a relationship.

6. In SQL, the _____ command is used to tie two tables together based on a relationship between fields.

7. A(n) _____ is the individual who builds, maintains, and is responsible for a database.

8. QBE stands for _____.

9. A(n) _____ is used to make entering data into a table easier.

10. A(n) _____ is the combination of two or more base tables.

11. _____ is the term for removing unneeded fields from a super table.

12. Storing the same data in more than one place is called _____.

13. A(n) _____ can be defined as one-to-one, many-to-one, or one-to-many.

14. Different users need different _____ of a database in order to properly see the information they need.

15. In SQL, the _____ command is used to pick the fields to show from the join of two tables.

Exercises

1. HAI! Adventure wants to expand into white-water rafting in Idaho. Do the needs analysis and physical database design for this plan. What existing tables should be used to build the database for this resort? What new tables would be needed? Could existing tables be modified for this purpose?

2. The white-water rafting has numerous classes each day. Each instructor has classes at varying experience levels. What tables need to be used and what fields need to be included to produce a report showing the clients in each class for each instructor?

3. Sketch what the GUI for the report in exercise 2 would look like.

4. Write the SQL statement needed to display the information for the report in exercise 2.

5. The Accounting department for HAI! wants to add information to the database for each employee. They want to add information on individual taxes and insurance to the **ASTeam** table. Why would you advise against this?

6. What solution would you offer to the Accounting department? What would you name the table? What relationships would you establish?

7. HAI! wants to set up a feedback form for its clients to fill out after an activity. What fields should be included? What should it be called? What relationships should be set up?

8. In preparation for the upcoming ski season, HAI! wants to send out promotional information to last year's clients. What tables and fields are needed to do a mailing?

9. What changes would you make if you decided to send out an email promotion instead of snail mail?

10. Write the SQL statement needed to display the promotional information.

chapter 17

SHHH, IT'S A SECRET

Privacy and Digital Security

learning objectives

> Explain what is meant by privacy; discuss the issues surrounding privacy of information

> List and explain the meaning of the OECD Fair Information Practices

> Compare privacy in the United States to the European Union privacy practices

> Discuss the issues of disagreement concerning privacy: Opt-in/Opt-out and compliance/enforcement

> Explain the security methods used in public key cryptosystems (PKCs), in particular, in the RSA system

> Perform simple encryption from cleartext to cipher text and perform the reverse decryption

SHHH, IT'S A SECRET
Privacy and Digital Security

I've never looked through a keyhole without finding someone was looking back.

—JUDY GARLAND,
COMMENTING ON HER LACK OF PRIVACY, 1967

PRIVACY is a fundamental human right. The United Nations Universal Declaration of Human Rights recognizes privacy in Article 12. The constitutions of Australia, Hungary, and South Africa, among others, state a right to privacy. Though privacy is not explicitly mentioned in the US Constitution, the US Supreme Court has accepted privacy as a right implied by other constitutional guarantees. And privacy is a right that matters to us all. No matter how exemplary our life may be, there are aspects of it we would prefer to keep secret. And they are no one else's business. When those aspects interact with information technology, the issues of electronic privacy and security become important. There is much more than our passwords that we want to keep to ourselves.

In this chapter we discuss privacy and security. To begin, we consider a business transaction as a basis for understanding the topic of privacy and for considering who has an interest in private information. We consider different definitions of privacy, adopting a clear, but abstract definition. We look at how private information can be kept private, and we list the principles of privacy, including the principles from the Organization for Economic Cooperation and Development. Then we explore the differences between how the principles are followed in the United States and in other countries, including a disagreement between the United States and the European Union over these principles. Next we consider how cookies can be abused to compromise Web users' security. Finally, we discuss the problem of identity theft.

The next topic is encryption. After learning encryption vocabulary, we study a simple encryption example. Public key cryptosystems (PKC) are studied as a means of achieving more convenient security for Internet-related situations. PKC systems seem at first to offer almost no protection, and then they seem to offer so much protection that it's impossible to decrypt what was encrypted. This dilemma is resolved for the RSA public key system. We explore the matter of compromising RSA's security, with the outcome that 100 billion computers wouldn't really help!

Finally, we consider how to keep your information secure from computer failures.

● PRIVACY: WHOSE INFORMATION IS IT?

Buying a product at a store generates a transaction, which produces information. The merchant can gather the date and time of the purchase, the product, the cost, and possibly information about other products in the same "market basket." Is this information connected to a specific customer? Paying with cash generally assures anonymity, that is, the buyer is not connected with the purchase, though cash payments in small towns or even in neighborhood stores where "everyone knows everyone" probably aren't anonymous. However, other transactions can definitely link the purchase with the customer:

> > Paying by check, credit card, or debit card

> > Purchasing through mail order or on the Internet

> > Providing a "preferred customer" number

> > Buying a product that must be registered for a service agreement or warranty

If you're buying socks, you probably don't care if this information is recorded. If you're buying *Dating for Total Dummies*, you probably do. You want your purchase of the book to be private.

But what is private? It's not easy to define; we'll give a formal definition later. For now, we'll examine the *Dating for Total Dummies* transaction.

How Can the Information Be Used?

The book merchant, who accepts your check for *Dating for Total Dummies*, can reasonably claim that gathering the transaction information is a normal part of conducting business (keeping a record until the check clears), and so the information belongs to the store, or at least doesn't belong to you alone. If the bookstore decides, based on the information from this transaction, to send you an advertisement—"*Improve Your Love Life* Spring Sale"—the store is using the information for the standard business practice of generating more business. You may even be happy to receive the advertisement. But even if you're not, using "customer information" is so established—it's probably been used since merchandizing began—that few would claim the store misused the information. If the merchant sells your name and lovelorn status to the local florists, movie theaters, restaurants, cosmetic surgeons, and so forth, has the information been misused? They are only trying to generate more business, too. Is it misused if the information gets to the campus newspaper, where it is published? Has the store broken the law? (The United States differs from Europe in this respect.) Can't you just be left alone to upgrade your dating skills in peace?

Modern Devices and Privacy

Justice Louis D. Brandeis would have sympathized with your wish. He described privacy as the individual's "right to be left alone." He also wrote (with Samuel D. Warren) in the *Harvard Law Review*:

> *The narrower doctrine [of privacy] may have satisfied the demands of society at a time when the abuse to be guarded against could rarely have arisen without violating a contract or a special confidence; but now that* **modern devices** *afford abundant opportunities for the perpetration of such wrongs without any participation of the injured party, the protection granted by the law must be placed upon a broader foundation. [Emphasis added]*

This argues that, in the past, it was hard for people's privacy to be violated without their knowledge, but using *modern devices*, people's privacy can be violated without their knowing it. The amazing thing about Warren and Brandeis' comments is that they were written in 1890. The modern devices they referred to were the first portable cameras and the faster film permitting short exposure photographs. They continued,

> *While, for instance, the state of the photographic art was such that one's picture could seldom be taken without his consciously "sitting" for the purpose, the law of contract or of trust might afford the prudent man sufficient safeguards against the improper circulation of his portrait; but since the latest advances in photographic art have rendered it possible to take pictures surreptitiously, the doctrines of contract and of trust are inadequate to support the required protection.*

What would Warren and Brandeis have thought about the ever-present surveillance camera? Their important point is that your image—and more generally information about you—deserves "sufficient safeguards against improper circulation." It's a nineteenth-century formulation of a twenty-first-century concern.

Controlling the Use of Information

The *Dating for Total Dummies* problem comes down to, "Who controls the use, if any, of the transaction information?" There is a spectrum spanning four main possibilities:

1. **No Uses.** The information ought to be deleted when the store is finished with it (for example, when the check has cleared the bank), because there is no further use of it.

2. **Approval or Opt-in.** The store can use it for other purposes, but only if you approve the use.

3. **Objection or Opt-out.** The store can use it for other purposes, but not if you object to a use.

4. **No Limits.** The information can be used any way the store chooses.

The spectrum, which ranges from No Uses to No Limits, includes other intermediate points, too.

There is also a fifth possibility, call it **internal use**, where the store can use the information to conduct business with you, but for no other use. "Conducting business with you" might mean keeping your address on file so that they can send you announcements about book readings. It would not include giving or selling your information to another person or business, but it may not require your approval either.

fitBYTE — **Australian Perspective.** The Preamble to the Australian Privacy Charter states, "A free and democratic people requires respect for the autonomy of individuals, and limits on the power of both state and private organizations to intrude on that autonomy . . . . Privacy is a basic human right and the reasonable expectation of every person."

If the transaction took place in Europe, New Zealand, Australia, Canada, Hong Kong, or several other countries, the law and standards would place it between (1) and (2), but very close to (1). If the transaction occurred in the United States, the law and standards would place it between (3) and (4), but very close to (4). Perhaps of greater concern, many Americans apparently *assume* that there is a privacy law that is close to the fifth case, internal use. We will return to these different standards in a later section, but first we must understand the concept of privacy.

A PRIVACY DEFINITION

As important as it is, privacy is difficult to define. It is more than Brandeis' right "to be left alone." Generally, privacy concerns four aspects of our lives: our bodies, territory, personal information, and communication. Of these only the last two concern us here. We adopt the definition

> **Privacy:** The right of people to choose freely under what circumstances and to what extent they will reveal themselves, their attitude, and their behavior to others.

The definition emphasizes first that it is the person who decides the "circumstances" and the "extent" to which information is revealed, not anyone else. The person has the control. Second, it emphasizes that the range of features over which the person controls the information embodies every aspect of the person—themselves, their attitudes, and their behaviors. Adopting such an inclusive definition is essential for covering situations of importance. For example, buying *Dating for Total Dummies* was an act, covered by behavior, included in our privacy definition. Notice that it doesn't automatically imply the No Uses classification. We may decide that the fact that the book was paid for with a check rather than cash—that is, with an identifying form of payment as opposed to an anonymous one—was evidence of a willingness by the buyer to reveal the fact of the purchase. Or we could decide that the form of payment has no bearing on whether the information should be revealed; permission to reveal it must be explicitly given.

Threats to Privacy

Now that we have the definition, what are the threats to privacy? There are only two basic threats: government and business. A third threat, snooping or gossiping private parties, will be handled by security, that is, by keeping the information private. Historically, the governmental threat—a regime spying on its citizens—worries people the most, probably because when it happens the consequences are so serious. The business threat is a more recent worry, and its IT aspects even newer still. There are two types of business threats: surveillance of employees and the use of business-related information, including transaction information, for other purposes.

Voluntary Disclosure

A person can in principle enjoy perfect privacy by simply deciding not to reveal anything to anyone; that is, to be a hermit, though that probably would mean living alone on a remote island, surviving on coconuts and clams. But most of us interact with many people and organizations—businesses, our employer, and governments—to whom it is in our interest to reveal private information. That is, we freely choose to reveal information in exchange for real benefits.

> We tell our doctors many personal facts about ourselves so they can help us stay healthy.

> We allow credit card companies to check our credit record in exchange for the convenience of paying with a card.

> We permit our employer to read email we send at work, understanding that we are using the employer's computer, Internet connection, and time; that the email system is there for us to use on the job; and that we have no need or intent to send personal email.

> We reveal to the government—though not in the United States—our religion, our parents' names and birthplaces, our race and ethnicity, and so on for the purposes of enjoying the rights of citizenship.

How private can we be when we reveal so much about ourselves, our attitudes, and our behavior?

FAIR INFORMATION PRACTICES

It is possible to reveal information about ourselves and still enjoy considerable privacy, but it depends on what happens to the information after we've revealed it to other people and organizations. If they keep the information confidential, use it only for the purposes for which they gathered it, and protect it from all threats, our privacy is not seriously compromised. We receive the benefits and preserve our privacy. It's a good deal.

But if those people or organizations are free to give or sell the information to anyone else, they are also revealing information about us. Our privacy is compromised. It's not enough to trust the people we give the information to. There must be clear guidelines adopted for handling private information, so that we have standards by which to judge whether the trust is warranted. For that we have the Fair Information Practices principles.

OECD Fair Information Practices

In 1980 the Organization of Economic Cooperation and Development (OECD)—an organization of 29 countries concerned with international trade—developed an eight-point list of privacy principles that became known as the Fair Information Practices. They have become a widely accepted standard, forming a reasonably complete solution to the problem of keeping information private while at the same time revealing appropriate information to businesses and governments. The public has an interest in these principles becoming law. The principles also give a standard that businesses and governments can meet as a "due diligence test" for protecting citizens' rights of privacy, thereby protecting themselves from criticism or legal action. The OECD principles are a practical implementation of privacy protection.

The OECD Fair Information Practices principles are as follows.

> **Limited Collection Principle**: There should be limits to the personal data collected about anyone; data should be collected by fair and lawful means; and it should be collected with the knowledge and consent of the person whenever appropriate and possible.

> **Quality Principle**: Personal data gathered should be relevant to the purposes for which it is used, and should be accurate, complete, and up-to-date.

> **Purpose Principle**: The purposes for collecting personal data should be stated when it is collected, and the uses should be limited to those purposes.

> **Use Limitation Principle**: Personal data should not be disclosed or used for purposes other than stated in the Purpose Principle, except with the consent of the individual or by the authority of law.

> **Security Principle**: Personal data should be protected by reasonable security measures against risks of disclosure, unauthorized access, misuse, modification, destruction, or loss.

> **Openness Principle**: There should be general openness of policies and practices about personal data collection, making it possible to know of

its existence, kind, and purpose of use, as well as the identity and contact information for the data controller.

> **Participation Principle:** An individual should be able to (a) determine whether the data controller has information about him or her, and (b) discover what it is in a timely manner, in an understandable form, and at a reasonable charge (if any). If the enquiry is denied, the individual should be allowed to find out why and be able to challenge the denial. Further, the individual can challenge the data relating to him or her, and if successful, have the data erased, completed, or changed.

> **Accountability Principle:** The data controller should be accountable for complying with these principles.

An important aspect of the OECD principles is the concept that the **data controller**, a person or office that sets the policies, must interact with individuals about their information, if any, and must be accountable for those policies and actions.

COMPARING PRIVACY ACROSS THE ATLANTIC

Despite being a fundamental human right, privacy is not enjoyed in much of the world at the OECD standard for both government- and business-held information. This is somewhat surprising because privacy is well understood, its IT implications are clear, and all that's left is to enact laws and enforce them. What's the problem?

Privacy often comes in conflict with private or governmental interests. For example, the United States has not adopted the OECD principles, despite being a major player in the OECD and having created earlier principles on which the Fair Information Practices are based. It can be presumed that this is because many US companies profit by gathering and collating information, or by buying and using information in ways that are inconsistent with the OECD principles. Similarly, the Chinese government isn't going to protect the right to privacy when it denies other basic human rights. The rights to privacy for these countries' citizens are thus diminished. Globalization may change that.

In 1995, in a landmark advancement for privacy, the European Union issued the European Data Protection Directive, a benchmark law incorporating the OECD principles. The member countries have enacted this law giving everyone in the EU the same high level of privacy.

Many non-EU countries, such as Australia, New Zealand, Canada, Hong Kong, and non-EU European countries have adopted laws based on OECD principles. This is important because one provision in the EU Directive requires that data about EU citizens be protected by the standards of the law even when it leaves their country. Non-EU countries that want information on EU citizens must show that they have privacy laws consistent with the OECD principles. Switzerland, a non-EU country, applied and was approved. The United States applied and was not. What sorts of laws protect US privacy?

---

fit **TTP**

Private Comparison. A good way to check your understanding of the OECD guidelines is to compare them with industry voluntary compliance guidelines, such as the Online Privacy Alliance, `www.privacyalliance.org/resources/`. Can you find differences? Can you find similarities?

US Laws Protecting Privacy

The United States passed the Privacy Act of 1974, a strong limit on the government's ability to invade people's privacy. (The US Patriot Act of 2002 has weakened its protections.) This covers half of the privacy problem—interactions with *government*. But the reason the United States failed to meet the requirements of the EU Directive concerns information stored by *businesses*.

By contrast to the "omnibus" solution of adopting the OECD list, the United States uses an approach called "sectoral," meaning that it passes laws to deal with specific industries (business sectors) or practices. Examples include:

> Electronic Communication Privacy Act of 1986

> Video Privacy Protection Act of 1988

> Telephone Consumer Protection Act of 1991

> Driver's Privacy Protection Act of 1994

To illustrate, the Driver's Privacy Protection Act makes it illegal for motor vehicle registration departments to make information publicly available. Mass marketers once used motor vehicle information to create mailing lists. (Driving an expensive car might imply that you have a large income.) Now, the DMV must *get permission from the registrant* before making the information available for any purpose other than registering cars.

---

fit **BYTE**

Don't Ask. When the Supreme Court upheld the constitutionality of the Driver's Privacy Protection Act, the *Wall Street Journal* quoted a mass marketing industry spokesman as saying it was "death to us . . . If you can't use information about a person without permission, that generally means you're not going to have a list of any great substance." That is, using information without permission is essential to mass marketing.

The sectoral approach, though it often provides very strong privacy protections in specific narrow cases, leaves much information unprotected. By contrast, an omnibus solution provides consistent protection to all information. Citizens do not have to wonder whether specific information is safe.

Privacy Principles: European Union

The differences in privacy laws between the US and the EU is a serious problem for multinational companies and Internet and Web-based businesses. A company cannot move data from a EU country to the United States until the United States meets the OECD principles. (Non-EU states subscribing to the OECD principles would probably object, too.)

The Federal Trade Commission and the EU have been negotiating for years to solve this problem. A tentative agreement was founded on a concept called a Safe Harbor, which means a US company that follows the rules of the agreement can receive information from the EU. The FTC Safe Harbor guidelines are much weaker than the OECD principles. There are two glaring points of disagreement—Opt-in/Opt-out and compliance/enforcement—that are causing most of the difficulties.

Opt-in/Opt-out refers to the approval and objection aspects of privacy as illustrated in our *Dating for Total Dummies* example. That is, when can an organization use information it collects for one purpose for a different purpose? "Opt-in" means the business cannot use it unless the person explicitly allows the new use. "Opt-out" means the business can use it unless the person explicitly prohibits the new use. Privacy principles as far back as 1972 have consistently required Opt-in for all changes in use because otherwise the person does not control the use of private information. (Opt-in is actually a longer-standing principle than stated. Warren and Brandeis' 1892 concept of a "special confidence" between photographers and their subjects protecting their privacy amounts to Opt-in. That is, the photographer would violate the confidence unless he or she asked for and received permission from the subject first.) It was the Opt-in requirement of the motor vehicle registration act that caused predictions of "death" by the mass marketing spokesman. The FTC guidelines, however, require Opt-in only for highly sensitive information like medical data; Opt-out is the standard in the US—and opposite of the OECD guidelines.

Compliance/Enforcement refers to how organizations meet their obligations under the principles, that is, how the role of the data controller is implemented. The EU and other OECD-subscribing countries have introduced offices to perform the duties of the data controller. There is no such person or office in the United States. The FTC proposes that US companies "comply voluntarily," as a result of "market pressure." Private firms like TRUSTe and private agencies like the Better Business Bureau would do the monitoring. These private agencies and firms would then report violations to the FTC, but privacy advocates point out that such a voluntary process amounts to no enforcement at all. The EU apparently agrees.

These privacy issues are important to both sides. Without Opt-in and enforcement, the OECD principles are badly eroded. But with those requirements, industries like direct marketing are by their own description, mortally affected. At last check, the stalemate continues.

fit BYTE

Voluntary Compliance? Privacy consultant Richard M. Smith discovered in November 1999 that Real Networks' JukeBox software was gathering music taste profiles based on users' unique IDs. The company had a privacy policy, but it did not mention the unique ID or the profiling activity, *until he caught them.* Further, Real Networks had hired the audit firm TRUSTe.

A Privacy Success Story

Americans' electronic privacy has become dramatically worse since 2000 with spam, spyware, identity theft, exploits, phishing, etc., but there is a success story. Unfortunately, the story also illustrates that, in the context of privacy, "voluntary compliance." doesn't work.

Consider the history of the Do-Not-Call List. In the 1990s households would receive numerous calls every evening from telemarketers trying to sell products. Though Americans hated the calls and heaped criticism and scorn on telemarketers, the calls only got worse. People didn't do anything about it. Why? Because the "industry self-policing" mechanism was a little-known system requiring a person either (a) to write a letter to the industry association—you couldn't even call, despite the fact it was a telemarketing association—or (b) to opt-out online by paying a fee using a credit card. That is, people had to pay to stop being harassed by the telemarketers! And even then, these actions only stopped the telemarketers that belonged to that association. Despite these difficulties, five million households put their phone numbers on the list.

Finally, the problem got so bad that the US government set up the Do-Not-Call List, a central place where people could simply give their phone number—by phone or online—to stop telemarketers. The list was an instant success! Ten million households opted-out on the first day of operation. Today there are over 80,000,000 households on the Do-Not-Call List. And, of course, the telemarketing business has largely collapsed.

fit CAUTION

Partial Success. Voluntary compliance has succeeded in getting Web sites to publish privacy policies. It's a small accomplishment, because the privacy policies don't imply any assurance of privacy, as the Real Networks example shows. A 2003 Annenberg survey found that 57 percent of those polled thought (mistakenly) that a site with a privacy policy does not share data with other organizations. But privacy policies are all different. Some are strong; others simply explain that information *is* shared with other organizations, often in terms that make it sound like that's exactly what you would like them to do. So, read the policies carefully, or for quicker results, search for "opt" to find the place where they tell you how to opt out of their data "sharing."

There was no economic incentive for telemarketers to make it easy for people to opt-out, though history proves it was easy to do. So, rather than setting up a way for Americans to be left alone—as Brandeis wished—to enjoy dinner without the interruption of telemarketing calls, the industry association "voluntarily complied" by making it difficult and ineffective to opt-out. There is no reason to think Internet information gatherers are any different.

● THE COOKIE MONSTER

Cookies are a standard computer science concept originally used by Netscape engineers to connect the identity of a client across a series of independent client/server events. Here's the problem cookies solve.

Recall the Web server's view of the client/server relationship, as shown in Figure 17.1. Imagine this is your bank's server, and you are paying bills online, which makes you a client. The server is helping many clients at once, and to know who's who, the server stores a **cookie**—a record containing seven fields of information that uniquely identify a customer's session—on your computer. Many sites use cookies, even when the interaction is not intended to be as secure as a bank transaction. For example, the National Air and Space Museum sent me this cookie

```
www.nasm.si.edu   FALSE / FALSE   2052246450   CFTOKEN   89367880
```

while I was writing Chapter 3. The meaning of the fields is unimportant, except to note that the first is the server and the last is the unique information identifying my session. Cookies are exchanged between the client and the server on each transmission of information, allowing the server to know which of the many client computers is sending information. Cookies are an elegant way for servers to give clients the illusion they are the only one being served.

*fit***TIP**   **Finding Cookies.** Locate the cookies stored on your computer by searching for files and folders containing the string `cookie` or `cookies`. The files, maintained by a browser, can be opened using a basic ASCII text editor like **Notepad**, **TextEdit**, or **BBEdit**. College computers are often "wiped clean" after each session, so you may have to surf for a few minutes before any cookies are stored.

The reason users need to know about cookies is that they can be abused using a loophole called a *third-party cookie*. In principle, a cookie is exchanged between the client and the server making the interaction private. This privacy is enforced because browsers don't allow servers to check to see what other cookies are stored on your computer. Why would a server want to know? An online business might want to know if a customer has visited other similar businesses in the last few minutes to evaluate its competition and see how often it's the first place customers visit.

But there is a loophole. If the Web server includes advertisements on its page, it contracts with an ad company to create and place the ads. While the browser is setting up your page, the server directs it to link to the ad company—a third party—to deliver the ad. At that moment, your computer is in a client/server relationship with the ad company, and can allow it to place a cookie on your computer. You may have never heard of the ad company or be aware that it's placing information on your computer. If you visit a different server that uses the same ad company, it will also exchange cookies when it places its ads. Since the ad company gets the same cookie from your computer that it placed moments before for a different company, it knows that you visited the other company. By this means it is possible to log considerable information about a user's behavior. Is that bad? It's up to you to decide.

*fit*BYTE | **Many Double Clicks.** In June 2000 Richard M. Smith, a privacy consultant, testified before Congress that in the previous six months his computer had logged 250,000 Internet transactions, roughly 10 percent of which was traffic to a single Web advertising company, DoubleClick, allowing them to track the URLs of the sites he visited.

So, cookies are useful and essential for Web interactions with online banks and brokers. But, they can be abused. What can be done? All modern browsers allow users to control how cookies are processed. One possibility is to turn them off entirely, forcing the browser to ask you every time a server wants to send you a cookie whether you will accept it. Though it may be annoying, it is also very interesting to turn off cookie acceptance for a while to see how many cookies are sent, and from what servers. You'll be surprised. Turning cookies off prevents you from being able to bank online, but you can turn cookie acceptance back on when you want.

Browsers also allow users to automatically accept cookies from the servers they visit, but not to automatically accept them from third parties. Such a setting allows cookies to work as they were originally intended, since we are usually willing to accept cookies from a site we choose to visit. Though cookies are not the worst computer privacy risk users take, it is also easy to manage the risk by simply setting your browser's cookie policy at your own comfort level.

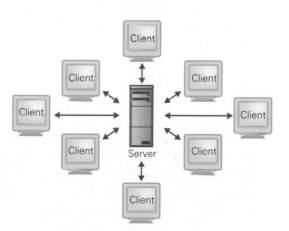

Figure 17.1. *Server's view of the client/server relationship.*

*fit***BYTE** | **Plain and Simple.** Companies that are serious about protecting your privacy say so simply, without complex and wordy privacy policies. For example, while Expedia.com is searching for airline flights in its database, it displays the message, "We do not lease or sell your information to anyone."

Identity Theft

We have focused most on the Use Limitation Principle of the Fair Information Practices, wherein a person decides whether to allow a use (Opt-in) that is different from the original use for which information was collected. But the Security Principle has become at least as important. The Security Principle states that those who hold private information are obligated to maintain its privacy against unauthorized access and other hazards. Americans do not enjoy protection from this principle either.

In February of 2005 the information broker ChoicePoint announced that personal data it holds on 145,000 Americans had been in the company's words "viewed by unauthorized parties." ChoicePoint keeps data on people's credit rating, and initially they only admitted that information on 32,000 people had been compromised. This smaller number apparently referred only to the Californians on the list, because California is the only state with a law requiring notification of security violations. Public pressure forced ChoicePoint to admit to and notify the larger population.

The Electronic Privacy Information Center (EPIC), a privacy watchdog, stated the situation more plainly, "ChoicePoint, which recently admitted it sold personal information on 145,000 Americans to identity thieves, also sold such information on at least 7,000 people to identity thieves in 2002." In an unrelated incident in March 2005 it was discovered that information about thousands of season-pass holders to Disney Japan had been stolen.

How can this private information be used? One possibility is **identity theft**—the crime of posing as someone else for fraudulent purposes. Because information from a company like ChoicePoint includes credit card numbers, social security numbers, bank account numbers, employers, etc., a thief has no more difficulty applying for a credit card or a loan than does the person whose information it actually is. It's the victim, however, who ends up with a ruined credit rating and large debts.

The identity theft issue has not yet been resolved. If the OECD guidelines were law in the US, ChoicePoint's failure to keep data secure from unauthorized access would be subject to penalties under the Accountability Principle; it is uncertain what penalties ChoicePoint faces under existing law. It is likely that identity theft will remain an issue for some time.

Identity Crisis. Chipmaker Intel introduced a unique ID for each Pentium III processor chip, but removed it under intense criticism. The ID would have greatly simplified the task of matching Web-collected data—it's like all .coms using the same cookie on a given machine.

Managing Your Privacy

Unfortunately our brief discussion about privacy threats has touched only a few high points. There are other assaults to our privacy to worry about. For example, **spyware**—software that monitors and records details of computer usage usually for some business—is a growing problem, about which you will want to consult your antivirus software vendor. What's a user to do about privacy?

The main obligation is to understand that in the US, protecting your privacy is your job; the laws are completely inadequate. Constructive actions can be recommended, however:

> Purchase up-to-date virus checking software, as described in Chapter 12, to minimize the unsavory critters that arrive by email.

> Adjust your cookie settings in your browser—they're under **Preferences > Security**—to match your comfort level.

> Read the privacy statement of any site to which you will give personally identifying information *before* you give it, including credit card information for a purchase. Though you may want to assume they will not share the information, a better assumption is that they will, until you see the place in their privacy policy where they say they do not.

> Review the five protections to avoid phishing scams given in Chapter 12, since being a victim of a phishing scam can make you vulnerable to identity theft.

> Patronize reputable companies for music, software, DVDs, and other downloaded files; file sharing is thought to be a major vector for spyware and other privacy-compromising software.

> Be skeptical. Paranoia isn't necessary, but skepticism is.

> Stay familiar with the current assaults on privacy; they're often announced in the national media, but it's a simple matter to find them at sites like EPIC (`www.epic.org`).

> As a final action item, perhaps Americans should be lobbying for US adoption of the Fair Information Practices.

Enter Your Salary. In a widely reported incident in 2000, Intuit was sued by customers of its Web-based Quicken mortgage software for disclosing to mass advertiser, DoubleClick, private information gathered when Web users computed mortgages at Intuit's site.

ENCRYPTION AND DECRYPTION

The best way to keep electronic information secret is to **digitally encrypt** it—that is, to transform the representation so it is no longer understandable.

Encryption Terminology

In Chapter 12 we saw encryption applied to passwords. We noted that if we forget our password, the superuser usually cannot tell us what it is because the software stores it in encrypted form—what we called scrambled. In a **cryptosystem**—a combination of encryption and decryption methods—the password is the **cleartext** or **plaintext**, that is, the information before encryption. The encrypted password is the **cipher text**, the encrypted form. Passwords use a **one-way cipher**—an encryption technique that cannot be easily reversed—because there's really no need to decrypt them: The system encrypts the password the user enters and compares it to the stored version, which is also encrypted. If they don't match as cipher text, they don't match as cleartext either. So, for password scrambling, the simple one-way encryption works.

Information is encrypted so it can be safely transmitted or stored. Transmitting or storing unencrypted information makes it vulnerable to snooping. Eventually, the cleartext must be recovered by reversing the encryption process, or **decrypting** the cipher text. In the diagram of the cryptosystem shown in Figure 17.2, the sender and receiver agree on a key, K_{SR}. The sender uses the key to encrypt the cleartext, and the receiver uses it to decrypt the cipher text. The key can be applied to the letters of the cleartext in various ways.

A common way is as follows: ASCII letters are treated as numbers using their bit representation and transformed by some mathematical operation with an inverse, say, multiplication, to produce the cipher text bits. That is, a few letters of the ASCII text are multiplied times the key and the resulting number is sent or stored. The cleartext can be recovered by applying the inverse operation (division by the key, in this case).

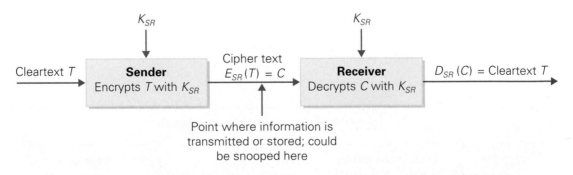

Figure 17.2. Schematic diagram of a cryptosystem. Using a key K_{SR} known only to them, the sender encrypts the cleartext information to produce a cipher text, and the receiver decrypts the cipher text to recover the cleartext.

XOR: An Encryption Operation

Exclusive OR, known as XOR, is an interesting way to apply a key to cleartext. XOR, which can be described as "*x* or *y* but not both," is written like an addition symbol in a circle, $\oplus$. It combines two bits by the rule: If the bits are the same, the result is 0; if the bits are different, the result is 1. Thus, if 0101 is the cleartext and 1001 is the key, then

```
  0101   Cleartext
⊕ 1001   Key
  ────────────
  1100   Cipher text
```

XOR produces 1100 for the cipher text. Applying the key to the cipher text again with XOR produces the original cleartext:

```
  1100   Cipher text
⊕ 1001   Key
  ────────────
  0101   Cleartext
```

Thus XOR is its own inverse.

Encrypting a Message. To illustrate encryption, imagine two students who have been writing messages to each other on the white board in the computer lab, but now they're worried that other people may be reading them, and so they decide to encrypt them. They agree on a key 0001 0111 0010 1101, and plan to encode pairs of ASCII letters by transforming them with the key using XOR. Here's what they do (see Figure 17.3).

Using the cleartext `Meet@12:15@Joe's`, they first write down the ASCII representation of these letters in pairs. (The ASCII representation is shown in Figure 8.6.) Next, they XOR each of these 16-bit sequences with their key sequence to produce the cipher text, which in this case has the ASCII equivalent of `ZHrYW`^F_S`%`$^E_\Sigma$`&`^C_N`WgxH0_`. This is the cipher text—a very strange sequence that should be secure to the casual observer in the computer lab. The cipher text can be easily decrypted using the same technique: XOR each of the ASCII equivalents of the cipher text with the key to produce the cleartext bits of the pairs. Then, look up the letters in the ASCII table. We can see that this scheme must always work by reviewing Figure 17.3 and using two facts:

> If any bit sequence is XORed with another bit sequence (the key) and the result is also XORed again with the key, that result is the original bit sequence.

> With XOR, it makes no difference whether the key is on the left or the right.

These facts mean that encrypting is moving from left to right in the figure, whereas decrypting would move from right to left.

Cleartext	Key	Cipher Text
Me 0100 1101 0110 0101		0101 1010 0100 1000 ZH
et 0110 0101 0111 0100		0111 0010 0101 1001 rY
@1 0100 0000 0011 0001		0101 0111 0001 1100 W^F_S
2: 0011 0010 0011 1010	⊕ 0001 0111 0010 1101 =	0010 0101 0001 0111 %E$_Σ$
15 0011 0001 0011 0101		0010 0110 0001 1000 &^C_N
@J 0100 0000 0100 1010		0101 0111 0110 0111 Wg
oe 0110 1111 0110 0101		0111 1000 0100 1000 xH
's 0010 0111 0111 0010		0011 0000 0101 1111 0_

Figure 17.3. *Encrypting the cleartext* `Meet@12:15@Joe's`, *using ASCII encoding of letter pairs, the key* `0001 0111 0010 1101`, *and the operation of exclusive OR to produce the cipher text* `ZHrYW`^F_S`%E`$_Σ$`&`^C_N`WgxH0_`. *(Decryption works in the opposite direction, as if the "⊕" and "=" symbols of the figure were exchanged.)*

Breaking the Code. How secure is the code? Probably not too secure, though being a cipher text of only 16 characters, a code cracker has very little to work with. The longer the text, the easier it is to decode, because once enough letters have been used, it's possible to notice what bit patterns show up frequently. Even in our short message there are two H's in the second position, corresponding to e's, and two W's in the first position, corresponding to @'s. Repeated W's are not very likely in a longer text, but repeated H's are.

As we know, *e* is the most common letter in English. Seeing these patterns and guessing that they correspond to *e* bytes, we can begin to figure out the cleartext from the cipher text by replacing each occurrence with *e*'s. (Naturally, **r** in the first position—the encoding of *e* with the first half of the key—will show up with roughly the same frequency.) In English, the 12 most common letters are e t a o i n s h r d l u. (Curiously, most people who remember this sequence do so by pronouncing it!) Other languages are different, of course. These dozen letters represent about 80 percent of the letters in the average English text. Using these letters, we can replace the dozen most frequently occurring (left and right) patterns. Decrypting that many letters of a cipher text would make decrypting the remainder a simple *Wheel-of-Fortune* endgame. We would have broken the code without ever knowing that the two students had used XOR as the encryption operation, or what the key was. The only property we used was that the students' code consistently replaced each letter with one of two patterns. Clearly they had better be smarter next time!

*fit***BYTE**

Tse Beht of Tnmeh. The frequency count for English is not fixed, of course. Different sources produce somewhat different results, even for large documents. For example, *A Tale of Two Cities* contains more than half a million letters that are distributed from greatest to least frequency: e t a o n i h s r d l u. That is, *n* and *i* are swapped, and *s* and *h* are swapped from the standard distribution.

Being smarter about byte-for-byte substitutions is easy to do. For example, grouping more than two bytes will help our student encoders. The harder problem is that the sender and the receiver have to agree on the key *ahead of time*. That is, they had to meet or at least communicate for the purpose of selecting the key. If they don't meet, but communicate instead, that communication isn't secure because there is no agreed upon key yet. Key exchange would be a showstopper for applications like Internet commerce, where credit card numbers should be kept secret, but the customer and the company cannot meet, perhaps because they are on opposite sides of the planet. The problem is beautifully solved using public key encryption.

PUBLIC KEY CRYPTOSYSTEMS

In a public key cryptosystem (PKC), people who want to receive secure information publish a key that senders should use to encrypt messages. For example, the key could be published on a Web page. Imagine that the key is 129 digits long and the senders are told to cube 32-byte groups of ASCII letters—yes, treat the bits like a 256-bit number and raise it to the third power—divide the result by the key, and send the remainder (that is, the bits smaller than the key that are left over from the division). The key was chosen so that the receiver, but not the general public or a code cracker, can decrypt it. If we change Figure 17.2 to a public key encryption, we get Figure 17.4.

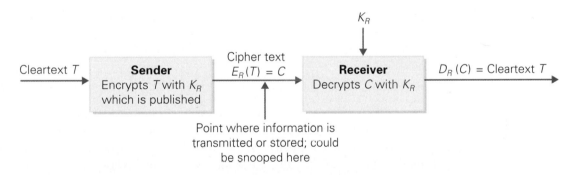

Figure 17.4. *Public key cryptosystem. The sender uses the receiver's public key K_R to encrypt the cleartext, and only the receiver is able to decrypt it to recover the cleartext.*

*fit*BYTE | **Public Spirited.** Computer scientists Whitfield Diffie and Martin Helman invented public key cryptosystems in 1976.

Code Cracker's Problem

The bad guy who is trying to snoop the communication by intercepting the cipher text and decrypting it knows the key, too, because it's published on the Web page. And it would seem the bad guy has the same ability to perform arithmetic on the cipher text that the receiver does. How much security can there be when so much information is known?

But cracking the code isn't so easy. All that was sent was the **remainder**—the bits that were left over from the division.

Recall from middle school that the definition for division, *a/b*, is to satisfy the equation

$$a = b \cdot c + d$$

for *divisor b*, *quotient c*, that is, the result of the division, and *remainder d*. Further, *d* will be smaller than *b*. For example, 30/8 becomes

$$30 = 8 \cdot 3 + 6$$

which is the same as saying, "30 divided by 8 is 3 with a remainder of 6." This is called the **quotient-remainder** form of division. Substituting the variables of our encryption situation, the equation becomes

$$T^3 = K_R \cdot c + d$$

for cleartext *T* and some quotient *c* that doesn't interest us. Only *d*, the remainder, is sent.

Snooping and Decrypting

If the code cracker had the quotient *c and* the remainder *d*, he or she could simply multiply the quotient by the key ($K_R \cdot c$) and add in the remainder to produce T^3. Using a calculator to find the cube root gives the binary number of the 32-byte sequences. Presto! There's the original cleartext, *T*. But the snooper didn't get both the quotient and the remainder, only the remainder. So snooping is a lot tougher.

But now it doesn't look so good for the receiver. The receiver didn't get the quotient either, only the remainder, so how is he or she supposed to figure out what was sent? It seems that the message is so well encrypted *no one* can figure it out! Happily, Leonhard Euler, an eighteenth-century mathematician, and a few enterprising computer scientists, came to everyone's rescue—except, of course, the cracker.

RSA PUBLIC KEY CRYPTOSYSTEM

The **RSA public key cryptosystem** is the best known of the PKC systems. Named for its inventors, Ron Rivest, Adi Shamir, and Len Adleman, the RSA scheme is basically the same as the PKC scheme we just described. We need to learn enough about how it works to retrieve the original cleartext. *Why* it works relies on very deep mathematics and computer science that will not be described here. But it does work. It has withstood formidable attacks and will continue to as computers get faster. We'll describe the assaults on RSA after we give it a try.

*fit*BYTE	**Secret Prize.** Rivest, Shamir, and Adleman were awarded the 2003 Turing Award by the Association for Computing Machinery, computing's Nobel Prize, for their creation of the RSA cryptosystem.

The RSA scheme relies on prime numbers. Recall from middle school that **prime numbers** can only be divided evenly—that is, without a remainder—by 1 and themselves. So, the first few prime numbers are 2, 3, 5, 7, 11, 13, 17, 19, 23, 29, 31, . . .

Mathematicians adore prime numbers because they have amazing properties. The rest of us only know that prime numbers are the basic "atoms" of a whole number. Any number can be **factored** into primes in only one way. The factors of a number x are just whole numbers that when multiplied together give x. So, factors of 30 are

$1 \times 30 = 30$
$2 \times 15 = 30$
$3 \times 10 = 30$
$5 \times 6 = 30$
$2 \times 3 \times 5 = 30$

but only {2,3,5} are the prime factors of 30.

Choosing a Key

The secret of the RSA scheme, of course, is that the receiver didn't publish any random 129-digit sequence as the public key, K_R. The key has some special properties. Specifically, the public key must be the product of two different prime numbers, p and q,

$K_R = pq$

Because multiplying two numbers of roughly equal size produces a number twice as long, p and q must be about 64 or 65 digits long to produce the 129-digit public key of the example. Additionally, p and q, besides being long enough and prime, must also be 2 greater than a multiple of 3. It's a rather strange requirement, but essential, as we'll see in a moment. Many primes have this property. For example, 5 and 11 are 2 larger than multiples of 3, namely, 3 and 9. As a running example, take

$p = 5$
$q = 11$
$K_R = pq = 55.$

Encrypting a Message

To encrypt a cleartext, divide it into blocks—we'll use 6-bit blocks of the ASCII encoding for the running example, but they're usually many bytes long—cube the blocks, divide them by the public key, and transmit the remainders from the divisions. (We use 6-bit blocks just to keep the numbers small.)

Thus, to encrypt the amount of a credit card transaction,

****$0.02

the ASCII characters are expressed in their byte representation

0010 1010 0010 1010 0010 1010 0010 1010 0010 0100 0011 0000
0010 1110 0011 0000 0011 0010

and grouped into 6-bit blocks,

0010 1010 0010 1010 0010 1010 0010 1010 0010 0100 0011 0000
0010 1110 0011 0000 0011 0010

shown in white and blue.

Recalling from Chapter 11 that bits can be interpreted in any way that is convenient, our groups are interpreted as numbers

$T = 10, 34, 40, 42, 10, 34, 16, 48, 11, 35, 0, 50$

cubed,

$T^3 = 1000, 39304, 64000, 74088, 1000, 39304, 4096, 110592, 1331, 42875, 0, 125000$

divided by the key $K_R = 55$, and expressed in quotient, remainder form,

$$
\begin{aligned}
1000 &= 55 \cdot 18 + 10 \\
39304 &= 55 \cdot 714 + 34 \\
64000 &= 55 \cdot 1163 + 35 \\
74088 &= 55 \cdot 1347 + 3 \\
1000 &= 55 \cdot 18 + 10 \\
39304 &= 55 \cdot 714 + 34 \\
4096 &= 55 \cdot 74 + 26 \\
110592 &= 55 \cdot 2010 + 42 \\
1331 &= 55 \cdot 24 + 11 \\
42875 &= 55 \cdot 779 + 30 \\
0 &= 55 \cdot 0 + 0 \\
125000 &= 55 \cdot 2272 + 40
\end{aligned}
$$

And finally, only the remainders are kept to yield the cipher text

$C = 10, 34, 35, 3, 10, 34, 26, 42, 11, 30, 0, 40$

These numbers are the encrypted message to be sent. (The apparent coincidence that some of the cipher text numbers happened to be the same as their corresponding cleartext occurs because our example numbers (55) are so small. The result is still incomprehensibly scrambled.)

The Decryption Method

How does the receiver reconstruct the cleartext? First, we must compute the quantity

$$s = (1/3)(2(p-1)(q-1) + 1)$$

For our running example, this curious number is

$$s = (1/3) (2 \cdot 4 \cdot 10 + 1) = 81/3 = 27$$

To make s come out right, we added the requirement of "2 greater than a multiple of 3" when choosing p and q.

The amazing fact is that if the cipher text numbers C are each raised to the s power, C^s—that's right, C^{27} in our example—and divided by the key K_R, the remainders are the cleartext! That is, for some quotient c that we don't care about,

$$C^s = K_R \cdot c + T$$

which is *truly* the key to the RSA scheme.

Decrypting: $C = 10$. To demonstrate this amazing fact, take the first number of our cipher text

$$C = 10$$

and compute

$$C^s = C^{27} = 10^{27} = 1{,}000{,}000{,}000{,}000{,}000{,}000{,}000{,}000{,}000$$

which is not a binary number, but the huge decimal number of 1 followed by 27 zeros. Divide by $K_R = 55$ and express the result in the quotient-remainder form

$$1{,}000{,}000{,}000{,}000{,}000{,}000{,}000{,}000{,}000$$
$$= 55 \cdot 18{,}181{,}818{,}181{,}818{,}181{,}818{,}181{,}818 + 10$$

Thus, $T = 10$, so the first 6 bits of the cleartext must be 10 in binary, 001010, as can be checked.

Decrypting: $C = 3$. The numbers can get very large for us—encryption algorithms actually use several techniques, such as modular arithmetic, to avoid the large intermediate numbers—but let's try another example. The fourth term of the cipher text is

$$C = 3$$

which we can raise to the 27th power with a calculator to get

$$3^s = 3^{27} = 7{,}625{,}597{,}484{,}987$$

Dividing by the public key, K_R and expressing the result in the quotient-remainder form yields

7,625,597,484,987 = 55 · 138,647,226,999 + 42

implying that the fourth block of the text is binary for 42, or 101010, as can be verified. As a third example, we notice that everything works out right for the cipher text $C = 0$.

Why does the RSA work? Euler proved the following theorem in 1736. (This is the only occurrence of higher mathematics in this book. It isn't necessary to understand it. Simply accept that Euler's formula makes the RSA scheme work out.)

> **Theorem:** Let p and q be distinct primes, $K = pq$, $0 < T < K$, and $r > 0$. If $T^{r(p-1)(q-1)+1}$ is divided by K, the remainder is T.

For our use of Euler's formula, $r = 2$, because

$$(T^3)^s = (T^3)^{(1/3)[2\,(p-1)(q-1)+1]}$$
$$= T^{2(p-1)(q-1)+1}$$

Thus, when the cipher text—that is, the remainders—is raised to the s power and divided by the key, the cleartext is recovered.

Summarizing the RSA System

To summarize (our example version of the) RSA public key crypto scheme follows these steps:

1. **Publishing.** Select two different prime numbers, p and q, which are 2 larger than a multiple of 3, and define $K_R = pq$, the public key. Compute $s = (1/3)[2(p-1)(q-1)+1]$. Keep p, q, and s secret. Publish K_R where senders can find it.

2. **Encrypting.** Get the public key from the receiver, and break the cleartext bit-sequence into blocks according to the receiver's instructions, but less than K_R. Cube each block, divide each of the cubes by K_R, and send the remainders to the receiver as the cipher text.

3. **Decrypting.** Using the secret value s, raise each number in the cipher text to the s power, divide each result by K_R, and assemble the remainders into the blocks of the bit sequence of the cleartext.

Of course, humans don't do these calculations. Software does. And though the software is extremely sophisticated to perform these operations fast, the principles that the programs implement are embodied in these three steps.

RSA Security Challenge. Can RSA withstand attacks? Can anyone actually break the code? As far as is known, scientifically, a code cracker would have to figure out what s is to break the code. Constructing s is easy if the two primes p and q are known.

Factoring the Key. The problem of finding *s* reduces to factoring the public key K_R to discover *p* and *q*. But factoring large numbers is a computationally difficult problem, even for the world's fastest computers. It is the fact that factoring large numbers is so difficult that keeps the public key encryption schemes secure. Put another way, if the key is large enough, it can be published because there is no known way to factor it into its two prime components in any reasonable amount of time.

{ GREAT *fit* MOMENTS }

RSA's Challenge >>

In 1977, shortly after inventing their scheme, Rivest, Shamir, and Adleman issued a challenge to the world: Break the small cipher text they encrypted with their public key RSA129—the 129 refers to the number of digits of their key—and win $100. This was a bold challenge because, although there was no known way to factor a 129-digit key quickly, maybe someone could invent a better factoring algorithm. The best known method at the time wasn't much better than the grammar school technique of dividing consecutive prime numbers into the number, looking for one that divides evenly. If computer scientists were clever enough to come up with public key encryption in the first place, they could probably come up with better ways to factor.

In fact, in 1981 Carl Pomerance did invent a new factoring method that gave some hope, though all the while other computer scientists were trying to prove that the factoring process could never be improved much. Pomerance's algorithm was better, but it didn't crack the code. Eventually, Arjen Lenstra and Mark Manasse organized an effort, which in 1994, using better algorithms, the Internet, and the improved speed of computers, cracked the RSA129 cipher. Their strategy took eight months and used nearly a thousand computers from around the world. But this wasn't the end of public key cryptosystems. It only revealed the factors of a *single* public key.

Most of us don't have a thousand computers or eight months to spend trying to snoop a single credit card transaction. Even if the secret is extremely important—a missile code, for example, or the outcome of the final episode of a TV show—and the code cracker has the resources of the US government, the RSA scheme is still secure because all it takes to make things harder for code crackers is to increase the size of the key.

The difficulty of factoring increases dramatically as the key length grows. It has been estimated that increasing the key to 250 digits—that is, doubling its length—would increase the cracking time 100,000,000 times. Keys can be increased to 300 or 400 digits or more if one hundred million times harder is not enough. Larger keys do not seriously complicate the problem for the encryption and decryption processes compared to their impact on increasing the factoring time.

When RSA129 was cracked—an effort dubbed the largest computation of all time—everyone was waiting breathlessly to know what the secret message was. It turned out to be THE MAGIC WORDS ARE SQUEAMISH OSSIFRAGE.

Strong Encryption Techniques

Public key encryption techniques are known as **strong encryption**. The term is intended to convey the fact that a communicating party can use the technology to protect their communication so that no one else can read it. Period. From a national defense or crime fighting perspective, complete secrecy is of great concern. Agencies that protect society from internal and external threats have routinely snooped on those people and organizations that may cause harm. Because surveillance would be impossible if the "bad guys" got such technology, the US government has fought a long-running battle since the invention of PKC technology to keep it contained and out of the hands of "bad guys." This has never been a very realistic goal because papers describing the scientific foundations of the technology—including Diffie and Helman's original paper, "New Directions in Cryptography" (*IEEE Transactions on Information Theory* IT(22):644–654)—are published in scientific journals, which anyone with a respectable computer science education can read to build his or her own encryption software. On the other hand, security professionals probably have a point. It could be valuable to spy on people who are in the process of planning crimes or attacks.

Of course, most people don't write their own software—they buy it—and that probably includes most "bad guys." If cryptography software vendors had to give government agencies and law enforcement officials a way to break such codes, perhaps we could have both security and a defense against the "bad buys." How could that be? Doesn't breaking the code require earth-shaking discoveries in factoring? Not from the software vendor's point of view.

Two techniques that could be used are known as **trapdoor** and **key escrow**:

> **Trapdoor.** While the software is encrypting the cleartext, ways might be provided to bypass the security. When the cipher text is sent, the cleartext could also be sent to law-enforcement or security officials. The trapdoor would work like a telephone wiretap in that the "bad guys'" encryption software would be configured without their knowledge. Legal safeguards (a court-approved warrant) would be required to do so. Other trapdoor techniques exist.

> **Key escrow.** Knowing the key makes breaking the code easy, so a key escrow system would require encryption software to register the key (actually, the two prime numbers from which the key is created) with a third party, who would hold the primes in confidence. Then, if there is ever a need to break a code—law enforcement personnel having a court-approved warrant, for example, or your computer being toasted in a fire—the escrow agent could provide the two primes.

These two schemes could also be abused: Couldn't anyone with (legal or illegal) access to your computer open the trapdoor? Wouldn't the escrow company be a tantalizing target for criminals because it contains everyone's PKC keys? Neither of these schemes has satisfied security and other experts.

REDUNDANCY IS VERY, VERY, VERY GOOD

As the saying goes, "Life is uncertain; eat dessert first." Uncertainty poses physical security challenges for networking and computer use generally.

Uncertainty results from lightning strikes that cut power, earthquakes and other natural disasters, terrorist attacks, accidents, and simple entropy—the tendency of things to "run down." To the list of physical risks, add the potential logical problems of program bugs, operator errors—*How could I have done that?!*—computer viruses, worms, backdoor assaults, and many more. Each of us would like to avoid such disasters. Life is uncertain, so it makes sense to take precautions.

Businesses whose success depends on computers—that is, most businesses—archive files daily and store these backups off-site so the disaster that zaps the original information doesn't also zap the backup. These companies have a system recovery team to clean up after a disaster strikes. And often they have system redundancy, that is, multiple computers performing the same work, so that when one fails, another—a **hot spare**—is up and running.

> **fit TIP**
>
> **Alternate Superstition.** People can be superstitious, believing, for example, that thinking about a disaster can make it happen. Naturally, repressing such thoughts is sensible. But believing a different superstition—that taking precautions against disasters, like saving often, prevents them—may make more sense in IT. They're both superstitions, of course, but the second one reduces the harm when it turns out to be wrong, which it will.

A Fault Recovery Program for Business

Recovering information after a disaster is usually quite technical, beyond the scope of this book, but the basic idea is easy. Start by keeping a full copy of everything written on the system as of some date and time. This is a *full backup*. After that, create *partial backups* of the changes since the last full (or partial) backup. Eventually there will have been enough changes that another full backup should be made. How often partial backups are performed is usually decided by the cost, and grief, of losing all of the information since the last partial backup. It would be easier to have full backups every few minutes, but that's too much information to copy and save. However, too many partial backups can make reconstruction extremely tedious, so regular full backups are a good idea.

After a disaster, recover by installing the last full backup copy. Then re-create the state of the system by making the changes saved in the partial backups in order. Continue with each partial backup until the most recent. That's as close to "full recovery" as it's possible to get. All of the information since the most recent backup (full or partial) has been lost.

Backing Up a Personal Computer

Backups aren't just for business. If you work on a computer system that is managed by a professional staff (like most college systems), there is little need to worry about backups. The support staff nearly always takes care of backups, though you should check to be sure. However, backing up your own personal computer is your responsibility. There are two important points to think about regarding backups.

How and What to Back Up. First, to back up your own computer, you can buy software for the task. Such programs perform incremental backups, analogous to the full/partial strategy just discussed, and do so automatically. They usually write to your Zip drive or writeable CD. Such software can save a lot of headaches.

fit **CAUTION**

> **A Three-Line Sermon.** Disasters don't just happen to someone else. (I've had disk meltdowns writing each edition of *Fluency*.) Backups are truly important. Backup today. Amen.

Of course, you can do backups manually by simply copying your directories and files to a disk or CD. Remember, you do not have to back up information that:

> > Can be re-created from some permanent source, such as software

> > Was saved before but has not changed—last year's email archive, for example

> > You don't care about, like your Web cache or old versions of term papers

Most of us do not have much to back up if we do so every two or three months.

fit **TIP**

> **How Often?** No rule says when to back up. Organizations must follow a fixed schedule, but individuals can simply assess the risk of losing everything. Hard use makes laptops more likely to fail than desktops; very new and very old equipment is more likely to fail than a middle-aged system. There is always risk.

Recovering Deleted Information. The second thing about backups is that they prevent "delete from deleting." Here is why. An organization's support staff backs up files regularly, usually daily. They keep the information safe so fires and earthquakes will not harm it. And, they often keep it for a very long time so people can go back to find information that they deleted long ago. If you accidentally delete important files, file restoration is a very desirable and helpful service. So, deleting a file that is then archived means that it is not truly gone.

Of course, backups can save evidence of crime or other inappropriate behavior, too. Computer users have hastily deleted incriminating files in hopes of covering up undesirable activity only to learn later that the files can be completely re-created from the backups. Unlike paper files, digital copies of files are easy to create and cheap to store, so it can be difficult to eradicate all copies of digital information.

Email is especially dangerous if you're trying to hide inappropriate behavior, but it's especially helpful if you're trying to discover it: Two copies of email are produced immediately when the **Send** button is clicked—one in the sender's sent mail directory, and one somewhere else, which is probably impossible for the sender to delete. Further, if that mail is around more than a few hours it will probably be backed up. Of course, your own backups have this same permanence property. Perhaps the Information Age will promote better behavior.

---

fit **BYTE**

Gone, but Not Forgotten. Emptying trash on a personal computer is another example when delete does not truly delete. Computers keep a free list of available disk storage blocks, and take blocks from it whenever they write. Emptying trash usually adds the trashed files' blocks to the free list, allowing them to be reused but without changing their contents. Until the blocks are overwritten, experts can recover the information.

SUMMARY

After discussing a privacy scenario, we defined privacy as the right of individuals to choose freely under what circumstances and to what extent they will reveal themselves, their attitudes, and their behaviors. We learned that:

> Revealing personal information can be beneficial, so the people and organizations that receive that information must keep it private. The guidelines for keeping data private have been created by several organizations, including the Organization for Economic Cooperation and Development.

> Guidelines often conflict with the interests of business and government, so some countries like the United States have not adopted them. Because the US takes a sectoral approach to privacy, adopting laws only for specific business sectors or practices, much of the information collected on its citizens is not protected by OECD standards.

> There have been long-running negotiations between the EU and the United States regarding privacy standards. The dispute's two main sticking points are Opt-in/Opt-out and compliance/enforcement.

> The "third-party cookie" loophole allows companies to gather information; identity theft is an unresolved problem. The best way to manage privacy in the information age is to have OECD-grade privacy laws.

> Public key cryptography (PKC) is a straightforward idea built on familiar concepts.

> Computer scientists have not yet proved the invincibility of the RSA scheme, but it can be "made more secure" simply by increasing the size of the key. This has little effect on the encryption and decryption processes, but it greatly increases the problem of finding the prime factors that make up the key.

> Strong encryption methods worry defense and law enforcement officials, but to date the conflict between balancing those concerns with the interests of peaceful, law-abiding citizens has not been reconciled.

> Backing up computer files is an essential safeguard. It ensures that your files will survive for a long time, even if you don't want them to.

> Privacy and security topics have not been fully resolved in the public forum, and both pose daunting challenges. Laws and policies are still under construction. Privacy seems to be waiting for the broad adoption of the OCED safeguards for both business and government information gathering. Security seems to be waiting for a way for parties to communicate securely by mechanisms fully within their control, yet that can be compromised in extraordinary circumstances of public importance.

EXERCISES

Multiple Choice

1. For a business, the least restrictive use of private information is called
   A. No Uses
   B. Approval
   C. Objection
   D. No Limits

2. An individual faces the fewest potential invasions of privacy from the policy called
   A. No uses
   B. Approval
   C. Objection
   D. No Limits

3. Which of the following is an example of identity theft?
   A. taking a test for someone else
   B. swiping your older sibling's ID
   C. posing as someone you're not to vote
   D. all of the above

4. The Code of Fair Information Practices lacked
   A. methods for correcting mistakes
   B. legal penalties
   C. protection for children
   D. rules for gaining access to your own data

5. You discover that credit information on you is inaccurate. Which principle does this violate?
   A. Limited Collection
   B. Quality
   C. Security
   D. Openness

6. Which Fair Information Practice provides for ways to correct your faulty credit record?
   A. Quality
   B. Purpose
   C. Participation
   D. Accountability

7. Data on EU citizens is
   A. not as secure as data on Americans
   B. protected even outside of the EU
   C. not protected by OECD principles
   D. protected in Europe but not outside of it

8. The Driver's Privacy Protection Act
   A. prevents departments of motor vehicles from releasing private information
   B. prevents departments of motor vehicles from charging for information
   C. prevents departments of motor vehicles from releasing information without permission
   D. allows departments of motor vehicles to sell information, provided the buyer discloses how the information will be used

9. Information from people in EU countries can be shared outside of the EU, providing the business or government follows the principles of
   A. Don't ask, don't tell
   B. Safe Harbor
   C. Fair Information Practices
   D. Opt-in/Opt-out

10. If the cleartext is 1101 and the XOR key is 1001, the cipher is
    A. 1011
    B. 0100
    C. 0110
    D. 1110

11. XOR can be described as
    A. *x* and *y* or *x* or *y*
    B. *x* or *y*
    C. *x* or *y* but not both
    D. none of the above

12. Digital encryption is
    A. only used for passwords
    B. easily broken by computer experts
    C. the use of math to make communication unreadable to snoops
    D. all of the above

Short Answer

1. _____ is the right of people to choose freely under what circumstances and to what extent they will reveal themselves, their attitude, and their behavior to others.

2. In regards to information technology, privacy is primarily concerned with _____ and _____.

3. _____ is an anonymous form of payment.

4. The _____ serve as a guideline for protecting personal privacy in regards to international trade.

5. The _____ provides a benchmark by which businesses can measure how well they are protecting the privacy of individuals.

6. A(n) _____ is responsible for maintaining personal information and is held accountable for it.

7. The _____ is the European Union's law incorporating the OECD principles.

8. In the United States, _____ offers more protection than _____ for protecting personal information.

9. A(n) _____ is a combination encryption and decryption.

10. _____ or plaintext is information before it is encrypted.

11. Passwords generally use a(n) _____ because it's hard to reverse and there's little need to decrypt it.

12. The _____ cryptosystem is the best-known public key cryptosystem.

13. _____ is the crime of posing as someone else for fraudulent purposes.

14. _____ is software that monitors and records details of computer usage.

15. A(n) _____ is an incremental backup of all changes since the last backup.

16. A(n) _____ is the listing of available blocks that can be used to store files.

Exercises

1. What are the two types of business threats regarding privacy?

2. There are several national "sweepstakes" that deliver big prizes to the winners. To be a part of these contests, you must register and provide your address (so they can deliver your check on national TV!). What potential privacy concerns are involved with such contests?

3. Credit card companies track your transactions. How can they abuse this?

4. What flaws exist in a sectoral approach to privacy?

5. Based on existing legislation, who appears to have more influence, business or individuals?

6. Explain how a simple serial number stored in a cookie can be used to store personal information.

7. Is compliance without enforcement effective?

8. Discuss the different approaches to privacy taken by the European Union and the United States.

9. Discuss the loopholes between compliance and enforcement.

10. Using XOR and 10110110, determine the cipher for the ASCII text for THE MAGIC WORDS ARE SQUEAMISH OSSIFRAGE.

ALAN KAY is one of the earliest pioneers of personal computing, and his research continues today. In 1967–1969 Alan co-invented the FLEX Machine, one of the earliest modern desktops, and designed the "Dynabook," considered by many to be the prototype for the notebook computer. At Xerox PARC in the early 1970s Alan invented Smalltalk, the first complete dynamic object-oriented language, development, and operating system. There, he also invented the now ubiquitous overlapping window interface. Most of his contributions have been the result of trying to create better learning environments, mainly for children.

Alan has been a Xerox Fellow, Chief Scientist of Atari, Apple Fellow, and Disney Fellow. In 2002, he joined Hewlett-Packard as a Senior Fellow at HP Labs.

Alan has his BA in Mathematics and Molecular Biology with minor concentrations in English and Anthropology from the University of Colorado, 1966, and his MS and PhD in Computer Science from the University of Utah, 1968 and 1969.

You started out in show business. What led you to become a computer scientist?

I was a professional jazz musician with quite medium abilities for about 10 years and did some teaching of guitar in that period. My general background included an artistic and musical mother, a scientific and mathematical father, and a grandfather who wrote and illustrated many books. So I grew up interested in many things and didn't make much distinction between what are called the Arts and the Sciences. I came across a number of books about computers and how to build them as a teenager in the 1950s and when taking a computer aptitude test in the Air Force was an option, I took it, got a good score on it, and starting programming in the early 1960s.

In college I carried full majors in mathematics and biology and supported this by being a programmer at the National Center for Atmospheric Research in Boulder. I was also still playing jazz in clubs at this time.

I wound up at the University of Utah ARPA project for grad school in 1966 as a complete fluke without any planning or knowledge about ARPA. From the moment I got there and met Dave Evans I "got" what ARPA was trying to do and it was a huge stroke of "romance" that I responded to.

How does the musician in you continue to influence the computer scientist?

Analogies can often be misleading, but there are some interesting ones to be made between music and computing (and mathematics and biology). The big ones for me have been the large aesthetic content of music and math and a wish for computing to always be that beautiful, the textures of different kinds of things interacting over time, the incredible ratio of parsimony to effect, etc.

You are often talking about education and the art of teaching. Did someone in particular inspire your concept of the ideal teacher?

The initial ideas about "teaching people to think better—even qualitatively better" came from a number of science fiction novels, one of which led me to the General Semantics movement started by Alfred Korzybski. I also had one truly fantastic teacher in the fourth grade. She knew how to reach and realize the potential in the many different kinds of children in her classroom "without teaching," and she has been one of the main models for me for how to go about helping people learn.

You have said that "literacy is not just about being able to read street signs or medicine labels. It means being able to deal in the world of ideas." What does it mean to you for someone to be computer literate?

I like Frank Smith's general definition of literacy as something that starts with important ideas, finds ways to write them down in some kind of language, and helps develop more "readers and writers." The computer has ways of "writing" down representation systems of all kinds—it is a simulator and a metamedium. By metamedium, I mean that it is a holder of all the media you can think of, as well as ones you haven't thought of yet. Computer literacy is all about important ideas written and read as simulations. And the writing and reading are actually some kind of programming, where the programs—like mathematics or a musical score or an essay—are a means for expressing a powerful idea.

What many consider to be the prototype for the laptop computer is a machine you designed about 35 years ago, the Dynabook, yet, you often contend that the Dynabook is still a dream . . .

It is indeed now possible to not just make a physical Dynabook, but one with many more capabilities than my original conception. However, the physical part of the Dynabook is about 5 percent of the dream. In musical terms, we can now make the body of the violin but we are still struggling with the strings, fingerboard, and bow (the user interface that includes authoring) and we still only have a few instances of what the musical expression will be like (the content of the Dynabook). The other difficult part of the design is that we somehow want the early parts of the Dynabook experience to be a lot more value-laden and fun than learning to play the violin usually is. More importantly, we want users to keep experimenting, move on, and not get complacent as many do for example after learning to play three chords on the guitar.

What is Squeak?

Squeak is a vehicle for getting to better places in all the areas we've been discussing. It is derived from one of the last Xerox PARC Smalltalks and has been brought forward to twenty-first-century graphics, etc. It contains models of itself, which make it easy to port, and now exists on more than 25 platforms running "bit-identically" (exactly the same). From the computer science standpoint it is a little more interesting than most of the other stuff that is around but pretty much all of its ideas date from the 1970s, so its interesting features are more of a commentary on what didn't happen in computer science in the last 20 years.

We have now done and tested a child's environment that is working out pretty well, and contains a number of new language and structuring ideas. This has been used to implement a much more comprehensive adult/media authoring environment (a kind of super-duper Hypercard) that contains the child's environment as a subset. This is essentially what we think the Dynabook should be like, plus, you can now download it and use it for free.

You have said, "The best way to predict the future is to invent it." What advice do you have for students who are planning a career in the field of technology?

Gain wide perspective by majoring in something else while an undergraduate. Try to find partial answers to Bruner's 3 Mac OS questions: What makes humans human? How did we get that way? How can we become more so? In other words, try to understand civilization and the role that representation systems for ideas have played in the journey called "civilization."

part **4** PROBLEM SOLVING

OUR STUDY of information technology has already covered problem solving in several different forms. We have solved problems related to writing HTML, finding accurate information sources, answering research questions about Buckminster Fuller, debugging, designing a database for HAI! Adventure, and more. In all cases our main tool was logical reasoning applied to a specific situation. In Part 4 we'll become even more effective problem solvers.

Problem solving requires a problem and some medium or mechanism in which to produce a solution. For us, Web pages and familiar applications provide the problems, and JavaScript is our solution medium. The important part of our study—the part that transfers to other aspects of our lives—is neither the problems nor the solutions, but the process by which we find them.

Though problem solving is the "high-order bit" (i.e., most significant information), JavaScript is a programming language. Once you see how programs are written, you will have a better idea of how IT works, which will make you more operationally attuned, and a better user. And, the practical bonus from learning JavaScript is that it allows you to create much fancier Web pages.

18

GET WITH THE PROGRAM
Fundamental Concepts Expressed in JavaScript

learning objectives

> Tell the difference between name, value, and variable

> List three basic data types and the rules for specifying them in a program

> Explain the way in which the assignment statement changes a variable's value

> Write expressions using arithmetic, relational, and logical operators

> Write conditional and compound statements

chapter 18

GET WITH THE PROGRAM
Fundamental Concepts Expressed in JavaScript

Verbing weirds language.

–BILL WATTERSON, *CALVIN & HOBBES*

PROGRAMMING is a profession, yet we all need to know something about it to be effective computer users. This is analogous to medicine. Doctors and nurses are professionals, but we need to know something about their specialties—our bodies, disease symptoms, nutrition, first aid, and so forth—to care for ourselves and benefit fully from their care. In neither case do we need an expert's knowledge, and in both cases we could probably survive with near total ignorance. But knowing some of what the professionals know is unquestionably beneficial and worth learning, despite its technical nature.

What we need to know about programming is a fuller elaboration of the concepts already discussed in Chapter 10 on algorithms. These concepts are deep and subtle. We cannot expect to understand them fully the first time we meet them. Indeed, our goal is to change our thinking habits to be more "abstract." Just as we need experience writing, reading, and speaking a foreign language in order to acquire it, so too do we need experience writing, reading, and executing algorithms and programs to acquire the thought processes of computation.

After preliminary remarks, we present an example program. Though it might look like gibberish at the start, the plan is to introduce all of the concepts used in the program. We begin by explaining about names, variables, and declarations, giving ourselves the ability to refer to the program's data. Then we cover the types of data values: numbers, character strings, and Booleans. Next, we introduce assignment statements and expressions, so we can compute new values. The last concepts are compound statements for grouping and conditional statements for testing. With this list of concepts, we return to the program and work through its execution. By the end of the chapter, we'll be programming!

OVERVIEW: PROGRAMMING CONCEPTS

Programming is the act of formulating an algorithm or program. It entails developing a systematic means of solving a problem so that an agent—someone other than the programmer and usually a computer—can follow the instructions and produce the intended result for every input, every time. The agent must also be able to perform or execute the program without any intervention from the programmer. This means that all of the steps must be spelled out precisely and effectively, and that all contingencies must be planned for.

Programming actually requires thinking. But relying on thinking alone makes programming too difficult. Instead, in this and other chapters, we introduce basic programming concepts developed over the past 50 years. These are the tools you will need to formulate any computation. They are used daily by professional programmers. They not only simplify common programming tasks, but also help you write programs that are clear and complete and assist in managing the complexity of writing a program. When you understand these concepts, programming should be manageable, an interesting intellectual exercise like completing a crossword puzzle or figuring out whodunit in a murder mystery. It's really no harder than that.

Trying to program an algorithm precisely using English is hopeless. Natural languages are too ambiguous for directing anything as clueless as a computer. So, programming languages have been developed to help programmers in two ways: they are precise and they are specialized in using the concepts mentioned in the last paragraph. Using a programming language is actually easier than writing in English. We will use **JavaScript**, a recently developed programming language that is especially effective for Web applications. You won't become a JavaScript expert from reading this chapter, but you might learn enough to make a glitzy personal Web page.

This chapter introduces the following programming concepts:

> Names, values, variables

> Declarations

> Data types, numbers, string literals, and Booleans

> Assignment

> Expressions

> Conditionals

With just these few concepts, you will be able to write actual programs. The program in Figure 18.1 is an example. It probably looks like gibberish at this moment, but by the end of the chapter you'll be able to read and understand it. (We present it now to make it clear where we are headed, but skip it if it appears intimidating.)

Finally, in introducing the deep ideas of the chapter, we must set down the practical details of programming. These rules can be as burdensome as a chapter-long list of dos and don'ts. So, we skip the more obvious rules here—the ones you would guess intuitively—you can reference them in Appendix B. This allows us to emphasize the few rules that you cannot guess on your own. When in doubt, refer to Appendix B. All of the rules are listed there.

At the Espresso Stand

Espresso is concentrated liquid coffee produced by passing steam through finely ground coffee beans. Some people enjoy drinking espresso straight, but others prefer a café latté, espresso in steamed milk; a cappuccino, espresso in equal parts of steamed milk and milk foam; or an Americano, espresso in near-boiling water. Espresso drinks are sold in three sizes: short (8 oz.), tall (12 oz.), and grande (16 oz.). These drinks are made with a single unit of espresso, called a shot, but coffee addicts often order additional shots. The price of additional shots is added to the base price of the drink, and tax is figured in to produce the charge for the drink. The program to compute the price of an espresso drink is:

Input:

drink, a character string with one of the values: **"espresso"**, **"latte"**,
    "cappuccino", **"Americano"**
ounce, an integer, giving the size of the drink in ounces
shots, an integer, giving the number of shots

Output:

price in dollars of an order, including 8.8% sales tax

Program:

```
var price;
var taxRate = 0.088;
if (drink == "espresso")
    price = 1.40;
if (drink == "latte" || drink == "cappuccino") {
    if (ounce == 8)
        price = 1.95;
    if (ounce == 12)
        price = 2.35;
    if (ounce == 16)
        price = 2.75;
}
if (drink == "Americano")
    price = 1.20 + .30 * (ounce/8);
price = price + (shots - 1) * .50;
price = price + price * taxRate;
```

Figure 18.1. Sample JavaScript computation to figure the cost of espresso drinks.

NAMES, VALUES, AND VARIABLES

Though we are familiar with the concepts of a name (the letter sequence used to refer to something), and a value (the thing itself), in normal conversation we tend not to distinguish carefully between the two. Thus, when we use the letter sequences "Julia Roberts" or "Harrison Ford," we mean those specific movie stars. There are many people with those names, of course, and if your friend from geology class is also named Harrison Ford, that name has one value for you in the context of that class, and another in the context of the movies. People understand this distinction in everyday conversation. In everyday life we treat names as "bound to" their values.

Names Have Changing Values

Names and values are separable in programming. The best way to think of names and values in programming is to think of names as if they were offices or titles, or other designations purposely selected to have changing values. There are plenty of examples:

Name	Current Value (1/1/2005)	Previous Values
US President	George W. Bush	Bill Clinton, George Washington
US Supreme Court Chief Justice	William Rehnquist	Warren Burger, Earl Warren
James Bond	Pierce Brosnan	Sean Connery, Roger Moore
Queen of England	Elizabeth II	Victoria I, Elizabeth I
UN Secretary General	Kofi Annan	Boutros Boutros-Ghali, U Thant

The names used in the middle and right columns are, of course, the informal usage of names from everyday conversation.

The reason we focus on the case where the values associated with a name can change is because they change in programs. A program is a fixed specification of a process. As the process evolves and the program transforms data to produce new values, the old names must refer to these new values, i.e., the names have changed values. This is a natural result of the fixed specification of the process. So, for example, the US Constitution contains this specification of a process: "The President-elect will be sworn into office by the Chief Justice on the January 20 following the election." The intent of this command is to describe a process that applies no matter who wins the presidential election, that is, the value of "President-elect," and who is the senior justice of the Supreme Court on that date, that is, the value of "Chief Justice." We naturally interpret the US Constitution this way. The names "President-elect" and "Chief Justice" have changing values.

Names used in this way—a single letter sequence with a varying value—are an already familiar concept to us from our previous computing experience. The file named `EnglishPaper` changes its value every time you save a version of your composition. In computing, the name is always separable from the value and the value can be changed. It's a basic idea worth thinking about.

Names in a Program Are Called Variables

In programming terminology, the names just discussed are called **variables**, a term that reminds us that their values *vary*. For example, in the *Alphabetize CDs* program in Chapter 10, two variables, *Alpha* and *Beta*, were used. Nearly every step in that program changed the value of one or the other of those variables. That's typical. The most commonly used programming language operation is the command to change the value of a variable. That command is called **assignment**, and it will be discussed shortly.

> *fit***BYTE**
>
> **Names and Values.** We've seen one other example of names having multiple values over time. Memory locations—their names are called *addresses*—have different values at different times. This is not a coincidence. Variables *are* memory locations in the computer. Variables are simply a more readable and convenient way to reference computer memory than are the actual numerical addresses. The value of the address is the current contents of the memory location, and it is the value of the corresponding variable.

Identifiers and Their Rules

The letter sequence that makes up a variable's name is called the **identifier**. In every programming language, identifiers must have a particular form, although the form is somewhat different from language to language. Generally, identifiers must begin with a letter, followed by any sequence of letters, numerals (the digits 0 through 9), or the underscore symbol (_). (JavaScript permits slightly more general identifiers than suggested here, but throughout the book, tiny limitations are implied to make it easier to learn and to help avoid errors. There is no loss of expressiveness in programming.)

Identifiers are not allowed to contain spaces. The following are eight identifiers:

```
X
x
ru4it
nineteen_eighty_four
Time_O_Day
Identifiers_can_B_long_but_if_so_typing_them_can_be_a_pain
oO0OOo
elizaBETH
```

Notice two features of identifiers: The underscore symbol can be used as a word separator to make identifiers more readable, and identifiers in most programming languages, including JavaScript, are case sensitive, meaning that uppercase and lowercase letters are different.

*fit*BYTE   **Form Rules.** User IDs, logins, and email names follow similar rules, but with a few important differences. For example, login and email names often allow a dash (-), but variable names do not, because a dash could be confused with a minus sign.

A VARIABLE DECLARATION STATEMENT

Programs are usually written "starting from scratch." That is, when you begin to program, you can think of the computer as if it were newly manufactured; it knows nothing except how to understand the programming language. So the first thing to do when writing any program is to state what variables will be used. This is called **declaring variables**, and we do it using a command called a **declaration**. In JavaScript, the **declaration command** is the word **var**, short for *variable*, followed by a list of the identifiers to be declared separated by commas. For example, to write a computation that computes the area of a circle given its radius, we need variables **area** and **radius**. So we declare,

```
var radius, area;
```

This command *declares* that in the program we will use these two identifiers as variables. Notice that the first command in the espresso computation in Figure 18.1

```
var price;
```

is a variable declaration of this type. (The program uses other variables that will be explained momentarily.)

The declaration was just called a *command*, because it is commanding the computer to record which identifiers will be used as variables. But everything we tell a computer to do is a command, so we should call the declaration by its proper term, declaration **statement**.

The Statement Terminator

A program is simply a list of statements. Because we can't always write one statement per line as in a normal list, the statements are often run together, which means that each statement must be terminated by some punctuation symbol. The **statement terminator** in JavaScript is the semicolon (**;**). It's the same idea as terminating sentences in English with periods, question marks, or exclamation points. The main difference is this If I forget to terminate an English sentence, like I just did, you still understand—both from the meaning and from the capital letter beginning the next sentence—that the sentence is over, that is, terminated. The computer isn't that clever. It needs the semicolon. So, the rule is: Terminate every statement (including the statements introduced below) with a semicolon.

fit **TIP**

First Mistake. *Everyone* makes mistakes when programming. Everyone. One of the most common mistakes for beginners is to forget the semicolon. When the semicolon is missing the computer becomes confused and debugging is necessary. Remembering semicolons makes programming easier.

Rules for Declaring Variables

Every variable used in a program must be declared. JavaScript allows declaration statements anywhere in the list of program statements. But because variable declarations announce what variables *will* be used in the program, programmers like to place them first in the program. It's like saying, "Here's the list of variables I'll be using in the program that follows." We will declare variables first.

Undefined Values. The declaration states that the identifier is the name of a variable. But what is the name's value? It has no value at first! The value of a declared variable is not defined. It's a name that doesn't yet name anything. Similarly, when a group of people forms an intramural basketball team, say, Crunch, the intramural sports office can refer to the Crunch captain, even if the person who will be captain hasn't been chosen. The name is declared—it will be meaningful when the season is under way—but there is no value assigned yet. The value is **undefined**.

Initializing a Declaration. Often we know an **initial value** for the identifiers we declare. So JavaScript allows us to set the initial value as part of the declaration, that is, to **initialize** the variable. To declare that `taxRate` and `balanceDue` will be variables in the program, and that their initial values are .088 and 0, respectively, we write

```
var taxRate = .088;
var balanceDue = 0;
```

We don't have to declare and initialize just one variable at a time in the `var` statement. We can declare and initialize any number of variables by separating them with commas:

```
var taxRate = .088, balanceDue = 0;
```

The computer doesn't care which style is used. They're equivalent. Typically, programmers include several variables in a single declaration statement when the variables are logically related. This serves to remind programmers that the variables are related. For example, variables describing a person's features might be declared

```
var height, weight, hairColor, eyeColor, astrological_sign;
```

If the variables are not related, they are usually specified in separate statements. All approaches are equivalent; there is no "proper" way.

try it

The *Alphabetize CDs* program used two variables, *Alpha* and *Beta*. Give a JavaScript declaration statement to declare them.

Answer: `var Alpha, Beta;`

try it

What is the important difference between the preceding declaration and

`var beta, alpha;`

Answer: The use of uppercase and lowercase letters. Because JavaScript is case sensitive, the two statements declare different variables. (The order of the variables in a declaration is unimportant.)

THREE BASIC DATA TYPES OF JAVASCRIPT

We will use three types of data in our JavaScript programs: numbers, strings, and Booleans.

Rules for Writing Numbers

The values assigned to the variables `taxRate` and `balanceDue` are **numbers**. Like everything in programming, there are rules for writing numbers, but basically numbers are written in the "usual way." (Details are provided in Appendix B.)

One "unusual" aspect of numbers in programming is that there are no "units." We can't write `33%` or `$10.89`; we must write `0.33` and `10.89`. This explains why there are no dollar signs in the program in Figure 18.1 even though it is a computation to figure the price of a coffee drink in dollars. Standard computer numbers can have about ten significant digits and range from as small as 10^{-324} to as large as 10^{308}. (Numbers and computer arithmetic are unexpectedly subtle. Our uses of numbers will be trivial and avoid any difficulties. As a general rule, the "safe zone" is the range from 2 billionths to 2 billion plus or minus. Outside that range, we must learn more about computer arithmetic.)

Though computers frequently compute on numbers, they compute on other kinds of data as well.

Strings

For us, strings will be the most common kind of data. **Strings** are sequences of keyboard characters. For example, here are nine strings:

```
"abcdefghijklmnopqrstuvwxyz"        "May"   '!@#$%^&*()_+|}{:]['
"strings are surrounded by quotes"  " "     "M&M's"
'strings can contain blanks'        ""      '"No," she said.'
```

Notice that a string is always surrounded by single (') or double (") quotes.

Strings Can Initialize a Declaration. Like numbers, strings can be used to initialize variables in a declaration. For example,

```
var hairColor = "black", eyeColor = "brown",
    astrological_sign = "Leo";
```

We need strings when manipulating text, as when we're building Web pages, for example. The program in Figure 18.1 uses several string constants: `"espresso"`, `"latte"`, `"cappuccino"`, and `"Americano"`.

Rules for Writing Strings in JavaScript. The rules for writing strings in JavaScript, most of which can be seen in the examples above, are as follows:

1. Strings must be surrounded by quotes, either single (') or double (").

2. Most characters are allowed within quotes except the return character (Enter), backspace character, tab character, \, and two others (little used).

3. Double quoted strings can contain single quotes, and vice versa.

4. The apostrophe (') is the same as the single quote.

5. Any number of characters is allowed in a string.

6. The minimum number of characters in a string is zero (`""`), which is called the **empty string**.

Rule (3) lets us include quotes in a string. To use double quotes in a string, for example, we enclose the string in single quotes, as in `'He said, "No!"'`. If our string contains single quotes, we enclose it in double quotes, as in `"Guide to B&B's"`. Because the apostrophe is commonly used in English's possessives and contractions, it's a good idea to use double quotes as the default. This allows the free use of apostrophes. We change to single quotes only when the string contains double quotes. Both methods work, and the computer doesn't care which one we use.

Notice that by rule (6) the empty string is a legitimate value. That is, writing

```
var exValDef = "";
var exValUndef;
```

results in two quite different situations. After these two statements, if we ask the computer what kind of value `exValDef` has, the answer would be "a string," but the answer for `exValUndef` would be "an undefined value."

Literals. The numbers and strings discussed are known as either **string constants** or **string literals**. The term *literal* conveys the idea that the characters are typed literally in the program. So there are rules about how to write these values explicitly in a computation. However, when literals become the values of variables and are stored in the computer, the representation changes slightly, especially for strings.

String Literals Stored in the Computer. First, because the surrounding quotes or double quotes are used only to delimit the string literal, they are removed when the literal is stored in the computer. That's why the empty string `""` has a length of 0, rather than 2.

Second, any character can be stored in the computer memory. Specifically, although a prohibited character such as a tab character cannot be *typed* in a literal, it can be the value of a string in the computer. To do this we use the "escape" mechanism, which we discussed in Chapters 4 and 8.

For JavaScript, the escape symbol is the backslash (\) and the escape sequences are shown in Table 18.1. Thus we can write declarations such as

```
var fourTabs = "\t\t\t\t", backUp = "\b",
    bothQuotesInOne = "'\"";
```

which give values to the variables that cannot be typed literally. The escape sequences are converted to the single characters they represent when they are stored in the computer's memory. So, the lengths of the values of these three string variables are 4, 1, and 2, respectively.

Table 18.1. *Escape sequences for characters prohibited from string literals*

Seq.	Character	Seq.	Character
\b	Backspace	\f	Form feed
\n	New line	\r	Carriage return
\t	Tab	\'	Apostrophe or single quote
\"	Double quote	\\	Backslash

Boolean Values

Another kind of value is the **Boolean value (Booleans)**. Unlike numbers and strings, there are only two Boolean values: `true` and `false`. Boolean values have their obvious logical meaning. We should emphasize that although `true` and `false` are letter sequences, they are *values*, like 1 is a value, not identifiers or strings. Although Booleans are used implicitly throughout the programming process, as we'll see, they are used only occasionally for initializing variables. Examples might be

```
var foreignLanguageReq = false, mathReq = true, totalCredits = 0;
```

This last declaration illustrates that variables appearing in the same declaration can be initialized with different kinds of values.

> *fit* **BYTE**
>
> **It's True.** Boolean values get their name from George Boole. True. Boole was an English mathematician who invented true and false. False. True and false have been around since humans began to reason. Boole invented an algebra based on these two values that is basic to computer engineering and other fields.

The different kinds of values of a programming language are called its **data types** or its **value types** or simply its types. We have introduced three types for JavaScript: numbers, strings, and Booleans. There are several other types, but these are sufficient for most of what we will do in JavaScript. JavaScript is very kind to programmers with respect to types, as we will see later in the chapter.

> **try it**
>
> Declare variables (of your choosing) to describe literary personalities, and initialize them to values appropriate for Mark Twain: his real name, the century in which he wrote, whether he was a humorist, and a famous quotation.
>
> *Answer:*
> ```
> var real_first_name = 'Samuel', real_last_name = "Clemens";
> var humorist = true;
> var century = 19;
> var famous_quote = '"Nothing so needs reforming as other
>     people\'s habits."'
> ```
> Notice the use of escape apostrophe (`\'`) in `famous_quote`. It is required because the entire quotation is enclosed in single quotes to allow the text to include double quotes. In the computer's memory the value of `famous_quote` is the 54-character string:
>
> `"Nothing so needs reforming as other people's habits."`
>
> That is, the enclosing single quotes and the backslash are gone.

> *fit* **TIP**
>
> **Meta-Brackets.** In discussing programming languages, we often need to describe syntactic structures, such as declaration statements. To separate the language being defined from the language doing the defining, we enclose terms of the defining language in "angle brackets," (< >), known as **meta-brackets**. Thus, the general form of the preceding JavaScript declaration would be `var` *<variable name>* = *<initial value>*, where the symbols not in meta-brackets are written literally and symbols or words in the meta-brackets represent things of the sort indicated, as a kind of placeholder. Notice that these are *not* tags.

THE ASSIGNMENT STATEMENT

If variables are to change values in an algorithm or program, there should be a command to do so. The **assignment statement** changes a variable's value; it is the workhorse of programming.

An assignment statement has three parts that always occur in this order:

<variable> *<assignment symbol>* *<expression>***;**

Here *<variable>* is any declared variable in the program, *<assignment symbol>* is the language's notation for the assignment operation (discussed next), and *<expression>* is a kind of formula telling the computer how to compute the new value. Like any other statement, an assignment statement is terminated by a semicolon. JavaScript's *<assignment symbol>* is the equal sign (=), and we've already seen the assignment operation as the initializer for variable declarations.

Assignment Symbol

Different programming languages use different symbols for indicating assignment. The three most widely used symbols are the equal sign (=); the colon, equal sign pair (:=); and the left pointing arrow (←). There are others, but these are the most common. The := is considered a single symbol even though it is formed from two keyboard characters. Like JavaScript, most languages use = Pascal uses := and more mathematical languages like APL use ←. Regardless of which symbol the language uses, assignment is a standard and commonly used operation in every programming language.

An example assignment statement is

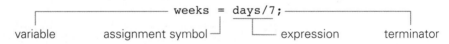

where **weeks** is the variable whose value is being changed, = is the assignment symbol, and **days/7** is the expression. Therefore, this assignment statement illustrates the standard form.

Interpreting an Assignment Statement

To understand how assignment works, you *must* think of a value flowing from the right side (expression side) of the assignment symbol to the left side (variable side). (This view makes the left arrow, ←, perhaps the most intuitive assignment symbol.) The **assignment symbol** should be read as "*is assigned*" or "*becomes*" or "*gets*." Therefore, our example can be read

> "the variable **weeks** *is assigned* the value resulting from dividing the value of the variable **days** by 7"

> "the value of **weeks** *becomes* the value resulting from dividing the value of the variable **days** by **7**"

> "the variable **weeks** *gets* the value resulting from dividing the value of the variable **days** by **7**"

*fit***BYTE**   **Get with the Program.** Most programmers prefer *gets* when reading assignments. It conveys the idea of filling a container, as in a "mailbox *gets* a letter" or a "flour tin *gets* refilled." The variable is the container.

Terms like *is assigned*, *becomes*, and *gets* emphasize the role that the assignment symbol plays, namely, to change the value of the variable named on the left side.

In an assignment statement, the expression (that is, everything to the right of the assignment symbol) is computed or evaluated first. If there are any variables used in the expression, their current values are used. This evaluation produces a value that then becomes the new value of the variable named on the left side. So, the effect of executing the example assignment statement

```
weeks = days/7;
```

is that the current value of the variable **days** is determined by looking in the memory (suppose it is **77**), and that value is divided by **7**, producing a new value, **11**. This is a new value that then becomes the new value of the variable **weeks**, that is, **weeks** is assigned **11**.

*fit***BYTE**   **Assignment to Memory.** In the computer, an assignment statement causes the value in the memory location(s) corresponding to the variable to be replaced by the new value resulting from the expression.

Three Key Points about Assignment

There are three key points to remember about assignment statements. First, all three of the components must be given; if anything is missing, the statement is meaningless. Second, the flow of the value to the name is always right to left. Thus the two variable names in the assignment statement

```
variable_receiving_new_value = newly_computed_value;
```

correctly show the motion of information. Notice that the expression can simply be some other variable; it doesn't have to be a complicated formula. Third, the values of any variables used in the expression are their values before the start of execution of the assignment. This point is extremely important because the variable being changed in the assignment statement might also be used in the expression.

For example, a program simulating a basketball game would probably use the assignment statement

```
totalScore = totalScore + 3;
```

for a basket from outside the three-point circle. When the expression on the right side of the assignment statement, `totalScore + 3`, is evaluated, the value of `totalScore` used in the computation is its value before starting this statement, that is, the score before the shot. When the assignment statement is completed, `totalScore` is the updated value reflecting the three-point shot.

Similarly, the program might contain the code

```
shotClock = shotClock - 1;
```

to implement the "tick" of the shot clock. Again, when evaluating the right side expression, the values used for variables are those before the statement is executed.

Repeating, because this is the most important of all of the ideas of this chapter: The role of = is to *assign* the value computed on the right side to be the new value of the variable named on the left side.

> **Programming Is Not Algebra.** Like algebra, many programming languages use an equal sign in assignments. In programming "=" is read "becomes," which suggests the dynamic meaning of right-to-left value flow. In algebra "=" is read "equals," which emphasizes the static meaning that both sides are identical. In programming, the statement "$x = x + 1$" means the value of x becomes 1 larger; in algebra, the equation "$x = x + 1$" is meaningless because there is no number that is identical to itself plus 1. The unknowns in algebra are names whose values do not change.

AN EXPRESSION AND ITS SYNTAX

Although programming is not mathematics, it has its roots in higher math. So, it is not surprising that one of the concepts in programming is an algebra-like formula called an **expression**. Expressions describe the means of performing the actual computation. As we've already seen (`days/7` is an expression), expressions are built out of variables and **operators**, which are standard arithmetic operations, such as addition or subtraction, found on the keys of a calculator.

The symbols of basic arithmetic are called the **arithmetic operators**. The actual symbols used for some operators may be different, depending on the programming language, so we limit ourselves here to JavaScript operators. Examples of expressions include

```
a * (b + c)
height * width / 2
pi * diameter
(((days * 24) + hours) * 60 + minutes) * 60 + seconds
```

Arithmetic Operators

Expressions usually follow rules similar to algebraic formulas, but not quite. Multiplication must be given explicitly with the asterisk (`*`) multiply operator; so, we write `a * b` rather than `ab` or `a · b` or `a × b`. As with algebra, multiply and divide are performed before add and subtract—multiply and divide have *higher precedence* than add and subtract—unless parentheses group the operations differently. Therefore, `a*b + a*c` is equivalent to `(a*b) + (a*c)` because multiplication is automatically performed before addition. Also, because expressions must be typed on a single line, superscripts, as in x^2, are prohibited. Some languages have an operator for exponents or powers, but JavaScript does not. If we want to compute the area of a circle, we must multiply `R` times itself because we can't square it. So

```
pi * R * R
```

is the expression for computing the area of a circle (πr^2), assuming that the variable `pi` has the value 3.1415962.

Operators like `+` and `*` are called **binary operators** because they operate on two values. The values they operate on are called **operands**. There are also **unary operators**, like negate (`-`), which have only one operand. (Language parsers can easily figure out whether the minus means negate or subtract.)

One very useful operator in future chapters will be mod. The **modulus** (mod) **operation** (`%`) divides two integers and returns the remainder. So, the result of `a%b` for integers `a` and `b` is the remainder of the division `a/b`. In particular, the result of `4%2` is `0` because `2` evenly divides `4`, whereas `5%2` is `1` because `2` into `5` leaves a remainder of `1`.

Relational Operators

Expressions involving addition, subtraction, and so on are similar to algebra, but programmers use other kinds of expressions. **Relational operators** are used to make comparisons between numerical values—that is, to test the relationship between two numbers. The outcome of the comparison is a Boolean value, either `true` or `false`. The operators are illustrated here with sample operands `a` and `b` that should be replaced with variables or expressions:

`a < b`	Is a less than b?
`a <= b`	Is a less than or equal to b?
`a == b`	Is a equal to b?
`a != b`	Is a not equal to b?
`a >= b`	Is a greater than or equal to b?
`a > b`	Is a greater than b?

Notice that the "equal to" relational operator (`==`) is a double equal sign, making it different from assignment.

Examples of relational expressions include

```
bondRate > certificateDeposit
temperature <= 212
drink == "espresso"
```

Notice that relational tests can apply to string variables, as in the last example, which is taken from the program in Figure 18.1. Both equal (==) and not equal (!=) can be applied to string variables.

> *fit***BYTE**
>
> **One Character or Two?** Several operators, such as <=, >=, and != are composed of two keyboard characters. They cannot contain a space and are considered a single character. They were invented years ago to make up for the limited number of characters on a standard keyboard. If programming language research started today, compounds would not be necessary because it's now easy to introduce new symbols that are not on the keyboard, such as ≤, ≥, and ≠.

Logical Operators

The relational test results in a **true** or **false** outcome; that is, either the two operands are related to each other as the relational operator asks, making the test outcome **true**, or they are not, making the test outcome **false**. It is common to test two or more relationships together, requiring that relational expression results are combined. For example, teenagers are older than 12 and younger than 20. In programming, "teenagerness" is determined by establishing that the relational tests `age > 12` and `age < 20` are both true. In JavaScript the "teenage" expression is

```
age > 12 && age < 20
```

Logical And.   The `&&` is the **logical and** operator, playing the same role AND plays in query expressions (Chapters 5 and 15). The outcome of *a* `&&` *b* is true if both *a* and *b* are true; otherwise, it is false. (The operands *a* and *b* can be variables, in which case they have Boolean values, or expressions, or a mixture.)

Thus, in the teenager expression, the current value of `age` is compared to 12, which yields a **true** or a **false** outcome. Then the current value of `age` is compared to 20, yielding another **true** or **false** outcome. Finally, these two outcomes, the operands of `&&`, are tested and if they are both **true**, the entire expression has a true outcome; otherwise, it is **false**. For example,

Value of age	age > 12	age < 20	age > 12 && age < 20
4	false	true	false
16	true	true	true
50	true	false	false

Notice that the operands for relational expressions must be numeric, but the operands for logical expressions must be Boolean (that is, `true` or `false`).

*fit*BYTE

> **Programming Is Still Not Algebra.** In algebra, the notation *12 < age < 20* would be used to assert "teenagerness," the static condition of an age within the indicated limits. In programming, both tests must be specified and the two results "anded" (combined using `&&`) to produce the final answer. The difference, again, is that in algebra we are just stating a fact, whereas in programming we are *commanding* the computer to perform the operation of testing the two conditions.

Logical Or. Not surprisingly, there is also a **logical or** operator, `||`. The outcome of *a* `||` *b* is `true` if either *a* is `true` or *b* is `true`, and it is also true if they are both `true`; it is false only if both are `false`. A "preteen" test expression

```
age == 11 || age == 12
```

illustrates the use of the logical operator `||`. Because `&&` and `||` have lower precedence than the relational operators, the relations are always tested first. To include 10-year-olds as preteens, we write an expression that states that either the person is age 10 or their age satisfies the previous preteen definition:

```
age == 10 || (age == 11 || age == 12)
```

Notice that the subexpression in parentheses produces a `true` or `false` value when evaluated, just like a relational test does. It doesn't matter how the operands of `||` are produced; it only matters that they are `true` or `false` values. Another way to achieve the same result is

```
(age == 10 || age == 11) || age == 12
```

Of course, it is also possible to test this definition of preteen with the expression

```
age >= 10 && age <= 12
```

which takes a bit less typing, and is like the teenager test. All of these expressions seem equally clear to a person, and the computer doesn't care which is used.

Logical Not. The **logical not** `!` is a unary operator—it takes only a single operand—and its outcome is opposite of the value of its operand. To command the computer to check if the age is not that of a teenager, write

```
! (age > 12 && age < 20)
```

It works as follows. The subexpression in parentheses tests whether the age qualifies as a teenager, that is, more than 12 and less than 20. The outcome of the test is either `true`, the age qualifies as a teenager, or `false`, it does not. By placing the logical not operator in front of the parenthesized expression, we have a new expression, which has the opposite outcome: The whole expression is `false` if the age is that of a teenager, and it is `true` if the age is not that of a teenager.

Operator Overload. Finally, we've reached **operator overload**. That might sound like the description of someone trying to learn too many new operators at a time—a state the reader has no doubt achieved!—but it is a technical term meaning the "use of an operator with different data types." The case of interest is +. Operators usually apply to a single data type, like numbers. So, we expect `4 + 5` to produce the numerical result of 9. And it does when the operands are numbers. But if the operands are the strings `"four" + "five"` the result is the string `"fourfive"`.

Concatenation. When we use + with strings, it joins the strings together by the operation of **concatenation**. In everyday writing, we simply place two strings together if we want them joined, but in programming, we command the computer to do the work, so we need the operator concatenation to tell the computer to put two strings together. We have "overloaded" the meaning of + to mean addition when operands are numeric and concatenation when the operands are strings. Though overloading is common in some programming languages, + is the only example we'll see here with our use of JavaScript.

---

fit **TIP**

Quote Note. When manipulating strings, as in the statement

`fullName = firstName + " " + middleName + " " + lastName;`

which creates a name from its parts using blanks as separators, it's easy to understand + as concatenation. But for a statement like

`colt = "4" + "5";`

the variable `colt` will be assigned the string `"45"`, not 9, because the operands are (length 1) strings. Thus, we must be alert for quotes that tell us the operand is a string rather than a numerical value.

A CONDITIONAL STATEMENT

The *Alphabetize CDs* program in Chapter 10 required many tests. For example, there was a test to determine if the titles of two CDs were in alphabetic order. A specific statement type, called a **conditional statement** or a **conditional**, has been invented to make testing simpler. The conditional statement of JavaScript has the form

```
if (<Boolean expression>)
     <then-statement>;
```

Here the <*Boolean expression*> is any expression evaluating to a Boolean `true` or `false` outcome, such as relational expressions, and the <*then-statement*> is any JavaScript statement, such as an assignment statement.

if Statements and Their Flow of Control

For example, an `if` statement that checks `waterTemp` in Fahrenheit

```
if (waterTemp < 32)
    waterState = "Frozen";
```

is a typical conditional statement. In a conditional the *<Boolean expression>*, called a **predicate**, is evaluated, producing a `true` or `false` outcome. If the outcome is `true`, the *<then-statement>* is performed. If the outcome is `false`, the *<then-statement>* is skipped. Therefore, in the example the value of the variable `waterTemp` is determined and compared to 32. If it is less than 32, the value of the variable `waterState` is changed to `"Frozen"`. Otherwise, the statement is passed over, and `waterState` remains unchanged. The following conditional

```
if (waterTemp >= 32 && waterTemp <= 212)
    waterState = "Liquid";
```

tests a range of values using relational operators and the and operator.

Some programming languages use the word *then* to separate the predicate from the *<then-statement>*, but JavaScript does not, because it is unnecessary. Writing the *<then-statement>* indented on the following line is actually only common practice, not a rule; the *<then-statement>* could be on the same line as the predicate,

```
if (waterTempC >= 0 && waterTempC <= 100) waterState = "Liquid";
```

It has the same meaning because white space is ignored in JavaScript. But programmers write the *<then-statement>* indented on the following line to set it off and emphasize its conditional nature for anyone reading the program. By the way, when you read a conditional statement you *say* "then" after the predicate.

Sometimes we need to perform more than one statement on a `true` outcome of the predicate test. We could just repeat the test for each statement, as in

```
if (waterTemp < 32) waterState = "Frozen";
if (waterTemp < 32) description = "Ice";
```

Repeating statements can become tedious, however.

Compound Statements

Programming languages allow for a sequence of statements in the `then` clause. The problem is that if there are several statements, how will we know how many to skip in case the predicate has a `false` outcome? The solution is easy: We group the statements by surrounding them with "curly braces," `{}`, which collects them to become a single statement known as a **compound statement**. Then they fulfill the requirements of the definition given above because now the *<then-statement>* refers to the single (compound) statement; it is skipped when the predicate outcome is `false`. For example,

```
if (waterTempC < 0) {
    waterState = "Frozen";
    description = "Ice";
}
```

Notice the location of the curly braces. One immediately follows the predicate to signal that a compound statement is next, and the other is placed conspicuously on its own line below the *i* of **if**. Programmers do this so that compound statement grouping symbols—which are easily overlooked by a person if they are in an unexpected place in a program—are easy to see. As always, the computer doesn't care where the curly braces are placed.

The "exception proving the rule" that every statement must be terminated by a semicolon is the compound statement. The closing curly brace, **}**, should not be followed by a semicolon.

fit **TIP**

Show Your Braces. Since compound statement braces have a huge impact on program behavior, always put them in the standard place, where they will be noticed.

Another example of the use of the compound statement is from the espresso computation of Figure 18.1:

```
if (drink == "latte" || drink == "cappuccino") {
    if (ounce == 8)
        price = 1.95;
    if (ounce == 12)
        price = 2.35;
    if (ounce == 16)
        price = 2.75;
}
```

This code illustrates an **if** with a compound statement containing three simple **if** statements. If **drink** is neither a **"latte"** nor a **"cappuccino"**, the three statements will be skipped. Otherwise, if **drink** equals **"latte"** or **drink** equals **"cappuccino"**, the three statements will be performed. Notice that at most one predicate of the three statements of the compound statement can be true, because **ounce** can have only one value at a time: 8, 12, 16, or something else. So, **price** will be changed at most once.

if/else Statements

Of course, performing statements when a condition is true is handy, but how can statements be executed when the condition's outcome is false? There is another form of the **if** statement known as the **if/else statement**. It has the form

```
if (<Boolean expression>)
    <then-statement>;
else
    <else-statement>;
```

The *<Boolean expression>* is evaluated first. If the outcome is true, the *<then-statement>* is executed and the *<else-statement>* is skipped. If the *<Boolean expression>*'s outcome is false, the *<then-statement>* is skipped and the *<else-statement>* is executed. For example,

```
if (day == 'Friday' || day == 'Saturday')
    calendarEntry = "Party!";
else
    calendarEntry = "Study";
```

The *<then-statement>* and *<else-statement>* are single statements, but several statements can be grouped into a compound statement with curly braces when necessary. For example,

```
if ((year % 4) == 0) {
    leapYear = true;
    febDays = febDays + 1;
}
else
    leapYear = false;
```

This example uses the mod operator `%`, so the outcome of `(year%4)` is the remainder of `year / 4`; that is, the result is 0, 1, 2, or 3.

A typical example sets the same variables in both parts of the conditional. Consider a coin toss at the start of a soccer game, which can be expressed as

```
if (sideUp == sideCalled) {
    coinTossWinner = visitorTeam;
    firstHalfOffensive = visitorTeam;
    secondHalfOffensive = hostTeam;
}
else {
    coinTossWinner = hostTeam;
    firstHalfOffensive = hostTeam;
    secondHalfOffensive = visitorTeam;
}
```

Notice that the opening curly brace for the *<else-statement>* is placed right after the `else`, and the closing curly brace is placed conspicuously on its own line directly below the *e* of `else`.

Nested if/else Statements

The *<then-statement>* and the *<else-statement>* can contain an `if/else`, but you have to be careful, because it can be ambiguous which `if` an `else` goes with. The rule in JavaScript and most other programming languages is that the `else` associates with the (immediately) preceding `if`. For example, the code

```
if (Pooh == "bear")                    Caution: This code is deceptive!
    if (Eeyore == "bear")
        report = "Pooh and Eeyore are the same kind of animal";
else
    report = "Pooh is not a bear";
```

has been *deceptively* indented so that it *appears* that the `else` associates with the first `if`. But white space is ignored. The JavaScript rule means that the `else` associates with the "inner" `if`, so that the following indentation matches the actual meaning:

```
if (Pooh == "bear")
   if (Eeyore == "bear")
      report = "Pooh and Eeyore are the same kind of animal";
   else
      report = "Pooh is not a bear";   Caution: This conclusion is wrong!
```

In fact, assuming Pooh is a bear and Eeyore is a donkey or any animal other than a bear, `report` gives the wrong answer. The best policy—the one successful programmers follow—is to enclose the *<then-statement>* or *<else-statement>* in compound curly braces whenever they contain an `if/else`. Thus the right way to express the statement is

```
if (Pooh == "bear") {
   if (Eeyore == "bear")
      report = "Pooh and Eeyore are the same kind of animal";
}
else
   report = "Pooh is not a bear";
```

The braces ensure that the `else` matches with its `if`. This policy saves a lot of grief.

As one final example of **nested conditionals**, consider the four outcomes from flipping two coins expressed by nested conditionals:

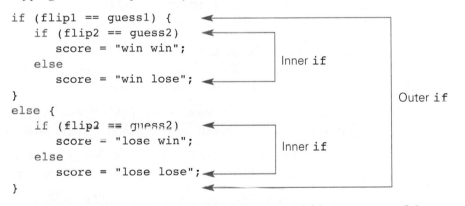

This example shows clearly the logic of the true and false outcomes of the predicates.

THE ESPRESSO PROGRAM

We now return to the program shown in Figure 18.1. The program computes the price of four kinds of espresso drinks based on the type of drink, the size of drink, and the number of additional shots, plus tax. The input variables are listed at the start of the program, as is the output.

Input:

drink, a character string with one of the values: "espresso", "latte",
    "cappuccino", "Americano"
ounce, an integer, giving the size of the drink in ounces
shots, an integer, giving the number of shots

Output:

price in dollars of an order, including 8.8% sales tax

Program:

```
1.   var price;
2.   var taxRate = 0.088;
3.   if (drink == "espresso")
         price = 1.40;
4.   if (drink == "latte" || drink == "cappuccino") {
4a.      if (ounce == 8)
             price = 1.95;
4b.      if (ounce == 12)
             price = 2.35;
4c.      if (ounce == 16)
             price = 2.75;
     }
5.   if (drink == "Americano")
         price = 1.20 + .30 * (ounce/8);
6.   price = price + (shots - 1) * .50;
7.   price = price + price * taxRate;
```

The input variables are assumed to be given; see Chapter 19 for details on how this is done with a GUI. Because the program will create the output, we declare the output to be a variable as the first statement of the program.

Statements 3 through 5 determine the kind of drink and establish the base price. These statements have been written to show different programming techniques:

> **Line 3:** If the order is straight espresso, the first shot is priced at $1.40. This is an example of a basic conditional statement.

> **Lines 4–4c:** These statements establish the base prices for lattés and cappuccinos using an **if** statement with conditionals in the **then** statement compound statement.

> **Line 5:** This line uses a basic **if** statement to compute the base price for Americanos.

> **Lines 6, 7:** Finally, the total **price** is computed in Lines 6 and 7. In Line 6 the cost of additional shots is added to the base price. In Line 7 the tax is added in. This is accomplished by multiplying the total price by the **taxRate**, then adding the result to the total price.

Notice that the `if` statements on Lines 3, 4, and 5 will always be executed, but because they apply to different drinks, the statement(s) of their `then` statements will be executed in at most one of the cases.

Execution for a Double Tall Latté

To see the espresso program in action, compute the price of a double tall latté, the second most common phrase used in Seattle after "it's still raining." A "double" means a total of two shots in the drink, that is, one extra shot. Thus the input variables to the program are

```
drink  ⇔  "latte"
ounce  ⇔  12
shots  ⇔  2
```

where ⇔ means "has the value of" or "contains." This notation allows us to give the value of a variable without using the equal sign, which would look like an assignment statement.

The first statements are declarations, which are like definitions. In particular, we should treat `price` as not yet having any value. The following lines are executed:

> **Line 3** is executed first. The test `drink == "espresso"` fails, because the variable drink has the value `"latte"`. As a result its `then` statement is skipped.

> **Line 4** is executed next. The test `drink == "latte" || drink == "cappuccino"` has a `true` outcome because the subexpression `drink == "latte"` is `true`; the relational test `drink == "cappuccino"` is `false`, of course, but because one of the operands of the `||` is `true`, the whole expression is `true`. This means that the `then` statement containing the conditionals 4a–4c will be executed.

> **Line 4a** is executed next. The test `ounce == 8` has a `false` outcome, so its `then` statement is skipped.

> **Line 4b** is nexecuted. (I made up *nexecuted* for "next executed." Isn't it a great word?) The `ounce == 12` test is true, so the `then` statement is executed, giving `price` its initial value, `price ⇔ 2.35`.

> **Line 4c** is nexecuted. The `ounce == 16` test fails, so its `then` statement is skipped.

> **Line 5** is nexecuted. The `drink == "Americano"` test fails, so its `then` statement is skipped.

> **Line 6** is nexecuted. This causes the value of `shots` minus 1 to be multiplied by `.50`, resulting in the value `.50`, which is added to `price`, yielding `price ⇔ 2.85`.

> **Line 7** is nexecuted. The current value of `price` is multiplied by `taxRate`, whose value was initialized on line 2 (`taxRate ⇔ 0.088`),

resulting in **0.25**, which is added to **price** to compute the final value of **3.10**, which is assigned to **price**.

Thus, **price** ⇔ **3.10**, so a "double tall latté" costs $3.10.

SUMMARY

In this chapter, we introduced enough programming concepts—and their JavaScript syntax—to read and understand basic programs. The chapter began by introducing the idea that a name can be separated from its value. Captain is a name for a team leader, but its value, that is, the person who is the captain, can change. In fact, the name exists, though with an undefined value, as soon as a team is formed. Names-with-changing-values is a familiar idea. File names work this way as we progressively update a file with, say, a word processor. Variables in programming languages have changing values, too. The reason is simple. A program is a fixed, finite specification for a computation written out in a few pages of code. Yet, when the computation is executed, many values may be created to produce the final answer. In the espresso computation, for example, the variable **price**, which is initially undefined, has three different values: the base price, the total price before tax, and the final price. At any point, the value of **price** is the price as computed so far, but the process of computing **price** continues until the program is finished.

In basic programming, we now understand that:

> Name–value separation is an important concept. It's one of the ways that programming differs from algebra.

> Letter sequences that make up a variable's name (identifiers), must be declared. Variables can be initialized when they are declared. Changing the value of a variable is possible by using assignment.

> An assignment statement has a variable on the left side of the symbol and an expression on the right side. The operation is to compute the value of the expression and make the result the new value of the variable. This makes information flow from right to left in an assignment statement. Statements like **x = x + 1;** make sense in programming, but not in algebra. This statement is a command to the computer to find the current value of the variable **x**, add 1 to it, and make the result of the addition the new value of **x**.

> There are three JavaScript data types—numbers, strings, and Booleans—we can build expressions to compute values of these types.

> Standard arithmetic operators and relationals compute on numbers, and logical operations on Booleans. (See Appendix B for a full listing.) In defining concatenation, we learned about "operator overload." Expressions "do the computing" in our programs, and are generally a familiar idea.

> As a rule, all programming statements are executed one after another, starting at the beginning. The conditional statements are the exception. JavaScript's two conditional forms are `if` and `if/else`. These allow statements to be executed depending on the outcome of a Boolean expression called a predicate. Using conditionals, we can organize our computations so that operations are performed when "the conditions are right."

> We must be careful to group statements within a compound statement to make it plain which statements are skipped or executed. We also must be careful when we are using `if/else` in a conditional so that the `if` and `else` associate correctly.

> The espresso program in Figure 18 1 illustrates most of the ideas of the chapter. The program uses both numeric and string data types, as well as the declaration, assignment, and conditional statement forms

> All that keeps us from running the program and demonstrating our knowledge is setting up the input to acquire the values for `drink`, `ounce`, and `shots`, and outputting the `price`. This requires a GUI written in HTML (the topic of Chapter 19).

chapter 19

THE BEAN COUNTER

A JavaScript Program

learning objectives

> Use the Bean Counter application as a model to

- Write input elements
- Create a button table
- Write an event handler in JavaScript
- Produce a GUI similar to that of the Bean Counter

> Trace the execution of the Bean Counter, saying what output is produced by a given input

> Explain event-based programming in JavaScript and the use of event handlers

THE BEAN COUNTER
A JavaScript Program

Programming today is a race between software engineers striving to build bigger and better idiot-proofed programs, and the Universe trying to produce bigger and better idiots. So far the Universe is winning.

—RICH COOK

MUCH OF MODERN programming requires two activities. The first is creating the algorithm that directs the computer to solve a problem. The second is creating a user interface to assist with the human/computer interaction; specifically, a way to enter the input and a way to display the computed output. JavaScript (JS) is designed for Web applications, which means that JavaScript code is included in Web page source code written in HTML. The Web page is the graphical user interface; the JavaScript does the computing.

In Chapter 18, we wrote a program to charge for espresso drinks. That program is the computational part of our solution. In this chapter, we focus on creating a user interface and connecting it to the espresso program. So, our main goal is to produce a user-friendly GUI for the program.

We will create the Bean Counter application. The first step is to make sure that the computation from Chapter 18 is correct. Then, after covering two preliminaries, we will follow these steps:

1. Review Web page programming, recalling some HTML basics, and introduce the idea of HTML input elements.
2. Build the GUI for the Bean Counter program, so that the graphic looks right. Only the picture will be complete; the buttons will not work yet.
3. Introduce the idea of event programming and connect the buttons to the program logic.
4. Test the Web page, evaluating it for its usefulness.
5. Revise the Web page and the logic to improve the solution to the problem.

When the Web page is complete, we will have created our first complete JavaScript program.

PRELIMINARIES

Recall from Chapter 4 that HTML files are simple ASCII text. The fancy formatting of word processors like WordPerfect, MS Word, or ClarisWorks simply confuses Web browsers, and must be avoided. Instead we'll use a basic text editor such as Notepad, SimpleText, WordPad, or BBEdit. The file format must be `text` or `txt`, and the filename's extension (the characters following the last dot) must be `html`. So, `bean.html` is an appropriate filename. The operating system knows that the file will be processed by a Web browser, and the browser will be able to understand everything in the file without becoming confused.

> **𝑓𝑖𝑡 TIP**
>
> **Build as You Go.** The best way to learn the ideas and the practical skills of this chapter is to build the program yourself as you read along.

To create your program, start by using the text editor to make a file whose first line is `<html>` and whose last line is `</html>`. To include JavaScript (JS) in an HTML file, enclose the JavaScript text in `<script language="JavaScript">` `</script>` tags. The information that you include between these tags is the subject of this chapter. When it's time to test your program, save it. Remember that the file format must be `text` and the file extension must be `.html`, but if you've specified the extension already, a simple **Save** should be sufficient. Then find the file on your computer and double-click it. Your Web browser should open the file and display the Web page you've constructed. It's that simple.

> **𝑓𝑖𝑡 TIP**
>
> **"Modern" Software.** The JavaScript in this book requires a "contemporary" browser such as Internet Explorer 4 or higher, Netscape 6 or higher, Mozilla, FireFox, or Safari. Because of browser inconsistencies, the figures shown in the text may appear slightly different from browser to browser.

To work through the mechanics of running a JavaScript program, we will ignore the user interface for the moment and simply run the computational part of the program from Chapter 18. This is mostly an exercise, because we will not be able to interact with the result, and all that we will see is one number printed out. We begin this way to make sure the Bean Counter code is working. We'll use this code later in the chapter. The program structure needed to run just the computation is shown in Figure 19.1. You should *accurately* type it into a file, save it as `beanV0.html`, and run it.

Because we have not yet built the user interface, we have no way to give inputs. So we fake the input. We declare and initialize three new variables—`drink`, `shots`, and `ounce`—as the first three statements of the JavaScript code. We'll take these out later, when we add the buttons. These initializers are for a "double tall latté," that is, a 12-ounce café latté made with two shots of espresso. After you type in and run the program, you should see the result shown in Figure 19.2.

```
<html>
  <head><title>Version 0</title></head>
  <body>
    <h1>Here's Version 0 of the Bean Counter</h1>
    <script language = "JavaScript">
      var drink = "latte"; //Temporary Decl. for Version 0;
                           //to be removed
      var shots = 2;        //Temporary Decl. for Version 0;
                           //to be removed
      var ounce = 12;       //Temporary Decl. for Version 0;
                           //to be removed
      var price;
      var taxRate = 0.088;
      if (drink == "espresso")
         price = 1.40;
      if (drink == "latte" || drink == "cappuccino") {
        if (ounce == 8)
            price = 1.95;
        if (ounce == 12)
            price = 2.35;
        if (ounce == 16)
            price = 2.75;
      }
      if (drink == "Americano")
        price = 1.20 + .30 * (ounce/8);
      price = price + (shots - 1) * .50;
      price = price + price * taxRate;
      alert(price);     //Temporary statement to print result;
                       //to be changed
    </script>
  </body>
</html>
```

Figure 19.1. *Version 0 of the Bean Counter program without the user interface, and with fixed inputs:* `drink="latte"`, `shots=2`, `ounce=12`.

Figure 19.2. *Web page displayed by Version 0 of the Bean Counter program of Figure 19.1.*

The `alert(price)` command prints out the amount that the program computed for the `price`. We verify that the program did produce the same price for a "double tall latté" that we computed in Chapter 18. (The answer isn't rounded to a whole penny, but we'll solve that problem later.) Our next step is to construct the graphical user interface.

BACKGROUND FOR THE GUI

This section covers two introductory topics that we need to understand to create the JavaScript graphical user interface. First we present a quick review of HTML. If you need more information, consult Chapter 4. Next we explain a new HTML tag, the `<input...>` tag. This allows us to create buttons and print output.

The Bean Counter GUI (see Figure 19.3) offers the user rows and columns of buttons, and a window in the lower right corner to display the total price of the espresso drink. The first column of buttons specifies the number of shots. The second column specifies the size of the drink, where S, T, and G stand for short, tall, and grande. The next column specifies the type of espresso drink. The meanings of the last two buttons in the rightmost column are obvious.

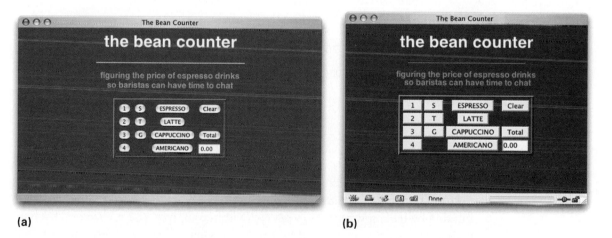

(a)   **(b)**

Figure 19.3. *Web interface for the Bean Counter program displayed using (a) Safari and (b) Mozilla.*

Review HTML Basics

Recall from Chapter 4 that HTML is a markup language that describes how a Web page should appear on a computer monitor, by using tags that surround the relevant text, images, and so on.

HTML Tags. An HTML file is enclosed in `<html>` `</html>` tags. It requires a head, which has the form

```
<head>
   <title>The Bean Counter</title>
</head>
```

and its body is surrounded by `<body>` `</body>` tags. All of the programming of this chapter is concentrated in the body of the document.

HTML has several levels of headings, such as the `<h1>` `</h1>` tags. Paragraphs are surrounded by `<p>` `</p>` tags, and text can be forced to a new line by the `<br>` tag. Text can be made italic using `<i>` `</i>` tags, or bold with `<b>` `</b>` tags. A horizontal line can be drawn with the horizontal rule tag, `<hr>`. The `<a href="`*fn*`">` `</a>` tags place a link to another Web page with filename *fn*. The tag `<img src="`*fn*`">` places an image contained in the file *fn* into the document.

Most tags have attributes that customize the document to the situation. For example, the background color for a page can be specified, as can its font color and typeface. Thus

```
<body bgcolor="#804000" text="#FF9900" align="center">
   <font face="Helvetica", "Arial">
   <h1 align="center">
      <font color="#FFFFFF">the bean counter</font></h1>
   <hr width=50%>
   <p align="center"><b>figuring the price of espresso
      drinks<br>so baristas can have time to chat</b></p>
```

gives us a coffee-brown background color (`#804000`), a terracotta text color (`#FF9900`), and a sans serif font (`Helvetica`). All of the HTML just presented will be part of our Bean Counter program in the file `bean.html`.

Tables in HTML. Often when we create interfaces for JavaScript programs, we organize the design as a table. We do this because tables give us some control over where information is displayed on a page. Recall that table definitions are enclosed by `<table></table>` tags and are a sequence of rows. Each row is surrounded by table row tags, `<tr></tr>`. Within each row, a sequence of table data items is given, each surrounded by `<td></td>` tags. There are several ways to make a fancier table, but our use of tables requires only these basics. Check Appendix A for more information.

Interacting with a GUI

Curiously, the input facilities like **buttons** and **checkboxes** are known as elements of **forms**. They were introduced into HTML to assist with activities like ordering products or answering survey questions. Users fill out the form by clicking on buttons or entering data in text windows. When the form is complete, it is sent to the computer for processing. Although our application doesn't involve questionnaires, we use the input elements, and so must use the form tags.

Forms.   The form tags `<form></form>` must surround all of the input elements. Though `<form>` has several attributes, we will use only the **name** attribute, which gives a name to the form. Thus, to allow us to use input buttons, the next item in our HTML program is the pair

```
<form name = "Bean">
</form>
```

The rest of our GUI programming will be placed between these two tags. The file ends with

```
    </body>
</html>
```

By the way, the name, like everything in JavaScript, is case sensitive. Figure 19.4 shows the code for the page as it looks so far.

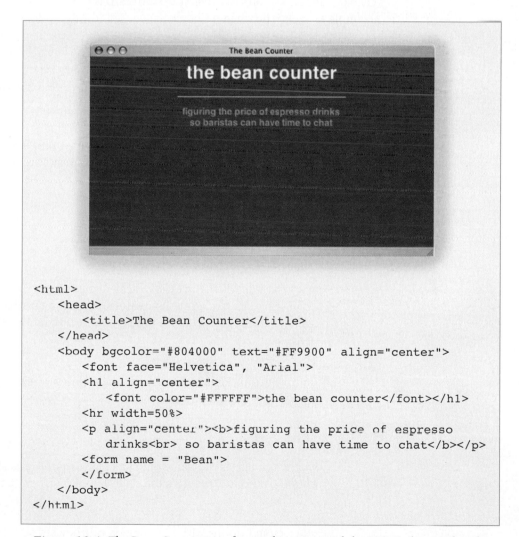

```
<html>
    <head>
        <title>The Bean Counter</title>
    </head>
    <body bgcolor="#804000" text="#FF9900" align="center">
        <font face="Helvetica", "Arial">
        <h1 align="center">
            <font color="#FFFFFF">the bean counter</font></h1>
        <hr width=50%>
        <p align="center"><b>figuring the price of espresso
            drinks<br> so baristas can have time to chat</b></p>
        <form name = "Bean">
        </form>
    </body>
</html>
```

Figure 19.4. *The Bean Counter interface to this point, and the HTML that produced it.*

Events and Event Handlers. When the GUI inputs are used, they cause an event to occur. For example, when the user clicks on a command button, he or she causes a "click event" to occur. An **event** is an indication from the computer (operating system) that something just happened (mouse click).

We want our JavaScript program to respond to that click—that is, perform the operation corresponding to the button command. When JavaScript finds out about the event, it runs a piece of program called the event handler for that event. An **event handler** is the program that performs the task to respond to an event. We will explain this concept further in a moment.

Three Input Elements

The **<input . . . >** tag specifies all of the input types, buttons, text boxes, checkboxes, and so on. The easiest way to learn the types is simply to study an example of each. The three input elements used in this book are the button, text box, and radio controls.

> **Button.** The form of the button input is
>
> ```
> <input type=button value="label" onClick=" event_handler ">
> ```
>
> where **value** gives the text to be printed on the button, and **onClick** gives the event handler composed of JavaScript instructions. When the user clicks on the button, the JavaScript code of the event handler is executed. Event handling will be discussed momentarily. The image for the button is placed in the next position in the text of the HTML program.

> **Text Box.** The text box can be used to input or output numbers or words. Its general form is
>
> ```
> <input type=text name="identifier" size=6
>     onChange=" event_handler ">
> ```
>
> where *identifier* is the name of the element and **onChange** gives the event handler's JavaScript instructions. After the user has changed the contents of the text window, the JavaScript program instructions are performed. The image for the text input is placed in the next position in the text of the HTML program.

> **Radio Button.** Radio buttons give a selection of preprogrammed settings. Their general form is
>
> ```
> <input type=radio name="identifier"
>     onClick=" event_handler ">label text
> ```
>
> where *identifier* is the name of the element, *label text* is shown beside the button, and **onClick** gives the event handler. When the user clicks on a radio button, the center darkens to indicate that it is set, and the JavaScript instructions of the event handler are performed. If there are other radio buttons with the same name, they are also cleared. The image is placed in the next position in the text of the HTML program.

For the Bean Counter application, we need only the text and button inputs. We will use radio buttons later.

CREATE THE GRAPHICAL USER INTERFACE

We are well on our way to creating the Bean Counter interface, as shown in Figure 19.3. The HTML in Figure 19.4 has the heading information, the horizontal line, and the slogan. "All" we have to do is create a table and fill in the entries. We should place the table between the form tags to ensure that the browser understands the inputs.

> *fit***TIP**
>
> **Focus Point.** When faced with a task, it's a good idea to "think it through" before starting. List the required steps in the order you will do them. Then you can focus your attention on one step at a time. This process, which is a main topic of Chapter 22, is illustrated here by writing down our plan before starting

Notice that the table in Figure 19.3 is a four-row, four-column table with two empty cells. (The columns are not all the same size, but the browser will take care of making them the right size.) Buttons appear in all of the occupied cells but one, so our table is mostly a table of buttons. This suggests the following algorithm for building the table:

1. **Create a button table.** Program the HTML for a four-row, four-column table with a generic button in each cell. This is a good strategy because we can build such a table quickly using **Copy/Paste**.

2. **Delete two buttons.** Two of the cells of the table should be empty. Delete the buttons, but not the cells.

3. **Insert text box.** Replace the button for the last cell and make it a text control.

4. **Label the buttons.** Pass through the table and set the value attribute of each button so that the label on the button is correct

5. **Primp the interface.** Check the interface and adjust the specification where it is necessary.

Once these five steps are complete, the picture of the Bean Counter interface will be finished. Consider each step in detail.

> *fit***TIP**
>
> **Table Trick.** A fast way to build a table in HTML is to create a skeleton first, then fill it in. This is easy because the skeleton can be constructed inside out using copy and paste. Begin with a generic cell such as `<td> </td>`; copy and paste it as many times as needed to build a row, and enclose the result in `<tr>` tags; copy and paste that for as many rows as needed, and surround the result with `<table>` tags. Finally, fill in the entries.

1. Create a Button Table

We use the "inside out" scheme to build the table. Given the information about the button input, we decide that the generic cell can have the form

```
<td>
    <input type=button value="b" onClick =' '>
</td>
```

Here **"b"** is a placeholder for the button label that we'll fix in Step 4, and **' '** is a placeholder for the JavaScript text of the event handler that we'll write later.

We make four copies of the cell in the file from Figure 19.4 and surround them by row tags. We make four copies of the row and surround them with table tags. We save the page and review it, and immediately notice that the table is left-justified. We want it centered, so we surround our table tags with ** ** tags. The result is shown in Figure 19.5(a).

2. Delete Two Buttons

In row 2, cell 4, and row 4, cell 2, we remove the **<input...>** because these cells must be empty. In HTML, we can leave a cell empty, but we still need to surround it with the **<td> </td>** tags for it to be a cell.

3. Insert Text Box

From the last section, we decide to name the text box **"price"** because that's the information that will be printed. The window should be five characters wide because no combination of drink inputs will result in a price of more than four digits plus the decimal point. What's more, **onChange** needs a placeholder. So the button in row 4, cell 4 should be replaced by

```
<input type=text name="price" value="0.00" size=5 onChange=' '>
```

which produces the result shown in Figure 19.5(b). This looks a little lopsided, but we haven't labeled the buttons yet.

4. Label the Buttons

The next task is to pass through the table cells and change the **value** attribute of each button from "b" to its proper button label. The first column is the number of shots (1, 2, 3, 4), the second column is the sizes (S, T, G), and the third column is the drinks (espresso, latté, cappuccino, Americano), which will be given in all uppercase letters.

Because of the row formulation of HTML tables, it is easiest to work row-wise through the table rather than column-wise. The result of our work is shown in Figure 19.5(c). We're close to achieving what we want, but we still need to fix the buttons a bit.

(a)

(b)

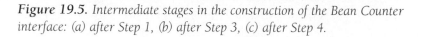

(c)

Figure 19.5. Intermediate stages in the construction of the Bean Counter interface: (a) after Step 1, (b) after Step 3, (c) after Step 4.

5. Primp the Interface

Our guess that the form of the form wouldn't be quite right was right. Looking at the design in Figure 19.5(c), we notice that that the buttons are left justified in the columns. This makes no difference for the first two columns, but the last two columns would look nicer if the buttons were centered. So, we add center alignment to the cells of the last two columns. For example, the ESPRESSO entry is revised as:

```
<td align="center">
   <input type = button value = " ESPRESSO " onClick=' '>
</td>
```

These changes will arrange the buttons so that they match the design shown in Figure 19.3.

The only remaining difference is that the table in Figure 19.3 has borders and colors. Giving the table a background color requires only that the attribute is:

```
<table bgcolor="#993300">
```

Adding the `border` attribute to the `<table>` tag would place a border around all the cells of the table. But we want the border around the table as a whole. So, we use a handy trick: We make a table with only one cell and make the existing table the table data for that cell; that is, we put the table we've just developed into a one-cell table:

```
<table border=2>
   <tr><td>

      existing table goes here

   </td></tr>
</table>
```

Finally, to outline the price text box with red, we simply add the attribute

```
<td bgcolor="red">
```

to that cell. Now our interface matches Figure 19.3 exactly.

EVENT-BASED PROGRAMMING

How should the Bean Counter program work? Like a calculator, something should happen as each button is clicked, that is, in response to user-caused events. The rest of the time nothing should happen. Programming the Bean Counter application amounts to defining in JavaScript the actions that should be performed when each button is clicked. This is called event-based programming. In this section we'll write the event-handling code.

The onClick Event Handler

The greatest part of the programming task is already done, because the action for the **Total** button is to compute the final price, and that computation, shown between the `<script>` and `</script>` tags in Figure 19.2, is already programmed. Because this code defines the action we want the computer to perform when the **Total** button is clicked, we make it the **onClick** event handler for the **Total** button. The input element for the **Total** button is now

```
<td>
   <input type = button value = "Total" onClick =' '>
</td>
```

where **onClick** is the **event-handling attribute** for the **Total** button. We insert the price computation code inside the quotes for the **onClick** attribute, as shown in Figure 19.6, and it becomes the **onClick** event handler.

```
<td>
<input type = button value = "Total" onClick =
'   var price;
    var taxRate = 0.088;
    if (drink == "espresso")
        price = 1.40;
    if (drink == "latte" || drink == "cappuccino") {
        if (ounce == 8)
            price = 1.95;
        if (ounce == 12)
            price = 2.35;
        if (ounce == 16)
            price = 2.75;
    }
    if (drink == "Americano")
        price = 1.20 + .30 * (ounce/8);
    price = price + (shots - 1) * .50;
    price = price + price * taxRate;
//one more assignment is required here
'>
</td>
```

Figure 19.6. The Total text box input element with the price computation inserted as the event handler. (Notice that the three temporary declarations of Figure 19.1 have been removed, as has the temporary "alert" command.)

Click Event

Here's what happens. When the barista clicks on the **Total** button, it causes a **click event** in the browser. The browser, designed to perform an action in response to the click event, looks for the `onClick` event handler in the `Total` button input tag. The browser should find the JavaScript instructions to perform the action associated with the button. The browser runs those instructions, implements the action, and then waits for the next event. That's why we move the price computation instructions—the JavaScript text of Figure 19.1 with the temporary assignments removed—to between the quotes of the `onClick` attribute. Doing so specifies what action the browser is to perform on the click event and how it is to be performed. The browser can now *handle* the click event. (One more instruction is required, as explained at the end of this section.)

Shots Button

Handling the click events for the other buttons is even easier. In each case, we ask what action should be performed when a particular button is clicked. For the first column of buttons—the shots buttons—the answer is to specify the number of shots the customer requests. For example, clicking on the `1` button should cause the `shots` variable to have the value 1. So, to handle the click event for the `1` button input, we need to assign `shots` as follows:

```
<td>
   <input type = button value = "1" onClick = 'shots = 1'>
</td>
```

Notice that the `2` button assigns `shots` the value 2, and so on. Thus the event handlers for the shots buttons require only one JavaScript command each: an assignment of the right number to `shots`.

Size and Drink Buttons

The buttons in the size and drink columns are similar. The action to be performed on a click event for the size buttons is to assign the `ounce` variable the appropriate value, 8, 12, or 16, as in

```
<td>
   <input type = button value = " S " onClick = 'ounce = 8'>
</td>
```

For the drink column, the `drink` variable gets the name of the drink quoted:

```
<td align="center">
   <input type = button value = " ESPRESSO "
      onClick = 'drink = "espresso"'>
</td>
```

Notice that single quotes surround the assignment statement, which uses double quotes. To plan for the use of double-quoted string literals, we chose single quotes for the event handler placeholder in the generic button of the last section.

Also, notice that drink was assigned the string `"espresso"`, not `"ESPRESSO"`, as written on the key. The reason is that when the JavaScript code computes the price, the `if` statement compares the value of drink with the string literal `"espresso"`, and since the comparison is case sensitive, the two strings have to be the same case to match.

> **Match Point.** You need to be careful when typing string literals like `"espresso"` because when the computer compares this value with the string literal in the `Total` button's event handler (Figure 19.6, line 5), they must match *exactly*. Misspellings (`"expresso"`), case differences (`"Espresso"`), or even unintentional blanks (`" espresso"`) will fail to match.

Clear Button and Initializations

Clicking on the `Clear` button should reset all of the variables (`drink`, `ounce`, and `shots`) to their initial values. When we think about what those initial values are, we realize that we haven't initialized them yet. In fact, we haven't even declared the variables yet. As is common in programming, working on the solution to one task—setting up the `Clear` event handler—reminds us that we have another task to do—declare the variables. So, we first handle the declaration with initialization, and then return to the `Clear` event handler.

The declarations should be placed at the beginning of the program, but we don't really have a single program. Rather, we have many little program pieces in the form of event handlers. So, referring to Figure 19.2, we place the declarations for the three variables at the start of the body just after the `<body>` tag. As usual, the declarations must be enclosed in `<script>` tags. (Notice that `<script>` tags are not needed for the event handlers, because they *expect* JavaScript.) The declarations are

```
<script language = 'JavaScript'>
   var shots = 1;
   var drink = "none";
   var ounce = 0;
</script>
```

The initial value for `shots` is 1 because every espresso drink will have at least one shot. The initial values for `drink` and `ounce` are chosen to be illegal values, so that if the barista forgets to specify either one, he or she will receive an error message, indicating that an input has been forgotten. Finally, the `Clear` button should make these same assignments, resulting in its `onClick` event handler being

```
<td>
   <input type = button value = "Clear" onClick =
     'shots = 1;
      drink = "none";
      ounce = 0;
      document.Bean.price.value = "0.00"'>
</td>
```

completing both the initialization and `Clear` event handler specifications.

The last assignment statement of the `Clear` event handler

```
document.Bean.price.value = "0.00"
```

is important. It places `0.00` in the `price` window, reinitializing it. The next section explains how the assignment statement works.

Referencing Data across Controls

The document that is displayed by the browser can contain one or more forms. Our document has a form named `Bean`. Forms can contain one or more elements. Our `Bean` form has an input named `price`. Input controls can have several attributes. The `price` input control has a `value` attribute, which was initially assigned `"0.00"`. (See *3. Insert Text Box* on page 556.) The `value` attribute of the `price` element of the `Bean` form of the `document` is displayed by the window.

When we program in JavaScript and want a statement in one element (e.g., the `Clear` button) to change a value in another element (e.g., the `value` attribute of the `price` text window), we must tell the browser how to navigate among the elements. For that we need the **dot operator**.

Dot Operator.   The dot operator provides a means of navigation to the proper object. So, the reference

```
object.property
```

selects the **property of the object**. We usually read this reference *right to left*, saying the dot as "of," as in "*property of object.*" So, the assignment in the `Clear` button event handler reinitializing the window

```
document.Bean.price.value = "0.00"
```

can be read "the `value` attribute *of* the `price` input *of* the `Bean` form *of* the **document** is assigned `0.00`." Said another way, when the `Clear` button wants to change the window of the `price` element, it tells the browser to find the `Bean` form in the `document`, and then within it, find the `price` window, and then within it, find the `value` attribute, and change it.

Changing the Window.   Because the `value` attribute is the content displayed in the `price` window, when the assignment changes the value back to `0.00`, the browser displays the assigned value. In this way, the event handler of one element can refer to an attribute of another input element.

Notice that when the `value` is reassigned, the window displays the `0.00` and thus acts as an output. The idea that something called an *input* is used to output information may seem strange. But the window can be seen from both the user's and the computer's point of view. If one side gets information (input) from it, the other must have put (output) the information. And vice versa. Input elements are for both input and output.

Displaying the Total. There is one other case where the event handler of one element must refer to the **value** attribute of **price**. The **Total** event handler, the one we built first, must output the price. It does this the same way the **Clear** button event handler clears the **price** window—by assigning to the **value** attribute of **price**. Thus the final line of the **Total** event handler—the one that is a comment in Figure 19.6 promising a revised statement—should be replaced by

```
document.Bean.price.value - price;
```

in order to display the final price. That change completes the **Total** event handler, which means we've finished the Bean Counter application. Run it!

CRITIQUING THE BEAN COUNTER

Every design must be critiqued to ensure that it meets the requirements of solving the problem and to determine if it can be improved. Therefore, the next task is to experiment with the Bean Counter application, trying a dozen or more sample values to see how well it works.

Does our design fulfill the barista's needs? We'll organize our analysis by topic.

Numbers versus Money

The most obvious and annoying problem with the Bean Counter application is that the final price is shown as a decimal number with several digits of precision rather than as currency with only two digits to the right of the decimal point. This problem can be almost completely fixed by changing the last line of the **Total** button event handler to

```
document.Bean.price.value = Math.round(price*100)/100;
```

The computation works as follows: The **price** is first multiplied by 100. This changes the price from a "dollars amount" to a "cents amount," that is, the **price** is expressed as the total number of pennies. That result is then rounded by using the built-in JavaScript function **Math.round()** to eliminate any digits to the right of the decimal point that now represent less than a penny. Finally, that result is divided by 100 again to convert back to a "dollars amount." The computation is a standard way to remove unwanted digits.

The solution doesn't quite solve the problem, because trailing zeros are dropped; that is, the price of $3.10 for a double tall latté would print as 3.1. But this is a small problem that doesn't come up much, so we'll ignore it. The full solution requires some advanced concepts, resulting in the assignment statement:

```
document.Bean.price.value =
    (Math.round(price*100)/100).toString().match(/[\.\d]{4}/);
```

Organization

The organization of the buttons is generally consistent with how the application will be used. Because espresso drinks are typically named with syntax of the form

<shots> <size> <kind>;

as in "double tall latté," the buttons are in a good order for the left-to-right cursor flow. It might make sense to put the `Clear` button on the left side to start the process, but because there is no obvious place for it and because the cursor will generally be positioned on the `Total` button at the end of the previous purchase—that is, on the right side of the table below the `Clear` button—the design is not inconvenient. We will leave the page organized as it is.

Feedback

One problem with the design is that it doesn't give the barista any feedback about the current settings of the variables. One principle of user interfaces from Chapter 2 is that there should always be feedback for every operation. For some browsers there is *a bit of* feedback because buttons are automatically highlighted when they are clicked. But once another button is clicked, the automatic highlighting moves to that button. Adding feedback—for example, a window above each column of buttons that gives the current setting—would be better.

RECAP OF THE BEAN COUNTER APPLICATION

The sample program of Chapter 18 is now a useful application. In the process, we learned the basics of event-based programming using JavaScript. Because this chapter focused on building the application, we didn't spend much time discussing the ideas generally. So let's review the major ideas now.

We created a graphical user interface for the Bean Counter application by first creating the HTML text to produce the picture of the interface, and then adding JavaScript—mostly in event handlers for inputs—to make the application work. Though we discussed programs in Chapter 18 as if they were single, monolithic sequences of statements, the Bean Counter application is actually many tiny code segments that are mostly one or two statements long. This is typical of event-based programming. Other, less interactive forms of computing are more monolithic.

Referencing Variables

The only problem that the many-tiny-code-segments property caused is that we didn't immediately know where to place the declarations for the variables, `shots`, `ounce`, and `drink`. Declarations are usually placed at the start of the program. With many event handlers, however, it's as though we have many program "starts." We placed the declarations right after the `<body>` tag, which is not the start of a JavaScript program, just the start of the body of the HTML program. That's why the declarations had to go inside `<script> </script>` tags.

Though any event handler can reference the globally declared variables, the same is not true for the values of the text elements, such as the `price`. The `value` property of this window is local to the element. So, if an event handler of one element needs to place a value in the window of another element, it must describe how to navigate to the item it wants to change. That was the purpose of this code:

```
document.Bean.price.value = "0.00";
```

It uses the dot operator to navigate from the enclosing document to the target element value, by naming the appropriate item at each step along the path. The dot operator is best read right to left and can then be pronounced "of." So the statement reads, "assign `0.00` to the `value` attribute *of the* `price` window *of the* `Bean` form *of the* `document`."

The Bean Counter application illustrates three different ways to reference data values in an event-handling program: as variables local to a handler (`taxRate`), as variables global to all the handlers (`drink`), and as a variable in another element (`document.Bean.price.value`). In the first two cases the reference simply requires the variable name because they are defined in the handler (in the case of locals) or in an "enclosing" program (in the case of globals). Only cross-element references require the dot operator.

Program and Test

The programming process for the Bean Counter application was incremental. We began by producing a minimal 14-line HTML program (see Figure 19.4), and then we tested it. We added a skeleton table and tested it. We improved the table one feature at a time, testing as we went. We wrote JavaScript to solve one event handler at a time. And, recognizing similarities among the various events, we developed their event handlers together. Finally, we critiqued the result.

The result is a 109-line program of nearly 3000 characters. Compared to other first programs, it's huge! This strategy—the result of breaking the task into tiny pieces and testing the program after each small milestone—had two advantages: At no point did we have to solve a complex task that taxed our brains, and the continual testing meant that we immediately knew where any errors were located, namely, in the part we just added. Though the program in Appendix C looks impressive, it is not hard to produce by the program-and-test method. Obviously the approach works generally, as we'll see again in Chapter 22.

Assess the Program Design

When the initial design was completed, we critiqued the result. We were not critiquing the programming. Rather, we were critiquing how well our solution fulfilled the barista's needs. This is an important part of any design effort, but it is especially critical for software. Since software can do anything, it should perfectly match the solution requirements. We found that our design did not give the barista feedback, and so violated one of the principles listed in Chapter 2. This shortcoming could be remedied by adding feedback windows.

SUMMARY

We created the Bean Counter application using the price computation of Chapter 18 and a GUI developed in this chapter. The result is a substantial program that performs a useful computation, at least if you are a barista. The application is analogous to the calculator applications provided by operating systems: the user uses the application by clicking or typing. The requested computation is performed immediately in response to the input events. In the process of creating our application we:

> Used HTML to set up a context in which event handlers perform the actual work. The setup involved placing buttons and other input elements on a Web page, so a user could enter data and receive results. This is the input/output part of the application and it is principally written in HTML.

> Wrote JavaScript code for the event handlers. This is the processing part of the application. We used the event-based programming style and the basic instructions we learned in Chapter 18. The style, which is ideal for interactive applications, will be used throughout the rest of the book. Though HTML and JavaScript are separate languages, that won't matter much. Generally, HTML will simply be the input/output part of a program written in JavaScript.

EXERCISES

Multiple Choice

1. HTML pages are made from
   A. JavaScript
   B. ASCII text
   C. word processing files
   D. any of the above

2. The first tag of a Web page is
   A. `<script>`
   B. `<head>`
   C. `<top>`
   D. `<html>`

3. Most of the content of a Web page goes inside the
   A. `<head>` tag
   B. `<body>` tag,
   C. `<content>` tag
   D. `<page>` tag

4. The `<bgcolor>` tag sets the
   A. text color
   B. background color
   C. border color
   D. link color

5. The `<p>` tag is used to
   A. insert a picture
   B. print a page
   C. insert a paragraph
   D. load a page

6. All of the following are input elements except
   A. print
   B. radio button
   C. text box
   D. checkbox

7. In JavaScript, `onClick` is a(n)
   A. variable
   B. event
   C. event handler
   D. button

8. The operating system signals that a mouse click has occurred. This is called a(n)
   A. handler
   B. event
   C. trigger
   D. action

9. When a button is clicked, the browser
   A. looks for an `onClick` event handler
   B. looks for the JavaScript program to download
   C. creates the button for the program
   D. none of the above

10. The GUI for a Web-based application is built with
    A. HTML
    B. JavaScript
    C. both of the above
    D. none of the above

Short Answer

1. The interface for a JavaScript program is a(n) _____.

2. The extension for an HTML page must be _____

3. The _____ tag is used to place a line horizontally across a Web page.

4. The _____ tag is used to place text in italic.

5. A(n) _____ is an indication from the computer that something just happened.

6. A(n) _____ is programming code that responds to an event.

7. A(n) _____ is used to change a value in another element.

8. In the line, `document.Bean.price.value = "0.00"` the input element is _____, the attribute is _____, and _____ is the form.

9. _____ elements are used for both input and output.

10. _____ is a function used in JavaScript to round numbers.

11. The _____ principle of user interfaces states that a computer should indicate when it has completed the action.

12. Java Script is used mainly for _____.

13. In HTML, _____ are used to place and display content.

14. A(n) _____ approach to programming breaks a task into small pieces and tests each piece along the way.

Exercises

1. How many inputs are needed for the Bean Counter program (Figure 19.1) to run correctly?

2. How many outputs does the Bean Counter program have?

3. Explain how variables are initialized. Why do variables need to be initialized?

4. Could radio buttons be used for this application? What would they be like?

5. What would the variable for storing a person's age be called? Create an input element that asks for a person's age.

6. The tax rate for the Bean Counter program is 8.8 percent. What needs to be changed if the tax rate drops to 7 percent?

7. What events are coded into the Bean Counter program?

8. Why won't you know how much your coffee costs until you click on the **Total** button?

9. Explain why none of these strings match:

   `'Espresso'`, `'espresso'`, `'ESPRESSO'`, `'Expresso'`, `' espresso '`

10. In layman's terms, explain what happens when the user clicks on the Tall button.

11. Why is a dot operator needed when referencing some variables and not others?

12. Can the user make this program crash?

chapter **20**

THINKING BIG
Programming Functions

learning objectives

> Apply JavaScript rules for functions, declarations, return values, function calls, scope of reference, and local/global variable reference

> Write JavaScript functions with the proper structure

> Build a GUI that contains functions, analogous to the Memory Bank Web page

> Explain how computers generate random numbers

THINKING BIG

Programming Functions

Civilization advances by extending the number of important operations which we can perform without thinking about them.

—ALFRED NORTH WHITEHEAD 1911

AS WE KNOW, an algorithm is a precise and systematic method for producing a specific outcome. If we want an algorithm that we can "carry around" and use in different settings—say while we're programming JavaScript—we put it into a function. A **function** is simply the standard package into which we place algorithms so they are useful in practice.

We have two motives for packaging algorithms into functions: The first benefit of functions is reuse; once we work out the details of how an algorithm produces its outcome, we'd rather not think about it again. Functions allow us to reuse our thinking over and over without repeating the actual thinking. That's a great advantage. The second benefit is to *reduce complexity*, that is, to simplify our thinking. Many times—we'll see a specific case in Chapter 22—problems get so complicated that we experience "brain fry" trying to figure out how to solve them. Functions allow us to encapsulate parts of the solution so that we can set them aside where they no longer confuse us. That's a great advantage, too.

In this chapter we learn how to create functions in JavaScript. While learning the syntax and operation of functions, we will show many simple examples. The task of learning about functions is not too difficult, so there is time at the end of the chapter to create the *interactive* Memory Bank Web page, a personal page where we can file away our functions as well as all those facts we need to know, but would rather not spend time remembering.

● ANATOMY OF A FUNCTION

Functions are packages for algorithms, which implies they have three parts:

> *Name*

> *Parameters*

> *Definition*

Together these parts form the **function declaration**; they are present in functions of all sorts, including JavaScript and other programming languages, spreadsheets, databases, mathematics, etc. As we consider each, let's use the process of converting from the Celsius to Fahrenheit temperature scales as a running example, since it's a computation many Americans struggle with. (We'll do the Fahrenheit to Celsius conversion, the one the rest of the world struggles with, later.) Recall that the relationship between Celsius and Fahrenheit is

Fahrenheit = ⁹/₅ Celsius + 32

This is an equation, not an assignment statement. It is this simple computation that we want to package up into a function.

---

*fit***BYTE**   **Alternate Function.** Functions are also known as *procedures* in both informal and computing languages. *Subroutine* is an antiquated computing term for the same idea. Another technical term is *method*.

Pick a Name

Obviously, the *name* is the identifier for the function, and it is common to use it to describe what the function does. Although computers would be happy with any unique name, it's best to try to pick meaningful names that will be useful to humans. And we are the humans of greatest interest. We will want a suggestive name to remind ourselves what computation the function performs when we encounter it weeks or years later.

Names in JavaScript follow the usual rules for identifiers, that is, they begin with a letter, use any mix of letters, numbers, and underscores (_), avoid reserved words (see Appendix B), and are case sensitive. Let's pick `convertC2F` for our conversion function.

Naturally, programming languages have a standard form for writing function declarations, and JavaScript's form is quite typical

```
function <name> ( <parameter list> ) {
    <statement list>
}
```

We have just picked the name; the other two parts will be described momentarily. Look at the punctuation. Parentheses always follow a function name, even if there is no *<parameter list>*. And the curly braces, although they can be positioned anywhere to enclose the *<statement list>*, should always be placed where they are obvious. Like the curly braces used with `if` statements, they are easy to miss. So programmers adopt the convention of placing them where shown so that everyone knows where to look for them.

Parameters

The *parameters* are the values that the function will compute on, the input to the function. For our example, the input is the Celsius temperature. In order for the statements of the algorithm to refer to the input values, they are given names. The *<parameter list>* is simply the list of names for the input values separated by commas. Parameter names follow the usual rules for identifiers in all programming languages. If we pick `tempInC` as the name for our one parameter in our conversion function, that is, the Celsius temperature we want to convert to Fahrenheit, then our definition so far is

```
function convertC2F ( tempInC ) {
     <statement list>
}
```

When writing our algorithm statements, the parameters are like normal variables; the only difference is that they begin with a value—the function's input—and they don't have to be declared. Because they're parameters, JavaScript automatically declares them for us.

Definition

The *definition* is the algorithm written in a programming language. A function definition follows the language's general rules for program statements, so for JavaScript, the rules that apply are those covered in Chapters 18–21 and Appendix B.

Because the definition is computing an algorithm—a precise and systematic method for producing a specified result—there must be some way to say what the result is, that is, some way to give the answer. Different languages do this differently, but JavaScript uses the statement

```
return <expression>
```

where the answer is whatever value the *<expression>* produces. We call the answer the function's result or value. For example, the function

```
function cheshireCat ();
    return "Smile!";
```

is a function that returns the letter string `Smile!`. It is also a function with no parameters.

Converting from Celsius to Fahrenheit is so easy—the answer we want to produce is simply ⁹⁄₅ *Celsius* + 32—that our entire function definition is a single line

```
function convertC2F ( tempInC ) {
    return 9/5*tempInC + 32;
}
```

First, notice that we use our parameter `tempInC`, which is the input to the function, as the variable in the conversion computation, and second, that we must write the multiply operation (*) explicitly, as is normal in programming.

That's it. We never have to think about how to convert Celsius to Fahrenheit again. This function will do it for us, saving our brainpower for more important stuff, like movies.

> **try it**
>
> **Q.** Write a JavaScript function to convert from Fahrenheit to Celsius. The equation for the relationship above implies that Celsius is ⁵⁄₉ (*Fahrenheit* – 32).
>
> **A.** The solution is completely analogous to the `convertC2F()` function:
>
> ```
> function convertF2C (tempInF) {
>     return 5/9*(tempInF - 32);
> }
> ```

The `convertC2F()` function defines the algorithm for converting from Celsius to Fahrenheit, but how exactly will we get the answers? We must *call* the function.

Calling a function is asking the computer to run or execute the statements of the function to produce the answers. We simply write the function's name and put the input values, known as **arguments**, in parentheses after, as in `convertC2F(38)`. The computer follows the definition of the function and returns the answer, `100.4`. Now, that's hot! Getting answers couldn't be easier.

Since we wrote our function in JavaScript, we will have to illustrate the function call by setting up a little Web page to host the JavaScript and to provide a situation in which to call the function. Figure 20.1 shows the page. It begins with the standard HTML; it gives the definition of the function—we say the function is *declared*—and it computes the result using an `alert()` call, as was used for version 0 of the Bean Counter computation in Chapter 19. (Of course, `alert()` is itself a built-in JavaScript function.)

*fit*TIP

Arguments versus Parameters. Notice that parameters and arguments are two different ways to refer to the same thing. In the function *declaration* we write `function convertC2F(tempInC)` and use the term *parameter* for `tempInC`. In the function *call* we write `convertC2F(38)` and use the term *argument* for 38. It's a parameter when the function's input is viewed from the "inside" of the function; it's an argument when the function's input is viewed from "outside" of the function. They are opposite sides of the same thing.

```
<html>
    <head><title>Function Execution</title></head>
    <body>
        <script language="JavaScript">
            function convertC2F (tempInC) {
                return 9/5*tempInC + 32;
            }
            alert( "38C is " + convertC2F(38) + "F");
        </script>
    </body>
</html>
```

> **JavaScript**
>
> 38C is 100.4F
>
> OK

Figure 20.1. *The* `convertC2F()` *function in JavaScript called from an* `alert()`.

Declaration versus Call

Figure 20.1 illustrates an important point about functions: A function's declaration (specification) is different from its call (use). To emphasize the distinction, let's review what we just did.

We *declared* the function right after the `<script>` tag by writing down its three parts in the form required by JavaScript. Functions are only declared once, because it's unnecessary to tell the computer more than once how the function works. Notice, for built-in functions like `alert()`, we don't even have to do that much: Some other programmer declared `alert()` while writing the JavaScript interpreter; all we have to do is call it.

We *called* the function `convertC2F()` in an `alert()` call as part of the composition of a string of characters for displaying the answer. Functions are typically called many times because the answers they give are needed many times. For example, we expect to call `convertC2F()` every time someone mentions a Celsius temperature we don't understand. *One declaration, many calls.*

The main problem with `convertC2F()` is that it is inconvenient to write a Web page to find out the answer, even a little one like Figure 20.1. The problem is that in present solution, the argument, `38`, had to be typed directly into an `alert()` call; to give a different temperature, we'd have to change the file and reexecute it. It would be more convenient if we had a Web page already prepared in which we just typed the Celsius temperature into an input text box, and the answer was returned. This is possible, of course, using forms like we used to display the total in the Bean Counter application.

Forms and Functions

The page we intend to construct looks like this:

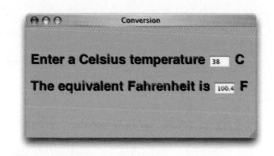

Most of the work has been thought out already. All that remains is to set up the forms.

Recall from Chapter 19 that

> forms must be enclosed in `<form>` tags, which have a name attribute

> text boxes are specified by an `<input type="text" . . . >` tag

> text boxes have a name, size, and other properties

> to refer to the contents of a text box named `tb` in a form named `fm`, we write `document.fm.tb.value`

> the main event handler of interest is `onChange`

The `onChange` event handler recognizes when a value is entered into the Celsius window (by the cursor moving out of the window) and handles it as we direct. Of course, the operation is pretty easy—we call the `convertC2F()` function with the number typed into the window as the argument. More specifically, let's set up the forms as follows

```
<form name="therm">
  <input type="text" name="tempIn" size=4
       onChange=''>                          For Celsius input
  <input type="text" name="tempOut" size=4>  For Fahrenheit output
</form>
```

The `tempIn` window will be where we type the Celsius temperature, and the `tempOut` window will show the result. (Recall that even though we use it as an output in this case, JavaScript uses the `<input . . . >` tag for both input and output text boxes.) So, with these names, we handle the `onChange` event with the function call

```
onChange = "document.therm.tempOut.value =
   convertC2F(document.therm.tempIn.value)"
```

In English, this line says, when the input window (`tempIn`) is changed, use the value in that window (`document.therm.tempIn.value`) as an argument to `convertC2F()` and assign the result to display as the value (`document.therm.tempOut.value`) of the output window. Putting some text around the text boxes yields the page we want, as shown in Figure 20.2.

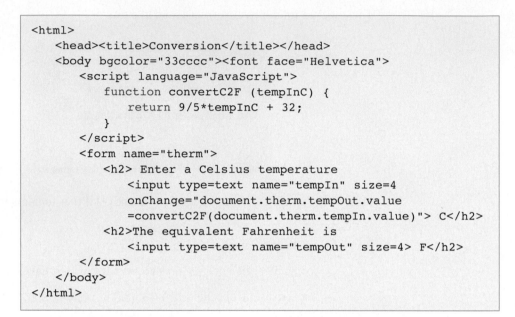

```
<html>
    <head><title>Conversion</title></head>
    <body bgcolor="33cccc"><font face="Helvetica">
        <script language="JavaScript">
            function convertC2F (tempInC) {
                return 9/5*tempInC + 32;
            }
        </script>
        <form name="therm">
            <h2> Enter a Celsius temperature
                <input type=text name="tempIn" size=4
                onChange="document.therm.tempOut.value
                =convertC2F(document.therm.tempIn.value)"> C</h2>
            <h2>The equivalent Fahrenheit is
                <input type=text name="tempOut" size=4> F</h2>
        </form>
    </body>
</html>
```

Figure 20.2. *The HTML/JavaScript source for the Conversion application.*

Calling to Customize a Page

In JavaScript there are three ways to get the result of a function call to print on the monitor, and we've just seen two: before the page is created, as we saw with the `alert()` call, and interactively after the page is displayed, as we saw with the **Conversion** page. The third case applies *while* the page is being created. Calling functions while the browser is creating the page is handy because we can customize pages on-the-fly.

First, we need to know how a browser builds a page. It begins by reading through the HTML file, figuring out all of the tags and preparing to build the page. As it's reading the file, it finds our JavaScript tags. The browser removes those tags and all of the text between them, that is, our JavaScript. Then it does whatever the JavaScript tells it to do. One thing that the JavaScript could tell the browser to do is to put some text back into the file, where the JavaScript just came from. There is a built-in function, `document.write()`, that does just that: It inserts the text of its argument into the Web page at the point of the JavaScript tags, as shown in Figure 20.3.

HTML Source File	HTML Used for Page

```
<html>
  <head><title>Explain</title></head>
  <body><p> The browser reads the
     HTML before it creates the page.
     When it comes to a script tag it
     processes it immediately. There
     may be document.write()s and
     if so, it writes the argument
     <script language="JavaScript">
        document.write("into the file");
     </script>
     at the point of the script tags.
  </body>
</html>
```

```
<html>
  <head><title>Explain</title></head>
  <body><p> The browser reads the
     HTML before it creates the page.
     When it comes to a script tag it
     processes it immediately. There
     may be document.write()s and
     if so it writes the argument

     into the file

     at the point of the script tags.
  </body>
</html>
```

Figure 20.3. *An HTML source file containing a JavaScript* `document.write()`*, and the HTML text used by the browser to create the page.*

We can use this idea to build a page on-the-fly. Suppose we want a table of temperature conversions for a Web page with a column for Celsius and a column for Fahrenheit (see Figure 20.4). It is easy to set up the page and specify the table tags using normal HTML. Place `<script>` tags where the table *rows* will go. Then, using `document.write()` within the JavaScript tags, create the rows of the table. A row will be composed of several components joined (concatenated) together. For example, the first row is built from

```
<tr align=center bgcolor="#00ccff">    Table row tag and attributes
<td>-10</td>                           Table data tags for first entry
<td>                                   Table data tag for second entry
   convertC2F(-10)                     Call to conversion function
</td></tr>                             Closing tags for data and row
```

Notice that the first table entry (−10) is also the value converted by the function call that creates the second table entry; that is, −10 is the argument to `convertC2F()`.

When the components are combined into a `document.write()` call with the proper quotes and concatenations, it has the form

```
document.write('<tr align=center bgcolor="#00ccff">'
   + '<td>-10</td><td>' + convertC2F(-10) + '</td></tr>')
```

All of the rows have a similar structure.

As the browser is setting up the page, it encounters the script tags. It does what our JavaScript program says and calls the `document.write()` functions. To call those functions the browser must construct its argument using concatenation. As it begins to build the argument string, it encounters our `convertC2F(-10)` function call with its argument (**-10**), and runs it. The Fahrenheit value is returned (**14**), it is included with the other parts of the argument string, and the **document.write()** function places the newly constructed row tags into the document. When the browser builds the page, the table is formed from our created-on-the-fly rows that used our conversion function to figure the Fahrenheit temperature.

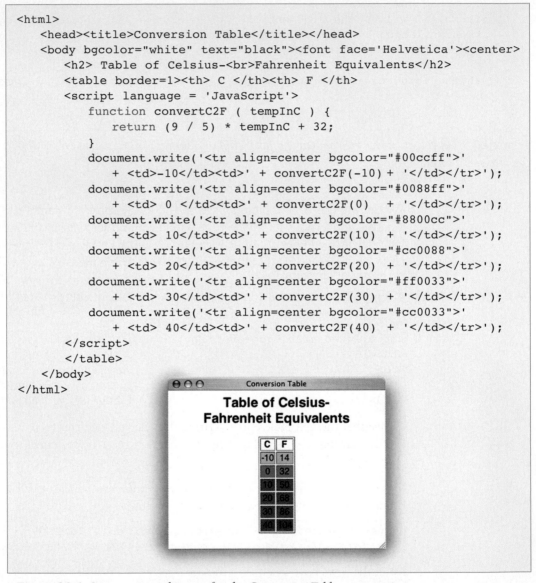

```html
<html>
    <head><title>Conversion Table</title></head>
    <body bgcolor="white" text="black"><font face='Helvetica'><center>
        <h2> Table of Celsius-<br>Fahrenheit Equivalents</h2>
        <table border=1><th> C </th><th> F </th>
        <script language = 'JavaScript'>
            function convertC2F ( tempInC ) {
                return (9 / 5) * tempInC + 32;
            }
            document.write('<tr align=center bgcolor="#00ccff">'
                + <td>-10</td><td>' + convertC2F(-10) + '</td></tr>');
            document.write('<tr align=center bgcolor="#0088ff">'
                + <td> 0 </td><td>' + convertC2F(0)  + '</td></tr>');
            document.write('<tr align=center bgcolor="#8800cc">'
                + <td> 10</td><td>' + convertC2F(10) + '</td></tr>');
            document.write('<tr align=center bgcolor="#cc0088">'
                + <td> 20</td><td>' + convertC2F(20) + '</td></tr>');
            document.write('<tr align=center bgcolor="#ff0033">'
                + <td> 30</td><td>' + convertC2F(30) + '</td></tr>');
            document.write('<tr align=center bgcolor="#cc0033">'
                + <td> 40</td><td>' + convertC2F(40) + '</td></tr>');
        </script>
        </table>
    </body>
</html>
```

Figure 20.4. *Source text and image for the Conversion Table computation.*

 Hot Tip. Notice that it's not hard to estimate Celsius temperatures in Fahrenheit. Remember a couple of pairs, such as 20°C is 68°F or 30°C is 86°F, and for each 10° in Celsius up or down, add or subtract 18° in Fahrenheit. So, 10°C is 50°F.

WRITING FUNCTIONS, USING FUNCTIONS

Though our knowledge of functions is not quite complete, it is good enough to write some functions for interesting computations. In this section we compute the Body Mass Index, a combined measure of height and weight, and we try flipping electronic "coins." Both computations give us further practice with functions.

Flipping Electronic Coins

How can a computer flip a coin? It seems impossible, except for robots, because computers have no moving parts. The answer is not to focus on the act of flipping, but on the fact that a coin flip is an unpredictable event whose two outcomes are "equally probable." We might guess that a computer could generate a random number between 0 and 1, and round to the nearest whole number; 0 could represent tails and 1 could represent heads. About half the time the outcome would be tails (the random number was less than 0.5) and the rest of the time it would be heads. The only problem is that computers are completely deterministic, as we learned in Chapter 9: Given a program and its input, the outcome is perfectly predictable. It's not random in any way. It would be possible to create truly random numbers based on an unpredictable physical process such as counting the particle emissions from a radioactive material like U_{238}, but computers don't have to be radioactive to generate random numbers. They can generate pseudo-random numbers.

fit **BYTE**

Flipping Out. The mathematician John von Neumann, one of the computing pioneers, once said, "Anyone who attempts to generate random numbers by deterministic means is, of course, living in a state of sin."

Pseudo-random numbers are an invention of computer science in which an algorithm produces a sequence of numbers that passes the statistical tests for randomness. For example, a sequence of pseudo-random numbers between 0 and 1 has the property that about half are closer to 0 and the others are closer to 1, that is, the sequence items, when rounded to the nearest whole number, behave like a coin flip. (It's still deterministic: If you know the algorithm and the starting point, you can perfectly predict the sequence; but you don't!) Because pseudo-random numbers are so good, we'll drop the "pseudo" part from here on.

Random numbers are important in many applications, so programming languages come with a built-in function for generating them. In JavaScript the random number generator is called `Math.random()`. It's part of a library of handy mathematical functions, which includes `Math.round()`. Each time `Math.random()` is called, it generates a random number between 0 and 1, which is never exactly equal to 0 or 1. So, a function to flip electronic coins—that is, to generate a 0 or a 1 with roughly equal probability—would have the form

```
function coinFlip() {
    return Math.round(Math.random());
}
```

When `coinFlip()` is called, it returns with equal probability a 0 or a 1, which can represent tails and heads.

The obvious improvement to the `coinFlip()` function is to return the text **Heads** and **Tails** rather than numbers. So, we create a new function

```
function flipText() {
   if (coinFlip()==0)
      return 'Tails';
   else
      return 'Heads';
}
```

Notice that we have called the previous `coinFlip()` function in the `if` statement test of the `flipText()` function. Calling functions from inside other functions is the most common way to use functions because it allows us to build more complex programs progressively.

Our flipping function would be even more useful if it gave the outcome in response to clicking a button on a Web page. As we learned in Chapter 19, buttons are inputs just like text boxes, so creating such a Web page is not too difficult. We will need a form, which we call **eCoin**, and the functions we've just finished programming. Figure 20.5 shows the image and source for this program.

```
<html>
   <head><title>Electronic Coin Flipping</title></head>
   <body bgcolor="#ccffcc" text="green"><font face="Helvetica">
      <script language="JavaScript">
         function coinFlip() {
            return Math.round(Math.random());
         }
         function flipText() {
            if (coinFlip()==0)
               return 'Tails';
            else
               return 'Heads';
         }
      </script>
      <form name="eCoin">
         <h2>Heads or Tails? <input type=button value="Flip"
            onClick='document.eCoin.ans.value=flipText()'>
         <input type=text name="ans" size=5></h2>
      </form>
   </body>
</html>
```

Figure 20.5. The JavaScript and image for the Electronic Coin-Flipping page.

fit **TIP** **Bug Report.** When you cannot figure out why a JavaScript program is not working, you can often find helpful information from Mozilla's JavaScript Console, where the browser informs us what it doesn't like about a JavaScript program:
Tools > Web Development > JavaScript Console.

The Body Mass Index Computation

The Body Mass Index (BMI) is a standard measure of a person's weight in proportion to his or her height. (A "normal" BMI is generally accepted to be in the range of 18.5 to 25, but as usual, experts disagree.) What is your BMI? The formula for determining BMI, using metric units, that is, height in meters and weight in kilos, is

Index = weight/height²

In the same way that it was easy to translate the Celsius conversion into a function, it is easy to translate the metric BMI into a function, though this time we need two parameters, one for weight and one for height. Also, let's take the height in centimeters and convert:

```
function bmiM ( weightKg, heightCm ) {   //Compute BMI in metric
    var heightM = heightCm / 100;        //Change cm to meters
    return weightKg / (heightM * heightM);
}
```

We have used **var** to declare an extra variable (**heightM**) for use in converting from centimeters to meters. In fact, the conversion is part of the initialization for the variable. Also, there's no "square" in JavaScript, so we must multiply **heightM** times itself.

For weight and height in English units, the formula is

Index = 4.89 weight / height²

where weight is given in pounds and height is given in feet. Of course, Americans give their height in feet and inches—that is, a person says, "I'm 5 feet, 6 inches" rather than "I'm 5.5 feet." But working with feet and inches is a little messy, so we take the height input in inches and convert it to feet before applying the formula. That strategy yields

```
function bmiE ( weightLbs, heightIn ) { //Compute BMI in English
    var heightFt = heightIn / 12;       //Change inches to feet
    return 4.89 * weightLbs / (heightFt * heightFt);
}
```

The two functions are quite similar.

It would be more universal if the function could compute the BMI in whatever units the user specified. That would require a new function with three inputs, one for the kind of units and the other two for weight and height. Such a function could use our previous functions—another example of calling a function within a function. The declaration for the universal BMI is

```
function BMI ( units, weight, height ) {
   if (units == 'E')
       return bmiE(weight, height); //Answer for English
   else
       return bmiM(weight, height); //Answer for Metric
}
```

Notice first that we check the `units` parameter to call the correct function. Second, we have simply passed the `weight` and `height` parameters as arguments to our previously programmed BMI functions.

---

fit **TIP**   **Counting Arguments.** A function must be given as many arguments as it has parameters, because they correspond one-to-one. For this reason, for multi-parameter functions, it is also important that the arguments are given in the right order.

How should the BMI function be used? Perhaps the most convenient way would be to have a Web page similar to the Conversion and Coin Flipping pages. For that, we need to define the functions, set up the forms, and define the event handlers, as we've done before. The final result is shown in Figure 20.6.

---

fit **TIP**   **Code Breaking.** Notice the structure of the Figure BMI page in Figure 20.6. Besides the HTML tags at the beginning and end, the program has two main parts: A section enclosed in script tags, where functions and other JavaScript computations are given, and a section enclosed in form tags, where input, output, and other text of the page are given. Most programs in this chapter (and this book) have that structure; recognizing it helps with understanding long sequences of text.

We have used radio buttons to select the units as English or metric. Recall from Chapter 19 that radio buttons, like command buttons, are specified with `<input . . .>` tags, and so must be placed within `<form>` tags. We name the form `mass`. The two new features of radio buttons are

> > all related radio buttons share the same name; that is, if when clicking on one the other should click off, then they must have the same name

> > radio buttons can be preset by writing `checked='true'`

The button has been preset to English units, but can easily be preset to metric.

In addition to presetting a radio button we must also write the `onClick` event handlers for them. What should happen when the user clicks on the radio button? Obviously, we need to remember the type of units chosen. But we are not quite ready to call the `BMI()` function—the other inputs are not yet available—so we need to store the values in a variable that we will pass to `BMI()`. At the start of the JavaScript code we declare and initialize

```
var scale = "E";
```

```
<html>
    <head><title>Figure BMI</title></head>
    <body bgcolor="#8888FF" text="white"><font face="Helvetica">
        <script language="JavaScript">
            var scale='E';
            function bmiM ( weightKg, heightCm ) {      //Metric BMI
                var heightM = heightCm / 100;           //Change to meters
                return weightKg / (heightM * heightM);
            }
            function bmiE ( weightLbs, heightIn ) {     //English BMI
                var heightFt = heightIn / 12;           //Change to feet
                return 4.89 * weightLbs / (heightFt * heightFt);
            }
            function BMI ( units, weight, height ) {
                if (units == 'E')
                    return bmiE( weight, height);       //Answer in English
                else
                    return bmiM( weight, height);       //Answer in Metric
            }
        </script>
        <form name="mass">
            <h2 align="right"> What units do you use:
                <input type=radio name="unit" onClick='scale="E"'
                    checked=true> English
                <input type=radio name="unit" onClick='scale="M"'>
                    Metric</h2>
            <h2 align="right">Enter your weight in <i>lbs</i> or
                    <i>kg</i>:
                <input type=text name="wgt" size=4></h2>
            <h2 align="right"> Enter your height in <i>in</i> or
                    <i>cm</i>:
                <input type=text name="hgt" size=4
                    onChange="document.mass.ans.value=
                        BMI(scale,
                        document.mass.wgt.value,
                        document.mass.hgt.value)"> </h2>
            <h2 align="right"> Your Body Mass Index is:
                <input type=text name="ans" size=4></h2>
        </form>
    </body>
</html>
```

Figure 20.6. The image and source for the Figure BMI page.

Thus, `scale` starts out with the value that was preset in the radio button. When the Metric button is clicked, we want

```
scale = "M";
```

as the response to the click-event. So, that becomes the `onClick` event handler for Metric. Similarly, when the English button is clicked we should assign `scale` the value `"E"` again.

Finally, notice that we call the `BMI()` function from the `onChange` event handler for the height (`hgt`) input. Since we assume the values will be filled in sequentially, all of the inputs will be available after the height has been entered. So the computation can be performed. The arguments to the call

```
onChange = "document.mass.ans.value=
        BMI(scale,
            document.mass.wgt.value,
            document.mass.hgt.value)"
```

require some explanation. As we learned in Chapter 19, the "dot notation" allows the browser to navigate among the different forms to locate the values in the other boxes. The `scale` variable, having been declared outside of any function or form is a global variable. No navigation is required, because it is known to all functions and forms.

Global variables, like `scale`, are considered in greater detail in the next section. It is the last topic we need to mention about functions.

Scoping: When to Use Names

There is one thing left to learn about functions: name scoping. Once we've learned about it, all that remains is practice.

The scope of a name—any name in a program—defines how "far" from its declaration it can be used. Every programming language has its own scoping constraints, but the general rule for scoping is fairly simple:

> Variable names declared in a function can be used only within that function. They are said to be *local to the function* and are called *local variables* or simply *locals*; parameters are considered local variables.

> Variable names declared outside any function can be used throughout the program. They are said to be *global to the function* and are called *global variables* or simply *globals*.

The consequences of this distinction are global variables can be used inside of functions, but local variables cannot be used outside of functions they are declared in. Examples will make this clear.

An Annotated Example. Consider the JavaScript program shown in Figure 20.7, which illustrates different cases of the above rule. The functions in the program are a variation on the BMI computation of Figure 20.6: Rather than choosing between English and metric each time, however, the page is customized to one kind of unit when it is created. (This is another way—besides presetting the radio button—to specialize the solution to the default settings of the common case when most users want the same units.) Since the page will have different text for each case, the forms are created with `document.write()` calls, which haven't been filled in because they are not important to our example. In addition, there is a test to see if the `height` is zero, so as to avoid a divide-by-zero error. If it is zero, the `reportErr` variable is checked to see if errors are supposed to be reported, and in that case `"Huh?"` is returned as the function's value.

```
<script language="JavaScript">
   var scale='E'; //Set to M for metric units      Declare global variable
   var reportErr=true; //Request error reports      Declare global variable
   function bmiM ( weightKg, heightCm ) {           Parameters are locals
      var heightM = heightCm / 100;                 Declare local, set w/local
      return weightKg/ (heightM*heightM);           Reference local variables
   }
   function bmiE ( weightLbs, heightIn ) {          Parameters are local
      var heightFt = heightIn / 12;                 Declare local; set w/local
      return 4.89*weightLbs/(heightFt*heightFt);    Reference locals
   }
   function BMI ( units, weight, height ) {         Parameters are locals
      if (height==0) {                              Reference local variable
         if (reportErr)                             Reference global variable
            alert("Height is 0!");
         return 'Huh?';
      }
      if (units == 'E')                             Reference local variable
         return bmiE( weight, height);              Use locals as arguments
      else
         return bmiM( weight, height);              Use locals as arguments
      }
      if (scale=='E') {                             Reference global variable
         document.write('<h1>BMI in English</h1>');
         ... Forms customized to English input
      }
      else {
         document.write('<h1>BMI in Metric</h1>');
         ... Forms customized to metric input
   }
</script>
```

Figure 20.7. *Annotated functions showing the scope of each variable reference.*

Figure 20.7 classifies all of the variable uses in the program as to whether they are local or global. The classification is simply an application of the scoping rule: The variables declared within a function—both the user-defined variables like `heightM` and the parameters like `heightCm`—are locals. The two global variables, `scale` and `reportErr`, are declared at the start of the JavaScript, outside of any function. `scale` and `reportErr` are referenced inside `BMI()`, illustrating that globals can be referenced from inside functions.

The only way to figure out the scoping information shown in the figure is to notice where the variables are declared and where they are used, and then apply the rule.

So, why is scoping so important? Local and global variables behave differently. *Locals come into existence when a function begins, and when it ends, they vanish. Global variables are around all the time.* So, if information must be saved from one function call to the next, it must be a global variable.

Global/Local Scope Interaction. There is one tricky case to consider. It's the case where a global variable and a local variable have the same name. For example

```
var y=0;
...
function tricky (x) {
    var y;
        y = x;
    ...
}
```

In the example, `y` is globally declared and can be referenced anywhere. The same name is declared as a local in the `tricky()` function. They are two different variables. Which `y` is being assigned the parameter `x`? It's the local `y` because it is declared in the function's scope, making it the "closest" declaration and hiding the global `y`.

Because programmers tend to reuse names, the `tricky()` case does arise. Luckily, programmers almost always intend for the reference to be to the local variable, so the program usually works right. When they don't, it's usually a tough bug to find!

Perhaps scoping is analogous to using pronouns—he, she, them—in natural language: When speaking it is always necessary for the speaker and the listener to know who a pronoun refers to, and it's the speaker's responsibility to make it clear. In the same way, the programmer and computer have to agree on what a variable name refers to, and it's the programmer's responsibility to get it right.

THE MEMORY BANK WEB PAGE

Remembering useless trivia is easy, probably because it's fun to know. For example,

> *Q: Who was the fifth Beatle?*

> *A: Stuart Sutcliffe was a founding member of The Beatles with Lennon, McCartney, and Harrison.*

Remembering useful stuff seems to be more difficult for some reason. So, in this section we create the Memory Bank Web page for remembering useful computations. It will be a place for us to store information in an interactive form. The Web page will also give us a chance to practice programming with functions.

Plan the Memory Bank Web Page

Figure 20.8 shows the HTML image for the initial Memory Bank Web page. Here is how it is supposed to work. Each row of the table will present a computation. Each text box in the row except the last will be an input to the computation; the last text box will be the output. The user types inputs into the text box(es), and when they are all filled, gets the answer back in the output text box by clicking.

We have started the page with a row for the BMI computation. It's a form of the Figure BMI program of Figure 20.6, except for one improvement: We now allow users to specify their weight and height in either order. (Recall that previously, weight had to be specified before height because we called the **BMI()** function from the **hgt onChange** event handler.) Now, we call it from both the **wgt** and **hgt onChange** event handlers if the other text box already contains a value; otherwise we do nothing, and wait for the other value. This is a more convenient way to present the computation to users.

Our plan is to add more rows to the table using the computations we've programmed, plus others. We will add embellishments to the page to make it more useful to us personally. The idea is to create a page to keep in our Web space that we can add to from time to time as we progress through college. After all, if functions save us some thinking, we might as well present them on a fancy Web page for convenience.

Random Additions

We begin by adding our coin-flipping computation to the Memory Bank page, so we can decide with our friend who buys coffee. (If we're going to use electronic money, we'll need electronic coins!) However, anyone who loses will be skeptical about the fairness of our electronic coin flip. (It's fair — computer theorists can prove it!) So, we will improve the computation by adding a count of the number of heads and tails that have been flipped. That way, a skeptic can click the **Flip** button a few times and verify that the outcomes are roughly split between heads and tails.

Revised Random Choice Function

Our previous coin-flipping procedure, **coinFlip()**, used the computation

```
Math.round(Math.random())
```

to choose evenly between 0 and 1. There is another way to pick evenly between 0 and 1: Multiply the result of **Math.random()** times 2, and throw away the digits

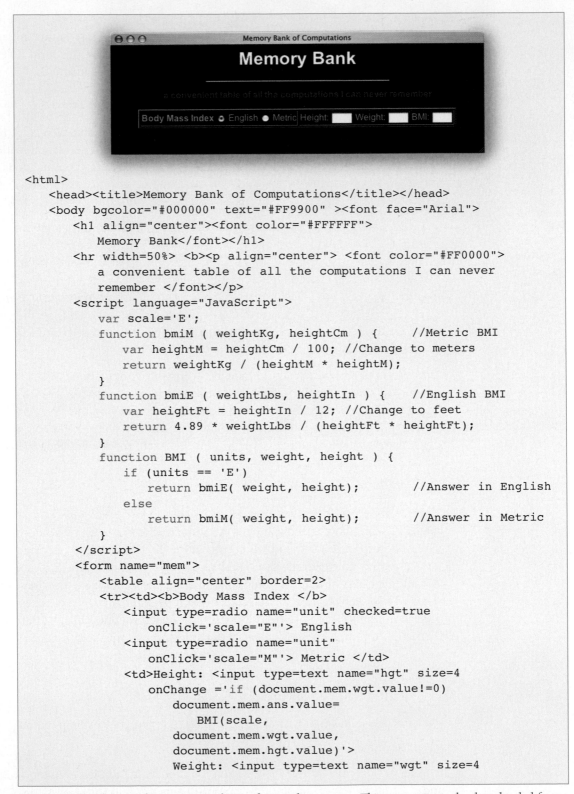

```
<html>
    <head><title>Memory Bank of Computations</title></head>
    <body bgcolor="#000000" text="#FF9900" ><font face="Arial">
        <h1 align="center"><font color="#FFFFFF">
            Memory Bank</font></h1>
        <hr width=50%> <b><p align="center"> <font color="#FF0000">
            a convenient table of all the computations I can never
            remember </font></p>
        <script language="JavaScript">
            var scale='E';
            function bmiM ( weightKg, heightCm ) {      //Metric BMI
                var heightM = heightCm / 100; //Change to meters
                return weightKg / (heightM * heightM);
            }
            function bmiE ( weightLbs, heightIn ) {     //English BMI
                var heightFt = heightIn / 12; //Change to feet
                return 4.89 * weightLbs / (heightFt * heightFt);
            }
            function BMI ( units, weight, height ) {
                if (units == 'E')
                    return bmiE( weight, height);       //Answer in English
                else
                    return bmiM( weight, height);       //Answer in Metric
            }
        </script>
        <form name="mem">
            <table align="center" border=2>
            <tr><td><b>Body Mass Index </b>
                <input type=radio name="unit" checked=true
                    onClick='scale="E"'> English
                <input type=radio name="unit"
                    onClick='scale="M"'> Metric </td>
                <td>Height: <input type=text name="hgt" size=4
                onChange ='if (document.mem.wgt.value!=0)
                    document.mem.ans.value=
                        BMI(scale,
                    document.mem.wgt.value,
                    document.mem.hgt.value)'>
                    Weight: <input type=text name="wgt" size=4
```

Figure 20.8. *The initial Memory Bank interface and its source. This program can be downloaded from* `www.aw.com/snyder/` *(continues next page).*

```
                onChange = 'if (document.mem.hgt.value!=0)
                    document.mem.ans.value=
                        BMI(scale,
                            document.mem.wgt.value,
                            document.mem.hgt.value)'>
                BMI: <input type=text name="ans" size=4>
            </td></tr>
            </table></b>
        </form>
    </body>
</html>
```

Figure 20.8 (continued). *The initial Memory Bank interface and its source. This program can be downloaded from* `www.aw.com/snyder/`

to the right of the decimal point. Since the "throwing away" operation is called `Math.floor()` in JavaScript, the computation becomes

`Math.floor(2*Math.random())`

That result is either 0 or 1 with roughly equal probability.

How does this work? `Math.random()` produces a result in the interval (0,1); that is, any number is possible within those limits (and the limits of the computer) except 0 and 1 themselves. When we multiply `Math.random()` by some number, say 2, we expand the interval over which the random numbers spread, say to (0,2). Generally, multiplying by *n* expands to the interval (0,*n*). The numbers are whole numbers with a decimal fraction. For example in (0,2) we'll have numbers like 0.21598895302006 and 1.84151605441332; a number starting with 2 cannot result, because the end points are not possible. If we throw away the decimal fraction, we get whole numbers, and when the interval is (0,2) we get either 0 or 1. Since `Math.random()` was fair on (0,1), this new technique is also fair.

Such reasoning motivates us to write a function that chooses random whole numbers in a range from 0 to *n*, not including *n*. For coin-flipping, the range will be of size 2, that is, the whole numbers 0 and 1. Since our new function handles situations that are more general than `coinFlip()`, we'll give it a new name:

```
function randNum (range) {
    return Math.floor(range*Math.random());
}
```

So, `randNum(2)` produces values 0 and 1 with equal probability, but the function picks from larger intervals too.

Q: How can `randNum()` be used to pick randomly for the game Rock-Paper-Scissors?

A: Assigning 0 to Rock, 1 to Paper, and 2 to Scissors, `randNum(3)` solves the problem. A function for the computation might have the form

```
function rps () {
    var choice = randNum(3);
    if (choice==0)
        return "Rock";
    if (choice==1)
        return "Paper";
    else
        return "Scissors";
}
```

The Coin-Flipping Row

The coin-flipping row of the table

is defined by text and text boxes of the form:

```
<tr><td><b> Electronic Coin Flip </b></td>
    <td> <input type=button value="Flip"
      onClick='flipCoin()'>
        Outcome: <input type=text name="oc" size=4>
        Heads: <input type=text name="nH" size=3 value=0>
        Tails: <input type=text name="nT" size=3 value=0>
    </td></tr>
```

The components are by now self-explanatory. All that remains is to program the event handler, `flipCoin()`.

To keep track of the numbers of heads and tails flipped, we will need global variables—`numHeads`, `numTails`—that can be incremented from the `flipCoin()` function each time the user clicks **Flip**. We choose global variables rather than defining local variables in `flipCoin()`, because local variables come into existence when a function is called and they vanish after the function returns; so they will not keep their values "across function calls." Accordingly, we add declarations

```
var numHeads=0, numTails=0;
```

just after the `<script . . .>` tag.

With the global counters defined, all that remains is to flip the coin, check the outcome, and update two of the three windows depending on the results of the flip. The following logic implements the function

```
function flipCoin () {
    if (randNum(2)==0) {
        document.mem.oc.value="Heads";
        numHeads=numHeads+1;
        document.mem.nH.value=numHeads;
    }
    else {
        document.mem.oc.value="Tails";
        numTails=numTails+1;
        document.mem.nT.value=numTails;
    }
}
```

Notice that the random number is generated in the test of the `if` statement. Also, the then clause and `else` clause must have curly braces around them because they involve multiple statements. By also adding the definition of `randNum()` to our accumulating HTML file, the newly added row is complete.

The I'm Thinking of a Number Row

The Rock-Paper-Scissors example reminds us that not all guessing games involve making a binary choice. We could choose a number from 1 to n. Since we have already programmed the new `randNum()` function that chooses a random integer from a range—although it is a range from 0 to $n-1$—it is a simple matter to shift the range by one: The computation

```
randNum(n)+1
```

does the job.

The row in the Memory Bank page is quite similar to the coin-flipping row, though it has a text box to set the upper end of the range.

```
<tr><td><b> I'm thinking of a number from 1 to </b>
    <input type=text name='limit' size=2 value=10
        onChange='if (document.mem.limit.value > 0)
                    topEnd=document.mem.limit.value;
                else
                    document.mem.limit.value="?"'></td>
    <td><input type=button value="Pick"
        onClick='document.mem.res.value=randNum(topEnd)+1'>
        a number from the range:
        <input type=text name="res" size=4>
```

As before, we need to declare a global variable, topEnd, that says what the limit of the range is. This value is initialized to 10, which is the default value shown in the limit text box. Changing the text box produces a new topEnd value if that value is greater than 0. Otherwise a question mark is displayed.

When the user clicks **Pick**, the randNum() function is called with the topEnd argument and the result is incremented to shift its range. That value is displayed.

IMPROVING THE MEMORY BANK PAGE

The Memory Bank page is useful, but it needs to be fancier and include some other cool features. In this section we program the Memory Bank page to splash new pages onto the screen. Opening a new window differs from linking to a new page, because a link replaces the page being displayed, while the new window allows both to be displayed. It's very easy to open a new window, and it's handy if we want a page to remain on the screen even when the Memory Bank page is closed.

Splashing a New Page

Figure 20.9 shows a revised Memory Bank page with two new rows. These differ from the rows above. They have a title on the left side, as usual, but they have a single button on the right. When the user clicks on the button a new page is displayed. The result of clicking on the **Convert** button is shown. The page is a variation of our Celsius and Fahrenheit conversions, but it is slightly improved. Specifically, rather than giving users two options—converting from Celsius to Fahrenheit or converting from Fahrenheit to Celsius—the new page simply gives two temperature text boxes. When the user fills one in, the other is filled in with the converted temperature. The program is shown in Figure 20.10.

It's easy to get a new page to display. All we need to do is open it. In order to open a page we must give the location of the page just as if we were using a `<a href= . . . >` or `<img src= . . . >,` as described in Chapter 4. If the HTML file for the page is in the same directory as the page from which it is being opened, then giving the name is enough. Otherwise, navigation to lower or higher (`../`) directories is necessary. And, it is possible to give a full URL.

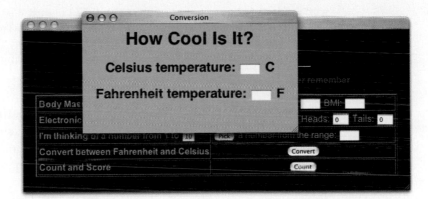

Figure 20.9. *The revised Memory Bank page and the Conversion page that displays when* **Convert** *is clicked.*

```
<html>
    <head><title>Conversion</title></head>
    <body bgcolor="#33cccc"><font face="Helvetica"><center>
        <h1>How Cool Is It? </h1>
        <script language="JavaScript">
            function convertC2F (tempInC) {
                return 9/5*tempInC + 32;
            }
            function convertF2C (tempInF) {
                return 5/9*(tempInF - 32);
            }
        </script>
        <form name="therm">
            <h2> Celsius temperature:
                <input type=text name="textTempC" size=4
                    onChange="document.therm.textTempF.value
                    =convertC2F(document.therm.textTempC.value)"> C</h2>
            <h2> Fahrenheit temperature:
                <input type=text name="textTempF" size=4
                    onChange="document.therm.textTempC.value
                    =convertF2C(document.therm.textTempF.value)"> F</h2>
        </form></center>
    </body>
</html>
```

Figure 20.10. *The file* `temperature.html` *for the new Conversion page in Figure 20.9.*

For the Memory Bank page the Conversion page from Figure 20.10 is saved in a file named `temperature.html`, which is in the same directory as `memoryBank.html`. So, the `Convert` line for the Memory Bank table is

```
<tr><td><b>Convert between Fahrenheit and Celsius</b></td>
   <td align='center'><input type=button value="Convert"
      onClick="window.open('temperature.html', 'jack',
      'resizable=yes')">
   </td>
</tr>
```

The `window.open()` function loads the page whose location is given as its first argument. The second argument is the window's name, and because we won't need the name for other purposes, we give any unique name. The third argument allows the page to be resized; there is a fourth argument, which we ignore. We always follow this form.

The last row of the Memory Bank page will reference a new page, which we will write momentarily. The new page will be stored in a file named `counter.html`. So, the HTML for the last row of the Memory Bank page is

```
<tr><td><b> Count and Score </b></td>
   <td align='center'><input type=button value="Count"
      onClick="window.open('counter.html', 'jill',
      'resizable=yes')">
   </td>
</tr>
```

If there are other pages we wish to display in new windows, we follow this same process.

A Counting Page

It is common when searching for things or watching sports to keep track of counts. It's easy enough to get a scrap of paper and tally the number, but it is equally easy to click a mouse. So, we write the Counter Assistant application

Its operation is pretty obvious: Clicking on the **Count** button increments the **Total** field; the **Meaning** field can be filled with any text to remind us which counter is which among several; the **C** button clears the fields.

The interest in the Counter Assistant page is that we write a function to create a row of the table, placing the entire HTML text in the function. The strategy requires us to use a sequence of `document.write()` functions. The program is shown in Figure 20.11.

```html
<html><head><title>Counter Assistant</title></head>
    <body bgcolor="#cc88ff" text="white"><font face="Helvetica">
        <center>
        <h2>Every Little Bit Counts!</h2>
        <script language="JavaScript">
            var count1=0, count2=0, count3=0, count4=0;
            function row(num) {
                document.write('<tr><td><input type=button value=Count' );
                document.write(' onClick="count'+num+'=count'+num+'+1;' );
                document.write(' document.win.arch'+num+'.value=count'
                    +num+'"></td>' );
                document.write(' <td><input type=text size=5 name=arch'
                    +num+'></td>' );
                document.write(' <td><input type=text size=20 name=what'
                    +num+'></td>' );
                document.write(' <td><input type=button value="C" ' );
                document.write(' onClick="document.win.arch'+num+'.value='
                    +"' ';" );
                document.write("  document.win.what"+num+".value=' ';" );
                document.write(' count'+num+'=0"></td></tr>' );
            }
        </script>
        <form name="win">
            <table>
                <tr><th>Save</th><th> Count </th><th> Meaning </th><th>Clear</th>
                <script>
                    row(1); row(2); row(3); row(4);
                </script>
            </table>
        </form></center>
    </body>
</html>
```

Figure 20.11. The Counter Assistant application, saved in a file `counter.html`.

Checking the code, we see that it relies on four global variables to keep track of the counts, `count1` through `count4`. After declaring these variables, the `row()` procedure is declared. It has a single parameter, which is the number of the row being specified. Then comes a series of `document.write()` calls in which the value of the parameter is concatenated with other text to produce the required HTML. The HTML is familiar, by now. The `onClick` event handlers for the two buttons perform the obvious operations. The **Count** button increments the correct counter; the **C** button overwrites the two text boxes with a space and reinitializes the proper counter to 0. The table is easily constructed by writing four calls to `row()`. A Counter Assistant with more rows could be constructed by editing the `counter.html` file so that more counter variables are declared, and more calls to `row()` are placed.

Recap: Two Reasons to Write Functions

Most of our functions—`convertC2F()`, `BMI()`, `randNum()`, and so on—are general. We wrote them for our application, but we hope that we will have a chance to use them again. Think of them as building blocks for programs that we may write in the future. But `flipCoin() and row()` are not building blocks.

Because `flipCoin()` and `row()` contain explicit references like `document.mem.oc.value`, they must run within a document with a form having a specific name, and that form must have within it, input controls *with specific names*. We do not expect this situation ever to happen again. Instead, we wrote these two functions to encapsulate the complexity of handling the `Flip` click-event and generating a table row. Packaging the event-handling operation and the row construction processes allowed us to get them out of the way.

So, we have had an opportunity to write functions that reflect the two reasons for packaging algorithms into functions: reuse and complexity management. The former are the building blocks of future programming, the latter help us to keep our sanity while we're solving problems.

ADD FINAL TOUCHES TO MEMORY BANK

To wrap up our discussion of functions and the Memory Bank page development, we add two finishing touches: a date and Web links. Both features are simple, but they make the page more useful. Also, we add one bonus feature.

Add a Date

The date can be added at the top after the red motto text, centered. JavaScript gives us many ways to manipulate dates, but here we use only the `Date()` function. We could write a function to insert the date into the HTML document, but it is only a single line, so we write the code

```
<script language = 'JavaScript'>
   document.write('<center>' + (Date().toString()) + '</center>');
</script>
```

placing it just after the motto line. Because the `document.write()` operation is a JavaScript statement, `<script>` tags must surround it, as usual.

The expression in the center of the string (`Date().toString()`) references the date object, which contains the current date and time in numeric form. The numeric form can be converted to a printable form using `toString()`. So the expression says, "Get the current date and time converted to a printable string."

Add Web Links

Our Memory Bank page has concentrated on programming computations, but it's a Web page, so we can include useful links, too. These links are probably book-marked in your browser, but by placing them on the Memory Bank page, they are available even when you're using a different computer or browser. What should those links be? Anything that is useful—an online dictionary and thesaurus for writing term papers, a link to the Fluency class's home page, a periodic table for chemistry class, and maybe the CIA's fact book of country information for geography class.

Where should the links be located? We could add another column to the table, placing one link per row. Because the links are highlighted with a different color, they would appear to be in their own column. But, why should the number of links match the number of rows of the table? And furthermore, it's cumbersome to add columns to HTML tables.

An alternative is to add another row at the bottom of the table that spans both columns, and fill it with the links. We choose this solution for two reasons. First, it gives us a free-form region in which to list the links and organize them by topic. Second, we can set it up so that adding more links is easy, encouraging us to include new ones. The HTML is shown in Figure 20.12.

Assess the Web Page Design

First, notice that to get the table data to span two columns, HTML's `colspan = 2` attribute is included with the `<td>` tag. Second, the links are grouped by topic, which uses the standard text color to stand out from the differently colored links. Third, a red bullet—a `.gif` image—is used to separate the entries because some of them are two or three words. (Of course, a file named `bullet.gif` must be in the same directory as this page, as explained in Chapter 4.) Finally, and most important, the link area has a very neat structure that makes adding new links almost trivial. The headings and entries all have a standard structure, and a schema has been developed and placed in a comment, so setting up for a new link is a simple **Copy/Paste** operation. This should encourage us to keep the content current.

We'll add one more feature to our Web page. See the *fit*BYTE, *Time of Your Life*, on the following pages.

With these additions, the Memory Bank page is complete for the moment. (An HTML and JavaScript listing is given in Appendix D.) More functions can be added in the future.

```
<tr>
<!-- The standard form for the links is...

    <br><b>topic name ...</b>
        <img src='bullet.gif'>
        <a href='http:// url goes here'>
            anchor term(s) here</a>


    So, just copy/paste/edit it.-->

<td colspan = 2> <center>IMPORTANT LINKS</center>
    <br>Resource Links ...
        <img src='bullet.gif'>
        <a href='http://dictionary.cambridge.org'>Cambridge Dictionary</a>
        <img src='bullet.gif'>
        <a href='http://www.wordsmyth.net'>Thesaurus</a>
    <br>Classes...
        <img src='bullet.gif'>
        <a href='http://www.cs.washington.edu/100/'>Fluency Class</a>
        <img src='bullet.gif'>
        <a href='http://www.chemsoc.org/viselements/pages/pertable_j.htm'>
            Periodic Table</a>
        <img src='bullet.gif'>
        <a href='http://www.cia.gov/cia/publications/factbook/'>Countries for
            Geography</a>
</td>
</tr>
```

Figure 20.12. HTML for the link area of the Memory Bank Web page.

{ *fit* BYTE }

Time of Your Life >>

Computers can easily work with dates because they usually keep track of dates and time with "UNIX dates." The UNIX operating system began recording dates as the number of milliseconds since 1 January 1970 at 00:00:00 Universal Time, that is, New Year's Day 1970 in Greenwich, England. Thus the number of milliseconds between any two dates after New Year's Day 1970 can be found by subtracting the two UNIX dates, making it much easier to compute than if time were recorded in years, days, and hours.

JavaScript uses UNIX dates. It also provides functions to refer to time as if it were recorded in days and hours, when that is convenient for us. We use these features to compute your age in seconds. (Of course, your age in milliseconds is just 1000 times more.) See Figure 20.13.

The JavaScript code, to be placed just after the `</table>` tag at the end of the Memory Bank program inside of script tags, is

```
var today = new Date();    // Get today's date
var myBdate = new Date();  // Get a date object to modify
var difference;            // Declare a temporary variable

myBdate.setFullYear(1984); // Set my birth year to 1984
myBdate.setMonth(6);       // Set my birth mo to July
                           // (mos start at 0)
myBdate.setDate(4);        // Set my birth day to 4th
myBdate.setHours(12);      // Set my hour of birth to noon
myBdate.setMinutes(0);     // Set my minute of birth to
                           // o'clock
myBdate.setSeconds(0);     // Set my second of birth on the
                           // hour

difference = today.getTime() - myBdate.getTime();
difference = Math.floor(difference/1000);
document.write("<center><font color=yellow> I'm " + difference
            + " seconds old. What <i>am</i> I doing with
            my life?</font></center>");
```

The code creates two date objects, one for today and one for your birthday. (Objects are a complex subject and will not be covered here.) In the six statements after the declarations, we set your birthday as if it were exactly noon, July 4, 1984. To do this, we use JavaScript functions that allow us to refer to the time using months and hours. Once your birthday has been set, we compute `difference`, the difference between the present time and that date. This computation uses UNIX dates. Then we divide the result by 1000 to convert it to seconds and print it out at the bottom of the Memory Bank page.

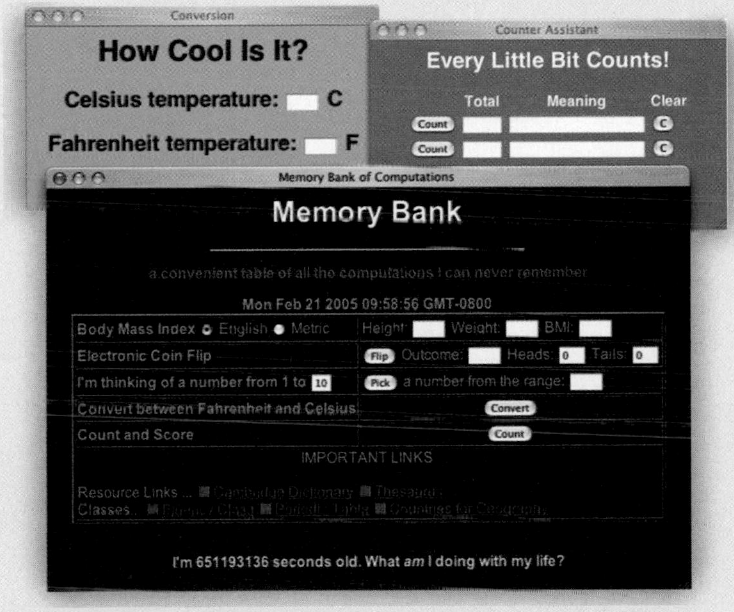

Figure 20.13. Final version of the Memory Bank, Conversion, and Counter Assistant pages.

SUMMARY

This chapter began by introducing the concept of a function as a package for an algorithm. Two motivations led us to study functions: They are a means of reusing our thinking and a tool for managing complexity. Both benefits were demonstrated in the chapter, specifically:

> The three parts of a function—name, parameter list, and definition—are specified in a function declaration using a standard form. We illustrated their use in defining `convertC2F()`, `bmiE()`, `randNum()`, and many others.

> The function declaration specifies to the computer how the function works, so we give it only once. To use the function—something we will likely do many times—requires that we give the function name and its input values, known as arguments. The arguments correspond one-to-one with the parameters of the function.

> Writing functions packages algorithms, but to get their benefit in JavaScript and HTML requires that we develop Web pages with which we give the inputs to the functions and get their answers displayed.

> We showed three different ways to display the results of a function in HTML, using `alert()`, interacting with a page that has text boxes, and using `document.write()` to include the results of a function while the page is being constructed. We used all three techniques repeatedly.

> We put all of our knowledge about functions into the Memory Bank page. It gave us the ability to apply functions directly, as for computing our Body Mass Index, and it gave us the ability to open a new page, as with the Counter Assistant page. We also decided to add a link repository for our hot list.

EXERCISES

Multiple Choice

1. The building blocks of programming are
   A. programming languages
   B. functions
   C. HTML and JavaScript
   D. variables and events

2. A curly brace, }, in a piece of JavaScript code
   A. must be placed on its own line to work
   B. indicates the end of the code
   C. should be on its own line for clarity
   D. all of the above

3. In JavaScript, a line beginning with // is a(n)
   A. assignment
   B. comparison
   C. comment
   D. function

4. In a function
   A. each argument must be supplied with a parameter
   B. each parameter must have an argument
   C. parameters are input values
   D. parameters are output values

5. The event associated with the input control is
   A. `onClick`
   B. `textChange`
   C. `onChange`
   D. `spareChange`

6. Radio buttons will work together when
   A. the `checked` attribute is set to `TRUE`
   B. they are on the same form
   C. when all of them are selected
   D. when all of them have the same name

7. Random numbers are generated by using
   A. `Math.random()`
   B. `Rnd`
   C. `Math.rnd`
   D. `Random.Math()`

8. The JavaScript `Date()` function
   A. returns the date as a string
   B. returns the current date and time as a number
   C. is displayed as a decimal
   D. none of the above

9. In HTML, `href`
   A. creates an image
   B. displays the answer to a JavaScript function
   C. creates a Web link
   D. is the extension for a Web page

10. UNIX is
    A. an international date standard
    B. a program
    C. an operating system
    D. a cookie

Short Answer

1. _____ is a process where simple steps are grouped together and given a name that describes the process.

2. _____ statement specifies what value results from a function.

3. A(n) _____ is all the code needed to create a function.

4. _____ are variables in a function that do not need to be declared with a `var` statement.

5. The _____ of a variable describes where and when it can be referenced.

6. Input values for a function are called _____.

7. When you divide by zero in JavaScript, _____ is returned as the answer.

8. Computer-generated numbers for a coin toss are technically called _____.

9. A random number generated in JavaScript is always between _____ and _____.

10. In JavaScript, time is tracked in _____, each of which is one one-thousandth of a second.

11. JavaScript keeps track of dates using _____ dates, which are expressed as the number of milliseconds since January 1, 1970 at 00:00:00 Universal Time.

12. What is the difference between a declaration and a call?

13. Describe how you would write a function for randomly picking "rock, paper, scissors."

Exercises

1. Describe how random numbers could be used to simulate the roll of a die. How could two dice be simulated using this function?

2. Identify the three parts of a function.

3. Describe how dates are tracked in JavaScript.

4. Calculate your age as a UNIX date.

5. How would the banking industry make use of the computer's ability to calculate the difference between two dates?

6. What are five words that cannot be used to name a function or a variable? What are five more?

7. Describe a function in terms of input, processing, and output.

8. Write a function to calculate your wages for a part-time job. (Don't worry about calculating overtime.)

chapter 21

ONCE IS NOT ENOUGH
Iteration Principles

learning objectives

> Trace the execution of a given **for** loop

> Write a World-Famous Iteration **for** loop

> Discuss the structure of nested loops

> Explain the use of indexes

> List the rules for arrays; describe the syntax of an array reference

> Explain the main programming tasks for online animations

ONCE IS NOT ENOUGH
Iteration Principles

There are three kinds of programmers: those who make off-by-one errors, and those who don't.

—ANONYMOUS

THE TOPIC of this chapter is iteration—the process of repetition. We are familiar with the English word *reiterate*, which means to repeat something, as in "The attorney reiterated her client's position." Because *iterate* means to repeat, *reiterate* sounds redundant. But repetition is redundant; that's what it's about. So, English has both words, and maybe it needs a third, *rereiterate*, meaning, perhaps, "repeated endlessly," as in "Beer commercials are rereiterated." Repetition is usually tiresome, but learning about it is not. And, iteration is the source of considerable computational power, making it a very important topic. By learning how to use iteration, we can make the computer perform the tiresome parts of programming.

In this chapter, we complete our study of programming concepts by learning about iteration and applying it to computational problems. We begin by explaining the `for` statement, one of JavaScript's iteration statements and the key to iterative computation. Then we explore iteration more deeply by discussing how its components can vary. The key to understanding iteration is to focus on how the iteration variable changes values. We mention the Fundamental Principle of Iteration and then we return to the topic of random numbers. After that, we consider the companion topics of indexing and arrays. Together, indexing and arrays can be used with iteration to perform almost unlimited amounts of computation, making them a major source of computing power. Finally, to bring all of these topics together, we study online animation, which allows us to add action to our Web pages. We work through the animation of a familiar icon to prepare us for more interesting animations.

ITERATION: *PLAY IT AGAIN, SAM*

There is a slight difference between the meanings of *iterate* and *repeat*. When your mother said, "I've repeated myself four times," she meant, strictly speaking, she'd said the same thing five times. Usually, the first time isn't considered a "repeat." Only the second through last are "repeats." If she'd actually said the sentence exactly four times, she should have used *iterate*. (Pointing this out to her would *not* have been smart.) We often ignore this difference in terminology in common speech. For example, "reps" (for *repetitions*) in weight training count the total number. In this book, we follow common usage and use *repeat* and *iterate* interchangeably, except where precision is essential, in which case we use *iterate*. When something is iterated five times, there are five instances; you can't be off by one.

The for Loop Basic Syntax

Iteration—probably the fourth most important programming idea after assignment, conditionals, and functions—means looping through a series of statements to repeat them. In JavaScript, the main **iteration statement** is the **for loop**, which has the following syntax:

```
for ( <initialization>; <continuation>; <next iteration> ) {
    <statement list>
}
```

Here the text that is not in meta-brackets must be given literally. (Notice the prominent position of the closed curly brace.) The statement sequence to be repeated is in the *<statement list>*, and the constructs in parentheses—which we'll explain in a minute—control how many times the *<statement list>* is iterated. The whole statement sequence is performed for each iteration. So, if the **for** loop

```
for ( <initialization>; <continuation>; <next iteration> ) {
    document.write('A');
    document.write('AB');
    document.write('ABC');
}
```

iterates three times, it will produce

```
A
AB
ABC
A
AB
ABC
A
AB
ABC
```

That is, the computer completes the whole statement sequence of the *<statement list> before* beginning the next iteration.

`The Iteration Variable.` The three operations in the parentheses of the **for** loop, *<initialization>*, *<continuation>*, and *<next iteration>*, control the number of times the loop iterates. They are called the **control specification**. They control the loop by using an **iteration variable**. Iteration variables are normal variables, so they must be declared. They are called iteration variables only while they are serving to control the loop. Here's a typical example in which the iteration variable is **j**:

```
for ( j = 1 ; j <= 3 ; j = j + 1 ) {
    <statement list>
}
```

To see how these statements work, imagine that the **for** loop has been replaced with the schematic form

General Form

```
<initialization>;
if (<continuation>) {
    <statement list>;
    <next iteration>;
}
```

Specific Example with **j**

```
j = 1;
if ( j <= 3 ) {
    <statement list>;
    j = j + 1;
}
```

The arrow means to go back to do the **if** statement again.

Here's what happens. The first operation of a **for** loop is the *<initialization>*. The **initialization** sets the iteration variable's value for the first (if any) iteration of the loop. Next, the **continuation** has the same form as the predicate in a conditional statement. If the *<continuation>* test has a **false** outcome, the loop terminates, the *<statement list>* is skipped, and it is as if nothing happened except that the iteration variable got assigned its initial value.

However, if the *<continuation>* test has a **true** outcome, the *<statement list>* is performed. The statement list can be any sequence of statements, including other **for** statements. When the statements are completed, the *<next iteration>* operation is performed. The next iteration expression changes the iteration variable. That completes the first iteration. The next iteration starts with the *<continuation>* test, performing the same sequence of operations. All following iterations proceed as the first one until the *<continuation>* test has a **false** outcome, terminating the loop. In this way, the statement sequence can be performed many times without having to write each of the statements to be performed.

*fit***TIP**

Terminator, Too. The second item among the control operations is called the *<continuation>* test here, because if its outcome is **true**, the iteration continues, and if its outcome is **false**, it ends. But the proper programming term for this test is **termination test** because it checks to see if the loop should terminate. However, as a termination test, the outcomes are backward **true** means continue, **false** means terminate! Both terms are useful. To remember the meanings of the outcomes, think of the test as asking "Continue?"

Following the Iteration Variable. In the `for` loop with iteration variable `j`, and in all `for` loops, the story is fully embodied in the operations involving the iteration variable. Consider the sequence of operations on `j` shown in Table 21.1.

Table 21.1. *The sequence of operations on `j` from the `for` loop with control specification (`j=1; j<=3; j=j+1`)*

Operation	Operation Result	Role
`j = 1`	j's value is 1	Initialize iteration variable
`j <= 3`	true, j *is less than* 3	First *<continuation>* test, continue
`j = j + 1`	j's value is 2	First *<next iteration>* operation
`j <= 3`	true, j *is less than* 3	Second *<continuation>* test, continue
`j = j + 1`	j's value is 3	Second *<next iteration>* operation
`j <= 3`	true, j *is equal to* 3	Third *<continuation>* test, continue
`j = j + 1`	j's value is 4	Third *<next iteration>* operation
`j <= 3`	false, j *is greater than* 3	Fourth *<continuation>* test, terminate

The loop iterates three times by beginning at 1 and, after assigning a new value to `j`, testing to see if it should continue. The statements of the *<statement list>* are executed between the *<continuation>* test and the *<next iteration>* operation. Notice that `j` counts from 1 to 4, but at 4, the test determines that `j` has counted too far, so it quits before performing the *<statement list>* again. Thus the *<statement list>* is performed the right number of times.

> *fit*BYTE
>
> **No Planning.** The `for` loop *might have been* designed to figure the number of iterations to perform before starting out, and then doing them. But iteration doesn't work that way. Instead, the computer just plods along, testing to see if it should continue before starting an iteration, doing the statement sequence, changing the iteration variable, and repeating. Plodding is more powerful, because it's not always possible to predict the number of iterations.

How a `for` Loop Works

To exercise our understanding of how `for` loops work, consider a computation on declared variables `j` and `text`,

```
text = "She said ";              //Set text to a string
for (j = 1; j <= 3; j = j + 1) { //Define a 3 cycle loop
    text = text + "Never! ";     //Concatenate on a string
}                                // ... end of loop
alert(text);                     // Show result
```

which produces the alert box shown on the next page.

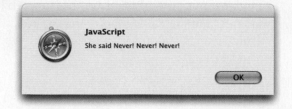

This **for** loop, which iterates three times, was used with two assignment statements to produce the value of **text** by appending three copies of the string `"Never! "`. To check the code's operation, notice that through the four continuation tests, **text** has the following values:

`"She said "`	*Before the loop is entered*
`"She said Never! "`	*After one iteration*
`"She said Never! Never! "`	*After two iterations*
`"She said Never! Never! Never! "`	*After three iterations*

So the **for** loop allowed us to build the phrase one word at a time. Of course, this phrase could have been typed out, `"She said Never! Never! Never! "`. But the more emphatic phrase in which she says `"Never! "` 1000 times would be much harder to type. Using a **for** loop, we can simply change the 3 to 1000. It's easy to be emphatic with **for** loops.

 ## JAVASCRIPT RULES FOR for LOOPS

A programmer would say that our "emphatic" **for** loop "iterates from 1 to 3 by 1." This is different from saying the **for** loop iterates three times. The programmer's description focuses on the most relevant feature of a **for** loop—its control. The key parts of the control are the starting point (1, in the "emphatic" loop), the ending point (3), and the step size (1).

In this section, we consider some of the possibilities:

> The iteration variable

> A starting point

> Continuation/termination test

> Step size

> Reference to the iteration variable

> A World-Famous Iteration

> Avoiding Infinite Loops

The Iteration Variable

Iteration variables are normal variables that help with an iteration. They must be declared, and they follow the usual rules for identifiers. Programmers tend to choose short or even single-letter identifiers for iteration variables because they are usually typed frequently, as we'll see. By far, `i`, `j`, and `k` are the most common.

A Starting Point

An iteration can begin anywhere, including with negative numbers. So, for example, in

```
for (j = -10; j <= 10; j = j + 1) { ... }
```

the iteration variable `j` assumes each of the 21 values from −10 to 10, that is, including 0. And, similarly, in

```
for (j = 990; j <= 1010; j = j + 1) { ... }
```

`j` assumes each of the 21 values around 1000. Finally, it's possible to start at a fractional number. So, in the loop

```
for (j = 2.5; j <= 6; j = j + 1) { ... }
```

`j` assumes the values **2.5**, **3.5**, **4.5**, and **5.5** because the continuation test will finally fail at **6.5**.

Continuation/Termination Test

If it's possible to begin an iteration anywhere, it must be possible to end it anywhere. The <*continuation*> test follows the rules for predicates—the tests in `if` statements. That is, the test is any expression resulting in a Boolean value.

The key point to remember about the continuation test is that to avoid an infinite loop (explained later in the section "Avoiding Infinite Loops"), it must involve the iteration variable. Other variables can be used as well as the logical operations and (`&&`), or (`||`), and not (`!`). For example, a loop that is supposed to stop at `j <= 6` could also be terminated by `((j < 6) || (j == 6))` or `j < 7`.

Step Size

The <*next iteration*> also allows considerable freedom. It allows us to specify an amount of change, known as the **step** or **step size**. For example, it's possible to step by units of 2, say, to iterate through the even numbers from 0 to 20:

```
for (j = 0; j < 20; j = j + 2) { ... }
```

In this case `j` takes the values of ten numbers because 20 is not included. The <*next iteration*> computation is often called the **increment** by programmers because, as we've seen, it almost always *increases* the value of the iteration variable. But it doesn't have to. The step can be negative, resulting in a **decrement**, and so we call it the <*next iteration*> computation to cover both the increasing and decreasing cases. For example, to count the 21 integers around 0, from *positive* to *negative* this time, we use the following:

```
for (j = 10; j >= -10; j = j - 1) { ... }
```

The successive values of j are 10, 9, 8, . . . , −9, −10. Notice that reversing the direction of the enumeration of the values means the *<continuation>* test has to be adjusted, too.

---

*fit***TIP**

> **Pluses and Minuses.** Because incrementing and decrementing by 1 are so common, JavaScript has a special "post increment/decrement" notation. Thus i++ means i = i + 1, and i−− means i = i − 1. (The variable can be anything, of course.) This notation is handy for the *<next iteration>* component of a `for` loop.

Reference to the Iteration Variable

As we will soon see, the iteration variable is often used in the computations of the *<statement list>*, which is why we focus on the values of the iteration variable during the looping. We care what these values are because we compute with them. So, for example, the iteration variable j is used in the statement that computes 5 factorial (5!):

```
fact = 1;
for (j = 1; j <= 5; j = j + 1) {
    fact = fact * j;
}
```

That is, it computes ((((1 * 1) * 2) * 3) * 4) * 5 ⇔ 120. Using the iteration variable in the computation is necessary and useful.

The World-Famous Iteration

Because JavaScript has the same `for` loop statement structure as the most popular programming languages (e.g., C, C++, and Java), thousands of `for` loops with the form just described are written every day—millions in the past decade. With so many loops, programmers have gotten in the habit of using one standard form most of the time:

```
for (j=0; j<n; j++) { ... }
```

Without a doubt this is the most frequently written `for` loop of all time, so we will call it the **World-Famous Iteration** (**WFI**). Of course, j and n can be replaced with other declared variables. It is worth taking a moment to study this form because you will see it again and again.

Notice first that the iteration variable starts at 0. You will soon see why starting at 0 is better than starting at 1. The iteration counts up from 0 in steps of 1 because the post-increment j++ is used. And the iteration ends when the iteration variable is no longer strictly less than n—that is, the loop's last iteration is for j ⇔ n−1. Thus the `for` loop *<statement list>* is performed n times: 0, 1, 2, . . . , n−1. When used in this stylized form, the variable or expression following the < symbol—the n in this case—is exactly the number of times through the loop, so we can see the iteration count in an instant without thinking hard about it. And this form saves on typing, which is important if you consider how difficult it is to type programming symbols. When you see JavaScript in the **Source** listing of the Web pages you download, chances are you will see this World-Famous Iteration. Nearly every iteration in the rest of this book has this WFI form.

Off Again. An extremely common error in computing—you've probably made it several times in *this* section—is to miscount by one. It's so common it has a name, *Off by One Error.* "Exam week is from the 3rd to the 10th," so how many days is it? We tend to subtract to get seven, but it's eight because it includes the end points. Figuring the number of iterations is similarly error prone. Happily, the World-Famous Iteration helps. The **n** following **<** in the WFI form is the *exact* iteration count.

Avoiding Infinite Loops

For loops are relatively error free, especially if we follow the world-famous form, but it's still possible to create infinite loops. To avoid this, think about what could go wrong. It's a fact that every loop in a program must have a continuation test or it will never terminate. As we learned in Chapter 10, the fifth property of algorithms is that they must be finite, that is, stop and report an answer, or stop and report that no answer is possible. **For** loops have a *<continuation>* test, so they meet the requirement of testing in each iteration. But just because there is a test, doesn't mean that it will stop the loop. It must test a condition based on a value that is changing during the loop, such as the value changed by the *<next iteration>* operation. If the test is based on values that don't change in the loop, the outcome of the test will never change, and the loop will never complete. Again, if we follow the rules, things will work out.

Nevertheless, it's not too difficult to make a mistake and create an infinite loop. For example,

```
for ( j = 1 ; j <= 3; i = i + 1) { ... }
```

looks almost like our earlier "emphatic" **for** loop, but it is broken and will loop forever. (Very emphatic, indeed!) The problem is that the variable being compared in the *<continuation>* test (**j**) is not the one incremented in the *<next iteration>* operation (**i**). Unless the iteration variable is changed in the loop—iteration variables should never be changed by statements in the *<statement list>*—the iteration will loop forever. Anyone carefully analyzing this **for** statement will spot the problem, but it's easy to miss. It's also easy enough to create, say, by making incomplete edits. (Imagine that the statement had previously used **i** as an iteration variable and was incompletely revised.)

Infinite Loops. Infinite loops happen. It's a fact of programming. Luckily, JavaScript is kind to programmers who make this mistake. Mozilla and Internet Explorer warn you that the script is running slowly and ask if you want to terminate it. Netscape and other browsers can simply be forced to close. In the past, you had to turn off the computer to stop an infinite loop.

try it

Try writing an infinite loop, then run it and force the browser to terminate so that you recognize the behavior.

EXPERIMENTS WITH FLIPPING COINS

To practice `for` loops, we experiment with flipping electronic coins. Recall that in Chapter 20 we wrote a function `randNum()` that takes an argument that is the range of integers from which to select. So, `randNum(2)`, which returns either `0` (tails) or `1` (heads), can be used for our experiments.

The first experiment is to find out how many heads and tails we get in 100 flips. We expect the numbers to be roughly equal. To run the experiment, we must set up an iteration in which our `randNum()` function is performed 100 times and statistics are gathered along the way. The code is

```
<html><head><title>Coin Flips</title></head>
<body><script language='JavaScript'>
var heads=0, tails=0;                    //Counters
var i;                                    //Iteration variable
for (i=0; i<100; i++ ){
   if (randNum(2) == 1)
      heads++;
   else
      tails++;
}
alert("Heads: " + heads + " and Tails: " + tails);
function randNum(range) {
   return Math.floor(range*Math.random());
}
</script></body></html>
```

(Because the output will be reported using `alert()`, the page doesn't matter, so we can compress the HTML.)

The `for` loop, which uses the WFI form, loops 100 times—i ranges from 0 through 99—and uses a conditional statement to check and record the outcomes of the random number generation. The post-increment (`++`) notation has been used three times, allowing us to replace statements like `heads = heads + 1` with the briefer `heads++`. Running the program gave me the results shown in the alert below the first time I tried it on my computer. But you should experiment on your computer; expect to get different results.

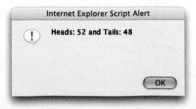

Running the program several times gives us different answers. My five runs ranged from a 50–50 outcome to a 57–43 outcome. This motivates us to run several trials.

Our trial will be the 100-sample iteration just described. To run several trials, we want to iterate them. That is, we will iterate an iteration. Think of the earlier iteration

```
for (i=0; i<100; i++ ){                     //Trial line 1
   if (randNum(2) == 1)                      //Trial line 2
      heads++;                               //Trial line 3
   else                                      //Trial line 4
      tails++;                               //Trial line 5
}                                            //Trial line 6
alert("Heads: " + heads + " and Tails: " + tails);
                                             //Trial line 7
```

as a unit called a Trial. (Notice that thinking of the loop as a unit is an *abstraction*, as discussed in Chapter 10.)

A Nested Loop

To iterate these statements, we create another **for** loop with the *<statement list>* containing this Trial unit and a couple of additional statements needed to make the whole process work out. The additional statements must reinitialize the counters, because they should begin at 0 for each new trial. The result is

```
var heads = 0, tails = 0;
var i, j;                                    //Iteration vars
for (j = 0; j < 5; j++){                     //Outer loop start
   for (i=0; i<100; i++){                    //Trial line 1
      if (randNum(2) == 1)                   //Trial line 2
         heads++;                            //Trial line 3
      else                                   //Trial line 4
         tails++;                            //Trial line 5
   }                                         //Trial line 6
   alert("Heads: "+heads+" and Tails: "+tails);
                                             //Trial line 7
   heads = 0; tails = 0;                     //Additional
}                                            //Outer loop end
```

This structure—a loop within a loop—is called a **nested loop**. Notice that another iteration variable, j, had to be declared because the outer loop cannot use the same iteration variable as the inner loop.

The behavior of the nested loop should be clear: The outer loop on j, which also uses the WFI form, iterates five times; that is, j assumes the values 0 to 4. *For each of these* j *values*, the whole *<statement list>* is executed; that is, the inner loop on i iterates 100 times, the alert is printed out, and the counters are reinitialized. That is a total of five trials of 100 flips each, or 500 total flips. Run the program, and see the range of results.

A Diagram of Results

Suppose we are interested in how far off from a perfect 50–50 score a trial is. Such information is easily displayed with a diagram. We compute the difference of the coin flip from 50–50 and show that number using asterisks. For example, the first trial, 49–51, is represented by a single asterisk because it differs from perfect by one coin flip. Either of the quantities `heads-50` or `tails-50` gives us the right number of asterisks, but one expression is positive and the other one is negative. JavaScript has a function `Math.abs()` for the absolute value; that is, it makes all numbers—positive or negative—positive, implying that `Math.abs(heads-50)` is the number of asterisks to display.

As with the raw data, the line of asterisks is added to `text` at the end of the inner loop. (Declare `text` and initialize it to `''`, the empty string.) But how do we include a variable number of asterisks? With another iteration, of course. We replace the previous `alert` statement with the statement sequence

```
text = text + 'Trial ' + j + ': ';
for (i = 0; i < (Math.abs(heads-50)); i++) {
    text = text + '*';
}
text = text + '\n';
```

The line for the *j*th trial result begins with the text `"Trial `*j*`: "`. Then, an iteration is performed in which asterisks are added one at a time, up to a total of `Math.abs(heads-50)`. We can reuse the iteration variable `i` because its previous use as an iteration variable is complete. It is also fine to put the math function in the *<continuation>* test. (Notice that the WFI form tells us immediately that we have the right number of iterations.) Finally, after the iteration, the new line character is added. Add `alert(text)` as the last line. My program generated the output shown here.

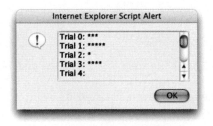

In the sample output, we notice that the successive values of `j` do indeed start at 0, that Trial 4 evidently resulted in a 50–50 outcome, and that Trial 1 had the widest variation, being 5 away from perfect, that is, either 45–55 or 55–45.

We can revise the program to print the Trials starting at 1 by changing the `text` assignment to

```
text = text + 'Trial ' + (j + 1) + ': ';
```

This is a very unusual statement because the + has two different meanings. The third + is addition, while the other three are concatenation. How does the computer know which one we mean? It looks to see if we are combining numbers (in which case it adds) or strings (in which case it concatenates). The special rule is that if there is one number and one string, it concatenates. So, we need the parentheses around $j + 1$ to cause the addition.

The final version of the coin-flipping program, as shown in Figure 21.1 uses three iterations, all in the WFI form.

Though it is only 21 lines long, the program performs hundreds of statements' worth of computation. We could easily change to 1000 sample trials, with no additional programming. And that's the value of iteration: it allows us to command the computer to do a lot of work with very few program lines.

INDEXING

If you're familiar with Elizabeth II, Super Bowl XXV, *Rocky 3*, and Apollo 13, you are acquainted with indexing. **Indexing** is the process of creating a sequence of names by associating a base name ("Apollo") with a number ("13"). When a new name is needed, the next number in sequence is used ("Apollo 14"). Each indexed item is called an **element** of the base-named sequence.

Index Syntax

Naturally, in programming, indexing has a special syntax. An index is enclosed in square brackets in JavaScript, for example, `Apollo[13]`. The index can be a constant, variable, or expression. It must evaluate to a non-negative integer, the index value. (See the section "Array Reference Syntax" for more information.) Indexing is important in computing because of its close link to iteration: Iterations can be used to refer to all elements of a name; that is, a notation like `A[j]` can, on successive iterations over `j`, refer to different elements of `A`.

*fit*BYTE

> **Index Terms.** The terms *indexes* and *indices* are both commonly used to refer to more than one index.

Index Origin

When indexing queens, Super Bowls, popes, and so on, we usually start counting at 1, though often the first item doesn't initially get an index; for example, Queen Elizabeth I was just called Queen Elizabeth until Elizabeth II came along. Yard lines in football begin indexing with 0 (goal = 0). Movie sequels start at 2 because there can't be a *sequel* to nothing. The point at which indexing begins, that is, the least index, is known as the **index origin**.

```
var heads = 0, tails = 0;              //Counters
var i, j;                              //Iteration variables
var text = '';                         //Output accumulator
for (j=0; j<5; j++){                   //"Trials" iteration ─
    for (i=0; i<100; i++){             //"Flips" iteration ─
        if (randNum(2))
            heads++;
        else
            tails++;
    } ◄
    text = text + 'Trial ' + (j + 1) + ': ';
    for (i = 0; i < (Math.abs(heads-50)); i++) { //"Stars" ─
        text = text + '*';
    } ◄
    text = text + '\n';
    heads = 0; tails = 0;
} ◄
alert(text);
function randNum(range) {
    return Math.floor(range*Math.random());
}
```

Figure 21.1. *The final version of the coin-flipping program.*

● ARRAYS

In programming, an indexed base name is called an **array**; arrays must be declared. In JavaScript, arrays are declared with the syntax

`var` *<variable>* `= new Array(`*<number of elements>*`)`

Notice that `Array` starts with a capital letter `A`. Also unlike queens, variables either are or are not arrays; they don't change. In the example declaration

`var week = new Array(7);`

`week` is the identifier being declared, and `new Array(7)` specifies that the identifier will be an array variable. The number in parentheses gives the number of array elements. *JavaScript uses index origin 0*, meaning that the least index of any array is always 0, and the greatest index is the number of elements minus 1. Thus, the array just declared has elements `week[0]`, `week[1]`, . . . , `week[6]`, that is, seven elements. The **array length** refers to the number of elements in an array. To refer to an array's length, we use *<variable>*`.length`. For example, `week.length` ⟺ 7.

Rules for Arrays

To summarize, here are the rules for arrays in JavaScript:

> Arrays are normal variables initialized by `new Array(`*<number of elements>*`)`.

> *<number of elements>* in the declaration is just that—the number of array elements.

> Array indexing begins at 0.

> The number of elements in an array is its *length*.

> The greatest index of an array is *<number of elements>* − 1 because of the 0 origin.

Array Reference Syntax

An **array reference** consists of the array name together with an index—a constant, variable, or expression—enclosed in brackets and evaluating to a nonnegative integer, the **index value**. The value to which the index evaluates must be less than the array's length. Thus, the statements

```
var dwarf = new Array(7);    //Declarations use parentheses
var deux = 2;                //Create value for examples
dwarf[0] = "Happy";          //References use brackets
dwarf[1] = "Sleepy";         //Index by a constant
dwarf[deux] = "Dopey";       //Index by a variable
dwarf[deux+1] = "Sneezy";    //Index by an expression
dwarf[2*deux] = "Bashful";
dwarf[3*deux-1] = "Grumpy";
dwarf[10-(2*deux)] = "Doc";
```

assign values to the array elements using a variety of index alternatives.

> *fit***BYTE**
>
> **Sub Standard.** The index is also known as a *subscript*. In mathematics, indexes, written below the line as in x_1 and y_1, are called subscripts. Programming inherits the same term but writes them in brackets.

When introducing the World-Famous Iteration, we said that the reason for indexing from `0` to `n-1` would soon be evident. Now we can see that 0-origin iteration is perfect for 0-origin indexing. Study the following version of the WFI:

```
for (j = 0; j < week.length ; j++) {
   week[j] = dwarf[j] + " & " + dwarf[(j+1)%7] + " do dishes";
}
```

The variable `j` ranges over all of the elements of the array `week`. By using *<array name>*`.length` in the *<continuation>* clause of the control, we set up to enumerate all of the array's elements. This iteration creates the values

```
week[0]  ⇔  "Happy & Sleepy do dishes"
week[1]  ⇔  "Sleepy & Dopey do dishes"
week[2]  ⇔  "Dopey & Sneezy do dishes"
week[3]  ⇔  "Sneezy & Bashful do dishes"
week[4]  ⇔  "Bashful & Grumpy do dishes"
week[5]  ⇔  "Grumpy & Doc do dishes"
week[6]  ⇔  "Doc & Happy do dishes"
```

for the array week by referring to a consecutive pair of elements from `dwarf`. The final pair—Doc & Happy—which must "wraparound," uses (*j*+1) *mod* 7 to index the `dwarf` array in the second reference. That is, `(j+1)%7` results in an index value of 0 because (6+1) divided by 7 has a 0 remainder, which is Happy.

> *fit* **BYTE**
>
> **Why So Famous?** Our focus on computing the index with an expression explains why the WFI is so popular. Because it's common to have to program *some* expression for the index values, it doesn't matter much whether the iteration variable counts starting at 0 or at 1 or at 14. The index expression can adjust the value as long as the *total* number of values is correct. The WFI does this, and does it better than other iterations.

THE BUSY ANIMATION

As we know, movies, cartoons, and flipbooks animate by the rapid display of many still pictures known as *frames*. Human visual perception is relatively slow—presumably because of the amazingly complicated tasks it performs—so it is fooled into observing smooth motion when the *display rate* is about 30 frames per second, that is, 30 Hz. In this section, we learn the principles of online animation—like the Dymaxion Map of Chapter 6—and practice using iteration, arrays, and indexing.

The animation we plan to construct is a familiar "busy" indicator, as shown in Figure 21.2. The 12 frames contributing to the animation are shown with their names. The rapid display of the frames makes the black bar appear to revolve. Creating this Busy Animation is the goal of this section.

> *fit* **TIP**
>
> **Fast Forward.** The quickest way to learn both the ideas and the practical skills of animation is to build the animation program yourself as you read along.

Before you can successfully program an animation in JavaScript, you must understand three concepts:

> Using a timer to initiate animation events

> Prefetching the frames of the animation

> Redrawing a Web page image

As the ideas are introduced, we program the Busy Animation.

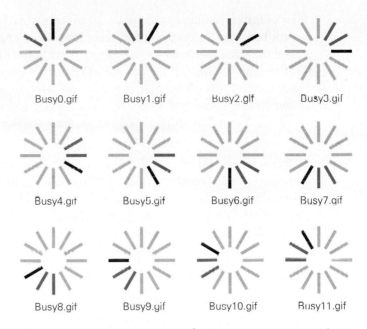

Figure 21.2. *The* `.gif` *images for the Busy Animation. These files are available at* `www.aw.com/snyder/`*.*

Using a Timer to Initiate Animation

The animation we produce will be displayed by a Web browser. As we know, Web browsers are *event driven*. That is, they are told to perform a task, they do it, and then they sit idle waiting for an event, which will cause them to do the next task. If browsers are idle when they are not working on a task, how can they animate anything? Animations require action every 30 milliseconds (ms). The obvious solution is to turn the activity of drawing the next frame into an event. The event will be the regular "ticking" of a clock. We'll use a timer analogy.

We set a timer to wake up the browser to tell it to display the next frame, and then set it again for 30 ms into the future. In 30 ms, we repeat the process. In this way, we draw the frames at regular intervals and create an animation. We use such a scheme for *online animations*. Animations like *Toy Story* apply these ideas differently. Not surprisingly, JavaScript comes equipped with all of the features, for example, timers needed to implement online animation.

Setting a Timer. Computers have extremely fast internal clocks, which are too fast for most programming purposes. Instead, programmers' timers typically "tick" once per millisecond. Timers are pretty intuitive. In JavaScript, the command to set a timer is

`setTimeout("`*<event handler>*`", `*<duration>*`)`

where *<event handler>* is a string giving the JavaScript computation that will run when the timer goes off, and *<duration>* is any positive number of milliseconds.

For example, to display a frame in 30 ms using the function `animate()` as an event handler, we write `setTimeout("animate()", 30)`. Thirty milliseconds later, the computer runs the `animate()` function and displays the frame. Of course, the last step for the `animate()` function must be to set the timer so that it "wakes up" again. Otherwise, the animation stops. ("Every 30 ms" is different from 30 times a second, of course, because 1000/30 = 33.333 ms. We can set the timer to 33 ms, but animation is not an exact science and 30 is close enough.)

Using a Handle to Refer to a Timer. Unlike mechanical timers, computer timers can keep track of many different times at once. How does the computer keep the settings straight? When we perform `setTimeout()`, we get back a special code—it's called a **handle**—that the computer uses to identify our timer. We can use the handle to refer to our timer, say, to cancel it. For example, if we declare a variable, `timerID`, with which to save the handle, and write

```
timerID = setTimeout("animate()", 30);
```

we can cancel the timer by writing

```
clearTimeout(timerID);
```

and the computer will know which of the timers it's tracking should be canceled.

Using Buttons to Start/Stop the Animation. Because timers can be set and canceled, we will include two buttons to start and stop our animation. Their definitions are

```
<input type=button value=Start onClick=
    'setTimeout("animate()",30)'>
<input type=button value=Stop onClick='clearTimeout(timerID)'>
```

The `Start` button sets the timer for the first time. The animation keeps going on its own thereafter. Each time `animate()` sets the timer, the handle is stored in `timerID`. Then, when the `Stop` button is clicked, its event handler clears the timer and stops the animation.

Prefetching Images

Next, we'll consider displaying images. Recall from Chapter 4 that to keep our Web pages tidy, we keep the `.gif` and `.jpg` images in a separate directory or folder. So, assume that the graphics files shown in Figure 21.2 are in a folder `gifpix`. The first of the images would be displayed on a Web page with the HTML

```
<img src="gifpix/Busy0.gif">
```

We begin with the skeleton HTML page that includes the `<form>` tags and the two buttons:

```
<html><head><title>Busy</title></head>
   <body><center>
      <img src=gifpix/Busy0.gif> <!-- Initial Frame -->
      <form>
         <input type=button value=Start
            onClick='setTimeout("animate()",30);'>
         <input type=button value=Stop
            onClick='clearTimeout(timerID);'>
      </form>
   </center></body>
</html>
```

We would like to overwrite that single image with all of the other `.gif` files in `gifpix` in sequence, one every 30 ms. But we can't do so directly. The problem is that loading the images is generally too slow to allow us to show a new image so quickly. Web images must be transferred from the Web server across the Internet, where they encounter all sorts of delays. (We don't notice this while we're developing a Web application on our computers because all of the files are already stored locally.) Consequently, the strategy is to get the images first, store them locally so they are available in the computer's memory, and then display them. The process of loading the images ahead of time is called **prefetching**.

Where will the 12 images (`Busy0.gif` through `Busy11.gif`) of the `gifpix` folder be put? Because they are indexed already, it's logical to use an array. We'll name the array `pics` and declare it

```
var pics = new Array (12);
```

indicating that it will have 12 elements.

Initializing to an Image Object. In order for the elements of the array to store an image, they must be initialized to an **image object**. An image object is a blank instance of an image (Chapter 2). Think of an image object as a skeleton that provides places for all the information needed to store an image, such as its name, size of its two dimensions, and its actual pixels. To initialize the 12 array elements to image objects requires an iteration and the new `Image()` operation,

```
for (i = 0; i < pics.length; i++) {
   pics[i] = new Image();
}
```

Notice that `Image()` begins with a capital `I`.

Using the src Component. Among the places in the image object is a field called `src` where the image's source is stored—that is, the file name of the file containing the image. This is the string that we give in the `<img src="...">` tag. When we assign to the `src` field using dot notation, the browser saves the name and gets the file, storing it in memory, just as we require. Thus,

```
pics[0].src = "gifpix/Busy0.gif"
```

parallels our earlier explicit fetch of the initial frame. Because there are 12 images in total, we use a loop,

```
for (i = 0; i < pics.length; i++) {
   pics[i].src = "gifpix/Busy" + i + ".gif";
}
```

which constructs the filenames on-the-fly. That is, we build up filename `Busyi.gif` using the iteration variable and concatenation.

There is an important difference between the prefetching by assigning to the `.src` field of an image variable, and using `<img src="...">` in HTML. The former is not visible on the screen, whereas the latter is. This works to our advantage both ways. The image variable, which is just a part of our JavaScript program, is not visible because it hasn't been placed on the page. But that's fine, because we don't want the user to see the prefetch happening anyway. The `<img src="...">` tag places an image on the page, and so is visible. We need both.

Redrawing an Image

To animate the initial frame that we placed earlier with `<img src="...">`, we need to overwrite it with the images that we just prefetched at a rate of one every 30 ms. How do we refer to the initial frame in order to overwrite it? Interestingly, Web browsers keep in the HTML document an array of the images that is just like our `pics` array. As the `<img src="...">` commands are encountered, the browser fills its images array just like we filled `pics`. So, `document.images[0]` is the name of the first image—that is, our initial frame `Busy0.gif`. Any additional `<img src="...">` images are indexed with higher numbers in sequence. The browser's images array elements have the `src` property too, and assigning to it overwrites the image. Thus, to change the initial frame, we write the assignment

```
document.images[0].src = pics[i].src;
```

which replaces the initial frame with the *i*th element of the `pics` array, causing it to be displayed. All that needs to happen to animate the Busy icon is to sweep through all of the `i` values, cyclically, one every 30 ms.

Defining the animate() Event Handler. The `animate()` event handler overwrites the image, sets up for the next frame, and sets the timer to call itself again:

```
function animate () {
   document.images[0].src = pics[frame].src;
   frame = (frame + 1)%12;
   timerID = setTimeout ("animate()", 100);
}
```

We set the timer for 100 ms rather than 30 ms because it makes the bar appear to revolve at a nice pace.

The whole Busy Animation, including the familiar `Start` and `Stop` buttons, is shown in Figure 21.3, with the concepts explained. As a postscript to the Busy Animation, the reader is encouraged to click **Start** several times, followed by an equal number of **Stop** clicks. Can you explain what happens?

```
<html><head><title>Busy</title></head><body bgcolor=white><center>
<img src=gifpix/Busy0.gif>
<script>
var i, frame = 0;                              //Iteration vars
var timerID;                                   //Timer handle
var pics = new Array (12);                     //Array to prefetch into
for (i=0;i<pics.length ; i++) {                //Init. array for images
    pics[i] = new Image();
}
for (i=0;i<pics.length; i++) {                 //Prefetch images
    pics[i].src = "gifpix/Busy" + i + ".gif";
}
function animate () {                          //Draw pic, call self
    document.images[0].src = pics[frame].src;  //Change pic
    frame = (1+frame)%12;                      //Move to next frame
    timerID = setTimeout("animate()", 100);    //Schedule next tick
}
</script>
<form>
<input type=button value=Start onClick='timerID=setTimeout("animate()",30)'>
<input type=button value=Stop onClick='clearTimeout(timerID)'>
</form>
</center></body></html>
```

Figure 21.3. *The Busy Animation image and program, assuming that the 12* `.gif` *files are stored in a directory* `gifpix`.

SUMMARY

We studied the fundamentals of programming to understand the sources of power in computation. The concepts of this chapter—iteration, indexing, and arrays—account for much of it. There is much more to say about programming, but we'll leave the rest of it to the experts. In this chapter we discussed:

> The basics of **for** loop iteration. The control part of a **for** statement is written in parentheses and the *<statement list>* is enclosed in curly

braces. With each iteration, the entire statement list is performed. The number of iterations is determined by assignments to, and tests of, the iteration variable as specified in the control part.

> In the JavaScript `for` statement, the *<initialization>* component is executed first. Then, prior to each iteration, including the first, the *<continuation>* predicate is tested. If it is `true`, the *<statement list>* is performed; otherwise, it is skipped, and the `for` statement terminates. After each iteration, the *<next iteration>* operation is performed.

> The principles of iteration ensure that every iteration contains a test and that the test is dependent on variables that change in the loop.

> The `for` statement is very flexible. The *<initialization>* can begin anywhere, the *<continuation>* test can stop the loop anywhere, and the *<next iteration>* operation can increment by various amounts and count upward or downward.

> Programmers routinely use the World-Famous Iteration (WFI)—a stylized iteration that begins at 0, tests that the iteration variable is strictly less than some limit, and increments by 1. There is no obligation to use the WFI, but it allows us to quickly determine the number of times around the loop—it's the limit to the right of `<`. Because it is common to make errors figuring out the number of iterations, programmers use the WFI to recognize the number of iterations quickly.

> In indexing, we create a series of names by associating a number with a base name. If we need more names, we count out more numbers. Indexed variables are known as **arrays** in programming. Like ordinary variables, arrays must be declared, but they use the `new Array(`*<length>*`)` syntax, in which *<length>* is the number of elements of the array.

> Array elements—referenced by giving the name and a nonnegative index in brackets—can be used like ordinary variables. Arrays and iterations can be effectively used together.

> Basic concepts of online animation. All animations achieve the appearance of motion by rapidly displaying a series of still frames.

> When animating information displayed by a Web browser, we should prefetch the images so that they are readily accessible for rapid display. The key idea is to use a timer to create events, and then use the timer-event handler to redraw an image that has been placed on the Web page by the `<img src="...">` tag. These are referenced as the elements of the document's images array.

EXERCISES

Multiple Choice

1. In JavaScript the `for` statement is used for
   A. assignment
   B. increment
   C. iteration
   D. selection

2. If your mother told you four times to clean up your room (or in the computer age, to clean up your Desktop), there were
   A. four repetitions
   B. four iterations
   C. three iterations
   D. five iterations

3. In a `for` loop, the iteration value is changed by
   A. the *<continuation>* test
   B. the *<next iteration>*
   C. a false *<continuation>* test
   D. the end of the statement sequence

4. A `false` outcome for a termination test means
   A. terminate the loop
   B. terminate the program
   C. continue the loop
   D. do not enter the loop

5. The command to display an alert box in JavaScript is
   A. `write.alert`
   B. `display.alert`
   C. `alert()`
   D. `alert = "text"`

6. The maximum number of times a loop can iterate is
   A. 1024
   B. 65,536
   C. 1,048,576
   D. infinite

7. `i++` means
   A. add the value of `i` to itself and store the result in `i`
   B. add 1 to `i`
   C. multiply `i` by itself
   D. check to see if `i` is positive

8. For the statement below, which of the following is true?

   ```
   for (j = 0; j < n; j++) {...}
   ```

   A. the loop starts at 0
   B. the loop increments by 1
   C. the loop stops after **n** iterations
   D. all of the above

9. Array elements cannot be numbered with
   A. negative numbers
   B. decimals
   C. numbers greater or equal to their number of elements
   D. all of the above

10. The timer in JavaScript is called
    A. `setTimeout`
    B. `Math.Timer`
    C. `Timer`
    D. `setTick`

11. Given the line below, which of the following is a valid array reference?

    ```
    var cols = New Array(9)
    ```

    A. `cols[0]`
    B. `cols[4.5]`
    C. `cols[9]`
    D. `cols[10]`

12. Loading an image ahead of time is known as
    A. buffering
    B. prefetching
    C. caching
    D. backlogging

Short Answer

1. _____ means to loop through a series of statements to repeat them.

2. The _____ statement is used to start a loop in JavaScript.

3. A **for** loop is controlled by a _____.

4. _____ is the first operation of a **for** loop.

5. The first step of the second iteration of a loop is the _____ test.

6. The shortcut to subtract 1 from **i** is _____.

7. A loop that never ends is known as a(n) _____.

8. A loop inside a loop is called a(n) _____.

9. In JavaScript, the command to force a new line is _____.

10. `Math.abs()` is used in JavaScript to find _____.

11. _____ is the creation of a sequence of names by associating a base name with a number.

12. An indexed item is called a(n) _____.

13. The number of elements in an array is its _____.

14. A(n) _____ is an array name with its index.

15. The _____ is the number of frames per second that is displayed in an animation.

Exercises

1. You're making cookies (the real ones) and the directions say to stir until thoroughly mixed. Explain how a loop like this works.

2. What property of a loop ensures it will terminate?

3. Write the code for a loop that starts at 0 and iterates seven times.

4. Write the code for a loop that starts at your birth year and iterates for each year of your age.

5. Young lovers often use a daisy to determine the true feelings of the other. With each petal they count, they alternate "She loves me" and "She loves me, not." Generate a random number up to 25 and then use that to determine if your girlfriend (or boyfriend) loves you. Even numbers mean love. Other numbers mean not. Display the process.

6. Use nested loops to "count" from 1 to 100. Use the inner loop for the ones digit and the outer loop for the tens digit. Concatenate them to display the "number."

7. What would it take to "count" to 1000 in exercise 6?

8. Create a loop to display a set of asterisks to create a set of "stairs."

9. Create a loop to display a set of "stairs" that go down instead of up.

10. Compile a list of everyday items that make up an array.

11. Explain why loops can use negative numbers and decimals but an array cannot.

12. Explain how an animation uses still images and loops to create the illusion of motion.

chapter 22

THE SMOOTH MOTION

Case Study in Algorithmic Problem Solving

learning objectives

> State and apply the Decomposition Principle

> Explain the problem-solving strategy used in creating the Smooth Motion application

> Explain the use of the JavaScript operations for iteration, indexing, arrays, functions, animation controls, and event handlers in Smooth Motion

> Explain how mouse events are handled in Smooth Motion

THE SMOOTH MOTION

Case Study in Algorithmic Problem Solving

*All parts should go together without forcing. You must remember that the parts
you are reassembling were disassembled by you. Therefore, if you can't get them
together again, there must be a reason. By all means, do not use a hammer.*

                                              —IBM MAINTENANCE MANUAL (1925)

THE PROGRAMMING that we've learned indicates how computers solve problems and demonstrates the source of their speed and versatility. We've learned
enough programming to be able to embellish our Web pages, making them more
adaptive and dynamic. But the great value of the knowledge we've learned is neither insight nor embellishment. Rather, we can apply the programming ideas to
general problem-solving situations. Processes, procedures, instructions and directions, decision-making, and so forth are phenomena we meet in daily life beyond
the sphere of computers. Our knowledge applies in all of those cases, making us
more effective at learning, performing, and planning tasks. In this chapter we
apply this knowledge by solving a more substantial task.

Though the ideas have broad application, our interest and preparation are still
with IT. Accordingly, the task at hand is a Web application we'll call Smooth
Motion, for testing a user's coordination at manipulating a mouse. How smooth
are you? The application will use event programming, including "mouse events,"
animation, controls, more sophisticated HTML, functions, iteration, indexing, and
arrays. Smooth Motion is a generic application that allows us to focus on the problem-solving activity. By patiently following this fully worked case study, we will
have opportunities to discuss when and how to apply the ideas we have learned.

THE SMOOTH MOTION APPLICATION

Step 0 in solving any problem is to understand what must be accomplished. (Almost everything in this chapter is 0-origin!) The Smooth Motion application is a coordination test. (Try Smooth Motion at `www.aw.com/snyder/`.) The graphical user interface is shown in Figure 22.1. Naming the components from top to bottom we have these parts:

> **Heading:** The text "Smooth Motion"

> **Grid:** The 7 × 20 grid of squares

> **Keys:** The row of seven brown/orange boxes

> **Controls:** The buttons and radio settings

> **Instructions:** The text at the bottom

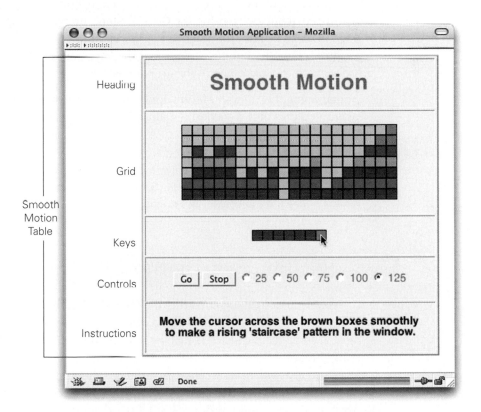

Figure 22.1. *The Smooth Motion application user interface. Try it at* `www.aw.com/snyder/`

Further, the components are enclosed in a one-column table with a border and a colored background.

How the Smooth Motion Application Should Work

Smooth Motion works as follows. The application starts up automatically five seconds after it is loaded. It begins filling the grid from the right with stacks of blocks of random height. The blocks move steadily to the left at a rate determined by the controls. Examples of the random stacks of blocks are shown in the left half of the grid in Figure 22.1.

The random stack generation continues until the user places the mouse cursor over one of the brown keys. At that point, the user is in control of the stacks of blocks displayed in the grid. If we call the leftmost key, key 1, and the rightmost key, key 7, then when the mouse hovers over key *n*, a stack of *n* blocks appears in the grid. Figure 22.1 shows the seven-block stack being selected by the cursor on key 7.

The user's goal is to move the mouse across the brown keys as smoothly as possible. When the user has moved the mouse smoothly enough to create a perfect staircase rising to the right in the grid, the action stops. The process can be started or stopped at any point using the **Go** and **Stop** buttons. The speed selections are given in milliseconds and describe the rate at which the blocks move left. The test requires a smooth mouse motion across the keys from left to right at a rate corresponding to the frame rate of the grid animation.

Programming the Smooth Motion application is a substantial project, but surprisingly it requires only a modest amount of HTML and JavaScript.

> *fit* **TIP**
>
> **Smooth Move.** How would you program Smooth Motion? Before reading about problem solving in this chapter, spend five minutes thinking about how you would create the Smooth Motion application. Truly, thinking about your own solution first will help you to understand the chapter more readily.

● PLANNING SMOOTH MOTION

The goal is to design and construct the Smooth Motion application. Achieving such a goal entails a substantial design with several functions and some intricate logic. A complicating factor is that we have both timer events for the animation and mouse events for the controls happening simultaneously. Most of us would never succeed with such an effort by trying to "brain it out." The complications of the project would overwhelm us. Instead, we will succeed by approaching it in a methodical step-by-step way, applying a standard divide-and-conquer technique to simplify our work. By breaking the project into convenient, manageable pieces, we will succeed.

Apply the Decomposition Principle

A fundamental strategy for solving complex problems is the following principle:

Decomposition Principle: Divide a large task into smaller subtasks that can be solved separately and then combine their solutions to produce the overall solution.

Of course, the subtasks may not be small enough to be worked out easily, so the Decomposition Principle can be applied again to each of the subtasks, producing even smaller subtasks. Eventually the components become small enough that it is possible to figure out how to solve them directly. When the subtasks are all solved, we begin the assembly process, combining the most primitive components to produce the more complex components, and so on until the overall problem is solved. The Decomposition Principle is little more than common sense, but when applied judiciously, it is a powerful technique for achieving significant results.

List the Tasks

The Smooth Motion application has several parts that provide an obvious beginning point for applying the Decomposition Principle:

Task	Description
Build GUI	Create a Web page with the table and its five parts: title, grid, keys, controls, and instructions
Animate Grid	Move the block stacks to the left
Sense Keys	Handle the mouse events and transfer the control information to the grid animator
Detect Staircase	Recognize, when among a stream of events, the user has "met the test"
Build Controls	Implement the actions to control the application
Assemble Overall Design	Build the automatic random start-up, handle the starting and stopping, set the speeds, and interconnect the other components
Primp the Design	Make the page attractive and functional

Only the Build GUI task is simple enough to be solved directly, and even it is fancier than the other Web pages we've constructed so far. All of the other tasks will require further decomposition when we start to solve them.

Decide on a Problem-Solving Strategy

Decomposing the problem into tasks is step number one in solving it. Step number two is to strategize how to solve each of the parts. The strategy is concerned mostly with the order in which we'll solve the parts.

Build a Basic Web Page First. First, because JavaScript programming usually needs a Web page to host the computation, it makes sense to begin with the Build GUI task rather than any of the others. Such an approach gives us a place to test and save the solutions to the other tasks. The page becomes an organizing structure, a location where we record our progress by adding our JavaScript code to it.

fit **CAUTION**

> **Total Waste.** One pitfall to avoid in any JavaScript design is spending hours constructing a splashy Web page only to discover that it doesn't fit well with the solutions to the other tasks. Such a mistake won't happen here—this is a "textbook example" after all—but it is an error to avoid on your other projects.

So, we begin by building the host page, but to avoid wasting time on a splashy-but-inappropriate page, we will build only the basic primitive page, and wait to embellish the design until after the parts are all working. Thus we're splitting the GUI construction into two parts.

Though our problem is too small to illustrate it, there is a problem-solving strategy that creates a working prototype first before completing the whole design. This strategy is smart because it is easier to add to an already-working primitive design. Our plan to focus on the basic Web page and leave the cosmetic features to the end is in the spirit of this approach.

Solve Independent Tasks before Dependent Tasks.
Deciding the order in which to solve the other tasks requires us to consider the **task dependencies**. That is, some tasks—for example, Detect Staircase—*rely on* or *depend on* the solution of other tasks, such as Sense Keys. Tasks that do not rely on the solution of any other tasks are *independent*, and should be done first. Tasks that depend on the independent tasks are done next, tasks that depend on them follow, and so on. All of the tasks could be mutually dependent, though this is rare. In that case the dependent tasks are started, pushed as far as possible until they absolutely need the results of another task, and then are interrupted to work on the other task. For us, GUI construction is the independent task, and the Animate Grid task is dependent only on it. So, we'll schedule it second. Sense Keys is also dependent only on the GUI, but it is easier to test when the Animate Grid task is completed. It will be our third task.

PERT Chart. Keeping track of many dependencies can be confusing, so systems engineers and managers draw a **task dependency graph**, or **PERT chart**. Standing for Program Evaluation and Review Technique, PERT charts were developed by the US Navy in the 1950s.

There are several ways to draw them; we place tasks in circles and use arrows to show dependencies. In Figure 22.2 we have placed an arrow between two circles so that the task at the head of the arrow depends on the task at the tail of the arrow. In this (very common) form of a PERT chart, we begin with circles that have no incoming arrows. From any circle, the arrows show which tasks can be done next when the task in the circle is completed.

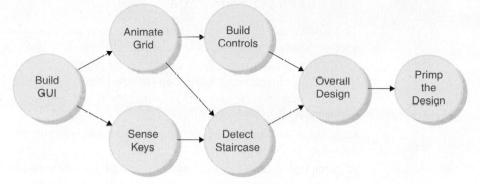

Figure 22.2. *A task dependency diagram, also known as a PERT chart. Tasks are in circles and arrows are read as "task at head of arrow depends on task at tail of arrow."*

✔ check LIST >>   Our strategy is to solve the tasks in this order:

- ☑ *Build GUI, to give us the basic Web page.*

- ☑ *Animate Grid, which is dependent only on the Build GUI task.*

- ☑ *Sense Keys, which is dependent only on the Build GUI task.*

- ☑ *Detect Staircase, which is dependent on Animate Grid and Sense Keys.*

- ☑ *Build Controls, which is dependent on Animate Grid.*

- ☑ *Assemble Overall Design, wrapping up those parts not yet complete.*

- ☑ *Primp the Design, embellishing the Web page.*

Usually each of these tasks would be further simplified using the Decomposition Principle until all of its subtasks were simple enough to solve directly. Doing so ensures that the decomposition has produced a practical solution. For our purposes, we will use a slightly different strategy, choosing instead to assign a section of this chapter to each task and to apply the Decomposition Principle at the start of the section.

BUILD THE BASIC WEB PAGE GUI

The full graphical user interface for Smooth Motion will have a table with constituent parts: heading, grid, keys, controls, and instructions. For now, we'll create the basic structure. We'll call this the structural page. The "basic" features include the table, heading, and instructions as well as the background color, font style and color, and the centering of the application on the page. We'll improve it later when the application is completely working.

The Structural Page

The structural page contains a five-row, one-column table; the text for the Smooth Motion heading and instructions are placed in the first and last rows. As we learned from making the Bean Counter Web page in Chapter 19, it is easiest to build tables "inside out," using **Copy/Paste**. That is, we construct a generic table cell with `<td>` tags, replicate that to make a row which we enclose in `<tr>` tags, and then replicate the row to make the whole table which we enclose in `<table>` tags. Then we fill it in. Because the present table has only one column, it's not necessary to replicate the cells to make a row for this situation. For us, the "generic" table cell is centered and contains a single blank character, that is, `<td align="center"> </td>`. The "basic" table has a border.

The Structural Page Heading

For the heading text, we use an `<h1>` heading, and for the instructions, we use a paragraph tag. Because the instructions text has a different text color than the other text on the page, we must set its font color.

The graphic and the HTML for the structural page definition are shown in Figure 22.3. Notice that the middle three rows of Figure 22.1 are empty in Figure 22.3 because they are white space. However, they are defined in the HTML, providing a site for our next programming step, the Animate Grid task.

ANIMATE THE GRID

The Animate Grid task must animate the 7 × 20 = 140 grid of blocks moving from right to left. This task is much too complicated to solve directly, so we apply the Decomposition Principle again.

First Analysis

The Busy Animation of Chapter 21 illustrated the basic steps of animation:

> > Define and place the initial image.
>
> > Prefetch the frames for updating the image.
>
> > Set a timer and build a timer event handler, which updates the image.

These are the starting decomposition for the Grid Animation. But these three steps don't fully solve the problem. We need to think and strategize further.

Frames for the Columns of Blocks. How will we organize the rapid redrawing of 140 images, keeping track of each block's trajectory? Reviewing how the application is supposed to work, we first notice that it only discusses

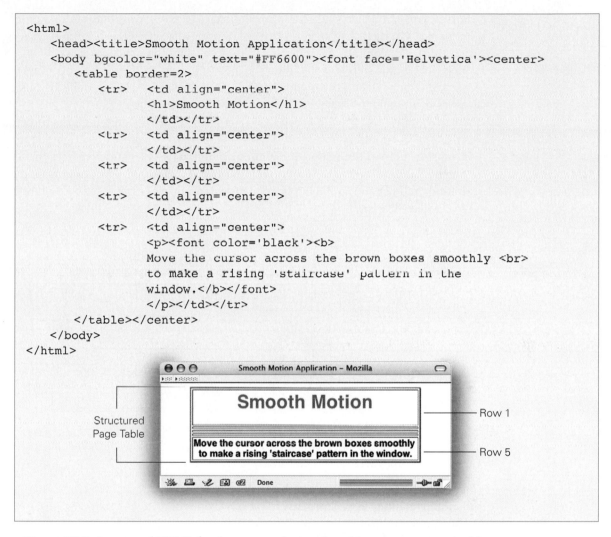

```
<html>
    <head><title>Smooth Motion Application</title></head>
    <body bgcolor="white" text="#FF6600"><font face='Helvetica'><center>
        <table border=2>
            <tr>    <td align="center">
                    <h1>Smooth Motion</h1>
                    </td></tr>
            <tr>    <td align="center">
                    </td></tr>
            <tr>    <td align="center">
                    </td></tr>
            <tr>    <td align="center">
                    </td></tr>
            <tr>    <td align="center">
                    <p><font color='black'><b>
                    Move the cursor across the brown boxes smoothly <br>
                    to make a rising 'staircase' pattern in the
                    window.</b></font>
                    </p></td></tr>
        </table></center>
    </body>
</html>
```

Figure 22.3. Image and HTML for the structural page; the table appears compressed because rows 2–4 contain nothing. Remember, your browser image may be slightly different.

"stacks" of blocks. This implies that there is no "motion" of images vertically, only horizontally. (This is obvious by the color scheme, too.) And, the horizontal motion is limited only to moving from right to left. From these observations we can conclude that we don't have to animate individual squares at all. The images can be whole columns. That simplification reduces the total number of images in the grid to 20, that is, the number of columns. Of course, we will need a frame image for each stack of blocks: a 0-stack, a 1-stack, . . . , and a 7-stack, resulting in a total of eight frames. So, a new subtask to add to our list of three is to define and organize the column frames.

`Indexing Columns Left to Right.` Next we consider the "motion of an image." On each time step, a given column is replaced by the column to its right. If the 20 columns are indexed left to right, then the image in column *i* of the grid at a time step is replaced on the next time step by the image in column *i*+1 (see Figure 22.4). (The columns will be indexed from 0, left to right, because, as was mentioned in Chapter 21, when browsers place images on a page, they record them in the array `document.images` in the order encountered; that order is the construction sequence of an HTML page, top to bottom, left to right. So, the leftmost column of the grid is `document.images[0]`.) The action replaces the contents of `document.images[i]` with the contents of `document.images[i+1]`. Shifting each column to the left is quite easy, and it leaves only the last column to be handled differently.

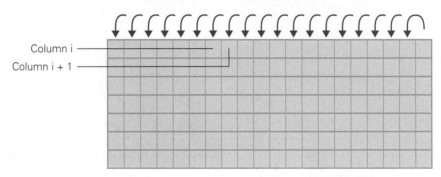

Figure 22.4. *With column 0 at the left, the image in column i should be replaced by the image in column i + 1 to implement the left-moving motion for the Grid Animation event handler.*

Handling column 19 (last) is easy because we only need to assign a new image—that is, one of the eight frames. Which frame do we assign? If we are in the random start-up phase, it should be a random frame. If we are in the user-controlled phase, it should be whichever frame the user has specified by the mouse position, if any. We will leave this choice of the frame open for the time being because the Assemble Overall Design task will set the frame selection properly.

Second Analysis

From our first analysis it seems that we should add subtasks for defining an image-shifting process and for defining a column-19 fill process, but it's not necessary. Both activities will be part of the timer event handler, which is already on our list. So, our subtask list for the Animate Grid task has increased by only one new item:

1. Define and organize the eight columnar frames.

2. Define and place the initial images, 0 through 19.

3. Prefetch the eight frames for updating the image.

4. Set a timer with an event handler that shifts the images in columns 1 through 19 to columns 0 through 18, respectively, and introduce a new frame into column 19.

We'll assign a subsection to each subtask.

Subtask: Define and Organize the Frames

The eight frames for the Smooth Motion application are shown in Figure 22.5. The files are available online (**www.aw.com/snyder/**) so we don't need to create them here. Notice that they have names indexed in accordance with the block height. Also, the images have the necessary colors and lines that will be placed densely side-by-side to construct the grid.

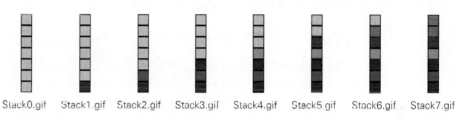

Stack0.gif   Stack1.gif   Stack2.gif   Stack3.gif   Stack4.gif   Stack5.gif   Stack6.gif   Stack7.gif

Figure 22.5. *The eight frames required for the Smooth Motion application.*

If the **gif** frames had not been available, we would have had to create them. Numerous tools are available for this purpose, from simple paint programs to sophisticated image editing facilities. Though the tools vary in capabilities, convenience, and sophistication, there are only two guidelines to follow when creating frame images for JavaScript animations:

> Ensure that all images overwriting one another have the same dimensions in pixels; an easy way to meet this constraint is to create an initial "blank" frame, save it, and use it as the base for creating all of the other frames.

> Ensure that all files are saved using either the **.gif** or **.jpg** formats, and that they are used consistently; that is, only overwrite **.gif**s with **.gif**s.

To use images in HTML, it is recommended that they be placed in a separate directory, simply as an organizing technique (Chapter 3). Following that advice, the stack **gif**s of Figure 22.5 are saved in a directory called **gifpix**, meaning that their names relative to the HTML file are **gifpix/Stack0.gif**, **gifpix/Stack1.gif**, etc.

Subtask: Define and Place Initial Images

This subtask constructs the grid in the second row of the structural page (see Figure 22.3). The initial state of the grid is created from 20 copies of **Stack0.gif**. As usual, to place an image on a page, we use the **<img src="...">** tag. But the

20 images will require 20 such tags. This calls for a loop. To use JavaScript's **for** statement, we place the **<script>** tags inside of the second row's **<td>** tags, and within them we write the necessary JavaScript. To have the images appear on the structural page, we must place them using the **document.write()** function.

The iteration can use the World-Famous Iteration form and must declare an iteration variable. The necessary code to implement these objectives is

```
<script language='JavaScript'>
   var j;                             //Declare iteration var
   for (j = 0; j < 20; j++) {        //Initialize grid images
      document.write('<img src="gifpix/Stack0.gif">');
   }
</script>
```

which completes the image initialization.

Subtask: Prefetch the Frame Images

As explained in Chapter 21, animating with images fetched from across the Internet is not likely to work because of delays that the **.gif** files might encounter during transfer. So, prefetching is necessary, and it is the goal of this subtask. (Review prefetching from the Busy Animation of Chapter 21, if necessary.)

Relative to the creation of the Web page, the prefetching activity can be performed at any time prior to the start of the animation. Because the prefetching also requires JavaScript code, we decide to place it with the code from the initialization subtask just completed, say, after the declaration. This is a good location because to prefetch the frames, we need an eight-element image array to prefetch into, and so we need another declaration for that array.

The three steps of prefetching are:

1. Declare the array into which the images will be fetched.

2. Initialize the array elements to be image objects; that is, define the image structure for each array element using the **new Image()** specification.

3. Assign the names of the files to the **src** fields of the image objects, causing the browser to record the names and get the files, thus implementing the prefetch.

The file names are those given in Figure 22.5. We call the array **pics**, and use a separate iteration for the second and third tasks, though combining the two operations into a single iteration is equivalent. The resulting code

```
var pics = new Array(8);           //Declare array for gifs
for (j = 0; j < 8; j++) {          //Make the elements images
   pics[j] = new Image();
}
for (j = 0; j < 8; j++) {          //Name source file & prefetch
   pics[j].src = "gifpix/Stack" + j + ".gif";
}
```

is inserted within the previous `<script>` tags, after the declaration. Notice that the file names are constructed on-the-fly to save us from typing separate statements.

Subtask: Set Timer and Build Timer Event Handler

The subtask is mostly concerned with writing the event handler to move each of the grid's images one position left, obliterating the 0 image and assigning a new image to position 19. So we begin by constructing that event handler, called `animate()`. As we work on it, several additional details arise that require our attention.

The timer event handler `animate()` has three operations:

1. To move all images but the first, one position left.

2. To assign a new frame to image 19.

3. To schedule itself for sometime in the future.

The mechanism for choosing the new frame is not yet worked out, but the Assemble Overall Design task will resolve it. For the moment, we simply assign a random frame as an easy way to have something different happening on each tick. And, assigning random frames is the way the application is to begin anyway.

Recall that browsers store the details of the images they display in an array called `images`, that the array is referenced as `document.images`, and that the source field, `src`, is the relevant one to change if we want to display a new image. We use `document.images` and we program the three steps of the `animate()` function as

```
function animate() {
   for (j = 0; j < 19; j++) {                              //Shift left 1
      document.images[j].src = document.images[j+1].src;
   }
   document.images[19].src = pics[randNum(8)].src;//New image
   timerId = setTimeout("animate()", duration);   //Set timer
}
```

We have used the `randNum()` function developed in Chapter 20

```
function randNum (range) {
   return Math.floor(range * Math.random());
}
```

so we must include its declaration in order to reuse it. Also, we add a variable `duration` to the accumulating list of declarations:

```
var duration = 125;
```

To get the process started automatically after five seconds, we include the additional statement before the function definitions

```
timerId = setTimeout("animate()", 5000);
```

which sets the `animate()` function to be run 5000 ms after the browser starts. As with the Busy Animation, we save the handle received from the `setTimeout` function in a variable `timerId` (it must be declared!) so that the animation can be stopped. And, with that code, the Set Timer subtask is completed, completing the Animate Grid task. Figure 22.6 shows the state of the structural page at this point.

```html
<html>
    <head><title>Smooth Motion Application</title></head>
    <body bgcolor="white" text="#FF6600"><font face='Helvetica'><center>
        <table border=2>
            <tr> <td align="center">
                <h1>Smooth Motion</h1></td></tr>
            <tr> <td align="center">
                <script>
                    var j;                               //Declare iter var
                    var duration = 125, timerId;         //& other vars
                    var pics = new Array(8);             //& prefetch array
                    for (j = 0; j < 8; j++) {            //Initial img array
                        pics[j] = new Image();
                    }
                    for (j = 0; j < 8; j++) {            //Prefetch images
                        pics[j].src = "gifpix/Stack" + j + ".gif";
                    }
                    for (j = 0; j < 20; j++) {           //Place grid imgs
                        document.write('<img src="gifpix/Stack0.gif">');
                    }
                </script></td></tr>
            <tr> <td align="center"></td></tr>
            <tr> <td align="center"></td></tr>
            <tr> <td align="center">
                <p><font color='black'><b>
                Move the cursor across the brown boxes smoothly <br>
                to make a rising 'staircase' pattern in the window.</b>
                </font></p></td></tr>
        </table></center>
        <script language='JavaScript'>
            timerId = setTimeout("animate()", 5000);     //Initial timer
            function animate() {                         //Animate eh
                for (j = 0; j < 19; j++) {               //Shift images L
                    document.images[j].src = document.images[j+1].src;
                }
                document.images[19].src = pics[randNum(8)].src; //Place random img
                timerId = setTimeout("animate()", duration); //Set timer for next
            }
            function randNum (range) {                   //Rand No. from
                return Math.floor(range * Math.random()); // Chapter 20
            }
        </script>
    </body>
</html>
```

Figure 22.6. *HTML, JavaScript, and image for the Smooth Motion implementation after the completion of the Animate Grid task (continues next page).*

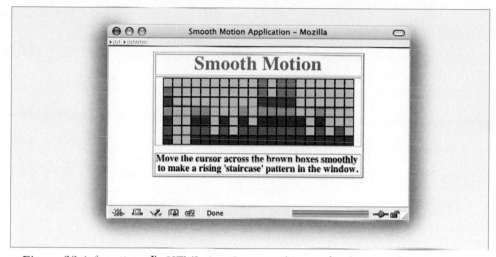

Figure 22.6 (continued). *HTML, JavaScript, and image for the Smooth Motion implementation after the completion of the Animate Grid task.*

THE BEST LAID PLANS...

The next step in our task decomposition strategy is to solve key sensing. However, now that we have the grid animation worked out, we find it very cumbersome not to be able to start and stop the animation on demand. It would be very helpful to have the controls available to stop the animation so that we don't have to kill the browser application each time to do so. But the Build Controls task is planned for later. Perhaps it makes more sense to solve it now to simplify our work. As Robert Burns noted, plans don't always work out, no matter how hard we try. (Burns put it more poetically: *The best laid schemes o' mice and men gang aft agley*.) Adjusting the order of tasks is very typical of large projects because it isn't always possible to figure out ahead of time all of the relevant interactions. So, we proceed to the Build Controls task.

BUILD CONTROLS

Inspecting the GUI in Figure 22.1, we see that the controls entry of the table contains seven input controls. Thus the fourth row of the table must contain `<form>` tags so that we can specify the controls. (Chapters 20 and 21 covered `<form>` tags.) The only challenge is how to handle the click-events. As always, we ask, "What should happen when the control is clicked?" There are three scenarios:

> **Go button click-event.** Start the animation with `setTimeout()`, keeping track of the handle.

> **Stop button click-event.** End the animation by clearing the timer using the handle.

> **Radio button click-event.** Set the timer interval by assigning to
> `duration`.

None of these activities is more than a single statement, so rather than creating
functions for the event handlers, we simply place the code in an input control:

```
<form>
    <input type=button value=Go
       onClick='animate()'>
    <input type=button value=Stop
       onClick="clearTimeout(timerId)">
    <input type=radio name=speed onClick="duration=25"> 25
    <input type=radio name=speed onClick="duration=50"> 50
    <input type=radio name=speed onClick="duration=75"> 75
    <input type=radio name=speed onClick="duration=100"> 100
    <input type=radio name=speed
       onClick="duration=125" checked=true> 125
</form>
```

We place the code in the fourth row of the structural page table (see Figure 22.6).
Notice that the last button is `checked` to indicate that `duration`⇔`125` is the
default.

fit **TIP**   **Easily Repeated.** We could have used a `for` loop to place the radio buttons, though
only the first four have the consistent structure suitable for a loop. Looping would
require `<script>` tags, `document.write`, and so on. With so few repetitions, it's
simpler to use **Copy/Paste/Edit** rather than a loop.

Having completed the Build Controls task, we can start and stop the animation.
"We now return to our originally scheduled program."

● SENSE THE KEYS

The Sense Keys task implements the ability to recognize when the mouse hovers
over a given key. The task requires us to understand how mouse motions are
sensed, a topic that has not yet been introduced. But, it's typical when solving a
large problem not to know the details of the constituent parts and to have to learn
a new concept, system, or operation to solve the task. That's our situation with
respect to sensing mouse motions. So, before attempting the task decomposition,
we find out about mouse motions.

Actually, sensing mouse motions is very easy. Browsers recognize events on the
objects of a Web page, such as images, just as they recognize events caused by
controls. For example, if we click on an image, we cause a click-event, which we
can process with an event handler. We specify the event handler by using the
`onClick` attribute of the image tag, as in `<img src="..." onClick=`
`"doSomething()">`. This enables a mouse click on an image of a Web page to be
recognized.

The browser, with the help of the operating system, keeps track of where the mouse pointer is at any moment. (After all, it's the operating system that is drawing the mouse pointer in the first place.) When the mouse pointer moves over an image or other Web page object, a *MouseOver* event is recognized. When the mouse pointer moves off of the object, a *MouseOut* event is recognized. We need these two events in order to follow the mouse cursor across the Smooth Motion keys. The keys are images, so we write an event handler for each of the two mouse events. We specify them to the browser by the `onMouseOver` and `onMouseOut` event handler specifications in the `<img src="...">` tag defining the key's image.

With that information, we can decompose the Sense Keys task by asking, "How should key sensing work?" First, we notice that there are no keys yet (see Figure 22.6), so we have to define them. Second, after thinking about their operation—they change their color from brown to orange on MouseOver and then change back to brown on MouseOut—it's clear that the keys are effectively another animation. The difference between other animations we've written and the keys' animation is that the former are updated by a timer, whereas the latter are updated by mouse motions. This observation is a tremendous help in our planning, because we have solved animation problems before. So, we begin our problem decomposition with the standard animation decomposition used for the Animate Grid task:

1. Define and organize the necessary frames.

2. Place the initial images and create the keys.

3. Prefetch the frames.

4. Build the event handlers.

This is a sufficient strategy to solve the problem.

Subtask: Define and Organize the Frames

The first subtask involves only two images, ■ and ■. They are named `BrownBox.gif` and `OrangeBox.gif` and are stored in the `gifpix` directory with the `Stack` images. Moving the files to that directory completes the first subtask.

Subtask: Place the Initial Images

Placing the images creates the keys. Seven images will be placed in the center of the third row of the structural page's table. They are all `BrownBox.gif`. As before, we write a JavaScript loop to iterate the `document.write` of the `<img src="...">` tags. The resulting code, which is still incomplete—but will be fixed momentarily—is

```
for (j = 0; j < 7; j++) {                              //Incomplete
    document.write('<img src="gifpix/BrownBox.gif">');
}
```

This completes the placement subtask for the time being.

Subtask: Prefetch the Frames

Prefetching the frames is also completely analogous to our earlier animations, and by now its three-subtask sequence is becoming familiar. There are only two frames to prefetch, leading to the declaration of a small array:

```
var keypix = new Array(2);
```

We add simple code for image initialization,

```
keypix[0] = new Image();
keypix[1] = new Image();
```

and prefetching,

```
keypix[0].src = "gifpix/BrownBox.gif";
keypix[1].src = "gifpix/OrangeBox.gif";
```

because it isn't worth writing loops. These lines complete the prefetch subtask.

Subtask: Build the Event Handlers

Finally, we build the two event handlers, **here()** for **MouseOver** and **gone()** for **MouseOut**. They're not difficult to build.

As with any event handler, we ask, "What should happen when the mouse moves over a key?" First, the key must change color to give feedback to the user that the mouse is on or off the key. This involves simply updating the key's image with the **OrangeBox.gif** or the **BrownBox.gif** image. But how do we refer to the key's image? We know that it is listed in the **images** array that the browser keeps of the images on the page. Because the keys come after the grid, the key images are obviously stored in the array after the grid images. The grid images are **images[0]**, . . . , **images[19]**, so by the preceding loop, the keys must be **images[20]**, . . . , **images[26]**. Of course, if we know the position of the key, say, **pos**, we can refer to the image as **images[20+pos]**. We conclude that we need to record the position of each key in the sequence.

Next, the mouse-sensing event handlers must tell the Grid Animation event handler which new **Stack** image to draw in the last position of the grid. All that event handler needs is the key's position, so if we assign it to a global variable, say, **frame**, we've done the job. These observations lead us to declare a variable **frame** and to define the two mouse event handlers:

```
function here (pos) {
    document.images[20+pos].src = "gifpix/OrangeBox.gif";
    frame = pos + 1;
}
function gone (pos) {
    document.images[20+pos].src = "gifpix/BrownBox.gif";
    frame = 0;
}
```

We have made the key's position a parameter.

Notice how `here()` solves a problem of mismatched indices. The keys are 0-origin indexed (i.e., 0, 1, . . . , 6); `pos` will have one of these values. The stacks of blocks are 1-origin indexed (i.e., `Stack1.gif`, `Stack2.gif`, . . . , `Stack7.gif`); `frame` should have one of these values. That is, the mouse over `key[0]` means draw `Stack1.gif`. The `here()` function makes up for this mismatch with the assignment

```
frame = pos + 1;
```

Also, notice that for `gone()`, we don't know where the mouse is moving to. It could be moving to another key, or it could be moving off the keys entirely, which should draw the `Stack0.gif`. The safe thing is to set `frame = 0`. If the mouse moves to another key, its `MouseOver` event handler will be called immediately, setting `frame` to the right number.

Combine the Subtasks

With the two mouse event handlers defined, we return to the image initialization subtask to add the event handler specifications to the `<img src="...">` tags. The revised and final form of the initialization is

```
for (j = 0; j < 7; j++) {
    document.write('<img src="gifpix/BrownBox.gif" ' +
    'onMouseOver = "here(' + j + ')" ' +
    'onMouseOut = "gone(' + j + ')">');
}
```

The two mouse event handler functions have their position parameters specified by the `for` loop's iteration variable `j`. To test the Sense Keys task solution, we make one tiny change in the Grid Animation event handler, `animate()`, namely, to change the `frame` assigned to the last column from the random choice to the frame variable. The new line has the form

```
document.images[19].src = pics[frame].src;
```

allowing us to test the code.

Having completed the Sense Keys task, Figure 22.7 shows the code entered into the structural page in the third row. (The two declarations—`keypix` and `frame`—are included with the earlier declarations, and the event handling functions are included with the previously defined functions.)

STAIRCASE DETECTION

When the user has manipulated the mouse in such a way as to create a rising "staircase" of blocks in the grid, the animation should stop. How do we recognize the "staircase"? It's not possible to look at the grid, of course, so we must identify it by other characteristics. Observe that the user will have created a staircase when the `frame` values for seven consecutive `animate()` calls are 1, 2, 3, 4, 5, 6, 7.

```
<script language = 'JavaScript'>
   var keypix = new Array(2);                //Array declaration
   for (j = 0; j < 7; j++) {                  //Image Placement
       document.write('<img src="gifpix/BrownBox.gif" ' +
       'onMouseOver = "here(' + j + ')" ' +
       'onMouseOut = "gone(' + j + ')">');
   }
   keypix[0] = new Image();                   //Image initialize
   keypix[1] = new Image();                   //
   keypix[0].src = "gifpix/BrownBox.gif";  //Prefetch images
   keypix[1].src = "gifpix/OrangeBox.gif"; //
</script>
```

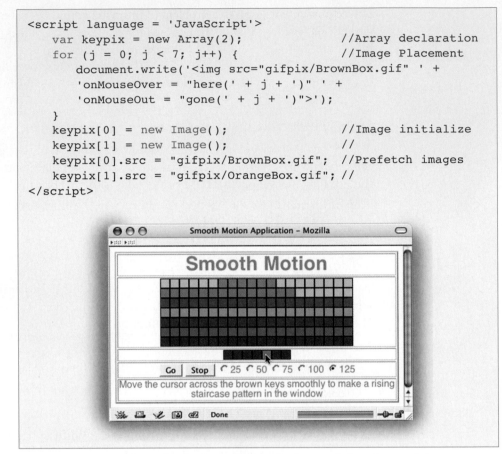

Figure 22.7. *JavaScript for the Sense Keys task; the two declarations and the two event handlers are not shown.*

This is true because the value of `frame` tells the `animate()` event handler which `Stack` frame to display, and if it is directed to display the seven frames in order on seven consecutive ticks, there will be a staircase in the grid.

Subtask: Recognizing the Staircase

How do we recognize the seven consecutive `frame` values? There are many techniques. Some involve keeping an array of the seven most recent frame values and checking each time to see if the desired sequence occurs. Another involves looking at the `src` fields in the last seven images of the grid—it's almost like looking at the picture—to see if they have the right sequence of file names. But the technique we will employ requires slightly less programming and seems cleverer. The idea is to keep predicting the next `frame` value.

Subtask: Recognizing Continuity

Notice that we are trying to recognize continuity across a sequence of events, that is, seven events in which the value for **frame** is 1, 2, 3, 4, 5, 6, 7. By analogy, imagine you are sitting at a bus stop trying to determine if seven consecutive buses ever pass by with the last digit of their license numbers making the sequence 1 through 7. But you have no paper to write down the data and your memory isn't so good. You have exactly seven coins—your bus fare—so you put one coin in your left pocket. That's a prediction that the next bus has a license ending in 1.

As a bus arrives, you check to see if the last digit of its license plate is equal to the number of coins in your left pocket. If so, and you still have coins, you add another coin to your left pocket. If not, you put all the coins, but one, back in your right pocket. If you ever try to add a coin, but have run out, it happened! What you are doing with the coins in your left pocket is predicting the number on the next bus' license plate. If the prediction is right, you make the next prediction by adding another coin; but if not, you start back with 1. It's an easy idea for keeping the continuity of a series of events.

Implementing the bus analogy, we modify the **animate()** function at the point where it is about to set the timer for the next tick, because if the staircase is found, there should be no next tick. Additionally, we'll declare another variable, **next1**, that corresponds to the coins in your left pocket, that is, as if predicting an event. Implementing the steps of the process

```
if (frame == next1)                    //Is the prediction correct?
   next1 = next1 + 1;                   //Yes, make next prediction
else                                    //No
   next1 = 1;                           //Go back to the start
if (next1 != 8)                         //Are we still looking?
   timerId = setTimeout("animate()",duration); //Yes, set timer
```

Notice that the test in the last **if** statement compares to 8 rather than 7 because **next1** was already incremented previously, and so the condition of "no more coins left" is equivalent to **next1** ⇔ 8. With that addition to **animate()** we have completed the Detect Staircase task.

ASSEMBLE OVERALL DESIGN

With the Build Controls task performed out of order and parts of the Assemble Overall Design task performed ahead of time, there is not much left to do to complete the programming of the Smooth Motion application. Nevertheless, this is the point at which we make sure that the whole application works as planned.

Reviewing the description at the start of the chapter, we notice that the display of randomly selected stacks of blocks isn't presently working. Originally we generated random stacks when we solved the Animate Grid task. But we took that feature out to test the keys. Now we want to put it back in.

Basically we should set image 19 to `frame` or `randNum(8)`, depending on whether or not the user has ever passed the mouse over a key. How will we know? The `MouseOver` event handlers will recognize the situation, but at the moment, they are programmed only to return a `frame` value from 1 through 7. So, if we started out with frame initialized to some erroneous number, say, –1, and test it in the `animate()` event handler before using the `frame` value, we could recognize the two situations: –1 means the mouse has not yet passed over the keys for the first time; anything else means the mouse has passed over the keys the first time. Thus we must change the initialization of `frame` in its declaration to

```
var frame = -1;          //Set for initial random generation
```

and rewrite the assignment to the last column of the grid one more time:

```
if (frame == -1)
   document.images[19].src = pics[randNum(8)].src;
else
   document.images[19].src = pics[frame].src;
```

This last change to `animate()` makes it quite cluttered with `if` statements, as shown in Figure 22.8. The clutter obscures the simple two-part logic of shifting the grid and checking for the staircase. So, we relegate both operations to functions. The resulting solution is no shorter—in fact, it is longer by four lines—but it makes the important `animate()` event handler clearer, making the exercise worthwhile.

After checking the operation of the Smooth Motion application, it seems that we've taken care of all of the design elements, except the fancy GUI, which is the last remaining task.

PRIMP THE DESIGN

The structural page we've built our application around can be made more attractive. In fact, the task of improving the aesthetics of Web pages is probably an unending task. We recognize the following improvements that will produce the page shown in Figure 22.1:

> Table background color

> Cell padding

These are considered advanced features of HTML and will not be covered here, because at the stage when a page is being enhanced, we usually have to familiarize ourselves with the advanced features again, having forgotten them since the last time we enhanced a Web page. For the record, the two enhancements can be programmed using attributes of the `<table>` tag:

```
<table border=2 cellspacing="3" cellpadding="20%"
   bgcolor="#FFFF99">
```

An explanation of how `cellpadding` and `cellspacing` work is found at `www.w3c.org/TR/REC-html40/struct/tables.html#h-11.3.3` and nearby pages. It's left to the interested reader to explore alternative styles.

Assessment and Retrospective

When we are asked to design a solution to someone else's problem, we are usually finished when we verify that we've done what we've been asked to do. If the design is to achieve a goal of our own choice, however, an assessment step remains. When we pick a goal, we usually do not have a fixed target like Figure 22.1 to work toward. Rather, we design a solution to our original "best guess"; then we consider whether the result is the best possible solution. (We have used such assessments in Chapters 16 and 19.) Generally, having a working solution suggests many worthwhile improvements.

In this chapter, the first case applies, and so we are finished. Instead of an assessment, consider the ideas from earlier chapters applied in this chapter. There are three primary topics:

> > Loops
> > Parameterizing functions for reuse
> > Managing complexity with functions

Applying these ideas has produced a better program. Consider how.

Loops. The Smooth Motion application used several `for` loops. These saved us from tedious activities like writing 20 `<img src="...">` statements in a row. Such loops simplified the programming. But at times, when we might have used loops, we chose not to. For example, we explicitly wrote the instructions for defining the radio buttons and for prefetching the key images. We used copy, paste, and edit rather than a loop, because it was easier to program. Had there been more iterations, or had the specification been slightly simpler, we might have used a loop. The computer does the same work either way; we decide which method is convenient.

Parameterized Functions for Reuse. The `here()` and `gone()` functions each use a single parameter that is the position of the key in sequence. The actual value is passed to the functions in the event handler specifications. For example, the third key from the left is defined by a `document.write` that produces

```
<img src="gifpix/BrownBox.gif"
    onMouseOver = "here(2)" onMouseOut = "gone(2)">
```

where the "**2**" indicates the key's 0-origin number. The parameter customizes the event handler for each key. We could have written separate functions in which the key's position is used explicitly everywhere `pos` occurs, but this would create a proliferation of almost-identical functions. The parameter says where and how the event handlers differ from each other, and their use produces a more abstract—and easier to understand—solution.

Managing Complexity with Functions. The functions
`shiftGrid()` and `checkStairAndContinue()` shown in Figure 22.8 are examples of creating functions to manage complexity. Both functions "package" program logic allowing us to *name them* and *move them* out of the way, revealing the simple two-part logic of the `animate()` function.

```
function animate() {
   shiftGrid ();
   checkStairAndContinue ();
}
```

```
function animate() {
   for (j = 0; j < 19; j++) {
      document.images[j].src = document.images[j+1].src;
   }
   if (frame == -1)
      document.images[19].src = pics[randNum(8)].src;
   else
      document.images[19].src = pics[frame].src;
   if (frame == next1)
      next1 = next1 + 1;
   else
      next1 = 1;
   if (next1 != 8)
      timerId = setTimeout("animate()",duration);
}
```

becomes

```
function animate() {
   shiftGrid ();
   checkStairAndContinue ();
}
function shiftGrid() {
   for (j = 0; j < 19; j++) {
      document.images[j].src = document.images[j+1].src;
   }
   if (frame == -1)
      document.images[19].src = pics[randNum(8)].src;
   else
      document.images[19].src = pics[frame].src;
}
function checkStairAndContinue() {
   if (frame == next1)
      next1 = next1 + 1;
   else
      next1 = 1;
   if (next1 != 8)
      timerId = setTimeout("animate()",duration);
}
```

Figure 22.8. *Revision of the function* `animate()` *to encapsulate portions of the computation into functions.*

As with loops and parameters, functions clarify to humans how the animation function works; it's all the same to the computer. Humans will see our choice of function names—for example `shiftGrid()`—and correctly interpret them as describing what the function does. If people need to know how the program shifts the grid, they can check the function; otherwise, it's out of the way, replaced by a succinct statement of what it does (its name). This role of shifting the grid might have been expressed as a comment at the start of the code sequence, but comments are often overlooked. The abstraction —naming the function and giving its definition—creates a new concept in our minds, raising our level of understanding of Smooth Motion's animation process. Though these two functions will never be used again, the goal of simplifying the program justifies our effort to define them. See Appendix E for a complete listing of the Smooth Motion application.

Thus we see that programming is as much about teaching viewers of our program how we solved the problem as it is about instructing the computer. Even for programs that are not textbook examples, helping humans understand programs is essential. It helps with debugging—an important concern for us—and by organizing the solution in an understandable way, we instill confidence in others about the correctness of our solution.

SUMMARY

We have programmed a substantial application that would have been too complicated to achieve directly. To succeed, we applied the Decomposition Principle, first to create the high-level tasks that guided our overall solution, and then again, when it came time to solve the tasks that were still too complicated. Though it is mostly common sense, the Decomposition Principle provides a strategy that works to solve all difficult problems. To solve the problem at hand we:

> Defined the tasks and strategized about the order in which to solve them. Because there were dependencies among the tasks, we defined a feasible plan to solve them.

> Used a dependency diagram to show which tasks depended on others and to assist us in strategizing. We planned an order consistent with the diagram—that is, no task was scheduled ahead of the tasks it depended on— and produced a workable plan.

> Considered other features, such as ease of testing, and adjusted the schedule to address these aspects.

> Developed the actual solution of the Smooth Motion program directly. We decomposed each task into four or five subtasks. There was similarity among these subtasks. For example, the timer-driven animation and the key-driven animation used a similar set of subtasks.

> Decided to solve the tasks out of order from our original schedule, to give ourselves the ability to start and stop the animation. Convenience

motivated us to depart from our original schedule, but originally it was not possible to predict the benefits of the alternative plan.

> Learned about mouse events, a topic we had not previously encountered. This was not a difficult concept to grasp, but it illustrated a common feature of any large task—that it is often necessary to learn new information to solve a complex problem.

> Used the programming facilities covered in earlier chapters—loops, functions, parameters, and so on—as tools to instruct both the computer and humans looking at the program. Those facilities clarified the program, making it plain how the problem was solved.

> Developed an IT application with techniques that have wide application. We can expect to use decomposition in other problem solving, to abstract the components of a solution by giving them names and precise definitions, and to reduce the complexity of a solution to an understandable level.

> Learned powerful problem-solving techniques.

EXERCISES

Multiple Choice

1. The first step in problem-solving is
   A. develop an algorithm
   B. understand the problem
   C. create the interface
   D. determine the functions needed

2. The second step in problem-solving is
   A. break the problem into smaller tasks
   B. plan how to solve the problems
   C. design the interface
   D. build the functions

3. The Build Controls task is dependent on
   A. Overall Design
   B. Detect Staircase
   C. Sense Keys
   D. Animate Grid

4. Before the Animate Grid task can be completed, the
   A. Build Controls task must be completed
   B. Detect Staircase task must be completed
   C. Build GUI task must be completed
   D. Sense Keys task must be completed

5. The Detect Staircase task is not dependent on
   A. Build Controls
   B. Sense Keys
   C. Animate Grid
   D. Build GUI

6. Which of the following is an example of the World-Famous Iteration form?
   A. `for (j = 0; j < 10; j++)`
   B. `for (i = 1; i <=5; i = i +1)`
   C. `for (k = 10; k > 1; k--)`
   D. `for (j = 1; j++; j<=5)`

7. To use a graphic that has been prefetched
   A. the `href` command must be used
   B. the `src` command must be used
   C. a specific image must be placed in a specific location
   D. none of the above

8. To get the browser to delay 5 seconds, you need to set the `setTimeout` function to
   A. 5
   B. 500
   C. 5000
   D. .5

9. It is worthwhile to write a loop to do a repetitive task when there are
   A. 2 or more tasks
   B. more than 3–5 tasks
   C. more than 8–10 tasks
   D. 20 or more tasks

10. A meaningful name for a function
   A. makes the code easier to read
   B. raises the level of understanding for those who read the code
   C. means as much to the computer as a meaningless name
   D. all of the above

Short Answer

1. The _____ is used to break a task into smaller, easy-to-solve tasks.

2. _____ is the second step in problem-solving.

3. _____ are the relationships between tasks that determines the order in which the tasks in a program are solved.

4. When solving a problem, the _____ should be solved first.

5. PERT stands for _____.

6. A(n) _____ can be used to visually keep track of which tasks depend on another.

7. The _____ task must be completed before the Sense Keys task can be completed.

8. The Animate Grid task and the Sense Keys task both must be completed before the _____ task can be completed.

9. An array called _____ is where a browser stores information about the images on a page.

10. Clicking on a button on a Web page will trigger a(n) _____.

11. _____ are objects that, when placed in a group, work together to allow the user to select one item from the group.

12. The unit used for timing JavaScript events on the computer is called a _____.

Exercises

1. Describe the Decomposition Principle.

2. Apply the Decomposition Principle to cooking a meal.

3. Create a PERT chart for the preceding exercise.

4. List the dependent tasks and the independent tasks for cooking a meal.

5. On the Smooth Motion Web page, what objects are used for user input?

6. Explain why it's a good idea to create the GUI early in the process, but not finalize it until the end of the process.

7. What is the advantage of prefetching images for an animation?

8. How would you modify the Smooth Motion code to keep track of how long the user can keep the animation running and display it at the end?

9. Explain how the `onMouseOver` and `onMouseOut` events work.

chapter **23**

COMPUTERS CAN DO ALMOST {□ EVERYTHING, □ NOTHING}

Limits to Computation

learning objectives

> Explain what the Turing test was designed to show

> Discuss the issue of a computer being intelligent and able to think; refer to Deep Blue

> Discuss the issue of computer creativity; refer to computer-generated Mondrian-like art

> State the meaning of the Universality Principle

> State the way in which the amount of work in a program is related to the speed of the program

COMPUTERS CAN DO ALMOST
{☐ EVERYTHING,☐ NOTHING}

Limits to Computation

The real danger is not that computers will begin to think like men, but that men will begin to think like computers.

-SYDNEY J HARRIS

Artificial Intelligence is no match for natural stupidity.

-ANONYMOUS

Rules have no existence outside of individuals.

-HENRI MATISSE

COMPUTERS have achieved sustained speeds of well over 30 trillion additions per second. On a pocket calculator, at one operation per second, it takes 1000 lifetimes (assuming 60 years of daily calculating for 14 hours each day) to perform a trillion operations. But so what? Everyone knows computers are amazingly fast at arithmetic. Shouldn't we be more impressed if a computer ever had an original thought, no matter how trivial? Absolutely! But it probably won't happen. As we have learned, for a computer to do anything, it must be programmed to do it, and so far "thought" in the sense we usually mean the term, has eluded researchers. So, we have a curious situation. Computers can be truly awesome at some tasks and completely hopeless at others. Because they're so different from humans, it's reasonable to wonder what computers can and cannot do.

This chapter addresses philosophical issues. First we ask whether a computer can think. Thinking about thinking leads us to the famous Turing test. Chess—a game requiring smarts—became a *de facto* goal of artificial intelligence research. We explore how computers play chess, summarize the advancements, and report the victory of Deep Blue. We also speculate on how creative computers can be. Next, we consider the easy-to-understand but significant idea—the Universality Principle—that asks how different computers can be. Any "new and improved" computer will be faster or larger, but not more capable. How important is more speed? We explore how fast computers can solve various problems by revisiting the *Alphabetize CDs* algorithm from Chapter 10. Finally, there are problems that cannot be solved by a computer even in principle, not because they are too nebulous to specify for a computer, but because to do so would be a contradiction.

CAN COMPUTERS THINK?

The inventors of electronic computers thought that they were discovering how to "think with electricity." And to the extent that operations like addition and multiplication require humans to think, it's easy to see their point. Previously, electricity had been used directly as an energy source for driving motors and powering light bulbs. With the digital computer, electricity switched complex circuits, implementing logical operations. The power was applied to manipulate information. The phenomenon was truly new.

Today, electronic devices that manipulate information are so common, we are less impressed by them. It is difficult to regard a pocket calculator as "thinking." But our view of what constitutes thinking has changed over time, too. In the Middle Ages, when very few people could read or reckon, as performing arithmetic was called, anyone who could add and multiply was thought to have special powers, divinely or perhaps mystically conferred. Reckoning was a uniquely human activity. It took centuries for addition and multiplication to be codified into the algorithms that we all learn in elementary school. Is a capability, once classified as thinking and believed to be a divine gift, no longer thinking when it turns out to be algorithmic? It required thinking when we learned it. Maybe all thought is algorithmic. Maybe it's thinking only as long as no one understands how it's accomplished.

*fit*BYTE

Sub Text. Computer scientist Edsger Dijkstra is quoted as saying, "The question of whether a computer can think is no more interesting than the question of whether a submarine can swim." But he seems to be in the minority.

The Turing Test

The problem of defining thinking for the purposes of deciding whether a computer thinks concerned Alan M. Turing, one of the pioneers of computation. Turing was aware of definitions like "thinking is what people do," and the tendency for people to call an activity "thinking" until it turns out to be algorithmic. So, he decided to forget trying to define what thinking is and proposed a simple experiment that would demonstrate intelligence. Turing designed the following experimental setting, which has since become known as the **Turing test**.

> **Turing test:** Two identical rooms labeled A and B are connected electronically to a judge who can type questions directed to the occupant of either room. A human being occupies one room, and the other contains a computer. The judge's goal is to decide, based on the questions asked and the answers received, which room contains the computer. If after a reasonable period of time the judge cannot decide for certain, the computer can be said to be intelligent.

Thus, the computer is intelligent if it acts enough like a human to deceive the judge.

Passing the Test

Turing's experiment not only sidestepped the problem of defining thinking or intelligence, but it also got away from focusing on any specific ability such as performing arithmetic. The judge can ask any questions, so as to explore the entire range of thought processes. Apparent stumpers for the computer like

In Hamlet's famous soliloquy, what metaphors does Shakespeare use for "death"?

might not be so hard if the computer has access to online sources of Shakespearean criticism. Apparent "gimmes" for the computer like

What are the prime factors of 72, 914, 426?

might be answered in more human-like ways such as being slow or refusing to answer such questions at all. When Turing proposed the test in 1950, there was little prospect that a computer could deceive the judge. Nevertheless, it emphasized the important point that thinking is a process; how it is accomplished—with synapses or transistors—shouldn't matter.

Advances in the last half-century have definitely improved the computer's chances of "passing" the Turing test, though perhaps they are still not very good. Researchers reading Turing's paper in 1950 might have conceded that computers could be better than people at arithmetic, but probably all of them would have believed that "natural language"—a true human invention—was beyond the abilities of computers. For example, when Turing conceived the test, no algorithmic process was known for parsing (analyzing) English into its grammatical structure, as word processors' grammar checkers do today. Nor was "machine translation"—converting text from one language into its semantic equivalent in another language—anything more than science fiction. Nor was recognizing semantically meaningful information something a computer could perform, as Google does today.

{ GREAT *fit* MINDS }

Grand Turing >>

Englishman Alan Mathison Turing (1912–1954) was probably the most brilliant of all of the computer pioneers. In addition to the Turing test, he invented the first theoretical computer, now known as the Turing Machine, and discovered the Universality Principle (explained later in this chapter). During World War II he worked at the British Government's Code and Cipher School at Bletchley Park breaking Germany's Enigma Code. The Cambridge educated mathematician and marathon runner was awarded the Order of the British Empire (OBE) and was a member of the Royal Society. He died in 1954 of potassium cyanide poisoning under suspicious circumstances.

Admittedly, computers are still a long way from being perfect at any of these tasks, but they are pretty good at all three—at least good enough to be the basis for useful applications. More important, they are good enough at these language tasks that we can imagine a day when computers are better than most humans. And then, like reckoning, the tasks of parsing, translation, and semantic searching in natural language will have been reduced to algorithmic form. Does it add to our admiration of computers that they are closer to passing the Turing test? Or does it detract from our opinion of ourselves, suggesting that instead of computers being more like people, perhaps people are just computers. The questions are truly profound.

Motto. IBM, the dominant computer manufacturer of the 1950s–1970s, used "Think" as its corporate motto. It was common to see the command in computer rooms and on programmers' desks. Perhaps one of the best signs employed "negative space" to get the reader's brain working.

ACTING INTELLIGENTLY?

Anyone with even passing experience with grammar or spell checkers knows that these programs don't "understand" the sentences. They know the parts of speech such as prepositions and verbs, concepts like subject/object agreement, passive voice, and so on, but they don't understand complete sentences. Such concepts are not trivialities. It takes tremendously complex software and substantial dictionary resources to implement grammar and spell checking, and they're occasionally good enough to be helpful. But they definitely do not "understand" English.

The distinction between being intelligent and being programmed to seem intelligent concerned researchers in the 1950s and 1960s. The Doctor program (also known as Eliza) developed by MIT researcher Joseph Weizenbaum demonstrated this difference clearly. Doctor was programmed to ask questions in a dialog like a psychotherapist and a patient:

User: I'm depressed.
Doctor: Why are you depressed?
User: My mother is not speaking to me.
Doctor: Tell me about your mother.
User: She doesn't want me to major in engineering.
Doctor: No?
User: No, she wants me to go into medicine.

Doctor was programmed to keep the dialog going by asking questions and requesting more information. It would take cues from words like mother, including a reference to them in its next response. It would also notice uses of negative sentences, but the dialog was essentially preplanned. It may have appeared to be intelligent, but it definitely was not. What would a computer have to do to be intelligent or to demonstrate that it "understands" something?

As the research field of artificial intelligence (AI) came into existence, a consensus grew that to exhibit intelligence, a computer would have to "understand" a complex situation and reason well enough to act on its "understanding." Moreover, the actions could not be scripted or predetermined in any way. Most complex situations require the ability to understand natural language and/or require much real-world knowledge. Both properties badly handicapped computers of the day.

Playing Chess

Playing chess, however, was much cleaner. It offered a challenging task that humans were both good at and interested in. The rules were clear, and success could be easily defined: beat a grand master in a tournament. Indeed, in the initial exuberance over computing, it was predicted as early as 1952 that a computer would beat a grand master "sometime in the next decade." Though it took more than a decade before computers could do much more than know the legal chess moves, the problem was well established as a litmus test for AI.

*fit*BYTE   **A Modest Proposal.** Claude Shannon, a pioneer in information theory, was first to propose how a computer might play chess in 1949.

The Board Configuration. How does a computer play chess? First, like all computational problems, the information must be represented in bits. The chess "world" is especially easy to represent because it is completely defined by an 8×8 checkered board, 32 pieces of two colors and six different types, and a single bit indicating whose turn it is to move. Because details are unimportant, think of the graphic of a chessboard as printed in game books or newspapers; see Figure 23.1. Call it a board configuration, or simply a board.

The Game Tree. Next the computer must decide on a move. It does this in roughly the same way we do, by exploring moves to determine,

> *"Will a move of this piece to that position make me better off or worse off?"*

"Better off or worse off" are determined with respect to winning, of course, but it is very difficult to "compute" such information. Humans use intuition and experience. A computer uses an **evaluation function**, a procedure that assigns a numerical value to each piece and, taking into account things like captures and board position, computes a score for the move. If the score is positive, it's better; if it's negative, it's worse. Then, starting from the current board configuration, the computer checks the evaluation function on the result of every possible single legal

Figure 23.1. *A chessboard configuration.*

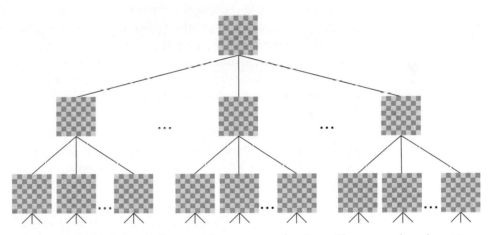

Figure 23.2. *A schematic diagram of a game tree for chess. The current board position is at the top (root). The boards produced in a single move are on the layer below, those reachable in two moves are on the layer below that, and so forth.*

move, as shown in the **game tree** of Figure 23.2. One of these moves—suppose there are 28 legal moves—will give the highest score, which might be the one that the computer should pick.

Using the Game Tree Tactically. Before picking a move, the computer should consider what the opponent might do. So for each of these "1-move" board configurations considered so far, the computer considers every possible next move from each and evaluates them. These boards are two moves away from the current board configuration. Furthermore, because the opponent makes the second move, the interpretation of the evaluation function is reversed. That is, the best move for the opponent is presumably the worst move for the computer, so the computer assumes the opponent will choose the move with the most negative score in the computer's evaluation function. This process is known as "look ahead." Clearly, the further ahead the computer looks—it's described as *deeper* in chess because of the tree formulation—the more complete is the computer's knowledge about possible outcomes of the game.

It would seem that the computer, being very fast, could look all the way to the end of the game, find a winning path, and follow that. But checking the whole game tree is generally impossible because of the geometric increase in the number of boards that must be considered. For example, if there are 28 moves possible from the current position, and an average of 28 from each of those, and each of their descendents, and so on, then considering only six moves deep (i.e., three for each side) generates

$$28 + 28^2 + 28^3 + 28^4 + 28^5 + 28^6 = 499{,}738{,}092$$

which is a half billion boards. It's infeasible for a computer to look 50 moves into the future.

Which move should the computer select? Picking the best move at the first level is not the best strategy, because the evaluation function is generally a static assessment of the board configuration. If in that one move the computer could reach a checkmate, the evaluation function would be very positive and the computer should pick it. But if not, the situation needs more strategy, because the most positive evaluation might come from a capture that would give the computer a piece advantage, whereas another choice, though less desirable at the moment, might lead in a few moves to a win. To play an intelligent game—that is, to strategize, to sacrifice pieces, to force the opponent into specific behaviors—requires the computer to analyze the game tree much more carefully.

Using a Database of Knowledge.   Finally, in addition to representing the game and making moves, the computer needs some knowledge. In chess, this takes the form of a database of openings and endgames. Because chess is interesting and has been studied for so long, much is known about how to start and finish chess games. Providing this database is like giving the computer chess experience. Because learning is probably even harder than being intelligent, loading the database saves the computer the need to "learn from experience." It's analogous to aspiring chess players reading books by grand masters.

Using Parallel Computation

Slowly, as the basic logic just discussed got worked out, chess programs got better and better. Eventually they were beating duffers, then serious players, and then masters. Progress came as a combination of faster computers, more complete databases, and better evaluation and "strategizing" functions. In time, **parallel computation**—the application of several computers to one task—and custom hardware allowed computer researchers to entertain the possibility of beating a grand master in tournament conditions.

The Deep Blue Matches. In 1996, reigning grand master Garry Kasparov trounced an IBM computer dubbed Deep Blue. Deep Blue was a parallel computer composed of 32 general-purpose computers (IBM RS/6000 SP) and 256 custom chess processors, enabling it to consider on average 200 million board positions per second. In one of the six games of the match, the computer played very well and won. Kasparov saw himself as victorious in defending the human race, but AI researchers were also ecstatic. At last a computer had played world-class chess in tournament conditions. A rematch was inevitable. On May 11, 1997, Kasparov lost 3.5–2.5 to an improved Deep Blue, achieving the "in the next decade" goal of the 1950s in a mere 45 years.

Interpreting the Outcome of the Matches

Did Deep Blue settle the question of whether computers can be intelligent? Not to everyone's satisfaction. To its credit, it answered one of the greatest technical challenges of the century. To do so required a large database of prior knowledge on openings and endgames, but that's analogous to reading books and playing chess. It also required special-purpose hardware that allowed rapid evaluation of board positions, but that's probably analogous to synaptic development in the brains of chess experts, giving them the ability over time to encapsulate whole board configurations as single mental units. But disappointingly—at least to some observers, and probably the AI pioneers who made the predictions in the first place—the problem was basically solved by speed. Deep Blue simply looked deeper. It did so *intelligently*, of course, because the geometric explosion of boards prevents success based simply on raw power. And that may be the strongest message from the Deep Blue/Kasparov matches. Intelligence may be the ability to consider many alternatives in an informed and directed way. Deep Blue surely demonstrated that.

The Deep Blue experience may have demonstrated that computers can be intelligent, or it may have demonstrated that IBM's team of chess experts and computer programmers is very intelligent. In the final analysis, the hardware was simply following the instructions that the programmers and engineers gave it. Such an objection has been raised in the "intelligence" debate since the beginning. It is a weak criticism because we can imagine intelligence, or creativity, or any other intellectual process being encoded in a general form, so that once started on a body of information, the program operates autonomously, responding to new inputs and realizing states not planned by its designers. Deep Blue operates autonomously in this sense and thus transcends its designers.

The main cautionary note regarding Deep Blue is that it is completely specialized to chess. That is, the 256 chess processors only evaluate board positions and are not useful for any other purpose. The 32 general-purpose processors can run other programs, of course, but none of Deep Blue's "intelligence" is transferable to another computation unless a programmer abstracts the ideas from Deep Blue and incorporates them into that computation. The "intelligence" isn't formulated in any general-purpose way. Thus Deep Blue speaks only indirectly to the subject of general-purpose intelligence.

Another View. John Searle, an outspoken critic of AI, offers a widely quoted criticism: The Chinese Room Argument. A monolingual English speaker is locked in a room and given rules in English for correlating symbols in three batches of Chinese text to produce translations. Ignorant of Chinese, the occupant follows the rules. The format is designed to mirror AI programs. The occupant is amazingly good, but unaware of his role. Amazed Chinese believe he's a native speaker. Is he intelligent? Or only following rules like a computer? Much has been debated on both sides.

ACTING CREATIVELY

An alternative approach to understanding the limitation and potential of computers is to consider whether they can be "creative." For example, can a computer create art? It's not a question of whether a computer can be the art medium—artists have manipulated computers to produce art for decades. Rather the question is whether a computer can prevail in, perhaps, a "graphic version" of the Turing test: A judge visits an art gallery and decides whether a person or a computer produced the art. Could a computer be successful at fooling the judge? The task may be more daunting even than the original Turing test because creativity is by definition a process of breaking the rules, and computers only follow rules. How could they ever succeed at being creative? Perhaps there are rules—**metarules**—that describe how to break the rules or, perhaps, transcend existing rules. A computer could follow those. To see how this might be, let's first look at a program to create fine art.

There has been something of a fad recently in writing Java applets to create graphic designs after the famed cubist Piet Mondrian (1872–1944), whose paintings are exhibited in the great art collections of the world (see Figure 23.3).

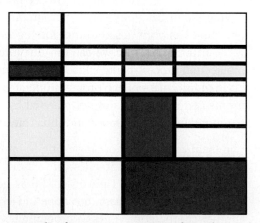

Figure 23.3. *Example of a computer-generated graphic in the style of Piet Mondrian. (Finding current examples only requires a Web search on terms like mondrian AND java; other geometrically regular graphics, for example, Moorish designs, can also be found.)*

The programs display a new Mondrian-like picture with each mouse click. Inspecting the code, we find that the programs use random numbers to steer a deterministic process for placing lines and filling regions with color. That is, the program encodes a set of rules for creating graphics in the style of Mondrian, using what looks to the casual observer like the same design elements, same colors, and so on. The graphics are new in the sense that they have never before existed, but as art critics love to say: "The work is derivative."

Mondrian is famous not because he created pleasing pictures with strong lines and bold primary colors, but because he had something to say about his world that he expressed through art. That is, he's famous for a body of work from which the program's rules have been (reasonably faithfully) abstracted. The program only produces variations on the application of the rules using random numbers. But to many, creativity means inventing the rules in the first place.

Creativity as a Spectrum

Computer scientist Bruce Jacob distinguishes between the form of creativity that comes from inspiration—"a flash out of the blue"—and the form that comes from hard work—"incremental revision." Inspiration remains a mystery; in Jacob's view the hard work is algorithmic. (This is reminiscent of Thomas Edison's famous description of genius: 1 percent inspiration, 99 percent perspiration.)

To organize our discussion, think of creativity as a spectrum ranging from "flash out of the blue" to "Mondrian in a click." To be creative in fine art at the "flash out of the blue" end, the computer would have to step outside of the "established order," inventing its own rules, whereas at the applet end of the spectrum, the computer just randomly assembles parts by the rules some programmer gave it, never extending or modifying them. Between those two extremes, there are still alternatives.

The Hard Work Forms. Jacob illustrates the hard work form of creativity using canons (musical compositions that have the incremental-variation-on-a-theme property).

Jacob has developed a music composition system, Variations, which attempts to create canons by extending a repertoire of base themes by (randomly) generating new themes, assessing them as "good" or "bad," and discarding the "bad" ones. Interestingly, Jacob points out that because the program must work within the underlying characteristics of the base themes, getting a random variation to "fit" within those constraints "sometimes requires creativity!" That is, forcing a random variation on the constraints imposed by a set of rules produces new techniques.

Calling Jacob's work **computer creativity** may seem difficult, because the program appears to embody much of the designer—the test for "bad" for instance—and there is a certain "stumbling onto a solution" quality from the randomness. Nevertheless, this and similar efforts, which span creative pursuits from inventing typefaces to making analogies, focus on the rule-making aspect of creativity and demonstrate that incremental revision is algorithmic. So, the conclusion seems to be that creativity ranges from the startling "flash out of the blue" end to the mechanical Mondrian-in-a-click end.

> *fit***BYTE**
>
> **Classical Question.** At a recent University of Oregon demonstration, three pianists played three different pieces of music in the style of Bach, one composed by Bach, one composed by Steven Larson (a UO professor), and one composed by EMI, a computer program. The audience voted on who they thought wrote which piece. Larson's composition was thought to be the program's, Bach's composition was thought to be Larson's, and EMI's composition was thought to be Bach's.

What Part of Creativity Is Algorithmic?

When the Turing test was invented, "Draw a picture in the style of Mondrian" would have been a request that a computer would have utterly failed at. Today it is a three-page Java program.

AI researchers have demonstrated in various contexts that the "hard work" form of creativity is algorithmic. If the matter of whether a computer can be creative is not taken to be a yes/no question, but rather is seen as an expedition into the process of creativity, we find our answer. The more deeply we understand creativity, the more we find ways in which it is algorithmic. Will it be found to be entirely algorithmic at some point in the future? Will there be rules for breaking the rules? Will it become like reckoning? Or will there necessarily be a non-algorithmic part at the inspirational end? No matter how it turns out, aspects of creativity are algorithmic. To the extent that creativity is algorithmic, a computer can be creative. But who needs a computer? If creativity is algorithmic, we can all be creative by following the rules. Progress in understanding creativity can benefit us, too. And how it is accomplished—with synapses or transistors—shouldn't matter.

> *fit***BYTE**
>
> **Fill in the Blank.** In an essay on creativity published in *Science*, Goldenberg, Mazursky, and Solomon report that, in one study, 89 percent of award-winning advertisements contain a use of one of six "creativity templates," that is, follow-the-rules techniques, and that one simple template, *Replacement*, accounted for 25 percent of all award-winning ads.

● THE UNIVERSALITY PRINCIPLE

Another problem that concerned Turing and other computer pioneers was to determine what makes one computer more powerful than another. Their amazing discovery was that any computer using only very simple instructions could simulate any other computer. This fact—known as the **Universality Principle**—means, for example, that all computers have the same power!

***fit*BYTE**

All Computers Are Created Equal. Though computer scientists have found different fundamental instruction sets, the six instructions `Add` (as described in Chapter 9), `Subtract`, `Set_To_One`, `Load`, `Store`, and `Branch_On_Zero` are sufficient to program any computation.

It goes without saying that every computer has these primitive instructions and much more. From the commercial point of view, the Universality Principle means that Intel and Motorola cannot compete with each other to build a computer that can compute more computations. Every computer the two companies have ever made is equivalent to all other computers in terms of what they can compute. The Universality Principle says that all computers compute the same set of computations. It's surprising.

The Universality Principle has deep theoretical implications, but there are important practical consequences, too.

***fit*BYTE**

Getting Down to Basics. Another startling consequence of the Universality Principle is that programs, in effect, reduce *all* computation—playing chess or checking grammar or figuring income tax—to the point where it is expressible with only a half dozen different kinds of instructions.

Universal Information Processor

Perhaps the most important aspect of universality is that if we want to do some new information-processing task, we don't need to buy a new computer. The computer we have is sufficient if we can write or buy the software for the task.

This is quite different, say, from wanting to perform a new task in the kitchen or the shop, where we would have to buy a new gadget. Machines that transform material must be specialized to each activity, requiring us—or enabling us, if you like to get new gadgets!—to buy a specialized device. By contrast, there is only one information-processing machine, the computer.

Because computers are general purpose, people play a greater role in setting them up and configuring them for a specific task—installing software, for example—than they do for single-purpose machines like food processors or table saws. This greater role in customizing the general-purpose device to our needs is one reason why it is important to become Fluent with IT.

Practical Consequences of the Universality Principle

The Universality Principle says that all computers compute the same way, and their speed is the only difference. Unfortunately, the Universality Principle's claim that any computer can simulate any other computer has the disadvantage that simulation does the work much more slowly.

{*fit*BYTE}

Competing Machines and the Universality Principle >>

To understand why all computers are equivalent, imagine two computers, the ZAP^2 and the BXLE, and suppose they have the same hardwired instructions, except that ZAP^2 has one additional instruction. Its manufacturer claims, contrary to the Universality Principle, that the new instruction enables new computations on the ZAP^2 that are not possible on the BXLE. "Baloney," says BXLE's CEO. "Using the instructions already in BXLE, we will program a function that performs the operation of ZAP^2's special hardwired instruction. Then, in any program, we will replace every use of their special instruction with a call to our function. Anything ZAP^2 can do, BXLE can do, too." For a schematic diagram, see Figure 23.4.

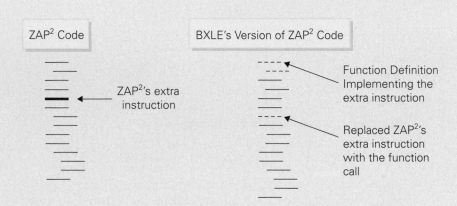

Figure 23.4. *Schematic diagram showing a revision of ZAP^2's program to run on the BXLE, in which the special instruction has been replaced by a function call.*

In effect, ZAP^2 performs the instruction in hardware while the BXLE performs the instruction in software, that is, by using a function. The argument holds up as long as the special instruction can be programmed with the basic instructions of the BXLE, which we can be confident will be possible. But the skeptic needn't accept that on faith. Rather, it's possible to write a program for the BXLE to simulate circuits and to simulate the entire circuitry of ZAP^2. Simulating ZAP^2 by the BXLE is possible because ZAP^2 is built from (zillions of) two-input logic gates. There are only 16 different gates, and they can be trivially simulated with the six basic instructions, which the BXLE surely has. Because BXLE can exactly duplicate the ZAP^2 operation in the simulator, it is possible to do all of the same computations, too. Notice that this solution also solves the problem in software.

Because all computers do the same computations, the main basis for technical competition among manufacturers is speed.

In the first solution of the ZAP^2/BXLE example, BXLE was only slower on the special instruction, which presumably takes several basic instructions to implement. The second case was much slower because each instruction of the ZAP^2 might take thousands of logical operations, and the BXLE must simulate each of these. So, although both computers can realize the same computations, they perform them at different rates. For that reason, manufacturers *do* include special instructions for tasks such as digital signal processing, graphics, and encryption, hoping that their frequent use will speed up their computer.

The Universality Principle seems to conflict with our everyday experience, however. Three obvious difficulties arise:

> > Macintosh software doesn't run on the PC and vice versa; if Macs and PCs are the same, why not?

> > People say old machines become outmoded; how so, if they're all the same?

> > Is it really true that the computer in my laptop is the same as the one in my microwave oven?

Despite these apparent problems, the Universality Principle is a practical fact. Consider each objection in turn.

Macintosh versus PC. PC and Mac processors are different—Intel's Pentium and Motorola's PowerPC—implying each has a different **combination** of instructions, though they include the six most basic ones mentioned earlier. These instruction sets are encoded differently, they operate slightly differently, each has instructions the other doesn't have, and so on. None of these differences is fundamental. It is possible to write a program for each machine to perform the instructions of the other machine, just as was argued earlier. It is not only possible in principle, computer scientists write such programs frequently.

But consumer software relies heavily on operating system facilities, too. OS software extends the basic instruction set of the computer—as we learned in Chapter 9—so it can perform useful operations like booting itself up and locating files on the hard disk. And this is the real difference between the Mac and PC: These operating systems do things very differently. None of the differences is fundamental, and it's possible in principle to simulate each OS on the other platform. Business considerations keep the two separate.

The alternative solution, which software companies like Adobe, Microsoft, and Oracle use, is to translate their programs to each computer family, as explained in Chapter 9. The software is written in a programming language like Basic, C, or Java, and then it is compiled—that is, translated—into the machine language of each processor type, Pentium or PowerPC. Special care is taken to ensure that operating system incompatibilities are removed. The result is that rather than simulating the software of one computer on another computer, there is a separate custom version of the software for each vendor's computer. (And, of course, it won't run on another vendor's computer.) In that way, any application software can run on any computer and not be slowed by simulating another machine. So, the Universality Principle is applied daily, but not along the lines of our original discussion.

Outmoded Computers. As noted, speed is the main difference among computers. Often, the reason why someone buys a new computer is that they own new software, doubtless loaded with slick new features, that runs slowly on their old machine. With the new software doing more, it is not surprising that a faster computer would help. But, for those who are patient, there is no need to upgrade.

People usually give two reasons in support of their claim that older computers become "outmoded." The first reason is that hardware and/or software products are often incompatible with older machines. For example, input/output devices, such as modems and printers, are often incompatible with older computers because of other internal parts, such as the system bus. (See the computer components diagram, Figure 9.2, in Chapter 9.) As a result, it is not possible to connect the new devices. However, these parts are not closely connected with instruction execution.

The second reason is that software vendors simply don't support old machines. As explained, software vendors compile their programs to each platform—usually a processor/OS combination—to sell to customers. But, if there are too few customers running an old processor/OS combination, the vendor may decide that it isn't profitable to sell and maintain a version for that machine. Thus new software is often not available for old computers. This is a business decision; there is no technical impediment.

The Laptop and the Microwave. The computers embedded in consumer products like microwave ovens, brakes, and other devices are there not because the task of running a microwave is so complex that it needs a computer. Rather, it's cheaper to implement the system with a computer and a read-only memory (ROM) chip containing a fixed program than it is to implement it with custom electronics. It's a matter of economics, not a technical requirement.

Embedded computers have a rich enough instruction set to run any other computer application. Their main handicap as computers is usually neither their instruction repertoire nor their speed. Rather, embedded computers are, well, embedded. The program is fixed—giving only options like popping popcorn or defrosting dinner—and it is connected to a very limited set of input/output devices, usually only the sensors and actuators of the system they control. If the embedded computer were connected to a keyboard and a monitor, as is the personal computer we're accustomed to, it could run the software just fine.

So, the Universality Principle is not only a theoretical fact, it is a practical fact, too.

MORE WORK, SLOWER SPEED

When we use computers, they are simply idling most of the time, waiting for us to give them something to do. For tasks like word processing, even including continuous grammar and spell checking doesn't keep them busy. So we listen to MP3 tunes too, which still doesn't stress them. Eventually, perhaps when we are manipulating digital images, we notice that certain activities, like making the image brighter, are computed very fast, but others, like rotating the image, are noticeably slower. This is curious when we think about it, because the image has the same number of pixels in both cases. What causes some tasks to take longer to compute?

Comparing *Alphabetize CDs* with *Face Forward*

The obvious and correct answer is that it takes more time to do more work. Recall the *Alphabetize CDs* example from Chapter 10. If the CD rack were smaller, the algorithm would complete sooner because fewer CDs would have to be considered. The point is even easier to see for a task like making sure the CDs all face forward.

The *Face Forward* algorithm requires only that we start at the beginning, inspect each CD to see which way it faces, and if it is not facing forward, reorient it and return it; in either case, we then move on to the next CD. If the rack holds 24 CDs, the algorithm takes 24 iterations of the inspect-and-reorient sequence because only one pass through the rack is sufficient. If the rack contains 48 CDs, 48 iterations will be required. The amount of work is proportional to the amount of data.

Cases of this type, where the amount of work is directly proportional to the amount of data, are said to be **work-proportional-to-*n*** algorithms. That is, the running time is at most the number of basic steps devoted to each item times the number *n* of data items. We say "at most" because all of the steps may not be necessary on each data item. If some CDs are already facing forward, there will be no need for a reorient step. In the worst case, all CDs are facing backward, and it takes the maximum predicted time.

Orienting the CDs to face forward is an easier task than alphabetizing them. Recall that the *Alphabetize CDs* algorithm did not solve the problem in "one pass" through the rack. In fact, for each CD referenced by *Alpha*, all of the CDs after it had to be considered; we called this a *Beta* sweep. So, if there are 24 CDs in the rack, 23 CDs must be considered to get the first CD into position in the front because *Alpha's* reference doesn't change, but *Beta* references the other 23 CDs. Thus the "In Order?" test must be made 23 times to locate the alphabetically first CD. Then *Alpha* moves to the second position, referencing the next slot, and *Beta* must visit the 22 CDs after it. This continues until the last step, when *Alpha* references the next-to-last CD and *Beta* references only the last slot—that is, only one interchange of CDs is considered at the very end. Adding these numbers yields

$$23 + 22 + \ldots + 1 = 276$$

That is, we test 276 times to put the CDs in order in a 24-slot rack. In the same way, if the CD rack contains 48 CDs, locating the alphabetically first CD would require 47 CD references in the first *Beta* sweep, finding the second would require 46, and so on. Adding these numbers we get

$$47 + 46 + \ldots + 1 = 1128$$

which is surprising because the rack is only twice as large, but the number of tests is more than four times larger. Clearly the repeated *Beta* sweeps of *Alphabetize CDs* require more work than the single sweep of the *Face Forward* algorithm.

{GREAT *fit* MINDS}

Brainy Kid >>

At age seven, Johann Karl Friedrich Gauss (1777–1855), the mathematician whose face graces the Ten Deutsche Mark note, was asked by his teacher to add the numbers 1 to 100. He found the answer 5050 immediately by noting that adding the first plus last numbers (1 + 100) equals 101, adding the next-to-first and next-to-last numbers (2 + 99) also equals 101, etc., and that there are 50 pairs summing to 101. Young Gauss's idea always works, so adding numbers from 1 to n is $(n + 1)n/2$.

Work Proportional to n^2

Thus, although the *Face Forward* computation took only one pass through the rack, *Alphabetize CDs* took many passes. In the former case, the number of repetitions is proportional to n for an n-slot rack, and in the latter case, the number of repetitions is proportional to $(n + 1)n/2 = (n^2 + n)/2$. Whereas *Face Forward* is said to be a **work-proportional-to-n algorithm**, *Alphabetize CDs* is said to be a **work-proportional-to-n^2 algorithm**. (Computer people don't worry about the other terms of the equation, only the most significant term, the n^2 here.)

Thus, if there are $n = 1000$ pieces of data, and a problem can be solved by a work-proportional-to-n algorithm, it will take about a thousand times the amount of work needed to do the task on one data item. But, if the problem is solved by a work-proportional-to-n^2 algorithm, the amount of work will be about a *million* = 1000×1000 times the amount of work needed to solve the problem on one data item. So, when we observe that one computation is taking more time than another despite requiring the same amount of data, it is generally because the algorithm does more work to solve the problem.

Notice that the explanation is that "the algorithm does more work to solve the problem," not that the problem *requires* more work to be solved. That is, the algorithm the programmer chose to solve the problem may not be the fastest. The fastest known algorithm is rarely the solution of choice. For example, there are faster ways to alphabetize CDs than the solution presented, though none with work proportional to n. And the alternatives are somewhat more complicated. Complexity and other factors contribute to a programmer's decision, and besides the computer is idle most of the time anyway.

HOW HARD CAN A PROBLEM BE?

With algorithms requiring work proportional to n and proportional to n^2, it is a good guess that there are algorithms requiring work proportional to n^3, n^4, and so on. There are, and they are all considered practical for computers to solve, though as the example of the last section made clear, the exponent does matter a lot to the user sitting and waiting for the answer.

NP-Complete Problems

There are much more difficult computations, many of which are important to business, science, and engineering. In fact, one of the most significant discoveries of the 1970s was that many problems of interest—for example, finding the cheapest set of plane tickets for touring n cities—don't have any known "practical" algorithmic solutions. Such problems are known by the rather curious name of **NP-complete** problems. In essence, the best-known algorithms do little more than try all possible solutions, and then pick the best. It seems that there should be cleverer algorithms than that. If there are, the person who discovers one will enjoy tremendous fame. In the meantime, such problems are said to be **intractable**—the best way to solve them is so difficult that large data sets cannot be solved with a realistic amount of computer time on any computer. Computers can solve them in principle, but not in practice.

*fit*BYTE | **Hard Problems.** Steve Cook of the University of Toronto and Dick Karp of UC Berkeley discovered NP-completeness. They also discovered the amazing fact that if anyone finds a better algorithm for just one NP-complete problem, their algorithm will improve *every* NP-complete problem.

Unsolvable Problems

Perhaps more surprisingly, there are problems computers cannot solve at all. It's not that the algorithms take too long, but that there are no algorithms, period! These are not problems like being intelligent or creative, but precisely definable problems with a clear quantifiable objective. For example, it's impossible for an algorithm to determine if a program has a bug in it, like looping forever. Such an algorithm would have been quite handy in Chapter 21 in our study of looping, when we messed up the *<next iteration>* step, causing infinite loops. We'd simply give our program to this imagined Loop-Checker algorithm, and it would tell us whether or not our program loops forever. Notice that the Loop-Checker would be especially useful for computations having, say, work proportional to n^4 because we have to wait a long time for the results. While we're waiting, we'd like to be sure we're going to get a result eventually, rather than have the program caught in an infinite loop, forcing us to wait forever.

The Nonexistent Loop Checker.   But the Loop-Checker can't exist. Suppose it did. That is, suppose there is a program `LC(P, x)` that takes as its input any program `P` and input data `x`, analyzes `P`, and answers back "Yes" or "No" as to whether `P` will loop forever on input `x`. This actually seems plausible, because `LC` could look through `P`, checking every loop to see if the *<next iteration>* and *<continuation>* tests are set right. And then it could follow the execution of `P` on `x`, looking to see if anything could go wrong. It seems plausible, but it's not. Here's why.

Create another program, `CD(P)`, that also takes as input a program `P`. `CD` is an abbreviation for "contradiction." The program works according to the flowchart shown in Figure 23.5. What does `CD(CD)` compute? We're not sure what the assumed `LC(CD,CD)` will answer back, but suppose it says "No," `CD` does not loop forever when the `CD` program is its input. In that case, the left arrow out of the diamond is taken and `CD` loops forever. So, `LC` would have been wrong. Perhaps `LC` answers "Yes," that `CD` will loop forever when `CD` is its input. In that case, the right arrow out of the diamond is taken and the program doesn't loop forever, but just stops. Wrong again. The Loop-Checker cannot answer correctly—neither "Yes" nor "No" is the right answer. This problem cannot be algorithmically solved.

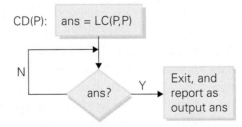

Figure 23.5. *The logic of the CD program, given the assumed program* `LC`.

The Halting Problem.   The Loop-Checker is trying to solve a famous computation known as the **Halting Problem**. Alan M. Turing was the first to recognize the impossibility of creating the perfect debugger, like the theoretical Loop-Checker. It's too bad one can't be created, because having such a debugger would be handy. Interestingly, debugging—the topic of Chapter 7—is something that humans can do, admittedly with great difficulty sometimes. In fact, it requires considerable intelligence to figure out what has gone wrong when an IT task doesn't work out. It's something that computers won't ever be able to do in any general way. So, maybe we were looking in the wrong place for capabilities that are uniquely human. Making computers solve our problems *properly* is something only humans can do!

SUMMARY

We have explored the limits of computation. We began by asking a question that has puzzled people since computers were invented—can computers think? The question challenged us to define what thinking is. In this chapter we:

> Identified a tendency for people to decide that an intellectual activity isn't considered thinking if it is algorithmic. Thinking is probably best defined as what humans do, and therefore something computers can't do.

> Discussed the Turing test, an experimental setting in which we can compare the capabilities of humans with those of computers.

> Studied the question of computer chess and learned that computers use a game tree formulation, an evaluation function to assess board positions, and a database of openings and endgames. Deep Blue became the chess champion of the world in 1997, a monumental achievement, but not one that closed the book on the algorithmic nature of intelligence.

> Studied creativity, deciding it occurs on a spectrum: from algorithmic variation (Mondrian-in-a-click) through incremental revision to a flash of inspiration. The degree to which the activities along the spectrum are algorithmic has advanced over the years.

> Presumed that there will be further advancement, but we do not know where the "algorithmic frontier" will be drawn. It's too early to tell if creativity, like reckoning, is entirely algorithmic. Computers will be creative insofar as creativity is algorithmic. And so will we all.

> Considered the Universality Principle, which implies that computers are equal in terms of what they can compute. This is not only a theoretical statement. We benefit from its practical consequences daily.

> Discussed that software companies can write a single application program and translate it into the machine language of any computer, making it available to everyone regardless of the kind of computer they own. This implied that computer vendors could only compete on speed, which led us to consider how fast computers can solve problems.

> Discussed that the many proportional-to-n computations require less work than the proportional-to-n^2 computations even though both require n data values. Such computations are practical and form the large part of computing.

> Learned that important problems—the so-called NP-complete problems—require much more computational work. Many of the problems we would like to solve are NP-complete problems, but unfortunately the NP-complete problems are intractable—large instances are solvable by computer only in principle, not in practice.

> Learned the amazing fact that some computations—general-purpose debugging—cannot be solved by computers, even in principle. If it were possible, we could solve the Halting Problem, and that's not logically possible. We should remember this when it seems computers can do anything!

EXERCISES

Multiple Choice

1. Computers can
   A. think
   B. manipulate information
   C. be creative
   D. all of the above

2. For the computer, chess is a series of
   A. algorithms
   B. computations
   C. possible moves reduced to an evaluation of the "best" move
   D. all of the above

3. Creativity can be
   A. "a flash out of the blue"
   B. incremental revision of existing work
   C. hard work
   D. perhaps some of each, depending on the definition

4. The ability of any computer to imitate another computer is known as
   A. mimicry
   B. the Imitation Principle
   C. the Universality Principle
   D. the Turing Test

5. The fastest computers can calculate up to
   A. ten billion instructions per second
   B. a trillion instructions per second
   C. a million instructions per minute
   D. ten trillion instructions per second

6. Work-proportional-to-n algorithms
   A. increase processing time proportionally to the data
   B. process data in roughly the same amount of time regardless of the amount of data
   C. work so fast that modern computers spend most of their time idling
   D. geometrically increase in processing time as the amount of data increases

7. The *Alphabetize CDs* algorithm is a
   A. work-proportional-to-n algorithm
   B. work-proportional-to-n^2 algorithm
   C. either A or B, depending on the initial order of the CDs
   D. A XOR B

Exercises

1. How many 0's in a trillion?

2. How long would it take a human to do a billion calculations?

3. Explain how computer art is derivative and not creative.

4. Where on the list does a chess algorithm fall for solving computer problems?

5. What type of algorithm is needed to solve a problem of finding the best route to take for a cross country trip?

6. Explain how a game tree could be used for card games.

7. Describe why the argument on whether computers can think has little impact on our daily lives. Use your word processor to answer this.

8. What does a computer have to do to pass the Turing test?

chapter **24**

CLICK TO CLOSE
A Fluency Summary

learning objectives

> Discuss the differences in remembering IT details and ideas when you are Fluent

> Discuss lifelong IT learning through finding new uses, asking for help, and noticing new technology

> Discuss the benefits of achieving Fluency now and in the future

CLICK TO CLOSE
A Fluency Summary

Whatever a man prays for, he prays for a miracle . . . "Great God, let not two times two make four."

—IVAN TURGENEV, 1862

WE HAVE COME to the final chapter. There has been no miracle—two times two still makes four—and IT makes sense. It has been a substantive and, at times, challenging tour. But our ability to apply IT has dramatically improved. We have acquired basic information about a broad spectrum of topics. We're not experts, but we know enough to know when we need to learn more. As our study proceeded, we integrated the basic information into a powerful intuitive IT model. As we acquire new knowledge, this model gives it a place to "fit into."

In this chapter we wrap up our Fluency study by summarizing two of several repeating ideas. Then we consider the two most pressing matters: How much of the information in this book do we have to remember, and how do we learn the technology that hasn't yet been invented? Both topics have unexpected outcomes. Finally, we reflect on the fact that in the world of IT, we can shift for ourselves.

TWO BIG IT IDEAS

Thinking back over the chapter summaries, several ideas have recurred in our IT study. Two examples are information structuring and strategies for nonalgorithmic tasks. We consider each in turn.

Information Structuring

In Chapter 5 we learned that collections of information are structured hierarchically—that is, organized by descriptive metadata into groups and subgroups—in order to assist us in locating specific items. In Chapter 8 we found that the *Oxford English Dictionary's* digitization includes metadata structural tags that enclose the constituents of each definition. Knowing the purpose of each part of the *OED's* content (headword, citation, etc.) allows the computer to perform complex searches and analysis. In Chapters 13–16, specifying the structure of the information gave the same powerful advantage when we built spreadsheets and databases. Specifying the characteristics of the data stored in a table—its type, whether it is key, etc.—allowed for sophisticated queries and prevented erroneous uses that would have produced garbage.

The idea is that *specifying structure is as essential as specifying content*. This idea comes up again and again because the value of information depends on how effectively we can use it, and all of the powerful applications rely on the computer's knowing the structure. The truth of this observation is clear from our studies. But we can learn more from it!

As we become increasingly more effective users, we will acquire a growing collection of personally important digital information. Years of old email correspondence, digital photos, collections of MP3 tunes, etc., will fill our hard disks. As our collections grow, we may eventually decide to move certain information into databases or other structured archives in order to manipulate them efficiently. But along the way, while we accumulate the information as independent files, it's smart to keep it structured; simply by the way we arrange it in directories and subdirectories. We should assign our MP3s and JPEGs to their own directories—substructured perhaps into folders based on content—so that we can find files when we want them. This simple directory structure organization is not as effective as the examples above because the computer does not know the structure. But *we* know it and it will assist us in a manual navigation of our collections.

Strategies for Nonalgorithmic Tasks

Algorithms have been an important topic in our Fluency study. We learned the placeholder technique for reformatting text (Chapter 2), an insertion sort for alphabetizing CDs (Chapter 10), an effective query construction (Chapter 15)—build a supertable with joins and then trim it down using `Select` and `Project`—and many others.

But perhaps the most significant content of our study concerned capabilities that are not algorithmic. Finding accurate information (Chapter 5), satisfying our curiosity through research (Chapter 6), debugging (Chapter 7), formulating a password (Chapter 12), designing a database (Chapter 16), testing and assessing a user interface (Chapter 19), and programming a complex Web application (Chapter 22) are all examples in which there are no deterministic, guaranteed-to-yield-a-solution rules. In each case we could only give guidelines. For example, debugging is facilitated by these guidelines:

check LIST >> Debugging Guidelines

- ☑ *Make sure that you can reproduce the error.*

- ☑ *Determine exactly what the problem is.*

- ☑ *Eliminate the "obvious" causes.*

- ☑ *Divide the process, separating the parts that work from the parts that don't.*

- ☑ *When you reach a dead end, reassess your information, ask where you may be making wrong assumptions or conclusions, and then step through the process again.*

- ☑ *As you work through the process from start to finish, make predictions about what should happen and verify that the predictions are fulfilled.*

The steps prescribe a rational approach to the task, but they don't form an algorithm.

The nonalgorithmic capabilities have been presented as though they form a separate knowledge base, and they do, in the sense that they each entail a separate list of guidelines. But generally the capabilities are all applications of logical reasoning in service of achieving some higher goal—true information, correct program, convenient application, etc. Reasoning is the key. It is applied in small ways on nearly every page of the book. Indeed, an overarching theme of this text is that *precision and the directed application of logical reasoning can solve problems great and small, algorithmic and nonalgorithmic.* The more we apply such thinking, the better we become at it!

FLUENCY: LESS IS MORE

In reviewing the material covered in the book, it is sobering to realize the enormous amount of detailed information that we've covered. We've learned about anchor tags in HTML, the `if/else` statement in JavaScript, the Vacation Message, the Nyquist Rule, SQL SELECT commands, and on and on. How can we ever remember it all?

Recall that the Fluency knowledge is compartmentalized into three components:

> Skills—competency with contemporary IT applications like word processing.

> Concepts—understanding the foundations on which IT is built, like the Fetch/Execute Cycle.

> Capabilities—facility with higher-level thinking processes like reasoning.

These three kinds of knowledge are co-equal and interdependent. But when we analyze the three types of knowledge from the point of view of how much we have to remember, we realize that they are very much *unequal*.

> The skills all require much detailed knowledge. For example, are field names in SQL expressed as *<table name>.<field name>* or *<field name>.<table name>*? It is impossible to write SQL without knowing which is correct. Furthermore, an annoying property of this detail is that the computer demands that we are *exactly right*; it is unforgiving. We can't use computers without knowing such facts.

> The concepts might be quite detailed, but the "basic ideas" are not. We know a computer's Fetch/Execute Cycle is an infinite process for interpreting instructions, but now that we understand the core idea, we don't really need to remember that the third of the five steps is called Data Fetch. It's the concept of an instruction execution engine that is important. IT concepts are like other scientific information. Ideas must be explained in full detail to be understood; but after they're learned, only the ideas themselves, not the particulars, are important for the non-specialist.

> The capabilities are the least detailed of all. Capabilities are mainly approaches to thinking. For example, problem decomposition, in which a complex task is broken into smaller tasks that are either solved directly or are themselves broken into smaller pieces still, is simply a rational way to tackle complex problems. Debugging—thinking objectively about a faulty IT application—is mostly a matter of being a good detective. Yes, there are guidelines on how to proceed, but debugging mainly comes down to forcing yourself to look at a situation the way it is rather than the way it seems so far. The capabilities require you to remember almost no detail whatsoever.

So there is a spectrum of detail from skills through concepts to capabilities.

Curiously, our Fluency study allows us to remember less, rather than requiring us to remember more. How can this be? We remember less *detail* because we remember the *basic ideas* instead.

The clearest example—much of our Fluency study works this way—was our discussion of what the digerati know (Chapter 2). The chapter seemed to cover necessary skill-level information about how to use a GUI, what's behind the **File** and **Edit** menus, how to use shift-select, and so on. But the chapter is really about the capability of *thinking abstractly about technology*, and how we learn to think abstractly. We asked sweeping questions like:

> How do we learn technology?

> How do software designers, indeed any tool designers, expect users to learn to use their new creations?

> When we're confronted with a task that requires technology, how do we figure out what to do?

The answers to these questions was not "Memorize thick, boring manuals." Rather, we pointed out that thinking abstractly about technology implies an adaptive approach to learning. Tool creators exploit consistent interfaces—every tape and CD player uses the same icons—so we should look for the consistency. Look for metaphors. When presented with a tool, explore it by "clicking around" to see what the inventor provided. Wonder what you're expected to do. And finally, simply "blaze away," trying things out and watching what happens, knowing that the garbage created when mistakes are made must be thrown away (at no cost) before starting over. In other words, we don't memorize the tool's details. Rather, we learn the details as we need them. If we use software frequently, we will become adept at the specifics, memorizing the details through use. If we use software rarely, we will forget the specifics. But even that's fine. We will know abstractly what to do and how to figure out the details again.

Thus the higher-level capabilities make us rational people, approaching IT tasks thoughtfully, enabling us to proceed in a directed and disciplined way toward the goal, solving problems as they arise, figuring out what to do as required, logically figuring out what's wrong when a bug has us blocked. We've learned how to learn IT. Fluency doesn't require that we use our heads to memorize details. It only requires that we use our heads.

LIFELONG IT LEARNING

Information technology learning is a process of lifelong learning, but that doesn't mean you have to read 20 pages of *Programming in XML* every night before bed. In fact, it doesn't mean that you have to do much at all. To learn IT throughout life requires only that you engage in three activities:

> Pursue new IT uses that fulfill your personal needs.

> Be rational about asking for help.

> Notice new ideas and technology as they arise.

There's no course of study to attend.

Pursuing New Uses

While studying Fluency, you have had to learn many new and unfamiliar applications. Though learning new skills may initially have been daunting, the process should have become steadily easier as your experience broadened and your facility with "clicking around" and "blazing away" developed. This success, and the fact that learning becomes easier the more you know, should give you confidence that you can learn IT on your own. And that's the best way to advance your knowledge. When you are engaged in information processing tasks—addressing envelopes, paying bills, or looking up Manila's time zone—determine whether you should use information technology to help you. If so, be confident that you can learn the new application, and take the time to do so. Expanding your IT use is the best way to continue to learn.

If you think objectively when you ask the question, "Can IT help in this situation?" the answer will not always be "yes." If the occasions when you address envelopes are limited to Mother's Day and Father's Day, IT will not help. Besides, do you want address labels on their greeting cards? If the envelope addressing occurs once a year for holiday greeting cards and you have only a modest list, again it may not pay. For the monthly reminders for the members of your book club—even if there are only five of them—it might be worth it to set up a postcard printing application. You'll send 60 reminders during the year, and once you've set up the announcement document and the address list, running the cards through the printer twice (two sides) might be beneficial. In summary, apply IT only if it can help, but if it can help, don't hesitate to apply it.

Asking for Help

One goal of our study is to convert you into a self-reliant computer and information user. Does that mean that you should solve all of your problems yourself? Of course not. In fact, it is certain that there are problems that are beyond your knowledge now, and there always will be. We always need experts. So, eventually we need to get assistance from someone more knowledgeable than we are.

But acknowledging that we need help doesn't mean that the moment things go awry we throw up our hands in desperation. Fluency has taught us how to troubleshoot our problems, and our experience has given us some perspective. We should assess whether the problem is probably due to our own stupidity—and eagerly fix it on our own to save the embarrassment of revealing that stupidity to someone else—or something more fundamental that requires greater expertise. Only after we've applied reasonable efforts to solving the problem ourselves will we need to ask for help. But when we do need assistance, we should ask. Of course, one reason to limit our asking professionals for help is that it usually takes longer to solve the problem than we are willing to wait.

As a contributor to lifelong learning, trying to solve our own problems and asking for help when we're truly stuck can contribute to a greater understanding of IT. If we figure it out ourselves, we're at least more experienced at troubleshooting. If someone else helps us, we may learn some facts we didn't know. Either way, we win.

Noticing New Technology

If the technological changes of the last half-century are any guide to the changes to come, IT will be quite different at the end of the next half-century. To learn about and apply the upcoming advances requires attention. Is the "advance" being touted in the press a fundamental leap forward that's potentially beneficial to me, or is it just hype about an old product in a different package? The latter is far more common than the former. We must be attentive and skeptical.

When there is a fundamental advancement—it happens more like once a decade than once a month—we need to be willing to learn about it. The media often covers the "science" of new technologies; following these technologies should be easy now that you've learned the concepts taught in this book. Using the technology might require taking a class, but more likely it won't. After all, thinking about technology abstractly, we know that those eager to deploy a new technology will prepare a "migration path" for those of us who are competent, daily users of the current technology. Innovations will likely be harder to use than the mature technologies with which we are familiar, of course. But if, as Fluent users, we don't have the background and experience to overcome those difficulties—that is, if we can't succeed with a new technology—then it isn't ready.

It often happens that technologies—small advances as well as large ones—are rushed to market before they're ready, so there is considerable risk in being an early adopter. But waiting involves risks too. One of technology's defining characteristics is that it steadily improves. Inventing technology is a difficult creative activity, and engineering it to perfection the first time never happens. So, there are steady improvements—automobiles improved throughout the entire twentieth century. There will always be a next-generation technology that is more convenient, more functional, and more versatile with better price performance, and so on. But waiting for perfection might require a hundred-year wait, and during that time you won't benefit from the technology. The lesson: Adopt a technology as soon as there's a high probability that it will assist you, but expect it to continue to improve.

SHIFTING FOR YOURSELF

Ted Nelson, the inventor of hypertext, tells a story of his first meeting with a software development team for a project he was to direct. He was depressed to find that everyone on the team drove a car with a standard transmission (a car requiring the driver to shift gears manually). Nelson's point in telling the story is that software should be as easy for people to use as automatic transmissions are, and that programmers who enjoy shifting their own gears may not produce such software. Whether his point is correct or not, his story gives us a valuable—if different—perspective.

Fluency enables *us*, the users, to shift gears. It doesn't give us the ability to build a car, to repair it, or to modify it. But, we can control IT to extract its full power, to be in command, and to reach our destination. Nelson may be right regarding builders, but for users, the ability to manipulate the levers of IT is not an ability to deplore.

Whatever the IT equivalent of the automatic transmission is, it is still on the drawing board. It took 60 years for cars to come equipped with automatic transmissions. With IT's 60th birthday still years away, we can't wait. We'll shift for ourselves.

EXERCISES

Multiple Choice

1. Specifying structure is
   A. more important than specifying content
   B. less important than specifying content
   C. just as important as specifying content
   D. the same as specifying content

2. Examples of nonalgorithmic tasks include all of the following except
   A. finding information
   B. using placeholders to reformat text
   C. database design
   D. creating a password

3. The first step in debugging is to
   A. determine what the problem is
   B. reproduce the error
   C. eliminate obvious causes
   D. divide the problem into smaller parts

4. Debugging is
   A. algorithmic
   B. procedural
   C. ordinal
   D. none of the above

5. Problems can be solved by approaching them
   A. through the use of algorithms
   B. by applying more and faster computers to the problem
   C. by using logical reasoning
   D. through trial and error

6. Which of the following is not a component of Fluency knowledge?
   A. Skills
   B. Capabilities
   C. Content
   D. Concepts

7. Put the three Fluency components in order from the least detailed to the most detailed.
   A. Capabilities, Concepts, Skills
   B. Concepts, Capabilities, Skills
   C. Skills, Concepts, Capabilities
   D. Skills, Capabilities, Concepts

8. Thinking Fluently involves the use of
   A. memorization
   B. repetition and practice
   C. abstract thinking
   D. attention to detail

9. You should adopt technology when
   A. the price/performance ratio is in your favor
   B. as soon as you can get your hands on it
   C. only after most of the rest of the public has adopted it
   D. when there is a high probability that it will prove beneficial to you

10. Fundamental advances in IT come along
    A. daily
    B. monthly
    C. yearly
    D. less often than that

Short Answer

1. _____ is involved when there is no deterministic, unfailing method to solve a problem.

2. _____ is a series of steps that, when taken, guarantees the successful completion of a task.

3. Debugging is not algorithmic, but, rather, it is _____.

4. Of the three Fluency components, the ability to use email is considered a _____.

5. Of the three Fluency components, the understanding of networking principles is considered a _____.

6. Of the three Fluency components, the understanding of algorithmic thinking is considered a _____.

7. _____ is the process of asking questions, pursuing ideas and interests, and being curious.

8. A list of files provides _____ for storing them, but it gives no indication of their _____.

9. Examples of _____ include the Smooth Motion program, the insertion sort, and query construction.

10. With Fluency, _____ are to details what _____ are to the "big picture."

Exercises

1. Explain how knowledge of program debugging can be used to solve other problems.

2. Describe the debugging process as a loop. What condition allows you to end the loop?

3. Describe how the development of the GUI is like the shift (pardon the pun) from manual to automatic transmissions.

4. Why are computers very good at structure but very poor on content?

5. Why is the best technology often the most overlooked?

6. Why is structure as important as content?

7. At what point should you be satisfied with your knowledge of IT?

8. How are skills tied to details while capabilities are tied to the "big picture?"

TIM BERNERS-LEE is the Director of the World Wide Web Consortium (W3C) and Principal Research Scientist at MIT's Laboratory for Computer Science. In 1989, while working at the European Particle Physics Laboratory CERN, Tim invented an Internet-based hypermedia initiative for global information sharing, commonly known as the World Wide Web. A year later, he wrote the first Web client and server. Tim received his degree in physics from Oxford University in 1976.

You earned your first degree in physics. Why did you later pursue your PhD in Computer Science?

After my physics degree, the telecommunications research companies seemed to be the most interesting places to be. The microprocessor had just come out, and telecommunications was switching very fast from hardwired logic to microprocessor-based systems. It was very exciting.

How did your foundation in physics influence your design of the Web?

When you study physics, you imagine what rules of behavior on the very small scale could possibly give rise to the large-scale world as we see it. When you design a global system like the Web, you try to invent rules of behavior of Web pages and links and things that could create a large-scale world as we would like it. One is analysis and the other synthesis, but they are very similar.

You've often said that the Web is simply "not done yet." What do you envision it to be like when it is done?

As I say in my book, *Weaving the Web*, I have a dream for the Web . . . and it has two parts.

In the first part, the Web becomes a much more powerful means for collaboration between people. I have always imagined the information space as something to which everyone has immediate and intuitive access, and not just to browse, but to create. Furthermore, the dream of people-to-people communication through shared knowledge must be possible for groups of all sizes, interacting electronically with as much ease as they do now in person.

In the second part of the dream, collaborations extend to computers. Machines become capable of analyzing all the data on the Web—the content, links, and transactions between people and computers. A "Semantic Web," which should make this possible, has yet to emerge, but when it does, the day-to-day mechanisms of trade, bureaucracy, and our daily lives will be handled by machines talking to machines, leaving humans to provide inspiration and intuition . . . This machine-understandable Web will come about through the implementation of a series of technical advances and social agreements that are now beginning.

Once the two-part dream is reached, the Web will be a place where the whim of a human being and the reasoning of a machine coexist in an ideal, powerful mixture.

And what does that mixture look like?

There is just one Web, whatever your browser, it's always available, and anyone can access it no matter what hardware device, software vendor, geographical position, disability, language, or culture.

What do you find most challenging about your work?

When two groups disagree strongly about something, but want in the end to achieve a common goal, finding exactly what they each mean and where the misunderstandings are can be very demanding. The chair of any working group knows that. However, this is what it takes to make progress toward consensus on a large scale.

What challenges are you facing in trying to achieve the Semantic Web?

Technically, there are many standards to make in the area of rules of query languages and Web services, and at the same time there is the job of working out how these will all fit together as logical systems.

Commercially, it is difficult to find a short-term business model for anything Web-like, because its value depends on the extent to which others are also using it.

Legally, the threat of patents hangs over any standards area until everyone involved has agreed to make the common infrastructure royalty-free.

These are three of the larger challenges we are facing, but overcoming them is the excitement, creativity, and business wisdom of many people who are working together in different ways.

What do you think students should be aware of as Web technology advances?

Be aware that what you can make with communications and computing technology is limited only by your imagination. Be aware also that while technology gives us more choices as to what we do, it does not change the essential nature, limitations, and strengths of a human being.

appendix

A

HTML REFERENCE

The following brief descriptions form an alphabetical list of the HTML tags used in this book. Check Chapter 4 for further explanation or consult `www.w3.org/hypertext/WWW/MarkUp/MarkUp.html`

HTML Document Structure

Every HTML source file must contain the following tags in the given order:

```
<html>
    <head>
        All header content goes here
    </head>
    <body>
        All body content goes here
    </body>
</html>
```

HTML Tags

Anchor (`<a> </a>`): Defines a hyperlink using the `href="`*fn*`"` attribute, where *fn* is a file name. The text between the two tags is known as the link and is highlighted.

```
<a href="nextPage.html">Click here for next page</a>
```

fit **CAUTION**

Text Only! Remember, HTML source files must contain standard keyboard text (ASCII) only. Word processors include fancy formatting that confuses browsers. Use simple text editors only, such as Simple Text, BBEdit, or Notepad. Also, the file name extension—the characters after the last dot in the file name—must be `html`.

Body (`<body> </body>`): Specifies the extent of the body of the HTML document (see the "HTML Document Structure" section for an example). Useful attributes include:

> `background="`*fn*`"` fills the page background with the image (possibly tiled) from the file *fn*

> `bgcolor="`*color*`"` paints the background the specified *color*

> `text="`*color*`"` displays text the specified *color*

> `link="`*color*`"` displays links the specified *color*

Bold (`<b> </b>`): Specifies that the style of the enclosed text is to be a bold font.

`<b>This text prints as bold</b>`

Caption (`<caption> </caption>`): Specifies a table caption, and must be enclosed by table tags (see "Table" for an example).

Comment (`<!--`*comment goes here*`-->`): The comment text is enclosed within angle brackets; avoid using angle brackets in the comments, which can confuse browsers.

`<!-- This text will not be displayed -->`

Definitional List (`<dl> </dl>`): Defines a definitional list, which is composed of two-part entries, called the definitional-list term (`<dt> </dt>`) and the definitional-list definition (`<dd> </dd>`). Terms are on separate lines and the definitions are on the following lines. A useful attribute is `compact`, which displays terms and definitions on the same line.

```
<dl>
   <dt>First term</dt>
   <dd>First definition goes here</dd>
   <dt>Second term</dt>
   <dd>Second definition goes here</dd>
</dl>
```

Font (`<font> </font>`): Defines a range of text in which the font style is to be adjusted from the prevailing style. Useful attributes include:

> `color="`*color*`"` displays text the specified *color*

> `face="`*type*`"` displays text the specified *type* face

`<font face="Helvetica"> This text is sans serif</font>`

Header (`<head> </head>`): Defines the extent of the header of the HTML document, which must include a title (see the "HTML Document Structure" section for an example).

Headings (`<h1> </h1>` ... `<h8> </h8>`): Specifies that the enclosed text is to be one of eight heading levels. The smaller the number the larger and more prominent the text.

```
<h1> Heading level 1 </h1>  Most prominent
<h2> Heading level 2 </h2>
...
<h7> Heading level 7 </h7>
<h8> Heading level 8 </h8>  Least prominent
```

Horizontal Rule (`<hr>`): Defines a line that spans the window, though it can be reduced in size using the `width="p%"` attribute. The attribute `size="n"` specifies the (point) thickness of the line.

```
<hr width="75%">
```

HTML (`<html> </html>`): Defines the beginning and end of the document (see the "HTML Document Structure" section for an example).

Image (`<img>`): Causes an image—specified by the `src="fn"` attribute—to be placed in the document at the current position. Positioning information uses the `align` attribute to specify the position on the line—`top`, `middle`, `bottom`—and the position in the window—`left`, `center`, `right`. Also, `height` and `width` attributes specify the displayed image's size in pixels.

```
<img src="prettyPic.html" align='left' height='200' width='140'>
```

Italics (`<i> </i>`): Specifies that the style of the enclosed text is to be italic.

```
<i>This text is emphasized by italics</i>
```

Line Break (`<br>`): Ends the current line and continues the text on the next line.

```
This text is on one line.<br> This text is on the next line.
```

List Item (`<li> </li>`): Specifies an entry in either an ordered or an unordered list (see "Ordered List" and "Unordered List" for examples).

Ordered List (`<ol> </ol>`): Specifies the extent of an ordered list, whose entries are list items. The list items are prefixed with a number.

```
<ol>
   <li>First list item</li>
   <li>Second list item</li>
</ol>
```

Paragraph (`<p> </p>`): Specifies the extent of a paragraph. Paragraphs begin on a new line.

```
<p> This text forms a one-line paragraph</p>
```

Title (`<title> </title>`): Defines the page title; it must be given in the header section of the HTML source.

```
<title> Title displays at the top of the browser window</title>
```

Table (`<table> </table>`): Defines a table of table rows; the rows contain table data. Optionally, the first row of the definition can be formed with table heading tags. A useful attribute is border, giving the table a border.

```
<table border>
   <caption>Description</caption>
   <tr>
      <th>Head Col 1</th>
      <th>Head Col 2</th>
      <th>Head Col 3</th>
   </tr>
   <tr>
      <td>Row 1, Cell 1</td>
      <td>Row 1, Cell 2</td>
      <td>Row 1, Cell 3</td>
   </tr>
   <tr>
      <td>Row 2, Cell 1</td>
      <td>Row 2, Cell 2</td>
      <td>Row 2, Cell 3</td>
   </tr>
   <tr>
      <td>Row 3, Cell 1</td>
      <td>Row 3, Cell 2</td>
      <td>Row 3, Cell 3</td>
   </tr>
</table>
```

Table Data (`<td> </td>`): Specifies a cell in a table, and must be enclosed by table row tags. A useful attribute is `bgcolor="`*color*`"` (see "Table" for an example).

Table Heading (`<th> </th>`): Specifies a cell in the heading row of a table, and must be enclosed by table row tags. A useful attribute is `bgcolor="`*color*`"` (see "Table" for an example).

Table Row (`<tr> </tr>`): Specifies a row in a table, and must be enclosed by table tags. A useful attribute is `bgcolor="`*color*`"` (see "Table" for an example).

Unordered List (`<ul> </ul>`): Specifies the extent of an unordered list, whose entries are list items. The list items are prefixed with a bullet. A list item can enclose another list.

```
<ul>
   <li>First list item</li>
   <li>Second list item</li>
</ul>
```

RGB Colors

Table A.1 shows the hexadecimal coding for commonly used colors that are consistently displayed by all browsers. The numbers, when used in attribute specifications, should have the form "#*dddddd*".

Table A.1. Web-safe colors for Web page design

990033 153:0:51	FF3366 255:51:102	CC0033 204:0:51	FF0033 255:0:51	FF9999 255:153:153	CC3366 204:51:102	FFCCFF 255:204:204	CC6699 204:51:153	993366 153:51:102	660033 102:0:51	CC3399 204:51:153	FF99CC 255:153:204	FF66CC 255:102:204	FF99FF 255:153:255	FF6699 255:102:153	CC0066 204:0:102
FF0066 255:0:102	FF3399 255:51:153	FF0099 255:0:153	FF33CC 255:51:204	FF00CC 255:0:204	FF66FF 255:102:255	FF33FF 255:51:255	FF00FF 255:0:255	CC0099 204:0:153	990066 153:0:102	CC66CC 204:102:204	CC33CC 204:51:204	CC99FF 204:153:255	CC66FF 204:102:255	CC33FF 204:51:255	993399 153:51:153
CC00CC 204:0:204	CC00FF 204:0:255	9900CC 153:0:204	990099 153:0:153	CC99CC 204:153:204	996699 153:102:153	663300 102:51:102	000099 102:0:153	000099 153:51:204	660066 102:0:102	9900FF 153:0:255	9933FF 153:51:255	9966CC 153:102:204	330033 51:0:51	663399 102:51:153	6633CC 102:51:204
6600CC 102:0:204	330066 51:0:102	9966FF 153:102:255	6600FF 102:0:255	6633FF 102:51:255	CCCCFF 204:204:255	9999FF 153:153:255	9999CC 153:153:204	6666CC 102:102:204	6666FF 102:102:255	666699 102:102:153	333366 51:51:102	333399 51:51:153	330099 51:0:153	3300CC 51:0:204	3300FF 51:0:255
3333FF 51:51:255	3333CC 51:51:204	0066FF 0:102:255	0033FF 0:51:255	3366FF 51:102:255	3366CC 51:102:204	000066 0:0:102	000033 0:0:51	0000FF 0:0:255	000099 0:0:153	0033CC 0:51:204	0000CC 0:0:204	336699 51:102:153	0066CC 0:102:204	99CCFF 153:204:255	6699FF 102:153:255
003366 0:51:102	6699CC 102:153:204	006699 0:102:153	3399CC 51:153:204	0099CC 0:153:204	66CCFF 102:204:255	3399FF 51:153:255	003399 0:51:153	0099FF 0:153:255	33CCFF 51:204:255	00CCFF 0:204:255	99FFFF 153:255:255	66FFFF 102:255:255	33FFFF 51:255:255	00FFFF 0:255:255	00CCCC 0:204:204
009999 0:153:153	669999 102:153:153	99CCCC 153:204:204	CCFFFF 204:255:255	33CCCC 51:204:204	66CCCC 102:204:204	339999 51:153:153	336666 51:102:102	006666 0:102:102	003333 0:51:51	00FFCC 0:255:204	33FFCC 51:255:204	33CC99 51:204:153	00CC99 0:204:153	00FFCC 102:255:204	00FFCC 153:255:204
00FF99 0:255:153	339966 51:153:102	006633 0:102:51	669966 102:153:102	66CC66 102:204:102	99FF99 153:255:153	66FF66 102:255:102	99CC99 153:204:153	336633 51:102:51	66FF99 102:255:153	33FF99 51:255:153	33CC66 51:204:102	00CC66 0:204:102	66CC99 102:204:153	009966 0:153:102	339933 51:153:51
009933 0:153:51	33FF66 51:255:102	00FF66 0:255:102	CCFFCC 204:255:204	CCFF99 204:255:153	99FF66 153:255:102	99FF33 153:255:51	00FF33 0:255:51	33FF33 51:255:51	00CC33 0:204:51	33CC33 51:204:51	66FF33 102:255:51	00FF00 0:255:0	66CC33 102:204:51	006600 0:102:0	003300 0:51:0
009900 0:153:0	33FF00 51:255:0	66FF00 102:255:0	99FF00 153:255:0	66CC00 102:204:0	00CC00 0:204:0	33CC00 51:204:0	339900 51:153:0	99CC66 153:204:102	669933 102:153:51	99CC33 153:204:51	336600 51:102:0	669900 102:153:0	99CC00 153:204:0	CCFF00 204:255:102	CCFF33 204:255:51
CCFF00 204:255:0	999900 153:153:0	CCCC00 204:204:0	CCCC33 204:204:51	333300 51:51:0	666600 102:102:0	999933 153:153:51	CCCC66 204:204:102	666633 102:102:51	999966 153:153:102	CCCC99 204:204:153	FFFFCC 255:255:204	FFFF99 255:255:153	FFFF66 255:255:102	FFFF33 255:255:51	FFFF00 255:255:0
FFCC00 255:204:0	FFCC66 255:204:102	FFCC33 255:204:51	CC9933 204:153:51	996600 153:102:0	CC9900 204:153:0	FF9900 255:153:0	CC6600 204:102:0	993300 153:51:0	CC6633 204:102:51	663300 102:51:0	FF9966 255:153:102	FF6633 255:102:51	FF9933 255:153:51	FF6600 255:102:0	CC3300 204:51:0
996633 153:102:51	330000 51:0:0	663333 102:51:51	996666 153:102:102	CC9999 204:153:153	993333 153:51:51	CC6666 204:102:102	FFCCCC 255:204:204	FF3333 255:51:51	CC3333 204:51:51	FF6666 255:102:102	800000 102:0:0	990000 153:0:0	CC0000 204:0:0	FF0000 255:0:0	FF3300 255:51:0
CC9966 204:153:102	FFCC99 255:204:153	CCCCCC 204:204:204	999999 153:153:153	666666 102:102:102	333333 51:51:51	FFFFFF 255:255:255	000000 0:0:0								

B JAVASCRIPT PROGRAMMING RULES

This appendix summarizes in brief statements the "rules" for writing JavaScript and the rules that JavaScript follows when executing programs. The chapter in which each rule was introduced is given in brackets. Notice Tables B.1 and B.2.

Program Structure

White space is ignored [18]. Any number of spaces, tabs, or new line characters can generally separate the components of a program. Avoid breaking up identifiers and literals such as numbers and strings.

Place declarations first [18]. Declarations should appear before other statements. If there are multiple blocks of JavaScript code, place global declarations at the beginning of the first block.

First-to-last execution [18]. Program statements are all executed from first to last, unless specifically commanded to skip using conditional **if** statements or told to repeat using **for** statements.

Terminate statements with semicolons [18]. Every statement, including those on their own line, must be terminated with a semicolon (**;**), except the compound statement (i.e., the curly brace (**}**) is *not* followed by a semicolon).

Slash slash comment [18]. Text from **//** to the end of the line is treated as a comment. For example,

```
x = 3.1; //Set rate
```

Slash star-star slash comment [18]. All text enclosed by the symbols **/*** and ***/** is treated as a comment, and so can span several lines. For example,

```
/* The text in a Slash Star-Star Slash comment can spill across
lines of program, but the Slash Slash comment is limited to the
end of one line. */
```

Data Types

Four rules for numbers [18]. Numerical constants:

1. Keep the digits together without spaces, so `3.141 596` is wrong, whereas `3.141596` is right.

2. Don't use digit grouping symbols of any type, so 1,000,000 is wrong, whereas `1000000` is right.

3. Use a period as the decimal point so `0,221` is wrong, whereas `0.221` is right.

4. Use no units, so `33%` and `$10.89` are wrong, whereas `0.33` and `10.89` are right.

Six rules for strings [18]. When typing string literals:

1. The characters must be surrounded by quotes, either single (') or double (").

2. Most characters are allowed within quotes except new line, backspace, tab, \, form feed, and return.

3. Double-quoted strings can contain single quotes and vice versa.

4. The apostrophe (') is the same as the single quote.

5. Any number of characters is allowed in a string.

6. The minimum number of characters in a string is zero (`""`), which is called the empty string.

String literal escape characters [18]. Table B.1 gives the escape sequences for the special characters of string literals that cannot be typed directly. For example, `"\b\b"` is a string of two backspaces.

Boolean data type [18]. There are two Boolean values: `true` and `false`.

Table B.1. Escape sequences for characters prohibited from string literals

Seq.	Character	Seq.	Character
\b	Backspace	\f	Form feed
\n	New line	\r	Carriage return
\t	Tab	\'	Apostrophe or single quote
\"	Double quote	\\	Backslash

Variables and Declarations

Identifier structure [18]. Identifiers must begin with a letter and may contain any combination of letters, numerals, or underscores ( ). Identifiers cannot contain white space. For example, `green`, `eGGs`, `ham_and_2_eggs` are three identifiers.

Case sensitivity [18]. JavaScript identifiers are case sensitive, so `y` and `Y` are different.

Reserved words [18]. Some words, such as `var` and `true`, are reserved by JavaScript and cannot be identifiers. Table B.2 lists these words. To use a word in the list as an identifier, prefix it with an underscore (for example, `_true`), but it's safer (and smarter) to think up a different identifier.

Declare variables [18]. All variables must be declared using `var`. Do not declare any variable more than once.

Variable declaration list separated by commas [18]. For example,

```
var prices, hemlines, interestRates;
```

Variable declaration initializers can be expressions [18]. For example,

```
var minutesInDay = 60 * 24;
```

Expressions

Operators [18]. A selection of JavaScript operators is given in Table B.3.

Use parentheses [18]. Though JavaScript uses precedence to determine the order in which to perform operators when no parentheses are given, that feature is for professionals. To be safe, parenthesize all complex expressions.

Operator overloading [18]. Plus (+) means addition for numerical operands; it means concatenation for string operands. If + has an operand of each type (e.g., `4 + "5"`), the number converts to a string and returns a string (e.g., `"45"`).

Arrays and Indexes

Array declarations [21]. Arrays are declared using the `var` statement and the `new Array (<`*elements*`>)` designation, where `<`*elements*`>` is the number of array elements. For example,

```
var zodiacSigns = new Array (12);
```

Arrays are 0-origin, meaning the least index value is 0, and the largest index is `<`*elements*`> - 1`.

Array references [21]. Array elements can be referenced by the syntax

`<`*array_name*`>[<`*index*`>]`

where `<`*array_name*`>` is a declared array and `<`*index*`>` is any integer value from 0 to `<`*elements*`> - 1`. An array reference, e.g., `A[i]`, is a variable and can be used wherever variables can be used.

Index values [21]. An index value can be any expression, including a constant (e.g., `3`), a variable (e.g., `i`), or an expression involving operators (e.g., `(i+12)%5`) that evaluates to an integer in the range from 0 to the highest index of the array, `<`*elements*`> - 1`.

Table B.2. *Reserved words and property terms in JavaScript. These words cannot or should not be used as identifiers.*

abstract	eval	moveBy	scrollbars
alert	export	moveTo	scrollBy
arguments	extends	name	scrollTo
Array	false	NaN	self
blur	final	native	setInterval
boolean	finally	netscape	setTimeout
Boolean	find	new	short
break	float	null	static
byte	for	number	status
callee	focus	Object	statusbar
caller	frames	open	stop
captureEvents	function	opener	String
case	Function	outerHeight	super
catch	goto	outerWidth	switch
char	history	package	synchronized
class	home	Packages	this
clearInterval	if	pageXOffset	throw
clearTimeout	implements	pageYOffset	throws
close	import	parent	toolbar
closed	in	parseFloat	top
confirm	infinity	parseInt	toString
const	innerHeight	personalbar	transient
constructor	innerWidth	print	true
continue	instanceof	private	try
Date	int	prompt	typeof
debugger	interface	protected	unescape
default	isFinite	prototype	unwatch
defaultStatus	isNaN	public	valueOf
delete	java	RegExp	var
do	length	releaseEvents	void
document	location	resizeBy	watch
double	locationbar	resizeTo	while
else	long	return	window
enum	Math	routeEvent	with
escape	menubar	scroll	

Statements

Assignment statement [18]. The assignment statement (e.g., `lap = lap + 1`) updates the value of a variable on the left side of the = (e.g., `lap`) by computing the value of the expression on the right side of = (e.g., `lap + 1`) and making it the new value of the variable. The value flow is from the right side to the left side.

Compound statements [18]. A sequence of statements enclosed by `{ }` is a compound statement and is treated as one statement, say, for purposes of the *<statement>* in `if`, `if/else`, iteration statements, and function declarations. The compound statement is not terminated by a semicolon, though statements it contains must be.

if statement [18]. The `if` statement, or conditional statement, has the form

```
if (<Boolean expression>)
    <then-statement>;
```

If the value of the Boolean expression is `true`, the *<then-statement>* is performed; if the Boolean expression is `false`, the *<then-statement>* is skipped.

if/else statement [18]. The `if/else` statement, or conditional statement, has the form

```
if ( <Boolean expression> )
    <then-statement>;
else
    <else-statement>;
```

If the result of the Boolean expression is `true`, the *<then-statement>* is performed and the *<else-statement>* is skipped. If the Boolean expression is `false`, the *<then-statement>* is skipped and the *<else-statement>* is performed.

Conditional within a conditional [18]. If a conditional's *<then-statement>* or *<else-statement>* contains another conditional, make it a compound statement (enclose it in `{ }`) to avoid ambiguity as to which `if` statement the `else` associates with.

for loops [21]. The `for` statement has the syntax

```
for ( <initialization>; <continuation>; <next iteration> ) {
    <statement list>
}
```

The *<initialization>* is an assignment to the iteration variable, the *<continuation>* is a Boolean expression like those used in `if` statements, and the *<next iteration>* is an assignment to the iteration variable.

for loop operation [21]. A `for` loop works as follows: The initialization assignment is performed first, followed by the continuation test. If the test result is `false`, the *<statement list>* is skipped and the `for` loop ends. If the test result is `true`, the *<statement list>* is performed followed by the next iteration assignment. That completes one iteration. At the completion of an iteration, the process repeats with the continuation test.

World-Famous Iteration [21]. The World-Famous Iteration (WFI) is a `for` statement that has the following standard form:

```
for ( <iteration var> = 0; <iteration var> < <limit> ; <iteration var>++ ) {
    <statement list>
}
```

The *<iteration var>* is any declared variable, and the *<limit>* is any expression or variable. An example is

```
for ( j = 0; j < n ; j++ ) {
    <statement list>
}
```

The number of iterations—the number of times the loop loops—is **n**.

Functions

Function declaration [20]. Functions are declared using the following syntax:

```
function <name> ( <parameter list> ) {
    <statement list>
}
```

Notice the conspicuous position of the closed brace on its own line, below the *f* in function. The brace is not followed by a semicolon. An example is

```
function prefixTitle ( familyName, mORf ) {
    if (mORf = "M")
        return "Mr. " + familyName;
    else
        return "Ms " + familyName;
}
```

Function names are identifiers [20]. Function names, e.g., `prefixTitle`, follow the rules for identifiers. It is best if the chosen name says what the function does.

Parameters are identifiers [20]. Function parameters, e.g., `familyName`, follow the rules for identifiers.

Parameters are not declared [20]. Function parameters should not be declared because the JavaScript interpreter automatically declares them.

Return statement [20]. A function completes when it reaches a `return` statement:

```
return <expression>
```

The result of the function is the result of *<expression>*, which could simply be a variable.

Guidelines

Programmer's rules: Professional programmers have a set of good programming practices, including:

> Choose meaningful identifiers for variables. For example, `interestRate` is better than, say, `p`.

> Insert white space liberally to improve code readability. For example,

```
if(input!="")name=first+last;
```

is poor, while

```
if ( input != "" )
    name = first + last;
```

is preferred.

> Comment programs liberally, saying what the variables mean and what the logic is doing.

> Align code—especially when the statements are logically related—and be consistent; it helps to locate errors.

Wrong:

```
    able="a;
baker = 'b';
        charlie = "c";
```

Right:

```
able    = "a";
baker   = "b";
charlie = "c";
```

Table B.3. *JavaScript operators used in this book*

Name	Symbol	# of Operands and Data Type	Example	Comment	Result of Example
Addition	+	2 Numeric	`4 + 5`		`9`
Concatenation	+	2 String	`"four"+"five"` `6 + "pack"`	1 numeric operand implies concatenate	`"fourfive"` `"6 pack"`
Subtraction	–	2 Numeric	`9 - 5`		`4`
Multiplication	*	2 Numeric	`-2 * 4`		`-8`
Division	/	2 Numeric	`10/3`		`0.33333...`
Modulus	%	2 Numeric	`10%3`	Remainder	`1`
Increment	++	1 Numeric	`3++`	See Chapter 20	`4`
Decrement	--	1 Numeric	`3--`	See Chapter 20	`2`
Less Than	<	2 Numeric	`4 < 4`		`false`
Less Than or Equal	<=	2 Numeric	`4 <= 4`		`true`
Equal	==	2 Numeric 2 String	`4 == 4` `"a" == "A"`		`true` `false`
Not Equal	!=	2 Numeric 2 String	`4 != 4` `"a" != " a"`		`false` `true`
Greater Than or Equal	>=	2 Numeric	`4 >= 4`		`true`
Greater Than	>	2 Numeric	`4 > 4`		`false`
Negation	–	1 Numeric	`- 4`		`-4`
Logical **Not**	!	1 Boolean	`! true`		`false`
Logical **And**	&&	2 Boolean	`true && true`		`true`
Logical **Or**	||	2 Boolean	`false || true`		`true`

Note: The examples use literal data (actual numbers) to show the operation; in practice the operands are variables.

C

BEAN COUNTER PROGRAM

The final HTML and JavaScript code for the Bean Counter application in Chapter 19 is as follows. Note that variations in Web browsers will affect how closely it matches the sample output in the figure.

```html
<html>
  <head>
    <title>The Bean Counter</title>
  </head>
  <body bgcolor="#884000" text="#FF9900" align="center">
    <font face="Helvetica", "Arial">
    <h1 align="center">
    <font color="#FFFFFF">the bean counter</font></h1>
    <hr width=50%>
    <p align="center"><b>figuring the price of espresso drinks<br>
    so baristas can have time to chat</b></p>
    <form name = "Bean">
    <center>
```

```
<table border=2>
<tr><td>
<table bgcolor="#993300">
<tr>
  <td>
    <input type=button value="1" onClick ='shots=1'>
  </td>
  <td>
    <input type=button value="S" onClick ='ounce=8'>
  </td>
  <td align="center">
    <input type=button value="ESPRESSO" onClick ='drink="espresso"'>
  </td>
  <td align="center">
    <input type=button value="Clear" onClick =
       'shots = 1;
       drink = "none";
       ounce = 0;
       document.Bean.price.value = "0.00"
       '>
  </td>
</tr>
<tr>
  <td>
    <input type=button value="2" onClick ='shots=2'>
  </td>
  <td>
    <input type=button value="T" onClick ='ounce=12'>
  </td>
  <td align="center">
    <input type=button value="LATTE" onClick ='drink="latte"'>
  </td>
  <td>

  </td>
</tr>
<tr>
  <td>
    <input type=button value="3" onClick ='shots=3'>
  </td>
  <td>
    <input type=button value="G" onClick ='ounce=16'>
  </td>
  <td align="center">
    <input type=button value="CAPPUCCINO" onClick
        ='drink="cappuccino"'>
  </td>
  <td align="center">
    <input type=button value="Total" onClick ='var price;
      var taxRate = 0.088;
      if (drink == "espresso")
          price = 1.40;
```

```
                    if (drink == "latte" || drink == "cappuccino") {
                        if (ounce == 8)
                            price = 1.95;
                        if (ounce == 12)
                            price = 2.35;
                        if (ounce == 16)
                            price = 2.75;
                    }
                    if (drink == "Americano")
                        price = 1.20 + .30 * (ounce/8);
                    price = price + (shots - 1) * .50;
                    price = price + price * taxRate;
                    document.Bean.price.value = Math.round(price*100)/100;
                    '>
            </td>
        </tr>
        <tr>
          <td>
            <input type=button value="4" onClick ='shots=4'>
          </td>
          <td>

          </td>
          <td align="center">
            <input type=button value="AMERICANO" onClick ='drink="Americano"'>
          </td>
          <td bgcolor="red" align="center">
            <input type=text name="price" value="0.00" size=5>
          </td>
        </tr>
        </table>
        </td></tr>
        </table>
        </center>
        </form>
    </body>
</html>
```

D

MEMORY BANK CODE

The following HTML and JavaScript code produces the Memory Bank page in
Chapter 20 (Figure 20.13).

Main *Memory Bank* Page

```
<html>
  <head><title>Memory Bank of Computations</title></head>
  <body bgcolor="#000000" text="#FF9900" ><font face="Arial">
    <h1 align="center"><font color="#FFFFFF">Memory Bank</font></h1>
    <hr width=50%> <b><p align="center"> <font color="#FF0000">
        a convenient table of all the computations I can never remember
        </font></p>
          <script language="JavaScript">
            var scale='E', numHeads=0, numTails=0, topEnd=10;
            document.write('<center>' + (Date().toString()) + '</center>');
            function bmiM ( weightKg, heightCm ) {    //Metric BMI
                var heightM = heightCm / 100; //Change to meters
                return weightKg / (heightM * heightM);
            }
            function bmiE ( weightLbs, heightIn ) {   //English BMI
                var heightFt = heightIn / 12; //Change to feet
                return 4.89 * weightLbs / (heightFt * heightFt);
            }
            function BMI ( units, weight, height ) {
                if (units == 'E')
                    return bmiE( weight, height);//Answer in
                else
                    return bmiM( weight, height);//Answer in
            }
            function randNum (range) {
                return Math.floor(range*Math.random());
            }
            function coinFlip () {
                if (randNum(2)==0) {
                    document.mem.oc.value="Heads";
                    numHeads=numHeads+1;
                    document.mem.nH.value=numHeads;
                }
                else {
                    document.mem.oc.value="Tails";
                    numTails=numTails+1;
                    document.mem.nT.value=numTails;
                }
            }
          </script>
          <form name="mem">
            <table align="center" border=2>
            <tr>
              <td><b>Body Mass Index </b>
                  <input type=radio name="unit" checked=true
                      onClick='scale="E"'> English
                  <input type=radio name="unit"
                      onClick='scale="M"'> Metric </td>
```

```
    <td>Height: <input type=text name="hgt" size=4
        onChange ='if (document.mem.wgt.value!=0)
                    document.mem.ans.value=
                            BMI(scale,
                                document.mem.wgt.value,
                                document.mem.hgt.value)'>
        Weight: <input type=text name="wgt" size=4
            onChange = 'if (document.mem.hgt.value!=0)
                        document.mem.ans.value=
                                BMI(scale,
                                    document.mem.wgt.value,
                                    document.mem.hgt.value)'>
        BMI: <input type=text name="ans" size=4></td></tr>
<tr>
   <td><b> Electronic Coin Flip </b></td>
   <td><input type=button value="Flip" onClick='coinFlip()'>
       Outcome: <input type=text name="oc" size=4>
       Heads:   <input type=text name="nH" size=3 value=0>
       Tails:   <input type=text name="nT" size=3 value=0>
   </td></tr>
<tr>
   <td><b> I'm thinking of a number from 1 to </b>
       <input type=text name='limit' size=2 value=10
          onChange='if (document.mem.limit.value>0)
             topEnd=document.mem.limit.value;
          else
             document.mem.limit.value="?"'></td>
   <td><input type=button value="Pick"
       onClick='document.mem.res.value=randNum(topEnd)+1'>
       a number from the range:
       <input type=text name="res" size=4>
   </td></tr>
<tr>
   <td><b>Convert between Fahrenheit and Celsius</b></td>
   <td align='center'><input type=button value="Convert"
          onClick="window.open('temperature.html', 'jack',
             'resizable=yes')"></td></tr>
<tr>
   <td><b> Count and Score </b></td>
   <td align='center'><input type=button value="Count"
          onClick="window.open('counter.html', 'jill',
             'resizable=yes')"></td></tr>
<tr><!-- The standard form for the links is...
      <br><b>topic name ...</b>
         <img src='bullet.gif'>
            <a href='http:// url goes here'>
            anchor term(s) here</a>

      So, just copy/paste/edit it.-->
```

```
<td colspan = 2> <center>IMPORTANT LINKS</center>
    <br>Resource Links ...
        <img src='bullet.gif'>
            <a href='http://dictionary.cambridge.org'>
            Cambridge Dictionary</a>
        <img src='bullet.gif'>
            <a href='http://www.wordsmyth.net'>
            Thesaurus</a>
    <br>Classes...
        <img src='bullet.gif'>
            <a href='http://www.cs.washington.edu/100'>
            Fluency Class</a>
        <img src='bullet.gif'>
            <a  href='http://www.chemsoc.org/viselements/pages/pertable_j.htm'>
            Periodic Table</a>
        <img src='bullet.gif'>
            <a href='http://www.cia.gov/cia/publications/factbook/'>
            Countries for Geography</a>
        </td></tr>
    </table>
    </form>
    <script>
        var today = new Date();       // Get today's date
        var myBdate = new Date();     // Get a date object to modify
        var difference;               // Declare a temporary variable

        myBdate.setFullYear(1984);    // Set my birth year to 1984
        myBdate.setMonth(6);     //Set my birth mo to Jul (mo.s start at 0)
        myBdate.setDate(4);           // Set my birth day to 4th
        myBdate.setHours(12);         // Set my hour of birth to noon
        myBdate.setMinutes(0);        // Set my minute of birth to o'clock
        myBdate.setSeconds(0);        // Set my second of birth on the hour
        difference = today.getTime() - myBdate.getTime();
        difference = Math.floor(difference/1000);
        document.write("<br><center><font color=yellow> I'm "
            + difference + " seconds old. What <i>am</i> I "
            + "doing with my life?</font></center>");
    </script>
  </body>
</html>
```

How Cool Page of `temperature.html`

```html
<html>
    <head><title>Conversion</title></head>
    <body bgcolor="#33cccc"><font face="Helvetica"><center>
        <h1>How Cool Is It? </h1>
        <script language="JavaScript">
            function convertC2F (tempInC) {
                return 9/5*tempInC + 32;
            }
            function convertF2C (tempInF) {
                return 5/9*(tempInF - 32);
            }
        </script>
        <form name="therm">
            <h2> Celsius temperature:
                <input type=text name="textTempC" size=4
                    onChange="document.therm.textTempF.value
                    =convertC2F(document.therm.textTempC.value)"> C</h2>
            <h2> Fahrenheit temperature:
                <input type=text name="textTempF" size=4
                    onChange="document.therm.textTempC.value
                    =convertF2C(document.therm.textTempF.value)"> F</h2>
        </form></center>
    </body>
</html>
```

Every Little Bit Page of `counter.html`

```html
<html><head><title>Counter Assistant</title></head>
    <body bgcolor="#cc88ff" text="white"><font face="Helvetica">
        <center>
        <h2>Every Little Bit Counts!</h2>
        <script language="JavaScript">
            var count1=0, count2=0, count3=0, count4=0;
            function row(num) {
                document.write('<tr><td><input type=button value=Count' );
                document.write(' onClick="count'+num+'=count'+num+'+1;' );
                document.write(' document.win.arch'+num+'.value=count'
                    +num+'"></td>' );
                document.write(' <td><input type=text size=5 name=arch'
                    +num+'></td>' );
                document.write(' <td><input type=text size=20 name=what'
                    +num+'></td>' );
                document.write(' <td><input type=button value="C" ' );
                document.write(' onClick="document.win.arch'+num+'.value='
                    +"' ';" );
                document.write("   document.win.what"+num+".value=' ';" );
                document.write(' count'+num+'=0"></td></tr>' );
            }
        </script>
```

```
    <form name="win">
        <table>
            <tr><th>Save</th><th> Count </th><th> Meaning </th><th>Clear</th>
            <script>
                row(1); row(2); row(3); row(4);
            </script>
        </table>
    </form></center>
  </body>
</html>
```

E

SMOOTH MOTION PROGRAM

The following HTML and JavaScript code produces the Smooth Motion program in Chapter 22 (Figure 22.1).

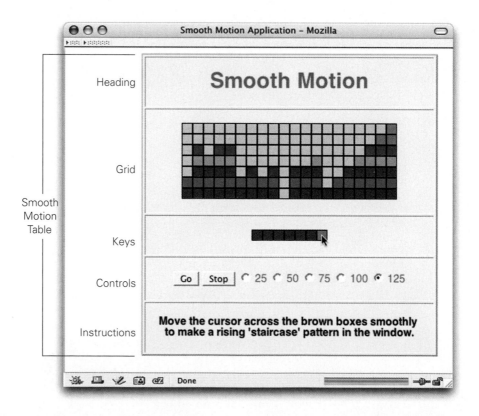

```html
<html>
    <head><title>Smooth Motion Application</title></head>
    <body bgcolor="white" text="#FF6600"> <font face='Helvetica'>
    <center>
    <table border=2 cellspacing="3" cellpadding="20%" bgcolor="#FFFF99">
        <tr> <td align="center">
            <h1>Smooth Motion</h1>
        </td></tr>
        <tr> <td align="center">
            <script>
                var j;      //Declare iter var
                var duration = 125, timerId;          // & other vars
                var pics = new Array(8);              // & prefetch array
                var keypix = new Array(2);
                var next1 = 0, frame = -1;
                for (j = 0; j < 8; j++) {             //Initial img array
                    pics[j] = new Image();
                }
                for (j = 0; j < 8; j++) {             //Prefetch images
                    pics[j].src = "gifpix/Stack" + j + ".gif";
                }
                for (j = 0; j < 20; j++) {        //Place grid imgs
                    document.write('<img src="gifpix/Stack0.gif">');
                }
            </script>
        </td></tr>
        <tr> <td align="center">
            <script>
                keypix[0] = new Image();
                keypix[1] = new Image();
                keypix[0].src = "gifpix/BrownBox.gif";
                keypix[1].src = "gifpix/OrangeBox.gif";
                for (j = 0; j < 7; j++) {
                    document.write('<img src="gifpix/BrownBox.gif" ' +
                    'onMouseOver = "here(' + j + ')" ' +
                    'onMouseOut = "gone(' + j + ')">');
                }
            </script>
        </td></tr>
        <tr> <td align="center">
            <form>
                <input type=button value=Go
                    onClick='timerId=setTimeout("animate()",duration)'>
                <input type=button value=Stop
                    onClick="clearTimeout(timerId)">
                <input type=radio name=speed onClick="duration=25"> 25
                <input type=radio name=speed onClick="duration=50"> 50
                <input type=radio name=speed onClick="duration=75"> 75
                <input type=radio name=speed onClick="duration=100"> 100
                <input type=radio name=speed
                    onClick="duration=125" checked=true> 125
            </form>
```

```
        </td></tr>
        <tr> <td align="center">
            <p><font color='black'><b>
            Move the cursor across the brown boxes smoothly <br>
            to make a rising 'staircase' pattern in the
            window.</b></font></p>
        </td></tr>
    </table></center>
        <script language='JavaScript'>
            timerId = setTimeout("animate()", 5000);            //Initial timer
            function animate() {
                shiftGrid ()
                checkStairAndContinue ();
            }
            function shiftGrid() {
                for (j = 0; j < 19; j++) {
                    document.images[j].src = document.images[j+1].src;
                }
                if (frame == -1)
                    document.images[19].src = pics[randNum(8)].src;
                else
                    document.images[19].src = pics[frame].src;
            }
            function checkStairAndContinue() {
                if (frame == next1)
                    next1 = next1 + 1;
                else
                    next1 = 1;
                if (next1 != 8)
                    timerId = setTimeout("animate()",duration);
            }
            function here (pos) {
                document.images[20+pos].src = "gifpix/OrangeBox.gif";
                frame = pos + 1;
            }
            function gone (pos) {
                document.images[20+pos].src = "gifpix/BrownBox.gif";
                frame = 0;
            }
            function randNum (range) {                      //Rand No. fcn from
                return Math.floor(range * Math.random());   // Chapter 20
            }
        </script>
    </body>
</html>
```

GLOSSARY

1-way cipher, *see* one-way cipher

A

absolute pathname, navigation information for locating files in HTML using complete URLs

absolute reference, an address or pointer that does not change; in a spreadsheet, a cell with an absolute reference does not change even if copied

abstract, to remove an idea, concept, or process from a specific situation

abstraction, the central idea or concept removed from a situation

ADC, *see* analog-to-digital converter

administrative authority, having the ability to access all functions of a computer or software system, including overriding passwords; also called *superuser*

administrator, one who has complete access to a computer system; also called *superuser*

algorithm, a precise and systematic method for producing a specified result

algorithmic thinking, devising algorithms that achieve specific goals and solve problems effectively

alphanumeric, describing characters or text as being composed solely of letters, numbers, and possibly a few special characters like spaces and tabs, but not punctuation

ALU, *see* arithmetic/logic unit

analog signal, a continuously varying representation of a phenomenon, e.g., a sound wave

analog-to-digital converter (ADC), in digitizing sound, takes the continuous sound wave and samples it at regular intervals, outputting binary numbers that are written to memory for each sample

anchor, the HTML tag that specifies a link, or the text associated with the reference that is highlighted in the document

append, to add to the end of an existing structure

applet, a small application program, often written in Java, which is executed on a client

argument, an input value provided for a parameter in a function call

arithmetic/logic unit (ALU), a subsystem of a computer that performs the operations of an instruction

arithmetic operators, the symbols of basic arithmetic

array element, an indexed item; also called an *element*

ASCII (American Standard Code for Information Interchange), a standard for assigning numerical values to the letters in the Roman alphabet and to typographical characters, pronounced AS·key

assembly language, a symbolic form of a binary machine language

assignment statement, a programming command expressed with a variable on the left and a variable or expression on the right of an assignment symbol, usually =

asynchronous communication, indicates that the actions of senders and receivers occur at separate times, as in the exchange of email

attribute, in HTML, a parameter used within the tags to specify additional information; in a database, a property of an entity; also called a *field*

automated reply, a function of mail servers that allows a user to set up a message saying that he or she is temporarily away and unable to reply to emails; also called a *vacation message*

B

b, abbreviation for bit, e.g., Kb is kilobits

B, abbreviation for byte, e.g., KB is kilobytes

backdoor access, a program that enters a computer and configures it so that it can be controlled remotely without the user's awareness

bandwidth, the bit-transmission capacity of a channel, usually measured in bits per second

base, the number that is raised to various powers to generate the counting units of a number system; e.g., the base of the decimal system is 10 and the base of the binary system is 2; also called *radix*

binary, having two related components

binary number, a quantity expressed in radix 2 number representation

binary operator, an operator such as addition (+) having two operands

binary system, any information encoding using symbols formed from two patterns; also called *PandA representation* in this book

bit, basic unit of information representation having two states, usually denoted 0 and 1

bit-mapped, as in bit-mapped display, indicates that the display's video image is stored pixel-by-pixel in the computer's memory

blazing away, assertively trying unfamiliar software by exploring its features

Boolean, having the property of being either true or false

boot, to start a computer and load its operating system

broadcast, a type of transmission of information from one sender to all receivers

browsing information, on a Web page, used for casual perusing; contrast with navigational information

bug, an error in a computer, program, or process

byte, a sequence of eight bits treated as a unit

C

cable, a bundle of wires carrying power and/or signals between computer components; also called *cord* or *wires*

card, a small printed circuit board plugged into a motherboard to provide additional functionality; also called a *daughter board*

cathode ray tube (CRT), a video display technology

cell, in a spreadsheet, the intersection of a row and a column

cell range, in a spreadsheet, a naming scheme that allows the user to refer to a group of cells by naming the first cell and the last cell and placing a colon (:) in between

CGI, *see* Common Gateway Interface

channel, the physical medium, e.g., wires, overwhich signals are sent; in silicon technology, the area under the gate of a transistor

character, an uppercase or lowercase Latin letter, Arabic numeral, or English punctuation; can be used generally to include the alphabet and punctuation for other natural languages

cipher text, in a cryptosystem, an encrypted form of the cleartext

classifier, a component of an optical character recognition system that ranks characters by the probability that they match a given set of features

cleartext, information before encryption or after decryption

click event, the result caused by a user clicking a command button

clicking around, exploring a user interface

click-with-shift, a GUI command in which the shift key is pressed while the mouse selects an item to avoid deselecting the items already selected; also called *shift-select*

client, a computer that receives the services in a client/server structure

client/server structure, a relationship between two computers in which the client computer requests services from the server computer

clock, in computing, determines the rate of the Fetch/Execute Cycle

CMOS (Complementary Metal Oxide Semiconductor), the most widely used integrated circuit technology, pronounced SEE·moss

collating sequence, an ordering for a set of symbols used to sort them; for example, alphabetical ordering

command button, a synthesized image of a GUI that appears to be a physical button used to cause an operation to be performed; the HTML button input control

Common Gateway Interface (CGI), an extension to HTML allowing browsers to cause a Web server to run programs on their behalf with specific data

compile, to translate a programming language into a language a computer can interpret (machine language)

compliance/enforcement, how organizations meet their obligations regarding privacy issues

compound statement, in programming, a group of statements surrounded by curly braces to become a single statement

compression, encoding information with fewer bits than a given representation by exploiting properties of regularity or unimportance

compression ratio, the factor by which compression reduces an encoding from its uncompressed size

computable, a task that can be performed by a computer; algorithmic

computer, a device that deterministically follows instructions to process information

concatenation, in programming, to join strings

conditional, a programming statement, usually identified by if, that optionally executes statements depending on the outcome of a Boolean test

continuation test, a Boolean expression to determine whether an iteration statement will execute its statement sequence again; also called a *termination test*

control, a subsystem of a computer that is the hardware implementation of the Fetch/Execute Cycle

cookie, information stored on a Web client computer by an HTTP server computer

copyright, the legal protection of many forms of intellectual property

cracker, a person who attempts to break a code

crawler, a program that navigates the Internet, cataloging and indexing Web pages by the words they contain for use by a query processor

CRT, *see* cathode ray tube

cryptography, the study of encryption and decryption methods

cycle power, to turn a computer off, wait a moment, and then turn it back on

D

DAC, *see* digital-to-analog converter

daemon, a program that periodically "wakes up" to perform a system management task

data controller, in Fair Information Practices, the person who sets policies, responds to individuals regarding information, and is accountable for those policies and actions

Data Fetch (DF), the third step in the Fetch/Execute Cycle; the action of retrieving the instruction's operands from memory

data types, the different kinds of values of a programming language; also called *value types*

database query, an operation that creates a database view

database scheme or **schema**, the declaration of entities and relationships of a database

database view, a restructured version of the data designed for a specific user

daughter board, a small printed circuit board plugged into a motherboard to provide additional functionality; also called a *card*

debugging, the act of discovering why a system does not work properly

declaration, in programming, the command used to declare variables

declaring variables, stating what variables will be used in a program

decrement, an amount by which a variable is decreased; a negative increment

decrypt, to recover the original information from a digitally encrypted representation; also called *digitally decrypt*

definiteness, a property of algorithms requiring that a specific sequence of steps is defined

definitional list, in HTML, a list form usually comprising a sequence of terms and their definitions

device driver, software that enables a computer to communicate with a peripheral device

DF, *see* Data Fetch

digitally decrypt, to recover the original information from a digitally encrypted representation; also called *decrypt*

digitally encrypt, to transform a digital representation so that the information cannot be readily discerned; also called *encrypt*

digital signal, a discrete or step levels representation of a phenomenon, varying instantaneously

digital subscriber line (DSL), a dedicated connection to an Internet service provider

digital-to-analog converter (DAC), in playing sound, creates an electrical wave by interpolation between the digital values; the signal is input to a speaker, which converts it to a sound wave

digitize, originally to encode with decimal numerals, now to encode in bits

directory, a named collection of files, other directories, or both; also called a *folder*

directory hierarchy, the complete file structure of a computer

discrete, distinct or separable; not able to be changed by continuous variation

disk, a magnetic medium (floppy or hard)

display rate, in animation, the frequency with which images are changed

DNS, *see* Domain Name System

domain, in networking, a related set of networked computers, e.g., .edu is the set of education-related computers

Domain Name System (DNS), the collection of Internet-connected computers that translate domain addresses into IP addresses

dot operator, in JavaScript, provides a means of navigation to the proper object

drop-down, menu type in a GUI; when selected, a menu drops down and is displayed; also called a *pull-down menu*

DSL, *see* digital subscriber line

dual booting, loading two operating systems at once

E

eCommerce, electronic commerce; the use of electronic data communication to conduct business

effectiveness, a property of algorithms requiring that all instructions are performed mechanically within the capabilities of the executing agent

element, an indexed item; also called an *array element*

email attachment, a file that is sent with an email message

emoticon, a character sequence that is common in email and that expresses an emotion by its physical form, e.g., the "smiley face" `:)` to express happiness or humor

empty string, a character sequence of zero length

empty table, in a database, a table with name and column headings, but no rows

encrypt, to transform a digital representation so that the information cannot be readily discerned; also called *digitally encrypt*

entity, something that can be identified by a fixed number of its characteristics

entity-relationship diagram (ER diagram), a visual illustration of some or all of a database schema in which relationships are drawn as arrows between boxes that represent entities

ER diagram, *see* entity-relationship diagram

escape symbol, a character, often `&` or `\`, that is a prefix to another character or word used to enlarge a character's encoding, e.g., `&infinity` to encode ∞

evaluation function, in computer games, e.g., in chess, a procedure that assigns a numerical value to each piece, accounts for captures and board position, and computes a score for the move

even parity, a property of binary numbers in which the number of 1-bits is even

event handler, the program that performs the task that responds to an event

event, an indication from the operating system that a mouse click or other action has occurred

event-handling attribute, in JavaScript, tells the browser how to respond to an event; e.g., `onClick`

EX, *see* Instruction Execution

Exchange Sort, a standard algorithm that compares pairs of items chosen in a particular way

execute, to perform the instructions of a program, usually by a computer; to run a program

exploit, in computer security, a program that takes advantage of a vulnerability or security hole in software

expression, in programming, a formula-like description of how to compute a value

Extended ASCII, improved standard character representation with 256 symbols, enough to encode English and Western European languages

Extensible Markup Language (XML), a W3C standard for structured information encoding

F

factor, in arithmetic, any number that divides a given number evenly, i.e., without a remainder

factor of improvement, the amount by which a first measurement must be multiplied to be equivalent to the second measurement when computing scale of change

fail-safe, in software, a program that stops operating to avoid harm

fail-soft, in software, a program that continues to operate but provides possibly degraded functionality

fair use, a concept in copyright law in which copyright limitations are waived for explicitly listed, socially valuable purposes

feature, a component of a character in an optical character recognition system

feedback, in a GUI, an indication that the computer is working or has completed a request

Fetch/Execute Cycle, the basic instruction execution process of a computer

field, in a database, a property of an entity; also called an *attribute*

field effect transistor, in semiconductors, a device used to control conductivity

field inputs, character input, such as telephone numbers, with a specific structure

file structure, the directories and files of a computer

filling, in a spreadsheet, automated copying and pasting; allows the user to replicate the contents of a cell

fill tab, in a spreadsheet, used to drag a selection to extend a series or fill a selection

finiteness, a property of algorithms requiring that they terminate with the intended result or an indication that no solution is possible

flame-a-thon, email battle; also called a *flame war*

floppy disk (drive), a storage device that provides persistent memory using (removable) diskettes

folder, a named collection of files, other directories, or both; also called a *directory*

for statement, a common programming structure for iterating a sequence of instructions over a regular range of index values

foreign data, data from another application that one wants to import into a spreadsheet

foreign key, in a database, a field in a record that points to a key field of another database record in another table

form, in HTML, used to collect user input, e.g., when ordering a product on the Web

formal language, a synthetic notation designed for expressing algorithms and programs

formula, in a spreadsheet, an expression that indicates how data in a specific number of cells should be calculated

frame, in animation, one of many images rapidly redrawn to create the illusion of motion

frame grabber, in OCR, an electronic device that recognizes when to snap an image and send it to a computer for processing

freeware, software available on the Web at no cost

frequency, in sound, the number of waves per second

full backup, a complete copy of a body of information usually performed at a specific point in time

function, a programming structure with a name, optional parameter list, and a definition that encapsulates an algorithm

function body, the definition of a function's computation

function declaration, the specification of a function, including its name, parameters, and body

functional composition, the ability to create software by combining other software

functions, in a spreadsheet, for computing common summary operations such as totals, maximums, averages, etc.

G

game tree, a conceptualization of the possible future configurations of a multiperson game

garbage, in a database, inconsistent data

generalize, to formulate an idea, concept, or process so that it abstracts multiple situations

GIF (Graphics Interchange Format), file extension, e.g., picture.gif, that specifies a graphic image format; pronounced with either a soft or hard g

giga-, prefix for billion; pronounced with a hard g

global variable, a variable declared outside the scope of a function, usually at the start of a program

graphical user interface (GUI), the synthesized visual medium of interaction between a user and a computer; pronounced GOO·ey

GUI, see graphical user interface

H

Halting Problem, determining if a computation halts for a given input; a problem that cannot be solved by a computer

handle, in programming, a binary value returned by a function or server to be used for subsequent references

haptic device, an input/output technology that interfaces with the sense of touch

hard disk, a high-capacity, persistent peripheral storage device; also called a *disk* or *hard drive*

hard drive, see hard disk

hardware, the physical implementation of a computer, usually electronic, which includes the processor, memory, and typically its peripheral devices

hard-wired, in a computer, operations done directly with wires and transistors

heuristic, a guideline used to solve a problem that usually results in a solution; for example, "when looking for a lost item check the last place you had it"

hex digit, one of the sixteen numerals of hexadecimal, 0, 1, 2, 3, 4, 5, 6, 7, 8, 9, A, B, C, D, E, F

hexadecimal, radix 16 number representation

hierarchical index, a structure for organizing information using descriptive terms that partition the information

hierarchy, an organizing structure composed of a sequence of levels that partition all items so that those of one level are partitioned into smaller groups at the next level

high-level programming languages, used in all software programming today; programs are compiled into assembly languages, which are then assembled into binary

hit, in a Web search, a match to a query; for a Web site, a visit

hop, in networking, the transfer of a packet or message to an adjacent router

HTML, see Hypertext Markup Language

HTTP, see Hypertext Transfer Protocol

hyperlink reference, the recipient Web address of a hyperlink

Hypertext Markup Language (HTML), a notation for specifying the form of a Web page to a browser

Hypertext Transfer Protocol (HTTP), the rules governing the interaction between client and server on the Web

Hz (Hertz), cycles, or repetitions per second

I

IC, see integrated circuit

ID, see Instruction Decode

identifier, a legal sequence of letters, numerals, or punctuation marks forming the name of variable, file, directory, etc.

identity theft, the crime of posing as someone else for fraudulent purposes

IE, *see* Instruction Execution

if statement, a programming structure that allows the conditional execution of statements based on the outcome of a Boolean test

IF, *see* Instruction Fetch

image object, a blank instance of an image

inconsistency, in a database, the same information stored differently in rows or tables

increment, in JavaScript, the next iteration computation; it almost always increases the value of the iteration variable

index, in information structures, an organizing mechanism used to find information in a large collection; in programming, the number that together with an identifier, forms an array reference

index origin, the number at which indexing begins; the least index

index value, the result of evaluating an index expression; the number of an array element

indexing, in programming, the mechanism of associating a number and an identifier to locate an element

infix operator, a binary operator, e.g., +, whose syntax requires that it is written between its operands, as in 4 + 3

initialization, in JavaScript, the first operation of a `for` loop

initialize, in JavaScript, setting the initial value of a variable as part of the declaration

input, information put into a communications system for transmission or into a computer system for processing

Input Unit, a subsystem of a computer transferring information from the physical world via an input device to the computer's memory

input/output (I/O), in a computer, transferring data between the memory and a peripheral device

instance, the current values of an entity, table, or database

Instruction Decode (ID), the second step in the Fetch/Execute Cycle; the action of determining which operation is to be performed and computing the addresses of the operands

Instruction Execution (EX), the fourth step in the Fetch/Execute Cycle; the action of performing a machine instruction

Instruction Fetch (IF), the first step in the Fetch/Execute Cycle; the action of retrieving a machine instruction from the memory address given by the program counter

instruction interpretation, the process of executing a program

integer, a whole number; in programming, a data type for a whole number, either positive or negative

integrated circuit (IC), a complex set of electronic components and their interconnections that are etched or imprinted on a computer chip

integration, in silicon technology, the ability to fabricate both active and connective parts of a circuit using a family of compatible materials in a single complexity-independent process

intellectual property, creations of the human mind that have value to others

Internet, the total of all wires, fibers, switches, routers, satellite links, and other hardware used to transport information between named computers

Internet Protocol address (IP address), a unique address given to each computer connected to the Internet composed of four numbers in the range 0–255

Internet service provider (ISP), a utility that connects private and business computers to the Internet

interpolation, filling in intermediate values between two points

interpret, to follow a computer program's instruction

intractable, a description for computations solvable by computer in principle, but not in practice

intranet, local network that supports communication within an organization and connects to the Internet by a gateway

invocation (of a function), to call the function

IP, acronym for Internet Protocol

IP address, *see* Internet Protocol address

IP packet, a fixed quantum of information packaged together with an IP address and other data for sending information over the Internet

ISO, acronym for the International Standards Organization

ISP, *see* Internet service provider

iteration, in programming, looping through a series of statements to repeat them

iteration statement, in programming, a loop that repeatedly executes a statement

iteration variable, any variable controlling an iteration statement, e.g., a `for` statement

J

JavaScript, a programming language

JPEG, acronym for Joint Photographic Experts Group, a committee of the ISO; pronounced JAY·peg

JPG, file extension, e.g., `picture.jpg`, for JPEG encoding

K

key, in a database, field(s) that make the rows of an entity (table) unique; in cryptography, selectable code used to encrypt and subsequently decrypt information

key escrow, in encryption software, registering a secret key with a trusted third party

kilo-, prefix for thousand; if prefixing a quantity counted in binary, e.g., memory, prefix for 1,024

L

LAN, *see* local area network

latency, the time required to deliver or generate information

LCD, *see* liquid crystal display

length (of an array), the number of elements in an array

lexical structure, a specification of the form of character input; e.g., telephone numbers in North America are formed of ten Arabic numerals with a space following the third and a hyphen following the sixth

liquid crystal display (LCD), a video display technology

list-server, a mailing list application

local area network (LAN), a network connecting computers within a small physical space such as a building; acronym usually pronounced

local variable, a variable declared within a function

logical and, in programming, the operator `&&` that represents "and"

logical operator, a connective (*and, or,* or *not*)

logical or, in programming, the operator `||` that represents "or"

lossless compression, the process of reducing the number of bits required to represent information in which the original form can be exactly reconstructed

lossy compression, the process of reducing the number of bits required to represent information in which the original cannot be exactly reconstructed

M

machine language, computer instructions expressed in binary, respecting the form required for a specific machine

many-to-one, in a database, a relation where many rows of one table refer to one row of a second table

mask, in fabrication technology, a material similar to a photographic negative containing the pattern to be transferred to the silicon surface in the process of constructing a chip

MB, *see* megabyte

mega-, prefix for million; if prefixing a quantity counted in binary, e.g., memory, prefix for 1,048,576

megabyte (MB), 1 million bytes

megahertz (MHz), 1 million cycles per second

memory address, a whole number that designates a specific location in a computer's memory

memory, a device capable of storing information, usually in fixed-size, addressable units; a subsystem of a computer used to store programs and their data while they execute

menu, a list of available operations from which a user can select by clicking on one item

metadata, information describing the properties of other information

metarules, in programming, rules that describe how to operate on other rules

MHz, *see* megahertz

microprocessor, component of a computer that computes or performs instructions; also called a *processor*

mnemonic, an aid for remembering something

moderator, a person responsible for deciding what is to be sent to a mailing list

modulus, in JavaScript, divides two integers and returns the remainder

monitor, a computer's video output device or display; also called a *screen*

monolithic, a computer having all its devices bundled together, e.g., an iMAC or a laptop

MOS, a transistor made of metal, oxide, and semiconductors (cross sections, top to bottom)

motherboard, contains the processor chip, memory, and other computer electronics; also called a *printed circuit*

MPEG (Motion Picture Experts Group), a committee of the ISO; pronounced EM·peg

MPG, file extension, e.g., `flick.mpg`, for MPEG encoding

multicast, a type of transmission of information from one sender to many receivers

N

name conflict, the attempt to give a different definition, e.g., variable declaration, to an identifier with an existing meaning

navigation, in searching, following a series of links to locate specific information often in a hierarchy

navigational information, on a Web page, used to find specific data; contrast with browsing information

nested conditionals, in JavaScript, an `if` statement as the `then` or `else` statement of another conditional

nested loop, the condition of a loop (inner loop) appearing in the statement sequence of another loop (outer loop)

netiquette, Internet etiquette

new line, in word processing, represented by ↵ or ¶

NP-complete, a measure of difficulty of problems believed to be intractable for computers

Nyquist Rule, a digitization guideline stating that the sampling frequency should exceed the signal frequency by at least two times

O

OCR, *see* optical character recognition

one-way cipher, a form of encryption that cannot easily be reversed, i.e., decrypted, often used for passwords

operand, the data used in computer instructions; the value(s) that operators operate on

operating system (OS), software that performs tasks for the computer; it controls input and output, keeps track of files and directories, and controls peripheral devices such as disk drives and printers

operationally attuned, applying what one knows about how a device or system works to simplify its use

operator, in programming, a symbol used to perform an operation on some value

operator overloading, a property of some programming languages in which operators like + have different meanings depending on their operand data types, e.g., + used for both addition or concatenation in JavaScript

optical character recognition (OCR), a computer application in which printed text is converted to the ASCII letters that represent it

Opt-in/Opt-out, the choice of approving or objecting to a use of information

OS, *see* operating system

output, the information produced by a program or process from a specific input

Output Unit, a subsystem of a computer that transfers information from the computer's memory to the physical world via an output device

overflow exception, an error condition for operations such as addition, in which a result is too large to be represented in the available number of bits

P

PageRank, in Google, computing the importance of a Web page based on its relevancy, determined by links to that page

PandA, in this book, a mnemonic for "present and absent encoding," the fundamental physical representation of information; also called *binary system*

paragraph symbol (¶), represents a new line in some word processing programs

parallel computation, the use of multiple computers to solve a single problem

parameter, an input to a function

parity, refers to whether a number is even or odd

partial backup, new information copied to another medium that has been added to a system since the last full or partial backup

partitionings, in hierarchies, a classification where leaves appear only once

password, a sequence of characters that one must input to gain access to a file, application, or computer system

pathname, the sequence following the IP address; tells the server which file (page) is requested and where to find it

PC, acronym for program counter, printed circuit (board), and personal computer

peripherals, devices connected to a computer, usually for I/O purposes

PERT (Program Evaluation and Review Technique) chart, a task dependency graph used by systems engineers and managers in project management; acronym pronounced

photolithography, a process of transferring a pattern by means of light shown through a mask or negative

photoresist, a material used in a silicon chip fabrication process that is chemically changed by light, allowing it to be patterned by a mask

physical database, in a database, the tables stored on the disk drive

picture element or **pixel**, the smallest displayable unit of a video monitor

pins, stiff wires in a cable's plug that insert into sockets to make the connection

pixel, contraction for picture element

place value, in decimal numbers, positions representing the next higher power of 10, starting from the right

placeholder technique, a searching algorithm in which strings are temporarily replaced with a special character to protect them from change by other substitution commands

plaintext, synonym for cleartext

point-to-point communication, a type of transmission of information from one sender to one receiver

pop-up menu, a menu that is displayed at the cursor position when the mouse is clicked

power cable, connects a computer system to a power supply

power switch, in a monolithic computer system, turns the system on and off

precedence, the relationship among operators describing which is to be performed first

predicate, the Boolean expression in a conditional statement that is evaluated to produce a true or false outcome

prefetching, in online animation, the process of loading the images prior to beginning an animation

preformatted, in HTML, text that is enclosed between `<pre>` and `</pre>` tags

primary key, the column in a database table that always has a unique value for every row

primary source, a person who provides information based on direct knowledge or experience

prime number, a number that can only be divided evenly by itself and one

printed circuit, a stiff composite board containing the processor chip, memory, and other computer electronics; also called a *motherboard*

privacy, the right to choose freely the circumstances under which and the extent to which people will reveal themselves, their attitudes, and their behaviors

processor, the component of a computer that computes, i.e., performs the instructions; also called a *microprocessor*

processor box, in a component system, houses the computer and most of its parts (hard disk, floppy disk drive, and CD drive

program, an algorithm encoded for a specific situation

program counter, a register in a computer that stores the address of the next instruction to be executed

protocol, a standard procedure for regulating data transmission between computers

public domain, the status of a work in which the copyright owner has explicitly given up rights

public key, a key published by the receiver and used by the sender to encrypt messages

pull-down, menu type in a GUI; when selected, a menu drops down and is displayed; also called a *drop-down menu*

Q

QBE, *see* Query by Example

Query by Example (QBE), a method for defining queries in a database

query, database command defining a table expressed using the five database operators

query processor, the part of a search engine that uses the crawler's index to report Web pages associated with keywords provided by a user

quotient-remainder form of division, a means of expressing the division of a/b as the solution to the equation $a = b \cdot c + d$, where c is the quotient and d is the remainder

R

radix, the number that is raised to various powers to generate the counting units of a number system; e.g., the radix of the decimal system is 10 and the radix of the binary system is 2; also called *base*

RAM, *see* random access memory

random access memory (RAM), a subsystem of a computer used for storing programs and data while they execute; acronym pronounced

random access, referencing an item directly; contrast with sequential access

reachable configurations, in software, the possible configurations that a program can define

read only memory (ROM), permanently set memory; acronym pronounced

reboot, to restart a computer by clearing its memory and reloading its operating system

redirection, on the Web, the substitution of one URL for another

redundancy, used to resolve hardware failures by having computers perform computations of a safety critical system and make decisions based on majority vote; in databases, duplicated information

reference, in HTML, the displayed and highlighted portion of an anchor tag

refresh rate, the frequency with which a video display is redisplayed

relational operator, one of six operators ($< \leq = \neq \geq >$) that compare two values; in JavaScript, one of the six operators (`<  <=  ==  !=  >=  >`)

relationship, a correspondence between two tables of a database

relative pathname, navigation information for locating an HTML file on the local site

relative reference, an address or pointer that changes when the target item is moved or the relationship to it has changed; in a spreadsheet, a cell with a relative reference changes its formula when copied

remainder, the whole number less than the devisor that is left after completing a division

replacement string, in editing, the letter sequence that substitutes for the search string

Result Return (RR), the fifth and final step of the Fetch/Execute Cycle, the action of storing in memory the value produced by executing a machine instruction

RGB, red, green, blue; name for a color encoding method

ROM, *see* read only memory

root server, one of several Internet DNS servers that contain the IP addresses of the top level domain registry organizations that maintain global domains (`.com`, `.net`, `.org`, `.gov`, `.edu`, etc.)

row, a set of values for the fields of a table; also called a *tuple*

RR, *see* Result Return

RSA, a public key encryption method invented by Rivest, Shamir, and Adelman

run, what a computer does to a program when one asks it to perform a task

run-length encoding, a representation in which numbers are used to give the lengths of consecutive sequences of 0's or 1's.

S

safe software, the goal of software programs to be reliable in safety-critical situations, such as life support

sample, to take measurements at regular intervals, as in sound digitization

sampling rate, the number of samples per second

schema, the abstract structure of an entity or entities; the metadata of a database's tables

scope, in programming, the range of statements over which a variable or other defined object is known

screen, a computer's video output device or display; also called a *monitor*

scroll bar, a slider control appearing at the side and/or bottom of a window when the information cannot be fully displayed

SCSI (Small Computer System Interface), acronym pronounced scuzzy

search engine, a software system composed of a crawler and a query processor that helps users locate specific information on the Web or on a specific Web site

search string, the series of characters sought in a text search

search text, in searches, a sequence formed by tokens

seat, to firmly insert a plug into a socket after an initial alignment

secondary source, a person providing information without direct knowledge of or experience with the topic

sequential access, a memory reference pattern in which no item can be referenced without passing (skipping or referencing) the items that precede it; contrast with random access

series, in a spreadsheet, results from the automatic incrementing of data by adding one to days, dates, times, etc.

series fill, in a spreadsheet, allows the user to enter a series of numbers or dates into a range of cells

server, a computer providing the services in a client/server structure

shareware, software available on the Web, paid for on the honor system

shift-select, a GUI command in which the shift key is pressed while the mouse selects an item, to avoid deselecting the items already selected; also called *click-with-shift*

signal, an electrical or light pulse or frequency in a wire, fiber, or wireless transmission; refers to anything that is generated and transmitted (power, data, control systems)

slider control, a synthesized slot in which a bar can be moved to select a position within a continuous range

software, a collective term for programs

software license, generally allows use of the software; the ownership remains with the party who markets the program

source, on the Web, the HTML or other text description of how a Web page should be displayed

specification, in programming, a precise definition of the input; how the system should behave and how the output should be produced

SQL, *see* Structured Query Language

standard functionality, the basic operations that all PC applications should be able to perform

statement, in JavaScript, a program instruction

statement terminator, in JavaScript, the semi colon (`;`) used to end each statement

string constants, in JavaScript, numbers or strings; characters typed literally in a program; also called *string literals*

string literals, in JavaScript, numbers or strings; characters typed literally in a program; also called *string constants*

string, in searching, a sequence of characters; in programming, a data type for a sequence of characters

strong encryption, public key encryption technique; a communicating party can use the technology to protect communications so that no one else can read it

structure, something made up of a number of parts that are held or put together in a particular way, e.g., a hierarchy

Structured Query Language (SQL), a standard notation for defining tables from tables in a database; sometimes pronounced SEE·quel

subscript, an index

substitution, in searching, the result of replacing a substring of a character sequence with another string

superuser, having the capability to access all functions of a computer or software system, including overriding passwords; also called *administrative authority*

symbol, an information code formed from a specific sequence of base patterns, for example, 01000001 is the ASCII symbol for *A* formed from patterns of 0's and 1's

synchronous communication, requires that both the sender and the receiver are simultaneously active, e.g., a telephone conversation

T

tab, in word processing, a formatting character often represented by →

tab-delimited text, in a spreadsheet, how foreign data is imported; each cell's entry ends with a tab and each row ends with a return

table, an organizing mechanism for database entities

tag, a word or abbreviation enclosed in angle brackets, usually paired with a companion starting with a slash, which describes a property of data or expresses a command to be performed; e.g., `<italic>You're it!</italic>`

task dependencies, when solving tasks, the fact that some tasks rely or depend on the resolution of other tasks

task dependency graph, used by systems engineers and managers in project management; also called a *PERT chart*

TCP/IP, acronym for Transmission Control Protocol, Internet Protocol

template, the structural information of a document with placeholders for content that is later filled in to produce a complete document

tera-, prefix for trillion; in prefixing, a quantity counted in binary, e.g., memory, prefix for 1,099,511,627,776

termination test, a Boolean expression to determine whether an iteration statement will execute its statement sequence again; also called a *continuation test*

test, in algorithmic thinking, included in a loop to determine if the instructions should be repeated

text, a sequence of characters; in searching, the material being searched

text editor, basic software to create and modify text files; contrast with word processor

tiling, in graphics, copying a small image repeatedly to create a background pattern

toggling, reversing the state of an item, e.g., toggling between selected and deselected

token, a symbol sequence treated as a single unit in searching or in languages

top-level domain, in an IP address, `.com`, `.net`, `.org`, `.gov`, `.edu`, etc.

transducer, a device that converts waves of one form into waves of another, usually electrical

transistor, a connection between two wires that can be controlled by a third wire to allow or disallow a charge to flow

translate, in graphics, to move an image to a new position unchanged; in programming, to compile a programming language into a language that the computer can interpret (machine language)

trapdoor, in encryption software, incorporated by the programmer as a way to gain access to particular cleartext; works like a telephone wiretap

tree, a graphic representation of a hierarchical directory

triangle pointers, small triangles indicating hidden information; clicking on the triangle pointer displays the information

Trojan, a useful and apparently innocuous program that takes its name from the Trojan Horse of Greek mythology; it contains hidden code that allows the unauthorized collection, exploitation, or destruction of data

troubleshoot, in computing, determining why something does not work due to malfunctioning hardware or buggy or outdated software

tuple, a set of values for the attributes of an entity; also called a *row*

Turing Test, an experimental setting to determine if a computer and a person can be distinguished by their answers to a judge's questions

U

unary operator, an operator such as negation (-), with a single operand

undefined, in JavaScript, the value of declared variables before they are assigned

Universal Resource Locator (URL), a two-part name for a Web page composed of an IP address followed by the filename, which can default to `index.html`

universality, a property of computation that all computers with a minimal set of instructions can compute the same set of computations

URL, *see* Universal Resource Locator

V

vacation message, a function of mail servers that allows a user to set up a message saying that he or she is temporarily away and unable to reply to email; also called an *automated reply*

value types, the different kinds of values of a programming language; also called *data types*

variable, a named quantity in a programming language

virtual, a modifier meaning not actually, but as if

virtual reality, a digital representation of the world

virus, a program that infects another program by embedding a (possibly evolved) copy of itself

virus-checking software, programs that check for known viruses, worms, etc.

W

W3C, *see* World Wide Web Consortium

WAN, *see* wide area network

Web, short form of World Wide Web

Web browser, a software application that locates and reads HTML pages. Modern browsers can display sound and video as well as text and graphics (although plug-ins may be required for multimedia)

Web client, a computer requesting services from a Web server; a computer running a Web browser

Web server, a computer providing pages to Web clients; a computer hosting a Web page

WFI, *see* World Famous Iteration

white space, in HTML, space inserted for readability

wide area network (WAN), a network connecting computers over a wider area than a few kilometers

window, an area of a computer screen that displays its own file or message independent of the rest of the screen

word processor, software to create and modify text files that include formatting; contrast with text editor

work-proportional-to-*n*, a description of the time required to solve a problem with input of size *n*

World-Famous Iteration (WFI), in JavaScript, the most frequently written `for` loop used by programmers

World Wide Web (WWW), the collection of all HTML servers connected by the Internet and their information resources

World Wide Web Consortium (W3C), a standards body composed mainly of companies that produce Web software

worm, an independent program that replicates itself from machine to machine across network connections

wrap, in HTML, when there is insufficient window space for the full sequence of text, the browser continues the text on the next line

WYSIWYG (what you see is what you get), pronounced WHIZ·ee·wig

X

XML, *see* Extensible Markup Language

ANSWERS TO SELECTED QUESTIONS

Chapter 1

Multiple Choice

1. A. Monitors use bit-mapped technology generated by the computer whereas TVs use recorded images.
3. C. A laptop has an LCD display and uses RGB color.
5. D. Follow the acronym, PILPOF, plug in last, pull out first.
7. A.
9. D.

Short Answer

1. microprocessor
3. screen saver
5. 786,432 or 1024×768
7. tip of the arrow
9. Execute *or* run
11. abstraction
13. word processor
15. generalization

Chapter 2

Multiple Choice

1. A. Those with computer skills are sometimes called digerati.
3. D. Both A and B are correct. Ease of use is one of the driving forces behind software development and one of the reasons for the popularity of some software.
5. B. You'll find all except door handles in a typical GUI.
7. B. In Windows, you can close a subwindow, such as a spreadsheet or word processing file, and the application will keep running.
9. B. Operations that can be applied immediately are shown in solid color and operations that are not available at the moment are shown in a lighter color or "grayed out."
11. C. Use nothing.

Short Answer

1. digerati
3. analogies
5. Triangle pointers
7. menus
9. Help
11. drop-down menu
13. gray
15. command

Chapter 3

Multiple Choice

1. D. The Internet is a great medium for asynchronous communication.
3. B. The ability to create and publish Web pages has made it easier for people to express their opinions and creativity.
5. C. For every *n* computers attached to the Internet, an additional computer adds *n* connections.
7. B. The right side shows the domain. That will get the message to the correct location. From there, the mail server will have to get it to the correct address. This is very similar to the postal service.
9. C. The government, educational institutions, and big business put together the first system in the late 1960s.
11. D. The client/server relationship is very efficient; the server can handle hundreds or thousands of requests at a time.
13. C. Most countries allow people access to the Internet with few restrictions.
15. D. A wireless hub can be used to connect wireless devices to a network and the Internet.

Short Answer

1. electronic commerce
3. multicast
5. peers
7. channel
9. gateways
11. Web servers
13. FTP
15. Hypertext Markup Language
17. blog

Chapter 4

Multiple Choice

1. C. The commands used in HTML are called tags. They are enclosed in < >.
3. A. The first one has the tags properly paired.

5. C. These are paragraph tags and put a double space around the text to set it off from the rest of the page.

7. D.

9. A. `img src = "filename.ext"` will get the image. Then use `align` = and enclose the proper alignment in quotes.

Short Answer

1. Web authoring software

3. `<br>` *or* `<pre>`

5. attributes

7. relative

9. Graphics Interchange Format

11. `#000000`

Chapter 5

Multiple Choice

1. A. Some use the Web for their own gains and slant their content accordingly.

3. D. Libraries have large online collections and services for Internet users. Resources are free and open to everyone.

5. B. The query processor looks at the search information and performs the search.

7. C. Google was the first search engine to get its keywords from the anchor tags of Web pages to identify content on a page and to find pages to crawl.

9. C. Use the minus sign (–) in front of the word to exclude pages that have that word.

Short Answer

1. library

3. Single links

5. Google

7. logical (or Boolean) operators

9. hierarchy

11. hits

13. AND

15. InterNIC

Chapter 6

True/False and Multiple Choice

1. F. A tertiary source is removed from the source by time or space. A tertiary source reports what happened but isn't an eyewitness.

3. D. In addition, mistakes in print tend to stay mistakes.

5. B. An eyewitness and a participant are examples of primary sources.

7. C. We obtain online information from primary and secondary sources. It is important to check the credentials of online authors, especially those who are secondary sources of information.

Short Answer

1. Curiosity-driven research
3. History
5. primary source

Chapter 7

Multiple Choice

1. B. The computer doesn't understand the information it was given. This usually means the user didn't understand what the computer wanted or the user simply entered the wrong information.
3. B. See if the error repeats itself. If it doesn't, then you're in the clear. If it does, then you need to work through the debugging process.
5. A. Look again for the error. See if you can duplicate the problem.

Short Answer

1. Field inputs
3. ~~b~~
5. bug
7. workaround

Chapter 8

Multiple Choice

1. C. 6 times 6 is 36 and 6 times 6 times 6 is 216.
3. D. The Tab key can work alone. The other keys are used in conjunction with another key.
5. A. A clock with hands is analog. If the clock displays digits, it is digital.
7. D. It's called a syllogism. From the two statements, I can deduce the third statement.
9. A. The coating on floppies and hard disks is an iron compound that can store a magnetic charge.

Short Answer

1. molecules
3. Present and Absent
5. collating sequence
7. escape character
9. Bit
11. Hex
13. ASCII code

Chapter 9

Multiple Choice

1. A. The computer executes its instructions literally. There is no allowance for free will, creativity, or intuition.

3. D. The fastest personal computers can sustain speeds even higher than that, and each generation of computers is faster.

5. B. The ALU performs instructions.

7. B. Branch and jump make the computer switch tasks so it doesn't always grab the next instruction.

9. B. The correct order is thousands, millions, billions, trillions.

11. C. Assembly language is the most primitive software level that humans work with, and rarely used.

Short Answer

1. Computers

3. RAM

5. deterministically

7. information processing

9. keyboard

11. Programming

13. Instruction interpretation

15. gate

17. high-level

Chapter 10

Multiple Choice

1. C. There are five basic requirements: inputs specified, outputs specified, definiteness, effectiveness, and finiteness.

3. A. A natural language lacks the rigorous structure and precise meaning of the others.

5. C. These steps must be repeated in order to put the whole set of CDs in order.

7. A. You took a specific example and generated an idea from it.

9. D. After the *Alpha* sweep, the algorithm is complete.

Short Answer

1. algorithm

3. algorithm, program

5. *Beta* sweep

7. nonredundant

9. loop

Chapter 11

Multiple Choice

1. B. Each intensity has a range from 0–255. That gives you 256 possible settings for each color or 16,777,216 possible colors.

3. B. Analog information is not discrete. It can always be divided into a smaller sampling.

5. D.

7. A. MP3 is the audio layer of MPEG movies.

9. C. A supermarket uses UPC codes, the little sets of numbers and black and white lines on packages.

Short Answer

1. black
3. Interpolation
5. ADC
7. ISO
9. optical character recognition (OCR)
11. virtual reality
13. Haptic devices
15. Bias-free Universal Medium Principle

Chapter 12

Multiple Choice

1. B. Multicasting means you can send the same email message to more than one person at a time. Each of the other options is a limitation of email.
3. B. Take some time to cool down before you reply. Or take the high road and don't reply at all.
5. B. Although it can happen, messages for a list-serve are seldom edited or censored.
7. C. The first was accidentally released in 1988.
9. D. Under the "fair use" policy, educational and scholarly use of small parts of a copyrighted piece is allowed.

Short Answer

1. Netiquette
3. asynchronous, chat sessions
5. moderator
7. virus
9. Intellectual property
11. public domain
13. fail-soft
15. Phishing

Chapter 13

True/False

1. F. It will spill over into the cell to the right if that cell is empty. If text is in the cell, it will display as much as possible. If a number is in the cell, it will display cross-hatches (#).
3. T.
5. F. It is used to fill other cells with the contents of the selected cell.
7. F. You should use the dollar sign ($).
9. T.

Multiple Choice

1. C. It is sometimes called a range as well..
3. D. All of the above are valid ranges.
5. C. There are six rows and three columns for a total of 18 cells.
7. C. The results are displayed in the cell. Look at the formula line at the top of the spreadsheet to see the formula.
9. A. When the dollar sign is used in a cell reference it makes that part of the reference absolute.
11. A. The dollar sign in front of the G makes it absolute. Without the dollar sign, the 5 is relative.
13. C. The Return and Enter keys will both create a carriage return.

Short Answer

1. atomic or monolithic
3. row
5. fill handle
7. absolute
9. max or maximum
11. series
13. Pmt or payment
15. Concatenate

Chapter 14

Multiple Choice

1. D. A set of entities is information. It can be almost anything.
3. A. A tuple is a row in a database and contains information defined by the other three.
5. A. Customary naming of a field name consists of the table name and the field name, so this field is named with both the name of the table and the name of the field.
7. C. Often a phone number is shared. Students in a dorm or those sharing an apartment often share a phone number.
9. B. The `Project` operation takes selected fields from a table and creates a new table from them.
11. B. The `Product` operation adds the fields together and multiplies the rows to create a new table.

Short Answer

1. database
3. picture, structure
5. Attributes
7. primary key
9. Test
11. concatenation
13. common field
15. relational database

Chapter 15

Multiple Choice

1. C. SQL, sometimes pronounced "sequel," is a popular commercial database system.
3. B. Relationships define the connection between entities in a database.
5. C. A row in one table should have a row in the other table that corresponds to it.
7. B. Tables can be physical tables that actually store information or logical tables that are created each time they're needed.
9. B. SQL is a language designed to let users extract information from databases.

Short Answer

1. view
3. redundancy
5. garbage in, garbage out
7. logical database
9. `FROM`
11. `ON`
13. one-to-one

Chapter 16

Multiple Choice

1. D. The needs analysis is the first step. The physical design is the next step.
3. B. The `Clients` table stores information on each individual.
5. C. Social Security numbers are not suitable for a key field.
7. D. `CustomerID` maintains the relationship between the two tables.
9. B. The relationship between the two is one-to-one.
11. C. The `Union` operation joins two tables together.

Short Answer

1. needs analysis
3. many-to-one
5. infinity sign
7. database administrator
9. form *or* GUI
11. Trimming
13. relationship
15. `SELECT`

Chapter 17

Multiple Choice

1. D. There are few limits on how businesses can use the information.
3. D. Each is an instance of using another's identity for personal profit or gain.
5. B. According to the Quality principle, your personal information should be accurate.

7. B. The EC requires others to follow its guidelines when information on EC citizens is used outside their countries.
9. C.
11. C. XOR means you can have x or y, but not both.
13. D. Each is an instance of using another's identity for personal profit or gain.

Short Answer
1. Privacy
3. Cash
5. due diligence test
7. European Data Protection Directive
9. cryptosystem
11. one-way cipher
13. Identity theft
15. partial backup

Chapter 18

Multiple Choice
1. B. JavaScript is used mainly for the Web.
3. C. An underscore can be used to separate words in a variable name. That makes the variable name easier to read.
5. C. When declared, the value of a variable is undefined. Be sure to assign a value to it before you use it.
7. C. The values of the variables before the start of the statement are used in a calculation.
9. C. Multiplication and division are done before addition and subtraction.
11. B. Both must be true for the operator to work.

Short Answer
1. program
3. declaration
5. initialize
7. operators
9. unary
11. !
13. conditional statement
15. {} or curly braces

Chapter 19

Multiple Choice
1. B. HTML pages are saved as ASCII code.
3. B. The `<body>` tag holds the body of the page, what the viewer will see.
5. C. The `<p>` tag starts a new paragraph.
7. C. When there is an event, it is handled by an event handler.
9. A. A click triggers an `onClick` event handler.

Short Answer

1. Web page
3. `<hr>`
5. event
7. dot operator
9. Input
11. feedback
13. tags

Chapter 20

Multiple Choice

1. B. Functions are used to solve simple tasks. When put together, they solve complicated tasks.
3. C. Two slashes are used to start a comment.
5. C. `onChange` is used. When the input is changed, the event is triggered.
7. A. `Math.random()` returns a number greater than 0 and less than 1.
9. C. Links are created using `href`, short for hypertext reference.

Short Answer

1. Abstraction
3. declaration
5. scope
7. infinity
9. 0, 1
11. Unix
13. Assigning 0 to rock, 1 to paper, and 2 to scissors, `randNum(3)` solves the problem.

Chapter 21

Multiple Choice

1. C. The for statement is used for iteration.
3. B. The *<next iteration>* changes the value of the iteration value.
5. C. The `alert()` command is used.
7. B. It means to add 1 to i.
9. D. All of the above are elements with invalid numbers.
11. A. The array starts at 0, ends at 8, has nine elements, and does not have any with decimals.

Short Answer

1. Iteration
3. variable
5. continuation or termination
7. infinite loop
9. `"\n"`

11. Indexing
13. length
15. display rate

Chapter 22

Multiple Choice

1. B. You must understand the problem before you can do anything else.
3. D. The Animate Grid task must be completed before the Build Controls task can be completed.
5. A. Build Controls is not dependent on the Detect Staircase task.
7. B. Graphics are placed using the `src` command.
9. B. Usually, when there are 3 to 5 tasks or more, it becomes useful to use a loop.

Short Answer

1. Decomposition Principle
3. Task dependencies
5. Program Evaluation and Review Technique
7. Build GUI
9. `document.images`
11. Radio buttons

Chapter 23

Multiple Choice

1. B. Computers are great at manipulating information, but that's about it.
3. D. Creativity is hard to define and hard to explain.
5. D.
7. B. Regardless of the order the CDs are in, the computer must make a pass to check it.
9. C. Getting computers to work properly is the only thing humans can do better than computers.
11. C. Checkers is a much simpler game than chess so the algorithm is much simpler.
13. A. The process is called deeper.
15. B. Six basic instructions are sufficient.
17. A. A program debugger can detect syntax errors, but it cannot find logical errors.

Short Answer

1. Deep Blue
3. artificial intelligence
5. specialized
7. Universality Principle
9. computer
11. business
13. compatibility and support
15. NP-complete problems

Chapter 24

Multiple Choice

1. C. The value of information depends on how we use it.
3. B. The first step is to make sure the error happens again. If you cannot duplicate the error, then there probably isn't a bug.
5. C. Logical reasoning can be applied to most problems with successful results.
7. A. The Capabilities component has the broadest range. Skills has the most detail.
9. D. There are risks to being too early or too late with new developments.

Short Answer

1. Nonalgorithmic thinking
3. heuristic
5. Concept
7. Lifelong learning
9. algorithms

INDEX

CREDITS